SILICON ALLEYS

Selected Metro Silicon Valley Columns,
2005-2020

Gary Singh

Cameron,
From the Alleys
to YOU♡
GARY SINGH

Published by Anti Man About Town Press.
San Jose, California, USA

Every word originally published in Metro Silicon Valley, 2005-2020
Foreword © 2020 *Rudy Rucker*
Cover design by *Kara Brown*
Author Illustration by *Rick Geary*
Interior design by *Sean George*

ISBN: 978-1-7350688-0-0 (paperback)
ISBN: 978-1-7350688-1-7 (epub)
ISBN: 978-1-7350688-2-4 (mobi)
Library of Congress Control Number: 2020904027

*For Alice Singh, who taught me how to read
when I was two years old*

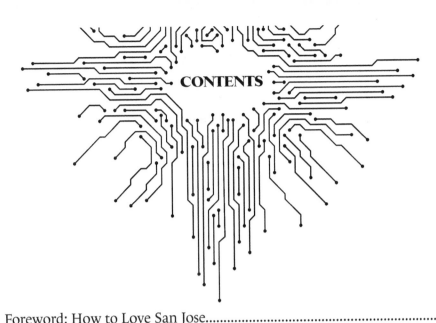

CONTENTS

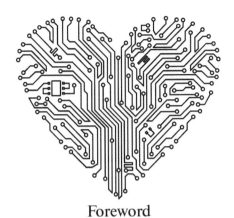

Foreword

How to Love San Jose

I met Gary Singh a few years after moving to our beloved, gets-no-respect burg of San Jose. My true job was, as always, writing avant-garde science-fiction novels, popular science books, and whatever journalistic pieces I could sell. But my family needed for me to have a salaried job as well, and I'd found a pleasant niche as a professor of computer science at San Jose State.

Sometime in the late 1990s, Gary appeared in my office on the third floor of MacQuarrie Hall on a by-now-turfed-over block of San Carlos Street. Immediately I sensed him to be a kindred soul. He has a captivating style of speech, he bursts with fresh ideas, and his voice is a confiding, well-modulated baritone. I always feel like Gary is letting me in on important, unknown facts. Somehow it's like listening to a magic talking crow. I'm all ears.

His visit had little to do with my expertise in CS—no, he was there because of my rep as a semi-underground cult novelist. Gary was writing a Master's thesis for a project in—well, I never did quite understand what the field officially was. He'd majored in Music at SJSU, and his Master's project was an absurdist, surreal, transreal, SFish novel about a character who builds a device called a Ridiculometer. Gary felt that, obviously, it would be handy to have a ridiculometer to calibrate how effing ridiculous everything is.

Gary is a striking figure: tall, dark, with piercing eyes, an aquiline nose, a curly shock of black hair. He's a bemused prophet, energetically depressed, cautiously hilarious, a man of parts, with none of the parts quite matching. Over and over my wife and I encounter him at events around our strange and disparate San Jose—or we might spot him trucking along an empty-as-usual downtown sidewalk.

Often, when seeing Gary, I silently misquote an inspiring Bob Dylan lyric to myself: "I dreamed I saw Saint Augustine, as live as you or me / Tarrying through these quarters with the utmost empathy."

Over the years I've had a number of journalist friends. They're a bit different than novelists. Novelists are like farmers or like builders. We're boring, we're out in the field day after day, season after season, nursing our crops, hammering our frames, worrying about the rain, fitting in windows. Journalists are more like hunter-gatherers. Or hyenas. Gary goes somewhere cool (or uncool), merges into the scene, notices anomalies, snaps up choice quotes, goes home to his laptop, and has at it.

Or, wait, maybe Gary's like a graffiti artist with a tote bag full of spray cans, a virgin wall to defile, and one glorious night to do it in. Or like a cameraman shooting a portfolio of photos. Or like a poet, whittling his experience down to a few *mots justes*. Or, hell, he's like Gary Singh and none other.

By the way, Gary is in fact a photographer, with works in galleries, and a poet, with screeds hither and yon. One of Gary's favorite poems, which he refers to several times in this collection, is Allen Ginsberg's short 1954 work "In Back of the Real," taken from his seminal Howl, and composed, one imagines, while he was visiting our local Beat icon Neal Cassady in downtown San Jose. (See Gary's 2018 column, "Neal Cassady's Old House on Santa Clara Street.")

> *railroad yard in San Jose*
>
> *I wandered desolate*
>
> *in front of a tank factory*
>
> *and sat on a bench*
>
> *near the switchman's shack.*
>
> *A flower lay on the hay on*
>
> *the asphalt highway*
>
>   *...*
>
> *Yellow, yellow flower, and*
>
> *flower of industry,*
>
> *tough spiky ugly flower,*
>
> *flower nonetheless,*
>
> *with the form of the great yellow*
>
> *Rose in your brain!*
>
> *This is the flower of the World.*

One of Gary's specialties, which I enjoy exceedingly, is to visit some seemingly dull, blah, forgettable or even ugly precinct of San Jose—and totally get into it, like he's an alien visiting from Mars, and then describe the hell out of it. When in this mode, Gary refers to himself as "the urban blight junkie." As recently as 2019, with his ridiculometer running full bore, Gary walked a few blocks along San Carlos Street. Let me quote *in extenso* from "Urban Blight Junkie Returns to San Carlos Street," with a few editorial annotations.

This stretch of road takes us to a different era. The streetscapes are left over from decades ago, when San Jose wasn't entirely filled in with suburbia…

Falafel's Drive-in was jammed at lunchtime on a Saturday. There was a Faction sticker on the front window, right underneath the Zagat designation—a yin-yang of punk and luxury. It doesn't get any more San Jose than that.

[As Gary explains in a 2018 column, "The Faction and Lars Frederiksen at The Ritz," the Faction is a San Jose skate-punk band founded in the early 1980s, and skate-punk is one of the numerous indigenous San Jose movements that San Ho doesn't get much credit for. Back to Gary now.]

A slew of beautifully disfigured facades highlighted the next mile, including San Jose's celebrated row of antique shops. As always, each one featured its own janky panache and each one was doing business when I slithered in. Believe me, the experience of hearing 'Green, Green Grass of Home' by Tom Jones while exploring the labyrithine confines of a San Carlos Street antique shop is more necessary than anything WeWork will provide.

[WeWork being the short-term-office-rental biz, which is just the kind of 21st C development that's likely to tweak Gary's ridiculometer. Back to the man himself.]

Neighborhood bars are important, too. If your hands are shaking pre noon, like mine used to be, Alex's 49er Inn remains a highlight on this strip. …. At these legendary watering holes, you will not find $17 artisan pickle sandwiches or craft brew hipsters bathing in beard oil. Instead, you'll find heroic denizens of the gritty underbelly with stories to tell.

Gary's "Silicon Alleys" *Metro* column hasn't missed a week yet, and by now it's been running for fifteen years. It's wonderful to have so many of his pieces assembled here. You sense the epic sweep of history—characters emerge, caper, and a few years later Gary's memorializing their death. Also there's the intimate history of Gary Singh himself. As a true and deep writer, his columns are about himself as much as they're about our SJ quarters. He's looking through a two-way mirror, with his solemn, amused visage overlaid upon our scenes.

San Jose isn't like any other city I've known. First of all, we're incredibly diverse, so much so that, at times, the familiar race or ethnicity or gender categories don't always apply. And in terms of income, we have our share of entitled one-percenters (the guy in the Tesla doing a U-turn in a busy two-lane street), but we have a ton of old-school working types as well. In certain locales you might think you're in Nebraska or El Paso or Saigon or, rather, all three at once. And that's when it gets real San Jose.

Beats, skaters, punks, acidheads, coders, chip etchers, transrealists—all have left their mark here. But often as not it feels like nothing is going on. Where's the action? We count on Gary Singh to find it—in his persona of "the anti-man-about-town." An incurable romantic. A brooding, sarcastic hipster. You have to have lived here awhile to understand his attitude.

Does Gary hate San Jose? Short answer: No. Longer answer: see the following words from his 2005 column, "Hitting Rock Bottom."

Occasionally folks get into a tizzy-fit when they interpret something I write or say as "disrespectful to San Jose." It doesn't matter what the topic is. With the phlegm-spittle of a rabid gopher, they usually wind up saying, "Well, if you hate San Jose so much, then why don't you just leave?" ...

"Maybe it's love," I say. "Inverted love. I don't know."

Thank you, Gary, for showing us the way.

—*Rudy Rucker, March 11, 2020*

Introduction

In the Beginning

In 2005, the editors of *Metro Silicon Valley* gave me a weekly column so I could document the San Jose condition from a perspective only a native wacko could offer. With no expectations, I took them up on it. At the time, I already navigated the guts of the city in various other sections of the paper, writing art reviews, music pieces, cover stories, streams of consciousness and whatnot, yet they saw a potential I didn't know existed. In order to open up the paper each week with bizarre ruminations on something, anything, the editors turned me loose to write whatever I wanted. I figured it would last maybe a few months.

Ultimately, no one could have predicted the Pandora's box that would explode on the Silicon Alleys page. The column became more popular as every year unfolded, spreading almost entirely by word of mouth, so there was no way to stop writing. Over time, the missives began to feel like offspring, with me putting my own bent spin on every local subject I could possibly find, for as long as I could keep plugging away. People began to compliment me on the street wherever I went, often multiple times a day. I did not expect this. I wasn't accustomed to being liked.

Yet that's what happened. Over and over again. And for better or worse, each column seemed to trigger a craving to write another one. The dopamine rush wouldn't stop. As long as I was engaged in the process of writing, my spirits improved and I became happy. No matter how many times I fell deeply for a woman that only wanted to be friends, if I just kept writing, then I could surmount any degree of pain and heartbreak, regardless of the situation. I became able to communicate with my fingers on a keyboard much better than I could ever do in conversation. Even better, people actually wanted to read the stories. Go figure.

For once in my life, I'd found a way to harness my entire life-matrix of experiences, interests and perspectives and tap into my own innate talents. No one had ever asked me to do that. No one had ever wanted me to do that.

Of course, each week was different, depending on what mood the muses were in and how they decided to string me along. If the muses were happy, then the column was a happy one. If the muses were in a difficult mood, then the column either became more pessimistic or devolved into me taking my own inadequacies out on something else. In any case, I always at least tried to provide a subversive sense of humor. Over the years, many others told me that even when scraping the bottom of the barrel of cynicism, even when bashing the city up, down and sideways, I always seemed to offer a sense of hope, somehow. They pointed out that underneath the darkness, hope existed. Whether they were talking about the city of San Jose or me personally, I don't know. But this was probably the best compliment I could ever ask for. I have nothing but gratitude.

Subjectwise, my home town gave me a wide open palette, from punk rock to high art, from dive bars to luxury digs, from literary fixations to local history, plus arts criticism, business profiles and abstract mystical screeds. Sometimes I even wrote journalism. In 15 years, I rarely figured out the column more than a week in advance. It's just how I rolled. And once I began the mechanical process of writing, I often felt like I had no conscious command over where the words came from, as if I was channeling the columns from somewhere else, or at least the first drafts. That's not a cliché. It really felt that way sometimes. As I went back to select the columns you now have in front of you, there were many instances in which I couldn't remember how or why I wrote what I did.

The Silicon Alleys page thus became my ever-changing impermanent self, my true nature, my natural voice. It was me. It reflected the trials and tribulations of however my brain was operating on any given week. Nevertheless, as long as I found an ability to elevate the ignored people and stories of San Jose, then I was content. In a sense, the city of San Jose will always be ignored and disregarded by everyone else in the world. Most natives know this. So much that the whole city itself seems terminally "off the beaten path" and thus always ripe for zonked-out column fodder. I was sitting on a gold mine.

As a result, I have the editors to thank first and foremost: Dan Pulcrano, for giving me the space when I didn't realize what I even had to offer, plus all the editors I've ever worked with at that newspaper, in alphabetical order: Corinne Asturias, Mike Connor, Michael S. Gant, Dean Hinton, Stett Holbrook, Traci Hukill, Todd Inoue, Eric Johnson, Josh Koehn, Steve Palopoli, Nick Veronin, Traci Vogel, Jennifer Wadsworth and Heather Zimmerman. All of them somehow managed to put up with me. Plus, I cannot leave out several other employees over the years, not just those that helped lay out and design the book you now have in your hands, but some of those who toiled away uploading the columns to the website, designing the pages, selling the ads, shooting the photos, proofreading my screeds and other heroes that tolerated the chaos of me trying to love San Jose every single week: Sean George, Kathy Manlapaz, Kara Brown, Gordy Carbone, Jim Carrico, John Haugh, Dave Miller, Jimmy Arceneaux, Tabi Dolan, Felipe Buitrago, Harry Allison, Allie Gottlieb, Sarah Quelland, Vrinda Normand, Greg Ramar, Jeanne Sullivan, Richard Von Busack and Anne Gelhaus. Special super-duper thanks goes to Lisa Thomas, who facilitated the process for me to interview at Metro in the first place. To all those I'm forgetting, my hat goes off to every one of you!

Subjectwise, it would take another 450 pages to recognize everyone. I will say this, though: Just because you or your predicament did not make it into any of these columns does not mean you were unworthy of coverage. Quite the opposite. Everyone is worthy. There is simply too much to write. I can only hope that my journey has inspired others to take up their pens, or keyboards, and engage their own cities in brand new ways. Don't ever give up. Never say die!

Years ago, I began to understand the city of San Jose as a character in one long story, told via *Metro* columns each week. So herein you will find a small 400-page overview of that city, my home town, as I've come to know it, warts and all.

2005

◇

Alien Notion: Jacques Vallee

Besides being a successful Silicon Valley venture capitalist, Jacques Vallee has researched the UFO phenomenon perhaps more than any other person currently alive. He has written almost a dozen books on ufology, and he was the real-life model for the French UFO scientist in *Close Encounters of the Third Kind*. Vallee lives in San Francisco, but he recently infiltrated Silicon Valley to summarize his four decades of research in a public presentation at the Institute of Transpersonal Psychology in Palo Alto.

The reason Vallee has irked so many ardent UFO believers for decades is that he doesn't believe UFOs are nuts-and-bolts machines from outer space or spinning silver disks operated by aliens from another universe. Crudely simplified, he was the first scientist to suggest that UFO experiences are in fact interactions with interdimensional beings that have always existed among us—invisible hands toying with human society from a different level of consciousness. It's not just a physical phenomenon. It's a sociological, spiritual and psychic experience all wrapped up into one.

Vallee also suggested in several books that many of these so-called "abduction" tales are the result of manipulation, either by the government or the interdimensional beings themselves. Even though his work was documented in former Metro scribe Jonathan Vankin's *80 Greatest Conspiracies of All Time*, Vallee has commanded a huge amount of respect over the years, even from UFO debunkers. As he's been quoted everywhere, "The UFO Phenomenon exists. It has been with us throughout history. It is physical in nature, and it remains unexplained in terms of contemporary science. It represents a level of consciousness that we have not yet recognized, and which is able to manipulate dimensions beyond time and space as we understand them. It affects our own consciousness in ways that we do not grasp fully, and it generally behaves as a control system." He has also theorized that UFO experiences echo those of traditional contact with nonhuman consciousness in the form of elves, fairies or demons throughout several cultures for millennia.

Since Vallee has spent decades filtering out the lunatic fringe on this matter, he didn't want any advance press about his lecture, and I went along with that. He understandably didn't want kooks with preconceived conclusions showing up and turning the whole presentation into a circus. Instead, he wanted to keep the lecture purely a scientific one.

So it only makes sense that the event was hosted by the Foundation for Mind-Being Research (FMBR), a 25-year-old Silicon Valley-based organization of scientists, engineers, spiritualists, artists, philosophers, psychics and psychologists devoted to establishing consciousness studies as a bona fide science. One of FMBR's main principles is that the four-dimensional space-time world of ordinary human experience may be inadequate to accommodate the physics of the mind sciences. Vallee's research throughout the last four decades intertwines with that theory.

"This lecture was an experiment," he explained via email afterward. "I am staying away from the media and public presentations because the field has become so polarized between different ideologies that anything I would say as a scientist would be lost in the noise. The FMBR group is unique because it is open-minded and understands the nature of research. Thus it provided an opportunity to test my current conclusions about the phenomenon before a responsive, yet critical audience."

In the presentation, he explained that the entire UFO discourse has degenerated into a confrontational and polarized situation between the hard-core skeptics and the extraterrestrial believers, and we need new radical hypotheses. So Vallee and others are going back underground and returning to the days of the *Invisible College*, the title of his 1975 book about a group of scientists researching UFOs while keeping their names and activities out of the press.

"The phenomenon presents great opportunities to learn about the world and human nature," he explained. "I continue to do research, but I do it with my own resources, in communication with a small network of scientists and investigators around the world. Good progress can be done this way, in an environment of trust rather than confrontation or hype."

Kepler's 50th Anniversary

Long before Barnes & Noble, Borders and Amazon, there was Kepler's Books in Menlo Park. As of right now, the independent bookstore is turning 50 years old. World War II conscientious objector Roy Kepler first opened the place in May of 1955. Several other South Bay bookstores have come and gone in the meantime, but Kepler's still reigns supreme. The stories are endless.

It seems odd now, but back in the '50s, most publishers (as well as the general public) didn't consider paperbacks to be "real" books. Roy Kepler, along with Fred and Pat Cody in Berkeley, and Lawrence Ferlinghetti at City Lights in San Francisco, changed all that. Bay Area bookstores became the leaders of the "paperback revolution."

Kepler himself drew considerable attention for his antiwar efforts, and in 1960 he was arrested at the Lawrence Radiation Laboratory for anti-nuclear weapons protesting. Throughout the '60s, Kepler's blossomed into a counterculture mecca. According to Grateful Dead historian Dennis McNally, "The Grateful Dead started here. Jerry Garcia was a fixture at Kepler's in the early '60s. He got his education stealing things off the shelves."

In John Markoff's wonderful book, *What the Dormouse Said: How the '60s Counterculture Shaped the Personal Computer Industry*, he says Kepler's "served as a beacon for an eclectic group of intellectuals who were outsiders in a community that was largely split in its economic dependence among Stanford, a fledgling electronics industry, and large military contractors like Lockheed."

According to former store manager Betty Sumrall, "If you had long hair, you could come in—there were places at this time where you could not even go if you had long hair. If you were too poor to buy a book, you could come in and read. Anyone, radical or not, was welcome."

Kepler's didn't endure the '60s without problems, of course. There were arson attempts and bomb blasts, due to the antiwar nature of the place. In 1968, someone blasted out the front windows in the Los Altos store.

An ad from the time read: "It's hard to say which is growing faster—the peninsula war industries or Kepler's Books. Unlike the Stanford Research Institute, Kepler isn't planning an underground shelter yet, but with books lining the walls and floors, we may be forced underground, too."

After moving around a few times, the store eventually made it to its current location at 1010 El Camino Real in Menlo Park. It continues to be one of the most successful independent bookstores around. A huge public party Saturday afternoon (May 14, 1-4pm) will feature live music, raffles, games, prizes and book bags filled with the best books from the last five decades.

Which leaves us with one burning question: Why on earth can San Francisco, Berkeley, Menlo Park and Santa Cruz support independent bookstores, but San Jose can't? I've posed that question to several San Joseans over the years and no one seems to have an answer.

Clark Kepler, who currently runs the store, said he wasn't qualified to analyze San Jose's situation, since he doesn't know the community well enough, but he said folks should demand an alternative to the nauseating strip malls.

"The phenomena of big box retailing and chains are ones that are very seductive to the consumer," he explained. "The perception of having everything there—convenience, low pricing, to be on every corner, the strip mall look—is something I think a community wants an alternative to. I think a lot of times people like the idea of an independent bookseller or grocery store, and the question is whether you want to shop it and give it your business all the time. That's the key component in being able to maintain a community, a downtown that is local."

So call your favorite real estate mogul and demand lower rents and more independent bookstores in San Jose. Tell them you need better places besides Barnes & Noble in which to slug coffee, lurk in the occult section and hit on New Age women.

Neighborhood Art at Singh's Laundromat

Now it has been said that journalists are lazy bastards and that much of what appears in print is within walking distance of the journalist's office. That theory is only partly true, but when I saw the flier for a MA-CLA-sponsored movie at the dive Laundromat at Second and William streets around the corner, I nearly broke out in tears from laughing so hard.

That dump?

You've got to be kidding me, I thought. For years, I saw more haggard toothless hookers parading around that corner than anywhere else in downtown San Jose. People with no shirts or shoes would be in the place doing their laundry while crackheads peddled their wares outside. The place was riddled with graffiti, garbage and unsavory characters. So when MACLA, two doors down from *Metro*, decided to paint the place and show a community screening of an animated film, I had to get the skinny. That sounded too ridiculous to be true.

It turned out the place is called Singh's Laundromat (no relation, I swear), and MACLA had the same reaction to it that I did.

"We walked by the Laundromat and said, 'Wow, that's ugly,'" says Tamara Alvarado, MACLA's executive director.

But the whole project is part of MACLA's effort to get in touch with the local community and encourage neighborhood folks to get to know one another.

"At MACLA, we've always been involved with different neighborhoods, but not necessarily our own neighborhood," explains Alvarado. "We started doing a couple of different focus groups in the neighborhood, and said, 'What d'ya all wanna see in your neighborhood?' And how we can serve as a connector, if you will, between the different types of residents that live in the neighborhood now as opposed to 10 years ago?"

So they painted the inside of the place and put up vinyl lettering, and voila, a movie house was born. Local residents were then invited to wash their clothes and eat popcorn while watching a movie in the middle of the day.

"We just said, 'Hey Singh, we noticed a lot of malarkey goes down at your Laundromat and are you willing to work with us?'" Alvarado says.

"Part of our project is to work with small business owners. And he said, 'Go for it.'"

About 15 people showed up, and some even asked if MACLA would show movies every week.

"We know a little paint goes a long way," Alvarado said. "We're not done with the place yet. We're thinking about having a poetry night there. Like doing something at nighttime. It's experimental. The people who were there loved it."

After all, the Laundromat is perhaps the ultimate public space. A Laundromat can be a lonely space or a people-watching space, but it is an anonymous space. No one talks to each other. You just hate it when folks look at your dirty laundry. That's not good. There's always a sock left behind that no one wants to pick up and throw out. And MACLA is changing all this.

"A lot of conversations that we've had with people have centered around the fact that people don't know each other," Alvarado said. "Time and time again, people have said, 'We want to get to know our neighbors.' It comes up every single time we've had a formal focus group or an informal thing."

So there you have it. Something should be said for taking a dumpy Laundromat and doing something artistic with it. At Wash America on Santa Clara Street, you get blind-sided by the distorted classical music, but not at Singh's Laundromat.

The idea is that the more public spaces there are, the better, as more people will establish a sense of community. Even in Laundromats. Everyone has a Laundromat idea, so all you panty-stealing perverts out there, get ready. And Laundromats represent the last frontier when it comes to anarchically taking over a public space without regulatory difficulties and authoritarian intervention. Being the radical art movement that it is, MACLA figured this out. And no, I'm not just writing about this because the place is around the corner from my office.

Cloak and Dagger: Barry Eisler

Menlo Park author Barry Eisler has finally admitted that he used to work for the CIA. Until now, all he would divulge was that his "checks came from the U.S. State Department Foreign Service." In any event, he's created a whopping-good noir thriller series, all centering around the exploits and mind-states of a Japanese-American assassin named John Rain. It's a "killer thriller" series and even if you're not interested in underground Japanese culture, you'll get a kick out of these novels, as Rain is the most interesting assassin around these days.

Eisler spent years working in Japan and he places scenes in the labyrinth of Tokyo streets with astonishing detail. Just like *Lost in Translation*, if you've actually been to Tokyo, Eisler's novels—at least the first two—

will take you right back. You've got whisky bars, smoky jazz joints, hostess bars, fight clubs, thugs, mobsters and all sorts of seedy goings-on in several Tokyo districts. Eisler describes the dark atmospheric underbelly of Tokyo with precision and flair.

He even includes the Almond Cafe, a main pickup spot in Tokyo's heavily foreign Roppongi neighborhood. In the immediate area, expatriates abound due to the plethora of embassies, and Roppongi is where many young Japanese go to practice their English.

But enough of that. In the books, assassin John Rain is "a freelancer, a straddler, connected to many worlds, but a part of none"—pretty much exactly what it's like being a freelance journalist. Rain has perfected the art of assassination, but makes it look like the target died of natural causes. Inspired partly by assassin Nicholai Hel in Trevanian's 1979 international espionage masterpiece, *Shibumi*, John Rain represents the romantic concept of the assassin as poet, as artist. But not without the emotional backlash, of course.

Shibumi is an untranslatable Japanese concept referring to the understated beauty that underlies everything in life. It represents an active spiritual tranquility, a personality of overwhelming calm, an effortless state of perfection and a natural urge to find harmony in all action. You can apply it to chess, ikebana flower arranging, architecture, gardening, Japanese rope bondage (*nawa shibari*) and, especially, martial arts. Just like Nicholai Hel, John Rain applies it to the art of assassination. Of course, Eisler himself is also an accomplished practitioner of mixed martial arts. He holds a black belt from the prestigious Kodokan International Judo Center in Tokyo.

Eisler appears at Kepler's in Menlo Park (1010 El Camino Real) on Thursday, June 23, to launch his tour for the fourth John Rain book, *Killing Rain*. The first three, *Rain Fall*, *Hard Rain* and last year's *Rain Storm*, don't necessarily have to be read in order, but it helps. And since Eisler has changed his "status," allowing him to divulge his former CIA employment, he's got a lot to say about current world events that you don't hear from all the scream-head circus entertainers on the cable networks.

Killing Rain draws inspiration from recent events in Iraq and Afghanistan—where the U.S. government's bounties on Osama bin Laden and other terrorist figures have spawned a huge private effort to track down these targets. When asked why the CIA can't directly infiltrate Al Qaeda, Eisler says: "The problem is that there are certain things the CIA can't do. Al Qaeda and other terrorist organizations undoubtedly have a test for new initiates that involves killing. It's similar to the mob's concept of 'making your bones.' Why does the mob use murder as a prerequisite to becoming a full member? Because no matter how deep undercover a government law enforcement agent might be, there's no way he can commit a murder. The same holds true for the CIA vis-à-vis Al Qaeda. An undercover agent who tries to infiltrate a group like that will, at some point, be faced with a similar initiation. That's why private organizations are somewhat better positioned to infiltrate these groups. They don't have to explain to Congress how they got in."

Counterculture A.D.

Inside the old Camera One Theater on South First Street, the chairs are gone and the screen is nowhere to be found. Behind it, weeds grow out of the concrete, flyers from nearby clubs litter the parking lot and an empty pint bottle of Jack Daniels sits on the air compressor. Shattered glass covers the back porch. The place is gutted and Brian Eder of Two Fish Design is tearing out what's left of the front counter with a crowbar. It's pure manly destruction on a hot Wednesday afternoon, reminding me of when I used to work in the Spartan Bookstore receiving department in my college days, smashing old store fixtures on the receiving dock off San Fernando. The store always seemed to be in a state of remodeling, so we always had a wealth of old junk to physically destroy and throw into the dumpster—that is, the stuff we didn't take home and use for furniture. A co-worker would show up and work a 3-5pm shift—at $7 an hour—and do nothing but break shit out on the dock. God bless Spartan Bookstore.

Downtown is likewise in a constant state of remodeling and Eder, along with his partner Cherri Lakey, is moving their Anno Domini art gallery operation into the old Camera One building—a perfect return of counterculture to the SoFA district. It's about freakin' time. The district was always supposed to be a Bohemian artsy nexus and now that Anno Domini is moving on up (yep, start belting out the *Jeffersons* theme), the district will only get better. Actually, it hardly makes sense to call it a "district," since it's just two measly blocks—the equivalent of calling Market and San Carlos the "Hotel District." Only in San Jose ...

But anyway, Anno Domini represents the only counterculture arts operation around these parts and it has hosted several noteworthy shows, film screenings, performances and overall subversion over the years. For example, legendary San Francisco illustrator Barron Storey closes out his show with an artist talk this Thursday the 21st. Anno Domini has hosted Guerrilla News Network a few times and they once even convinced legendary S.F.-based countercultural publisher V. Vale from RE/Search to infiltrate the San Jose Museum of Art for a panel session. Who else would have pulled that one off? Vale would never have visited San Jose in his life if it weren't for Anno Domini.

Now, the word "counterculture" is problematic at best, and I'm using it loosely. This is not to say that Anno Domini is necessarily "counter" to any other establishments in the neighborhood. With the San Jose Institute of Contemporary Art, MACLA, the SoFA Lounge and the new locale for the Quilt Museum, the strip could finally revert back to the originators' artsy intentions. (Don't trash the Quilt Museum, by the way—they're a nice bunch of folks. Sure, they're displacing what used to be the best thrift store anywhere in San Jose, but that's another story ...)

And will Anno Domini's clientele clash with the furs and suits attending the California Theatre across the street? No. A resounding no. Folks from every part of the social and antisocial spectrum attend shows at the gallery and the artwork usually sells. The whole point of all this, for chrissakes, is just to support the artists, and folks who go to the opera or the symphony just might find a piece of artwork at Anno Domini they like. In fact, I know they will.

According to Eder, the new place will feature two galleries, a studio space and a permanent home for Anno Domini's collection of zines. The First Friday receptions will continue, but the monthly shows will now last a little longer. It's a much more lucrative location than their current one—some old brick building by the train station. And, most importantly, it will be a catalyst for bringing the insurrectionary disruptive culture-jamming mind-set back to South First. I can't freakin' wait.

Michael Ochs: 1000 Record Covers

Terminally unimpressed cynics like me pointed out in the '80s that CDs would just be a transition between vinyl and something else. Whether or not iPods eventually become that something else, we'll see. I sold off a good portion of my records long ago, but about a thousand of them still inhabit boxes in my mom's garage. And because of the new version of the Michael Ochs book *1000 Record Covers*, I'm just inclined to sniff through all those boxes and whip out Meat Loaf's *Bat Out of Hell* just to look at the artwork on the cover.

Ochs is the kingpin at Michael Ochs Archives, a gargantuan library of millions of music photographs and records in Venice, Calif. Basically, if you're a journalist or graphic designer and you need to access a photo of, say, Wendell Packard & the Half Notes, Ochs is the guy you get it from.

1000 Record Covers is one of several re-releases to celebrate publisher Taschen's 25th anniversary. Taschen is renowned for publishing over-the-top glossy art books, and this one is no different. But most importantly, it brings up a discussion that is taking place more and more often in these days of ubiquitous iPods and youngsters who've never seen a vinyl LP in their lives: the entire concept of the album cover as an art form has fallen by the wayside. Of course, this discussion is not new—pissed-off graphic designers were complaining back in the '80s that with CDs, cover art was now reduced from 12 inches to 5 inches. Nowadays, folks are downloading a zillion tunes and either burning them onto their own CDs or filling up iPods. The whole concept of cover art has been decimated. Folks don't realize that with LPs, the cover artwork and the packaging were completely part of how one experienced the music. Who could imagine listening to *Sgt. Pepper* without knowing what the cover looked like?

Enter Michael Ochs again. Last year he came to SJSU to speak at an art show he curated with designer Craig Butler. The show was titled "The Greatest Album Covers That Never Were." Here's what Ochs and Butler did: they contacted 100 established graphic designers and fine artists and asked them to paint or draw a hypothetical album cover for their favorite artist. No boundaries were to be imposed on the work at all. The artists had free reign to do whatever they wanted. It was an ingenious concept.

"Much to our surprise, the response exceeded our expectations," Ochs explains on his website. "Many of the most renowned artists in the graphic and fine arts fields loved the concept and came on board. For generations, the 12-inch album cover was the standard iconography for music and it was more sorely missed than we thought."

Ochs says it's "life in the past lane" and the nostalgia will not go away. Mark Pothier, a senior assistant business editor at the *Boston Globe*, shared that nostalgia in an uproarious piece for the *Mercury News* recently. In an article I really wish I had written, he lamented the days when you could go home with a potential lover and then scope out the person's record collection to determine whether you wanted to continue the relationship.

"It used to be easier to judge people unfairly," he said. "A cursory scan of their record collection revealed secrets. Telltale copies of REO Speedwagon's *Hi Infidelity* were known to wither budding relationships overnight. Soul-deep conversation and physical attraction could not compensate for the nagging doubt planted by *Frampton Comes Alive*. 'I must have been really drunk at the time' did not explain away *Air Supply's Greatest Hits*."

So what's the next step? Well, think about it. If people are going to download 20 Jimi Hendrix tunes and burn them onto their own CD, why not download cover art and packaging also? Well, that's exactly the grandiose scheme that Ochs has, but he said he doesn't know if it will ever happen.

So next time you see someone walking down the street with an iPod and those evil white cords stuck in his ears, don't rip the cord out of his face and strangle him with it. Instead, go down to your favorite thrift store and drop one dollar for a vinyl LP just for the cover. Don't even listen to the music, just buy it for the cover. Please.

Hitting Rock Bottom

Occasionally folks get into a Mayberry-style tizzy-fit when they interpret something I write or say as "disrespectful to San Jose." It doesn't matter what the topic is. With the phlegm-spittle of a rabid gopher, they usually wind up saying, "Well, if you hate San Jose so much, then why don't you just leave?"

My answer is that "hatred" has nothing to do with it. Instead, it's frustration. There are many of us—many more than this town realizes—who really wish it could become more than a sleepy suburb. Perhaps, maybe in some fantasy utopian future, a place with a thriving counterculture, several live music clubs, street pranks, world famous neighborhoods, historical landmarks that people under 70 actually care about, skyscrapers, a functional public transportation system, killer Russian delis, 100 art galleries, a million different things to do past midnight and cops who don't act like power-hungry meatheads who couldn't make the football team in high school.

If that makes me a dreamer, then so be it. Like John Lennon said, "I'm not the only one." I just want my hometown to be something I'm not embarrassed about.

But, alas, I've finally come to grips with my denial in this matter, and as much as I want to pretend this is not one more ridiculous "I wish we were San Francisco" complex, it is. I will now admit to having the same identity complex about San Jose that I ridicule everyone else for having. Instead of SJICA standing for the San Jose Institute of Contemporary Art, the acronym should instead stand for an association called San Jose Identity Complexers Anonymous, like Alcoholics Anonymous or Gamblers Anonymous. I've hit rock bottom and I need to get clean.

The main frustrating thing is that there do exist a lot of interesting bizarre characters in this valley to converse with—whether in scientific think tanks or dive bars. But unlike San Francisco, you have to go search them out. It's not as obvious here. There's a phrase I use elsewhere in this week's issue—"nauseating boredom"—to describe what it was like growing up here if you were someone beyond the pale. It fits. To use a milk carton metaphor, this city is long past its sell-by date and even *they* know it.

Whenever someone accuses me of "hating San Jose," Henry Miller's novel Nexus comes to mind immediately. During one exchange, a woman was accusing him of a being a dreamer. Miller's answer was that we're all dreamers but few of us wake up long enough to put it down in words. She then said Miller was someone trying to live a thousand lives in one—someone eternally dissatisfied with life and with everything, including himself.

"You're a Mongol," she told him. "You belong on the steppes of Central Asia."

As was the case when I first read this passage years ago, I was vicariously right there with the author. So allow me to quote in full the rest of that passage because it sounds disturbingly similar to a conversation I just had a few days ago. But I'll substitute "San Jose" for "America" and "Gary" for "Henry." Here we go—this is Henry Miller writing in the first person:

"You know," I said, getting worked up now, "one of the reasons why I feel so disjointed is that there's a little bit of everything in me. I can put myself in any period and feel at home in it. When I read about the Renaissance I feel like a man of the Renaissance; when I read about one of the Chinese dynasties I feel exactly like a Chinese of that epoch. Whatever the race, the period, the people, Egyptian, Aztec, Hindu or Chaldean, I'm thoroughly in it, and it's always a rich, tapestried world whose wonders are inexhaustible. That's what I crave—a humanly created world, a world responsive to man's thoughts, man's dreams, man's desires. What gets me about *this* life of ours, this San Jose life, is that we kill everything we touch. Talk of the Mongols and the Huns—they were cavaliers compared to us. This is a hideous, empty, desolate land. I see my compatriots through the eyes of my ancestors. I see clean through them—and they're hollow, worm-eaten ..."

I took the bottle of Gevrey-Chambertin and refilled the glasses. There was enough for one good swallow.

"To Napoleon!" I said. "A man who lived life to the fullest."

"Gary, you frighten me sometimes, the way you speak about San Jose. Do you really hate it that much?"

"Maybe it's love," I said. "Inverted love. I don't know."

Tripping Through Silicon Valley: Sacred Elixirs Conference

I crouched over the bar at Gordon Biersch one recent afternoon and shared beers with a Western yogi of many years. We discussed entheogens, psychotropic substances and breathing—none of which I know how to do. Eventually he whipped out a vial of *Salvia divinorum* tincture that he had purchased from a website and then squirted one drop of the stuff underneath his tongue. Right there at the bar. He explained that this particular extract from a psychotropic plant from the Oaxaca region of Mexico is a bona fide legal hallucinogenic. He had never once consumed the extract in a public place, but decided the time was right since I had just given him the lowdown on probably the most interesting conference to hit downtown San Jose in recent years: Sacred Elixirs: Drug Plants in the History of Religions, which takes place in the Montgomery Theater over the weekend of Oct. 22 and 23.

The yogi in question is correct in that *Salvia divinorum* is completely legal. Google it if you wish—there's info everywhere. It's not a party drug like LSD or marijuana. It's something that shamans in Mexico have used in spiritual and/or healing rituals for a few thousand years now. Think self-reflection, meditation or inner peace. The substance is something this yogi implied you might want to ingest while lounging alone among the redwoods or in your millionaire friend's outdoor spa in the hills of Woodside. The yogi, 64, tells me stories of how Salvia makes you much more self-aware, and how it's a cheap ticket to a reality outside the shallow-breathing, three-dimensional lives most people unschooled in yoga lead. The "trip," he says, lasts only 10 to 15 minutes or so, unlike LSD. He calls the stuff "Sister Salvia."

The online user's guide for *Salvia divinorum* says it's for older, mature, more philosophically minded folks, and that it's not addictive whatsoever. The yogi hadn't known about the Sacred Elixirs conference, and instead of scribbling the website down on a cocktail napkin like I would have done, he whipped out a digital voice recorder and uttered a quick sound bite to remind himself.

In order to find out more about the Sacred Elixirs conference, I just had to hook up with the organizer, Welshman Mike Crowley, a former Silicon Valley software engineer who is currently working on a book called *Secret Drugs of Buddhism*. He actually footed the bill for most of the conference himself—there has never anywhere been an academic gathering solely devoted to the role of drugs in religion.

Crowley and I met at a downtown San Jose Starbucks and grabbed an outside table that had just been vacated by four policemen. He argued that scourges of fundamentalist kooks are using religion to stamp out drugs, but the reality of it all is that drugs have been an integral element of all faiths everywhere.

"There's a kind of knee-jerk reaction, an anti-drug message, and it's especially tied to religiosity," he explained. "And one assumes if you're religious, you're against drugs. Well, this is a gross distortion of the historical position. All religions seem to have a favorite drug. In Christianity it's wine. In Hinduism, Shiva devotees, for instance, take cannabis—or marijuana as it's called in this country—except it's drunk as kind of a milkshake."

The Sacred Elixirs conference will feature several renowned speakers. Alexander Schulgin, 81, is probably the foremost psychedelic chemist in the world. "He's discovered about 200 psychedelic drugs," Crowley explained. "And that's about 198 more than most other psychedelic chemists."

Ralph Metzner, one of the earliest LSD researchers, will also make an appearance. John Winslow will host a panel discussion called "What Was Soma?" that explores that sacred psychoactive something-or-other from the Rig Veda of ancient India. There will also be books, artwork, psychoactive plants and entheogenic elixirs available for purchase.

Coming back to *Salvia divinorum*, Crowley was adamant in not recommending it for beginners. "[It's] very, very potent and very, very strange," he said. "If you're going to do it, you need a sitter. Somebody who can sit there with you and make sure that you don't do anything dangerous. It's very unusual for people to actually freak out on it, but it's not unusual for people to try and walk through a door which they see is there but isn't there in reality."

Nashville: 1,000 Points of Live

Every time someone from out of town asks me where to go see some original live music, I have to bite my tongue and explain that there's hardly anywhere in the valley to do so. Maybe three or four places. The emergence throughout the last decade of a mass clientele who prefer DJ clubs and vapid cover bands pretty much slaughtered any chance for original music to flourish here. Wanna be a songwriter? Go somewhere else.

Since it's fruitless to complain, I left town and journeyed straight to a place at the polar opposite end of the live music spectrum from San Jose: Nashville, Tennessee. You see, Nashville has over 1,000 live music venues. Now, to be fair, that includes every dive bar, theater, cafe, coffee shop, restaurant, nightclub, airport, concert hall and more. Wherever you go in Nashville, there's live music, even at 10 in the morning. It really is Music City USA—a songwriter's mecca, as they say. Many an aspiring tunesmith flocks to the city with nothing but a backpack and a guitar, hoping that someday Garth Brooks will pick up one of his songs. Hundreds of songwriters from California have moved to Nashville over the recent years.

The city has several music strips where bands play all night for nothing but tips and beer, just hoping that someone walks in and discovers them. One such joint is Tootsie's Orchid Lounge, probably the most famous country music club in the world. Movies have been filmed in the place. Willie Nelson, Roger Miller, Patsy Cline, Kris Kristofferson, Mel Tillis and Waylon Jennings were some of the original customers in the late '50s and early '60s.

Another legendary joint is the Bluebird Cafe, an intimate place where the audience encircles a small group of performers, who trade off playing their own songs. Cover tunes are not allowed. Seven nights a week, folks pile into this small joint to hear original tunes. Our party ate and drank for a few hours while four musicians took turns belting out their own songs. It turned out one of them was Alan O'Day—the guy who wrote Helen Reddy's "Angie Baby" and who also wrote and sung "Undercover Angel" in 1977. He also played a novelty tune, "Suite California," about California cities washing away in an earthquake, a song that contained the line: "Do you know the way to San Jose/ They say it was here just yesterday."

Now, if you had run into Alan O'Day playing "Undercover Angel" in a restaurant in San Jose, you'd immediately have thought, "Oh, how the mighty have fallen." But not in Nashville. This kind of stuff happens all the time in that city. It's not uncommon to find yourself drinking in a bar with some guy who wrote a few No. 1 smashes for other people—but you have no idea who the guy is.

And of Nashville's 1,000 live music venues, more than 200 of them have music at least four nights a week. So the city got an idea to identify those 200 clubs by installing sculptures of giant guitar picks in front of the clubs. On the picks, it says, "Live Music," so tourists and locals can quickly find the places that showcase original talent on a more regular basis.

Over dinner I told several locals that San Jose has maybe four places that showcase original talent. Their jaws all dropped to the floor in utter bewilderment.

Most of all, Nashville is not just about country music. This is important, as when you mention Nashville, folks who aren't in the know automatically think *Hee Haw*, which is nonsense. The city has blues, rock, metal, gospel and all sorts of stuff. The city has about 10 different equivalents of what used to be San Jose's Cactus Club. Classical music is also widely popular. When the Nashville Symphony Orchestra played at Carnegie Hall a few years ago, 1,100 local fans flew to New York to attend the show. How's that for a music scene?

Comparing San Jose to Nashville would be a thoughtless exercise in futility, so I have to do it. By 2002 estimates, the Nashville area is the 24th largest city in the United States and they have over 1,000 music venues. Here in San Jose, we've all had it beaten over our heads now that S.J. is the 10th largest city in the country, yet there exist about three or four places to see original live music, even on a semiregular basis. People in this valley just don't support it. I told this to some folks in Nashville and they all shook their heads in utter disbelief.

Northside Neighborhood Association

This has been a year of many anniversaries, and one in particular stands out for a few locals. San Jose's Northside Neighborhood Association (NNA) celebrated its 40th anniversary this year. Founded in 1965, it is the city's oldest neighborhood association. Especially nowadays with almost every other 1-square-mile section in San Jose breaking up into its own "neighborhood," the NNA can call itself the granddaddy of them all. Covering the area bounded by Julian on the south, Hedding on the north, Sixth Street on the west and Coyote Creek on the east, the NNA is constantly engaged in some sort of community building effort. They are a community that binds together like Eastman adhesive and bends over backward to improve the neighborhood. They've built gardens, refurbished parks and eradicated blighted areas. They've encouraged family businesses, home improvement and committee-based work. Their website contains a wealth of stories from old-timers and wonderful historical information about the neighborhood, going back almost 100 years. Above all else, the neighborhood is a great locale in which to saunter around and look at all the old houses.

According to their bylaws, the NNA's mission includes many community-boosting endeavors—everything from flea markets to litter removal to other social functions. After listing their goals, their statement says those goals include "any other lawful purpose which generally benefits Northside or its membership."

Speaking of "lawful purposes," my fondest recollection of living in the Northside Neighborhood is back in 1990 when I shared a run-down house near Backesto Park with way too many roommates. A classic example of our maladjusted overgrown-teenage behavior was the VHS movie-switching pranks we used to perpetrate at a local Northside Neighborhood corner market. It was called One Stop's Market. That's right—with an "apostrophe s." The facade said in hand-painted letters: Cold Beers, Hot Movies, *TV Guide Magazine*—as if someone would suddenly pull over and stop in solely because the store sold *TV Guides*. Inside the place you'd find moldy bread, cans of chili with an inch layer of dust on them, and coolers chock-filled with bottles of malt liquor and cheap beer. There was no cold storage in the back of the place whatsoever, so by the time the beer made it to the regular cooler, it tasted like it had sat in the trunk of someone's car for months. One Stop's was your quintessential dive corner market, but it fell by the wayside years ago.

The store's video rental section contributed the most to its diveness. The movies were located off in the back of the store and the porno section had its own side entrance around the corner, through a rickety half-broken door. Back in those days of rental movies in VHS format, usually there would be a small silver sticker with massive adhesive draped over the edge of the tape, warning you to not to remove the sticker under penalty of law. This was to prevent you from simply renting the movie, removing the title labels off the tape and putting them onto a different tape when you returned it—in order to keep the real movie for yourself. None of the rental movies in this Northside Neighborhood market had those preventive silver stickers, so we engaged in movie switcheroos on a regular basis. We'd rent a flick, switch the labels with a spare VHS tape that contained either another movie, news footage or just scrap recordings—and then return the tape. So the next time someone else came in and tried to rent that movie, they'd take home the wrong flick. Since the proprietors knew us as regulars, we simply gave them 2 bucks for each rental and signed a receipt. No ID, no nothing.

I think we did this primarily just to envision the looks on people's faces when they popped the tape in and didn't get what they expected. For example, if someone else rented *Pretty in Pink*, they would get four hours of *Perry Mason* episodes I had recorded years earlier. Sometimes the best pranks are the ones where you don't actually get to see the result, and I guess this was one of those times.

That, along with consuming too much lousy beer from that market over the fall/spring semesters of 1990-1991, is my contribution to the local history of the Northside Neighborhood. Of course, there were endless midnight runs to the righteous liquor stores on 13th Street and a few forgotten nights at the Derby, one of the Northside Neighborhood's best dive bars. To heist the Derby's motto, the Northside Neighborhood is a wonderful down-home place "where friends meet."

George Best in San Jose

George Best, one of the greatest soccer players in the history of the sport, is no longer with us. The Northern Ireland native passed away last Friday after almost two months of hospitalization. Even a controversial 2002 liver transplant could not stop him from drinking and he always said that alcohol was the only adversary he could never beat. He was right.

During his heyday for Manchester United in the latter days of the swinging '60s, Best was universally known as the Fifth Beatle and fans followed him wherever he went. Thousands of 14-year-old girls screamed whenever he touched the ball. The entire concept of the rock-star-millionaire-womanizing-boozing-sports-figure—Best practically invented it. There had never previously been such a flamboyant persona that combined a show business lifestyle with sheer genius on the pitch. He was the first and greatest rock star footballer. The chicks loved him and he did things on the field that no else could do. He was worshipped by millions. You think Dennis Rodman is an "outrageous" celebrity basketball player? Well, Rodman couldn't hold a punk candle to George Best's antics in his day. Upon hearing of Best's passing, Prime Minister Tony Blair even chimed in with a tribute from the road.

But if there was ever such a thing as a flawed genius, that would be George Best, and he was often lambasted for squandering his talent and his money over the years. He was quoted countless times as saying that he spent his millions on women, booze and cars—and that he wasted the rest.

By the time Best came to play for the San Jose Earthquakes of the old North American Soccer League in 1980, he was more than past his prime, but he still showed occasional flashes of incomparable genius. In 1981 he scored a near-impossible, bordering-on-frightening goal that people are still talking about to this day. He was called for a questionable foul and booked for verbally assaulting the ref afterward. Clearly angered at the referee's incompetence, and after *calling the goal in advance*, he took a pass and then went through six Fort Lauderdale players in 25 yards all by himself and blasted home the goal. He even beat one guy twice. Most who attended that match say it was the greatest goal they've ever seen and it was the 1981 NASL goal of the year. For those of us who were at that game, we will never forget that goal, and he himself said it was the best one he ever scored.

Best was on hand when the first Britannia Arms opened up in Cupertino in 1981. In fact, he was usually in the bar 30 minutes before the games most of the time. The famous "George Best Pub Crawl" took place whenever game time drew near and nobody knew where the hell he was. They had to go from bar to bar in search of the guy. Best will be remembered by many locals who are still left from those days, and he had many friends here. But that goal was the fondest memory for so many people. The goal was shown, among several others, in many newsreels after he died.

San Jose was also the place where his first marriage fell apart, due to alcoholism and adultery. In his second autobiography, *Blessed*, Best had this say: "Even if [Angie and I] had a hope of sorting out our life together, it was not going to be in San Jose, which turned out to be the worst place ever for me, in just about every aspect of my life." He also says that San Jose is where he really hit rock bottom. "I hated San Jose and although we had a nice house, which we filled with beautiful furniture, it was situated in the middle of nowhere. And while I tried to help around the house and get things ready for the new arrival [their son], I soon got bored and would head off on another bender. ... And nothing was going to stop me drinking, not even when Angie started hiding the car keys and all our money."

Angie went on to write a book about it all (www.angiebest.com) and their son Calum, who was born here when Best played for San Jose, is now a famous model. After Best left the Quakes, he went back to the U.K. for the 1983 season, but that was it. The last professional goal he ever scored was for the San Jose Earthquakes.

House of Siam

House of Siam on Market Street in San Jose was always the greatest place to surreptitiously rummage around for the lost exotic half of yourself. I say "was" because as of Dec. 1, it's no longer there. The two sisters who ran the joint decided to concentrate primarily on their newer House of Siam locale on Second Street instead. But the memories will live on—for me, primarily, because our particular cabal of troublemakers spent hundreds and hundreds of dollars at House of Siam for most of the '90s. Back in our postgraduate days at SJSU, we were "the crew" or "the boys" at House of Siam during the first few years after they opened. We were the notorious gang who always showed up and spent three hours carrying on at high volume over way-too-spicy food and what was then cheap Thai beer. (Now they charge $4.75 for a Singha. When they first opened in 1993, a Singha was $3.) Many times, folks at the table next to us would move across the restaurant because we were too loud. Then the waitress for that table would walk up and hit me on the head with a serving tray.

It was a quintessential family restaurant, a subtle combination of formality and informality. You always felt like Thai people were the Italians of Southeast Asia whenever you gorged at House of Siam. The owners always came up and talked to you. The newer establishment on Second Street is much more of an upscale place, which is fine, but back during the mid-'90s or so, the original one on Market was the place to be. They would always give some extra special attention to the regular customers, even if those customers were loud, obnoxious, long-haired grad students.

I remember one time in particular. A pal and I were dining at a two-person table near the back door. It was after closing time and we were the only ones left. We had been there two hours, eaten and consumed several beers and we were not going to stop. It turned out they were getting the carpets cleaned after hours that night, so the staff began removing all the tables and chairs. They never once asked us to leave, even when our table was the only one physically left in the building. The entire place was empty, literally, except for the two of us still sitting at this one table. All the other tables and chairs were moved outside. With my shoulders shrugged and my hands in the air, palms facing upward, I turned to the waitress and said, "What, are you trying to tell us something?"

That was the kind of eatery House of Siam was, and speaking of rummaging around, I just happened to slide into the place last week, in order to witness the aftermath of the dismantling process. Only a few dozen chairs, piles of broken wood and some leftover decorations remained. The owners, Somsamai Perreira and Nuttawee Ritprasert, and I sat there, pondering the past and rehashing old memories. My compadres and I were their favorite customers during those first few years or so, they said. Our group would always insist on the food being so spicy that the entire charade of us dining there turned into a complete spectacle for everyone else. It was theater. I once described their food as "A culinary dominatrix that flogs your taste buds." And as we sat there, the sisters even pulled out a bottle of Singha from the wreckage behind the bar and gave it to me. Yep, I drank the last beer at the original House of Siam. If that ain't local flavor, I don't know what is.

Back in the day, we had pretty much codified the dinner arrangements. It was like something you'd see in a spy flick—I'd call a friend and this would be the conversation:

"Hello."

"House of Siam. Seven o'clock."

"I'm there."

"See ya."

Click.

I could go on all night about House of Siam memories—and I have. The place took one straight to Thailand, so much that I just had to go out and purchase a copy of Michael Ziesing's book, I Walked Away: *An Expatriate's Guide to Living Cheaply in Thailand*. One reviewer hailed the author as an "anarcho-Taoist beer-mystic." I like that term. House of Siam brought out the anarcho-Taoist beer-mystic in all of us.

The Secret Steinholders

The Secret Holy Fraternal Order of Gordon Biersch Steinholders convened for a holiday get-together on Tuesday, Dec. 13, 2005, in the Pilsner Room of that brewery on San Fernando Street. The event was not open to the general public, and only Steinholders were allowed to attend. From the street, you'd never even know the Pilsner Room existed, as it's located in a secret sacred celebratory space off the back patio—perfect for such a hush-hush cabal of imbibers like the Steinholders.

The steins themselves are half-liter German-style chalices with pewter lids that you flip open with your thumb. Each Steinholder has his or her name etched into the lid and onto the museum-style cabinet in which the steins are kept behind the bar. You really feel like you've discovered the Holy Grail itself when the bartender opens the cabinet and pulls the stein off the shelf—the shelf with your name on it.

Whenever an out-of-towner or a nonregular arrives at the brewery, he or she always asks, "How do I get one of those?" What no one seems to understand is that no one will ever answer that question because nobody really knows. Those of us who have the steins just give whatever fake answer we can think of whenever someone asks us. One Steinholder might facetiously say, "You have to spend at least $10,000 a year at the bar in order to get one." Another might say, "We don't know. The bartenders all have to get permission from the supreme grand master of the San Fernando Street chapter of the West Coast Lodge of the Secret Holy Brotherhood of Steinholders." My particular response is usually, "You must have traced your bloodline all the way back through Charlemagne, Fulk the Black, Godfrey de Bouillon and eventually Jesus Christ and Mary Magdalene"—which I've actually done, on my mom's side. (I can't vouch for its accuracy, of course, but the need for mystery is always greater than the need for an answer, as Ken Kesey always said.)

Thus, the mere mortals dining at Gordon Biersch always depart the place pondering just who the hell these Steinholders are, which is precisely the intention. As I've always said, if you can make it look like you're important, then that's actually more important than being important. And only a few people in Palo Alto are blessed with secret knowledge about the exact origins of the Steinholders themselves. I have no idea. Maybe it goes all the way back to the mystery schools of ancient Egypt—like the Rosicrucians.

But we do know that Gordon Biersch first opened in Palo Alto in 1988 and that the San Jose locale emerged in 1990. There exist Steinholders who have been there ever since. The private get-together last week found several of them gathered around tables in the Pilsner Room, clutching their lager-filled Holy Grails like the grog-swilling monks of Thélème Abbey in François Rabelais' debaucherous Renaissance classic, *Gargantua and Pantagruel*. The lager flowed and the food just kept on coming. The only thing missing was a harem.

This is exactly what Silicon Valley needs more of: secret grog-swilling cabals dedicated to celebrating the pleasures of uninhibited excess. We need to revive Sir Francis Dashwood's Hell-Fire Club, a.k.a. The Monks of Medmenham, those 18th-century dilettantes who gathered in satirical meetings to rejoice in all forms of licentiousness and to ridicule all religious morals of the current day. Rabelais provided the main influence, of course.

The Steinholder parties take one right back to those times and even further back to the Thélème Abbey itself, that fictional place in Rabelais' novel where, upon the portal, it said, fay ce que vouldras, or "Do as you will." And, throughout the course of last week's Steinholder party, no one else in the entire restaurant even knew that way back out there in the Pilsner room, the Secret Holy Fraternal Order of Gordon Biersch Steinholders were tipping their chalices and filling their bellies in pure Rabelaisian fashion. A classic exchange from *Gargantua and Pantagruel* adequately sums it up:

"Here boy, be a good lad, please, and fill her up."
"Crown here till she's cardinal red on top."
"*Natura abhorret vacuum.* Nature abhors a vacuum."
"Do you think a fly would find any leavings here?"
"Breton fashion, bottoms up!"
"Fall to! Don't leave a drop!"
"Gulp it down; it's medicine!"

Spies and Shibumi

Trevanian, author of *The Eiger Sanction, Shibumi* and *The Summer of Katya*, is no longer with us. He died on Dec. 14 in London. Even when he was alive, no one knew who he was, because Trevanian was merely a pseudonym. Rodney Whitaker was his real name, and he published both fiction and nonfiction under multiple pen names. He may be the only person who can claim to have sold millions of books worldwide without making one single promotional appearance or doing one single booksigning or live interview. The editor of Trevanian's website (www.trevanian.com) had this to say: "There are few geniuses in the world and now there is one less." Due to the wildly divergent genres of both his fiction and nonfiction, a myth eventually developed that the books were all written by a group of authors under the same pen name. But, alas, it was only a myth.

Trevanian never explored the same genre more than once, and those who are old enough to have followed his career from beginning (I'm not) always waited in anticipation to see what the hell he was going to write about next. His first novel to infiltrate the general public was *The Eiger Sanction* back in the '70s, and hardly anyone realized it was actually a spoof. However, for many of us, his 1979 international espionage masterpiece, *Shibumi*, was the real deal and is by far the most revered book among his fans. There was so much deep philosophical material buried among *Shibumi*'s myriad threads that it went completely over the heads of some who read it as just a straight-up spy novel.

The main character is Nicholai Hel, born of Russian and German parents but raised in Japan during World War II. The quintessential part-Eastern-part-Western anti-hero, Hel strives to be the world's most artful lover and the world's highest paid assassin—all to achieve Shibumi, an untranslatable Japanese concept referring to the understated beauty that underlies everything in life. It represents an active spiritual tranquility, a personality of overwhelming calm, an effortless state of perfection and a natural urge to find harmony in all action. You can apply it to chess, ikebana flower arranging, martial arts or gardening. Hel applies it to assassination, and in the novel a supermonolith of international espionage known only as the Mother Company is trying to take him out. Hel lives in a Basque village in the Pyrenees with an expensive concubine and hangs out with all sorts of bizarre, unforgettable characters. Sounds like fun, doesn't it? The book is a vulgar, nasty, sarcastic, politically incorrect and downright glorious assault on the status quo, all of Western civilization and global capitalist sleaze, while functioning as top-notch espionage fiction at the same time. It's a perfect example of how a character with both Eastern and Western roots has a totally different perspective on the world.

Of course, many folks hated the book—primarily because it didn't fit into any one classifiable genre and therefore shattered their expectations—but it nailed several world issues that continue to dominate the landscape: the rise of the military-industrial complex, national government corruption, bumbling intelligence services and the Western idiocy of looking at the world in a black-or-white fashion.

Basically, *Shibumi* was an ingenious spoof of itself. Like the movie American Beauty, the characters were deliberately exaggerated and, as a whole, many folks just don't go for elitism as black humor. Trevanian had this to say about the book: "After the definitive exercise of the genre that was *Shibumi*, there was no point in me writing further in this genre … or anyone else, for that matter."

How does all this relate to Silicon Valley? It doesn't, except that I spent many a long Sunday afternoon over beers discussing *Shibumi* with a certain bearded Vietnam veteran who is now '86ed from nearly every bar in downtown San Jose. I'm exactly half Eastern and half Western myself, so I completely identified with the main character, which is why the veteran turned me onto the book in the first place, all those years ago.

You see, Trevanian's fans have always been referred to as The Others and this is what Trevanian himself had to say about them: "The Trevanian Buff is a strange and wonderful creature: an outsider, a natural elitist, not so much a cynic as an idealist mugged by reality, not just one of those who march to a different drummer, but the solo drummer in a parade of one."

2006

Bravo, Taco Bravo

When Katie Bloom's in downtown San Jose finally succumbed to the war on nightlife, Metro exposed the farmer's-town machinations of the Downtown Nightlife Prevention Bureau. But now it looks as if the war on nightlife has shifted to the suburbs, as some pretty shady maneuverings nearly took place over in Campbell. This time, however, nightlife won.

Here's what happened: Twenty puritanical knuckleheads were trying to prevent the legendary late-night eatery Taco Bravo from staying open until 3am. They wanted Campbell's longtime cultural icon to shut its doors at 11pm instead. Blasphemy, I say! The issue came before the City of Campbell Planning Commission on Dec. 13, but the petitioners were not successful.

You see, folks have chowed down on post-midnight grub at Taco Bravo for 30 years now. People come from all over the valley—as far away as Los Gatos—for those late-night come-down-off-the-booze feasts. If any musician or band comes to town, where do you think they go to scarf after the show's over? Taco Bravo. A lot of non-Campbell residents would never even think of visiting that city if it weren't for Taco Bravo. Forcing the place to close at 11pm would destroy the business completely. Everyone knows that. As local celebrity Lex van den Berghe told the *Campbell Reporter*, asking Taco Bravo to close at 11 would be like asking a donut shop to open only after lunch. He also said that when it comes to landmarks in Campbell, more people know Taco Bravo than the water tower or the Ainsley House. He's right. Everybody has a Taco Bravo story of some sort. Don't even get me started ...

In any event, Taco Bravo is one of the most famous bastions of late-night revelry in all of the South Bay. Even in the thriving world-class metropolis of downtown San Jose, you don't find late-night attractions like Taco Bravo. In fact, since downtown San Jose doesn't have many late-night places, some folks take their business to Campbell instead. One Campbell club owner was recently reported as saying something like,

"I hope they keep screwing up downtown San Jose. It just brings more business over here."

The '30s-era gospel tent crusade against Bravo's closing time began over two years ago. "In April of 2003, there was one neighbor back there who complained," said proprietor Dennis Wuollet. "Some police chased one guy from down here—I don't know whether it was from Der Weinerschnitzel or Taco Bravo or anywhere, but they chased him about a block down the street and handcuffed him. So the neighbor got a petition going and stated that he wanted Taco Bravo to close and that no legitimate business should be open after 11. I don't know where he was coming from, but he got 20 people to sign it."

It just makes you wonder what planet such people live on. I guess they just have a little too much time on their hands. I don't know the exact history, but Taco Bravo is pretty much the place that originally spearheaded late-night usage in the entire city of Campbell.

"When I was younger and I first took the place over, we used to go and put fliers on all the cars at the bars and the factory and the Pruneyard, all over, just trying to get a bar rush, because this store was pretty slow," Wuollet said. "And we succeeded. We got some really late-night business and we've been staying open till 3 ever since."

And of course, not one person who signed the petition actually showed up at the Planning Commission meeting.

"I guess it's easy to sign something but then when you have to put your face in front of it, they don't want to do it," Wuollet said.

Instead, Taco Bravo supporters jammed Campbell's City Hall for the meeting on Dec. 13. "We packed the place," Wuollet recalled. "One of the councilmen said, 'This has gotta be a record. I've never seen this many people in this place before.' ... I was amazed at the amount of people that came to support this restaurant. It brought tears to my eyes. I got a little glisteny there. It was just awesome."

Taco Bravo is now on a six-month conditional use permit and it is allowed to stay open until 3am. I applaud all those who showed up to the Planning Commission meeting on Taco Bravo's behalf. Wiser heads apparently prevailed. In the constant war on nightlife, this was one battle that just had to be won. Long live Taco Bravo!

The Lawrence Hotel

One of the greatest archaeological digs one can possibly perform in San Jose is not even underground. It's in the second story of the Lawrence Hotel building, located at 69-81 E. San Fernando St., above Cinebar and Stratta, and where Inca Gardens, Mandrake Shoe Repair and Twice Read Books used to be. Twice Read Books closed down in 2004 after nearly an 80-year run, and those who remember the place know it was literally a labyrinth of stuff. A zillion books stocked the homemade shelves.

But guess what? The old Lawrence Hotel upstairs, which later became the Lawrence Apartments (basically a flophouse), contains to this day even more books than were actually in the bookstore when it existed. Twice Read Books' previous owner, Craig Thush, also owned the entire building, and touring the place is like a twisted step back in time while doubling as a keen insight into how he organized all the books. The building itself is a 30-room former hotel dating back to the late 19th century, and now looks like a dilapidated miniversion of the Winchester Mystery House. The entire place is a maze of doorways, aisles, leaky roofs, peeling walls, bizarre cupboards, broken plumbing, furniture and garbage. And there are boxes of books and magazines in every room, piled halfway to the ceiling. You could get lost in the place.

One enters from a locked stairway that empties out onto the sidewalk right next door to Twice Read Books. When you get to the top of the stairway, your jaw drops to the floor and you just gaze around in utter amazement. One room might contain boxes of old *Playboys* from the '60s, while another might house 600 copies of *Popular Mechanics* from the '50s. There are thousands and thousands of books—all kinds.

William Cureton, uncle of Malcolm Durham, one of the new owners, showed me around one fine afternoon—a tour that should be included in every brochure of the San Jose Convention & Visitors Bureau. For example: One particular cabinet door still holds the original manager's keys to all the rooms. Tacked to the door one finds a typewritten note dated Nov. 29, 1974, warning the manager not to rent a room to one Earl Julian Moncrief who was known for passing bad checks. One particular room, mostly filled with vinyl LPs and sports magazines, overlooks San Fernando, and you can tell it was used for the manager's office because there's a small square window overlooking the stairway. "It was so they could see who's coming up the stairs," Cureton explained. Another room facing San Fernando contains boxes and boxes of books along with a few old couches and chairs. If the window actually opened, you could reach out and touch the neon Cinebar sign. Some of the rooms are so dark that you can't even see anything. Others are illuminated by skylights.

Cureton is working in the building on a purely voluntary basis to help liquidate some of the books. When I was there, he had just boxed up a set of 20 paperback porno novels from the '70s that someone had paid $170 for. There was also a box of 25 incest paperbacks from the '70s that I was going to offer him 10 bucks for, but after hearing the $170 figure, I didn't even bother.

After continued navigation through all the mysterious hallways of books, suddenly another man emerged from around the corner, scaring the hell out of me. I didn't even know he was there. "This is only half of the books that were here," he ascertained.

Twice Read Books was an institution in San Jose, but it was always hard to shop there since Thush had a ridiculous philosophy of selling items at outrageous prices solely based on how old the items were. I once went in there as a teenager to buy some *Mad books*. He'd pull out a cardboard price list and say that the ones from the '80s were 6 bucks, the ones from the '70s were 8 bucks, and the ones from the '60s were 10 bucks. Or something ridiculous like that. I'd tell him that was insane and I could just go right around the corner to Recycle Books and get them for 75 freakin' cents. Then he'd just throw his hands into the air and rant and rave.

On the way back down the staircase, I asked Cureton if he had any occult books and he said he didn't know. "If I see any, I'll save 'em for you."

Unibroue Synchronicities

According to Ellie Crystal's metaphysical and science website, "Synchronicities are people, places or events that your soul attracts into your life—to help you evolve or to place emphasis on something going on in your life. The more 'consciously aware' you become of how your soul creates, the higher your frequency goes and the faster your soul manifests. Each day your life will become filled with meaningful coincidences—synchronicities—that you have attracted or created in the grid of your experiences in the physical."

I've always been interested in this concept, since several instances have occurred when two people I hadn't seen in years were sitting around talking about me, and then all of a sudden I walked into the scene—whether it was in a restaurant, or at the beach, or whatever. Here's another example, as the Russian newspaper Pravda recently told it: "A ship sunk near the shores of Wales on December 5, 1664. Another ship went down on the same location on December 5, 1785. A third ship sunk to the bottom of the sea on the same location on December 5, 1866. Each of the shipwrecks had only one survivor. In all the three cases, the survivor's name was Hugh Williams."

This topic is on my mind these days because a recent personal synchronicity occurred just a few weeks ago. But in order to explain it, let me first take you to the village of Chambly, Quebec, about 30 miles east of Montreal.

The last time I infiltrated Montreal was September of 2004, and I just had to check out the Unibroue brewery in Chambly, since those famous Belgian-inspired Quebecois brews are some of the best gourmet beers anywhere. In San Jose, you can only get them at Beverages & More and Cost Plus. They are strong and expensive as hell, but well worth it. And they're famous not just for the recipes, but for the elaborately designed labels based on classic Quebecois mythology. For example, the label for their beer, La Fin Du Monde—which translates as "The end of the world"—features a glowing relief map of Quebec and is dedicated to the great explorers, who believed they had reached the end of the world when they discovered Quebec. And Unibroue's masterpiece brew Maudite—which translates as "the damned one"—features a smiling Satan against a red backdrop of passengers in a flying canoe. An ancient Quebecois legend has it that a group of lumberjacks struck a deal with the devil to fly home in their canoes, guided by Satan himself, to make it home in time for Christmas.

The folks at Tourisme Québec set me up with a tour, and the folks at the brewery told me I was the only American journalist who had even been granted a solo tour of the place. But, by far the most bizarre fact I learned was that a Pakistani guy, Asaf Mirza, is the one who designs these elaborate labels. There we were, in Chambly, Quebec—where everyone is French-Canadian and there are no minorities anywhere—and it's a Pakistani chap who's behind these magnificent and highly creative labels. No one in Quebec even knows who this guy is, let alone in the United States.

And then one day a few Saturdays ago, I was sitting around in a San Jose bar over a glass of Pyramid Snowcap—one of my faves—and the subject of gourmet beer came up. As soon as I mentioned Unibroue, the woman sitting next to me turned and said, "Oh yeah, my dad's the one who designs the labels."

My jaw dropped. I looked at her incredulously and said, "What? You're kidding."

"I'm not," she said. "Asaf Mirza."

"I've been to your dad's office," I said, blown away.

She was equally incredulous and it turns out she lives in Morgan Hill. It was the craziest synchronicity I've ever experienced. It is said there are no coincidences. This mind-blowing occurrence was something beyond the laws of nature. I know it.

Robert Mueller Comes to San Jose

The past, present and future of information security descended upon San Jose last week via the RSA Conference at the McEnery Convention Center. If you're even remotely interested in cybercrime or the future of crime in general, this was the place to be, as the annual gathering is possibly the hugest get-together for industry professionals who deal with cryptography, network protection, crime-over-IP and more.

One of the initial highlights was Bill Gates calling for the end of passwords. The gist of his speech was that the future of the Internet will see it functioning as a "trust ecosystem" and, by then, "multifactor authentication" will have replaced passwords, making everything more secure somehow.

But Gates was not the most powerful man present. FBI director Robert Mueller spoke at a town hall meeting titled "Top Cops Versus Cyber Criminals," which took place in the Civic Auditorium. That Mueller himself actually showed up to this event is curious enough. At the talk, convention delegates jammed the floor while Secret Service chaps with spiral phone cords in their ears oversaw the action from the balcony level. Robert Holleyman, president and CEO of the Business Software Alliance, introduced Mueller and said that that cybercrime is the FBI's No. 3 priority after terrorism and counterintelligence. Mueller then took the stage and said that the FBI's work has changed dramatically with the rise of cybercrime. "Information technology has become a force-multiplier for criminals," he declared, "from online fraud to exploitation to identity theft. And with the advent of the information age, our world has become smaller, our world has become smarter, but the threats we face have become equally more diverse, equally more dangerous. Cyberspace has been likened by some to the Wild West—an open and largely unprotected frontier with seemingly limitless opportunities. Like any new frontier, there will be those who seek to stake their claims, whether by legal means or by illegal means. Like the outlaws of the Wild West, the outlaws of this new world operate without boundaries and without barriers. And they are moving as fast and as far as the technology will take them."

To "show how far we've come," Mueller then recalled one specific case from when he was working as a prosecutor in the U.S. attorney's office in San Francisco. A hacker had broken into the network of a high-tech company and had unleashed a "zombie" attack—using that network to target other computers. Mueller then wanted the FBI to monitor the company's system—with their permission—in case the intruder showed up again. But, at that time, according to Department of Justice policy, the FBI was not allowed to do that. Since the situation required them to move immediately without delay, Mueller became frustrated with the DOJ bureaucracy. He said that, now, thanks to the Patriot Act, the FBI can now go ahead and do this without the court order—as long as the company grants them permission. It just makes you wonder ...

After concluding his speech, Mueller exited the stage and didn't stay around to take any questions. The town hall panel session followed and featured three guests who did take questions, including Arif Alikhan, senior counsel to the deputy attorney general at the DOJ, where he oversees the Computer Hacking and Intellectual Property Program. He explained that cybercrime is getting much more organized. Now that we're in an Internet marketplace, cybercrime is a much more lucrative business.

Back at the conference, at one booth on the exhibition floor, one got a chance to see the past of code-breaking and cryptography. Jennifer Wilcox, assistant curator of the National Cryptologic Museum, showed off an original Enigma encryption machine—the one used by the Germans in World War II. The all-seeing emblem of the National Security Agency adorned the barrier behind her. Since I myself have never been secure, I eventually left the convention floor. But it was a damn good show, and one with a hell of a lot of security.

Larry Tritten: Writing for a Living

This time, the lurid yarn actually begins in the year 2000, or somewhere around there. At that juncture, I found myself plunging toward the point where I would have no steady income except for a few periodic freelance writing gigs. And that's when the synchronicity happened.

As I sat around depressed at the prospect of being a fulltime freelance writer, constantly pitching story ideas to a billion different outlets on a daily basis, a friend told me that the first piece Stephen King ever published was a porno story for Swank. So, to cheer myself up, I went down to the liquor store and snagged an issue of Swank for further research. I got home and for some reason threw the mag on the futon without even opening it up.

Later that day, I found myself reading an article in *Writer's Digest* penned by San Francisco-based Larry Tritten, a veteran freelance writer whose byline has appeared in so many publications that it's impossible to keep track of them all. In the article, Tritten emphasized the wide variety of places that he's published—for example, he had just done some porno fiction for Swank as well as an informative nonfiction piece for a pet-related magazine. *Writer's Digest* slapped this bio statement onto the end of the article: "Larry Tritten has written on just about everything and has been published just about everywhere."

I pondered that sentence for quite some time. The comic strip bubble appeared in the air above my head and I thought, "Yeah! Someday I want to be able to say that." So this became one of my goals in life, and later that evening I cracked open the issue of *Swank*, only to discover that it contained the same exact story by Tritten that he had mentioned in the *Writer's Digest* article. Whoa, I thought. However inconsequential, this synchronicity was a defining moment in my decision to pursue writing as a career. I felt that somebody somewhere was trying to tell me something.

I'm only relaying this information now because I just recently crossed paths with Mr. Tritten, as we were both part of a pocket-size cabal of travel writers congregating in Vancouver, British Columbia. I ambushed him with this anecdote over dinner at O'Doul's, an upscale jazz restaurant. I told him he was an influence. He then recalled that he sold his first piece in 1960 for $100 and it was like being bitten by a vampire. He became a writer and never went back. I can relate, so I concurred by quoting Bukowski: "You don't choose writing. It chooses you."

Turns out Mr. Tritten is also a walking encyclopedia of word history, as he writes for a quarterly etymological journal. As we each devoured a 10-ounce rib eye with brandy and peppercorn sauce, he explained that the word "travel" can be traced back to the French word travail which has something to do with toil or labor. The word was meant to describe the performance of a laborious or tortuous task. (So, if you're considering being a travel writer, you might want to think again. It's not just, "Me and Aunt Helen went to the Uffizi," or whatever. It should involve some seriously tortuous self-reflection.)

The next afternoon we infiltrated Wild Rice, a swank Chinese fusion eatery in Vancouver's Chinatown. As we devoured plates of wild boar braised in rice wine, maltose sugar and autumn spices, Tritten informed us that the word avocado can be traced back to the Nahuatl word *ahuakatl*, which means "testicle." Now that's useful information.

Later, on the ferry to Victoria, we talked about the freelance writing life and I shared Tritten's concerns that a growing amount of people just don't have the attention span for narrative text anymore when it comes to mainstream magazines. If you open up one of those lad mags like *Maxim*, it's mostly graphic-based articles and lowest-common-denominator twaddle like, "Five ways to steal your buddy's girlfriend." What's a full-time freelance writer to do? Tritten says he will carry on as he always has, since he wouldn't know what to do if he wasn't a fulltime writer. It's all he's ever done.

Back in San Jose, I contemplated all this over cheap beers at a dive bar. I agree with Tritten. At this juncture in time, I just have to write.

Verbal Abuse Rocks Your Liver

Last week the *San Francisco Chronicle* ran a schmaltzy, syrupy lamentation stating that this year is the 25th anniversary of Journey's Escape album. They called that slab "one of the most popular records produced by a Bay Area band." With slap-happy tippy-toe euphoria, several fans chimed in with their own sugar-coated recollections of who made out with whom during "Open Arms" or who cruised in his vintage Buick while blasting "Don't Stop Believin'." Apparently the memories are endless.

Speaking of memories, allow me to willfully debase this entire dialogue by recalling another Bay Area band who are celebrating a similar anniversary this year. Booze-fueled punk rock legends Verbal Abuse are rereleasing their seminal 1986 classic album, *Verbal Abuse Rocks Your Liver*. This is the one whose cover featured a gorgeous full color hand-drawing of the band members as rats wearing denim vests, sitting around a table getting hammered at 491 Guerrero in San Francisco, an address that actually makes an appearance in one of the tracks.

Now, this was not the original incarnation of the band, as a slightly different assemblage of sots made noise in the early '80s, but since I didn't stumble into the fold until way later, my memories of Verbal Abuse gigs come from the late '80s. *The Rocks Your Liver* album was a prime mover for me during a very trying time of my unstable late-teenage youth. If all these folks can carry on about Journey's Escape album, I can definitely seethe poetic about *VA Rocks Your Liver*, which has now been remastered.

VA dive-bombed upon San Jose one particular time in the late '80s, playing at a dump on Coleman Avenue called the Stagecoach Inn. Hardly a sober person was in the establishment. During their infamous cover of the Elton John tune, "Saturday Night's Alright (For Fighting)", instead of singing the refrain, "Saturday, Saturday, SATurday," frontman Scott Wilkins screamed, "San Jose, San Jose, SAAAAN Jose." Facetiously speaking, it was the first time I ever felt proud to be a San Josean and I have Scott to thank for it, in some insane way.

I saw those guys here and in San Francisco, Oakland and Berkeley many times, and one time I even drove from San Jose all the way to Nevada City, near Grass Valley, just to see one of their gigs. It wasn't that I was a lunatic stalker or anything. I was just a dorky fan who had nothing else to do that day and the few friends I had weren't around, so I impulsively took off and went. I got blasted with the band afterward and I wound up driving behind their painted-black ice cream truck back down the freeway toward S.F. But I didn't make it all the way. They ended up offloading me at the Denny's in Davis, where I crashed out with my face and arms down on the counter—an image perfectly depicting the aftermath of a Verbal Abuse gig.

Then there was the time when they opened up for Motorhead at the Omni in Oakland. To steal a phrase from *Sanford and Son*, I got so carried away, I had to be carried away. A few years before that, there was a gig at Pony Express Pizza in Redwood City, a place about the size of my cubicle. The band played, literally, right in our faces.

All this came at a time—and here comes my equivalent of the schmaltzy syrupy part—when I really didn't know what I wanted to do in life. My father had died a few years earlier and I was a self-destructive monster in my late teens who didn't care if he even lived to be able to drink legally. And I played that album to death. This was also at a time when punk was "crossing over" with metal, a phenomenon that people on both sides are still complaining about. Verbal Abuse was right in the middle of it all and I had a blast during those days.

So there you have it. You can quack all you want about how you conceived your kid while playing Journey's *Escape album*. 2006 is the twentieth anniversary of *Verbal Abuse Rocks Your Liver* and I have my own dark demons to commemorate. Cheers.

24th Street Rocks

The stretch of McLaughlin Avenue that becomes 24th Street going north from 280 to Santa Clara Street should be in every brochure of the San Jose Convention and Visitors Bureau. It beats out Bonfante Gardens and the Niles Canyon Railway by a landslide. Whoever wins the District 3 City Council race should dedicate a monument to the cross-section of San Jose culture that this promenade exudes. Visitors from as far away as Story and King might come check it out.

I descended upon the locale just last week and couldn't stop scribbling down details on the ambience of the entire surroundings. The voyage began at 527 McLaughlin: a place called San Jose Trailer Park, which dates back to 1937. Rundown mobile homes dot the landscape, trash overflows out of the dumpsters and beat-up '80s minivans abound. Since placards inside warned that the locale is monitored by electronic surveillance, I escaped back out to McLaughlin and my gaze went straight to an old Hispanic man with crutches who was waiting for the 72 across the street. He had a neat cowboy hat.

Venturing northbound on McLaughlin, one finds a few taquerias, Laundromats and a dive car wash before it turns into 24th Street. There you see a classic strip mall with nothing but Mexican places, oddly titled Grewal Center—Grewal being a Punjabi surname. Then you have a few auto repair places and tire shops that precede the railroad tracks. A glaring sign warns, "Tracks out of service." I glanced down the tracks and watched two guys walking along them until they disappeared over the horizon. Everyone knows that defunct railroad tracks are an integral part of any urban exploration.

As the glaring sun beat down on the pavement, I then found myself at Clean Carts Sales and Service, an industrial yard filled with nothing but hundreds of shopping carts, all painstakingly organized in tidy rows. A yellow Penske rental truck was dropping off more carts, and they crashed to the ground as they fell off the lift-gate. Only then was I distracted by a young Mexican girl walking down 24th Street in a skimpy white shirt that said, "Midnight Cowgirl."

Continuing north toward Santa Clara Street takes you through a more residential neighborhood where neatly restored Victorian homes are juxtaposed with dive apartments. And then, like a diamond in the rough, as you approach Santa Clara, you find brand spanking-new cookie cutter condos right across the street from an old shack that houses an ice cream vendor operation—you know, those Hispanic guys who push the carts around with bells ringing.

Finally, when you hit Santa Clara, you have Ponderosa Westernwear, a few Mexican restaurants and a rundown building with piñatas hanging in front that houses a party supply shop. Then, all you have to do is segue left and you'll hit Al's Furniture with some Chinese characters on the sign, and a Vietnamese eatery called Binh Minh with white bars on the window. Man, what a rocking neighborhood.

You see, people in San Jose just aren't interested in urban exploration anymore. They think having to walk four blocks to go somewhere is an arduous task. Since San Jose is basically 30 small towns duct-taped together, no one really goes out of their way to explore other parts of the city besides their own neighborhood. As I've said, nobody in Evergreen cares what goes on in Willow Glen and nobody at Foxworthy and Meridian gives a rat's ass about 24th Street. I once got an email from someone who said she hadn't been downtown in 30 years. That blew me away.

The politicians must decide whether or not this is all a good thing for the future of the 10th largest city in the United States. Whoever becomes mayor must figure out what to do with the wreckage of suburban sprawl that he or she will inherit.

And because of that sprawl, it seems like every other block has its own freakin' "neighborhood organization." And, yes, there actually exists a 24th Street Neighborhood Association. They meet on the second Tuesday of every month and apparently it begins with a potluck from 6:30 to 7pm. What a merry-making bash that must be. I just might check it out myself.

Tour the Underbelly With Lisa Dewey

Local musician, songwriter and celebrity Lisa Dewey runs her own sightseeing tours of San Jose because she's sick and tired of listening to her friends from out of town bash the place. At her home recording studio, she's hosted folks from as far away as Germany and taken them on explorations of what she calls "cool industrial wacky way-old-school San Jose stuff." That could mean dilapidated buildings in Japantown, the former site of the old brick roundhouse where Lenzen Avenue meets the railroad tracks or a hill at the Heritage Rose Garden just south of the airport. That last particular mound of grass, she told me, used to be a great place to bring a girl on a date, drink wine, chew tobacco and just get wrecked. As we stood on that mound, she pointed across the street to where a large oak tree used to be and complained that it was no longer there. She said she used to visit this mound, lie back and watch the planes fly immediately overhead. "It sounded like *Star Wars*," she recalled.

Now—full disclosure—Lisa and I go way, way back. We both graduated with music degrees at SJSU in the spring of 1994. I was in her senior recital and she was in mine. We also had three mutual friends pass away in a short amount of time during those days—a sequence of events that still lingers in both our psyches.

These days she has her own record label, Kitchen Whore Records, and several bands have rocked out at the 24-track recording studio in her house, which she calls the Dewey Compound. She has at least four albums out and has toured all over the country numerous times but remains steadfastly cemented in San Jose. If people can walk around Manhattan talking about a local place that made it into a Suzanne Vega song, then I can definitely have Lisa Dewey drive me around while we explore the bowels of San Jose. Also—and this is a another thing I always bring up whenever I run into her fans—on Oct. 28, 1993, I had Lisa onstage in a ski mask, while a dozen of us took sledgehammers to an amplified Honda Civic.

Dewey's tour of San Jose's underbelly took me mostly between and around downtown and Willow Glen. Turns out one of her favorite buildings is a ramshackle rundown heap on Sixth Street in Japantown. "The architecture in Japantown is very interesting," she said. Another main stop on Dewey's tour is the industrial wasteland that inhabits Bassett Street just west of Highway 87. Proceeding north on Terraine Street from the Fallon Statue, one is taken past empty warehouses, vacant lots, chain-link fences and weeds. Turning left underneath Highway 87 onto Bassett, the road ends at what has to be one of the best deadend streets in all of San Jose. There you can feast your eyes upon an old brick building that used to be the warehouse for Hart's Department Store—probably about 40 years ago. In fact, on the back of the building facing the railroad tracks, it still says "Hart's. San Jose's Big Department Store. Warehouse No. 2." You can either see this from the freeway if you're driving south on 87, or you can walk back behind the place and check it out, while segueing from the broken car parts, tires, rusty machinery, unearthed tree stumps and piles of clothes. The tour also includes a site inspection of the Dewey Compound itself, a place with two black cats and a '58 Chevy pickup. I was going to ask to see the bedroom, but I chickened out.

Throughout our tour, Lisa could not stop complaining about the driving habits of everyone else on the streets of our hometown. She constantly cussed everyone out. "The drivers in San Jose have gotten progressively worse," she said as we exited 280 onto Bird Avenue, headed toward Willow Glen, our final destination. We wound up kicking it at Taqueria Tlaquepaque No. 2 at the desolate intersection of Willow and Delmas. Even though she owns real estate, Lisa says she still likes to take dates to cheap taquerias. And her band, Lisa Dewey & the Lotus Life, will headline the San Jose Gay Pride Festival on Sunday, June 11.

Bret Michaels Live at Gordon Biersch

Bret Michaels, lead singer of the seminal '80s hair-metal band Poison, descended upon San Jose a month ago with his own solo band to play at a superprivate party. The restaurant where it all went down shall go unnamed and, as far as I know, I was the only member of the general public to infiltrate the event. I conned the general manager into sneaking me through the kitchen and into the section of the property where the show took place. The entire event had been planned for quite a while, and the gig was kept so under wraps that even the employees of the restaurant were not allowed to attend. Arena-style security goons decked out in yellow polo shirts lurked everywhere and black drapes blocked off any possible view from outside.

But here's the real love story: The aforementioned general manager told me that the party was thrown by a woman for her husband's 40th birthday. Poison was her husband's favorite group from the '80s, so she apparently flew in Bret Michaels just for the occasion. Even though only about 60 people comprised this party, the band spent all afternoon loading in all the goods: a lighting truss, two Marshall stacks and a 48-channel soundboard just for the monitor mix. And they spent a few hours doing an arenalike sound check. You just wanted to scream, "Dude! There's only going to be about 60 people here. Why do you need all this equipment?" And during the show, folks crowded the stage and threw their hands into the air just like at an arena show as Michaels held his microphone into the small group so they could sing along.

But that's rock & roll and that's definitely '80s hair-metal. To all the Poison fans in Silicon Valley, I have this to say: I hope you are thoroughly crushed that you missed this intimate gig. I was there and you were not and I hate this freakin' music.

Michaels played all the Poison classics plus a bunch of '70s rock covers. He even did "Sweet Home Alabama"—one of the most overplayed songs in human history—and he did it *twice*. He also announced the Poison Twentieth Anniversary Tour, which hits the Chronicle Pavilion on June 30. Personally, I can't think of anything in the world more unnecessary than a "Poison Twentieth Anniversary Tour," but I guess there exist folks who will show up.

To see Mr. Michaels at a private party was a prime experience indeed. Even if you despise the music, he's a seasoned frontman who knows how to rock out and please the crowd. His website even says this: "Michaels, Poison front man and primary singer/songwriter, and a lifelong juvenile diabetic, has survived 20 years in the entertainment business. He has not only sold over 22 million records and had fifteen top 40 singles. After nineteen years and twelve albums, he continues to sell out arenas and amphitheaters worldwide."

At the party, Michaels also announced that on Poison's 20th anniversary tour, they will be playing the ancient Grand Funk Railroad tune, "We're an American Band," a track that Bay Area punk legends Verbal Abuse covered with 8,000 times more balls and grit 24 years ago—and, ironically, a band I had just written about a week before I showed up at this secret Bret Michaels gig.

On the good side, at least Michaels has finally given up the '80s glam metal look—the pink lipstick and a hairdo that looks like it was done in a washing machine. Now, apparently, he's a cowboy and crossing over into the country realm ("Every Rose Has Its Thorn" does not count, and you know it). It just makes you want to say: Jesus Christ, the inhumanity of it all.

Lastly, for this private gig, one good thing is that the band did not supply a ridiculous rider asking for no brown M&Ms the way Van Halen notoriously did back in the day. The event planner at the restaurant told me that all the band required was beer and food. And at the party, both were both indeed plentiful. Unfortunately, I walked out with that dim-witted turd of a song "Unskinny Bop" stuck in my head for weeks. Thank you, Bret Michaels, and rock on.

The Ron Gonzales Gong Show at City Hall

Last week, media everywhere reported on the "historic" San Jose City Council meeting where most of the council emotionally asked Mayor Ron Gonzales to throw in the towel. Following Gonzo's recent indictment on several charges including bribery and conspiracy, the councilmembers unleashed a last-minute agenda to thrash out the details of what they should do in case he doesn't resign. More than the usual amount of television cameras, reporters and security guards filled City Hall for this "special meeting." Every possible emotion—joy, sorrow and disgust—was thrown right in your face.

By the time you read this, everyone will already have written, screamed and blogged about it, so allow me to furnish an alternative description of the clown show that this was: You see, back in the '70s, America was blessed with an ingenious TV program called *The Gong Show*. Legendary game show impresario Chuck Barris went out and solicited the worst acts he possibly could, put 'em onstage and paid three celebrities to get drunk and judge the whole thing. If the celebrities deemed an act absolutely atrocious, they would stand up and bash a huge gong, signaling the end of the performance. The concept of the "gong" thus forever ingrained itself in American pop culture.

This special session of the City Council should have been an episode of *The Gong Show*. Here are a few of the highlights: At the onset, Gonzo defiantly declared: "I plan to complete my term as your mayor." One person booed, and one person applauded. About 20 members of the Gonzales family were in the audience and he directed them all to stand up while he explained that this whole ordeal was about preserving the Gonzales family name and the family pride. Someone in the audience immediately yelled, "Save it for the jury!"

As the grumblings from the crowd escalated, the mayor reminded the audience that they must remain quiet until the public session commenced. He then asked his staff to stand up as he bragged that their combined efforts added up to two centuries of public service—a claim about as meaningless as a tag-team pro-wrestling duo being ticketed at a "total combined weight" of 750 pounds.

Councilmember Forrest Williams—one of two along with Madison Nguyen who didn't vote for Gonzo's resignation—went on to compare the efforts of those calling for Ron's removal to the 1933 lynching in St. James Park. I immediately thought, Where's the bloody gong when you need it?

Councilmember Linda LeZotte, on the other hand, did not deserve a gong. In a poignant attack, she told this to Gonzales: "I am judging as I can under the charter your fitness for office and whether or not the 10th largest city in the country deserves a mayor with your obvious lack of judgment and the ability to lead under this cloud. Your refusal to resign speaks volumes about your arrogance, and of your failure to recognize your ethical shortcomings, not about your guilt or your innocence. Today is not about you. It's about what is best for this city. So again I ask you to do the honorable thing and resign, for the good of the citizens of San Jose." Hear, hear!

The public session constituted the main attraction of this episode of *The Gong Show* and many folks actually defended Gonzo, blasting the council for originally assuming they could simply sit down and remove the guy from office. Bill Chew went to the podium, sans the roller skates, and accused the council of being a lynch mob. Several Latinos also took center stage and played the race card, saying things like, "This didn't happen to the last white mayor." The lack of a gong really became apparent when a Bible-thumping zealot took the podium and compared Ron Gonzales' adultery to King David's adultery. He then blasted Gonzo for supporting gay marriage and voting to give health benefits to fornicators.

Lastly, let me point out that a regular on the original *Gong Show* was the Unknown Comic, that famous comedian who wore a paper bag over his head. There's a metaphor here somewhere, although I just don't know what. Let's just redo this whole City Council meeting with Chuck Barris as the emcee. I'll volunteer to be one of the judges.

Grads and Monsters: Annalee Newitz

I first met Annalee Newitz in the summer of 1997 while working on a few crazed treatises in grad school at SJSU. Computer Science professor and science fiction novelist Rudy Rucker sat on my committee, and after I complained to him that no one would listen to all my crazy ideas, he told me to contact Newitz. She had recently interviewed Rucker for her online magazine, Bad Subjects, so he kicked me in her general direction.

"So I'm the one that's supposed to be receptive to all your crazy ideas?" she said over the phone.

"I guess so," I answered.

So I drove my 1970 Plymouth up to Berkeley, where she was working on her Ph.D. dissertation on images of monsters, psychopaths and capitalism in 20th-century American pop culture. Over coffee, we talked about resisting the power of late capitalism by engaging in shadow tactics of ridicule and anonymity inspired by the 19th-century East Indian strangulation cult, the Thugs, in their resistance to authoritarian British colonial rule. Since the Thugs would engage in human sacrifice for the goddess

Kali, I suggested using human sacrifice as a metaphor for artistic expression via transgressive ridicule in cyberspace, and Newitz turned me on to René Girard's *Violence and the Sacred*, a fantastic exploration of the alliance between violence and religion. I still have the notes and flow charts she drew during that conversation. They contain boxes and arrows showing me how to focus the ridicule I was attempting to express in that particular essay. It was precisely this sequence of events—a series of conversations with Rucker and then one with Newitz—that pretty much made me want to be a writer. Yep, it's all their fault.

Why am I weaving this lurid yarn? Because Newitz just published a new book about monsters, apparently the result of her original Ph.D. work. *Pretend We're Dead: Capitalist Monsters in American Pop Culture* argues that the slimy killers and zombies who grace us with their presence in slasher flicks exemplify the brutal contradictions of capitalist culture. She takes example after example from over a century's worth of film creatures and uses them to contend that our capitalist culture turns every single one of us into absolute monsters. It's an academic work, but not so much as to render it unreadable for the masses.

Here's a morsel from the introduction: "In this book, I deal with five types of monsters: serial killers, mad doctors, the undead, robots, and people involved in the media industry." That alone should tell you all you need to know. Newitz supplies a completely unique analysis, one that should elicit the attention of economists, anthropologists, cinema freaks and serial killers alike. Who else would take F. W. Taylor's methods of rationalizing the labor process—where each part of the body functions by itself to perform some routine factory task—and apply it to autonomous decapitated body parts in the movie *Re-Animator*?

It doesn't stop there. In the last chapter, she assails the producers and consumers of mass media and declares them hideous monsters: "We find countless stories about how producers, actors, and directors become cruel demigods; how fans are reduced to mindless zombies who live only to consume mass culture or obey its commands; and even how pop narratives gain the monstrous power to suck people inside their dangerous, fictional realms."

With a book like this, just perusing the bibliography is gratifying in itself. The sheer variety of resources Newitz turned to for this thing is impressive indeed. Who would have imagined seeing *The Red Badge of Courage* in the same bibliography as Michael Heim's *The Erotic Ontology of Cyberspace*? Rudy Rucker even makes an appearance in the chapter on robots, rightfully so. Newitz discusses his original cyberpunk novel *Software*, which came out, ugh, 26 years ago. To celebrate the release of *Pretend We're Dead*, I considered sending Rucker an email with the subject line, "You, me and Annalee," but that sounded too much like a country song, so I abandoned the endeavor.

46

Got Elk?

The San Jose Elks Lodge No. 522 sits on a wonderfully desolate stretch of Alma Avenue. Everyone has driven by the place for years, but no one knows what's inside, so I just had to find out. To begin the adventure, my intrepid guide and I donned Hawaiian shirts and he took me through the parking lot, which doubles as an RV park. About 40 RVs call the place home. There's even a 100-year-old caboose propped up at the far corner of the lot.

Inside, one finds a huge swimming pool, a few bars and furniture that must date back at least 40 years. We enter through the front, the guide using a purple membership card to trigger the door. In the lobby, there's ratty black furniture, '50s décor and dozens of photos of past "Exalted Rulers" dating back to 1899. My guide likens the nomenclature to *The Flintstones*. Then I'm escorted into the "reading lounge," the room where prospective new members go through the questioning process, usually in front of about 15 people. My guide tells me he was inebriated when he went through the process, but he survived.

You see, when you fill out a membership for the San Jose chapter of the Benevolent and Protective Order of Elks of the United States of America, you must answer several questions about yourself. The membership application posted on the Elks' website offers a wealth of puzzling inquiries. Question No. 6 asks this: Are you willing to assume an obligation that: (a) will not conflict with your duties to yourself, or your family, or your religious or political opinions, and that (b) will bind you to uphold the Constitution and laws of the United States of America? Of course, that's only after they ask if you're a citizen of the United States and whether you believe in the existence of God. Other questions pry into your previous residences and ask for the names and addresses of at least two citizens of any city in which you have resided during the last five years, where a Lodge of this Order is located.

As if that wasn't enough, question No. 7 offers a wonderfully convoluted inquiry: Are you now a member of the Communist Party or directly or indirectly connected or affiliated with the Communist Party or with any organization or group advocating or believing in the overthrow of the government of the United States by force?

I wouldn't know how to answer that one, except to say, "Isn't everybody?" My guide tells me that he originally stated on the form that he didn't believe in God, but the Elks called him on the phone and asked if he could change that to say he believed in a higher power. He told me he replied and said, "Sure. If there's a swimming pool and two bars in the place, I'll believe in a higher power."

Along with that pool and two bars, they've got a card room, six pool tables, a Ronald Reagan calendar and a gym that smells like it hasn't been aired out in decades. On the door to the gym, a sign cautions: "Use this facility at your own risk." After leading me into the gym, my guide points to a treadmill that's been sitting in the same state of disrepair for years. "The guy fixing it just got up and vanished into thin air in '95 or so," he explained.

He went on to explain that the Elks are a club for just regular folks. It's not like some stuffy Swim & Racquet club where everyone brags about their social status: "As much as we bitch-slap the place, it's a home where you can come and swim, and drink and hang out. There's some empty bar stools and you can just hang out. No one here's going to ask what kind of car you drive."

Hey—with 25 cent popcorn and a giant elk's head above the juke-box, I think he's right. My guide also said the Elks let him bring how-ever many outside guests as he wants. "This place is for people just like you and me," he continued. "The pool is nice. That's really why we're here. Memorial Day and Labor Day, this place is packed. Aside from that, there's nobody here."

Tom Lehrer's Lunch Spot

In 1965, Tom Lehrer sang these lyrics for a San Francisco audience: "The breakfast garbage that you throw into the bay/ They drink at lunch in San Jose." I didn't come into this world until a few years after that, but I had to recently revive all my Tom Lehrer memories because Theater on San Pedro Square just finished its run of *Tomfoolery*, a theatrical exposi-tion of that singer's classic tunes.

If you don't know who Tom Lehrer is, you should. As early as the late '40s, Tom Lehrer was sitting there at his piano and performing ver-bally acerbic songs that unabashedly ridiculed just about everything. To the annoyance of my mother, my dad turned me on to those records when I was a kid. Whenever I tell people that I grew up listening to Tom Lehrer albums, people always say, "Ah, so that's what happened."

And my Tom Lehrer experiences go all the way back to the Boy Scouts. Troop 347 met every Tuesday in the early '80s in an historic building at the corner of Union Avenue and Los Gatos-Almaden Road. A women's group called We and Our Neighbors owned the place and let our troop use the facilities. An old piano sat inside and since I had started playing by age 9, I always wanted to sit there and tickle the ivories before, during and after the Boy Scout meetings. But the scoutmaster would never let me play the piano because the old ladies who owned the place had instructed him to say that. They understandably didn't want a bunch of kids bashing on the thing and ruining it. But I actually knew how to play, and I tried to explain this, but the scoutmaster wouldn't go for it. A great portion of my comprehensive hatred for the Boy Scouts came from them not letting me play the piano in that building at Union and Los Gatos-Almaden. The building is still there and that blasted piano probably still is, too.

Tom Lehrer factored in the equation because while I was in Boy Scouts, all I wanted was to sit there and play his song, "Be Prepared," on that piano, and they wouldn't let me. You see, that song was a glorious mockery of everything the Boy Scouts have ever stood for, and, at that juncture, I believe I was the only kid my age who had even heard of it, let alone being able to play it on the piano. Lehrer, who's now pushing 80, always said that of all the songs he ever sung, "Be Prepared" was the one he had the most requests not to play. The very first verse tells Boy Scouts to be prepared to hold their liquor pretty well, and not to write naughty words on walls if they can't spell. It also advised a young Boy Scout not to pimp out his sister unless he gets a "good percentage of her price." And then the infamous passage at the end: "If you're looking for adventure of a new and different kind/ And you come across a Girl Scout who is similarly inclined/ Don't be nervous, don't be flustered, don't be scared/ Be prepared!"

That song prepared me for life more than the Boy Scouts of America were ever able to do. And it ignited what was then my natural-born distrust for all authority figures worldwide.

But it wasn't all negative. I had a chemistry teacher in high school who used to play us a Tom Lehrer song called "The Elements," where Lehrer set the names of the chemical elements to a melody by Arthur Sullivan. It was a highly effective way to inflict rote memorization of the periodic table. And the teacher was blown away that I already knew who Tom Lehrer was. He even asked me to loan him the LPs because he had an old cassette copy of the song and wanted to rerecord the albums.

That's right—I was 16 years old and a high school chemistry teacher was asking *me* to loan *him* Tom Lehrer albums. It was one of the first times in my life where I actually respected authority. God bless Tom Lehrer and God bless Theater on San Pedro Square for celebrating one of the most brilliant songwriters in human history.

Surrealism on Stockton Avenue

Ever since RE/Search Publications released their compendium of quotes from world-shattering futurist author J.G. Ballard, I've been turning to that tome for inspiration. So many of his utterances can be mapped onto the terrain of San Jose, especially the chapter dealing with the suburbs.

Since Ballard has always championed Surrealism and the imagination, allow me to insert San Jose where he talks about his own hometown of Shepperton, England: "There are people who are constantly rediscovering the world on a second-by-second basis, for whom every minute is a new excitement. Whether it's a sort of naiveté or not I don't know, but I've always been one of those. I wake up in the morning and look out at San Jose, and I'm always amazed and think, 'What is this?'"

And since some of the best travel writing can be done right in your own hometown, that's what I decided to do. This time the voyage took place on Stockton Avenue, just outside of downtown San Jose.

Stockton Avenue should be in every travel guide to Silicon Valley. Even if you're not interested in thundering airport noise, rundown towing yards, industrial wastelands, dump trucks, dive bars and the Salvation Army like I am, you should get of the house once in a while and explore. Vacate the suburbs and the bedroom communities and have a look-see. It's good for you.

I began my journey where Stockton dead-ends at Emory Street, right behind Bellarmine High School and right at the College Park Caltrain Station, which was mentioned in one of Jack London's novels. It can be a beautifully desolate intersection at times. Graffiti-stained blockades warned me that as of July 2005, Stockton Avenue is permanently closed at this point. The railroad tracks disappeared over the horizon and underneath the freeway. Litter from homeless adventurers completely covered the landscape. Glaring signs warned me not the cross the tracks due to high-speed trains.

Continuing south, I paraded in front of Central Concrete Supply Company, a great place to look at a dozen cherry-red dump trucks getting their fill. The modern dump truck is a masterpiece of 20th-century automotive design. I was so enthralled that I wanted to segue across the street and grab a beer at what used to be a bar called the Shark's Tooth, but it isn't there anymore. It's now a piano-moving warehouse instead. Oh well.

This trek eventually led me to the Salvation Army store at the corner of Taylor and Stockton, another San Jose institution. Across the street, I saw more Royal Coach Tour buses in one place than I've ever seen. They are indeed San Jose's leading shuttle service and their headquarters exists right next to San Jose Boiler Works, who've been serving Northern California with commercial and industrial Boiler Sales, Rentals, Service, Parts and Engineering Assistance since 1922. You just don't see this stuff in travel guides, folks.

After passing by the old rundown location of Renegades, a popular gay bar, I descended upon the most gorgeous eyesore of the entire neighborhood: the archaic dilapidated Westinghouse plant at the corner of Stockton and Julian, a San Jose landmark if ever there was one. It is one of the most elegant examples of unoccupied falling-to-pieces urban decay anywhere in San Jose. I couldn't even tell you what decade it was last open. Go check it out.

Where Stockton hits Santa Clara, I wound up at another masterpiece of urban decay: the former Vietnamese restaurant/barbecue joint that is now fenced off. It went through a zillion incarnations, none of which ever succeeded. The most happening thing on that corner is the cheap car wash across the street.

And if you continue south of there, you can inspect the bowels of the Diridon Caltrain Station: the 6-foot-tall weeds, the gravel, the chain-link fence and the graffiti. And there, Stockton Avenue—and this adventure—ends.

Bad Planning, No Donut

A strip of road that adequately represents a microcosm of all things San Jose is the entire length of Auzerais Avenue, from the Children's Discovery Museum straight over to Meridian. My local travelogue began right there on Auzerais underneath Highway 87, just a stone's throw west of the light rail tracks at the Discovery Museum. I eagerly inspected the fenced-off construction area and all its wonders: Piles of unused steel girders, pallets of wooden planks, heaps of gravel, knocked-over stacks of cones, discarded pieces of rebar, a lone pickup truck and one portable bathroom. What a sight, and the chain-link fence was erected by Thompson & Thompson Fence Company in San Lorenzo. I don't know who the Thompsons are, but I like 'em already.

Venturing westward, I came to the corner of Delmas, where the building that used to house Lou's Living Donut Museum sits. It is a travesty of justice that Lou's is no longer in existence. The only thing gracing the storefront is an untouched rack of *Auto Mercado* magazines.

The next few blocks of Auzerais are highlighted by a few rundown trailers, a panel wagon from the '40s, a slew of dilapidated houses, the San Jose Fire Station No. 30 and a handful of auto repair shops. Continuing, I just had to stop and gawk at a beautiful local market from the old days. The sign above the place says this: Mi Rancho Grocery Beer Wine Vegetables. Someone should do a photography exhibit of dive corner markets in San Jose before they're all gone. Across the street, I just had to feast my eyes upon Janco Welding Supplies, housed in a building that is God knows how old. And at 525 Auzerais, I looked at an unidentifiable building with three blue awnings and a "closed" sign on the door. A glaring red sign on the black iron gate said: Herman's New Location. I know nothing of Herman, but I like him already, too.

After that, one of the best vacant lots in all of San Jose beckoned me over to have a look-see. Like a glove, the 6-foot-tall weeds completely enveloped the broken-down chain-link fence that looked like a truck had backed into it. On the other side of the fence, I saw abandoned cars, empty 12-packs of beer, a shipping container and a rotten wood fence that connected the lot to the dilapidated Victorian next door. Yeah! From there, I just had to keep on trucking across Bird Avenue, past Hitchcock's Construction Lawn And Garden Equipment and the bags of mulch that occupy a section of Orchard Supply Hardware across the street. The water tower from the old Del Monte Cannery stood above it all, beaming down like an ancient relic from the past that just refuses to die.

Just a stroll down the road sits one of the all-time fortresses of old-school San Jose: Paradiso's Delicatessen. I couldn't even tell you what decade it opened, but the Royal Crown Cola sign still holds court out there in front. If that place goes away, I'll blow up the new City Hall.

Now, to clarify: I'm not some crotchety old-timer against all progress—I just believe "development" should just be something that looks and feels freakin' real, for crying out loud. And speaking of that, as soon as I carried on down Auzerais and crossed the creek, the "new days" arrived. KB Homes is putting up yet another gargantuan mess of homogeneous condos. Passing them up without even looking, I passed by some wonderful abandoned warehouses at Sunol and made it to Lincoln, a gorgeous intersection graced by AJ's, the dancing girlie place, and Rossetta's Rain Gutters and Sheet Metal.

Finally, I came to where Auzerais dead-ends into an embarrassing minicity of hideous cookie-cutter condos between Race and Meridian, near where the Saddlerack used to be. I escaped through to Meridian and then segued left into the parking lot of Paramount Imports, where I bought my first music T-shirts 24 years ago. Standing there in that famous long skinny parking lot, looking at the doors of the building behind the place, I gazed at a sign above those doors that perfectly befitted the end of this journey: Lost Horizon.

Rucker's Prime

Los Gatos-based science fiction author Rudy Rucker has a new book out called *Mathematicians in Love* (Tor Books; $24.95) and only he would come up with the following passage: "'Two to the eighty-sixth is the largest power of two that doesn't have any zeros when you write it out in decimal,' said the other cockroach, who'd flopped down on his belly to goggle at Paul, still lying on his surfboard. 'Lemme ask you this. What's the biggest Mersenne prime you got? I'm only asking for the lizard's sake, mind you. My name's Osckar and I'm a hierophantic logician from— whaddya, whaddya, call it Galaxy Z.'"

For 20 years now, Rucker has been tapping out fiction and nonfiction from the Los Gatos Hills, but his work goes all the way back to the late '70s, when he, along with a few other mutant futurists, came up with the "Cyberpunk" subgenre of science fiction. And more than a few times now, he's placed San Jose, Los Gatos and Santa Cruz in his books.

The body of work this dude has produced would take pages to even attempt to describe. Yours truly first accosted Mr. Rucker when he was still at San Jose State University, hacking in C++ and teaching classes in software development. I had an idea for a novel in mind and wanted to consult a freak show of professors to get advice. It was pretty much hanging and talking shop with Rucker that made yours truly want to find a way to utilize my warped multifaceted background and get paid to write about it all.

Three years ago, I penned a cover story for *Metro* about a rerelease of his book *The Hacker and the Ants*, where he sets scenes all over downtown San Jose and Los Gatos. The dumpy apartments lining San Salvador Street across from the university are actually in the book, as is Super Taqueria on Tenth Street, as is the Wells Fargo on North Santa Cruz Avenue in Los Gatos.

We also talked about San Jose in general and used a mathematical artificial-life puzzle called Conway's Game of Life to analyze San Jose's redevelopment strategies for downtown. I don't think there exist two other people on Earth who could have collectively come up with that except Rudy and myself.

But Silicon Alleys this week is not about yours truly, it's about Rudy, as he is reading from *Mathematicians in Love* on Thursday, Jan. 11, at the Capitola Book Café (1475 41st Ave., Capitola), and you should make the trip over the hill. It's worth it. At least the Santa Cruz area can support an independent new bookstore (several, actually)—something San Jose just can't. In these days, when San Jo likes to make it as difficult as possible to run any independent business, whether it's a nightclub or whatever, Santa Cruz should be celebrated, and the town shows up all throughout *Mathematicians in Love*.

As with all of Rucker's writings, *Mathematicians in Love* contains eight zillion different things going on all at the same time, a quality that I share and probably owe to him personally. In this book, you've got deep mathematics, helicopters, time warps, cone shells, punk rock, bat wings, cockroaches, Natural Bridges State Beach, Sanskrit, parallel words, Tarot cards and number theory. And that's just in one freakin' chapter. Which was always the best thing about Rucker's novels anyway: you'd find deep high-tech physics right amid LSD, '60s beatnik radicalism, the counterculture and four-dimensional jellyfishes. Or something like that.

With *Mathematicians in Love,* he takes what's essentially a zonked-out romantic comedy and runs it through the usual Ruckeresque loony mill. No one else can combine Santa Cruz surf culture with cutting-edge mathematics and find some way to ridicule Republicans, all in the same paragraph. And you don't at all have to understand the math to enjoy the story. Rucker is out of town for the holidays, so I didn't want to bug him on his cell, but he would gladly have talked about Java Applets, electric eels, Japanese porn, beach trips, the Pixies, marijuana, the fourth dimension and Los Gatos yuppies—all in the same conversation. All I can do in his behalf is thank him for his inspiration.

2007

The Heather Takeover

A recent advice column in the *Mercury News* ran with a magnificent headline: "Boozy sex is no basis for a solid relationship." To sum it up, someone was chiming in for advice after hanging out with a woman a few times and then going home with her. Describing the predicament, the person said this: "We're obviously attracted to each other but can't seem to take the next step. When we're out drinking and having fun there aren't any barriers, but when that's over, it's back to normal. Should I let this go?" The advice columnist replied, saying that if "normal" is to have nights of drinking, then neither of them is ready for the "next step" in the relationship.

Right or wrong, I just couldn't get that exchange out of my head as I was beckoned into a bar at 10:30am by one of the Heathers, a San Jose-based female boozing club. By now it's not even a "club" any more. It's blossomed into almost a secret society of sorts. Gals in their 20s all over San Jose who like to drink are calling themselves Heathers but they don't even know the original origins.

Over that 10:30am knockback—and the next, and the next—we talked shop, and the Heather in question schooled me on how it all began. She explained that one night a bunch of gals were out on the town getting ruined and they all wound up at an obnoxious ultralounge. She explained that "A bunch of gross guys were hitting on us, so we all used the same fake name: Heather." Thus, the Heathers as a drinking society were born. They even have secret code names for each other, like Deather and Queather, depending on what their real first initials are.

But ultralounges are not the usual locales where you'll find the Heathers. Thankfully, they tend to infiltrate the punk rock crowds, the dive bars and the underbelly places, God bless 'em. If a particular dump serves up extra heavy Jack and Cokes, then you'll find the Heathers, and I have a scary feeling that after this article their membership will either increase or decrease tenfold.

But it's a great story nevertheless. Their blog even contains an application in case you want to date a Heather, saying that they prefer skater guys, tortured artists and dudes with emotional problems. The blog also states that you must be comfortable with all the Heathers making out with each other in a bar, and if you're a commit-o-phobe, then that's a good thing. A scholarly analysis is beyond the scope of this column.

The Heathers have a refreshingly disruptive mind-set, and as I sat there in the bar at 10:30am with that one Heather, we exchanged poignant tales of pranksterism and culture-jamming, especially the Brides of March, a legendary counterculture event that takes place during that month in San Francisco where several folks—men and women—don wedding dresses, go bar-hopping all day and mess with the tourists. It is a gorgeous event. Unlike downtown San Jose, no one needs to cruise up and down the street, blasting their car stereos, harassing women and looking for a fight. Instead, you have peacefully disobedient folks who just want to ridicule all mainstream culture, get tanked and make out with each other in public while wearing wedding dresses. It doesn't get any more wholesome and civilized than that.

In any event, it's safe to say that if I were a female in my 20s, I would join the Heathers immediately. That's right—I'll go out on a controversial limb and encourage it all. Parents, warn your teenage daughters now. It's not a group that you either join or don't join. It's a society. To paraphrase my old prankster pals the Cacophony Society in San Francisco, if you think you want to be a Heather, you may already be a member.

Adrienne Barbeau at Fangoria's Weekend of Horrors

Since this author grew up watching reruns of the '70s sitcom *Maude*, I just had to lurk in the shadows when Adrienne Barbeau rolled back into San Jose a few weeks ago for *Fangoria* magazine's Weekend of Horrors convention. She was filling in for famed horror director George Romero, who had to cancel his appearance, to the dismay of many conference attendees. Why she filled in for him, I'll never know, but since they had worked together on the 1982 flick Creepshow, I'm guessing they've been friends ever since.

Basically, she just sat onstage and had everyone ask her questions, most of which were about what it was like to work with all the people she's worked with in her 40-year career. The event was a blast, and to my knowledge, there had not been a horror convention in San Jose in about 15 years.

Not someone you usually see at horror cons, Barbeau has a long, varied career, and not many people in this neck of the swamp know that she actually went to junior high and high school in San Jose. She began her entertainment career here in the early '60s and went to Foothill College. That alone is worth celebrating.

Sitting there in the audience, I asked her which high school she went to and she said Del Mar. A few groans emanated the crowd, for whatever reason. She said she graduated in 1963 and that her sister still teaches high school somewhere in the Alum Rock district. She briefly talked about Del Mar and how in those days it was considered a flagship school for its time, with a sunken football field, an amphitheater and the whole nine yards. After apparently wondering about the groans, she then asked if the school was still there. We all nodded our heads. That was a weird exchange, I must admit.

Believe it or not, Barbeau has more than enough zonked stories to tell. When she was married to director John Carpenter, she appeared in his 1980 film *The Fog*, and when someone in the crowd asked her if she had seen the remake, she said no, and that she probably wouldn't ever go see it. That brought resounding applause from the audience. Barbeau also played Rizzo in the original stage version of *Grease* in 1972. When someone asked her what she thought of the movie version, she said she'd never even seen it. Again, resounding applause. I have much more respect for horror nerds after witnessing that.

Anyway, you can wax unpoetic all you want about that one scene in *Swamp Thing*, or that famous Barbeau poster, which this author confesses to having owned, or that she had twins at 51, but it is the sheer variety of stuff she's done that merits at least some amount of attention. Her career is absolutely one worth exploring. After all is said and done, any woman who took part in *Cannonball Run, Maude, Creepshow, Fiddler on the Roof, The Match Game, The Drew Carey Show* and *Cannibal Women in the Avocado Jungle of Death* is down in my book. Totally. If I lose friends for fessing up to this, then so be it. Just casually reminiscing about Barbeau's career with the convention attendees made me want to get back onstage and start playing wacky lounge tunes again, which is what I used to do as recently as four years ago.

Last year she released an autobiography titled *There Are Worse Things I Could Do*, which will soon be out in paperback. And what better quote can you find than this: "I went from being a musical comedy performer to a sitcom actress to a scream queen to a mother and a TV talk-show host and a book reviewer and a voice-over performer, and then back to the stage and back to musical comedy and back to television and concert halls and more films, and even into the recording studio for a CD and into my office to write this book." Hallelujah. I guess variety really is the spice of life.

Roberto Tinoco Duran: Our Poet Illaureate

When music professors talk about medieval music, they often tend to downplay the role of the Goliard poets, those vagrant, wandering scholars of the 12th century who, for one reason or another, gave up their training and priesthood in favor of a nomadic lifestyle. They roamed from university to university, gathering their acolytes and singing praises of the flesh and the drink. Deprecated by the church, they were relegated to social outcasts and rambunctious pests.

The Goliards were a diverse bunch at first, ranging from ambitious youths with a lust for learning to stout-hearted men with unsophisticated but crusading hymns. However, as time wore on, an increasing faction of these wandering scholars found the practice of parody more invigorating than mere song. By heisting the Latin staves of the vernacular and changing the words to create songs that celebrated every vice imaginable, their tactics offended the pious in unprecedented degrees. This increased almost exponentially. What began as harmless parody quickly blossomed into vile, blasphemous tactics, designed to bastardize anything ecclesiastic and completely ridicule the authors of all such material. "God Be With You" became "Fraud Be With You." Original texts from sacred masses became springboards for ritualized celebrations of drinking, whores or anything that mocked the liturgical ceremony. These nomadic scholars appropriated the material inflicted upon them and utilized it in a gorgeously unnerving fashion. They gradually became the singing advocates for all that irritated and disrupted the pious.

The Goliard Poets eventually ceased operations and disappeared sometime during the 13th century, gradually being written off as petty trifles and foul-mouthed babblers. If you actually study classical music in college, most history textbooks devote about a paragraph to them at the most; however, their laudable tactics of bashing their ultimate adversary of "righteousness" have continuously resurfaced in a million different arenas.

And speaking of that, I decided to hook up with one of San Jose's own favorite local Goliardesque poets, Roberto Tinoco Duran, since he has a new book out, Dark Spark, which is chock-filled with his definitively short, quick poems that viscerally explore everything about life in San Jose, Calif.: the Chicano experience, race, ethnic and social divisions, the police department, the "10th largest city," Silicon Valley, Ron Gonzales and more.

Duran is a combustible dude—not someone you invite to parties for pleasant chit-chat. To steal a phrase from Trevanian, he's wilder than a cat crapping razor blades and this book proves it. If anyone should be San Jose's poet illaureate, it's him. In one particular nugget, he says that his mind belongs on death row but his body isn't willing to go yet. And consider this little gem:

When I'm abrasive
It just means
I'm fine sanding
understanding.

That's the whole epic and that's the kind of stuff he does. His poems are like quick sound bites that smack you in the face. Here's another one, a blast that I really wish I had written:

Even
when
I
was
wasted
the
words
were
not

Read that again 100 times. What else could one possibly add to that? Duran elicits the Goliard in us all and San Jose needs more people like him.

San Jose Avenue Walking Tour

When I eventually write a travel guidebook to the industrial wastelands of San Jose, I will definitely include the area bounded by Alma Avenue to the north, Curtner to the South, Almaden Expressway to the west and Monterey Highway to the east. It is indeed primo territory through which to slither.

To gather material, I began an escapade at the corner of Monterey Highway and Alma and proceeded westward down Alma, a beautifully dilapidated stretch of road. The dive corner markets, vacant lots and feral cats just brightened up my day like a thousand suns. Instead of turning south down Little Orchard Street, I ambulated all the way to Almaden and drooled over the famous Bear's Cocktail Lounge and its spinning sign on the corner. Man, what an institution. There aren't too many watering holes with spinning signs anymore. Quickly passing by the new condos going southbound on Almaden, I ventured left on San Jose Avenue, one of the all-time legendary drags in this town. It is true industrial heaven. What greets you at that corner is Esmerelda's Tires and Wheels, and then a residential house with a sign that says Bruno's Tiling. After that, you're graced with an RV repair joint, various auto repair shops, a fenced-off yard filled with CO_2 gas tanks, Bobcat Batteries and more wreckage of all sorts. At 201 San Jose Ave., I found Bay Rag, a recycled clothing warehouse. The front door boasts a sticker that says "office" and two placards, one that says Bay Rag and the other the numerical address. An old man with a cigarette scurried out of the back door as I scoped it out.

Continuing east on San Jose Avenue, I nearly got run over by both a Snap-On tool truck and an empty San Jose Unified School bus, both of which were barreling down the street. But I did eventually make it to Duke & Racacho Cabinetry, a glorious warehouse that would make any carpenter proud. You could just smell the sawdust.

San Jose Avenue then ends at Monterey Highway, right where you find the Bold Knight steakhouse and San Jose Honda Sony, yet two more storied San Jose institutions. Nowhere else in the world will you find a Honda Sony shop, which is why their motto is "The One and Only."

From there, a quick jaunt south on Monterey brings the traveler to the next phase of the journey: a right turn westward onto Barnard Avenue, where the industrial wilderness continues. At the outset, a long stretch of light blue cookie-cutter warehouses sits across the street from a huge recycling plant. Then, smack in the middle of it all, I found Cottage Trailer Grove, a quintessential trailer park. Just outside is a green picket fence with a sign that says "Please don't feed the cat here thank you." Man, what an awesome street.

Barnard eventually reaches its end about 10 feet from the curve of Almaden Expressway, where it takes one of those 15 mph turns and becomes Stone Avenue as it goes south alongside the expressway. And on that road, you find even more of the industrial mecca. Loayza's Pools, Spas and Landscaping is yet another place to stare at pallets of every brick imaginable. Horizon Irrigation, right near there, is yet another place to gawk at every length and size of PVC piping imaginable. This is prime stuff, folks.

But at that point, I found it best to segue east through a nearby residential neighborhood and descend upon Little Orchard Street for the home stretch of this voyage. Heading south, I breezed by a slew of business complexes and a vacant lot where a mattress had been discarded. From behind the chain-link fence, another feral cat stared me down. I passed by a place called Old Orchard Mobile Park, a mobile home community, except an "A" was missing, so it said Old Orchard Mobile P rk. Within spitting distance of that mobile park, Little Orchard Street ends—right at the entrance to Oak Hill Cemetery, a fitting conclusion for this adventure.

Lars Frederiksen and My Refrigerator

While progressing through life, everyone develops a personal attachment to something, whether it's a favorite car, letters from your first girlfriend or something else that you just can't get rid of. For me, it was my first refrigerator.

This anecdote directly involves Campbell's most favorite son, Lars Frederiksen. By now, everyone knows that Frederiksen jams out some great tunes for a world-renowned punk band called Rancid, and because of their track "Roots Radicals," the entire planet Earth now knows about VTA bus route No. 60.

But how is Gary Singh's refrigerator related to all this? I'll tell you. At the very beginning of 1991, Lars was in a band called the Knowhere Men, and they played a gig in my back yard at 351 N. Tenth St. in San Jose. Actually, it wasn't really in the yard itself—it was in a garage separated from the house that we converted into a space where bands could play when we hosted parties—stage and all.

Don't get me wrong, I'm not trying to ride on the coattails of his success—you see, the tale is much more profound than that. At that house we had a majestic maroon refrigerator—the same one that I grew up with in my parents' house. When I moved to Tenth Street, I dragged the refrigerator with me and it subsequently became a bulletin board for a zillion stickers: punk bands, grunge bands, defunct radio stations and a few San Jose Earthquakes stickers from the old days. It was like an umbilical cord: I was finally out of home, but I still kept the fridge with me. It was dear to my always-aching heart.

Of the several stickers on that fridge, we had many cartoon ones of the Portland-based punk band Poison Idea, including their longhaired drummer, Slayer Hippy. After the Knowhere Men's set at that party, Lars observed that Slayer Hippy quite closely resembled the Knowhere Men's guitar player, Brendan Hallett, so he walked up and hand-wrote "Brendan" on the sticker. Lars' chicken-scratch stayed on that sticker throughout the entire course of the fridge's life. After its reign at the Tenth Street house, the fridge wound up at my flat on Sixth Street. The stickers continued to build up and, like a Timex, the fridge just kept on ticking. Yeah!

To make a long story short, the fridge eventually died a natural death at a later house on Seventh Street after it sat in our back yard for three years, primarily because I just couldn't get rid of it. In the end, we paid 18 bucks to have it hauled away to the dump.

I loved that fridge, and if I had known that Lars would later become famous, I would have saved the thing and sold it on eBay. Some 12-year-old punker would have begged his parents to buy it, and the fridge would have eventually made its way to the San Jose Rocks Hall of Fame. I can easily see it behind a glass case 30 years from now.

Since there were so many memories associated with that icebox, tears came to my eyes as we stood there in the front yard and watched the folks hoist it onto the back of a flatbed. Geez. All those stickers and all those splendid memories. Gone. It was finally over. The end of an era. All good things must pass. Only the good die young. Choose your cliché, that's what I felt like as we watched them take my fridge away. The only topper would have been my roommates and I, arms around each other's shoulders, singing that line from "Me and Bobby McGee": "Freedom's just another word for nothing left to lose"—the fridge being the last thing I lost, of course. When Lars finally writes a song about all this, then I will splurge and buy a Rancid CD.

Lorin Partridge Live at The Improv

As you read this, a group called 1stAct Silicon Valley is envisioning how to turn downtown San Jose into a world-class, creative urban Mecca. But forget all that for now, because San Jose already has a thriving downtown, as was evidenced by the sheer genius that went down at the Improv Comedy Club last week: A Circus Peanut-eating contest.

Now, almost everyone knows of Circus Peanuts—those pasty orange coma-inducing chunks of vapid emetic-disguised-as-candy that taste like sweaty Styrofoam dipped in stale banana food coloring. Perhaps the foulest candy ever devised, Circus Peanuts apparently have a following, yet I don't know a damn person on the planet who actually enjoys them. Cecil Adams in *The Straight Dope* frothed about Circus Peanuts a decade ago and one inspired reader chimed in with this star-studded riposte: "I think they are the horror that is the circus, that flat tin taste of fear and clowns and little lost children amid the cotton candy stink and the piles of elephant doo-doo and the clamor of the midway and the tinny sound of the circus band endlessly wheezing its way through yet another soulless circus fanfare."

That said, what better place to stage a Circus Peanut-eating charade than San Jose? My old accomplice in absurdity 10 years running, Lorin Partridge, rolled back into San Jo last week from Denver, and, along with fellow provocateur Sid Pink, staged the first and hopefully last Circus Peanut chow-down in this city's history. At similar eating challenges, the contestants are at least given enough H²O to help wash down the food, but such is not the case with Partridge and Pink's Circus Peanut-eating contest. The only fluid given to each competitor is orange soda.

I infiltrated the scene ahead of time. On the stage sat a table for the four contestants, complete with four Easter baskets filled with the Circus Peanuts and four martini glasses for the orange soda. Upstairs in the Green Room, the MC prepared himself for the show by drinking a mixture of tequila and Pepto-Bismol. The said MC and Partridge and Sid Pink decked themselves out in über-Vegas-style lounge lizard attire, giving the whole shebang a Playboy-era steak-and-martini feel that San Jose fatally lacks these days.

The entire spectacle was intertwined with a few films of Pink and Partridge's exploits back in the Mile High City, and completing this theater of the absurd was the house band, Beachkrieg, San Jose's only surf band. They don German World War I uniforms, smoke cigars and insult the French all night while the frontman shreds on a Farfisa organ. Scrunched down in my chair in the audience, I let it all sink in: the Circus Peanuts, the vomit, the lounge outfits, the martinis, the Farfisa and the Pepto-Bismol. With my shoulders shrugged and my hands in the air, palms facing upward, I uttered a statement disguised as a question: "And people think there's more to life than this?"

In short, it was good ol' American sideshow depravity at its finest. Had Partridge been crucified the following day, I would have equated the feast with the Last Supper. In the end, the winner was Denver's own Handsome Adam, who trounced the other contestants and managed to wolf down 94 Circus Peanuts, beating his own record of 80. And yes, it was easy for this author to predict the particular bodily function that would result from such an endeavor. The organizers even provided a pail for Adam in which vomit onstage in front of everyone else when all was said and done. The orange fluid poured out of his mouth like it was a fire hydrant.

Thank God my hometown decided to save the old Jose Theater and convert it to the Improv, providing a legitimate venue for such a refreshingly psychotic adventure as this. Just seeing Partridge's name on the marquee above Tommy Davidson was ridiculous enough to spike anyone's interest. Downtown San Jose is alive and well. All hail the creative urban mecca!

Walking San Carlos

Many folks older than me have declared that the stretch of San Carlos Street between downtown San Jose and Valley Fair should be transformed into a grand promenade, not unlike Melrose or Santa Monica Boulevard in that City of Angels down south. After all, there exist long stretches of road in L.A., especially in the more nauseating parts like Carson or Torrance, that completely resemble San Carlos Street, but with just more strip clubs and adult bookstores.

So, being the adventurous type, I had to hit the pavement yet again and go re-explore some of that road's most compelling locales, beginning with, of course, two San Jose institutions: Falafel Drive In at the corner of San Carlos and Revel, and Just Leather, which is right across the street. That small gray motorcycle has been parked in front of Just Leather for at least 20 years. At Falafel, businessmen packed the place as I scoped it out.

From there, I ambled eastward to the intersection of San Carlos and Bascom, one of Silicon Valley's most beautiful junctions. You've got the Pink Poodle and Alex's 49er Inn, one of San Jose's legendary cocktail lounges. You've also got Saver's thrift store and—bada bing—Babyland. And don't forget Time Deli with that renowned clock that everyone's driven by for the last two decades. Alex's also now has prime rib dinners on Tuesdays for $10. That's a smokin' deal. Upon arriving at the scene, I sauntered behind the place since dive bars are always more fun to enter through the back. Two ice machine repairmen were working on something outside, and over behind the vacant building next door, someone had dumped a broken refrigerator and an old mattress.

It's only a hop, skip and a jump to the next locale where it's more fun to enter through the back: Y Not Adult Toyz. But since a rack of *Metros* occupies the front, I had to enter through that side instead. I poked around and then left. Y Not, I heard somewhere, was a bar at one time, which is why the "Y" resembles a martini glass. Also, there's nothing like seeing a pink banner that says, "San Carlos Street Business District" right across the street from Y Not Adult Toyz.

Moving even further eastward, I investigated a few vacant lots and then found Burbank Pet Hospital. The place has two doors. One says "Cat Entrance" and the other says "Dog Entrance." Man, there were so many establishments on that street to check out that I had to finally infiltrate a third place at which it's more fun to enter through the rear: The Red Stag, another legendary watering hole. Yeah, they fixed it up, but it's still a rockin' place anyway.

Speaking of the San Carlos Street Business District, there's even a brochure and a website: www.san carlosstreet.com. In the directory of businesses, Red Stag, Alex's, The Pink Poodle and Y Not are listed in the "Entertainment" section.

But this expedition did not stop there. I felt it necessary to pause for a moment at the corner of San Carlos and Willard where Fiesta Lanes used to be. The sign is still there, but the war on bowling alleys continues, I guess. Another great dive bowling alley bites the dust. The next recommendation as one continues east from there is a place that has the most ridiculous name anywhere: Casa De Mini Storage. I take all visitors to that place and I think someone once took a picture of it and the picture wound up on Johnny Carson, Letterman, Jay Leno, or some other show. I forget.

After all the antique shops, car lots and bizarre retail that line that strip, there is one and only one way to finish the sojourn: The Diamond Laundry and Cleaners building just west of Highway 87. It is a masterpiece, and the sign is one of San Jose's classic old-school oddities.

Apologies go out to all those places not mentioned here due to lack of space. San Carlos Street definitely rules.

Loss of Innocence

Last week, I carried on about the stirring efforts of South Bay Live, a grass roots endeavor to reshape, again, a live music scene here. But here's an angle that no one wants to talk about, at least when it comes to the underground rock & roll slice of this whole perverted pie: How about all the folks in the live music scene who have died throughout the last 20 years? There are way too many to mention here, but I'll gloss over a few, including one that happened last week.

First things first: I've been around death for pretty much my entire life. My dad died when I was 16. My cousin ran his truck off the road and died a few years earlier. Another cousin killed himself around 1991 or so. My best friend in college, Mike Andrade, died pretty much right in front of me in 1996. Two other good friends in college also died that same year. I've been through a lot.

But back to the now, and allow me to convey a small number of other sordid tidbits. A longtime pal, known as Rockin' Rob Dapello, died inside the Cactus Club at a show in 2001. He was the brother of Lars Frederiksen of Rancid, and a huge tribute concert with 20 bands was staged in his memory shortly thereafter.

A wide variety of bands played. At the time, I had a lounge duo named Gary & Babs, and we opened the whole thing, although hardly anyone was in attendance yet. Old friends from out of the woodwork came to that gig, and hundreds partied inside and outside the club. Rob and I were huge soccer fans and would carry on all night about either that sport or bands like Motorhead or G.B.H. For that tribute show, they made shirts and stickers that said, "Never Forget Rockin' Rob."

Another dude lurking in the shadows of the club scene was a guy named Big Tom Laughlin. He was a skateboarder and a wacky artist who died in 2004. A memorial concert was held for him at the Blank Club, and they made shirts that said, "Never Forget Big Tom." Just last week, an anniversary gig was held, and brand-new shirts were made.

And then there's Pat Dooley, yet one more longtime San Jose scenester. He ended his life just a few years ago, and I still have my "Never Forget Pat Dooley" T-shirt. I've worn the thing a dozen times without washing it; I've spilled beer on it, and that's exactly what he would have wanted.

Basically, you don't have to have any connection to the rock & roll underground club gig scenario—or whatever you call it—to understand that there's a story here. This is community of people—a local community for that matter—who all support each other and party and grow older and strive to try and just eke out a rockin' life in a suburban wasteland.

And last week was the ultimate capper. She was universally known as Choley (rhyming with holy) but her real name was Nichole. After everyone found out she was dead, the amount of drinking that went down, myself included, was ugly. People went on benders for days. She had many, many friends, and if you remember the column I wrote on the Heathers, the female drinking club, she was one of the two damsels who beckoned me into the bar, which led to that story. If you unearth the Feb. 14, 2007, issue of *Metro*, where the cover story was called "MySpaced Out," she's on the cover on the left. At her funeral, the motorcade should be 10 miles long.

In the words of Menlo Park author Barry Eisler: "It's strange that we think of sexual experience as involving a loss of innocence. I don't see it that way at all. ... It's when you first experience death—and it's the end and it's real and it's final—that's when you really lose your innocence."

The Pigeon Invasion

With all the recent hoopla surrounding peregrine falcons nesting at the new San Jose City Hall and the webcam capturing the whole scenario, folks are getting the birdwatching itch again. Silicon Valley has always been a birdwatching hotbed, with expeditions extending out into the nearby wilderness and some folks merely tromping through their own back yards to identify, say, an oak titmouse (*Baeolophus inornatus*) or a California thrasher (*Toxostoma redivivum*). Since I know little of such things, I decided to embark on my own birdwatching adventure and gawk at all the dead pigeons underneath the overpass at the Lawrence Expressway Caltrain station in Sunnyvale. In Latin, we shall call them Mortuus pigeons procul *syrma constituo*.

You see, there has always been a tremendous pigeon problem at the Lawrence Station. The trains run underneath the overpass, perpendicular to the expressway, and hundreds of pigeons were setting up shop on a network of green steel girders that support the overpass. The horizontal girders run underneath the overpass and have lips jutting out on which the pigeons would sit while pooping all over the tracks and the station platform, including anyone sitting on the benches there. So somebody somewhere found a temporary answer and a massive wire mesh grid was installed, blocking off all access by the pigeons to the girders. But several still managed to find their way inside and get to the girders in order to nest. Unfortunately, many who got inside had not much room to fly around and ended getting themselves stuck in the wire mesh, either crushing themselves or choking to death. So there you have it—a dozen dead pigeons stuck in a wire mesh underneath an expressway overpass. At least that's what it looked like had happened.

But there's more. The pigeons also apparently used to sit on the exposed girders outside, the ones that run the length of the overpass, just below street level. As a result, massive spikes were installed on these girders so the pigeons could no longer sit there anymore. I watched one pigeon perched on a steel support cable, just a foot away from the spikes, and he was looking down at them with a very sad and confused look on his face, like he didn't know what to do, as if he had just lost his home. Even the most tactless, unfeeling person would have felt something for these dead pigeons. I freakin' hate pigeons and I still felt a peculiar sense of guilt about all this. If peregrine falcons had swooped in and eaten the pigeons—like they do at the new San Jose City Hall—then it would have seemed a lot more natural.

However, the Sunnyvale anti-pigeon counteroffensive doesn't stop there. All throughout the station, one finds small, electronically controlled devices hidden in various nooks and crannies. These small boxes randomly emit shrill, pulsating blasts of electronic sound designed to drive the pigeons away. And they work.

Out on the outside portions of the platform away from the overpass sit the actual booths where folks can buy their tickets and then sit down. The roofs of these booths are made of wooden rafters and the pigeons would inhabit them obsessively. But not after the electronic noise–generators were installed. The pigeons now pretty much leave the booths alone. Sure, anyone sitting there waiting for the train has to endure the piercing sounds, but at least no one gets pooped on. The entire picture is downright bizarre.

San Jose's answer to its own pigeon predicament at the Federal Building downtown was to install fake owls everywhere to scare off the pigeons. "They don't work," one security guard told me. I told him maybe they should hire more peregrine falcons instead.

Anyway, this entire pigeon scenario should be included in any bird-watching guide to Silicon Valley: Hundreds of pigeons flying all over the place, in and around an overpass while the dead ones remain stuck in a wire mesh grid. I may have to install a webcam myself.

In Praise of Meridian And Hamilton

San Jose City Councilmember Pierluigi Oliverio recently waxed poetic about his own District 6, howling praises about that constituency's three "viable business districts." He specifically pinpointed Lincoln Avenue, the Alameda and West San Carlos Street, the latter of which this author also recently went into raptures over. However, Silicon Alleys must admonish Mr. Oliverio for the slipshod fashion in which he brutally ignored the wondrous variety of overlooked commerce that bursts forth from the intersection of Meridian and Hamilton.

We begin with the Campbell Moose Lodge No. 1811, which is quite visible when driving down either Hamilton or Meridian. It sits right there, scrunched in between Bank of the West and Bally Fitness, with a gigantic brown sign with white capital letters that say "MOOSE." Many folks have cruised by that intersection wondering what exactly the hell that place is. I always thought it was a dive bar named Moose—which would have been something to brag about even more—until I actually walked up to the joint about 15 years ago and realized that it was indeed a fraternal order of some sort.

According to their website, "The Loyal Order of Moose is a fraternal and service organization founded in 1888, with nearly 1 million men in roughly 2000 Lodges, in all 50 states and four Canadian provinces, plus Great Britain and Bermuda." And they probably won't let you in the Antler Room unless you're a dues-paying member. Out in front, a white sign says that they have Bingo on Sundays at 6:30. It just doesn't get any better than that. But it's not just for men. There exists a "Women of the Moose" unit as well. Both are subsidiaries of Moose International Inc.

Across Meridian from the Moose Lodge sits one of the all–time institutions in San Jose: Gunther's Delicatessen. Sure, it's only been there since 1971, but the sheer amount of chow one gets at that place is downright staggering. Gunther himself, probably now in his mid–70s, still holds court in the kitchen. If you actually order a sandwich, they give you two pickles instead of one. Now that's old-school.

All one has to do then is amble north across Hamilton into what's called "Giant Plaza," for some strange reason. The sign has to be at least 40 years old. There one finds the Goodwill Store and a place right next door called Pine Dollar Store. Like any Goodwill franchise, there's always that unique–to–Goodwill aroma and the nauseating light rock music blasting from the stereo with a good deal of static mixed in. Other highlights of Giant Plaza include Vucko's Liquors and a brand spanking new breakfast and lunch spot called Cafe San Jose. Also in that same shopping center sits Dick's Bakery, another San Jose legend 60 years running, and it turns out they were on *Bay Area Backroads* just last weekend.

You see, these are the absolute gems of that neighborhood, and the particular milieu is indeed a viable business corner to destroy all corners, despite all the nearby hideous eyesores like Safeway, Starbucks, Burger King and RiteAid. And at the northeast corner of that intersection, one finds a beautifully bare and unadorned sign next to a cobbler shop that offers these words: Shoe Repair, Keys Made, Bootmaker. There is nowhere else in the South Bay, for whatever reason, where one can glimpse a sign that says that. Throw in a taqueria, a mobile/wireless/phone shop and a bizarre clean water outlet and the backdrop is complete.

Of course, one can float southward down Meridian to what used to be the main post office, but not without passing a few side streets that sport breathtaking suburban names like Cherry Grove and Willowhurst. Just segue down those streets and you'll see houses the architectures and landscapes of which will transplant you into a *Brady Bunch* episode—in a good way, of course. In any event, San Jose is a city of neighborhoods and the intersection of Meridian and Hamilton is one of many such rocking junctions. It must not be ignored.

Jennifer Field of Dreams

Now this could only happen to a guy like me; And only happen in a town like this

—Sinatra, "My Kind of Town"

Chapter Seven of Clifford L. Linedecker's sensationalist paperback on Richard Ramirez, the '80s serial killer known as the Night Stalker, is titled *Satan's Work*. The chapter opens with this quick bit:

"The Night Stalker had a theme song—an anthem. The media loved it. With their usual thirst for sensationalism, and eye on circulation and rating buildups, newspaper and television reporters latched on to the 'Satan Connection' and played it for all it was worth. 'Did the devil make him do it?' one newspaper asked in a headline."

The tune in question would be "Night Prowler" from AC/DC's *High-*

way to Hell album and this is right where Jennifer Field, Miss San Jose Grand Prix 2006, comes into this week's adventure.

You see, both she and I were simultaneously on the covers of two different publications, standing in exactly the same place—right out in front of San Jose's City Hall. I was on *Metro*'s cover for a story about the industrial wastelands of San Jose and she was decked out in her orange Grand Prix jumpsuit on the cover of *Area Chica*, a glossy sports and entertainment periodical.

So I just had to prowl around and try to get a photo op. It was too ridiculous to pass up. I mean, it would be her standing there, holding the *Area Chica* issue with her on the cover, right next to me holding the *Metro* issue with me on the cover. And I'd have my back turned, just like the cover. It had to work. It was a killer idea.

The event where I initially envisioned this happening was the Miss San Jose Grand Prix Swimsuit Competition, which took place last week at Taste Ultralounge, a place that used to be Club Deep, Blue Tattoo, Club Ecco, Hamburger Mary's and God knows what else. The Laundry Works? Hmmm.

Doing my best stalker imitation, I showed up with said copies of *Metro* and *Area Chica* in hand, hoping, praying, begging and urging for a ridiculous-on-purpose photo shot of me right next to the lovely Ms. Field.

I made it to Taste Ultra Lounge and no one there knew who I was at all. Whether that was a good thing or a bad thing, I guess I'll never know, but all the Grand Prix fans from parts unknown gathered on hand to gawk at the current Miss Grand Prix competitors flaunting their skin. Thumping house music rocked the joint and people swilled overpriced beers like there was no tomorrow. People also took primo advantage of their cell phone cameras and copped many photos of the bikini-clad beauties as they paraded their stuff on the makeshift walkway.

Even before the show started, I realized my function in society immediately. One dude, upon realizing that I was on the cover of *Metro*, asked me to autograph it, but then he suddenly decided to run off to a nearby Walgreen's so he could purchase a disposable cameras in order to come back and photograph all the Grand Prix chicks instead. That, in short, is the story of my life, however you want to interpret it.

So the ridiculous-on-purpose photo op with the lovely Ms. Field never happened, as she was by far the rock star of the entire event. I couldn't get her alone for five seconds without 6 billion other people intruding on the conversation. I suffered from an extreme case of Wannabe Rock Star Instant Jealousy Disorder (WRSIJD), which will hopefully be documented in the fifth edition of the *Diagnostic and Statistical Manual of Mental Disorders*.

The Other Campbell Ave

The website for Campbell's main street says this: "In Historic Downtown Campbell you'll find tree-lined walkways with charming sidewalk cafes and coffeehouses, fabulous restaurants, wonderful shops, and stylish boutiques. Explore Downtown Campbell and discover our boutiques featuring the latest trends in clothing and jewelry."

That's a pretty damn good description, but that street is not the only Campbell Avenue in this valley. A much more rocking street is the Campbell Avenue in Santa Clara that takes you through the industrial backwater behind Santa Clara University. Sure, the Campbell Avenue in the city of Campbell may offer a "vibrant shopping and entertainment district featuring many historical landmarks and over 100 shops, services, and restaurants for you to explore and enjoy," but this other Campbell Avenue offers piles of lumber, granite, a commercial laundry warehouse, empty blocked-off office buildings and unmarked facades with barbed-wire fences.

To get there, all you have to do is circle up the Alameda, and right where it turns the curve around the university and becomes El Camino, you hang a right onto Campbell Ave. The first sign you see is the one that says "Not a Through Street," signaling that there are only good things to come. Dead-end streets are some of the best places to investigate, and this one is yet another quintessential mixture of old and new.

The escapade commences right there at Stephen Schott Stadium, the university's baseball diamond. From there, the stroll takes you past T. W. Smith Wholesale Plumbing Supplies, a spectacular and groovy place to check out hundreds of lengths of pipe for what seems miles on end. It's in the same building as Kitchen and Bath Showplace, a rocking spot to sniff out some fixtures, sinks, tubs and other bathroom accessories.

Then be sure not to miss Blue's Roofing, a great yard in which to scope out piles of lumber and granite. A. J. Commercial Laundry also sits right there, in an ominous-looking warehouse building. A sign on the front warns visitors to enter the yard at their own risk.

You continue down a street that 20 years ago was entirely an industrial wasteland, then, all of sudden, everything changes. Right along the eastern side of the street are nothing but rows and rows of—you guessed it—condos. What is it with these people that insist on building hideous cookie-cutter bile and olive green condos right smack in the middle of an awesome backwater alley that is not far from the railroad tracks? The new street that circles through the first set of these condos is called Dahlia Loop. Ugh.

On the western side of Campbell Avenue, one notices a few side streets that used to go off Campbell and through the nearby residential neighborhoods, but medians have been installed to prevent that, thus a few more dead-ends.

As Campbell begins to meander its way to its end, one finds more bile-colored bungalows and a few unmarked facades. Highlights in the final stretch include Alberto's Concrete and Landmark Sign Company. Then the road dead-ends at a grassy median at Newhall where it used to actually go through. This is why these adventures are better off on foot, because that way you can just step over the median and turn left down Newhall, where it dead-ends at the railroad tracks. But before you do that, you can quickly segue right on Elm Street and trip through one more block of desolate industrial wasteland before it dead-ends at Highway 880. In fact, this entire adventure was nothing but one dead-end after the next.

On your way back out of the neighborhood, make sure you pass by the sign at the Encanto condos at Dahlia Loop. The sign says this: "Thank you for visiting Encanto Bungalow Community. Established 2006. San Jose, California." I thank no one except the person in charge of creating the piles of lumber and granite. Now that was something worth visiting.

A Tribute to ADD

Recently, while flipping through my shelf of books on Attention Deficit Disorder, I recalled a journal entry I wrote nine years ago, when I was diagnosed with that marvelous condition. It was me describing a typical day in the life of someone who has ADD, and it went a little somethin' like this:

"I work on a college campus and I live two blocks down the street, above a supermarket. A typical morning consists of me daydreaming at my job and then I suddenly remember my unpaid phone bill, so I run back home to search for my checkbook. Once I got home and find the bill, I get a fabulous idea. I have to do laundry. Since the washing machine down the hall takes only quarters, I go downstairs to the supermarket to get some change. I pull a crumpled up one-dollar bill out of my front pocket and the lady gives me four quarters. I come back upstairs, put the quarters down on the living room table and go surf the Internet for 45 minutes.

"I pick up the phone bill again and then pace back and forth in my apartment wondering how to make the day go by faster. An hour later, I grab the quarters, along with a few dirty towels. Down the hallway I go to load up the washer and pop in 75 cents.

"Back in my apartment, the pacing resumes. A thought comes to me: Well, I could go back to work and buy a stamp for the phone bill on the way. There you go—two birds with one stone. So I grab the bill and go back to my office on campus. I get all the way there and realize that I forgot my checkbook, which was the initial reason for going back home in the first place.

"I throw the phone bill down on my desk, lock my office up, and head across campus to the coffee stand. A drop-dead gorgeous woman named Rochelle, who's married, works there, and I grab some change out of my pocket just to buy a cup of coffee so I can talk to her for a second. Only then do I realize I already had quarters and I didn't need to go get change for the laundry in the first place. But ...

"Before going home again, I need lunch. Since it's boring sitting there in the burrito place with nothing else to do except eat, I decide to pick up something to read. I spend an hour in a nearby used book shop and drop seventy-five bucks. While flipping through one of the books and not actually reading it, I only end up eating half of the burrito.

"As soon as I get back up to my apartment, I put the books down on the floor and start looking for my checkbook again. Usually it's directly underneath a stack of parking tickets, unopened bills and a beer stein filled with pennies, but not today.

"So I sit down and peruse one of the books I just bought. I fall asleep on the couch and wake up around 9pm. I turn on the TV, flip through the channels for half an hour, and then turn it off. Then I phone an amazing babe that I have the hots for and ask her if she wants to go bowling. I don't even know how to bowl and she declines the offer anyway.

"The next morning, while leaving for work, I remember that I left my laundry in the washer the day before. So I go into the laundry room and find out that someone has taken my stuff out and thrown it all over the tops of the machines. I didn't have any quarters left for the dryer because yesterday I spent them on that last cup of coffee in order to talk to Rochelle. So I leave my wet laundry sitting there and I go to work."

The impulsivity reigns free, here and now. Let us explode.

Dove, Actually

Of all all the topics I've sashayed through in this column, there exists one in particular that will elicit opinions from every corner of San Jose's social spectrum—a topic that makes you either grit your teeth in annoyance, flip tables over in sheer anger or just laugh uproariously: pigeons.

In my May 30 column, I expounded on the presence of dead pigeons underneath the overpass at the Lawrence Expressway Caltrain Station. Netting had been placed underneath the overpass to prevent them from nesting, only to result in the strangulation of some birds upon their attempts to squeeze through the netting.

I received emails from all across the United States on that one, including manufacturers of pigeon repellent products, afraid that it was their netting that had caused these deaths. And one local resident left me a four-minute-long rambling voicemail that cut off before she was able to finish. Apparently everyone has something to say about pigeons. Local gadfly Steve Cohen, for example, made a nuisance of himself a few years back for constantly firing off calls and emails to then City Councilmember Cindy

Chavez's office about the abundance of pigeon poop on the sidewalks of downtown San Jose. According to him, the city refused to deal with it.

I used to count myself among the pigeon-haters, but I recently did a complete about-face after reading Andrew D. Blechman's, Pigeons: The Fascinating Saga of the World's Most Revered and Reviled Bird, a masterpiece of pigeon defense, the paperback version of which is out this week. The book is a snap to read and you will never look at pigeons the same way again after completing it. Blechman, an award-winning journalist whose work has graced the pages of Smithsonian Magazine, The New York Times, The New York Observer and Newsday, culled several known and unknown facts about pigeons, one of which is that the dove and the pigeon are the same bird. It's just that the former is equated with peace and tranquility while the latter is equated with disease and feces. Blame the French if you must, as "pigeon" is merely a French translation for the English word "dove," and it was French settlers, according to Blechman, who imported the bird to the New World for meat in the early 17th century. Now the bird overpopulates nearly every city in the Western Hemisphere.

Blechman reminds us: "It was a pigeon that delivered the results of the first Olympics in 776 B.C.E., and a pigeon that first brought news of Napoleon's defeat at Waterloo more than 2,500 years later. Nearly a million pigeons served in both World Wars and are credited with saving thousands of soldiers' lives."

He also calls to our attention to the fact that "pigeon droppings were once considered a semiprecious commodity. In ancient Egypt, it was highly prized manure, and for centuries in England pigeon feces were declared property of the Crown. The valuable dung was used to manufacture saltpeter, a critical ingredient for making gunpowder."

And furthermore: "Pigeons are athletes of the highest caliber: While racehorses receive all the glory with their 35 mph sprints around a one-mile racetrack, homing pigeons—a mere pound of flesh and feathers—routinely fly more than 500 miles in a single day at speeds exceeding 60 mph, finding their way home from a place they've never been before, and without stopping."

Lastly, I'll add this: pigeons are a key visual component of many of the world's most famous town plazas, like St. Mark's Square in Venice, Trafalgar Square in London and the defunct Albertson's parking lot in downtown San Jose. Who could imagine any of those locales without a smattering of the world's oldest domesticated bird? San Jose should celebrate the presence of these divine and peaceful creatures.

Little Saigon: Political Theater Of the Absurd

This week, an acid rain shower of absurdities for y'all. The Anti-Man-About-Town (AMAT) infiltrated San Jose City Hall once again last

Tuesday to witness the spectacle surrounding the council's decision to rename part of Story Road "Saigon Business District."

Usually AMAT has no difficulty entering City Hall and overseeing the circus, no matter what issues are being thrashed out, what bones of contention lay on the table or who isn't allowed to wear roller skates. For example, if William Garbett is at the podium addressing the council, I can usually weave and bob my way through the snoring audience and find a seat to collapse into.

But not this time. I couldn't even make it to the bloody elevator, as the entire place was overtaken by a shrieking battery of Vietnamese-Americans who wanted to name the stretch of Story Road "Little Saigon" instead. In fact, "battery" barely even described it, really. It was hard to navigate through it all and I had to swim upstream and hightail it out of their way.

Don't get me wrong. I'm all for witnessing hundreds of folks verbally abuse the City Council, especially when they have bullhorns and especially when it's in a language I can't understand. But due to the overwhelming masses, there was no way for me to even get my foot in the chambers, so I ventured elsewhere.

With all due respect to both sides of this confrontation—and it is a confrontation—I cannot help but willfully debase the entire dialogue. Look at it this way: San Jose first belonged to the Ohlone Indians, then to the Spanish and Mexicans, and then to Thomas Fallon and then to Tom McEnery, who still thinks it belongs to him.

Nowadays we have both a thriving Mexican-American and a Vietnamese-American community. What's the big deal? I love it all.

How about this: 30 years from now when 200 Iraqi-American businesses exist on Lincoln Avenue between Willow and Minnesota, should we rename it Little Fallujah, Ba'ath Party West or the Fifth Dynasty of Ur? In fact, I'd love to see the looks on faces of Willow Glen residents if that actually happens. I hope it does.

And then some of the protesters at the City Council meeting had the audacity to call Councilmember Madison Nguyen a communist for not supporting their particular side. Give me a break.

Look, in my day I've been called a "communist" by more than a few right-wing Bible-thumping bigots, so I know what it feels like. I may be a post-Nietzschean anarcho-Taoist beer mystic, but I ain't no stinking communist.

And neither is Madison.

Now some of these same folks want to recall her. Since the entire charade has degenerated into nothing but an irrational farce, AMAT will now describe the spectacle as a revamped version of le Theatre de l'Absurde, a la Samuel Beckett and Eugene Ionesco, since the French trying to reoccupy Vietnam is partly what created this whole stinking mess in the first place.

As Beckett famously said, "To find a form that accommodates the mess, that is the task of the artist now."

Anti-Man-About-Town over and out.

Meet Me at Count Five Place

Since the San Jose Rocks Hall of Fame project continues to spur all sorts of ideas, allow me to add one more: The renaming of streets after local musicians who've gone big time. You see, with San Jose's hare-brained hick-town penchant for naming buildings after politicians that aren't dead yet, they at least owe us a little rock & roll. Imagine Doobie Brothers Boulevard or Count Five Place. If that sounds implausible, then let me give you a few examples from progressive, forward-thinking communities like Oklahoma City and Bakersfield where similar things were recently done. The legendary Oklahoma City band the Flaming Lips have been known for their surreal neopsychedelic costumed rock madness for over 20 years now, so the city—apropos of the band's career—took a dirt-filled back alley littered with dumpsters and renamed it Flaming Lips Alley. Debates raged for a year about whether it was a tribute or an insult. The band's singer Wayne Coyne, who still lives in that city, overwhelmingly dug the idea.

"Any time you've got an alley with dumpsters and trucks loading beer out of the back, I thought about that—maybe that's a little better," he said. "I like to think that, in fact I almost prefer, that we're one of these great little secrets—that people sort of stumble upon us—while looking for something more obvious."

And he applauded Oklahoma City for stepping up to the plate and acknowledging the band's accomplishments. "It's not just a typical, 'Give them a street, give them a statue, give them a handshake,'" he said. "It's like some little secret special thing. So many bands despise their hometowns. I guess we're just lucky or it never felt that way to us. Oklahoma City never rejected us." Hallelujah.

And then there's Bakersfield. Legendary '90s heavy metal band Korn hails from that community and in 2006 the city showed its appreciation by naming a back access road to Rabobank Arena after the band. The street was designated Korn Row and the sign sits spitting distance from the railroad tracks behind the arena. A few hundred folks showed up for the unveiling ceremony, which, like the equivalent scenario in Oklahoma City, received national attention, with both MTV and VH1 covering the event.

Korn singer Jonathan Davis was teary-eyed about the whole affair. "This [city] was a place that I dreaded as a teenager because there wasn't much stuff to do, but it's always going to hold a special place in my heart," he said. "It's a little bit too much to handle. Like, what are these politicians doing here saying they like us?"

I can probably guess the answer to that question and I recall desperately suggesting in this space in 2005 that San Jose should do something similar. In that column, I reminded folks that a few years earlier New York City had renamed the corner of Second and Bowery Streets Joey Ramone Place. It's located right near CBGB where the Ramones and much of New York punk rock began. Since there was probably never a rock band more inherently "New York" than the Ramones, officials in the Big Apple had enough class to rename a corner in Joey's memory—even if they had to go down to the Bowery to do it. That's what a real city does. Thousands of fans filled the streets for the dedication ceremony.

Obviously, one would expect no less from a world class city like New York, but even in a town like Bakersfield, the politicians can at least temporarily ditch the farmer's town overalls and do something to show that their city a rocking place. The only remaining question is, can San Jose?

Hail Trapezoid

Despite the maneuverings of developers to slaughter everything original in this town, there still exist local occult centers of primal activity that continue to radiate their hidden powers. So for this week's sermon, allow me to proselytize about yet one more: A hallowed area that I will now christen as "The Saratoga/Kiely/Stevens Creek Trapezoid." Strip mall aficionados have always worshiped the seven deadly sins that emanate from this locale.

You see, even a casual glance at a road map shows that the area bounded by Saratoga Avenue, Stevens Creek Boulevard, Kiely Boulevard and Northlake Drive forms a trapezoid, and those schooled in the occult arts and sciences know that trapezoidal symbology pops up in many hidden philosophies. We'll get back to that in a second. But for now we shall begin by summoning the occult powers of the legendary San Jose establishments that inhabit this trapezoid.

First there's Harry's Hofbrau, one of S.J.'s great meccas for cheapskate carnivore fundamentalists. Harry's has graced Saratoga Avenue with Gluttony for years now. This particular branch is one of four left in the Bay Area, and together they supposedly go through a combined 1 million pounds of turkeys each year. You cannot enter this trapezoid without conjuring the gods of Harry's Hofbrau, nor can you ignore another San Jose institution right across the parking lot, the Garden City Casino, that beautiful bastion of Greed and Envy. The history of Garden City is way beyond the scope of this column, but it's safe to say that, from the outside, the building looks like a combo of a chateau and a church, probably contributing to its overall holiness.

Also in that parking lot sits an empty space that used to be the Cabaret, an infamous '80s rock club that encouraged all the sins you'd expect from the devil's music, including Sloth and Wrath. In case you're counting, that's now five of the Seven Deadly Sins, and if you throw in the Tinker's Damn gay bar and Hot Stuff adult toy place, which are kitty-corner across the intersection, those would appropriately constitute Lust, leaving us with just one more sin: Pride.

Across the street the other way, one finds Saratoga Plaza, a classic suburban strip mall with signs going back decades. We must make sure that it remains off the redevelopment radar enough so that it won't get remodeled and defaced with the standardized faux-Southwestern color scheme of rustic brown, bile-colored olive green, beige and faded canary that you see on almost every other post-2000 strip mall around here. Since the developers really are the self-proclaimed deities of this town, I'm left with no other choice in my reactionary paranoid rage but to give the devil his due here and prevent them from destroying the wonderful seven sins of this sacred territory.

In "The Law of the Trapezoid," Church of Satan founder Anton La Vey explains that contrary to pyramids—which are seen as "pleasing" objects, as finished symmetrical forms that are godlike to the eye—trapezoids can represent deliberate aberration and misdirection. They can provoke anxiety and disturbances. He then extends this to explore how subtle aberrations in topographical symmetry can elicit unconscious revulsions in even the most tranquil of individuals.

Such metaphors are common in magical rituals, so we should expand on this by using the trapezoid of Saratoga, Kiely, Stevens Creek and Northlake to instill emotional imbalance, hardship and tragedy in the spirits of those godlike developers who are secretly meditating on prayer beads to baptize it anew with their next phase of hideous uniform abodes. Long live the trapezoid!

2008

The Spartan Barber

As of last Monday, Frank Annino has operated the Spartan Barber Shop for exactly 50 years at 487 S. Fourth St. in San Jose. The original health permit, dated Dec. 31, 1957, graces the wall opposite the front window, and the rest of the place looks exactly what you would expect from an old school barber shop: Faded checkerboard flooring, archaic barber chairs, photos of Joe DiMaggio in his prime and dated posters of haircut styles from the early '60s. One such placard offers choices like "Butch," "Ivy League," "Flat Top With Fenders" and "Forward Brush." Annino says a duplicate of this same placard can be seen on the wall of Floyd's Barber Shop in an episode of *The Andy Griffith Show*, and he still gets requests for those cuts.

San Jose State University spent *mucho dinero* hyping the school's 150th anniversary in 2007, and Frank has now chopped hair right there in his shop around the corner for one-third of that time span. It's one thing for a restaurant to withstand the constantly changing scenarios of this valley for a half-century, but for one man to go it alone for that long is a rare feat. We do not see many Frank Anninos these days. Over the years, he has trimmed the hair of both the Smothers Brothers as well as quarterback Jeff Garcia, all of whom were SJSU students.

Originally, Frank ran a shop on Willow Street; he then got drafted into the army, where he was stationed in France and cut hair for 35 cents a head. Upon returning home to San Jose, he bought the Spartan Barber Shop for $750 in 1957, and the rest is history. Over in the corner of the place, you can even see one of the antique cash registers he originally used, with a $1 slot for the haircut.

Obviously, much has changed since then, but one gets a completely different perspective when seeing it all through a barber's eyes. "Once the Beatles came around, a lot of the barbers went out of business," Annino said. "There were a lot of barbers around the campus at that time, but many had to close." Annino then used some leftover bucks form his G.I. Bill to supplement his income. "I stuck it out," he said.

Like any old-timer, Annino has much to tell about how his neighborhood has changed over the years. "Fourth Street used to go both ways in the old days," he recalled. "Then it went one-way going north, and then they put 280 in there in '67 and then eventually it went one-way going south again." Annino also has photos on the wall from back when the train tracks went straight down Fourth Street and dropped the college students off. "The tracks are now underneath the street," he said. "They built over them."

These days, men come from all over the neighborhood and even from across town to get their cut of choice at Frank's place. Antony Nispel, a substitute teacher, has been getting his shag lopped at Frank's since 1984.

"I'm not usually a very talkative person," he said. "But as soon as I would walk in there and sit down, there would always be conversation of some sort. You would get the local news, or whatever the Spartan Football team was doing, or anything else. Frank is just a really easy guy to talk to."

Nispel also added that Frank's place has always been a multigenerational establishment: "People walk in there and he remembers cutting their dad's hair." It's true and there exist SJSU professors who've had their mops trimmed at Frank's for 20 years running.

Once in a while, some audacious creep might saunter in and ask Frank if he wants to sell the place. "I always say no," he told me.

When Naglee Met Doobie

San Jose's Naglee Park Neighborhood has always exuded a quaint historic charm and character. Among its environs one finds many a mansion and distinguished home, classic in style, the fertile ground on which generations can reminisce about the grand communities of times past. Many of the homes in Naglee Park have historical significance, so it makes sense that the current locals would assemble an "historic inventory" of those houses where famous people once dwelled. But one place they haven't bothered to officially document yet is the domicile at 285 S. 12th St., which once was occupied by the only rock band in San Jose history to play a cameo gig on an episode of the legendary '70s black-culture sitcom, *What's Happening*. I'm talking about, of course, the Doobie Brothers, and this house is where they began. It should be in the Naglee Park Historic Inventory for that TV appearance alone.

Those of us who worshipped *What's Happening* will always cherish that episode where Rerun got busted for bootlegging the Doobie Brothers show and the message it taught all of us. Rerun was the lovable bulb-shaped dufus character and he couldn't get into the show, so a few thugs set him up with free tickets in trade for illegally taping the show. And the tape recorder fell out of his overcoat during the song, "Taking It to the Streets." That's right—back in the '70s you could actually go to jail for recording somebody's show. That entire episode is now, ironically, available on YouTube.

The 12th Street house sits right behind what's now the Naglee Park Garage, a small restaurant in the corner of the plaza at 11th and San Carlos, which includes a legendary downtown 7-Eleven and which functions as the western gateway to Naglee Park. Back in the early '70s, the Doobies lived, partied, rehearsed and did who knows what else in this house. Singer and guitarist Tom Johnston used to park his motorcycle on the porch of the place. Bikes were constantly out front. Skip Spence from Jefferson Airplane and Moby Grape also held court. According to the Doobies' Pat Simmons, Stevie Nicks, later of Fleetwood Mac, lived next door.

The house was an institution in downtown San Jose during those years and it should be in all the books. And speaking of that, Johnston himself actually appears in the San Jose City Directories at this address for the years 1971–1973, so the info is right there in the public domain for everyone to see.

Steven Seaweed of 107.7 The Bone says he lived in the house immediately before the Doobies did. On the Bone's website he says, "We lived in a house on 12th street by San Jose State, right behind the 7-Eleven. Matter of fact, we even put a gate in the back fence leading directly into the parking lot of Slurpee Heaven (not that we ever got cravings or anything)."

In short, the stories about this historical landmark of San Jose's Naglee Park will continue to inhabit the annals of history, even if it currently sits on a pretty nondescript block—just the type of street where the sun might come up on a sleepy little town down around San Antone. (Insert wince or rimshot here.)

Madison Avenue

The Circus that is the Little Saigon debate isn't going away, and people are still congregating in front of City Hall every Tuesday to protest San Jose City Councilmember Madison Nguyen because she and others voted to rename a part of Story Road "Saigon Business District" instead of "Little Saigon."

Since the entire scenario is bordering on surreal, I have to suggest a solution that will satisfy everyone: just rename the street Madison Avenue.

We're talking about the stretch of Story Road that runs from Highway 101 all the way to Senter Road, which is a grand esplanade if ever there was one, and since this area has a baffling tradition of naming streets after politicians who are still alive, it shouldn't be a problem.

But in order to reassure myself that such a progressive idea makes sense, I conjured up the urban blight exploration junkie once again and walked the entire length of the area in question, beginning at Story and Via Ferrari, which is just west of 101. A gorgeous industrial grade-A recycling plant began the journey.

The next breeze-by had to be the Story Road Animal Hospital, a neat-looking tiny hamlet of a building. It's old-school architecture at its jazziest. The yellow sign out on the sidewalk is one of those archaic traditional signs that just begs to be photographed. It stands there like royalty, with the hospital sign perpendicular to the slanting vertical pole. A black dog is standing on its hind legs, trying to climb the pole and get to a cat that sits on top of it. Many folks have documented and/or photographed old-school San Jose signs, but this one often gets lost among the nearby Asian shopping malls, empty retail buildings and graffiti-laden placards. It rules. And the building has paw imprints painted all along the edge of the roof.

As the journey proceeds westward even further, the junkie then comes to the crossroads of Story and McLaughlin—one of those legendary congested East Side intersections where at least five cars run the red light in every direction to avoid getting stuck in a second or third cycle. And don't even get me started on the clowns who consistently try and make U-turns on McLaughlin when there's obviously not enough room. You can stand there and count the people who end up driving over the curb.

There are good things about this intersection, though. We have three liquor stores, a Save Mart, a Burger King, a bunch of killer Vietnamese and Mexican stuff and a barber shop right next to a place that says, "Cleaners. Alterations. Libreria Christiana." I guess you can get both your suit tailored and your Biblical fix in the same place.

But the journey couldn't stop there. Continuing westward, one finds the Grand Century Shopping Mall, which is Vietnam central—an awesome place to hang out. The food court is a thoroughly rocking place. Right across the street, one finds the now-ubiquitous Lee's Sandwich shop with a noble, imposing sign that says, "Got hot baguette."

And one couldn't possibly traverse this length of road without mentioning the KLIV/KRTY building that sits right in the middle of it all. This recently replaced what used to be a decades-old landmark radio building. You can look up the photos.

As the urban blight exploration junkie reaches the end of this now hotly contested stretch of Story Road, he then passes the Taco Bell at Roberts Avenue and crosses to a green meadow which is basically a fenced-off landfill on the other side of the creek from the sheep at the Happy Hollow Zoo. Man, what a stretch of road. The entire thing is a grand, majestic, all-inclusive, distinguished promenade worthy of being renamed Madison Avenue. This is the future of San Jose, right here and now.

Groundwerx Wants Downtown to be Disneyland

A brand new downtown San Jose beautification adventure called Groundwerx debuted last week. Two different teams, the Ambassadors and the Clean Team, will soon hit the streets to sanctify the downtown experience. The Ambassadors, wearing uniforms and green hats, will hit the streets either on foot, bicycles or Segways and will serve as roaming concierges of sorts. They will tell you where to catch the right bus, direct you to restaurants, monitor the panhandlers, report graffiti and also serve as extra eyeballs for the police. The Clean Team, decked out in uniforms and orange hats, will power-wash the sidewalks, eradicate graffiti, monitor refuse receptacles, remove gum from the benches and basically empty the trash more frequently than before. They will utilize eco-friendly motorized street sweepers that basically look like lime-green Zambonis with sirens attached. So look out litterbugs—they're coming to getcha!

"Our goal is to make this look like Disneyland," said Groundwerx honcho Chuck Hammers at the press conference. He then said that if someone tosses his or her Starbucks cup onto the ground, we can be sure that the Clean Team will be right there to pick it up. I was probably the only one in the crowd who rolled his eyes upon hearing this, as for 15 years now I've been verbally attacking the dignity of San Jose powers-that-be for trying to convert downtown into a manufactured Disneyland-like false paradise instead of letting it grow organically. But now Mr. Hammers finally came out and invoked ol' Walt's nom de plume for everyone to hear. There you have it. Of course, I realize he meant "Disneyland" in the sense that they're merely shooting for ultra spic-and-span sidewalks to make the environment more user-friendly, but I sure am tempted to summon the grand old philosopher Jean Baudrillard and quote his *Simulacra and Simulation* on Disneyland being a hyperreality—that is, people think it actually is the reality it's supposed to be simulating. And seeing these guys in the orange hats with the green Zambonis on the streets of downtown—yeah, it pretty much evokes a theme park state of mind. You're just waiting for the calliope music to kick in.

But to be fair, the city, the Downtown Association and the Redevelopment Agency have been laboring over this Roving Concierge/Team-Street-Maid combo idea for a long time now, and we'll just have to see if it works. Other cities have apparently achieved success with similar programs, so cross your fingers. We could have a squeaky-clean Disneyland downtown before you know it. And no public tax dollars are being tapped. Downtown property owners voted to basically assess themselves up to 7.5 cents a square foot to fund the whole thing. Support exists from across the board.

That said, it doesn't take a Ph.D. in semiotics to have some fun with this. I went and looked up a bunch of quotes from Walt Disney himself and all you have to do is basically substitute the word "downtown" for "Disneyland" and it completely works. Here we go:

- "Disneyland will never be completed. It will continue to grow as long as there is imagination left in the world."
- "I first saw the site for Disneyland back in 1953, In those days it was all flat land—no rivers, no mountains, no castles or rocket ships—just orange groves, and a few acres of walnut trees."
- "We did it [Disneyland], in the knowledge that most of the people I talked to thought it would be a financial disaster closed and forgotten within the first year."
- "Disneyland is a work of love. We didn't go into Disneyland just with the idea of making money."
- "I don't want the public to see the world they live in while they're in the Park (Disneyland). I want to feel they're in another world."

Count Dante: Beer, Blood & Cornmeal

Pretty soon, you'll be seeing a book titled *Beer, Blood & Cornmeal: Seven Years of Strange Wrestling*, penned by Count Dante, who was a high flyer during those rocking days when people in Sasquatch costumes appeared in the ring and also shared gigs with punk bands and started riots.

Dante hails from them thar wastelands of the S.F. peninsula, and he has quite a lot to say about the suburban droopiness of growing up around such locales as "Shallow Alto." It just makes you want to don a leopard skin and get paid 20 bucks to go in the ring and beat up a dude in a chicken suit. In fact, this book is probably one of the best descriptions I've ever read of what I myself was like as a teenager in the suburbs: collecting action figures, watching wrestling on a Saturday morning, driving beater cars and going to gigs in San Francisco.

Throughout the book, Dante, a.k.a. Bob Calhoun, takes readers into a world they most probably never knew existed, unless they're the type who naturally enjoy bouts between the Christians and the Abortionists. In Chapter 7, Calhoun refers to the "force field" complex that prevents people from finally leaving the suburbs for good. Instead, they wind up at rock & roll bars all over San Francisco instead and then drive back home to their mom's house afterward.

"I was captive of apathy and chickenshit fear," he explains in the book. "I was going on five (or was it six?) years at a two-year college. Sooner or later, you actually take those statistics and math classes you were avoiding and transfer to State. You finally have decisions to make. You don't really want to just manage the Kinko's copies or sling coffee at the local bookstore/espresso house. You want to be somebody and a dirtbag in the city seems so much more spectacular that a loser in the 'burbs. I didn't have an Obi-Wan Kenobi to deactivate my own personal tractor beam, but eventually, the city exerted a far greater gravitational pull on me than suburban security, sterility and convenience."

Aside from the raucous wrestling tour tales, which chart his saga up through the Vans Warped sideshow in 2001, the book also sheds light on a lot of forgotten San Francisco rock joints like the I-Beam, the Farm and the Paradise Lounge. Those of us who drove up to those places during our teenage youth in the '80s tend to get a little starry-eyed when it comes to that stuff.

And speaking of things "Incredibly Strange," V. Vale from RE/Search wrote the foreword for this thing and I agree with him when he says his favorite low-budget musical film is *The Incredibly Strange Creatures Who Stopped Living and Became Mixed-Up Zombies* by Ray Dennis Steckler. Vale kick-started the whole "incredibly strange" phenom with his books, *Incredibly Strange Films* and *Incredibly Strange Music, Vols. One and Two*. So someone made the right move by asking the dude to write the foreword.

Dante himself was also managed for a time by legendary San Jose disc jockey Dennis Erectus, who is also a wrestling connoisseur. In fact, in the book there's a great photo of him smashing a chair over Dante's back. Man, what a show.

Backwater Renaissance

In the tradition of world-class cities that preserve historical buildings and convert them to artists' spaces, along comes a project called the BackWater Arts Gallery, located in a historical San Jose home dating back to 1877. You wouldn't even know the two-story New England–style house exists, as it lies at the end of Quinn Avenue, a side street off Senter Road, buried at the back of what's now an industrial wasteland just west of Coyote Creek. If you veer off Senter down Quinn, you will dead-end at the house. The dwelling is a quintessential forgotten treasure with a long, long history. If you're out there on Senter, among the homogeneous strip-mall developments just north of Tully, you'd never even realize that a short venture down a nondescript little side street would bring you to an ancient house going back 130 years.

Back in those days, an Irishman named William Quinn came to this part of San Jose and purchased several acres of land on both sides of that section of Coyote Creek. Quinn Avenue is named after him. Another bloke named Frederick G. Wool sauntered onto the scene and acquired some of Quinn's property west of the creek and built this house. He later founded the F.G. Wool Packing Company in 1903, and the company was family-owned and -operated straight up until 1989, making it the longest continuously family-run cannery anywhere in the United States, if not the world.

The old brick cannery building still sits behind the house, along with a water tower and the whole nine yards. Although the surrounding area has long since been taken over by computer warehouses, trucking yards and the likes thereof, the original two-story home, along with a garden and a dilapidated greenhouse, remains right smack in the middle of it all—the last hanger-on from a long-forgotten era. You feel like you've left San Jose and stepped right into an episode of *Green Acres* and you're just waiting for Eddie Albert to walk out with a pitchfork.

One of Wool's descendants, Page Wool Hamilton, lived in the house straight up until she passed away in December of 2006 at the age of 93, and then everyone's favorite real estate developer with the cowboy hat got his hands on the property. And now, two innovative artists, Anne Sconberg and Sarah Cole, have started a project to turn the historic home into a gallery and a live/work space, which is already hosting art shows, performances, workshops, animation and short films—basically, a colony where artists can just show up and congregate, a place the likes of which San Jose fatally lacks these days. Thus, BackWater Arts is alive and well, and as of right now, 10 different artists either live or rent studios in the house. A fundraising art auction will take place this Saturday from 6 to 10pm. The world is invited.

Sconberg and Cole modeled the idea after the Brewery Arts Colony in Los Angeles, a huge outpost of hundreds of art studios nestled in what used to be the former Pabst Blue Ribbon and Eastside Beer breweries, as well as a historic power plant. Many artists flock to the Brewery to live in residence while they create their work, and the waiting list to rent one of the lofts is a mile long. Sconberg and Cole have a similar idea in mind with this house, one that should be a registered historic landmark, one that should be saved before the rezoning czars pounce in with plans for more hideously uniform condos that nobody anywhere wants or needs.

And again, you wouldn't even know this house was even there at the end of Quinn Avenue unless you were looking for the place. It's that secluded. "That's why we have the whole idea of BackWater Arts as our name," Cole explained. "It's indicative of our situation here, both on this property and as an arts organization in San Jose, and the river, and that this property is a great secret little place anyway."

Shamrock Arena

I recently wound up at mixed martial arts legend Frank Shamrock's studio in south San Jose near Oakridge Mall. Shamrock was the five-time UFC Middleweight World Champion before he retired undefeated. After a mishmash of other endeavors, he returned to his lifeblood, mixed martial arts. In 2005, he opened his first academy where he trains his students in kickboxing and submission wrestling.

Now that it's a legally sanctioned sport, mixed martial arts is generating all sorts of hoopla these days, and on March 29, Shamrock battles his crosstown rival, Cung Le, at the HP Pavilion. At a press conference last week, Shamrock walked right out of a sparring session and immediately hammed it up for the cameras.

"My new goal is to be a superdelegate," he quipped. "I have no idea what they are, but they have 'super' attached to it."

Reporters asked him about the crosstown rivalry and upcoming battle against Le at the Pavilion.

"It's my arena," he declared. "In my opinion, it's a fight for the entire city. Call it a predator rivalry, but only one guy can be the King of San Jose. I'm the one who brought mixed martial arts to San Jose in 1997, and as far I'm concerned, that should be me."

Fair enough, but aside from all the fighting, the martial arts and the theatrics, Shamrock has a colorful assortment of characters working in his entourage, and he inspires them all.

Tony Demaria, Shamrock's boxing coach, is a former rock singer and was one of a small city of rotating members in the legendary San Jose band Daddy-O, although unfortunately he was not in the lineup that performed on the Gong Show in 1979. But as a boxing coach, Demaria, 59, is a lifelong San Jose dude and has nothing but rapturous admiration for Shamrock as an athlete.

"He's got a lot of dignity," Demaria said of him. "He's very, very honest, and of all the guys I've ever got to work with in my life, he's been not only the most talented but by far the most intelligent and very much sincere. All I can sing are the kid's praises. If he was a custodian, he'd still be a superstar. He has super, super, super charisma, and super energy. ... He's just a monster. Whatever he did in life, he would be the very best at. ... He's the Muhammad Ali of mixed martial arts."

Standup comedian Mary Van Note used to work in Shamrock's office and says he even inspired her comedy. She originally posted an ad on Craigslist.com for an office receptionist job and Shamrock answered it himself.

"It totally freaked me out because I knew who he was and I was a fan," she explained over the phone following a recent performance at the Bridgetown Comedy Festival in Portland. "At the time I don't think they were really ready to hire somebody, but I was very adamant about getting that position, so I kind of showed up, sat around and kind of bothered them about it. And they ended up giving me the position. I became his assistant."

Van Note is now known throughout YouTube-land for alternative and wonderfully foul-mouthed comedy videos featuring X-rated language that isn't suitable even for this newspaper. And it all began at Shamrock Marital Arts Studios on Winfield Boulevard.

"I actually edited my first few videos on his computer," she said. "He would let me stay after work and use his camera. So he was just totally cool about letting me, you know, do my comedy stuff."

There you have it. My vote goes to renaming HP Pavilion Shamrock Arena. What do you think?

Paging Silicon Valley

I've been saying for years that what will finally put San Jose on the map is not the fact that we're the 10th largest city, the fifth cleanest big city, the eighth most walkable city or whatever twaddle the politicians are regaling us with this week. It will take authors who place San Jose locales in their novels. That's what will do it.

Take local writer Lynn Rogers for example. Aside from co-authoring the Arcadia Publishing photo book on Alviso, she also writes novels that take place in the industrial wastelands of the South Bay and feature beautifully marginalized antiheroes of the suburbs, from alcoholic veterans at the Salvation Army on Stockton Avenue to runaway goth kids who sneak into empty warehouses. Her newest romp, *A Valley of Ashes: Homeless in a Nuclear Warehouse*, is her fifth book and heavily features the abandoned 55-acre General Electric plant on the corner of Monterey Highway and Curtner, the one now flattened and replaced by a gargantuan retail mall.

"I definitely felt that the characters overtook me in this case," she explains. "They had a life of their own. I've known many fine writers, ironically, who had come out of the old GE plant. ... I found that it was a place of vanishing history, and that whole area out at Monterey Road became compelling to me."

That GE plant was San Jose's definitive dilapidated Cold War-era splotch of blighted industrial wilderness, and now it is forever immortalized in Rogers' book, which is available from Inkling Press (www.inklingpress.com). The site should now attract literary travelers from across the globe, much like that house in Pigott, Ark., where Hemingway wrote parts of *A Farewell to Arms*, the street corners of Cairo that Nobel Laureate Naguib Mahfouz wrote about, or that one church in San Damiano, Umbria, where St. Francis di Assisi first received his calling from God.

"The so-called blight and the marginalized people are the heart of the valley," Rogers told me. "That's the true voice of our valley right now. It cannot be found in Willow Glen yuppies' voices, and it can't be found amongst SUVs. It's out there. And if you're so blessed to hear the voice, it captures you. It just took me over."

When yakking with Rogers, it becomes apparent that her experience with blighted areas and marginal people in society borders on the spiritual.

"In general, I'm interested in people who the theologian Matthew Fox called the voiceless ones," she tells me. "And that's been true since I left Menlo Park and its affluence and took to the road as a teenager following some of those figures. Those who are on the fringe have no voice."

So she puts them in her books. Many of her books use real people and places in this valley, whether it's a dive bar on Monterey Highway or your everyday runaway goth hottie. Another one of her books, *The Rainbow's Daughter*, features a protagonist's true-life infiltration of a bizarre Menlo Park mystical Tupperware party powwow resembling EST, the legendary '70s New Age behavior improvement cult.

Rogers will read from her books and lecture at two upcoming events taking place in a suburban wasteland littered with uniform tract houses otherwise known as Cambrian Park. (I can say such things, I grew up there.) On April 16 at 1pm she will entertain the Kiwanis Club at the Cambrian Park Methodist Church at 1919 Gunston Way. A day later, she will headline a weekly gathering of scribes at 15272 Charmeran Ave. Both places exist in the 95124 zip code, and unlike Willow Glen, Cambrian Park feels no need to flaunt its zip code on its own T-shirts. For more information on each event, suburban blightophiles are encouraged to call 408.559.5995.

Missed It by That Much

Your birth is a mistake you'll spend your whole life trying to correct.
—*Chuck Palahniuk*

Part of being a respectable columnist is to exhibit a strong degree of self-confidence and integrity when admitting one's mistakes. Since I have committed more than my share of embarrassing howlers over the years, I feel the time is right to do just that. So here are a few to get us started.

In August of 2007, I suggested that both the Santa Clara County Fair and the Berryessa Flea Market should be moved into the empty retail space at City Hall. I thought it was a perfect idea, given that the futures of both the flea market and the fair are in jeopardy, and in pure downtown San Jose fashion, it really looked like nothing would ever move into the empty ground-level retail spaces of City Hall and the parking garage next door at Fourth and San Fernando. But since I had lumped both those buildings under the banner of "City Hall retail," it took a respectful call from Tom Manheim in the city manager's office to remind me that the garage building is not part of City Hall, that it's a completely different building. Fair enough.

In a similar faux pas, a column last January found me conversing with Jeffrey Deane Turner, the alleged Tiffany stalker and conspiracy theorist, one of the heroes depicted in Sean Donnelly's independent film *I Think We're Alone Now*. In the column I reported about Turner's take on the battle between the Illuminati and what I thought he referred to as the "Old secular right/international fascism." Well, that was wrong. Before Turner's autograph session at the Cinequest showing, he informed me that the Old Secular Right and the International Fascism strains of the conspiracy are not on the same side. They are actually at war with each other instead. "You missed that one," he told me.

In yet another colossal blunder, just three weeks ago, in a piece titled, "Backwater Renaissance," I mixed up Eddie Albert from *Green Acres* with country music legend Eddy Arnold. When describing a certain house, I said it was like "stepping into an episode of Green Acres and you're just waiting for Eddie Arnold to walk out with a pitchfork." This was a quintessential brain fart, as I absolutely knew the difference between the two, but some synapse in my brain just temporarily disconnected itself. One reader immediately chimed in with this gem: "I'm sure, however, that Mr. Arnold knows his way around a pitchfork a damned sight better than Mr. Albert." I totally agree and I think what happened is that I unconsciously mixed up Albert's character with that of Arnold the Pig, also a personality from *Green Acres*.

Finally, for the cover story on the Lake Cunningham Skate Park two weeks ago, I recklessly described the "fields of dandelions" surrounding the asphalt skatepark. Well, turns out they're not dandelions after all, and Arvind Kumar of the Santa Clara County Chapter of the California Native Plant Society informed me that "the lovely yellow flowers at the skate park are not dandelions, pesky invasive plants from Europe. They are California goldfields (*Lasthenia californica*), a lovely native annual that was once common in the Santa Clara Valley until the advent of agriculture, ploughing, orchards and later asphalt."

Touché. That was a gaffe of the highest order. I was nowhere near the mark on that one. I guess the only cornball explanation I can manufacture is this: Those skaters in that story, as well as myself, are originally from San Jose, Calif., so much of what we know, naturally, is concrete and weeds. In fact, we've been pesky, invasive dudes for most of our lives. We probably *are* the weeds in this town, for crying out loud. Ultimately, to err can be human and inhuman, natural and unnatural. In my case, it's probably all of the above.

Faber's Cycling Mecca

If you're one of the thousands who've trudged their way through the knee-high piles of bike parts in the yard of Faber's Cyclery over the years, you will be blown away by how clean and orderly the place is these days. Located at the corner of South First Street and Margaret, Faber's is one of the oldest buildings in the South Bay and it soaks in over a century of history. The place was a corner saloon in 1884 and has been a bicycle business since 1921.

Alexander La Riviere has owned the place for three decades, and is now right in the middle of hosting three Sunday Talks at Faber's in the back yard. The first lecture took place on April 13 and the next two will be this Sunday and the following Sunday, April 27 and May 4, respectively. The events are free of charge and you will learn more than you ever possibly imagined about all things related to the history, sociology, philosophy and probably theology of the two-wheeler. He'll break out historical photos, bikes and memorabilia no one else has.

Faber's has always been San José's mecca for vintage bike enthusiasts, and the place is like a ramshackle museum where you'll find brand spanking new boxes of components right next to a dusty 1941 Schwinn frame. People from all over the county show up to swap bikes, get their rig fixed, look for obscure parts or just revel in the sheer history of the place. It looks like a rundown shack from the road, but it's actually a gearhead's paradise on the inside. Whether you're looking to hotrod your '50s cruiser or just assemble a beater piece of junk to get you from dive bar A to dive bar B, Faber's has always been the place. These guys can probably cobble together a working bicycle from scratch parts faster than most people can take a new one out of the box.

Sunday Talks at Faber's are a joint effort between Faber's and artist Alex Clausen and are actually part of a larger endeavor called "The Distributed Exhibition," a collaborative project produced by Sara Thatcher and the San José Institute of Contemporary Art (SJICA), featuring several site-specific artworks at locales in the vicinity of SJICA.

One cannot yak with La Riviere without getting buried by his overwhelming and beautifully twisted encyclopedic knowledge of bicycles. He's also one of only a few qualified forensic experts in bicycle accidents in the country, and he often gets called upon to testify in court on such matters. With both him and his brother Anthony, sometimes it's hard to get out of that place in less than an hour because these guys are just so passionate about their trade that they can't stop talking about it.

For the lectures, La Riviere will discuss the entire history of bicycles, from 1791 to the present, how it parallels the histories of slavery and women's suffrage, and how the whole narrative intertwines with the rise of the blacksmith and sewing machine industries in the 19th century. He will pull out an entire 50-foot-long visual timeline and spread it across the front of the shed out back. He will display several bicycles circa 1880–1895, and he says it takes about three hours to set up everything for the show.

Sadly, everything in this town comes down to real estate, and the property upon which Faber's sits is on the chopping block, meaning that it's only a matter of time before some heartless inhuman monster swoops in, buys the property and flattens the place. Either that, or it will mysteriously burn down like other buildings that seem to prevent developers from having their way. La Riviere realizes that the fate of Faber's is out of his hands, but he at least wants to see the building preserved. "My hope is to make it a neighborhood learning facility that would promote history and cycling in general—not just San José, but for everything," he says.

Woolworth Museum in Oxnard

With all the recent spats about historical preservation and my fond retro-kitsch memories of downtown San Jose's old Woolworth Building, I felt like a higher cosmic intelligence was directing me southbound to fill the hole in my soul when I discovered a redevelopment mecca in Ventura County—the Woolworth Museum. Someone in downtown Oxnard, Calif., had restored that city's old Woolworth building and turned it into a museum, so I just had to make a spiritual trek and investigate the place. The place is a tour de force of historical preservation.

The Woolworth Museum is the brainchild of one Mr. David Feigin, who calls himself a "lunatic revivificationist"—that is, someone who "revives" old buildings, and then defends and nurtures their mystical eminence. And what better place to engage in such activity than an old Woolworth building? When Feigin first bought the empty, two-story, 16,800-square-foot structure, he brought in a lawn chair and sat alone for hours in the vacant cavernous place, just so he could "hear the building."

Many books are already published on all that was Woolworth, that famous variety store chain that gave the English language the term "five-and-dime." You could waltz in and do your cheap shopping while others mowed through greasy heart-stopper specials at the food counter. It was a place where graying waitresses would always refer to you as "honey." Sadly, the entire U.S. operation cashed in about 1997, and all Woolworths across the country closed. Feigin and his wife/business partner Nancy Greenfield gobbled up Oxnard's abandoned Woolworth's in 2002.

"It was the only one left that was still in its original state and hadn't been turned into something else yet," she told me.

The place is now subdivided and converted into, among other things, a new all-ages live music cafe, additional office space upstairs and, of course, the museum itself, which showcases all sorts of Woolworth ephemera —trinkets, postcards, old stamp machines, books, autographed photos, arcade games and the likes thereof. Almost any kitsch Woolworth artifact you can imagine is here. The cafe even features retro décor and a Woolworth-style lunch counter. Even though Feigin himself has nothing to do with the original Woolworth business, he decided not to slap some cheap hideous facade on the place. He tracked down a warehouse in New York that still had the original Woolworth gold-leaf lettering one used to see on the outsides of all the stores, imported it in and fashioned it for the front of the building, just like the old days. Still a work in progress, the museum intends to become a destination place, especially for those die-hard Woolworth fanatics.

Mike Driscoll, a travel writer based in Brookfield, Ill., has been collecting Woolworth memorabilia for 25 years. "I've always traveled to see them because of the Americana aspect," he said. "It used to be a lot of fun to go to towns like Lodi in the '70s. I would just trek through every town that I could. ... I would go to Palo Alto quite regularly. ... They all had that feeling. You just got a sense of America's past when you went there. So we used to trek to Woolworth's in every state."

Turns out Driscoll is only one of a vast underground network of Woolworth collectors throughout the United States and he says he's even traveled to Barbados and Southampton, England—places where Woolworths still actually exist. And he fully intends to visit Oxnard.

"Woolworth was Main Street America," he said. "You sort of have this feeling of the county courthouse across the street from Woolworth's when you go." There you have it. If San Jose wants to be a destination place, it needs to get some soul and build its own Woolworth Museum.

Mark Hager: Backstage Passing

With literary travel on the rise these days, more and more people are feeling the need to follow in their favorite authors' footsteps or to explore the locales that writers have placed in their novels. Longtime media consultant and video engineer Mark Hager is currently working on a novel about backstage life in Silicon Valley's corporate venues, and if I'm still around when this thing comes out, I will organize similar tours like the one he and I recently undertook.

Tentatively titled *Boom! Backstage Pass*, Hager's work in progress takes us through the chaotic circus of the house and backstage operations on show days at places like Shoreline Amphitheatre, the Mountain Winery, the San Jose McEnery and Santa Clara convention centers as well as HP Pavilion and the California Theatre in downtown San Jose. He claims to have a zillion stories from behind the curtains at all these venues, and he also says the novel is "the largest single collection of stagehand humor in one place, painstakingly collected from road crews from around the world."

So, just like others would jump at the opportunity to have Elmore Leonard himself point out skyscrapers in Detroit where certain characters of his shot each other, I couldn't resist when Hager graciously offered to escort me through the backstage confines of Shoreline Amphitheatre on a non-show-day and point out the locales he used in his unpublished novel.

(Full disclosure: There was a dark ulterior motive here on my part. I actually worked at Shoreline when I was a teenager. After surviving the first 16 years of my life as an only child in a dysfunctional family with an alcoholic father who had just died, I was way too emotionally immature to understand that I had no idea what a normal social relationship was and that I unconsciously just felt more natural surrounded by conflict. So I badmouthed everyone on the job, constantly snuck backstage where I wasn't supposed to be, stole alcohol from everywhere and basically abused every privilege until I got fired, not once, but three times. That was the late '80s, and I hadn't been back to Shoreline since, so it felt like a redemption to be actually invited backstage 20 years later. But that's another story.)

Anyway, there we were: Hager and I casually strolling through all the secret nooks and crannies of Shoreline that the general public never sees, most of which I can't even print here. But Hager's novel is not just some silly "backstage" exposé. Instead, he takes all the elements that come together when putting on a show at places like Shoreline from the crew's perspective—the load-in at 6am when the trucks back down the ramp, the running of the light trusses, the house PA, the band equipment, the iron workers, the stage riggers, the gophers, the production staff, the circus of everybody crisscrossing each other's spaces—and grafts it onto the structure of the novel. Each chapter is the equivalent of an act in a play with titles like Staging, Loading, Building, Rehearsing, Burning, Closing and Striking.

The novel also illuminates the cross-pollination of many different facets of Silicon Valley culture in ways that only a longtime audio/video crew insider can do. For example: the ways in which grand scale high-tech corporate culture has gradually merged with big-time rock-concert operations throughout the last 20 years; or, just as there's a rhythm that flows through the entire behind-the-scenes concert-day operations, there's a similar rhythm that buckles in, out and through the spider web of intersections between venture capital culture, high-end audio proliferation, suburban South Bay geography, Zen, computer hardware, chaos theory, fractals, rock music, backstage passes, Bluetooth and the Rosicrucians—and how all this represents the real Silicon Valley, and that it could only have happened here in Northern California.

Got it? Good. The second and final leg of the Hager literary tour finishes next week.

Hager Part Two: The Tao of Tech

Recently, I joined local video engineer Mark Hager on the first trial run of a literary tour through a slice of Silicon Valley underbelly that no one talks about. We'll call them the Ancient and Mystical Brotherhood of Union Stagehands (AMBUS) who toil away behind the scenes at all your favorite arena rock shows and grand-scale conventions and industrial events. Yes, the same crew of riggers, ironworkers, A/V techs, lighting designers and their ilk who bump into each other backstage at Shoreline Amphitheatre at least partly overlap with the folks running cable and troubleshooting satellite feeds behind the scenes at conventions and high-tech product launches. Hager, a Bellarmine graduate, is possibly the first one to ever write a book about the lifestyle. Boom! Backstage Pass is now complete and available at www.boombackstagepass.com. Aside from juicy gossip about high-tech celebs and rock stars, the book is filled with flashes of what life was like at the beginning of the dotcom bubble:

Data projectionists were suddenly so important because Silicon Valley had just discovered PowerPoint, the Microsoft presentation software. I discovered that I could make unbelievable amounts of money by just moving slides around, and leave the tweaking to someone else, so I quickly made myself a PowerPoint expert. This put me right in the crest of the Silicon Valley wave. A common joke asked, "How do you bring Silicon Valley to a standstill? Invent a virus that crashes PowerPoint." I saw all the best (and worst) business plans, marketing models, and sales projections, and they were all accompanied by the same pie charts. I saw the good and the bad, the truthful and the deceitful, the inspired and the expired.

For another leg of Hager's literary tour, he took me through the McEnery Convention Center and the backstage confines of the San Jose Civic Auditorium, both heavily featured in the chapter titled "Rehearsing." In that chapter, Hager tells the story of a rehearsal for the original launch of Microsoft's Explorer browser, which took place in those two venues. During those years, any new Microsoft product was certain to draw ridiculously large crowds, so even though Bill Gates was speaking to a crowd of 3,000 in the Civic Auditorium, Hager and the rest of the crew were required to set up and operate all the "overflow rooms" across the street in the Convention Center to accommodate media and/or VIPs who would either not make it inside on time or simply get locked out at show time.

Joey, Zed, Big Dick and I were the main crew for the biggest overflow room, Hall 2, which held several thousand. Dick was the job steward, I was in charge of the satellite feed from across the street, Joey was in charge of local computers, and Zed was in charge of the projectors. Yes, we broadcast by satellite just to go across the street. Such excesses were common. We had spent the whole day before building a full corporate stage with set pieces, curtains, sound system and event lights below two large screens that would show Bill from across the street. No one would ever speak from our stage, it was merely dressing for a signal that was bouncing though orbital space from across the street, all for an anticipated overflow audience that might not show up."

On a more philosophical note, Hager also explains that the hurry-up-and-wait rhythmic nature of setting up, working and tearing down a gig is just a microcosm of the larger-scale booming and busting of Silicon Valley itself. Everything is an organic, interconnected whole with the Tao flowing through it. "The best technician was like the ancient Taoist master, surrounded by the virtue of wu-wei, or 'non-action,'" he writes in the book. "In other words, 'doing nothing, yet leaving nothing undone.'"

Keep o1SJ Real

Last weekend, the o1SJ Global Festival of Art on the Edge took place in downtown San Jose and it was a mammoth cultural achievement, both for the city and SJSU, as well as the public and private sectors—true collaboration as only Silicon Valley can achieve. Some random notes:

• At the festival, the sense of community prevailed above all else. A wide mixture of artists took part—not just big names cruising into town on stipends and not just academics. Local talent was featured much, much more than last time and everybody intermingled. Legendary playwright Luis Valdez spoke at the opening ceremonies and proved he is the only dude anywhere who can defend Robert Graham's Quetzalcoatl statue in Plaza de Cesar Chavez as "art & technology." I didn't take notes, but it had something to do with how the Mayans, not the Hindus, invented the zero and that the statue's coil represents the sacred spiral dance. Imagine the scene: Luis Valdez—playwright, actor, producer, filmmaker, SJSU graduate and lifelong pal of Cesar Chavez—celebrating what's commonly ridiculed as the "poop statue" in the park named after Chavez—with all the politicos and corporate bigwigs in the audience. It just doesn't get any more "San Jose" than that, folks. Wow.

• S.J. has always been a place that looks to the outside for validation and approval while completely ignoring the subcultures and scenarios already existing here, and this festival has the potential to change all that. And to see the city of San Jose finally taking an interest in having a cultural signature of any kind is downright refreshing, to say the least. Walking around during this festival, knowing that this is only the second incarnation of something that will constantly change and grow and adapt, as it should, was awesome. You felt like San Jose was no longer just an adult city with diapers on.

• The SubZero street event all along South First Street on Friday night was by far the bohemian cyberlicious crème de la crème of the entire festival and easily the hippest thing to hit downtown San Jose since the first SoFA Street Fair in 1992. All the galleries showcased tech-related zonked-out works; bands performed on three stages; videos projected on buildings; interactive exhibits flanked three blocks and the widest possible variety of people showed up: kids, adults, corporate types, Burners, artists, politicians, programmers and the lunatic fringe. The entire vibe was high-tech, planetary, abstractly machinic and downright rocking.

• Unfortunately, during the run up to the festival, the phrase "pop culture" emerged in a few radio spots, and all of a sudden it was being billed as "Art, technology and pop culture" for some reason. I would hope that the organizers don't let this wonderful event degenerate into yet one more colorless dumbed-down "pop culture" event. If this thing winds up on MTV, or if I even start seeing o1SJ shirts on the wall in Hot Topic, then I will be very disappointed. It must continue to be a cutting-edge provocative zonked-out latticework of activity that asks questions, challenges assumptions and does all the things that new media art should do. I don't want to see a 01SJ jingle wind up in an Audi commercial.

• Now, will the 01SJ Global Festival of Art on the Edge eliminate San Jose's structural deficit or fill all the potholes? No. Of course not. Nobody anywhere is saying it will. That isn't the point. The important thing is that this festival at least helps foster a creative class and makes people actually want to be here and create here and work here and stay here. A healthy city needs such things. A healthy economy is at least somewhat intertwined with a healthy cultural environment. A lot of smart people live here and we deserve a better culture than what we already have.

History Must Go!

Last year, when my alter ego, the urban blight exploration junkie, decided to prowl around the industrial wastelands of Stockton Avenue in San Jose, fans of San Jose underbelly came roaring out of the woodwork to laud the elegant monstrosity of urban decay sitting at the corner of Julian and Stockton—that decrepit falling-to-pieces old Westinghouse warehouse. The building is famous, and several folks who appreciate the artistic value of urban blight photography have shot the place for their collections. *Metro* photographer Felipe Buitrago brilliantly captured it in the July 25, 2007, issue of *Metro*.

Along with many others, I assumed all these years that the building was unused, but boy was I wrong. Turns out the folks at History San Jose have been storing all sorts of dusty relics inside the building for 15 years and are now hosting an auction on the weekend of July 12–13 to get rid of it all. Technically, the auction is the final step of "deaccession," a method by which artifacts are permanently gutted from a museum's collection. It's a necessary practice museums go through in order to unload items that are in poor condition, already exist in great number, no longer have any relevance to the collection, or are just plain hazardous to keep. Media were invited for a sneak preview of the goods and believe me, this place is a treasure trove. Collectors of museum salvage, get ready. Here's a small example of what's inside the building: A 19th-century hearse. Bizarre medical equipment. Piles of Victorian architectural salvage. Old sinks, stoves and sewing machines. Ancient motor oil pumps. Busted farm gear. Vintage desks, armoires and vanities. A few sleighs. Old-fashioned printing press machinery. Heavy-duty sewer grates from 1887. And my two favorites:

(1.) An old machine for shock therapy, complete with dials and knobs for frequency control and settings that say things like, "surgery" and "therapy." (2.) An original '30s-era Thomas Alva Edison Voicewriter, complete with a box of wax cylinders.

97

We discovered a few potential diamonds in the rough, like an antique Steinway & Sons square piano, probably from the 19th century. Underneath the lid sits an old business card, dating from the '60s, that belonged to one Mr. Arlie R. Bolerjack, a piano tuner who worked at Ferguson's House of Rentals at 30 E. San Fernando St.

There's also a heavy gold-colored antique fireplace cover with an embossed Rosicrucian-looking Egyptian figure on the front. That piece will immediately get gobbled up during the opening live auction. Remains of a few antique cars are also there for the picking, including the carcass of an old Pierce-Arrow that somebody converted into a wooden popcorn truck. Yellow police caution tape weaves its way throughout the frame, complete with recent handwriting that says, "Do not move until termites are exterminated."

History San Jose claims that this sale has nothing to do with its current financial woes and that it just needs to get rid of stuff it no longer has a use for. The city owns the building and would rather it be a parking lot, so the stuff must go.

Auctioneer Frank Sunseri was present for the sneak preview, his voice booming throughout the warehouse as he advised the History San Jose folks how to effectively auction off the items, a daunting task given the amount of people that will probably show up. The final decision was to have the preview from 9 to 10:30am on Saturday, July 12, followed by a live auction. On Sunday, whatever is left will be sold off on a cash-and-carry basis. So bring your truck.

In short, this will be an awesome garage sale, to say the least. Restoration fanatics will drool over all the Victorian salvage. Antique auto collectors will be interested in the vehicle remains. And if you're the morbid type, you can even bid on the antique dust-covered gynecological table, complete with stirrups. There's something for everybody. Come on down! For info: www.historysanjose.org.

Local Chefs Say Eat Me

San Jose's own Joey Chestnut once again won the world-renowned Coney Island Hot Dog Eating Contest this last July Fourth, and his "bib sheet" on the International Federation of Competitive Eating's website rattles off an impressive list of his gluttonous conquests—records like 8.8 pounds of deep-fried asparagus spears in 10 minutes or 56 sausage-and-cheese kolaches in eight minutes. Advocates of clogged arteries from coast to coast are hailing the dude as a true hero and a national treasure. He's as American as apple pie.

But if you want to quack about local boys done good with their food, there's a much more wholesome rock & roll story you should know about. You see, Gordy Carbone and Gary Sunbury, two local pillars and swillers of the community, have now appeared on celebrity chef

Bobby Flay's newest show on the Food Network. The program, *Grill It! With Bobby Flay*, named after his recent *New York Times* bestselling cookbook, lets fans live out their ultimate culinary fantasy by cooking on television alongside Flay himself. Through audition videos and casting calls, Carbone and Sunbury competed with grillmeisters nationwide for 13 coveted guest spots, and they made it. If you were up at 6:30am last Sunday, you saw the debut of their episode, and it will now repeat again and again. Check your television schedules now.

(Chock-full disclosure: Both Carbone and Sunbury are old pals. Gordy is the throatman for the Forgotten, a local punk outfit on TKO Records that has been around 10 years and toured everywhere, while Gary is now the dude who changes the light bulbs above my desk.)

Years ago, the two blokes had already starred in their own homemade Internet cooking show called *Eat Me* (www.eatmetv.net), so they had plenty of source material with which to concoct their proposal when Sunbury first discovered the initial call for submissions on Craigslist. They both figured they had a unique package to submit: Two married punk-rock guys in their late '30s who cook a lot but can't afford $1,000 cutlery, have no need for gourmet parsley and who aren't concerned with the beta-carotene content of kale.

"I'm not going to talk shit on anybody who cooks, but I think what a lot of cooking shows lack is that they're not talking to the normal person," Carbone says. "When I emailed the show, I told them they were really missing the boat by not taking on what we've got to offer and from the get-go, it wasn't, 'Take Gordy and Gary,' it was, '*Take Eat Me.*' I said, 'When it comes to cooking shows, we're something you've never seen before.'"

So, with a punk-rock do-it-yourself aesthetic, Carbone and Sunbury fired off their home-edited submission complete with a soundtrack, and it worked. After all the contestants were whittled down, Flay's show contacted the two and informed them they had made the cut. A cameraman from Burbank even came to downtown San Jose in order to film Carbone and Sunbury in their environment. The guy spent seven solid hours shadowing the two while they shopped at Zanotto's, skated around town, cooked up their fare in the kitchen and then bickered with an old Vietnamese lady who regularly goes through their trash can.

Next step: Plane tickets, hotel rooms in New York City and the studio where *Grill It! With Bobby Flay* is filmed. On the show, Carbone and Sunbury grilled up homemade chicken quesadillas, a marinated flank steak and a surf 'n' turf salad. "This is a great example of teamwork," Flay said during the show. "You guys work very well together." The dress code for appearing on the set was not what they expected, as there exist certain stipulations about what works on camera. "We couldn't wear white or black or red or anything with stripes, or nothing with checkers, or pretty much, like, everything we own," Sunbury says. But both were absolutely blown away by Flay's dedication to his craft. "What impressed me the most about Flay was that he was just like us, he was a normal guy, but with him, it's food first," Carbone says.

And when Flay autographed Carbone's copy of *Grill It!*, he wrote: "Punk on. Thanks for the delicious quesadillas." In Sunbury's copy, Flay scribbled, "Eat San Jose alive."

St. James' Curse

The San Jose Redevelopment Agency has now released preliminary documents related to the relandscaping of St. James Park in downtown San Jose, a project intended to give the much-maligned park a new face-lift while preserving its historic character. Since this park was San Jose's original town square in the 1880s, I have a few thoughts on the park's crazed history.

By now, most folks know about the Brooke Hart lynching in 1933. It is San Jose's darkest moment. Two degenerate wastoids kidnapped and murdered the 22-year-old Hart, and law enforcement officials didn't have enough manpower to hold the killers in their cells, so the lynch mob prevailed and hanged the men from two different trees, an elm and a mulberry. The trees were later removed. Writing in a 1957 issue of *Modern Detective Magazine*, Edward G. Sullivan, who attended the lynching, described it harrowingly: "the mob rioted in frenzied glee under the two swinging bodies. Teenage schoolboys leaped and pranced back and forth on the grass, brandishing whiskey bottles and yelling in triumph. Women ... held their wide-eyed babies aloft to give them a good look. Laughing couples danced and embraced under the slowly dangling feet."

Now, I'll go out on a limb and suggest that there should be a plaque in St. James Park to designate this atrocity. We must never forget the dark side of human history. President William McKinley, for example, came to speak in the park in 1901 and was assassinated in Buffalo four months later. Presidential candidate Robert F. Kennedy came to speak in the park in 1968 and was assassinated in Los Angeles three months later. Monuments for both those individuals exist, but nothing regarding the lynching.

Jump to 2008. The Redevelopment Agency says that the funding available for the relandscaping is limited to the western half of the park, bounded by First Street, Second Street, St. James and St. John. The eastern half will not be dealt with for now, which, if you know San Jose, will definitely elicit some complaints.

You see, more than a few disgruntled east San Joseans objected to the new City Hall, arguing that the side of the building facing directly east—the solid, flat, rectangular Socialist-Gulag-looking side—is a callous and deliberate snub at east San Jose in general. Similar complaints emerged when one of the proposals to restore the clock tower on the Museum of Art suggested leaving off the particular clock face on the side of the tower facing east. So expect people to start screaming at the RDA for symbolically dissing the East Side by only redeveloping the west side of St. James Park. It's not as crazy as it sounds, believe me.

In any event, as part of this new landscaping plan, the landscape architect hired by the RDA asked a consulting arborist, one Mr. Michael Bench, to prepare an evaluation of all the trees in the park. In that evaluation, he says:

"During my visits to this site, I observed that police vehicles would routinely drive across the lawn between the trees in order to confront one or more individuals. On one occasion, I observed a City of San Jose maintenance vehicle being driven across the lawn. Apparently this is an accepted practice in this park. However, the use of vehicles no doubt contributes significantly to the soil compaction in the park. Soil compaction reduces the absorption of water into the soil, either by rainfall or by irrigation, and it reduces the drainage capability of the soil. The result is that absorbing roots die and require years to regenerate. Most trees react by slow decline. Some trees die. ... I recommend that police vehicles be driven primarily on the paved pathways except during an emergency."

So now we've come full circle. First Brooke Hart's killers were lynched from the trees because not enough officers were present to stop the angry mob, and now some of the current trees are dying because the cops keep driving across the grass. The fun just never ends in St. James Park and I wish the RDA nothing but luck in this endeavor.

Thollem McDonas: Key Witness

San Jose native and pianist extraordinaire Thollem McDonas is about to make history. The SJSU graduate was recently invited to compose for and record on the only piano that French composer Claude Debussy owned during the last 14 years of his life (1904—1918). Currently occupying the Labenche Museum of History and Art in Brive-la-Gaillarde, France, the instrument is a Blüthner piano, which uses the unique Aliquot stringing system. An extra set of resonating strings is included just above the usual sets, enriching the tone and giving the piano a luminous, iridescent sound in the higher registers. McDonas has invited legendary contrabassist Stefano Scodanibbio to join him for the Sept. 29 concert and contributions are currently being accepted to help fund the documentation of this historic project.

If you're not familiar with Debussy, at least dig this much: His revolutionary 1894 orchestral work *Prelude to the Afternoon of a Faun*, based on the Stéphane Mallarmé poem of the same name, is pegged by many as the beginning of modern music. The piece disregarded any adherence to standard tonality and was more of a continuous free-flowing tone poem than a customary orchestral composition. Although radical for its time, the piece was widely accepted and influenced generations of composers. Debussy himself drew heavy inspiration from the Symbolist poets and painters of his era and his music often evoked the shapes, colors and schemes of nature, but somehow on a more subtle and mystical plane. Conveniently, he also hung around all the prominent occult circles in turn-of-the-century France, of which there were many, and the conspiracy theories place him as the Grand Master of the Priory of Sion following Victor Hugo and preceding surrealist painter/filmmaker Jean Cocteau. With *Prelude to the Afternoon* of a Faun, Debussy claimed he had created music that "will no longer be professional rhetoric, but will be given a more universal and essential psychic conception." And when publishing music criticism under the pseudonym of *Monsieur Croche the Dilettante Hater*, Debussy blasted finicky academic analyses of composers' works, claiming that such nonsense "kills their mysteries." In short, Debussy was a mysterious, elusive personality who could never be pigeonholed, a special quality that, in my opinion, comes through in much of his music.

McDonas himself originally emerged from what's now San Jose City Council District 8 and was initiated into the piano-playing path almost from birth. After graduating 18 years ago with degrees in both piano performance and composition, he tripped around with various political and ecological movements before returning to music with full focus. These days, he spends his time perpetually touring back and forth between Europe and the States, mostly as a soloist, but also in collaboration with countless other individuals and groups. He's released over a dozen CDs and he's performed in theaters, art galleries, universities, elementary schools, concert halls, jazz and rock clubs, festivals, house concerts, forests, riots, and on TV and radio. This Saturday, he performs with a punk band in Milan, Italy, and the very next day he hops on a train to Paris and then to Brive-la-Gaillarde to record on the Debussy piano.

"It's an amazing opportunity that makes me equally terrified and ecstatic," he wrote me in an email from Italy. "There are thousands of pianists and composers who would probably be willing to break my legs to be in my position."

He added that Debussy's piano itself, due to the extra set of resonant strings, evokes a shimmering mystical quality. "In all of my travels, I've never played a piano like this," he said. "Six months ago, on my last French tour, I had an afternoon to play it, and immediately I was deeply connected to what felt like a supernatural energy."

Contributions are being solicited at three levels: $50/$150/$500 and can be made via PayPal to: thollem@yahoo.com or by postal mail to: Debussy Project, 1077 Fewtrell, Campbell, CA, 95008, USA.

Clampers on Parade

Last week's Veterans Day parade provided an opportunity to reacquaint myself with the Ancient and Honorable Order of E Clampus Vitus, Mountain Charlie Chapter No. 1850. The Clampers, as they call themselves, are a men's drinking fraternity of the absurd that doubles as a historical preservation society. They sport Old West duds and install historical plaques at various locales throughout California, swilling drinks in the process. The Mountain Charley chapter, our local faction, is named after "Mountain Charlie" McKiernan, the legendary Santa Cruz Mountain trailblazer and grizzly fighter. Every Veterans Day for the parade, the Clampers bring their own floats, one of which is a homemade wooden outhouse, complete with a shingled roof and all the expected accoutrements stuck to the outside: empty beer cans, a rusted toilet seat, a satellite dish, prospecting equipment, a "2 hour parking" sign, an American flag and more. In pure Clamper fashion, a beverage keg sits inside, routed to a tap on the outside of the structure. A pickup truck tows the whole thing. Another float, a wooden trailer complete with bales of hay and an ancient barber's chair for the imbibing, also made its annual appearance last week.

I arrived, coffee in hand, somewhere around 10am, as the rear fleet of parade floats maneuvered for position along Autumn Street next to the Shark Tank. A whorl of activity enveloped the scene. Harleys roared up from St. John Street. A float carrying the American Legion contingent appeared, complete with full regalia. Wandering firemen casually surveyed the scene on foot. Clampers gathered boisterously, all wearing their distinctive red long-sleeve shirts and black leather vests covered with buttons and patches. On the sidewalk by the Arena Green, they fired up a stove, the smell of propane filling the air. Hot dogs were flung onto the grill. The roar of a generator erupted in order to power the popcorn machine and the coffee maker. The men drank while the women operated the grill.

Another pickup truck eventually emerged, towing a mock old-school locomotive that the Clampers have hot-rodded with two stoves in order to cook sausage sandwiches during the parade. Unfortunately, they are no longer allowed to use the apparatus, due to the ban on flaming parade floats. Leave it to the San Jose Fire Marshall to ruin everything, as always. But the Clampers continued to shell out hot dogs for every passerby on the sidewalk. I wolfed down three myself. It was a free-for-all.

"We go alllll out," one Clamper told me as the golden beverages continued to flow. The vehicles then began to fall in line as the noon hour approached, signaling that they would soon embark on the parade route down Santa Clara Street toward Market. A few dozen Clampers parked their butts on the main float, using the bales of hay for seats, while raising their black and red mugs on high. The rest of the Clampers, along with their families, primed themselves to march on foot.

After the parade, the well-oiled fraternity made its way to Henry's Hi-Life, the legendary San Jose mecca for carnivore fundamentalists and the latest locale to be graced with an honorary plaque from E Clampus Vitus. Henry's boasts a century of gluttonous history, well described in the text of the plaque. As I approached from underneath the freeway overpass and watched the dedication ceremony mastered by Clamper Patrick Aloysius Sweeney, the scene was Dionysian. The plaque permanently rests outside on St. John Street, encased in brick, and the whole crowd of Clampers let out a raucous ovation while Sweeney, standing up above the masses, voiced the dedication. By 4pm, the bar area of Henry's Hi-Life was filled, elbow-to-elbow, with Clampers, many holding drinks in both hands. A delectable smell of barbecue emanated from the banquet room. Eventually I then slithered away as the sonic collage of clinking glass and high-octane conversation continued. As the Clamper creed goes, Right Wrongs Nobody. Support your troops!

Room of Secrets

You never know what you'll find in the California Room at the Martin Luther King Jr. Public Library. Every time I invade the place, I wind up staying at least an extra 30 minutes. The room is so utterly jammed to the gills with crackpot historical miscellanea that I never get out of there on schedule. I always wind up rummaging around for something I wasn't even planning on looking for in the first place. If you aren't familiar with the cargo of books, pamphlets, maps, old newspaper clippings and photographs within its timeless walls, you should be.

Now, to clarify: The California Room, located on the fifth floor of the main library, is their special collection of local history. Originally, about a century ago, it was composed almost entirely of history and travel books and works of local and state poets. Over the decades it grew into a massive collection of anything related to the lore of San Jose and Santa Clara County. For example, against one wall of the room, one finds entire rows of City Directories dating back to the early 1900s. If you want to know who lived at a particular street address in say, 1956, you can look up the address in the volume for that year. If you own a business and want to know what used to be at that location 30 years ago, the City Directories are the place to look.

Also, if want to see endless documentations of capital projects that never happened, the California Room is the locale. Need aerial photos of San Jose from 1921, press clippings about the Hart kidnapping or high school essays from the '70s about Agnews Developmental Center? Look no further.

You never know who you'll stumble into within the hallowed walls of this place. Years ago, when the main library was still on San Carlos Street, I was perusing a copy of David Ovason's book, *The Secret Architec-*

ture of Our Nation's Capital, in which the author theorizes that the founding of Washington, D.C., was directly linked to sacred geometry, astrology, zodiacs and Masonic ideology, right down to how they laid out the streets and the monuments. He gives diagrams of D.C. streets that were supposedly designed to synchronize with certain constellations.

I wondered if St. James Park and downtown San Jose were designed the same way. Why not? San Jose's first City Council included several freemasons, so maybe they also designed the streets according to Masonic principles. If you look at the original diagrams for St. James Park—the diagonal and peripheral walkways—there just might be some mystical symbology buried in there somewhere. It sounded like a plausible idea.

So I left my place on the bar stool and scurried over to the California Room to pore through two books titled *Fifty Years of Masonry in California*—enormous volumes from 1898 that weigh about 10 pounds each. Then, lo and behold, Jim Arbuckle, son of the late Clyde Arbuckle, the official San Jose historian, sauntered into the room and saw me leafing through the tomes.

"We have all those in the basement," he said of the books. "My dad was the historian."

That was the first time I had met Jim, and we became casual acquaintances. Jim admitted nothing of said Masonic ideology in the street layouts of downtown, but he later informed me in an email that Clyde, being at least a 32nd degree Mason himself, did indeed encode certain Masonic-related details within the pages of his legendary book, *Clyde Arbuckle's History of San Jose*.

So there you have it. Sadly, Jim Arbuckle passed away last year and I now have no one to pester with my zonked-out San Jose Masonic theories. But the California Room lives on. Try it sometime. You never know what you'll discover.

Shepard Fairey: Brush With Greatness

Most cities revel in their own pop culture landmarks or specific locales tied to things that celebrities did there. For example, much hoopla survives about the road where James Dean crashed, the hotel room where Sid Vicious of the Sex Pistols murdered his girlfriend, the garage that spawned Hewlett-Packard, the diner Suzanne Vega wrote a song about or that stretch of highway in Malibu where Mel Gibson got his infamous DUI. San Jose has a few similar sites, for example, the house on Jackson Street where Nirvana stayed in 1990.

I will suggest another local landmark which might possibly achieve similar notoriety: the city utilities box at the corner of Fruitdale and Southwest Expressway, where Shepard Fairey on Aug. 2, 2000, plastered a "promotional" poster for his art show at Anno Domini the next night. No one can vouch for how long the poster lasted, as the authorities painted over it soon thereafter. In fact, many of Shepard's other posters throughout San Jose that weekend were covered up or removed with impressive and extraordinary quickness. Little did anybody in San Jose know that eight years later, *Time* magazine would commission Shepard to create an image of president-elect Barack Obama for the cover of their 2008 Person of the Year issue—the one you see on the newsstands at this very moment.

Shepard is a world-renowned cultural provocateur who works with viral marketing and street art campaigns as forms of communication. He creates propaganda-style imagery that explores and confounds the role of subliminal advertising in our everyday lives. His most notable operation, "Obey Giant," began with just a few hundred stickers of the professional wrestler, Andre the Giant, containing the words, "Andre the Giant has a posse," including Andre's height and weight. The stickers, in themselves, meant absolutely nothing, but after Shepard and his friends started placing them around Charleston, S.C., an entire street art campaign exploded and the stickers began surfacing in major cities all across the country. Casual observers on the streets became confused. Some folks thought the stickers represented a religious cult, while others thought it was a gang. The campaign was a ridiculing of propaganda and a wiseass stunt to see how the populace would interpret the imagery, but it eventually grew into a worldwide movement, especially when Shepard added the "Obey" slogan to the stickers. "Obey Giant," as a brand, then went big time. "Obey" clothing lines, mural art and even musical instruments emerged and the iconography has infiltrated many facets of pop culture around the globe.

Then came Barack Obama's speech at the 2004 Democratic National Convention and Shepard was hooked. In what was seen by many as a departure from his standard inflammatory, anti-establishment tactics, Shepard, working independently, created the now-ubiquitous Obama "hope" poster, with the candidate's face silkscreened in red, white and blue. The picture became the iconic image of Obama's campaign. When the editors at *Time* chose the president-elect for their 2008 Person of the Year, they commissioned Shepard to create the cover image for the issue.

So there you have it. When Shepard came and plastered his street art over parts of San Jose eight years ago, the authorities either ripped 'em down or painted over them, and now he's getting paid to make Obama imagery for *Time* magazine. In fact, if you pull over and visit that hideous utilities box at Southwest and Fruitdale, right next to the 25 bus stop, you will see that two sides of the box appear to be still covered with paint and not the same color as the rest of the structure. The box just might be the only remaining landmark from Shepard Fairey's 2000 San Jose appearance. Think about that next time you look at *Time*'s 2008 Person of the Year issue. Even better, think about it whenever you drive by that intersection.

2009

Count Five Avenue

Last month saw the passing of John Byrne, lead singer of the '60s San Jose garage-rock band Count Five. He penned the immortal fuzzed-out 1966 hit *Psychotic Reaction*, which peaked at No. 5 on the *Billboard* charts and was listed in the Rock and Roll Hall of Fame's Top 500 songs that shaped rock & roll. A whole two years before Dionne Warwick sang that tune we all despise, the Count Five staged its famous promo picture, wearing Dracula-style capes in front of the Winchester Mystery House. Even though the band still commands an ample following among '60s garage-rock junkies all over the world, Count Five occupies an oddly secret slice of San Jose history. Byrne, originally from Dublin, Ireland, lived here for decades, but many locals have never even heard of the band.

Such were my thoughts when I wrote a Dec. 12, 2007, column titled "Meet Me at Count Five Place," suggesting that the city of San Jose name a street after the band. Aside from the fact that San Jose and Dublin are already sister cities, other locales have done similar things. For example, the legendary Oklahoma City band the Flaming Lips has been known for its surreal rock madness for more than 20 years now, so the city—apropos of the band's career—took an indistinguishable side street behind some clubs and renamed it Flaming Lips Alley. The band's singer, Wayne Coyne, who still lives in that city, dug the idea, actually preferring a back alley over a main street. "Any time you've got an alley with dumpsters and trucks loading beer out of the back, I thought, maybe that's a little better," he said. "I like to think that, in fact I almost prefer that we're one of these great little secrets—that people sort of stumble upon us—while looking for something more obvious."

Exactly. That would probably be the case for "Count Five Place" as well. But this is not a matter of being "secret" just to be secret. Renaming a street can be difficult due to the red tape involved. A lot of people have to be in the loop—the nearby residents, the postal service, the historians, the folks who make the maps, plus God knows how many layers of city bureaucracy. It's much easier to either create a new street and then name it, or just find an inconspicuous nonresidential road with a previous name that nobody would miss.

One such street in particular comes to mind, as suggested by the Blank Club, a live-music nightspot that sits on an older stretch of Almaden Avenue in downtown San Jose. You see, in this horribly planned city, there currently exists an Almaden *Expressway*, an Almaden *Road*, an Almaden *Boulevard* and an Almaden *Avenue*—a confusing mess that bugs the hell out of nonnatives looking for anything on one of those streets.

The parallel streets of Almaden Avenue and Vine run north and south, branching off from where Almaden Expressway ends at Alma. Before Park Center Plaza, the Center for the Performing Arts, the old library and the convention center all went in, those streets ran all the way north to Santa Clara Street and beyond. After the developments went in, Vine Avenue from 280 to Santa Clara Street was eventually widened and renamed Almaden *Boulevard.*

The Blank Club is located on one of the remaining stretches original Almaden Avenue just south of Santa Clara Street, the same side-street home to the Greyhound Bus Station and a popular dive bar called the Caravan, which also features rock bands three nights a week. Newcomers constantly get confused over the different Almaden streets, and since that entire two-block stretch has an edgy, back-alley punk-music kind of feel to it, I don't think anyone would complain if it was rechristened Count Five Avenue. I can't think of any better way to foster the San Jose/Dublin sister city relationship than to rename Almaden Avenue south of Santa Clara Street. No one lives there. No one would care. Let's do it.

On the Corner Music

Aside from Taco Bravo, the Recycling Center on McGlincy Lane and that large bear on top of Campbell Automotive, the other primary attraction in Campbell is a curious little bastion of activity called On the Corner Music. Located—you guessed it—on a corner of Campbell Avenue across from where Bradley Video bit the dust, this little record shop has peddled its wares for just more than two years now. Aside from offering an eclectic selection of vinyl LPs, the joint also regularly stages art openings, parties and happenings, the latest of which goes down this Friday (Feb. 27, at 8pm; 530 E. Campbell Ave.).

Aptly titled "We Love Music," the art exhibit will showcase 25 local characters who were asked to design unique art on used 12-inch LP covers. The artists include local skateboard legends, a DreamWorks animator, a tattoo artist, current and former club owners, horror-movie aficionados, refugees from the music scene and people who are already working painters, photographers and clothing designers. Individual names are being withheld in order to maintain the surprise bombshell nature of the show.

I grilled the show's organizer, Trisha Leeper, over the phone, and she revealed that each participant was issued a used LP cover and assigned to do whatever he or she wants with it. Some folks are using the artwork already on the cover and transforming it, a la billboard enhancement; some are painting over the original imagery; and others will produce more mixed-media assemblages or sculptures. All proceeds will go to the American Heart Association.

Now, of course, allow me to shed some light the historical context. With the rise of CDs and the ubiquity of iPods and other portable media players, LP covers are almost a forgotten art form. Those who didn't grow up in the era when vinyl reigned supreme tend to take jacket-cover art for granted. Before music videos came about, record covers constituted the only visual connection one had with the music, and many people actually did judge a record by its cover sometimes, identifying with an album through a singular image.

Cover design and packaging were an essential part of how one experienced the record. No one could possibly listen to *Sgt. Pepper's Lonely Hearts Club Band, The Dark Side of the Moon,* the Dead Kennedys' *Frankenchrist* or that one Telly Savalas abomination without at least visualizing what the cover looked like. Everyone can name at least a few albums that they bought primarily or initially just for the cover. When CDs became the dominant medium, graphic designers worldwide went apeshit as their canvases were now shrunk to accommodate the 5-by-5-inch CD cover as opposed to the LP. It appeared that cover art would lose a majority of its significance.

Then in the '90s, with the resurgence of space-age bachelor-pad tunes, crackpot exotica and the *Incredibly Strange Music* books from RE/Search, more and more folks continued rifling through thrift-store bins to purchase old LPs just for the covers. So, conceptually, the record cover as canvas didn't completely die when the LP format did, which is why these types of art shows are delicious fun for the entire family. There's nothing like a bunch of local underground celebrities producing objets d'art from cultural relics that society has thrown away like yesterday's newspaper and selling them for charity at the only existing vinyl shop in Campbell, Calif.

So next time you're poking around the Goodwill store on San Tomas Aquino Road, and you come across a seemingly unsalvageable copy of something like Alfred Hitchcock's *Music to Be Murdered By* (Imperial, LP-9052, 1958), or those wretched early '70s astrology records for each zodiac sign, or even the *Teach Your Parrot How to Talk* LP, don't let the store get rid of the things. Buy 'em and gobble 'em up. They just might serve as visual source material for the next art opening at On the Corner Music. God Bless Campbell, Calif.

Kites and Kicks

The legendary Herb Caen invented what was once called three-dot, or dot-dot-dot, journalism; that is, using the ellipsis to separate sections of his commentary. In my case, I'll call it splat-splat-splat journalism, which suits this week's musings—in honor of some local heroes.

As you read this, the world stage premiere of *The Kite Runner* will already be taking place at San Jose Rep (previews March 25–26, opening March 27). Adapted by SJSU professor Matthew Spangler, directed by David Ira Goldstein and based on the international bestseller by San Jose's Khaled Hosseini, the show runs until April 19. Crudely simplified, the story concerns two boys, Amir and Hassan, who grow up in the same household in Afghanistan but are immersed in different slices of the social and ethnic spectrum.

Amir is the son of a rich businessman and Hassan's dad is the servant of Amir's dad. When the Soviets invade, Amir and his father escape and later arrive in Fremont, where they deal with assimilation issues in what becomes a thriving Afghan community in that city. Amir then eventually returns to the homeland to make amends for failing to stick by his friend Hassan in times of trouble.

The novel includes vivid episodic passages immortalizing the Berryessa Flea Market, where the Afghan immigrant community has established its own little enclave, drinking tea and discussing politics and local gossip. Here is where Amir meets his future wife, Soraya, and I can't think of any more wholesome place in San Jose for that scene to occur, especially since the entire future of the flea market is still up in the air. In a now famous passage, Amir ponders the situation one evening after he gets home: "Lying awake in bed that night, I thought of Soraya Taheri's sickle-shaped birthmark, her gently hooked nose, and the way her luminous eyes had fleetingly held mine. My heart stuttered at the thought of her. Soraya Taheri. My Swap Meet Princess."

splat splat splat

Hosseini is not the only local hero currently putting San Jose on the map, however. Frank Shamrock, the Ultimate Fighting and mixed-martial-arts legend, is back in the news again, as he recently took over the top floor of the San Jose Athletic Club, the elite locale where executives and old-guard movers and shakers go to work out and swap stock tips in the sauna.

Originally the Scottish Rite Temple dating back to 1924, the building is a massive three-story neoclassical structure with Egyptian ornamentation. The timing was perfect. Shamrock's previous location on Winfield Boulevard was getting too small for the amount of classes he had, and the club finally decided to open the top level of the building after using it primarily for storage. Everything just fell into place. Shamrock now plans to use the Scottish Rite building for more classes as well as a head-quarters from which to franchise the business out to other locales.

If you climb the seemingly ancient stone steps past the red Frank Shamrock welcome mat, you arrive at the top level of the building. One can't help but wonder what secret Masonic rituals took place in that very room 80 years ago. From that same room, you can even sneak out onto the roof through a side door.

Shamrock was the dude who originally brought mixed martial arts to San Jose in 1997. However, exactly one year ago, he lost the middle-weight belt to another local, Cung Le, in a heated battle at HP Pavilion. Before that match, Shamrock touted that the arena belonged to him, so I suggested the city rename it Shamrock Arena. When he lost, a few Cung Le fans emailed and told me, in so many words, to go take a hike.

splat splat splat

So consider it the tale of two local heroes. In one corner, we have a SJSU professor adapting the Berryessa Flea Market for the stage at the San Jose Rep. In the other, we have the adaptive reuse of San Jose's most ornate building, the Scottish Rite Temple, for mixed martial arts and boxing lessons. Go San Jose.

Cesar Chavez Walkway

Last week, the San Jose City Council unanimously approved an official Cesar E. Chavez walkway, a five-mile route beginning downtown at the park named after the civil rights hero who founded the United Farm Workers of America. The route will continue east all the way down Santa Clara Street, almost to 680, and then south before looping back up and around to the Mexican Heritage Plaza.

Aside from those two plazas, five other landmarks along the route will be designated with simple signs: (1.) The Cesar Chavez Arch of Dignity, Equality and Justice, which sits right outside the Music Building on the SJSU Campus; (2.) The Mayfair Community Center; (3.) Cesar Chavez Elementary School; (4.) Our Lady of Guadalupe Church; and (5.) Chavez' former house on Scharff Avenue.

Now, as you would expect, any time the city of San Jose decides to establish an official walkway commemorating anyone or anything, the urban-blight exploration junkie needs to kill the pain at all costs and emphasize everything the city did *not* decide to highlight along the pre-scribed course. There is so much to see and do along Santa Clara Street between downtown and the East Side, it's hard to fathom. Of course, you have to temporarily bail from the four-wheeled cage and go tromp around for a few miles.

For example, one would probably have to be on foot to discover such hidden gems as Dulceria Mi Carnaval Party Supplies at 24th and Santa Clara streets. This corner shack is by far the best place to buy piñatas anywhere in San Jose. Anything that can be made into a piñata, you'll find it inside this place. It's a truly crackpot find.

If you keep going eastward from there, you'll pass by quite possibly the most bizarre variety of distinct old commercial buildings and facades—fixed-up, rundown or anything in-between. You'll discover a plethora of dime stores, cheap restaurants and other low-income mom-and-pop retail holes, comprising what seems like a completely discarded area of San Jose: a golden promenade between 24th Street and Highway 101 that time has simply forgotten.

For example, Valley Saw Inc. at 1269 E. Santa Clara is always a great place to stagger into. It's located in a cordial butterscotch-colored building that must be at least 60 years old. For bird feeders, band-saw blades and household fans, this is the place. There are fenced-off houses, functioning '50s gas stations, even a boarded-up lumber shop—all along the same stretch.

And just before you do arrive at 101, you'll descend upon one of the most precious hidden jewels anywhere in America's 10th-largest city: Kumar's Island Market at 1440 E. Santa Clara St. In one little hole-in-the-wall establishment, you can buy unusual cuts of meat and fish from Australia and Polynesia, as well as XXXXL-size Hawaiian shirts, fenugreek seeds, boxes of sarongs, Guam-logo hoodies, Samoan music CDs, magazines, canned goods, homemade bread and who knows what else. The current owner—my old drinking pal Suren from the Spartan Pub 18 years ago—will talk your ear off if you go in there, so allow some time.

While Kumar's provides an authentic island experience, the strip mall just east of King and Santa Clara offers a true destroyed urban-blight feel. This intersection, in fact, is a perfect place to soak in the yin-yang polar opposites of the social and economic spectrums. You have the Mexican Heritage Plaza, costing tens of millions and including the most state-of-the art theater in the whole city, and right across the street one sees a gorgeously decrepit, faded pink, infirmary-looking blighted strip mall—a splendid half-boarded-up paean to negligent landlords worldwide.

At the western corner of this blighted masterpiece sits a wrecked watering hole in all its devastated glory, aptly called Richard's Bar. Ten years ago, it was called Bob's Lounge. I guess Bob sold it. In any event, to all urban-blight photographers: this entire mall is your Shangri-la. Go for it. The blight junkie signs off for now.

Wild, Wild Walk

A few weeks ago, the San Jose City Council unanimously established the Cesar Chavez Memorial Walkway. I wholeheartedly applaud the effort, but if one actually peeks at the map of this thing, something just jumps right out and doesn't look right. At least not to me.

Here's what they did: They began the walkway, logically, at Plaza de

Cesar Chavez in downtown San Jose and then drew a path a few blocks east and up into SJSU, where the Arch of Dignity, Equality and Justice sits. This is a relatively new monument located between the Music Building and the cafeteria, facing what used to be Seventh Street. Those two markers—the plaza and the arch—constitute the beginning of the path.

Then the planners created five more spots in or near the Mayfair 'hood on the East Side, all of which make perfect sense but just happen to be nowhere near the first two downtown spots. Those markers are: Chavez's former home on Scharff Avenue just south of Alum Rock Avenue; Out Lady of Guadalupe Church; the Mayfair Community Center; Chavez Elementary School; and then the Mexican Heritage Plaza, the former site of a Safeway where the famous grape boycott took place.

Then the city just arbitrarily used a three-mile stretch of Santa Clara Street/Alum Rock Avenue—from downtown eastward all the way almost up to Jackson Avenue—and haphazardly connected these two neighborhoods. Maybe they're planning to eventually add more markers along Santa Clara, I don't know, but the whole thing looks disjointed at first, as if the city just decided to hurry up and make this thing official in time for the Cesar Chavez holiday—as opposed to waiting and doing a more complete job.

(Of course, this is standard operating procedure. For example, when it took five months to redo the light-rail station at Paseo de San Antonio, they finished half of it in time for the Grand Prix, made it look all spic and span and then held a press conference announcing they had finished it, when only one platform out of the two was actually completed.)

So what to do? Well, last week, the urban-blight exploration junkie filled in some of the missing highlights along this particular stretch of Santa Clara Street, so all I can do is add a few more, and as with any of these magnum expeditions, you must harbor a thriving passion for the absurd to fully appreciate the task at hand.

For example, we must consider it a travesty of justice, equality and dignity that the city did not include a rest-stop marker for the hole-in-the-wall greasy spoon diner named A Bite of Wyoming, which, incidentally, sits right at the corner of corner of Alum Rock and Scharff Avenue.

This is a legendary oddball obscure San Jose eatery that you'd never even notice the first time you drive by it. A friendly drawing of a bison graces the front door. The décor features rusted ranching tools from the Old West haphazardly strewn about the walls. Another bison's head sits on the back wall, and the booths are a rip-roaring blue shade of vinyl. There's probably no better place to get a $4.50 plate of spaghetti or a good old-fashioned cholesterol-filled heart-stopper special than A Bite of Wyoming. If on a weekend morning you actually try and traverse the entire Cesar Chavez Walkway from downtown three miles down Santa Clara Street to Scharff Avenue, you will probably be in dire need of some breakfast, believe me.

When you do get to the end of the path, after it circles through Mayfair and then winds up at the Mexican Heritage Plaza, you will have walked a total of five miles, apparently. If you decide to reverse your walk and then go all the way back down Santa Clara Street to downtown, you will probably drop dead of exhaustion in the process. Which is perfect, because another timeless San Jose landmark sits right at 11th and Santa Clara: the Darling and Fischer Mortuary—an appropriate conclusion if ever there was one.

Québec in Song

As you read this, Leonard Cohen will have just played three shows at the Paramount Theatre in Oakland, and if everything went as planned, I will have used my one ticket for the second show—rear balcony, Row Z, at the back, all by myself—to see the 74-year-old singer/poet/songwriter/novelist on his first U.S. tour in 16 years.

Since the majority of my interest in failed relationships, romantic disaster, loneliness, emotional isolation, distance, longing and loss has been righteously explored by Cohen in his lyrics throughout the last 40 years, I just needed to experience this famed saint from Montreal, Québec, in person. Since my deadline was long before the show, I will now share one particular scenario out of many where his lyrics have my sweetened my night.

During the summer of 2003, I was drinking on a Saturday night in a Québec City bar called Jules et Jim. Dark, smoky and its walls adorned with old movie photos befitting a place named after the classic François Truffaut film, the place is buried among the posh restaurants and hipster clubs of Avenue Cartier, away from the Old Town area where the tourists usually go.

In general, Québec City, looks, feels and operates like an old European capital. Sidewalk cafes and street performers abound. The drinking age is 18, and the bars remain open until 3 in the morning. Primarily a hangout for locals, Jules et Jim is a microcosm of the city itself: a mixture of old and new, a Francophone locale with unwavering *joie de vivre* and pride in *la belle province.* After ordering a pint of Boreal Rousse from the only bartender merciful enough to speak English, I took a seat at a knee-high table.

Luckily, a tipsy Irish woman at another table invited me over to her group solely for the purpose of English conversation, a rare occurrence at Jules et Jim. While Montréal is somewhat linguistically split, Québec City is almost entirely Francophone, with 98 percent of the population claiming French as their mother tongue.

I sat down next to a man drinking Bud Light. André was somewhere in his 50s, with short-cropped gray hair. Another woman, also in her 50s, with long gray hair down her back, drank Pernod out of the bottle and offered herself to every guy in the establishment. She got up and danced with one man, and then another. In English, Andre told me he liked Bill Clinton because he smoked out, he fooled around, and he's a musician—therefore a real person. "George Bush is not the American dream," he said.

The dancing woman then asked me to stand up and boogie with her, and I tried but failed miserably. "I have something to share with you," she kept repeating over and over. "I have something to share with you." A few drunken sentences in French were then broken up by the word "pussy."

Andre shook his head and motioned for me to dismiss her machinations. I hazily recalled a verse from the Cohen tune "Closing Time": "We're drinking, and we're dancing/ But there's nothing really happening/ The place is dead as Heaven on a Saturday night/ And my very close companion/ Gets me fumbling, gets me laughing/ She's a hundred, but she's wearing something tight."

You see, Québecers usually brag ad nauseam that their province produced Celine Dion—as if that were something to brag about—so whenever I'm there, I start yakking about Leonard Cohen, a much better representative. Apparently, I impressed them and one fellow turned from the bar and asked, "So are you Canadian?"

I said I'm American, and the chap next to him put his index finger to his mouth with a loud "Sssshhh"—the others immediately following suit. Thankfully, what would have been a confrontational anti-American conversation was then eased by more mutual recitation of Cohen lyrics: "There is a crack in everything/ That's how the light gets in." Andre and I continued carrying on into the night, in English, as the old dancing lady continued to approach every dude in the bar. Merci, Leonard Cohen.

Marc and Phoebe Aviles: Santa Clara Snapping

Since there aren't too many Filipino husband-and-wife photography duos based in San Jose who have won multiple awards in different hemispheres, I just had to infiltrate an operation called This is iT Photography on El Camino Real. Located in a newish-looking but nondescript retail complex just west of Lafayette Park, the studio of Marc and Phoebe Aviles technically lies within Santa Clara city limits, but the couple themselves actually live in San Jose proper. I can already imagine the two cities fighting over who gets to claim these folks. They are a humble yet powerful emerging force.

Originally, both were working as programmers in the IT industry in Singapore while shooting pictures on the side. But then Marc started winning awards for his photos, so he decided to eventually shift gears and devote more time to photography. The two moved to San Jose just over a year ago when Phoebe landed a job at AlphaSoft Services Corporation in Walnut Creek, where she still works. Marc runs the portrait studio full-time, and Phoebe shows up in the evenings and on weekends to do graphics and touch-up work.

As of right now, they specialize in wedding and portrait photography. Marc has a passion for landscapes, seascapes, rock formations, clouds and architecture—"Anything beautiful and unique," he says—while Phoebe prefers more edgy angles and juxtapositions.

In particular, they say ethnic weddings provide a perfect mixture of every scenario that photography is supposed to be all about: glamour; decked-out subjects in their preferred element; exotic locales; and the challenge that comes with a once-in-a-lifetime opportunity. As a result of their talents at capturing matrimonial merriment, Marc and Phoebe were featured as Wedding & Portrait Photographers International (WPPI) photographers of the month in its April 2008 newsletter. "Weddings are a challenge; you can't repeat the moments happening before your eyes," says Marc in the newsletter. "You cannot ask the couple or guests to hold on for a while—you must always be ready, attentive, observing and anticipating. Taking necessary prep steps is something we always labor over."

And last June, Marc received special honors at the 2008 WPPI 8-by-10-inch First-Half Print Competition. Two prints, one from Yosemite and the other from the Valley of Fire, near Las Vegas, out-and-out dazzled the judges. What's more, Marc's story is unique in the sense that, except for a high school class 20 years ago, he is entirely self-taught. Photography was always just a hobby until recently. "When he first started, he won awards right away," Phoebe tells me. "Then that's what motivated him."

Back in 2004 when Marc lived in Singapore, he won the PHOTOi/Nikon Best Photographer of the Year, a award for photographers local to that city. For the prize, he took home a snazzy Nikon D70. Not a bad deal, especially when he didn't even shoot with a Nikon in the first place. Perhaps the biggest award came in when Marc won the 2007 *Popular Photography & Imaging* Photographer of the Year Award—a gig that landed him a $5,000 prize and the auspicious title of "The Best Shooter on the Planet." For that one, hundreds of shooters from all over the world were narrowed down to 35 finalists, and Aviles prevailed.

Phoebe herself has likewise won a few accolades. She took home the 2006 best Storytelling Award from the National Geographic Channel and was also a 2007 finalist for *Digital Camera Magazine's/ Portrait Photographer of the Year.*

Now the husband-and-wife team sets up shop right here in little ol' Santa Clara, and Marc's high school alma mater back in Manila is even so proud of the guy that it held a contest named after him: The Marc Aviles Emerging Talent Photography Competition. It was a project of the San Juan National High School Alumni Association Inc., whose ambitious acronym is: SJNHSAAI. Whew.

Even though I am illiterate with a camera and even more conceptually removed from both weddings and portraits, I am inspired by these two individuals. You should be, too. Marc and Phoebe's work can be viewed on their website: www.thisisitphotography.com.

Conspiracy Convention in Santa Clara

With celebratory talk about the 40th anniversary of Woodstock reverberating throughout the land, no one seems to be bringing up the darker side of that era, especially since August will also mark the 40th anniversary of the Tate-LaBianca murders. There exist several local connections I could perhaps explore: Charles Manson spent time in San Jose on his way from the Haight-Ashbury to Los Angeles; Susan Atkins, a.k.a. Sadie, spent part of her childhood in Cambrian Park and, like me, went to Leigh High School; and local Homestead alumnus-turned–conspiracy theorist Jeffrey Deane Turner claims that factions of the Process Church of the Final Judgment, to which Manson may have had connections, eventually morphed into a more secret and sinister operation with tentacles still operating here in the South Bay. Whether or not there's any such thing as an accident—;and since the Conspiracy Convention 2009 just happens to hit the Santa Clara Convention Center this weekend—;I think I must probe a few seemingly connected spheres of influence. I originally met Turner in order to consider his claims that '60s sexpot Tuesday Weld is a descendant in a bloodline of druidic witches who indoctrinated her into the Illuminati, with whom she secretly unleashed nearly everything we currently know about the '60s counterculture. According to Turner, the Grateful Dead, the Jefferson Airplane, Moby Grape, the Who and many more were actually Weld's secret protégés, functioning as entertainment-industry fronts in her elaborately networked battle against the both the worldwide fascist network and another secret society, the All Nations Group, puppeteered by '80s pop star Tiffany.

I was introduced to Turner by his pal Douglas Hawes, a San Jose native who had appeared with Turner on *Untamed Dimensions*, an Internet radio show hosted by freelance investigative journalist Adam Gorightly. Originally writing for *Steamshovel Press*, Gorightly had been the first to break the story of Turner's paradigm-shattering claims. The essay, "Tiffany Overtakes Tuesday Weld," later appeared in *Secret and Suppressed II: Banned Ideas and Hidden History Into the 21st Century* (Feral House), as well as Gorightly's own compendium, *The Beast of Adam Gorightly: Collected Rantings (1992–2004)*. Gorightly will infiltrate Silicon Valley this weekend to cover Conspiracy Con 2009 for *Paranoia Magazine*. He will also be hawking an updated version of his book *The Shadow Over Santa Susana: Black Magic, Mind Control and the Manson Family Mythos*, to be released Aug. 8 by Creation Books, just in time for the 40th anniversary. According to the hype, it takes "readers on a black magic carpet ride from the Hollywood

'Beautiful People' scene of the late '60s through to the vast desert landscapes of a Death Valley gone mad—;with all the love-ins and murderous creepy-crawls that happened along the way." The book contains all the time-tested free-form 666-degrees-of-separation-alia: Manson's connection to the Beach Boys, the Hollywood S&M scene in the '60s, UFOs, Sammy Davis Jr.'s involvement in the Church of Satan, the Beatles' *White Album*, the Second Coming of Christ, Yul Brynner, the CIA and good old-fashioned satanic hippie love. The updated version contains new information on the possible whereabouts of Steve Grogan, a.k.a. "Clem," the only Manson Family member who was actually released from prison.

And getting back to the Process Church, Feral House will soon release *Love Sex Fear Death: The Inside Story of the Process Church of the Final Judgment*, written by former church member Timothy Wyllie. Judging by publisher Adam Parfrey's foreword, it looks to provide a more rational, thinking man's approach to the whole ball of wax, disproving the more hysterical fear-fueled sensationalism previously written on this cult.

How's that for a few meaningful coincidences? Seems like more sleuthing is in order, methinks. In the words of His Holiness the Dalai Lama, "I am open to the guidance of synchronicity, and do not let expectations hinder my path."

The Cambrian Era

I was recently invited back to one of the precincts that defined a good portion of my youth—those retail monstrosities occupying the legendary intersection of Camden and Hillsdale in Cambrian Park. Local sign maker Jere Avila has just given the hookah room at Blunt's Tobacco Shop a new intergalactic paint job, which is best viewed in 3-D using ChromaDepth® glasses. I advise you to check it out. It'll take you to a different planet.

Of course, returning to that area jarred some childhood memories, which forced me to do some soul-searching. You see, 25 years ago, this same beloved strip mall housed a defunct porno theater, the Cambrian Twin, plus a weird place called the Grecian Health Spa and one of the first Liquor Barn franchises, a pre-BevMo storehouse specializing in potent potables from around the globe.

In the mid-'80s, the theater reopened as a 75-cent nonporno establishment called the Hillsdale Twin and soon became the stomping ground for punk rockers, thrash-metal dudes or anybody beyond the pale of mainstream. If you grew up in that part of town, there was absolutely nothing else to do, so we just went to the theater and saw *Re-Animator* time and time again. Next door sat a Chinese fast-food place left over from the porno theater's tenure, aptly titled Fook Hing.

Even better was when Liquor Barn first opened. I remember walking through the aisles as a teenager, often staring for lengths of time at the varieties of booze from all over the world—the rums, the whiskeys, the beers, the wine, everything. It felt like an exotic, far-away place I had never visited—(all they sell is booze!)—and I opened up like a flower whenever I walked into that store. The entire world was there to greet me. The missing exotic half of myself instantly emerged. Although BevMo franchises eventually sprouted up across the landscape like weeds, nothing can replace the pure exoticism of the original Liquor Barn stores. Cambrian Park in the mid-'80s was textbook suburban-wasteland America, and for me Liquor Barn was a hall pass to get out.

Everything on that stretch of Camden/Hillsdale just sort of blended together like raw sewage into one gigantic strip mall. Cask & Flask Liquors was then and still is a fixture at Camden and Leigh. While in high school, I worked there as a stock boy—one of those hurry-up-and-wait jobs where you replenished shelves for 45 minutes and then did absolutely nothing for an hour. Stock, dust, sweep, sit, walk around, vegetate, fidget and then repeat—drudgery the likes of which would drive even the most assiduous employee completely bonkers. Every stock boy who worked there pilfered bottles at one time or another.

An old drunk lived down the street, and it was my job to deliver a fifth of Canadian Mist to the guy at least twice a week. He was a regular, so they didn't mind making house calls. He'd phone for another bottle, and I'd bag it up and tromp down Leigh Avenue to his home. He would then give me a $20 tip. That was my job at 17: running booze to an alcoholic down the street.

On a sweeter note, by far what defined the childhoods of many was Gemco—the quintessential pre-'90s one-stop discount department store, located where Target is now. Just like Costco, Gemco was membership-based; you had to flash your card upon strolling through the entryway. Kids were required to enter with their parents, and just about every aspiring teenage prankster alive tried to sneak in by randomly following behind an adult and pretending to be that person's kid. It was easy.

Gemco had it all: A dive snack bar, a sporting-goods section, electronics, appliances, a watch repairman older than dirt, a pharmacy with a separate entrance and a book section in the front corner, which is where I would usually hang out while my parents were shopping. Many folks would just dump their kids in the snack bar, but I always preferred the book section.

I thank Mr. Avila for reconnecting me with such convoluted times, and I especially want to thank all my friends on Facebook who chimed in with their own twisted memories of the Hillsdale Twin.

Farewell, Johnny V's

Turns out the address of 31 E. Santa Clara St. is steeped in history and a quick visit to the California Room at the Main Library filled in the gaps

This Sunday marks the final blowout gig at one of downtown San Jose's most popular dive bars and longstanding supporters of live underground music, Johnny V's. The address of 31 E. Santa Clara St. will never be the same.

Now, there are two threads I must embroider on this one. First, Johnny's has meant so much to so many of its bartenders and regular customers over the last six years that even by last week, several folks were already posting memories of the place on Facebook--bands they saw, friends they met, hookups that happened or gigs that went down. I can personally vouch for one Silicon Alleys column and one news story in particular that featured scenes in that bar. But even more, there exists a rich history behind that street address, going back to 1912, when Santa Clara Street was a dirt road.

Recently, Johnny's was the quintessential hole-in-the-wall dive where you could just pop in and see some loud bands a few nights a week. Touring rock acts would play for next to nothing. Every New Year's Day, Johnny's would open at 6am and cater to those who were still up partying. Legendary DJs like Rick Preston or Harry Whoo would usually be at the decks for what was a highly popular affair.

For me personally, some intrepid reportage I penned in 2005 would not have succeeded without Johnny V's. In what turned out to be a scream of a story, I hit the meat-market bars with a $50-an-hour paid female wingman from ladywingmen.com as an assistant to hit on women. After tripping through an art reception and then the jock bars, we wound up at Johnny V's, with her schooling me on pickup techniques as I scoped out the cute female bartenders.

One year later, in this space, I referred to Johnny V's as the "Beverly Hills of the Santa Clara Street block between First and Second." You see, I had just returned from some freelance business at the Beverly Hills Hilton and after flying back to San Jose, I went straight to a show by local punk legends, the Forgotten, at Johnny V's. So I compared and contrasted the corner of Wilshire and Santa Monica boulevards in Beverly Hills with the garbage, the bums, the homeless, the dealers, the halfway-house inhabitants and the urine and empty soup cans that comprised the corner of First and Santa Clara three years ago. At least for a few days, that column was on the wall inside Johnny V's.

From 1912 straight up until sometime in the mid-'80s, this address housed the Oyster Loaf Café. Croatian-born Frank Arnerich was the proprietor for the first 46 years of the eatery's existence until he retired and turned it over to new owners in 1958. According to a San Jose Mercury News column from the late '60s, one Mr. Jus Minjoulet had dined at the Oyster Loaf almost every day for 55 straight years.

Mr. Arnerich's story is quite an interesting one. According to a Sept. 20, 1975, obituary in the *Mercury News*, he came to San Jose in 1907 at the age of 18 and then opened the restaurant five years later. He went on to become both a civic leader and one of the best bowlers on the West Coast. He often told stories of how First and Santa Clara was a dirt intersection when he first opened the Oyster Loaf Café. He was a member of many fraternal organizations and his descendents still live in the area.

By the time the 1990s rolled around, an Irish bar and restaurant called Paddy's opened at the same location. To this author's recollection, it was the first nonsmoking bar in San Jose, before those laws even emerged. After that, the venue degenerated into an absolute dump called Tremor's before Johnny resurrected the place and brought in live rock bands. With glasses raised on high, I salute 31 E. Santa Clara St.

Giger Harvest

World travel is about continuous personal transformation, so before a recent trip to Switzerland, I checked out a copy of Richard and Iona Miller's *The Modern Alchemist: A Guide to Personal Transformation* from the main library here in San Jose before heading to Europe. Unlike most people, when I contemplate Switzerland, I don't think of army knives, watches or secret bank accounts. I think of Swiss psychologist Carl Jung writing about alchemy—transmuting base metals into gold as a metaphor for personal and psychological transformation.

As a result, I was especially transformed when I crept into the H.R. Giger Museum in the medieval village of Gruyères. Giger is the macabre Swiss surrealist best known for designing the creatures in the 1980 film *Alien*, for which he won an Oscar, but he also creates ghastly airbrush paintings, furniture, sculptures, album covers and graphic designs featuring imagery of violent biomechanical females, Lovecraftian nightmarescapes and erotic-occult-fantasy transmogrifications of the most intuitive sort. He says he paints whatever scares him.

Gruyères itself is a place that exists almost entirely for tourists, as thousands are regularly bussed in for the famous castle and cheese of the same name. Over time, Giger fell in love with the area, calling it a "beautiful cheek of Switzerland." In 1998, to the explosive annoyance of the locals, Giger acquired an old stone fortress, the Château St. Germain, and converted it into a permanent three-story museum of his work. Commendably, the place is staffed by Swiss goth hotties.

"When people go to Gruyères, they usually come for the castle and the cheese factory," explains my tour guide, with an angelic French accent. "Then they come in here and they get disgusted."

As we move through the museum, she provides a few stock details about Giger's life: His birth was unusually long and traumatic, with the doctor needing forceps to get him out of the womb; detractors blamed him for his first wife's depression and suicide; and as a teenager, he set his dad's pharmacy on fire by trying to melt lead. (Read: alchemy, transformation.)

We eventually arrive at a room with huge airbrushes of *The Spell*, I, II, III and IV—one on each wall. *Spell III* includes Giger's version of the Baphomet symbol at its center, complete with the Caduceus—the two snakes coiling into a figure 8 around a shaft. Baphomet and the snakes represent male and female energy or dark/light polarity.

Minutes later, she points out another famous Giger painting, *Anima Mia*, an otherwordly nightmarescape of flowing interconnected biomechanoids. Mia was Giger's second wife, and inspiration while he created this particular work. The title is a play on words: Anima means "soul" and is also a Jungian concept representing the unconscious feminine aspect of the male psyche. By sheer synchronicity—a Jungian term—I had just finished Chapter 3 of *The Modern Alchemist*, titled "Anima," while on the airplane. My own inner feminine slowly began to emerge.

Jung also provided some of the foundation for the mythopoetic "Wild Man" men's movement, that which tries to recapture of the fierceness of masculinity. By another synchronicity, I stayed at the Hotel Wilden Mann (Wild Man) while in Lucerne. Imagery of the Wild Man figure, the mystical savage, is intertwined with that city's history, and he is the symbol of untamed strength and resistance to all conventions. In the hotel, numerous mystical and symbolic medieval drawings, including Tarot cards, grace the walls of the salon, although most won't notice.

At journey's end, in Giger's hometown of Chur, I stood right in front of the building where he grew up, in a flat above his dad's pharmacy. It now boasts a bright yellow facade with a women's cosmetic shop on the ground level—the closing irony of it all, I suppose. In any event, after that trip I am personally transformed. To Giger, Jung and the San Jose Main Library, I say, *Tausend Dank!*

Rosicrucians Celebrate Harvey Spencer Lewis

Last week saw yet another intradimensional moment in San Jose history as the Rosicrucian Order AMORC held a special ceremony commemorating the 100th anniversary of H. Spencer Lewis' initiation into the Rosicrucian tradition in Toulouse, France. It was in 1909 that Lewis made contact with the European leaders of the Rosicrucian Order, and on Aug. 12 of that year, he officially received the mandate to lay the foundation for the order's resurgence in North America. So, in 1915, Lewis launched the Ancient and Mystical Order Rosae Crucis (AMORC) in New York and then briefly moved the headquarters to San Francisco and Tampa, Fla., respectively, before eventually relocating to San Jose in 1927, where AMORC's head office has been ever since.

On the 100th anniversary of Lewis' original initiation last Wednesday, AMORC actually opened up the temple in Rosicrucian Park to the general public for this special meditation and ceremony. The temple is nowhere near as exciting as one would expect from a secret order, but the place was built in 1949 and boasts décor resembling that of ancient Egypt. A triangular altar sits in the middle of the place, and the "Guardians" wear ceremonial aprons and walk only in right angles as they move through the facility.

Now, I am not a Rosicrucian, nor am I proselytizing, but I can at least tell you this much: They are not a religion or a sect but a community of spiritual seekers and philosophers who study and practice metaphysical and natural laws governing the universe. Their teachings, which they trace to the mystery schools of ancient Egypt, offer a nonmainstream route to esoteric Western spirituality and include lessons on the structure of matter, human consciousness, psychic centers, the nature of the soul, intuition, the space-time continuum, vibroturgy, radiesthesia, karma, sacred geometry and other esoteric subjects. AMORC's members include people from all creeds. In fact, some Rosicrucian members do not subscribe to any specific religious beliefs at all.

That said, a gong signaled the beginning of the ceremony and we all proceeded to fill the pews and watch a History Channel–style biography of H. Spencer Lewis and his original 1909 trip to France to get initiated into the Rosicrucian tradition. Following this, we listened to an audio recording of Julie Scott, grand master of the English Grand Lodge for the Americas, which led everyone in a group meditation, helping to visualize the most positive aspects of politics and government, economics, education, health care and healing, religion and mysticism. Scott lives here in San Jose, but was away in Toulouse, taking part in a similar commemorative ceremony with other Grand Masters from the throughout the world.

At the San Jose temple, the meditation/visualization asked everyone to actively participate in the positive transformation of our society and the world, in both mystical and material ways: "One of the ways that we will accomplish this is through the Mystical Law of the Triangle—by bringing two things together, thereby producing a third. There are many applications of this principle. One very powerful formula from an old Rosicrucian exercise is combing thought and projection, which manifest change. We energize and enliven our thoughts by projecting them powerfully into the world. We accomplish this by experiencing our visualization fully, including imagination and emotion. We then give it power through our breath and by the use of vowel sounds, thus sending the vibrations of our visualization into the world."

The recording then led everyone in chanting of specific vowel sounds—owm, rah, mah, ohm—to help "visualize the power of our government being used for good," to "envision an economic system that uses money as an expression of divine love and sharing," and "envision education that inspires our young people, educating the whole self and encouraging new ideas."

In the end, I will finish by leaving things open for the conspiracy theorists, since according to AMORC's own history, H. Spencer Lewis also originally went to France to accompany his dad, a genealogist who was doing research on behalf of the Rockefellers. So Mote It Be!

One Step Beyond Reunion

Last weekend saw another zenith in what seems like a long string of reunions celebrating San Jose's music scene of 20 years ago. This time, we're talking about the last half of the '80s and the legendary alternative club One Step Beyond. Known throughout the land as "One Step," the place was a haven for many alternative types in those days: punks, goth kids, '80s New Wavers, mods, rockabilly dudes, metalheads or basically anyone subjugated in high school by the jocks and cheerleaders and who wanted to fine-tune his or her teenage angst for use later in life.

Drawing folks from across the country, the event was like a family reunion, and it was all for a very worthy cause: The George Mark Children's House, a facility that treats children with life-span-limiting conditions. A young boy, Franco Louis Bastoni, passed away last year at the age of 4 due to an obscure brain-stem tumor, and since his mother, Corrina, has tons of friends from the One Step Beyond days, folks got together and organized the Sacred Leaf Benefit, a mini-Bacchanalian gothlike weekend among the custom-carved décor at Smoke Tiki Lounge.

Mary Zuchowski and Karl Holtz orchestrated the entire affair, and Stan Kent, the zany British crackpot who owned One Step, showed up from Los Angeles and emceed the event both nights. DJs played on Friday, and bands hit the outdoor patio stage on Saturday.

One Step was located on Martin Avenue in the industrial wasteland sector of Santa Clara, and thousands of folks have fond memories of driving up Lafayette, turning left near the Humane Society and heading on over to One Step.

It was a huge place with many different rooms for various goings-on, and the entire club occupies an important part in the alternative cultural landscape of San Jose history, since it was an all-ages venue. Sixteen-year-olds could go dancing and see national touring bands, while those of drinking age could imbibe.

Looking back, the list of bands that played there is downright staggering. This was also during the initial stages of the rave explosion, so One Step would stage underground after-hours events once all the bars closed. All in all, for a bunch of disenfranchised young people growing up in a suburban wasteland with absolutely nothing to do except hang out at the mall, One Step was pure heaven—Or pure Valhalla, depending on your perspective.

"It was like something that was inevitable, given the fact that so many kids had nowhere to go," Kent recalled. "But what was amazing to me, was that we actually pulled it off. ... What kept it going was all the bands that came in, and you had this amazing energy of kids that had nowhere to go, and you realized that you were their home. This was their home away from home. People met their loves there. People had their first sex there. It was an awesome place to be around."

The Ramones usually played at One Step every summer—often it was two nights—for usually about 8 to 10 bucks a show, and one year they even came back a few months later to play a two-day benefit for the Humane Society. Personally, I must have seen the Ramones at least six times at that club.

"Something I will always remember about One Step is that the Ramones were essentially our house band at the time," Kent said. "I can remember taking them out for dinner in their van, and we'd go for curry, because they liked vindaloo. And to me, I think I'll never forget that. It was like being in a dysfunctional family, and we had our dramas like any other club, but for me, the Ramones were the essence of One Step Beyond." At the end of the weekend, $1,800 was raised for the George Mark Children's House. Kent also said that a full-blown, higher-profile One Step Beyond reunion is planned for sometime next year. (For those who wish to donate, One Step Beyond T-shirts are still available for $15. Check the Sacred Leaf Benefit Facebook page.)

Walking Willow Glen

In case you weren't there, the urban-blight exploration junkie played his greatest hits on Auzerais Avenue, Stockton Avenue, 24th Street and in the parking lot of the Pink Elephant Center. The junkie had recently been in recovery, but after reading the wonderful book *Touring Historic Willow Glen: Ten Walking Loops*, he immediately relapsed and needed to kill the pain at all costs.

His journey through ignored Willow Glen began at 831 Malone Road, a hideous, rundown, boarded-up former hardware store and flooring company. The junkie looked through the windows and eyed the decades-old fixtures and rickety displays. You see, if one peeks at the original 1927 map of Willow Glen, Malone Road forms the southern border. Formerly known simply as "The Willows," the area incorporated as its own city in 1927 solely to stop the railroad from coming through. Thus began a long heritage of Willow Glen being identified with unapologetic NIMBYism—which only became worse when it got its own ZIP code 40 years ago. But since the dead hardware store still exists after 20 years of nonoperation, maybe the NIMBYs aren't so invincible after all.

Right across the street in Arnone's strip mall sits the PT Market & Liquor store, offering a gracious, affable and forthcoming environment. Unlike other liquor stores in the area, PT is not crammed to the gills with shelving and feels much airier than one would expect. There's even a Chinese Happy Buddha statue right there to greet you, and the young Chinese girl behind the counter tells you to rub its tummy for good luck—advice usually heeded by locals gobbling up throngs of lottery tickets.

After leaving the PT Market, the junkie made his way westward down Malone all the way to Lincoln, a corner housing the aptly named Lincoln Avenue Liquors. One can see what's left of an ancient neon sign directing visitors where to park. Unfortunately, this place has been getting flak from neighbors for what seems like decades now. One episode went down a few years back when the store began displaying X-rated cigarette lighters in glass cases, in full view of any adventurous minor who might be intrigued by such things. Residents brought the hammer down and coerced the owner to remove the lighters even though no one had actually purchased any of them.

At one time, this particular stretch of Lincoln Avenue was actually interesting, with a used bookstore, a used record store and a killer baseball card shop called Mike's Coliseum. Alas, no more.

From there, the junkie proceeded north all the way up into the heart of the neighborhood, the celebrated corner of Lincoln and Willow streets, also the site of Willow Glen Liquors. This is where many folks used to buy cheap wrestling tickets for bouts at the San Jose Civic, circa 1983. For eight bucks, kids could go watch the Magnificent Don Muraco (the bad guy) beat the crap out of Bob Backlund (the good guy), while our dads got embarrassingly plastered in the audience. Ah, the good ol' days.

If certain developers get their way, this classic liquor shop will probably bite the dust before too long, but the establishment is quintessential Willow Glen. You can tell because it carries brands of rotgut malt liquor that contain ginseng and amino acids.

Finally, the binge finished a few blocks up the road at one of the all-time distinguished landmarks of Willow Glen: Mr. T's Liquor Locker. The old-school neon sign is one of the most revered anywhere in the South Bay. Reviewer Martin "the butcher" B on Yelp.com gave it four stars: "I've talked to old timers who shoulder-tapped for drinks back in the early '60s. The original Mr. T is long gone but the Middle Eastern guy who owns it now doesn't seem to mind when I call him Mr. T."

He's actually Indian, not Middle Eastern, which proves one last thing: that reviewers on Yelp just cannot be trusted for accurate information.

Supercharged: Tim Brauch

Apropos of this week's issue—*Metro*'s annual Best Of installment—allow me to yak about a few events taking place this weekend honoring the legacy of world-renowned skateboarder and San Jose local Tim "Beans" Brauch, who departed this life 10 years ago. On May 9, 1999, at the young age of 25, Tim passed away of sudden cardiac arrest, but by that time, he had pretty much already conquered the skating universe.

Anyone who knew Tim Brauch will insist under oath that he absolutely belongs in any Best of San Jose compilation. Period. Those who made

Tim's acquaintance say that his motivation and kindness were infectious, that he inspired many, and that he was a role model for countless kids interested in skating, not just in San Jose, but throughout the world.

This weekend, the 11th Annual Tim Brauch Memorial Skateboard Contest will take place over two days: Saturday in Scotts Valley at the skatepark named after him and Sunday at the Lake Cunningham Regional Skate Park in San Jose. Also, a new documentary, *Supercharged: The Life and Times of Tim Brauch*, will debut Saturday night at the Camera 12 Cinemas in downtown San Jose. The first showing is sold out, with the second one going fast.

Tim's accomplishments are far too expansive to list in this column, but without a doubt, he put San Jose on the map all over the world. Sessions Skateboard Shop began sponsoring him at age 15. In 1998, Tim won the heralded Vans Triple Crown Street Competition in Huntington Beach, taking home the $15,000 prize and cementing himself as one of the most dynamic and consistent characters in the sport.

He also designed his own boards, co-founded Este Clothing and was later immortalized in the traveling Smithsonian exhibit "Sports: Breaking Records, Breaking Barriers," where he shared the honor of "More Than Sports Champion" alongside figures like Billie Jean King, Jim Thorpe and Roberto Clemente. For that project, a Smithsonian curator actually flew to San Jose and selected Tim's skateboard, his trophies and other belongings to be included in the show, which toured 2004–2007 and now permanently rests in the Smithsonian Museum.

Soon after Tim passed away, Sessions established the Tim Brauch Memorial Fund, which donates 100 percent of its proceeds to skateboard park development and scholarships. Tim always believed in giving back to the kids, as he was a people's skateboarder. On the Scotts Valley Skatepark's website, Sessions officially had this to say: "There are easily dozens of pro skateboarders today who won't give a kid the time of day at a demo. Tim was different. He knew that he was at the demos for the kids. Limbs willing, he wouldn't leave a demo until every trick that wanted to be seen was seen and every kid who wanted a moment of this time was given that and more."

Local photographer Jai Tanju took action shots of Tim for years. "When Tim skated, great skateboarders stopped to watch him, he was so good. He had something inside of him that came out when he was on the board that I could only compare to someone like Jimi Hendrix. It was like watching someone paint a masterpiece at top speed, with the biggest smile, which made you smile just watching him go."

The San Jose Contest this Sunday is also the ninth stop of the World Cup Skateboarding Concrete Bowl Series. A $5,000 purse will be split between categories: Pros, Grandmasters and Girls. The whole shebang gets going around 8am and admission is free.

Supercharged features interviews with Tim's friends and family, unseen footage of Tim skateboarding, stories of world travel and an exploration of the legend he left behind. Filmmaker Pete Koff originally met Tim in Lake Tahoe at a Harvey's Casino skateboard demo in 1991 and since then has included footage of Tim in his past five films. *Supercharged* also hopes to raise awareness of Wolff Parkinson White Syndrome, the cause of Tim's unexpected cardiac arrest. All of the film's profits will go to the Tim Brauch Memorial Fund.

Lunch With Tony

As you read this, the inaugural Silicon Valley Restaurant Week will have commenced. With such a variety of eateries in the valley, where does one begin? For me, the choice was easy: Alviso. Usually, this off-the-radar locale attracts lunchtime refugees from the concrete jungles of Cisco and TiVo right down the street, as high-tech development inches closer to what was once the last bastion of the simple life. Plus, a new restaurant called Lunch With Tony recently opened up, so off I went.

If you don't know Alviso, it was the South Bay's original port 150 years ago. To get there, just go all the way up First Street in San Jose until it ends near the salt flats. A primeval frontier from eons past, Alviso is a specimen pinned on the board, a discarded community that has irked San Jose's Department of Building, Planning and Code Enforcement for decades now.

Especially on a weekday at 10am when I recently visited, Alviso is the most desolate place anywhere around here. Bored seagulls hold court. Hallucinations of tumbleweeds begin to emerge. Sounds from roosters and distorted Mexican music emanate from unidentifiable places. It is the home of Vahl's, the celebrated throwback restaurant that makes O.J.'s look modern. And old-timers in these parts have detested San Jose ever since the city annexed Alviso in 1968.

Lunch With Tony occupies a parcel that can only be referred to as a microcosm of Alviso itself: A vacant lot sits across the street; taco trucks occupy the parking lot next door; across another road one finds the ever-encroaching cookie-cutter condos. The cafe is easy to find—you know, the 5200 block of First Street. Owner Tony Santos graduated with a business degree from Santa Clara University, but after becoming disenchanted with the corporate life, he went and got another degree from the California Culinary Academy.

"I knew right away who I was as a chef," he says. "No! to fine dining and white tablecloths. Yes! to gourmet, tasty but completely approachable food."

Tony comes from a legendary and colorful family of Alvisans. His grandfather Tony P. Santos served time as mayor and police chief way back when Alviso was still its own city. He passed in 2004 and a street now bears his name. Tony's uncle, Richard Santos, currently sits on the board at the Santa Clara Valley Water District.

After I showed up for some curried lentil and butternut squash soup, Tony's dad, also named Tony, rolled in with a pile of historic photos. Together, the father and son buried me with Alviso history, with the elder Tony managing to bash 40 years of San Jose politicians in a span of 15 minutes. It was fantastic.

"City workers have always been prejudiced against Alviso," the elder Tony told me, adding that if you grew up in Alviso, you were treated as a second-class citizen by folks in San Jose. "They could tell where you were from by the mud on your shoes," he said. "It was embarrassing."

I've heard some of these stories before. Alviso history is, um, awash in floods, environmental mismanagement, code violations, battles over slough restoration, property-owner soap operas, city and county neglect, economic conflicts of interest and much more. It goes way back. The Santos family owns mucho property in Alviso, and Tony loves to recount hostile exchanges with folks in the Planning Department, who he says are endlessly splitting hairs over nonsensical issues. Because they hate dealing with Alviso.

Anyway, the building now housing Lunch With Tony used to be a bar in the '40s, simply called Tony's. The current Tony eventually plans to cover one wall with the historic photos. When all is said and done, the people of Alviso just want the area to be properly preserved and attended to, while still retaining its small-town feel. However, the elder Tony cautioned, in some cases, that the seeds of progress just cannot be stopped.

"Vahl's now accepts credit cards," he said.

Thrillville With Will Viharo

Ever since Video Mania at Branham and Almaden Expressway bit the dust more than 20 years ago, there has not existed a public place in San Jose where aficionados of vapid B-movie trash can peacefully assemble and feel at home. Now everything has changed as Thrillville has finally hit San Jose. Will "The Thrill" Viharo has proudly brought his rolling blunder review of below-budget atrocities to the Camera 3 Cinemas in downtown San Jose, so fans of grimace-inducing bombs can get their fill while ingesting some killer rockabilly music and retro tiki culture at the same time.

Viharo is a Rat Pack–era steak-and-martini dude who usually dons a leopard skin fez and a smoking jacket, while his co-host/cohort, Monica Tiki Goddess, sports vintage muumuus of the most unassuming sort. Together, they have presented the Thrillville series of B-movie screenings in the East Bay for more than a decade now, and they've been faves of Bay Area cult film fans for years. But as of last summer, Thrillville officially started up on a regular basis at the Camera 3. B-movie buffs, *Mystery Science Theater* fanatics, lounge lizards and all other sordid supporters of schlock are encouraged to attend.

The first San Jose installment went down on June 18. As a spectacular bash celebrating the TV show *Creature Features* and dedicated to its late host Bob Wilkins, the evening included previously unseen outtakes and behind-the-scenes footage of Wilkins as well as of the late film critic Bob Shaw. Mr. Lobo from *Cinema Insomnia* made an appearance, as did John Stanley, Wilkins' eventual replacement on *Creature Features*. The San Jose band Aardvark dazzled the crowd with surf music while selected prizes were doled out to members of the audience. For the main spectacle, Will and Monica screened *The Horror of Party Beach*, perhaps the first monster panty raid movie—a god-awful 1964 romp in which radioactive monsters transformed by toxic waste get their fill at a swinging beach party.

The event was a huge success, with numerous underground scenesters and connoisseurs of high camp arriving to sample the evening's debauchery. Both Stanley and Mr. Lobo hawked videos and other swag at tables in the lobby, and the entire theater exuded a beautifully ridiculous aura of old-school iniquity. Other Thrillville installments soon followed, the most recent of which included a spectacular Mexican wrestling double feature, *Santo and Blue Demon vs. the Monsters* (1969) pairing nicely with *Wrestling Women vs. the Aztec Mummy* (1964).

And just in time for Halloween, the next affair takes place this Thursday (Oct. 22, 7:30pm). Aptly titled Thrillville's Gore 'n' Snorefest, the extravaganza will feature two supersleazy, sexy, spooky exploitation classics: *Hollywood Chainsaw Hookers* (1988) and *Zontar, the Thing From Venus* (1966). The former features veteran chainsaw virtuoso Gunnar Hansen plus '80s scream queens Linnea Quigley and Michele Bauer. One of the original grindhouse classics, *Hollywood Chainsaw Hookers* contains all the gratuitous nudity, violence and sad one-liners a director could possibly cram into 80 minutes. Don't miss Quigley doing the Virgin Dance of the Double Chainsaws. They just don't make 'em like that anymore.

Zontar, on the other hand, was a Z-grade designed-for-TV slaughtering of Roger Corman's *It Conquered the World*, which originally came out in 1956. In other words, it was a cheesy remake of an already cheesy-on-purpose catastrophe from 10 years earlier. Shot on 16 mm, it stars the quintessential B-movie staple, John Agar, whose abysmal talents graced numerous sci-fi washouts like *The Brain From Planet Arous* and countless others. *Zontar* is so painful to watch, even hardcore B-movie masochists might have difficulty with it. (For some critical insights, see Richard von Busack's piece in this week's film section.)

But that's not all you'll see at Thrillville. Like any true showman, Viharo sprinkles the entire evening with all sorts of other shenanigans, and since we're nearing All Hallows' Eve, no one knows what he has up the sleeves of that vintage leisure suit. He's promising trivia contests, prizes, dancing girls and other guaranteed bombs from the blue.

2010
◆

Finding San Jose: Josh Marcotte

For eight years now, Josh Marcotte has wandered around San Jose taking photographs of abandoned buildings, neon signs, empty storefronts, defunct railroad yards, discarded couches and graffiti-stained underpasses. His photo project, "Lost San Jose," captures every possible depiction of crumbling infrastructure he can find. His website, www.lostsanjose.com, describes his work as "insomnia, trespassing and a camera ... a view of a city that's hidden, overlooked and unwanted. It's a eulogy for my dying neighborhood."

But death is not the end. On Saturday, Feb. 6, Marcotte will launch a solo show of his photos at, of all places, the Blue Jean Bar in Santana Row. This is the hipster jeans place where you walk up to the counter and choose your material: dark, light or distressed—a concept perfectly fitting for the event.

Unlike most of us, Marcotte is a fourth-generation San Josean. His grandfather dropped out of Lincoln High School to fight in World War II. His great-grandfather worked for the railroad. Thanks to history lessons passed down from those earlier generations, Marcotte developed a keen sense of lost San Jose at a very early age.

"When I was growing up, every weekend I would go and mow my grandfather's lawn," Marcotte recalled over the phone. "He would always tell me all these great stories about the history of San Jose and downtown, and when he was a kid growing up. ... He would sometimes even drive me places and show me things that either were still there or no longer there. He was so fascinated with history, and he was such a fan of San Jose—and I just enjoyed going out with him so much."

When he arrived at San Jose State University in the late '90s, Marcotte found himself wandering alone downtown for the very first time. He would get out of class and just roam the streets. "I was trying to connect to what my grandfather had told me, and trying to piece things together," he said. "And what I found was that all of the buildings are empty, all the theaters were abandoned, all of the storefronts were boarded up; buildings were being torn down, hotels were being lifted up and moved across the parking lot. It was just chaos downtown, and everything seemed empty."

As a result, Marcotte was inspired enough to start documenting his travels. At that time, he worked at the Century Theatres on Winchester and often walked from there all the way down Stevens Creek and San Carlos to downtown San Jose, habitually writing up his perceptions of the city's seedy underbelly. To that point, his only experience with cameras was an intro to photography class at Del Mar High School, but he saved money, bought a camera and began to record his wanderings.

"It got to the point where so many things were disappearing," he said. "I wanted to document it. I wanted to have pictures of it, so I could remember it. ... I had pictures of Notre Dame High School being torn down; I had photos of the Santana Row fire; I had pictures of things that were starting to go away."

Marcotte takes most of his photos at night, since he often has insomnia and just wanders around the dark streets. The show will feature both new and old photos. His work will also be included in a group exhibit at Kaleid Gallery at Fourth and San Fernando streets, beginning Feb. 5.

"It's about trying to connect with the past generations of my family," Marcotte said. "Trying to document what I felt was being lost, trying to see if I was the only one out there who enjoyed San Jose and its nightlife and its underbelly."

Just like the Blues Jean Bar, Marcotte's photos have something for everybody—whether you're looking for dark, light or distressed material. I can't think of a better reason to visit Santana Row.

Chuck E. Cheese History

By mentioning the story behind the very first Chuck E. Cheese's Pizza Time Theatre a few weeks ago, the author knew he would hit it off with certain crackpot historians who share a passion for the ignored slices of Silicon Valley history. But he was not prepared for the assemblage of historical bric-a-brac located upstairs in the storage rooms of the Chuck E. Cheese's on Tully Road.

He found broken arcade games, old fixtures and signs, patches of original carpeting, piles of ancient tokens, decades-old electronics, benches, wires, vintage posters, giant tubing and pieces of long-defunct costumes. All it took was one source—we'll call him Seymour—to provide the author with unlimited access, completely unbeknownst to anyone else in the entire three-story building.

Back in 1977, Nolan Bushnell of Atari opened the first Pizza Time Theatre on Winchester and the second one soon followed on Kooser, where it still sits today. The Tully facility, originally the biggest one at the time, opened in the former Magic Village Toy Store, on a triangular parcel, right at the southeast corner of the Tully and Highway 101 interchange. To this day, a giant statue of Chuck E. Cheese stands on the west side of the building, facing 101.

Seymour led me through a labyrinth of stairways, crooked corridors and freight elevators. We prowled through probably a dozen rooms, including a former upstairs training kitchen, the current tech shop and several junk storage areas. "This is where old video games go to die," he explained. "Well, sort of. We still fix some of them."

Back when the Tully restaurant actually sold beer, Seymour told me, it was second only to the Flea Market in total beer sold in Santa Clara County. As we navigated past old fixtures and a dead Battlezone arcade game, he also pointed out that some of the building's circuit breakers actually still say things like "bicycles," from back when the place was Magic Village 35 years ago.

Just three years ago, a few dozen rabid Chuck E. Cheese's collector nerds from across the United States made a trip to California to celebrate the 30th anniversary of the place. Seymour was their point man for Silicon Valley. "Those guys were fanatics," he recalled, shaking his head in disbelief.

Speaking of history, the process of how Chuck E. Cheese himself has changed over the years is downright fascinating. The first and now collectible version of Chuck was much more gangsterlike than the sanitized mousey Chuck one now sees. "He began as a rat, and now he's a mouse," Seymour explained. "And he no longer has whiskers."

As we continued through the maze upstairs, we arrived at the obligatory storage room of ancient electronics. The Cyberamics Control System, for example, is what drove the pneumatic Pizza Time Theatre stage characters in the '70s. Moments later, we paused at a bay window overlooking the 101 and Tully interchange, where Seymour continued to rattle off stories nonstop.

"Back in 1981, a store opened in Capitola," he told me. "That was going to be their model store. But it only lasted for a few years." According to Seymour, the French version of *Playboy* even sent a reporter to that particular Chuck E. Cheese's to profile the whole place, along with its surfer-girl waitresses.

Thanks to Seymour and his tour of Pizza Time Theatre storage, the author is emboldened with still more appreciation for the ignored. Those who search out the forgotten history of Silicon Valley mustn't end their quest with the Atari 2600. If the author gets his way in some fantasy version of the future, this wreckage of past Chuck E. Cheese's oddities might someday be available for all to see. As he proclaimed once before, "If Greece and Rome can turn their ruins into tourist traps, then why shouldn't San Jose?"

Bob Tilley: Freelance Life

A few weeks ago, the anti-man-about-town went international and found himself in Chiang Mai, Thailand, at a spectacular haunt fittingly called the Writer"s Club and Wine Bar. Owned by British expat Bob Tilley and his Thai wife, Tong, the place is a big draw for traveling scribes of all sorts.

You never know who you'll run into. One day, someone will perch himself at the bar while working on a *Lonely Planet Guide*; the next day, a foreign correspondent might roll through town and stop in for a meal. All journalists are welcome. It's essentially the unofficial press club of Chiang Mai. An ancient Underwood typewriter sits on the bar, and several books by local authors, including Tilley, can be seen behind a case on the wall.

Tilley himself is up there in years. He has exactly five decades of experience as a stringer, mostly in Europe during the Cold War era, scavenging for stories for any number of newspapers. Like any true freelancer, he was a mercenary of sorts, often working for whichever publication had the dough. He wrote both for serious papers like the *Daily Telegraph* and also for tabloids like the *Sun* and the *Daily Mirror*.

Now writing pocket-size books under the pen name Bob Andrews, he recently released the riotous *No Mummy, No Money: Confessions of a Chequebook Journalist*, in which he spills lurid details of the freelance stringer's life. Self-published and available through his own outfit, the Writer's Club Chiang Mai (www.chiangmaiwritersclub.com), the whole thing is exactly 100 pages, and one can easily blow through it in an hour.

The reader takes home a side-splitting snapshot of the more lucrative aspects of Tilley's decades-long career: fabricating expense accounts, gate crashing, freeloading countless lunches at press conferences, simultaneously working for competing newspapers to pay the rent and phoning in stories from behind the Iron Curtain to clueless copy editors who can't spell umlaut.

In one chapter, Andrews gets an assignment to track down a preacher's daughter who had supposedly just slept with Mick Jagger. Another chapter explains a sting operation in which a bunch of British tabloid reporters were assigned to go to a bar in Germany and steal back an actual soccer ball from the 1966 World Cup Final, which was won by England. And there's more than one brutally honest confession of how much cheating is really done when a writer lands a gig updating a travel guide and the pay isn't enough to revisit the destination for as long as it takes to do the job right.

"There's this popular belief that journalists must be the guardians of honesty and probity," Tilley told me. "And we're not—at least, not the ones I worked with. From my experience, we're just a bunch of guys, and gals, trying to make a living while enjoying it."

But the book is not just about hackery. The author sheds light on the adrenaline rush that comes with every phone call, every new assignment, every new investigative adventure into the unknown: "That phone call," he writes, "however inconvenient, is an invitation to enter a world where anything can happen—and to enter it with complete immunity and impunity, equipped with press card and credit card, passport and overnight case, prebooked hotel rooms and hire cars, contacts waiting to welcome you and perhaps, if they're pretty and you're lucky, share your bed. There's the narcotic buzz of not knowing where you'll end up, whom you'll meet, with whom you'll be sharing your days and nights—and finally, the promise of applause for a job well done, the byline above a story you managed to unearth against all the odds."

As I write this column—in a business class seat on a China Airlines flight from Bangkok to Taipei—I can safely say that I am inspired by this book. I see at least one of my future selves. Tilley says he is already at work on a revised version of No Mummy, No Money. "One of the additional chapters I shall be writing is 'How to secure a business-class seat,'" he told me. "I wrote an article based on one or two experiences and Reader's Digest used it!"

At Linda Ronstadt's House with Dolores Huerta

Last week, an unprecedented liaison of creative minds took place in a house near the Sea Cliff neighborhood in San Francisco. The folks from CreaTV San Jose, a cable-access powerhouse, were on hand to film what turned out to be an inspiring, momentous occasion.

Activist and labor leader Dolores Huerta, co-founder and first vice president emeritus of the United Farm Workers of America, drove in from Stockton to meet with Linda Ronstadt and talk about what will be going down for this year's San José Mariachi and Mexican Heritage Festival. Huerta is now 80, but she exudes the same revolutionary attitude she did decades ago. Ronstadt, as most know by now, is the artistic director of the festival. At the meeting, Ronstadt and Huerta engaged in a conversation, parts of which will be streamed live from the festival's website (http://sanjosemariachifestival.com) within a few weeks. The house was then opened up to members of the press.

Since 2010 marks both the bicentennial of Mexico's independence and the centennial of the Mexican Revolution, the plans are only beginning to unfold. Ronstadt informed us that one of the themes this time around would be the Soldaderas, the female soldiers who fought in the Mexican Revolution. "I thought it was really important to see what this war was like from a woman's point of view," Ronstadt explained. "Because women and children are always the most horrifically cruel victims of war."

On another front, the festival is about connecting youth with their roots. Ronstadt said that in Mexican and Latin-American cultures, families are much more of an extended unit. The norm is for everyone, grandparents and grandkids, to all coalesce. The festival helps to give kids a sense of family history through the music. "Kids today don't know who they are," she said. "[The festival] gives them a chance to learn about who they are. Their background is Mexican—it resonates, it says 'Yes, you are; it's something to be proud of,' it connects them back to their grandparents. We don't have that so much here now. Everybody's living in their own little pod. There's a teenage pod, a toddler pod, a grandparents pod. They're not connected, and I think Mexican culture does that."

As an example, Ronstadt said that when she originally toured her *Canciones de Mi Padre* album more than 20 years ago, she didn't know who was going to show up. She had already done all the rock & roll gigs, for 40,000 people, summer after summer, year after year, but when she took the Mexican show out on the road, she had no idea what was going to happen. Were people going to scream for "It's So Easy"?

"People brought their children. They brought their grandmas. The whole family showed up," she recalled. "In all my rock & roll touring years, I'd never seen any little kids out there, or any grannies. Ever. I was thrilled. And the other cool thing [unlike rock audiences] is they know exactly where to yell in the music. They were my favorite audience I ever had." To this day, that album is the biggest selling non-English record in American history. Continuing, she said that the festival is designed "to create that resonance, so people can have a sense of who they are. And who you are has to be reflected back at you from the greater community."

Huerta added that mariachi music can have the same intricacies as classical music, as far as the rhythms and the way components interplay with each other. "The mariachi is an ambassador of goodwill," she said. "Especially when you think of all the racism that has been directed against people from Mexico—they're lazy and this and that—the mariachi is such an incredible statement of beauty. There's no one that can listen to Mariachi music without being thrilled."

World Cup Soccer: Made in Germany

On a recent European jaunt, the anti-man-about-town infiltrated Düsseldorf, Germany, just in time for the World Cup. Since I grew up watching German soccer on PBS, the scenario functioned as a catalyst for some good old-fashioned self-discovery and reflection.

As a child in the late '70s, I became particularly enamored with a now-legendary show called Soccer Made in Germany. Each hour-long show reprised news, games and highlights from the German Bundesliga. Many of us partly learned how to play soccer by watching that show.

The announcer, a colorful Brit named Toby Charles, was sort of like our teacher and our uncle at the same time. With him as our guide, we first learned about teams like Bayern Münich, Hamburg SV and Eintracht Frankfurt. In San Jose, the show was on Channel 9, and by the time I was 8 years old, I was familiar with the town of Düsseldorf. It was just a fun word to say.

These days, Düsseldorf is the capital of North Rhine-Westphalia, Germany's most populous state, with 18 million people. The city is one of those off-the-radar places most Americans wouldn't normally visit, but it has art, shopping, cuisine and music, with old and new architecture—only on a somewhat smaller scale than the more heavily trafficked German cities.

In just 15 minutes, an easy public transportation system takes people from the airport to the city center. The historical Old Town area (Altstadt) features at least 100 bars, restaurants, shops and outdoor cafes of seemingly every nationality. Strangely, the city's most upscale hotel, the Breidenbacher Hof, is the only one in Germany with a plastic-surgery clinic attached to it. The accommodation is frequented by travelers from the Middle East, usually primed for shopping outside on Königsallee, or "the Kö" for short. The city also boasts a mile of beer gardens along the Rhine River, an annual outdoor book fair, a definitive cream of mustard soup and even a Neanderthal Museum. I couldn't go wrong.

And as one would expect, soccer is an integral part of the social fabric. Each and every place with outdoor seating offered televisions for the World Cup. The German black, red and gold colors were ubiquitous, which was fun to witness, because it didn't use to be that way.

Germany hosted the last World Cup, in 2006, and during that tournament, an unprecedented cultural shift took place across the entire country. A fun and peaceful new brand of German flag-toting patriotism enveloped the nation. During previous decades, the German people usually felt discouraged to display national flags for any reason whatsoever. They felt conditioned not to openly show pride in their own country, or not to behave in any sort of fashion that could be interpreted as nationalistic, due to the country's sinister past. As simplistic as this sounds, the 2006 World Cup changed all of that. Gone was the stereotypical wooden, humorless German. Flags, colors and paraphernalia exploded everywhere. People painted their faces, and the nation appeared to be in a much better mood. This is a perfect example of why the World Cup is the greatest show on earth. According to the Germans who spoke to me, no other event would possibly have caused that to happen.

In Düsseldorf, when this year's World Cup began, there were Irish, Brits, Germans, Italians, Africans, Middle-Easterners and many others milling about all over Altstadt. A Brazilian samba procession snaked its way down the cobblestone path—the same people waving both Brazilian and German flags. An oompah band pounded out tunes around the corner. I saw national team shirts from at least a dozen countries. When England played the United States, I slithered into a local pub to watch the game and cheer on the United States. The Germans I met were also rooting for America in that game.

That U.S. game put everything into perspective. I grew up in San Jose watching Soccer Made in Germany. Now I was in Germany watching soccer made in America. The cycle was complete. And Düsseldorf is still a fun word to say.

San Jose People: Richard Alexander

Six stories up, in a building overlooking St. James Park in downtown San Jose, one finds the office of Richard Alexander, one of the city's best-known attorneys. Since I am always interested in hidden museums off the beaten path, when I heard that the walls of his office contained numerous artifacts related to the American Revolution, and the year 1776 specifically, I had to scurry over.

After all, that particular neighborhood is San Jose's most historical region -- St. James Park was the city's original town square a century ago and numerous ancient stories already circulate within its environs. About a minute after I appeared in the lobby, Alexander came thundering down the hallway. "Welcome to the Democratic version of the American Revolution," he declared, eventually pointing to a pristine model ship, the first thing one sees when stepping out of the elevator. Given to him by his wife as a 40th birthday present, it's a replica of the Bonhomme Richard, the famous Revolutionary War ship captained by John Paul Jones, the one where he supposedly uttered the phrase "I have not yet begun to fight."

Framed prints and etchings relating to the Revolutionary War hang from every wall throughout the office: Washington crossing the Delaware, the surrender of Cornwallis, the Battle of Bunker Hill, the first reading of the Declaration of Independence and even one print of the Battle of Québec. Several flags hang from poles throughout the front rooms, including a Bennington flag, the only one with white stripes at both the top and bottom.

As a personal-injury attorney, Alexander has handled more than his share of high-profile local cases, and his fight to hold big corporations accountable for their negligence is inspired by the American Revolution. When John Paul Jones uttered that famous line, little did he know that, a few hundred years later, a lawyer in San Jose would hold that phrase dear to his very practice. Alexander sees himself engaged in a struggle similar to that of the American colonists all those years ago.

"They were a small group of lawyers who organized and defeated the British Empire," Alexander tells me. "They understood natural inalienable rights, they were well versed in philosophy and they took on a monster. And that's what we do. We take on corporations like IBM and Ford."

Alexander's life story is far outside the scope of this column -- he has been married longer than I've been alive -- but one can easily see where his idea to collect this stuff actually came from: He went to Paul Revere Elementary School in Cleveland. He went to Nathan Hale Junior High. He went to John Adams High School. Nowadays, his current home address is 1776.

It doesn't stop there. Both his office phone and fax number end in 1776. He says he got the idea when working with the flamboyant attorney Melvin Belli in the early '70s. Back in those days, some telephone prefixes still began with a two-letter abbreviation, and Belli's famous number was YUkon 11849, invoking imagery of the Gold Rush. Belli's building on Montgomery Street in San Francisco was also located on the site of the first California meeting of Freemasons, in 1849.

That geographical fact, naturally, drove me to contemplate it all while staring out Alexander's sixth-story office window. A gaze northward provides an up-close shot of the Egyptian ornamentation of the San Jose Athletic Club building, originally constructed by the Freemasons. In fact, I have speculated in this space before about potential Masonic influence in the landscape design of St. James Park. Many on the first San Jose City Council were also Masons.

With that, I will leave things open for the conspiracy theorists. Several books already spell out Masonry's influence on the American Revolution. Another secret society, the Bavarian Illuminati, was revived in 1776 by Adam Weishaupt, a law professor. Perhaps Richard Alexander is one in a long line of heroes going back even farther.

Ramones Museum in Berlin

Literary travel is the rage these days, with more and more people jonesing to infiltrate the haunts of their favorite authors. That said, the ever-changing European cultural megalopolis of Berlin offers one such opportunity.

On a nondescript side street in the central borough, Krausnickstrasse 23 to be exact, sits the Ramones Museum, a collection of more than 300 artifacts devoted to the game-changing New York punk band that existed from 1974 to 1996. For 3.50, visitors enter a small labyrinth of Ramones clothing, posters, news clippings, set lists, backstage passes, cardboard cutouts, skate decks, album covers, handbills, pinhead costumes and other related ephemera. The entire collection emerged from the efforts and obsessions of Florian Hayler, a local Ramones fanatic.

Dee Dee Ramone, the band's original bass player and primary songwriter, spent some of his childhood in Berlin as an army brat. His mother was German, and his father was an American serviceman. His half-Germanness crept into several Ramones lyrics over the years.

The museum unfolds chronologically, including separate displays for each member of the band. Dee Dee's section features all of his books, including his notorious 2000 autobiography, *Lobotomy: Surviving the Ramones.*

Even better, another glass case commemorates the last show Dee Dee played with the band before he quit, which took place at One Step Beyond in Santa Clara on July 5, 1989. I am proud to say I was at that show and Santa Clarans can be proud that their city is thus recognized by an international museum. But this is literary travel. *Lobotomy,* originally released in the United Kingdom as *Poison Heart,* begins with Dee Dee's youth in Berlin. His father was a chronic alcoholic who regularly beat him. There was no familial unit, no emotional support, no nothing.

"I was disturbed," he writes, describing his failure in the first grade. "I had anxiety problems; I had no self-esteem. I was embarrassed, because of the fighting in my family. And I had never been taught anything by an adult. I had absolutely no guidance. Everything was a mystery."

Berlin itself is a city in constant flux. Dee Dee lived there for spells, before and after the wall went up in 1961. As a kid, he used to go wandering alone through bombed-out buildings.

Upon returning to Berlin later in the '60s, he realized the wall went directly through his old 'hood. Berlin was now a divided place, and he probably became a divided person, just like many of the natives.

Simply put, if one hails from a conflicted city, those conflicts often emerge in the person's creative work. And Dee Dee often said that if he had to identify a real home, Berlin would be it.

In 1995, the final song on the final Ramones album was titled "Born to Die in Berlin," penned by Dee Dee, even though he had long since left the band. The recording features him singing the bridge in German, which he submitted over the phone.

The man who essentially invented punk-rock bass playing also battled drugs for most of his life, beginning at an early age in Germany. Sadly, he lost that battle in June of 2002 in Los Angeles, dying of a heroin overdose at age 49—just four months after the Ramones were inducted into the Rock and Roll Hall of Fame and just days before he was supposed to play a solo gig at the Cactus Club in San Jose.

I contemplated it all during a long flight home on Air Berlin, which now flies straight from Germany to San Francisco. With all the vacuous, overdone "following in the footsteps" travel tours these days, Dee Dee's dysfunctional upbringing should be required reading if one goes to Berlin.

After all, it was most likely his messed up childhood in that city that drove him to drugs, near-madness and criminal activity, which in turn drove him to help invent punk rock and change the entire face of music and influence thousands of bands worldwide for decades thereafter. Long live Berlin and long live Dee Dee Ramone.

Chateau Liberté

The only San Jose band ever to make a cameo appearance on the '70s sitcom What's Happening, is currently celebrating its 40th anniversary. The Doobie Brothers began in 1970, releasing their self-titled debut the following year.

The cover of that album showed the band hanging out at Chateau Liberté, a now-legendary biker bar in the Santa Cruz Mountains, where the Doobies got their start. This year, the band releases a new album with a new track, "Back to the Chateau," dedicated to the venue, which existed until the mid-'70s.

"The Chateau," as the mountain ilk still say, was located on a muddy dirt path off Old Santa Cruz Highway, buried amid the gargantuan redwoods. The Hell's Angels ran the place for years, and the parties were over the top. Since the building was down the hill from the main road and somewhat difficult to reach, the sheriffs often just refused to drive all the way in.

Many bands played at the Chateau, including the earliest version of the Tubes and several offshoots of the Grateful Dead and the Jefferson Airplane. Skip Spence of Moby Grape, who had actually introduced the Doobie Brothers to each other, occasionally stayed in a van just outside the chateau. Hot Tuna recorded its live album, First Pull Up, Then Pull Down, at Chateau Liberté. In Jeff Tamarkin's book Got a Revolution, Jorma Kaukonen described the place: "It was a shit-kicking log cabin bar, an old stage stop in 1800s. It had very low ceilings and was down a muddy road. The sound was horrendous. We played there a lot and wanted to do this album there."

Previously, in the late 19th century, the building was a stop on the old Wells Fargo stagecoach line from San Jose to Santa Cruz. From 1920 to 1945 it was Chateau Boussy, a French restaurant and luxury hideaway for high-society types and politicians who needed a spot to bring their mistresses.

But many folks from the Chateau Liberté era still remain and continue to circulate their memories of the place. People of all shapes and sizes attended the festivities to eat, drink and listen to music. It was a communal atmosphere—a temporary autonomous zone of the most inspiring sort.

W.J. McKay, who first frequented the joint as a teenager, recalled how everyone seemed to get along: "You had people that were totally politically opposite, socially opposite," he told me. "Bikers and hippies were about as different as people could be, and yet they totally co-existed up there. They even had their own underground economy going on. Dope had an established exchange rate. Pot was worth so much in weight, for so many hits of acid. The hippies and the bikers totally worked together. They exchanged food, they worked on each other's vehicles, they did chores for each other."

Local real estate agent George Rabe currently owns and lives on the 72 acres where the Chateau sits. He restored the building and remains immersed in its history, so much that he went out of his way to give us a personal tour of the property. Oil painter Paul Berenson, who in 1973 lived in the redwoods right outside the Chateau, even drove up from Santa Barbara for the tour. It was the first time he'd been to the property in 37 years.

"It made me realize how much I didn't appreciate it back then." Berenson told me. "And how big of an influence it was on me. That was my first real appreciation of nature."

The Chateau Liberté scene was true counterculture in the sense that it could only have happened at that particular time and place. It was a uniquely Northern California scenario.

"It wasn't just a legendary rock & roll bar," McKay said. "It was an example of music and people breaking barriers, for better or worse, in one of the most beautiful natural coastal rain forests in the world. It was a scene that will never be re-created, and hopefully never forgotten."

Remembering Jim Nysted

Throughout its long bar-studded history, downtown San Jose never experienced a man, myth or legend quite as provocative, multidimensional and entertaining as James Martin Nysted, who passed away on July 22 at the age of 69.

He was an independently wealthy Vietnam veteran, mathematician, U.S. Chess Grandmaster, used-car collector, gadfly, conspiracy theorist, prolific writer, pianist, disputed Lutheran, art-class model, choir singer, homeless and mental-heath advocate and drinking buddy for anyone who would listen to him.

When he wasn't checking in at the VA Hospital in Palo Alto, practicing Beethoven's Moonlight Sonata in the Music Building at SJSU or purchasing yet one more used car from the Salvation Army on Taylor Street, he found his home in the various watering holes of the neighborhood, often just looking for other creative minds to chat with. He was known for reciting Edgar Allan Poe's "The Raven," by memory, in its entirety.

Conversing and drinking with Jim was sometimes just like reading his stream-of-consciousness manuscripts, which he often handed to everyone in the entire bar. Fantasy blurred with reality in the most poetic fashion. We spent days, perhaps years, philosophizing, arguing, conspiring, pontificating, complaining, lecturing, psychoanalyzing and diagnosing with each other.

We drank and laughed for hours on end, often holding court right inside the gate at Gordon Biersch on San Fernando Street, thoroughly perplexing the more civilized folks who ambled their way in. Several of those conversations provided source material for ideas I used in my own writings, this column especially.

Jim was also a chess grandmaster and although not completely invincible, he could usually destroy anyone who attempted to play him. At the old Katie Bloom's on South First Street, the bartender would set up a chessboard on the bar, and the matches would continue into the night. Even when hammered out of his mind, Jim could still beat most people. He adored the King's Gambit, he loathed castling queenside, and he would carry on all night about the Ruy Lopez opening. At the same time, though, he was deeply at war with himself over having lost the "killer instinct" for the game.

Over countless drinking sessions, Jim elaborated that the killer instinct at chess is what furnished him with a passageway to a different reality. That is, he could do things on the chessboard that he couldn't do in real life. For him, this was tangible proof that imagination could be made real.

Over at SJSU, Jim deliberately seeped into every circle of people imaginable. He was one of those characters from the '60s who just never managed to escape the sphere of the campus community. (There are many others—they either wound up in mental institutions or simply became SJSU employees for decades.)

But Jim, at least not recently, was never one for traditional concepts like "work." He had his pile—however much, he would never tell—and instead spent his time collecting used cars, parking them all over downtown and subsequently irritating police officers and meter maids throughout the land. His most famous line was "I started with nothing in life and managed to hold on to half of it."

There is no summary. Jim was a man who couldn't be reduced to any one essential theory or practice. He was totally postmodern, or perhaps more specifically, poststructuralist. There were multiple structures of thought in his brain, each one navigating its own trajectory, but all of which, somehow, were still connected. You can take any term from Deleuze and Guattari's A Thousand Plateaus and apply it to Jim. Easily. He was a glorious weed between the cracks of downtown San Jose public life.

"There are two things worth mentioning," he once told me. "One is that the imagination can be made real on the chessboard. The other is that chess is life. When both of these are gone, then it's time to quit."

Jack's Bar at Flugtag Long Beach

Last Saturday the anti-man-about-town jet-setted down to SoCal because the only Bay Area team competing in the Red Bull Flugtag at Long Beach was a handful of San Jose characters from Jack's Bar on Taylor Street.

German for "flying day," Flugtag is that ridiculous-on-purpose competition challenging lunatics of all sorts to build human-powered flying machines and pilot them off a 30-foot high pier. Many of the contraptions just dive-bomb and crash into the water, which is sort of expected, but a few wind up taking flight for about 50–90 feet or so. It is one helluva charade.

Flugtag debuted in 1991 in Vienna, Austria—home of Red Bull. The first flugtag in the United States was in San Francisco in 2002, and this year the circus hit Miami, Minneapolis–St. Paul and Long Beach—and then heads to Philly over Labor Day weekend.

Calling themselves the Flying Rocks, the San Jose team—Travis Walter, Larry Hoang, Matt Turney, Jordan Trigg and Charlie Mann—made the 36-team cut out of 300 who entered. They "designed" a papier-mâché boulder-looking contraption on a makeshift frame with four bicycle tires. Two spinning circular appendages provided, well, something.

According to a few team members, it took five rolls of duct tape to assemble the contraption plus 60 feet of chicken wire, a few packages of twist-ties and 127 issues of Metro for the papier-mâché. Faber's Cyclery helped out by donating tires, rims and PVC tubing. In that sense, it was a truly "San Jose" collaboration. Actually, the jerry-rigged craft looked more suited for Flugtag Alviso than Flugtag Long Beach, but I give 'em credit for trying.

As they towed it down the freeway to SoCal, the whole thing broke into pieces. They attempted to repair it on the road, and by the time they arrived—about 1:30pm Friday—the craft was destroyed. But they redid the papier-mâché and somehow got the contraption working again.

The Flugtag event itself is an absolute circus. One by one, each team rolls its contraption down the length of the pier in order to build up speed. When the team gets to the end of the pier, off the machine goes, with one person actually "piloting" it.

Each crew dresses up in homemade costumes to fit whatever theme suits its project and does its own choreographed dance out on the flight deck for all to see. Then they launch their contraption into the water. The teams are judged on distance, creativity of craft and showmanship.

Most teams also brought an equivalent "street team" to pass out T-shirts and solicit votes for the People's Choice Award. The Flying Rocks dressed up like cavemen and dragged about 50 folks from San Jose with them. During the lead-up to the event, each team displayed its respective machine in the street, and numerous passers-by stopped to have their photos taken, especially with the Flying Rocks. The caveman costumes were a big hit, wowing the SoCal crowd.

The takeoff pier protruded straight into Rainbow Harbor in Long Beach, surrounded by Parker's Lighthouse, Shoreline Aquatic Park, the shops and restaurants of Shoreline Village, the Queen Mary, the marina and dozens of boats. The setting drew an announced crowd of 105,000. People even parked on the 710 Freeway, essentially closing down the exit ramp to Long Beach. Celebrity judges included Cheech Marin and Tenley Molzahn from The Bachelor Pad.

In the end, the San Jose contraption went straight down into the water and didn't fly more than a few feet. But all agreed the entire process was worth it. Someone had to represent NorCal in this whole mess.

"It was great to great to represent San Jose and the Bay Area and Jack's Bar," Trigg said later that evening, as the crew partied in the rooftop pool at the Avia Hotel. "We had a wreck with the craft and everyone came out and helped us fix it. I felt like Mickey Mouse today, with all the pictures people took next to us. We had way too much fun."

Dalai Lama at the San Jose Convention Center

For the first time in San Jose history, the Dalai Lama will make two successive appearances in buildings on San Carlos Street. Next Tuesday, he will appear at the McEnery Convention Center, teaching on Geshe Langri Thangpa's Eight Verses of Training the Mind (lojong tsik gyema), organized by the Gyuto Vajrayana Center.

The next day he will show up at the SJSU Event Center to give an Amitabha Permission Initiation (opakmei jegang). The sold-out first appearance is presented as an interfaith event. That is, anyone connected to any denomination or nondenomination is encouraged to attend.

Now, I would not call myself a Buddhist, but Buddhist perspectives have always inspired me, especially the concept of Paticca-samuppada, or dependent origination—how nothing exists independently, how all beings and phenomena exist or occur because of their relationships with other beings and phenomena.

For me, this concept emerges in varying degrees, so the Dalai Lama's presence in my hometown drives me to ponder several interconnected milieus, a few of which I will unleash here. To paraphrase the interdisciplinary researcher and physicist Piet Hut, maybe I can view life as a laboratory, as an opportunity to examine myself and others, in the hope that it leads to something better.

Here we go: In 1998, I showed up at Todd Perreira's bachelor party, which took place in a secret upstairs room at a wonderful and now-defunct coffeehouse, Café Zucco. A San Jose native, Perreira married Somsamai Ritprasert, owner of the San Jose restaurant House of Siam, where I had spent hundreds of student loan dollars while at SJSU.

Their wedding took place at St. Joseph's Cathedral and was one of the happiest events I've ever attended. By any definition, it was an interfaith experience. They had a Western ceremony in the church, followed by a traditional Thai Buddhist ceremony at the St. Claire Hotel—true local flavor.

Just last week, I met with Perreira at San Jose's best Buddhist reincarnation of a gas station, Roy's Coffee in Japantown. Now a Buddhist scholar, he teaches in the comparative religious studies program at SJSU as he completes his Ph.D. research through Harvard.

Over coffee, we yakked about his current research on the genealogy of Chang and Eng Bunker, the famous Siamese twins and how their history might be intertwined with the first legit Buddhists ever to step on American soil. Perreira is connected to scholars in Bangkok currently at work on the goods as you read this.

We also discussed potential reincarnations of Frontier Village, a long-gone San Jose amusement park we both loved as kids. I mentioned that my life can be characterized by one gigantic loss after the next, Frontier Village being just one. We then laughed uproariously at the sadness of it all, just as those old Zen masters probably did.

And then there's the Dalai Lama, particularly known for his ever-growing interest in the resonances between Buddhist perspectives and quantum mechanics. He is not the only one. His former student, the scholar, scientist and ordained monk Alan Wallace, is striving to mainstream the conversation between Buddhism and Western science, in order to explore how the two should compare notes.

During the Dalai Lama's first teaching tour in the West in the late '70s, Wallace was his interpreter. These days, His Holiness attends or hosts academic conferences on consciousness studies and shows up at experiments in physicists' laboratories. No one is claiming that science "justifies" Buddhism or vice-versa; rather, they suggest that integrating methods of inquiry from both will give birth to profound new insights. Being half-Eastern and half-Western and naturally interested in anything "in-between," I am inspired by the approach.

Wallace's wife, Vesna—herself an accomplished Buddhist scholar and translator—is on Perreira's dissertation committee. How's that for connections? After last week's conversation with Perreira, I felt like I had finally come full circle. Now I feel dependently original and glad to be a San Jose native. The Dalai Lama's presence will indeed be significant in various degrees of unseparation. After getting my camera approved by the bomb squad, I will attend his teaching as an observer/participant and see what happens.

Sheepish in Scotland

Since one must often escape the confines of home to find inspiration, last week the anti-man-about-town bolted from Silicon Valley to Edinburgh, Scotland, a city fertile with culinary and literary backdrops. The muse emerged almost immediately.

First of all, no scribe worth his laptop would possibly infiltrate Scotland without consuming haggis, that country's traditional cuisine. Often described in more gruesome details than anyone wants to know, haggis, so it is said, contains a sheep's ground innards—pieces of the liver, heart, lungs or whatever is left—mixed with oatmeal and secret spices.

Traditionally, haggis is boiled inside a casing made from a sheep's stomach or bladder, presented on a plate and then ceremoniously escorted into the dining room, complete with a bagpipe player sounding off like there's no tomorrow. Scotch whisky is downed, and the ground haggis is then served in any number of formulations.

At the Balmoral Hotel, Edinburgh's famous historical landmark, we witnessed a haggis the shape of which defies any less-than-naughty description, even for this column. But as tradition goes, bagpiper Ian Grant, a local independent musician and storyteller, came thundering into the dining room, clad in complete Scots military attire, playing the pipes so loud we couldn't even think straight. It was fantastic.

Behind him, the chef carried in the plate of haggis and placed it on the table, flanked by two glasses of Glenmorangie. To complete the ceremony, Grant then recited the legendary "Address to a Haggis," a hysterical Robert Burns poem dedicated to the famed cuisine.

Delivered in old Scottish, the poem confounded a few members of our dinner party, who whispered that they had problems with Grant's accent. "No worries," he said. "Even the Scots can't understand the words."

Turns out all the horror stories I had heard about haggis were nonsense. The Balmoral's Michelin-star chef Jeff Bland prescribed tasty plates of haggis with "neeps and tatties" in the traditional style. The ground haggis is served with a separate layer of mashed potatoes on top, accompanied by turnips and a whisky sauce. Actually, the ground meat doesn't taste that much different from a microwave peroshki but with a fresher menagerie of spices. It was quite superb.

The Balmoral itself is one of the most famous hotels in all of Scotland. When it re-emerged anew in 1990, Edinburgh native Sean Connery showed up and officially reopened the property. The hotel is popular for business meetings or for older Europeans visiting their sons and daughters studying at Edinburgh University.

The Balmoral's famous clock tower is a reigning symbol, directional marker and dependable timepiece for the entire city. "People in Edinburgh see the hotel more as a monument," said general manager Ivan Artolli. "During the winter, the clock was broken for two days, and we had 575 phone calls."

Even better, as I began writing this column in room 542 at the Balmoral, I knew I was not the first scribe to take inspiration from this hotel. In a now-famous yarn, author J.K. Rowling moved into room 652 for a few months in order to complete the last Harry Potter novel, *Harry Potter and the Deathly Hallows*. When finished, she left a signed statement on a bust of Hermes, which is no longer there. No one will say how much she paid, but it's said she didn't get her deposit back after damaging the bust.

Rowling also famously wrote in a nearby cafe, the Elephant House, where she typed away in a back room overlooking the Edinburgh Castle. It was here that the first few Harry Potter novels came to light. A smattering of newspaper clippings adorns one wall of the cafe, documenting her presence.

In one article, Rowling explains she just sometimes has to leave her home in order to get inspired. I think I know what she's talking about. Now, if she would just write *Harry Potter and the Deathly Haggis*, then I will be inspired to read one of her books, and perhaps even wait in line at midnight when it goes on sale.

L'Amour Shoppe Local

This week, another fond memory of San Jose politics, porn and pile drivers. Basically, stories exist underneath every rock and pebble of this place, so when a friend offhandedly brought up the defunct adult novelty store, the L'Amour Shoppe, I decided to summon the Muses, the Nine Daughters of Memory.

A few of those adult shops still exist throughout California, but the San Jose store, which sat at 477 S. First St., remains intertwined with the memories of many a San Jose scenester from the old SoFA days.

During the late '80s and early '90s, when an alternative-music renaissance was cementing a Bohemian substratum along South First Street and providing a long-overdue alternative to bastions of blandness like Tapestry 'n' Talent, the L'Amour Shoppe was the last remaining vestige of adult-oriented retail left from the previous decades' worth of seedy porn underbelly. Everyone who went to the music clubs on South First stumbled into the L'Amour Shoppe at one time or another, in various states of sobriety.

It was a unique-to–San Jose sort of scenario. In the building now housing Liquid Agency, the L'Amour Shoppe occupied the street level, while a constantly rotating crew of colorful characters lived in the dump upstairs and threw notorious drunken rooftop parties.

Many local bands played gigs up there, with hundreds of people attending over the years. The entire building was named "Dinuba," and a few of the characters upstairs also worked in the L'Amour Shoppe downstairs. It was porn, booze and rock & roll, the likes of which San Jose will never see again. Unfortunately.

During that time, the city of San Jose was engaged in the first of many failed attempts at convincing the comfortable classes to move back downtown in search of inner-city recolonization. The City Council, drunk with rezoning power, was smashing all the porn. The L'Amour Shoppe was the last piece left and thus met its eventual fate in 1994. Like a lone soldier on the battlefield, the shop stuck it out until the very end.

It reminds me of the French World War II resistance tune "The Partisan," famously covered by Leonard Cohen. In the song, the narrator is a lone French soldier trying to remain free when the Germans invade: "When they poured across the border/ I was cautioned to surrender/ This I could not do." The Germans arrive at his door, and he disappears into the night.

To this day, the L'Amour business carries on, including stores in Salinas, Fremont and Sacramento. The Salinas store was and still is the headquarters of the entire company.

Nito Gomez, the former bodybuilder and professional wrestler, began working at the Salinas store in 1986, moving up from clerk to assistant manager and then to manager. After that, he managed the San Jose store until the Hammer of Susan came off the top rope with a forearm smash and took him out.

"Believe it or not, [the L'Amour owners were] actually a very good group of people," Gomez told me. "[They] had families, raised kids, worked hard and created a relaxed, fun environment that made a lot of people stay there for many years. Plus the owners paid well. Most managers received at least $2,000 per month salary, and the ones that were there for many years got upwards of 3 grand per month. And this was back in the late '80s and throughout the '90s. The clerks made at least $9 per hour to start, which was good for back then, at a relaxed type of job."

Just like the French resistance, the legends live on. One former L'Amour Shoppe employee, speaking under condition of anonymity, said the place attracted an entire ensemble cast of characters: "A group of guys would wait around for the new smut to roll in on Mondays and Thursday mornings. They would hang outside of the shop. ...The truck would arrive, they would go out, unload it, open the boxes and check the invoice for us and then discuss amongst themselves who gets to rent the new smut first. We labeled them as 'The Sharks.'"

In downtown San Jose, L'Amour is the Tenth Muse of Memory. It will never go away.

Hacienda Gardens Mall Malaise

In his day, the Urban Blight Exploration Junkie scored some legendary fixes all over town—the Pink Elephant Center, 24th Street, Stockton Avenue and the old FMC property by the airport, to name just a few.

However, of all his relapses throughout the last few years, nothing compares to the inevitable bender resulting from any survey of what's left at the Hacienda Gardens Shopping Center near Meridian and Hillsdale. It is perhaps the blight to end all blight, a gross disappointing failure by any definition of those words. If there existed such a concept as "shopping-center euthanasia," it would apply to Hacienda Gardens. The place is beyond help. Just take it off life support and let it die peacefully. Please.

Some background: Hacienda Gardens first opened for business in 1959 and eventually grew into a popular shopping center with department stores, clothing shops, two bookstores and many mom-and-pop places, all of which thrived as recently at the late '80s.

Van's Hobby Store was an awesome place for any inquisitive youngster who enjoyed learning things. Little Professor Bookshop was the definitive neighborhood store tucked away in the corner, with a decent magazine selection and loads of Cliffs Notes no one else had. By 1987, Hacienda Gardens was one of the Top 20 highest-grossing shopping centers in Santa Clara County, with $33 million in retail sales for that year.

After that, everything that could go wrong did. Some tenants went broke, while others simply bailed. Landlord neglect added fuel to the fire, and after phases of attempted renovations and/or extensions, pieces of the center were still left unfinished. Economies tanked, paperwork changed hands, people went bankrupt, loans were defaulted on and foreclosures loomed. It appeared that no one anywhere wanted to deal with the situation anymore.

There was thought to be "mixed-use" development on the way, thus hastening the next round of the suburban condopocalypse. Now, maybe a Walmart or a yogurt shop. Who knows? The recent demise of the Cardinal Lounge, formerly the Red Coach Coffee Shop, was essentially the last straw, regardless of the reason. A celebrated San Jose retro diner specializing in post-2am scarfing, the Cardinal is not replaceable. Those are impossible shoes to fill.

As of right now, Hacienda Gardens features empty pieces of the original complex, splotches of empty parking lots, piles of rubble and newer buildings painted with the same red, orange and olive color scheme one sees on every strip mall from Capitol Expressway to Mountain View.

It's almost as if the developer went to Home Depot, found the aisle labeled "San Jose Strip Mall Supplies" and bought a few prefab buildings. The entire area is depressing to look at, let alone drive by. No wonder some neighbors are frustrated. Who would want to live near an atrocity like this? How is anyone supposed to muster any sense of civic pride? They flattened the Marie Callender's, meaning even the comfort-food crowds lose out in this mess. Locals now have to drive all the way to Blossom Hill and Chesbro for that famous lemon meringue pie.

Like any addict, the Urban Blight Exploration Junkie's path to relapse begins with feelings of hopelessness. He begins to think that if no one else cares about any of this, then why should he? Due to low self-esteem imprinted since childhood, he starts to feel like he's losing all control of what goes on around him in San Jose.

The structure in his life is falling apart, and no one else in town can possibly know how he feels or what he's going through. He becomes irritable and overwhelmed with basic everyday inconveniences, avoiding anyone who provides honest feedback on his condition. A drug fix becomes the only perceivable way to make himself feel any better. All of which is even more common during the holiday season.

He then falls "off the wagon" and goes on a bender through any blighted wasteland he can find, only to realize once again how bad it really is out there. And each time, he keeps promising it will be the last time he relapses. It won't happen again, he says. Alas, with more and more rundown shopping centers and dead retail scattered all over this valley, the triggers for relapse will always be there. For the Urban Blight Exploration Junkie, it seems the struggle will never end.

2011

Syd Barrett, Twisted Genius

I have always been a fan of irregular people, so when a new biography of Syd Barrett emerged late last year titled *A Very Irregular Head*, I chose to consume the 400-page work over an entire weekend.

Author Rob Chapman succeeds at deconstructing many oft-exaggerated mythologies and much assumed wisdom surrounding Pink Floyd's original leader. He talked to ex-girlfriends and former grammar schoolmates, as well as acquaintances from art school who hadn't previously discussed their experiences with Barrett in public.

For the regular readers out there, Barrett was Pink Floyd's original frontman, songwriter and the twisted genius behind the band's first album, *The Piper at the Gates of Dawn*. He was an undisputed pioneer of the '60s English psychedelic scene and the driving force behind Floyd's early improvisational soundscapes.

The shorthand version of his story is that he became an acidhead, his mental faculties deteriorated and he could no longer contribute, so the band squeezed him out after one album. With the band's assistance, he then recorded more of his own material, completed two solo albums and then retired into obscurity for decades until his death in 2006. Significant portions of Pink Floyd's catalog—including *Dark Side of the Moon*, *Wish You Were Here* and *The Wall*—were admittedly about Syd.

Chapman digs even deeper and comes to a refreshingly sympathetic conclusion. Barrett, he deduces, wasn't really influenced by rock music that much at all. His lyrical influences came almost entirely from English children's literature by authors like Edward Lear, Kenneth Grahame, Hilaire Belloc and Lewis Carroll. Turns out each of those authors suffered the loss of a parent at an early age, as did Syd. In a drop-dead gorgeous passage, here's the author: "Certain themes recur throughout their work directly as a result of these early traumatic losses. Disembodied identity, a dreamlike sense of the self in limbo without place of purpose, rootlessness, restlessness, rejection, detachment, escapism, retreat into imaginary worlds, the past recounted in reverie, the lost grandeur of classicism and antiquity, faded or unreachable Arcadia, protracted childhood and the potency of myth—all crop up time and time again and in many guises, as they do through Syd Barrett's songs."

Barrett went to Camberwell College of Arts in south London and was primarily a painter influenced by collage methods, as well as the text-cutup techniques of sound poets like Bob Cobbing. At that time, Syd crisscrossed with AMM, the British pioneers of electroacoustic free-improvisation. In that group, Keith Rowe pioneered the use of prepared electric guitar, manipulating the strings with unorthodox techniques—an approach Syd identified with.

Barrett had an almost pathological aversion to discipline of any sort, and his disaffection with the pop star routine had much to do with an unguided, directionless life that didn't gel with the responsibilities of TV appearances, interviews and tours.

Drugs played a major role in his mental condition, of course, but Chapman paints a picture of someone who essentially just couldn't deal with the suffering caused by the pressures of fame. As a result, he retreated into anonymity and obscurity, where he felt more comfortable. It is sad story. Towards the end of his life, Syd returned to painting, his original love. After completing each painting, he would photograph the finished product and then burn the canvas.

By forces of habit and nature, I tend to relate everything to my own landscape, and San Jose's equivalent of Syd Barrett would undoubtedly be Skip Spence of Moby Grape. Skip was likewise an underappreciated musical genius, influencing many who went on to become much huger than he ever did. Like Syd, Skip also became disenfranchised with rock stardom and fell victim to drugs. As early as 1970, Skip was envisioning his own rock opera, to be performed in a geodesic venue. I hope that someday we can see a sympathetic portrait of him as well.

Drink to the Old Days: George Rich, RIP

Last Saturday, a faithful congregation showed up at the Caravan Lounge at Almaden Avenue and San Fernando Street in San Jose to pay tribute to deceased owner George Rich, who passed away recently at the age of 79. A preacher named Eddie performed the memorial service in the bar. Local barflies from decades past rolled in for the occasion.

Rich was one of the few remaining downtown San Jose bar proprietors from the "old days," whichever decade one identifies as the "old" one. The Caravan has always been one of San Jose's most storied and celebrated dive bars, that little ol' faded lady right down the block from the Greyhound Station, in which it used to be located.

Before he bought the Caravan from Tommy Thatcher, George operated Lenny's Cocktails on Santa Clara Street between Fourth and Fifth streets—an even seedier joint across from where City Hall now sits. That entire side of the block was leveled 10 years ago in order to sanitize the street for the eventual return of City Hall to downtown. According to one source at the city, many a classical musician would regularly show up at Lenny's after performing at the nearby Mother Olson's Inn. They were shattered when the place closed.

But the Caravan was George's recent lifeblood, as were its regulars—in the daytime and the nighttime. It's funny. Locals or old-timers who've driven by the Caravan for decades without venturing in probably wouldn't even realize that, for 20 years now, the bar has rocked at nighttime. A "younger" crowd of twenty- and thirtysomethings fill the place to see punk and metal bands or, essentially, just for somewhere to escape the jocks, the fashionistas, the amateur drinkers and the cologne-soaked frauds that infest most of downtown's other bars. It's a pleasantly seedy joint where folks are allowed to be themselves and listen to music, even if the bathrooms exude aromas unknown to mankind.

The Caravan's history, since the late '50s, is curiously intertwined with a few other institutions. The San Jose Greyhound Station moved to its current location in 1957. According to a May 1955 San Jose Mercury News article, Santa Clara University owned the particular parcel of land. It was bequeathed to the university by the late Isabel de Saisset, a member of a local pioneer French-American family, who requested that the university establish and maintain an art museum on campus in her family's name. SCU sold the land to Greyhound, upheld her request and built the de Saisset museum, which still exists to this day.

Originally operated by Leo Chargin, the Caravan Lounge was originally located inside the bus station, with an address of 58 S. Almaden. It was one of a large chain of Caravan Lounges doing business inside Greyhound depots throughout California. When Greyhound later booted the bar out of the station, Chargin relocated the business down the street to its current location, which was then a used car lot. Since the mid-'60s, the Caravan has been located at 98 S. Almaden.

Since SCU is a Jesuit institution, another San Jose newspaper clipping from 1955 added a humorous note to the land transaction, referencing cannon law from Bouscaren-Ellis: "The church ... sets forth very precise steps for disposition of property. An early step is an appraisal by at least two experts and a determination by high ecclesiastical officials that the sale is to be for the best interest of the church. All church property valued in excess of 30,000 gold francs ... must pass the review of several high church dignitaries before it can be sold. Therefore, the sale of the de Saisset-inherited property by the University of Santa Clara had to have the approval of the Province of the Jesuit Society Order in San Francisco and the Jesuit General of the Society of Jesus in Rome and the permission of the Pope himself."

So think about it. If that sequence of events actually happened, then it means Pope Pius XII approved the Greyhound Station in San Jose, Calif. The pope approved the Caravan Lounge. George Rich has been blessed and that bar will never go away. Ad maiorem Dei gloriam!

Antero Alli: To Dream of Falling Upwards

In Antero Alli's new film, *To Dream of Falling Upwards*, the elder magus of the Thelemic Temple of Horus dies of old age, intending to pass the torch to a younger adept, Jack Mason, a power-seeker whom the Magus has cultivated and trained to carry on the lineage of the temple.

Unfortunately, the elder magus' biological son, Michael Mallard, intrudes and inherits the temple instead. As a result, Mason employs an assassin/dominatrix who kills Mallard while making it look like autoerotic asphyxiation. And that's only the beginning.

Mallard soon reappears as a psychological demon with a straw hat and a Hawaiian shirt, plaguing Mason from then on. As a result, Mason heads to the desert, enlisting the help of two brujas, female mestizo witches, similar to characters straight out of Carlos Castaneda.

In the film, the Thelemic Temple of Horus, a secret initiatic order, takes its name from Thelema, a religion and/or philosophical system established by the notorious chrome-domed troublemaker Aleister Crowley more than 100 years ago. The goal is to find your own "True Will" through gradual "Knowledge and Conversation" with the Holy Guardian Angel, a slippery term resembling the underlying metaphysical self.

When it comes to this particular zone of "the occult," there are two roads. The path of the magus is anchored in the will to control and achieve power over others. The path of the heart, says Alli, is followed by one who serves and yields to mysterious forces rather than engaging those forces for his own power and control. Reflecting that concept, in the film, Mason must choose either the path of the magus or the path of the heart.

Alli says his own Holy Guardian Angel emerges as the Muse of Creativity. He writes: "Whereas the occult magickian strives to achieve knowledge and conversation with the Holy Guardian Angel to increase power, my aim as a filmmaker is to use similar methods to open up the playing fields of Creation and stimulate the Poetic Imagination."

I laughed throughout the flick, because over the last century-and-a-half, we've seen a glut of occult lodges, esoteric temples and secret orders, all with their respective warring spinoffs and branches, usually with everyone arguing over who has the proper authority to carry on the lineage of whomever. As myth and parody, the film lampoons all of the above.

And there ought to be clowns, as the song goes, so a backstory in the film also emerges, with two of Jack Mason's apprentices performing

156

as clowns in a version of Jack and the Beanstalk. In order to deliberately quash their own egos, Mason orders them to become professional clowns as part of their initiation into the next temple degree.

Campbell native and *Campbell Express* writer Duncan Cook plays both the human and demon forms of Michael Mallard. He says it was a challenge going from who the character was at the beginning to what he was at the end.

"Working with Antero, I knew he wasn't going to leave in a mediocre performance," said Cook. "I knew that whatever became of it would be top-notch. He didn't need to explain what he wanted; he just guided me through it. He wasn't puppeteering, he was sort of like guiding me toward a performance that would serve the movie. It was organic. He was like the sun guiding a growing plant, or something."

Alli himself claims never to have joined any occult orders but says he was privy to a wealth of insider scoops while hanging out with the late Dr. Christopher S. Hyatt, a self-made magus and author of many books on postmodern psychology, sex, tantra, kundalini, mysticism and brain exploration. In the closing credits, the following stipulation emerges: "Any similarities or likenesses with actual events, persons or organizations in this film are purely coincidental and not to be confused for synchronicity or any type of ill will towards any real life person, company or magickal order."

To Dream of Falling Upwards premieres Feb. 25 at 8pm at the Humanist Hall in Oakland, with an April San Jose showing at Anno Domini currently being planned.

The Chocolate Watchband

The only San Jose psychedelic garage-rock band ever to share a member with the Harvard-Smithsonian Center for Astrophysics just completed a brand-new album. Originally disbanding 41 years ago, the Chocolate Watchband has been back together for at least 12 years now, with periodic spells of activity, since lead singer David Aguilar sets up shop in Boston, where he teaches astrophysics and writes science books for *National Geographic*.

But now things are heating up. Just a few weeks ago, the band released a *Greatest Hits* album of tunes it rerecorded at KVP Studio in Santa Clara last year. The goal was to re-create the sound and energy they had on the first three Watchband albums in 1966, '67 and '68.

The group reproduced the reverb of the old "echo chamber." They used the exotic instrumentation—sitar, bouzouki, temple bells and a Theremin—that gave the original recordings their distinctive sound. The album is available on iTunes now.

"We really focused on listening to the original material and figuring out what the spirit, the heart and the magic was, and how to re-create that," said Tim Abbott, the Watchband's guitarist. "We used tape-emulation programs, we used a lot of tube stuff, tube amps, tube preamps, a lot of old-style vintage compressors, as much vintage gear as we could."

The Chocolate Watchband originally formed in San Jose in 1965. The band's music was a blend of garage and psychedelic rock, taking influences from blues and British R&B but with an experimental, multi-instrumental edge. The band incorporated elements of surf, jazz and '60s exotica, all under the umbrella of the drug-addled antiwar era.

The Watchband appeared in two films: 1967's *Riot on Sunset Strip and The Love-Ins*. Locally, the band gigged at a variety of places: Napredak Hall, the Continental Roller Rink, the San Jose Civic, the Spectrum in Redwood City, Homer's Warehouse in Palo Alto. Circa 1967, the group played every night at Winchester Cathedral in Redwood City with Sly and the Family Stone. At the Coconut Grove in Santa Cruz, the Watchband played at least once a month.

"There were free concerts everywhere," Abbott said. "San Francisco, up and down the peninsula, block parties, the park across from Stanford Shopping Center. There were venues everywhere. We were just playing our brains out. There was never a 'Hello, we gotta get a gig.' There were opportunities everywhere."

In those days, the legendary Stevens Music in Willow Glen supplied all of the band's equipment. The Watchband originally went for a Rolling Stones style, British-influenced sound, and the store provided all the Vox amplifiers.

Today, Abbott actually runs KVP Studio in Santa Clara, where the sessions went down. Rerecording the old material was just a prelude for the band's next step. Last month, the Watchband cut more than a dozen brand-new songs.

Abbott won't blow the whistle on everything yet, but he says the new work is essentially a biography of the Chocolate Watchband, including songs about the band itself. Aguilar wrote most of the lyrics, and the band collaborated on the songwriting.

"This is the next album that would have come out in the '60s, stylistically and soundwise," Abbott said, adding that a good amount of slide guitar and even sitar parts appear throughout the entire project. "It's going to have the full Watchband thing going on, with the different instruments and sounds. There's quite a range of moods."

Currently, the band will also be included on a multiple-CD tribute to Sky Saxon of the Seeds, who passed away last year. For that project, folks like Iggy Pop and Billy Corgan are also on board.

"We're still going," Abbott said. "We were 'back in the day,' but we're still doing it. The last 10 years, we've done some of the biggest shows we've ever done, bigger than the shows we did in the '60s. It's been good, but we're looking forward to being even better."

Cathleen Miller: Aiding Activism

Cathleen Miller is the only faculty member at San Jose State University ever to write about the horrors of female genital mutilation and have those words translated into 55 languages.

Fourteen years ago, immediately after completing her MFA at Penn State, Miller co-authored *Desert Flower*, the worldwide-blockbuster story of Somali supermodel Waris Dirie. To date, the book has sold 11 million copies. A recent film based on the book, already released in 27 countries outside America, premiered at Cinequest last week. National Geographic begins U.S. distribution of the film beginning March 18.

The book and film tell Waris' remarkable true story. Born into a nomad family in the Somali desert, she underwent the inhuman procedure of genital mutilation—a sickening tradition still practiced in many places today. Later, as a teenager, she fled from her family to London, where photographer Terence Donovan discovered her and made her a supermodel. She vaulted to international stardom on the catwalks of the world, but now devotes her time to fighting against female genital mutilation.

She has made a huge difference. Kofi Annan appointed her as U.N. special ambassador for the elimination of female genital mutilation. In 2007, French President Nicolas Sarkozy appointed her as a Chevalier de la Legion d'Honneur. Her Desert Flower Foundation raises millions for the United Nations. As a result, dozens of African countries have finally outlawed the practice of female genital mutilation, although 8,000 girls are still forced into the process each year.

Fresh out of graduate school, Miller settled for second billing on the book, which became an international bestseller, reaching No. 1 in several countries. In Germany, it remained in the Top 10 for 120 weeks.

When the project began, Miller was living on a farm in Zion, Penn., while trying to shop her own memoir around to a few publishers in New York. At the same time, Waris had made a snap decision to tell her life story but couldn't find any publishers to climb onboard and connect her with a co-author. William Morrow did agree and developed the contract before they even lined up who was going to write it. After a few potential collaborators didn't work out, Miller's agent came into the mix.

"As a brand-new author who hadn't published much, to see my name on a book that already had a contract to come out in hardback on William Morrow was a great opportunity," Miller told me, especially "to have it be involved with something that I immediately realized was a great humanitarian effort."

Miller then had six months to complete a manuscript, which proved to be difficult, since Waris was inherently erratic and unpredictable. Miller would take the train into Manhattan in order to meet Waris and tape the conversations, only to find out that Waris had left on a modeling assignment without telling her. Ultimately, Miller invited Waris to come stay with her at the farm in Pennsylvania, in order to have the necessary downtime to make the project happen on deadline. It was there that the two really got a chance to converse.

"I spent the week interviewing her, and I saw this as the moment to get the real grisly stuff," Miller said. "We were in a more tranquil environment there, without all of these interruptions." When it came to the genital mutilation scene, Miller made a conscious decision not to sanitize the passage in any respect. She wanted to capture the sheer horror of what was done to Waris.

"When I wrote it, I decided I was not going to make it easy on the reader," Miller told me. "There was a movement afoot at the time—this was 14 years ago, nobody even knew what this was, nobody talked about it—that this was an African cultural practice and Westerners really needed to keep their nose out of it. So I said, 'I'm going to write the scene in such a way that nobody is ever going to make that statement again.'"

As a result, Desert Flower continues to play a significant role in Waris' worldwide plight to eradicate this horrific practice.

George Best Gate at Buck Shaw Stadium

On a gloomy, rain-soaked evening two Saturdays ago, the San Jose Earthquakes unveiled George Best Gate for the public. Just in time for its 2011 home opener, the club rebranded Gate C at Buck Shaw Stadium in honor of the world-renowned legend from Belfast, Northern Ireland, who played for the Earthquakes in the old North American Soccer League in 1980 and 1981.

"George Best is one of the best soccer players to ever play, and we were lucky to have him in San Jose," said Earthquakes president David Kaval. "We have a proud history dating back to 1974, and George Best is a big part of that. We wanted to honor George at our stadium and also maintain the connection between the Earthquakes teams of the past and our current squad."

The cold, rainy and miserable circumstances were probably the worst home conditions the Quakes had ever played in. Some even quipped that San Jose had given way to Belfast weather in George's honor.

Rising to fame with Manchester United during the swinging '60s in England, Best was one of the most naturally gifted geniuses to ever step foot on the pitch. Unlike today, when most superstars tend to excel at specific aspects of the game—set pieces, dribbling, finishing, precision passing, ability in the air, vision or pure speed—Best was a maestro at all of those components. There really wasn't anything he couldn't do.

What's more, for those who dislike soccer due to the sissylike diving so prevalent today, well, Best embodied the opposite. He never resorted to such nonsense. Opposing players constantly tried to trip and kick the hell out of him, but he would always maintain balance. When he did go down, he would get right back up and somehow miraculously keep the ball anyway, often leaving defenders wondering, 10 seconds later, what on earth had actually just happened.

By the time he arrived in San Jose at age 34, Best was past his prime, but he still displayed flashes of incomparable genius. In the summer of 1981, he scored what many believe to be the best goal of his career. Those of us who attended that game love to brag about it.

Of course, genius always seems to have a dark side. In his heyday, Best was the very first pop-star footballer. With his good looks, impeccable style and women falling all over him, his party lifestyle quickly surpassed his football career and he wound up battling alcoholism for the rest of his life. Reflecting on his life many years later, George said: "I was born with a great gift, and sometimes with that comes a destructive streak. Just as I wanted to outdo everyone when I played, I had to outdo everyone when we were out on the town."

Even a controversial liver transplant in 2002 could not stop Best from drinking, and he eventually lost the battle in 2005, at the age of 59. The following weekend, a moment of silence preceded every single match in the Premier League of England. For Best's funeral, his coffin came off the airplane draped in a Manchester United flag. The city of Belfast gave him the equivalent of a State funeral, the streets closed, and an estimated 100,000 people stood in the miserable, pouring rain to watch the motorcade.

Following George's death, unprecedented public support led to the creation of the George Best Foundation, a charity whose aims are "chosen specifically to recognize aspects of Best's career, as well as soccer- and alcohol-related issues."

George's son, Calum, who was born in San Jose when Best played here, went on to a modeling career. His middle name is Milan, after Milan Mandaric, one of the original owners of the San Jose Earthquakes. Today, Calum is a patron for the National Association for Children of Alcoholics, a U.K. charity.

As the tempestuous rain poured from the sky two weeks ago, George Best Gate officially opened for the public in San Jose. I can't think of a situation more appropriate for a new beginning.

Joe Izzo: Finding 'Louie'

One of One of the first times I saw Joe Izzo's byline in Metro's food section was on a piece that celebrated a local institution known as Sam's Log Cabin. Izzo hailed the joint as "a landmark of rare historical significance with a life and character all its own."

Like most interesting places of similar stature in San Jose, Sam's is now gone, but I remember the moment when I first read that piece.

Little did I know, Izzo also wrote screenplays and even littler did I know that many years later I'd be learning of his new film, *Uncle Louie*, and its world premiere at the Buffalo Niagara Film Festival on April 14.

A fractured and mystical fairy tale situated in quite a few celebrated San Jose locales and streets, *Uncle Louie* is not a multimillion-dollar Academy Awardwinning tour de force by any definition of any of those words. In fact, Izzo and a menagerie of characters threw it together for less than the price of a new car. Call it a below-budget cult classic if you will. Joe Bob Briggs would probably give it a rave review. People who dig this film probably aren't the new-car types anyway.

The main character, Benny (Craig Ferriera), is waiting in limbo for his business plan to market a new product all over the world. Benny and his pregnant wife, Bernice (Michele Mangelli), are also in a predicament. They owe money to a rough character named Lester (Mikol Garcia), who won't go away until he gets paid.

Lester begins to swipe things—namely Benny's dog, Fidel—as collateral until he gets his dough. As a result, Benny and Bernice attend a voodoo ceremony to raise Benny's Uncle Louie (Nick D'Arpino) back from the dead for just 24 hours. Louie, a cigar-smoking Italian-American from Buffalo, was a professional hit man in life, so they plan on using his talents to help exterminate Lester.

What follows is a tale of karma and forgiveness. Louie brings back all sorts of moral stories from "the other side," including whether or not Jesus forgave Hitler. Now that Louie is temporarily walking the earth again, he educates Benny and Bernice with quite a few lessons from life and death. Is revenge worth it in the end? How does karma actually function? Is there an afterlife? Are people really better off on the other side, if it even exists at all? And where in San Jose can one get a decent anchovy pizza?

Since the film takes place in San Jose and environs, natives will recognize several celebrated landmarks. Rosicrucian Park, the Pink Poodle, the pedestrian tunnel under The Alameda, the Anno Domini gallery, Al Castello restaurant, the statue in front of Babe's Muffler, Tony & Alba's Pizza, Oak Hill Cemetery, as well as the clock at Time Deli all play significant roles in the narrative.

"We used those landmarks for their character, their colorful elements and wonderful old signs," Izzo told me. "Our locations, all of them, play themes of our story. The scenery burst with color. Over at the cemetery, we caught blasting fountains and lens flares galore. It was a cinematic dream."

When Louie appears from the dead, he smells like sulfur. Covered in leaves and twigs, it takes him awhile to realize what's happened.

"Voodoo is one of the only religions—and we did our research—

claiming to be able to reanimate the dead for determined periods of time," Izzo said. "It made sense. And I think we pulled it off."

Izzo even used local talent for the soundtrack. Booty Chesterfield chimes in with two ukulele tracks. The film opens with a twisted version of the old Guy Lombardo tune "Enjoy Yourself (It's Later Than You Think)," and then later on we hear a version of Dean Martin's "That's Amore." Both songs tie in to the film's themes.

And what would be a mystical karmic romp across the San Jose landscape via Buffalo, N.Y., without serendipitous resonance of some sort? Well, both of Izzo's parents grew up in Buffalo, and he himself vacationed in Buffalo every summer as a kid. He says the film premiering in Buffalo is "an event of extraordinary synchronicity." He also hopes to show the film in San Jose once the whole Buffalo adventure is over. We'll keep you posted.

From Chiang Mai to House of Siam

On a recent tear through Thailand for that country's Songkran Festival, its traditional New Year celebration, the author took in the searing heat, gave offerings to monks in saffron robes and infiltrated a multisensory cooking class. As with most travel, he returned with a heightened sense of awareness.

For Songkran, everyone throws water at each other in a festive spirit. People line up on the streets to hurl buckets or shoot water cannons, especially at foreigners. Even the monks bless people by sprinkling water.

For those who want to learn the local cuisine, tourist-driven cooking classes are the rage in Thailand, with several varieties available. In some instances, a family simply opens its kitchen for prearranged groups, while other institutions offer professional settings with cooking stations spread throughout an entire backyard.

In a suburb of Chiang Mai, the Baan Hongnual Cookery School offers the latter option, in a Lanna-style teak house. Guests learn how to cook four different dishes throughout the course of an entire morning or afternoon.

In our case, two women, our cooking teachers—Phantanan Jala, a.k.a. "Pam," and Siriporn Wongin, a.k.a. "Por"—first took us shopping at a local market, where we got a chance to buy galangal root, kaffir lime leaves, tamarind sauce, radishes, peanuts, chiles, holy basil and more. We were the only foreigners present at the market, located on a suburban side street. The facility even included an elaborate butchery room, where several older women sliced up piles of meat left and right. Everything seemed to be run by women.

Upon arriving at the Baan Hongnual compound, Pam and Por provided us with tea made from pandanus leaves—a perfect intro. We then received the lowdown on the four dishes we were going to cook: (1) Pad

Thai, (2) Tom Ka Gai—a coconut chicken soup, (3) stir-fried chicken with cashew nuts and (4) a dessert of pumpkin and coconut milk. Participants are to cook one dish, eat it and then move on to the next one.

Next came step-by-step hands-on instructions for each dish, beginning with the easy method for crushing garlic with a knife and running all the way to composing the final product. Each person manned his or her own cutting board and prep station, before migrating to a cooking setup, replete with a wok, vegetable oil, water, receptacles for ingredients and all the essentials.

"Do you want to know how to cook delicious food?" asked Pam. "Be happy and smile."

And that's what happened. She grinned from ear to ear and cracked up laughing at nearly everything we said. Pam also explained that she currently rents a room at Baan Hongnual while she continues to study English at Chiang Mai Rajabhat University. During the high season, the house operates two classes a day, one in the morning and one in the afternoon.

Throughout the lesson, aromas filled the atmosphere. For dessert, the pumpkin soaked in the coconut milk as the fragrance saturated the air. Everyone ate too much.

Baan Hongnual also features a garden with several herbs and fruits: pandanus, lichee, papaya, galangal and more. Some classes include picking herbs from the garden rather than going to the market, but the market is by far the way to go.

As always, I relate everything to my own landscape, even by chance occurrences. A few days after my return, in the throes of jet lag, I ad-libbed my way into House of Siam in downtown San Jose for some lunch. In what can only be described as a meaningful coincidence, I wound up sitting right next to two Buddhist monks in saffron robes.

The scene looked exactly like what I had just left in Thailand. I even had 100 Thai baht of currency still left in my wallet, which I offered, via the proprietor, to the monks. Affiliated with the Thai Temple in Fremont, the monks were on their way to City Hall to receive a ceremonial proclamation from the San Jose City Council for Songkran. It was a splendid way to return home, further reassuring me, as Buddhists claim, that everything is connected.

Soccer Signs: Vancouver–San Jose Synchronicities

Last week, in the city of Vancouver, British Columbia, a transdimensional mosaic of space-time continuum-shattering connections to the city of San Jose came to light. I was lucky to be there.

On a rainy and miserable evening, Vancouver Whitecaps FC hosted the San Jose Earthquakes of Major League Soccer. As I see it, just the relationship between those two clubs—currently and formerly—constitutes enough of an interstellar multiplicity to make one's head explode. So get ready.

This year, the Whitecaps came into the league as an expansion club—previously they competed in a lower-profile league—but, just like San Jose, they are using a moniker that goes back to the days of the old North American Soccer League (NASL) in the '70s.

Vancouver's NASL heritage is a major component of the club's entire brand today. It's part of everything the club does. The first thing one sees on the website is "Since 1974." The website makes it clear that the club's first match was against the San Jose Earthquakes in May of that year. Bob Lenarduzzi was on that 1974 team, and he is president of the current club. Throughout the temporary stadium, Empire Field, I saw posters, placards and gleaming white banners with the Whitecaps logo, underlined with: "Since 1974."

Before the game, in the media-command center, a few seasoned reporters carried on and told stories about those days. Current Whitecaps club ambassador, Carl Valentine, was also a star for some of those old Vancouver teams, and he was likewise carrying on about the NASL days, especially George Best.

Across the board, people seemed hip to the history, primarily because Vancouver brought home the NASL championship in 1979—the only title the city has ever won—so everyone who's old enough carries on about how 150,000 people showed up in downtown Vancouver to watch the victory parade. A video exists on YouTube if you desire to relive the moment. Both Lenarduzzi and Valentine played on that team. Everyone seemed to have much bigger hairstyles back then.

In those days, the club played in the former Empire Stadium, which was eventually torn down long after the NASL folded. Today, the Whitecaps' eventual permanent home, BC Place, is undergoing renovations, so the team is beginning its 2011 inaugural Major League Soccer season at a specially erected temporary stadium, Empire Field, at the exact same location of the former Empire Stadium that was torn down.

In fact, the first time I ever visited Vancouver—as a child on a family vacation in 1980—we attended a Whitecaps match at Empire Stadium. So, one can imagine how bizarre it was last week for me to attend my first Whitecaps match since 1980, at the same location but in a different stadium. The cycles of creation and destruction manifest themselves wherever I roam. To get there, we drove east from the postcard-picture skyline of downtown Vancouver, past the Scientology church, through the crackhead wasteland and straight up to the stadium. Yeah!

In the meantime, BC Place, site of the 2010 Winter Olympics Opening and Closing Ceremonies in downtown Vancouver, is undergoing the construction of a brand-new cable-supported retractable roof—the largest of its kind on earth. The Whitecaps will move in when the new stadium opens later this year.

The connections don't stop there. Current Quakes head coach, Frank

Yallop, grew up in Vancouver. His former childhood friend, roommate and teammate on the Canadian National Team, Colin Miller, is Vancouver's current assistant coach. One of Yallop's assistant coaches, Mark Watson, is also from Vancouver and likewise played alongside Yallop for the Canadian national side. Got all that? Of course you do.

And that's just soccer. The Sharks were on the radars of seemingly all Vancouverites last week, as locals watched San Jose eliminate Detroit, so it could play Vancouver in the NHL Western Conference Championship series. Sadly, my trip had to end on Sunday. The opening puck of game one dropped right as I flew back to the Bay Area.

Bascom Ave Dive Bar History

One of San Jose's most recognizable bastions of dive-bar architecture was the celebrated Bears Cocktail Lounge at the southeast corner of Alma Avenue and Almaden Expressway. It was there for a staggering 50 years. With a spinning sign outside and faded velvet curtains inside, and even a patio for smoking, Bears was a throwback to old San Jose, when Italian Gardens, right down the street, reigned supreme.

In the '70s, driving with my parents up Almaden Expressway on our way to San Jose Earthquakes games defined a good portion of my childhood. This included staring in wonder at the Bears every time we turned that corner. The place was an institution, that is, until a few years ago when the landlord destroyed the building in favor of an empty retail complex that will probably never get rented out. Which is quintessential San Jose, I guess.

I contemplated all of this while infiltrating the newer incarnation of the Bears at 1872 W. San Carlos St. It used to be the Glass Gecko, which used to be Bella's Club. At Bear's, Meghan poured me a fruit salad, and we contemplated a hypothetical, transdimensional, historical voyage down the seemingly endless corridor of South Bascom Avenue in search of legendary dive bars that no longer exist. From the Bears, it's only a quick stroll to the corner of Bascom and San Carlos, so my thoughts just naturally wandered in that direction.

Beginning at that intersection, where Alex's 49er Inn occupies closet 2241 of the appropriately named Business Circle, I envisioned a supernatural journey southward down Bascom, all the way to Los Gatos. Ghosts of dive bars from decades past emerged from the ether to greet me.

In 1960, a place called Hole in the Wall Tavern inhabited 860 S. Bascom Ave. I wasn't there, obviously, but it must have been awesome. As the fantasy continued, I recalled the defunct dive, Club Four, at 514 S. Bascom, right next to the celebrated Burbank porno theater. The bar went through many incarnations. A pickled old drunk in there once told me *Metro* was "left-wing propaganda." That's about all I remember.

If one soldiers on from there, the ghost of Murray's Bar soon appears.

Located for decades at 1015 S. Bascom, Murray's was a classic neighborhood joint. Workers from Valley Med regularly showed up, as did employees of Streetlight Records across the road. If one purchased goods at Streetlight and missed the bus afterward, Murray's was a logical place to kill time. Today, a vacant lot sits where Murray's used to be—a defining visual remnant of San Jose city policies.

After a few more miles, Bascom then bores through the gray area where San Jose morphs into Campbell and Los Gatos. Both Court's Lounge and the Escape still occupy 2425 and 2942 S. Bascom, respectively. They will never die.

But the ghosts do not stop appearing. Twenty-five years ago, the Pot Belly Saloon highlighted 2897 S. Bascom, at Shamrock. A legendary biker bar, it featured a gorgeous yellow sign. And then there was the Korner Club, located at Bascom and Union.

Even farther south, as Bascom turns into Los Gatos Boulevard, the ghost of a dive bar called Double Vision looms on the horizon. Formerly the Bascom Lounge, Double Vision died a natural death when the freeway was built. It sat right where 85 now plows through Los Gatos Boulevard. There was also Otto's Garden Room, a notorious biker bar, now the Boulevard Tavern at 15043 Los Gatos Boulevard. I made it to Otto's only once. I was legal, but too young to really fit in.

As Los Gatos Boulevard ends and turns the corner into Main Street in downtown Gatos, one only has to wander a few blocks up and around the corner to where the Last Call used to be. Basically, the Last Call was the place to go after one was cut off at every other bar in Los Gatos. Alas, Gatos is a place where folks hire chiropractors for their poodles and discuss real estate values while they get their weekly colonics, so a place like the Last Call was never going to survive.

There were many more dives on Bascom and Los Gatos Boulevard, which, incidentally, used to be called San Jose-Los Gatos Road, so this journey of the fantastic has only just begun. Bring on the ghosts!

Dan Fante: Writer's Legacy

Two years ago, Dan Fante and I shared war stories in the bowels of skid-row Los Angeles as part of another Esotouric™ guided bus adventure into the depths of secret L.A. The tour was dedicated to Dan's father, John Fante (1909–1983), a novelist who made his living as a screenwriter in the heyday of Hollywood.

Fante the elder was the author of *Ask the Dust, Dago Red, Dreams From Bunker Hill* and several others that inspired Charles Bukowski to do his thing. With brutal uncompromising style, Fante wrote about his life, his family, the Italian-American experience, booze, baseball and the frustration of the aspiring literary writer's existence—all with the underbelly of old Los Angeles as the backdrop.

Dan Fante, himself a novelist, and a sober one for more than 20 years, joined the Esotouric tour to provide insight into his father's old haunts and neighborhoods. Dan's own writing is likewise the brutal, confessional-from-the-gutter-type of stuff that, thankfully, will never be an Oprah's Book Club selection. His novel Chump Change makes Bukowski look like Mary Poppins.

That morning in 2009, as we talked, I noticed a tattoo on Dan's forearm, dedicated to his brother: NICK FANTE. DEAD FROM ALCOHOL, 1-31-42 TO 2-21-97. Normally I enjoy learning of someone I share a birthday with (Jan. 31), but in Nick's case, I wasn't so sure.

Now, in 2011, Dan's memoir is out on Harper Perennial. *Fante: A Family's Legacy of Writing, Drinking and Surviving* provides a schizo-slodge-podge of destroyed perspectives from life's urinals, barroom floors, drivers' seats of taxicabs, junkie hotels, mob drops, broken careers and family arguments—all directly from the lives of the Fantes, father and son. It is not for the weak, nor are any punches pulled, at least not from what I can tell.

Especially authentic are the dead-on descriptions of what it's like going through alcohol withdrawals when quitting cold turkey after years of being hammered every day. While trying to detox by himself in a hotel room, Dan's whole body shakes, he bangs his head against a wall, he thinks the TV is talking directly to him, he hallucinates and he can't force any food down without vomiting. He later returns to the practicing alcoholic life and repeats the cycle all over again.

The book also portrays with precisionlike accuracy the frustrations felt by John Fante, who knew he had literary talent but could barely sell novels and was forced to ply his trade penning B-grade screenplays and dealing with the backstabbing, jealousy and rage intrinsic to Hollywood.

It was only toward the end of his life that his novels were rediscovered and republished. It was only after his death that his work received the worldwide recognition it deserved. Many an aspiring writer can empathize with the sufferings of not being recognized enough.

And that is the framework of the story—the frustrations and resentments of both the father and son, played against each other. Throughout major portions of his life, Dan did not get along with his dad, but the two did eventually reconcile.

After his father's death, Dan came to the realization that his dad was a true hero, in that he never gave a shit if his work was commercial or not. In one scene, he gives Dan writing advice: "If what I write is good," said the elder Fante, "then people will read it. That's why literature exists. An author puts his heart and his guts on the page. A good novel can change the world. Keep that in mind before you attempt to sit down at a typewriter. Never waste time on something you don't believe in yourself."

In the epilogue, Dan explains he inherited his father's passion for writing, which, in addition to sobriety, has helped save his life: "I don't write clever tales or make up disposable yarns that lend themselves to re-hashed TV plots; I write about myself. The reason I write is not to change you but to let you know that you can change. I write about living and dying and falling in love and throwing it all away—then surviving it. I write about madness and death. I write for the survival of my heart. I am swallowed by, and in love with, the miracle of the human condition. My heroes are real people struggling to find their place on a planet. A planet where fitting in has become a disease as powerful as cancer."

Cambrian Era, Part Deux

Part of the human condition in San Jose, at least historically, involves decades of hick-town annexation spats, the most recent of which saw the sprawl kingpins at San Jose City Hall trying to bully the city of Campbell over the unincorporated "Cambrian 36" area.

San Jose basically wanted tax revenue from a 38-room hotel and a gas station on Camden, but residents living in the adjacent neighborhood didn't want to be incorporated into San Jose. They wanted to live in Campbell instead. After years of fighting the man, the residents won.

Cambrian 36 tips the scales at 103 acres, the southern boundary of which is Camden Avenue between Bascom Avenue and the freeway—an absolutely hideous stretch of road.

To save you all the trouble, I recently traversed that avenue for the first time in years. Aside from a few homeless dudes resembling Grizzly Adams and a bearded drunk having a loud conversation with himself at the Foster's Freeze, I was the only pedestrian in sight.

One of the most heavily trafficked, congested, fractured, patched-up, worn, beaten and downright ugliest stretches of wide-open concrete anywhere in San Jose, this portion of Camden is six lanes wide, but it seems like twice that much, with all the noise from semis, dump trucks, garbage trucks, roaring engines, car stereos and school buses. Sections of the street don't even have sidewalks. On the northern side, brand-new empty buildings sit right next to empty decrepit houses with weed-infested lots. There's an old auto stereo place, a carpet shop and a few gas stations.

In addition to the Foster's Freeze, the road is fast-food heaven, including a Wienerschnitzel, a Taco Bell, a Subway and a Jack in the Box. The camouflage-painted Sportsman's Supply bait, tackle and ammo shop has been there for decades. On the sidewalk in front of the place, the fake deer with the archery-supplies sign has also been there for decades.

As I sauntered my way down the road, the glaring sun beat down on the vast concrete landscape, since there's no shade anywhere. Fortunately, the area's only gem is the Royal Taj Indian restaurant—lunch buffet for $7.95 seven days a week—and it emerged like an exotic oasis amid the bland suburban topography. The egg curry was especially phenomenal.

Now, historically, Cambrian harbors great stories. About five years back, I released emotion in this very space about the most famous person ever to emerge from Cambrian Park: Susan Atkins. This is a fact every Cambrian Park real estate agent doesn't want you to know about. Atkins, a.k.a. Sadie Mae Glutz, member of the Manson Family and convicted murderer who died in prison two years ago, spent some of her childhood in Cambrian Park during the late '50s and early '60s.

In her now legendary autobiography written from prison in the '70s, *Child of Satan, Child of God*, Atkins, along with co-author Bob Slosser, talked a little about her time in San Jose. We see passages like this: "We moved into a good-sized but modest home in the suburban community of Cambrian Park near the Blossom Hills." And then later, this: "Our community sat right at the foot of the Blossom Hills, a part of the Los Gatos range. And our home was only about three and a half blocks away from those hills, rising gently to the east and covered with fruit trees and grape vines." It wasn't Cambrian 36, but it was close enough.

In that book, Atkins also writes that she became a regular at the Cambrian Park Baptist Church. Unfortunately, her mom passed away in 1964, after which her alcoholic father shuffled her off to Los Banos. A few years later she wound up in San Francisco, where she slept with Charles Manson—and the rest is history.

So perhaps the presence in Cambrian Park of someone who would go on to become one of the 20th century's most notorious murderers suggests that every neighborhood has its evil side, which leads us to the only rational conclusion, that the name Cambrian 36 probably harbors hidden significance. The sum of all integers from one to 36 equals 666, the Number of the Beast. That is, $1 + 2 + 3 + ... + 34 + 35 + 36 = 666$. A math person would say, Sum 36 = 666. I'll bet that all the targeted unincorporated areas in Santa Clara County also add up to 666, which would mean the San Jose Department of Planning, Building and Code Enforcement is the Great Satan. Ave Satanas!

Auguste Rodin Days

A recent visit to the venerable Cantor Arts Center at Stanford University proved to be inspiring in several ways. The new exhibition, "Rodin and America: Influence and Adaptation 1876-1936," explores the French sculptor Auguste Rodin's influence on a generation of American artists at the onset of the 20th century.

A variety of media is presented—sculpture, watercolors and more—by a wealth of famous folks, including Malvina Hoffman, Edward Steichen and Georgia O'Keeffe. Experiencing the show and perusing the catalog of essays definitely influenced my own pursuits in crackpot scholarship.

For example, in the exhibit catalog, art historian Jennifer Marshall writes about the etymology of the word influence, stating that, "[in] its earliest usage, during the 14th century, the word influence generally referred to astrological phenomena, the workings of the stars. Emanating from on high, an imagined ethereal fluid trickled downward to earth and then into the temperaments and behaviors of people."

It has the same etymology as *influenza*, and she quotes Harold Bloom, who defined influence as "a metaphor, one that implicates a matrix of relationships—imagistic, temporal, spiritual, psychological."

To wit, in the Cantor Center exhibit, one sees a miniature of Rodin's scandalous monument to French author Honoré de Balzac. The story is legendary. Commissioned in 1891 by the Sociéte; des Gens de Lettres, Rodin labored for years to produce a sculpture of Balzac highly unconventional for its time, a monument that captured Balzac's creative spirit, his soul, his inner conflicts and his tumultuousness. The work portrayed Balzac in a robe, bohemian yet domesticated, standing with one foot forward and his girth prominent.

Decrying the statue as grotesque, the backlash was near-violent. The Socie;te; rejected the work, which was simply too ideologically provocative for them to understand. As a result, Rodin kept the sculpture for himself, and it did not see the light of day until decades after his death.

Under the influence of such a hilarious tale, I unearthed a few tidbits intertwined with the whole affair. The tune goes a little like this: As Rodin began to miss deadlines for completing the Balzac monument, another sculptor, Anatole Marquet de Vasselot, fervently tried to weasel in on the action.

A Balzac fanatic, Vasselot was a contributor to the esoteric Salons de la Rose+Croix, a series of Rosicrucian-themed art shows in Paris. The Rosicrucians backed Vasselot to take Rodin's place and receive the commission. It was the mystics vs. Rodin.

Organized by the flamboyant novelist and mystic Joséphin Péladan, the Salons de la Rose+Croix occurred during the *fin de sicle* (end of the century) era of French symbolism, when occult interest was reaching a new apex. Composers, dancers, visual artists and various members of Parisian high society were becoming enamored with the aesthetics of mysteries and symbols. Vasselot even sculpted his own rendition of Balzac, cast as a winged sphinx, riddled with Rosicrucian symbolism. But to the dismay of the Rosicrucians, Vasselot didn't succeed in supplanting Rodin for the project. That was the end of it.

And then there's Aleister Crowley, the multidisciplinary English poet, philosopher and occultist troublemaker. Crowley actually defended Rodin against the critical backlash and subsequently befriended the sculptor a few years later.

Since the very mention of Crowley's name tends to upset the anthill, scholars seem to avoid him, but in 1907 he published a collaboration with Rodin. Titled *Rodin in Rime*, the book includes seven erotic watercolors that Rodin presented to Crowley, plus a few dozen of Crowley's poems dedicated to Rodin. Published in an extremely limited edition, the book today commands quite a price in antiquarian circles, but the text is available for free download at numerous websites.

So it was Auguste Rodin and Aleister Crowley vs. the Rosicrucians. What a story. To recap, the Salons de la Rose+Croix were esoteric art shows organized by Joséphin Péladan. Oddly enough, his mystical lineage can be traced to the same group of Rosicrucians who later initiated the American Harvey Spencer Lewis—the same chap who brought the Rosicrucian Order AMORC to the United States and, eventually, to our own San Jose, Calif. Whew.

Now I want to be an art historian.

I have the folks at the Cantor Center to thank. They have influenced me, and I have adapted.

Palomar Ballroom Atmospherics

The first time I infiltrated the Rock and Roll Hall of Fame and Museum in Cleveland, I spent hours amid the exhibits. The multistory building on Lake Erie provided a wealth of inspiration. I even lurked for quite awhile in the gift shop, especially the book section, where I flipped through Dominic Selerno's groundbreaking taxonomy of Burt Bacharach songs. Enlightenment ensued.

Titled Bacharach: Song by Song, the book breaks the composer's creative output into years. The section for 1968 includes an interview with Dionne Warwick, for whom Bacharach and Hal David wrote many hit songs. Reflecting on the tune, "Do You Know the Way to San Jose," Warwick was quoted as saying: "It's a beautiful little city. I was made an honorary citizen. I'm accused of putting it on the map and overpopulating it."

I contemplated that statement for a long, long time. She was accused of putting the city on the map. Not thanked, not congratulated, not applauded, but accused. For me, it put everything into perspective, since now, 40 years later, it often seems like many people in San Jose still don't want to city the be known for anything. They live here because they don't want it to be an interesting place.

In my opinion, the San Jose condition will always involve the conflict between urban and suburban, small town and big town, or what constitutes a "major city" and what doesn't. It seems like this creeps into everything that happens here: the arts community, the music scene, the convention and visitors bureau, sports, politics, the bars, the media, everything.

This is not a profound new insight on my part—just ask any old-timer—but that quote from Dionne Warwick just seemed to nail it. As I stood there, flipping through that Burt Bacharach book, while standing there in the gift shop at the Rock and Roll Hall of Fame and Museum, I felt like I had just received special psychic revelations from the Great God of Suburbia, commanding me to craft a column about my experiences.

That was three years ago, and since I just returned to Cleveland last month, the time seems right. Travel provides new models for contemplating one's own landscape and also helps to manifest a heightened sense of awareness. That is, certain connections will emerge that one cannot ignore. This time around, the Rock and Roll Hall of Fame set the ball in motion. Again.

In Cleveland, right outside the Rock Hall, one finds a historical marker designating the Birthplace of Rock & Roll. Legendary DJ Alan Freed organized what's referred to as the first rock concert, the Moondog Coronation Ball, on March 21, 1952, at the Cleveland Arena.

It was also the occasion of the first rock & roll riot, as thousands of counterfeit tickets were apparently sold. After waiting outside for hours, the overcapacity crowd shoved its way in, fights broke out, bottles flew and the riot ensued. Three of the acts didn't even get a chance to play. The arena itself was torn down decades ago, but the historical placard tells the story.

Standing there at that marker immediately made me think of San Jose's equivalent event, which took place four years later. The now legendary Fats Domino riot went down on July 7, 1956, at the celebrated Palomar Ballroom on Notre Dame Avenue, now the backside of the Axis luxury midrise condos. At that show, several folks were arrested and a few were admitted to the hospital with injuries. The event was a stain on the Palomar's legacy, one that included shows by Mel Torme, Doris Day, Louis Armstrong and many Latino performers.

Several folks over the decades have heroically referred to the Fats Domino show as the first ever rock & roll riot, which unfortunately isn't true. I wish San Jose could claim that one, but it can't. Cleveland, Ohio, is the place where it all went down that fateful night in 1952. And that town obviously has some class because they put a historical plaque right where the whole shebang took place—something San Jose would probably never do.

When the original Palomar Ballroom building was destroyed, the developers did absolutely nothing significant to acknowledge the magnificent history of that venue. I guess that would require class on their part. One of the new residents even recently complained about loud rock music on the patio of the De Anza Hotel. There you have it. So much for urban living. Dionne Warwick would be proud.

Hermann Hesse Museum

The anti-man-about-town has emerged in this space quite a few times over the years, but after experiencing the Hermann Hesse Museum and Foundation in Montagnola, Switzerland, he just may have found a new inspirational terrain.

The author of *Steppenwolf, Magister Ludi, Siddhartha* and others, Hesse was an original anti-man-about-town who often merged inner travel with outer travel, exploring his internal conflicts through his novels. And he won the Nobel Prize for doing it.

Born in Germany in 1877, Hesse spent the last half of his 85 years in Montagnola, a tiny village in Ticino, the Italian-speaking section of Switzerland. At exactly the age I am now, he separated from his family and country, moved to Montagnola and started all over again.

While en route to Ticino, he produced the short book Wandering, a juxtaposition of poems, prose and watercolor paintings of panoramic landscapes he found along the way. After settling in the Baroque-style Casa Camuzzi, he immediately wrote *Klein and Wagner*, followed by *Klingsor's Last Summer*. Both novellas are based on Hesse's conflicted life against the scenic backdrop of Ticino.

Today, the Fondazione Hermann Hesse includes a small museum in the tower adjacent to Casa Camuzzi, filled with many of the author's personal artifacts—his typewriter, desk, eyeglasses, books, watercolors and much more. One can peruse displays, posters, photos, plus audio accompaniment in Italian and German. A garden provides a regular setting where children take painting classes. Throughout the facility, collections of photos occupy the walls, accompanied by two different sets of texts. One set functions as explanatory material, while the other provides passages from Hesse's works that relate to the particular photographs displayed.

Regina Bucher, the museum's director, leads me around, explaining various components of the museum. Next door, the Boccadoro Literary Cafe hosts concerts, readings and other events. Patti Smith and Lenny Kaye recently showed up and performed together for a crowd of just a few hundred, while thousands jammed the cobblestone lanes outside.

"Our success is partly because we are very active," Bucher tells me. "Sometimes a museum is a calm, rather boring place. We try not to be boring."

In the main room, Hesse's typewriter sits atop his writing desk—quiet, calm and still, almost as if it is meditating. Hesse posters flank the walls on either side of the desk. This is the typewriter on which he wrote *Magister Ludi, Narcissus* and *Goldmund and The Journey to the East*. I imagine it's like experiencing the Bodhi Tree in India. But, Hesse did not write *Siddhartha* on this machine.

"*Siddhartha* he wrote by hand," says Bucher, as she leads me up to a small area on a landing. We then gaze at an original printed version of Siddhartha sitting behind a locked case. The book was one of a few dozen copied by the publisher and hand-bound by Hesse for his close friends.

"*Siddhartha* is a book that is even more important now than when it was originally published," Bucher says, adding that the novel's message needs to resonate with teenagers in our current fast-paced world. As a mother of a teen herself, she says teens have shorter and shorter attention spans these days. They're always online and communicating in a multitude of ways. They can't concentrate and focus.

From the museum, an official walking path takes one through the village and down to the cemetery where Hesse is buried. The graveyard is on the Swiss Inventory of Cultural Property of National and Regional Significance. Along the path, placards contain texts Hesse wrote while wandering down the exact same route.

One particular clearing presents a breathtaking, unreal view of Lake Lugano, as it disappears over the horizon, between jagged hills and snow-capped peaks.

At the cemetery, Hesse's grave sits in the far right corner. Tiny lizards dart back and forth across the thick gravel paths. There is no epitaph, just his name, along with the pertinent dates. On the bus back to Lugano, the anti-man-about-town could almost feel his inner conflicts beginning to resolve.

Blightings: Hacienda Gardens Relapse

Exactly one year ago, the Urban Blight Exploration Junkie relapsed at the crumbling remains of the Hacienda Gardens Shopping Center on Meridian Avenue between Hillsdale and Foxworthy.

Sure, there existed new components of a once-thriving center—replete with demoralizing San Jose strip mall color schemes of mustard yellow, brick red, olive and beige—but with the majority of those newer units remaining empty, the intended upgrade fell completely flat. The entire property remained a decrepit, postapocalyptic paean to landlord neglect, a result of botched urban planning, real estate greed, political indifference and suburban apathy—in other words, textbook San Jose.

Since Christmas season seems to be when troubled addicts relapse the most, the blight junkie was no exception, so his intrinsic feelings of hopelessness, isolation and unresolved abandonment issues again drove him to go on a bender by searching out the most rundown eyesore of dead retail he could find. That is, he needed to change the way he felt, so he resumed his craving for decrepitude and blight, consuming it all at Hacienda Gardens.

That was a year ago, and we are sad to report that another relapse has occurred. The junkie went on another binge at the ruined shopping center just last week. On the Meridian Avenue side, one of the newer signs proclaims that Panda Express is located therein.

The rest of the sign is hauntingly blank, as if the spaces designated for future tenants were just too premature. Another sign proclaims that BluRock BBQ and Hometown Buffet are the only two tenants in other parts of the complex. The older buildings, housing the Rite-Aid and Hometown Buffet, are feeble, decrepit and just plain uninviting. Behind the Rite-Aid, parts of the corner at Hillsdale and Yucca are fenced off. A trailer with a flat tire sits in the parking lot.

The sign for the Cardinal Coffee Shop still remains, but the facade of the former restaurant is falling apart and covered with graffiti. Old clothes, soaked from the rain, sit on top of a broken concrete garage receptacle in front of the place. Before the Wells Fargo moved across the lot to a new building, it sat next door, and one can still look through the dirty windows at what's left of the '70s-era d–cor inside. What a waste.

But even on a bender, the blight junkie can acknowledge the good things in life. He has learned to be grateful for what he has. Right across Foxworthy, a new grocery store finally moved into one of the abandoned buildings, providing cheap Listerine, frozen food, $9.99 flannel jackets and much more. The genius who owns the chain couldn't even come up with an interesting name, so it's called Grocery Outlet Bargain Market¨. Yes, you're reading that correctly—there's even a registered trademark symbol at the end.

Exploring the physical and cultural wreckage of a once-thriving set of buildings brought back numerous childhood memories for the blight junkie, as relapses often do. Perhaps the most fascinating place he could recall in Hacienda Gardens Shopping Center was Van's Hobby Shop, a jam-packed outpost of interesting stuff.

As a kid, the future blight junkie perused the shelves at Van's all the time, often without even looking for anything in particular. Like most curious people, he just loved to browse and look around, but unfortunately the old bats that ran the place did not want kids to browse. They followed him while he innocently looked around the shop. The bats repeatedly insisted on knowing why he was there, what he was looking for, his purpose, etc.

Apparently, they didn't understand that his journey of browsing and exploration was more important than the final outcome. The bats did not understand that, for him, life was not a problem to be solved; rather, it was a mystery to be experienced.

As the Urban Blight Exploration Junkie recalled this childhood memory, his spirits lifted. He felt more integrated, as if a missing part of him had finally been filled, enabling him to build a more complete identity. The old bats had been misguided. One needn't emphasize the goal, the outcome. Instead, curiosity and imagination were more important.

The experience of browsing in Van's Hobby Shop at Hacienda Gardens Shopping Center taught him that the journey was more precious than the final result. Now the junkie began to feel better about his current predicament. The road to recovery began. He was not going to let the present blighted state of Hacienda Gardens trigger him to relapse ever again.

2012

Film and Literary Tours, from L.A. to San Jose

The interstellar crossover between literature, old buildings and film industry history all converged last week at the inaugural Los Angeles Visionaries Association (LAVA) literary salon at the Musso & Frank Grill, the oldest restaurant in Hollywood.

Author and poet Dan Fante appeared and read from his memoir, *Fante: A Family's Legacy of Writing, Drinking and Surviving*. Fante's dad was the legendary John Fante, also known as the author who gave Charles Bukowski his entire shtick.

Fante the elder originally hung out at Musso & Frank for decades, as did many hard-boiled lions of American letters during the mid-20th century. Having hailed Fante in this space twice before, the anti-man-about-town grabbed a cheap Southwest flight, and an even cheaper hotel, just to be there.

LAVA co-founder Richard Schave has a thriving passion for books, old buildings and L.A. history, a bent menagerie of penchants that nurtured themselves when he studied with architectural critic Reyner Banham at UC–Santa Cruz.

Banham took him on driving tours of industrial wastelands right here in San Jose, and now Schave runs the Esotouric Bus Adventures into the secret heart of Los Angeles. From those L.A. tours, the idea for the LAVA salons emerged.

Taking place on a Monday, when Musso & Frank is normally closed, the salon provided the sold-out crowd of 90 with all the glorious and secret ribald history of golden-era Hollywood.

The decor of the place, as well as the menu, has barely changed in 50 years. Some of the bartenders have been there since the early '70s. The worn red booths evoke liaisons of past decades, and the wallpaper came directly from the hometown of chef Jean Rue, who presided from 1922 to 1976.

Perhaps the most lucrative component of Musso history was the exclusive "Back Room," a.k.a. "The Cocktail Room" or the "Algonquin West," an exclusive lair that no longer exists but was attached to the back of the restaurant, accessed through a private door and run by a separate maitre d'.

It was here that Hollywood's authors and screenwriters—folks like Faulkner, Fitzgerald, Saroyan, Nathanael West, Dorothy Parker and John Fante—would carouse and exchange perils of the trade. The Back Room raged from 1936 to 1955, after which Musso expanded its main room eastward, creating the two-parlor masterpiece that remains today.

Last week, before the salon started, one of our hosts led us through the restaurant, explaining where celebrities used to sit decades ago. Table #10, close to the restrooms, for example, was Mickey Rooney's favorite.

Table #1 was Charlie Chaplin's regular spot, while table #3 was Marilyn's main hangout. The chair at the end of the bar in the main room is where Steve McQueen always dined.

And get this: Radio and TV legend Ralph Edwards ate lunch at Musso's every single day from the late '50s until sometime in the '70s. He was the only person in history to have his own phone jack installed at the booth.

And even today, countless actors, screenwriters and high rollers of Hollywood frequent the place. So much, that no one is allowed to take photos inside. One can only scribble down notes and experience the ghosts and fables as they ooze from the hallowed confines. I think I heard the wallpaper speak at one point.

The scene reminded me of Buck's Restaurant in Woodside, steeped in Silicon Valley history, but instead of sitting at the table where Netscape was first dreamed up, one sits where Greta Garbo dined with Gary Cooper 80 years ago.

Bringing it all up to modern times, at least in Hollywood, is the LAVA Salon, and Dan Fante was possibly the most appropriate debut speaker.

Now pushing 70, Fante provides a direct link to the golden era of Hollywood's literary lore, since his father wrote screenplays for decades. Dan read from his memoir and weaved one tale of how his dad, after departing Musso & Frank one morning, had to rescue a drunken William Faulkner, whose lover was trying to set the apartment on fire.

A few Musso employees actually remember Fante the elder, so they reactivated John Fante's original account, #237, and gave it to Dan Fante, in his dad's honor. Only in Hollywood. The anti-man-about-town was overwhelmed at the end. History loves company and may Musso & Frank never die.

Metallica Art Show at Tony Alva's Gallery in LA

Whenever he roams, the anti-man-about-town seems to wind up in revelatory situations that directly relate to his teenage San Jose memories. No matter what lies buried and repressed within his personal unconscious, it always comes back.

This time he attended the "Obey Your Master" art show at Exhibit A Gallery, an exhibit of work inspired by Metallica songs. San Jose skateboard icon Steve Caballero contributed a painting to the show.

At the reception, without even trying, the anti-man-about-town recalled how, in 1985, he was possibly the only person in high school with a Metallica shirt. The band was not big yet. His conventional heavy metal friends hated the new extreme form of metal that Metallica was playing. To those friends, the band was "too close to punk." They didn't get it.

The only other miscreants at school who appreciated a Metallica shirt, oddly enough, were the skaters. At that time, Caballero was already a pro and a highly influential figure, especially in San Jo. A huge Metallica fan, he often skated to Kill 'Em All and Ride the Lightning, the band's first two LPs.

That was 27 years ago. Now, skip to 2012 at Exhibit A Gallery in L.A., conveniently co-owned by '70s skateboard icon Tony Alva.

Present at the reception were the four members of Metallica and their entourages, plus all the participating artists, rock celebs and aging skateboard legends that originally revolutionized the sport in the modern era.

Literally, it was Dogtown and Z-Boys meets the Metal Militia. I felt an overwhelming sense of counterculture kismet, like everything had come full circle in some odd fashion. It was surreal.

Across the board, the entire show characterized exactly the myriad influence one would expect Metallica tunes to inflict. Shepard Fairey supplied prints based on "Disposable Heroes."

He wrote: "Metallica first appealed to me because the aggression and rage in their music mirrored my own teenage feelings of frustration. I could vent my anger ... vicariously through Metallica, and directly by grinding curbs and coping on my skateboard."

Andy Biersack, who contributed a painting of deceased bass player Cliff Burton inspired by "Creeping Death," described the band as "equal parts darkness, intellect and vitriol."

Shawn "Clown" Crahan of the band Slipknot created a gigantic mixed media sculpture inspired by the tune "Damage Inc." Victor Castillo, who contributed an acrylic on canvas, said he first heard Metallica in Chile when he was 14.

Artist, photographer and filmmaker Chad Michael Ward created an original giclee print based on "The Unforgiven," and said he originally became smitten with two gorgeous stoner girls wearing Metallica shirts in junior high in 1986, and the rest was history. Caballero's painting of a monstrous robot was based on the track "Metal Militia."

Again, the reception was a revelation for the anti-man-about-town.

In 1985 in San Jose, the high school Metallica shirt scenario had a deep effect on his already-troubled psyche. He craved adventurous music, and, growing up in the valley's suburbia, it was difficult finding similar people to hang out with.

He was considered gifted as a youth, along with which came hyper-sensitive inclinations, and to be rejected by seemingly everyone for his forward-thinking musical taste felt catastrophic at the time. Rejected by everyone except for the skaters, that is.

But somehow, everything sorted itself out at the "Obey Your Master" reception. After all, he probably has Caballero to thank for the skaters originally digging his Metallica shirt when no one else would. And 27 years later, there they all were: some of the world's most revolutionary skateboarders—Caballero, Tony Alva and more, plus Metallica—all hanging out in Alva's own gallery. This mind-blowing space-time continuum-shattering circle of events was so extraordinary that the anti-man was finally able to dislodge the negative imprint from high school and the healing came from within.

He felt interconnected with all beings and phenomena. He no longer needed to repress the memories. Throughout the entire experience, including writing this column, he conquered the trauma of having no friends in high school that understood his Metallica shirt. His presence at this reception compensated for all the high school reunions he never attended.

If you harbor repressed memories from your teenage years in Silicon Valley, however insignificant, and they occasionally haunt you, stay positive. Things will work themselves out. Writing can help you discover hidden things about yourself. If it helped this dork from Leigh High School, it can help you too.

Kepler's 2020: Community Bookstore of the Future

Call it serendipity, but I slithered into Kepler's Books in Menlo Park on the very day the store announced its new venture to create the independent bookstore of the future. In fact, it was within a few hours. Get ready, as this idea could only have happened in Silicon Valley.

As most have figured out by now, the traditional economic model of an independent retail bookstore is essentially obsolete, thanks to the ease with which one can buy exactly what he or she wants much cheaper from online retailers. And Amazon has proven that after people buy e-readers, they end up purchasing way more e-books then print books.

Enter a brand-new idea: Kepler's 2020, the official transition phase into the community bookstore of the future. This will be a hybrid model, consisting of a community-owned bookstore that focuses on curating and retailing books and a nonprofit that focuses on events.

As the blog says: "When you know exactly what you want, an online retailer is a very efficient way to get it. What they aren't as good at is serendipity. Anyone who loves books can tell you about the gem they picked up while they were browsing at a bookstore—a staff pick, a personal recommendation or just a happy find. Bookstores also continue to excel at providing a community around writing and reading—author events, book clubs and literary gatherings."

Clark Kepler, whose dad opened the store 56 years ago, is not going away. He is retiring but will still function as chairman of the board. The store will still be called Kepler's, but leading the transition team is Praveen Madan, the "literary entrepreneur" who owns Booksmith on Haight Street in San Francisco.

Over the phone, Madan said that, unlike when Borders was going broke, with Kepler's, we are not witnessing the publishing industry pushing a business into bankruptcy. We are not seeing bookstore executives asking for bonuses as the company goes under.

At Kepler's, says Madan, the opposite is happening. An expression of grassroots love has emerged to innovate the next independent bookseller model. People are volunteering hours and hours of their own time.

"You just don't see that with any other commercial institution in this country," Madan says.

The particulars of the new model are still being hashed out, but the basic idea is to split off the community events and the author series into a dedicated nonprofit, which allows tax-deductible funding from corporate and individual donors.

Without the need to subsidize those events, the for-profit retail portion should be able to run more effectively and grow stronger.

The point is not just to save Kepler's; rather, this could be a revolution, an idea that should spread beyond Menlo Park to other independent booksellers. There is a future for this business, Madan believes.

"I do think there is a goal here, long-term," he tells me. "A lot of the ideas we've been talking about on the bookselling model, they are applicable to other independent bookstores in the rest of the country.

"As we've started to go public with the story and shared this with other people, we are already seeing interest from other independent bookstores. [They're] calling me, emailing me, and saying, 'Hey, how do we do this nonprofit thing? We've been thinking about this for years, but we just don't know how to do it, because it's so complex.'"

Madan himself comes from a tech background; he's a former software engineer and management consultant. The most interesting aspect of the plan is that he views the process as one of open-source innovation. Whatever the team learns from this endeavor will be given away in the hopes that it can help other independent bookstores. It's like a Wiki concept, allowing other bookstores to customize and adapt the plan to suit their own particular scenario. Anyone can port the idea to their own platform.

"It's like software," Madan explains. "And the people who get that immediately are the VCs. In fundraising rounds and meeting with entrepreneurs, the venture capitalists get that in the first five minutes of the conversation. They get it. There's like a multiplier effect here. You can totally scale this, but you don't scale it with a chain or by franchising it. Those are the old models. You do it by Wiki style or Mozilla style or Linux style. You give it away."

And we shall hope that serendipity still plays a role.

Laughing Yoga with Ramesh Pandey

Just talking to Yogi Ramesh Pandey on the phone makes me laugh. In this case, my laughter is a form of applause. I don't know how old he is, but he has an exuberant Indian accent and many stories to tell.

The mirth just oozes out of the phone, through my ear canal and into my brain, where it spreads down my spinal cord, through my destroyed nervous system and radiates outward. I can only imagine the utter hysteria that will transpire when he orchestrates an ensemble of laughing yoga at Satori Tea Company on April Fool's Day. Tea and yoga—what a combination.

Originally from the Himalayas, Yogi Ramesh began yoga at the age of 5 and has practiced every day for longer than I have been alive. He is the founder of the Universal Yoga Center in Palm Springs and even produces a television show, *Universal Yogi*.

He has performed international laughing yoga shows in Hawaii, Hong Kong, Japan, Korea and India. He has schooled doctors, teachers and patients. Everyone from Oprah to Roseanne Barr has elicited his mirth for the health benefits of their audiences. Now, for the first time in the current cycle of life, he will crystallize in downtown San Jose.

It all began, says Yogi Ramesh, in the Himalayas. His father never touched money, but he was always happy and laughing.

"From childhood I had a desire to awaken myself in heart, and soul, and teach about the spiritual life," he says. "Breathing, laughing, how to live healthy and happy by nature's way of healing."

After coming to the United States in 1984, he settled in the Los Angeles area and ran his own yoga studio for years, but it was not until he went up to the mountains and began dancing in the fog that he evolved into a laughing yoga teacher. It must have been the elevation.

"I started dancing and singing and said, 'Oh my God, I'm happy!'" His Indian accent becomes higher-pitched and squeaky as he tells the story. "I felt so good. So after 39 years of doing yoga, I got an idea of how to start laughing yoga. I'm happy! I'm relaxed!"

In fact, Ramesh sounds like a toy being wound up and spinning over and over again. The mirth is contagious. He says he teaches workshops all across the country. He appears at festivals, events and be-ins. He offers certification programs, in case others want to start teaching laughing yoga in their hometowns. Laughing really is the best medicine. It is a cure for stress, good for weight loss and leads to a more relaxed state of mind. It even helps cancer patients, he says.

"This is the best way to live until 100 and it's tax free," he says, laughing.

At Satori Tea Company, participants in the class are in for a treat, Ramesh promises. They will come away healthier, happier and more animated.

"Once they feel my energy, they will wake up," he says. "They will learn to clean their bodies, how to lose weight, how to get a clean heart and lungs. Laughing yoga helps inner sickness and stress reduction.

"I'll teach them how to do yoga anywhere at any time—at work, driving a car, taking a shower, on their cell phones, anywhere, anytime. It's good for everything, blood pressure, sinuses, diabetics, asthma, it's the best medicine. Everyone will be breathing, laughing and energizing their heart and mind."

The venue is a perfect match. After 18 months in business, Satori Tea Company has proven to be a unique spot in San Jose. You don't need to be geriatric or someone who carries a parasol. The esoteric alchemy of their ingredients will have a provocative effect on anyone's psyche.

If one walks in and asks something like, "What d'ya got for a destroyed nervous system?" the proprietors will brew a concoction unavailable anywhere else. They even carry ginger guayusa, which I refer to as the "hallucinogenic rainforest blend."

All in all, it's a healing combination, tea and laughing yoga. Only a fool would disagree.

Herman Vetterling and San Jose Trailer Park

If one contemplates the San Jose condition through a polarity of native and exotic, then interesting street-level phenomena will occasionally manifest themselves on a higher plane. Sounds ridiculous, I know, but a recent coincidence proved that things are seldom as they seem. Stories exist beneath every rock and pebble of our landscape.

Five years ago, when I conjured up a travel guide to ignored interstices of San Jose, aptly titled *Tour the Obscure*, I did not know that behind the shattered topography of San Jose Trailer Park at 527 McLaughlin, there lurked a secret esoteric history of the most exotic sort.

For that story, I arbitrarily began the narrative at that street address. Since most people throughout San Jose seem unfamiliar with the rest of the city outside their own neighborhood, San Jose Trailer Park just seemed like an obscure domestic place to launch the tour.

But now, five years later, thanks to the phenomenal research of Paul Tutwiler, Ph.D., a retired Catholic priest in Santa Cruz who specializes in oddball spiritual histories of our local region, I have learned that this exact same address was the home of one Mr. Herman Vetterling from 1901 to 1927. And who was he? I hear you ask.

Vetterling was known in oddball esoteric circles by his pseudonym, Philangi Dasa, as he was the guy who published the first Buddhist periodical anywhere in the United States, *The Buddhist Ray*, during the 1880s, from his home in the Santa Cruz Mountains.

He also wrote the controversial 1887 book *Swedenborg the Buddhist; or The Higher Swedenborgianism; Its Secrets; and Thibetan Origin*. In that eclectic work, Vetterling put forth a dream dialog tracing the ideas of the influential 18th-century Swedish philosopher and scientist Emanuel Swedenborg all the way back to ancient Buddhist monks.

Right or wrong, that book, along with *The Buddhist Ray*, was Philangi Dasa's definitive output before he moved to 527 McLaughlin Ave. in San Jose, which was then just outside the city limits.

Tutwiler connected all the dots in an article he wrote a few years ago for the Swedenborgian House of Studies at the Pacific School of Religion in Berkeley. With a drop-dead-gorgeous title—"Herman Vetterling, the Philosopher of San Jose; Philangi Dasa, the Buddhist of Santa Cruz"— the article elaborates on all phases of Vetterling's life and career, especially the time he spent as a physician and a farmer in San Jose.

Turns out Vetterling was also one of the folks who helped launch what evolved into the Humane Society Silicon Valley. The facts are not entirely clear, but according to his obituary, he tried to open an animal shelter in Willow Glen in 1928, but the natives put a stop to it. He then opened the shelter on Stevens Creek Road before resigning "because of differences over the terms of a gift of a $50,000." After he passed away in 1931, his caretaker remained at the same address, which was later listed as "San Jose Tourist Camp." I guess that was before trailer parks became common. Maybe that's how Team San Jose should market our city: build more tourist camps.

But while in San Jose, Vetterling eventually left his esoteric version of Buddhism and put the final decades-long touches on his magnum opus, a 1,500-page exploration of the Protestant mystic Jakob Boehme, aptly titled *The Iluminate of Goerlitz or Jakob Boehme's (1575-1624) Life and Philosophy: A Comparative Study*. Yes, he wrote most of this in San Jose, at 527 McLaughlin.

After ingesting Tutwiler's suburbia-shattering research on the life of Philangi Dasa, a.k.a. Herman Vetterling, I have a new appreciation for San Jose Trailer Park. When I chose that place to begin my tour of the obscure five years ago, I never knew there was a secret esoteric Swedenborgian Buddhist history beneath those environs.

Sometimes one feels a natural calling to investigate anything that is hidden, and this discovery was a revelation. Beneath the native lies the exotic.

According to natural law, one principle characterizing the San Jose condition is the law of polarity. Everything is a pair of opposites. All paradoxes of native San Jose and exotic San Jose shall be reconciled. From the darkest confines of suburbia at 527 McLaughlin, from the deepest mud, a lotus blooms.

'In the Valley of Digital Dreams: From Farming to iPad'

Born and raised in San Jose, Sheridan Tatsuno has lived and worked with the poorest and richest people of Silicon Valley. His life story is a combination of opposites. Emerging from working-class Japantown and San Jose High School to becoming one of Silicon Valley's top strategists since 1983, Tatsuno has consulted some of the most notable zillionaires this valley has known.

Now, he spills the beans, furnishing an e-book of insider tech stories, including his own. *In the Valley of Digital Dreams: From Farming to iPad in Silicon Valley* should be hitting the e-book markets any week now, so look for it. In the meantime, allow me to equip you with some insider previews.

Tatsuno begins by differentiating the "West Valley' from the "East Valley.' The western part of Santa Clara County, he writes, historically encompassed the wealthy Caucasian and now Asian suburbs where everyone goes to college and gets a nice job. This is the heart of Silicon Valley, he says, home to all the giants you know about—Facebook, Google, Apple, Stanford, etc.

However, the eastern half of the county, meaning San Jo, was quite different.

"Rarely told is the East Valley and San Jose,' Tatsuno writes, "which is heavily populated by working-class ethnic groups who toil as unsung line engineers, janitors, secretaries, shopkeepers and delivery people. These are the people I grew up with who provide the gritty foundation for Silicon Valley's rise to fame and glory. They are more like John Steinbeck's Joad family, not Leland Stanford's heirs.'

What follows is a local, and personal, rags-to-riches Silicon Valley story that could only have evolved as San Jose itself has. Tatsuno paints the scene decades ago, describing with vivid detail the San Jose of 1955, including the lonely four-lane Highway 101 with all of its stoplights and the hick-town airport that people said would never be "international' because no one would ever want to come here.

He depicts the oceans of vegetable fields surrounding San Jose, the whistles of the fruit-packing canneries, the frogs in the Guadalupe River and the dusty fields where kids played baseball. Decades of car-culture and endless subdivisions had yet to cannibalize suburban America, so in small working-class San Jose, children rode their bikes everywhere. And safely.

"We were the sons and daughters of farmers, farm workers, cannery workers and shopkeepers," writes Tatsuno. "Italians, Mexicans, Japanese, Chinese, Blacks, Filipinos, Portuguese, who grew up downtown in simple worker homes down the street from the elegant Victorians of bankers, lawyers and doctors lining avenues of maple trees."

Tatsuno's father and grandfather owned Nichi Bei Bussan, a shop in Japantown, the same shop Tatsuno's sister owns today. Their family helped fellow San Jose High graduate Norman Mineta in his rise to become the first Asian-American mayor of a major U.S. city, in 1971. The Bellarmine World Order had apparently receded from local politics at that time.

But only 25 pages later, as an employee of Dataquest in the '80s, Tatsuno helps Samsung put together its $5 billion DRAM market entry strategy. He testifies before a paranoid Congress about "Japanese threats" to the tech industry. He advises Intel on how to ditch its entire memory division in order to focus more on microprocessors. Tatsuno also boldly claims he anticipated technologies that led to Mosaic, Yahoo and YouTube but was unable to convince anyone else.

In telling the story, Tatsuno, who now lives in San Francisco, says above all else, he remains highly indebted and grateful to his father, who refused to leave downtown San Jose and move to the mostly Caucasian suburbs as the city gradually sprawled out and ate the hillsides:

"Years later, we would understand the wisdom of his decision. Many of our minority friends returned to San Jose, Berkeley and San Francisco after growing up in white suburbs, feeling totally alone, ignorant and alienated from their ethnic heritage. They only had white friends, while we had friends of all different colors and backgrounds. We were color-blind, not thinking about a person's color so much as their character."

As tech evangelist Guy Kawasaki says in the introduction, Silicon Valley is a place where anything can happen and usually does. Even from the eastern half.

KFJC: Month of Mayhem

This month, the sonic heroes at KFJC-FM (89.7) are programming their 32nd annual Month of Mayhem, a sordid menagerie of delightfully self-indulgent special programs that unfold all month long.

This eclectic station at Foothill College celebrated its 50th anniversary a few years ago, and the Month of Mayhem is always one of the highlights of the year. For 2012, the station will present specials on Hank Williams, the Rova Saxophone Quartet, Fela Kuti and John Cage. And that only scratches the surface. Throughout this month, almost 60 specials will go down.

For me, KFJC represents everything that college radio is supposed to be. That is, there are no Tom Shane commercials, no authoritarian formats and no mercy. If someone wants to play children's music from the '50s, followed by Yanni at the wrong speed, followed by a death metal band called Regurgitated Cattle Fetus, he or she is more than welcome to do that.

As a listener, one gets a fun glimpse into the DJ's head and some insight into the DJ's own twisted tastes. That's right—there's an actual human creature choosing what music gets played. What a concept!

With such a station, no expectations are possible or necessary. Listeners tune in precisely because they don't have any idea what will happen. That's why they listen. While the more mainstream folks might crave predictability and need their favorite hit songs repeated over and over again between insurance commercials, a KFJC fan is a natural iconoclast who despises such soul-sapping mediocrity.

I first discovered KFJC around 1985, and it changed my life for the better, so much that I can't even begin to estimate its influence. Thanks to KFJC, I learned how to purge the tortuous habituation effects of commercial radio and abandon all delusional expectations of what song should come next.

As a result, my musical taste matured, my life became richer and I discovered entire new realms of sonic possibilities. I developed much more appreciation for bands that prioritized constant change and exploration over those who insisted on releasing the same type of music for years and years.

In that sense, nowadays when I write a story on esoteric Buddhism, followed by a column on industrial wastelands, followed by a column on networked-computer art installations and then one applying Deleuze and Guattari to dive bars, I can definitely trace the influence back to KFJC. If I had to write the same stuff over and over again, serious depression would ensue.

This Month of Mayhem KFJC brings us yet still more eclectic programs. *Futurist Music and the First 100 Years of Noise* (May 17, 7pm) will concentrate on Luigi Russolo, who wrote the now-heralded *The Art of Noises* in 1913. He built his own noise machines, thus adding a sonic component to Italian Futurism, officially the first art movement to use propaganda as a weapon.

Any manifesto must declare the end of something else, and the Futurists wrote lots of them. Futurist painters and sculptors worshiped the dynamism of the industrial world and advocated the overthrow of just about everything.

Another Mayhem special will focus on Tiny Tim, one of the most ridiculed and misunderstood musicians of the twentieth century. Many probably do not know that Tiny was a respected musicologist and expert in early-20th-century song. His encyclopedic knowledge was impossible to contain.

During Mayhem, we will also experience tributes to Dutch techno, the Hammond B-3 organ, Sun Ra, the spoken word and even the saxophone's role in surf music. All that in one month. Throw in free improvisation, Welsh crooners and sludge metal and you've got one merry, merry month of May.

Perhaps most importantly, there will be a celebration of the late Jack Diamond, one of the all-time greats at KFJC, who passed away in 2010. About 20 years ago, Diamond introduced a whole new generation to what became revitalized as "space-age bachelor-pad music." He also featured tiki, lounge, exotica and anything appealing to connoisseurs of high camp. He will be dearly missed.

Memories of Jack Douglas, San Jose Historian

I cannot remember the first time I met Jack Douglas, the San Jose historian who passed away a few weeks ago at the age of 79, but it was probably at SJSU's old Wahlquist Library—right where the current Martin Luther King, Jr. Main Library now sits.

Jack ran the Special Collections room in that library. As an undergrad, I would often explore the massive quantities of old aromatic books in the various floors of that glorious building. Jack's place had all the secret stuff, seemingly.

The old Wahlquist Library was a crumbling relic of a place—in a magnificent way. Plaster intermittently tumbled from the walls, and it seemed like the elevators took five minutes to go up three floors. But the Special Collections room was a pristine oasis amid the ruins, where Jack kept track of so much historical ephemera that it was mind-boggling.

Unfortunately, you couldn't browse. Everything was located in the back, and you had to be sniffing for something in particular, pretty much like the current Special Collections room on the fifth floor of the MLK library.

Jack commanded an elderlike presence in that room. He was like the grand old man of local lore. It seemed like he knew the names of every faculty member who had ever taught at the university for 100 straight years.

It was not until much later that I would discover the books he himself had written about San Jose history. There were many. He penned a colorful taxonomy of characters and places, titled *Historical Footnotes of Santa Clara Valley*, and then just recently its sequel, *Historical Highlights of Santa Clara Valley*. Both of those volumes are jammed with crackpot yarns and forgotten stories. I've based several columns on info I originally learned from those books.

Another gem, a smaller paperback, *Historic San Jose: Tales of Naglee Park*, concentrates specifically on that neighborhood, its architecture and history, all of which go back to the 19th century. In gorgeous detail, Jack drills down into the histories of specific houses and the people who inhabited them, folks like Paul Masson and the first wife of John Steinbeck.

I still refer to those books all the time, and I will testify that they helped provide a foundation for me to find my own voice as a "crackpot historian," so to speak. It was in Jack's books that I first researched Astley (A.D.M.) Cooper, San Jose's most famous painter, who paid off his bar tabs with nude portraits of women.

Saloons up and down the coast carried Cooper's paintings. One local saloon keeper owned so many Cooper nudes that he named his watering hole the Louvre Saloon after the Louvre in Paris. Cooper died in 1924, and the Louvre Saloon was located at 53 N. First St. I would love to see that practice revived.

In any event, I did not even hang out with Jack until 2003, when he led a four-hour walking tour of downtown San Jose's historical buildings. I was easily the youngest one in the group, and I conjured up a screed in the July 3 issue of *Metro* that year.

Ever the cantankerous historian, Jack began the tour right where a restaurant exploded near First and Santa Clara streets in the early '60s. As the tour later crept down San Fernando, Jack told us the Cinebar was where all the left-wing SJSU faculty congregated in the late '50s and early '60s. Who would have thought that, a half-century later, one would see Frida Kahlo and punk bands painted on the walls of the place.

Over the years, I called Jack whenever I needed to fill in some obscure details on certain communiques I was conjuring up, and he always called me back. He was a treasured resource. After Clyde Arbuckle, Leonard McKay and a few others, Jack can be seen as the last of his generation of local historians. His are not easy shoes to fill.

Saturday afternoon, Jack's friends and family will host a public memorial service at Kelley Park. The stories will undoubtedly unfold. When Leonard McKay passed away, a celebration took place on the same grounds, with every old boy from every network making an appearance. The Ancient and Honorable Order of E Clampus Vitus, a.k.a. the Clampers, even brought their own Budweiser truck. For Jack's memorial, I do not know what will happen, but it will be historic.

Lost and Found: Josh Marcotte

For many years, the stretch of The Alameda extending east from the intersection of Race Street toward downtown San Jose could have been described as lost. It was a wasteland of decrepit roadside motels, empty retail storefronts, vacant lots and the occasional wandering transient.

All of which is why Josh Marcotte found the area ripe for shooting images. Two years ago, his photographs comprised the first official art show at the Usuals, a new clothing boutique on that exact stretch of The Alameda.

For that show, Marcotte exhibited photos of what the street used to look like, as well as its immediate surroundings. He presented shots of Plant 51 as it first morphed into condos and also the building that occupied the vacant lot now perennially slotted for Whole Foods. He captured Henry's Hi-Life and other legendary buildings.

Now Marcotte will exhibit more photos at the Usuals, beginning with a reception this Friday, featuring music by Seabright. Still under the nom de plume of Lost San Jose, his photos and work continue to depict the eternal cycles of creation and destruction that have characterized San Jose for decades. (His website is www.lostsanjose.com.)

When he first began to exhibit his photography, Marcotte concentrated primarily on the world-class San Jose landmarks we natives know and love: the statue of Babe the Muffler Man, the neon dancing-pig sign at Stephen's Meat Products and the time-forgotten thoroughfare of Monterey Highway.

Now his work is maturing. Marcotte explains that instead of concentrating on actual icons, he is beginning to develop his own personal relationship with the lost stories of San Jose's landscape as a whole.

"My work has evolved to not just documenting the historical and fantastical side of Silicon Valley but to the everyday," he says. "The emptiness, the sprawl, the clutter, the abandonment and also the people that wander these places. And I've also turned the camera on myself. I'm documenting my reflection and my shadow, out playing in the city streets, seeing the portraits as they come up."

Marcotte started this endeavor years ago, writing down his interpretations of what was left behind by the San Jose Redestruction Agency, while simultaneously taking amateur shots with throwaway cameras. He never imagined an audience that would identify with his perspective. After all, most people here seem to feel satisfied with chain restaurants, uniform condos and stripmalls. To most, this appears to constitute enough of a sense of place, so why explore any further than that? Why would anyone possibly be interested in historical architecture, crumbling ruins, local history and the stories beneath every rock and pebble?

"At one point, I just started putting these things online, and I didn't know if anyone would ever see it, or what the reaction would be," Marcotte recalls. "But people really connected with the project. They understood it from a historical standpoint, from a preservation standpoint. Some people saw the humor in the images, the odd day-to-day things you find when you take a minute to stop and look around. I was surprised at just how encouraging and supportive everybody was, that people understood the passion I have, and that other people shared that same passion."

As a result of Marcotte showing his work, other photographers began to contact him and swap clues to other hidden locales throughout the ruins of San Jose's underbelly—a universal quest, it seems, to locate forgotten stories between the cracks. His work has inspired others to explore and document and research the history of this landscape. A blight-junkie revolution is brewing, whether mainstream San Jose realizes it or not.

Over at the Usuals, they are selling shirts depicting the old Hart's Department Store. A new generation of locals is discovering the history of this town. Operated by a native San Jose brother and sister, the Usuals has helped spawn a minirenaissance along The Alameda. They sell a variety of goods for young urban folk. All the T-shirts and jewelry are by local designers. The clothing line is mostly from West Coast designers. The art exhibits go down once a month.

"They give the artists a lot of control as to what goes into their show," Marcotte says. "They pretty much let you do what you like. They encourage you to be creative."

Dennis Erectus, RIP

The radio world lost a unique individual on June 13, when former KOME legend Dennis "Erectus" Netto passed away at the physical age of 61. Dennis, in this author's opinion, was the originator of what's now commonly known as the "shock jock," and from 1977 to 1983 in particular, his beautifully indecent behavior vaulted KOME to mythical status. He was the lewd and crude genius who did things on the air that no one could possibly get away with today.

In what now seems like the vanishing Wild West, those years were essentially the heyday of FM radio's free-format era. The jocks had a lot more control and much more choice over what they played.

In Dennis' case, he could ridicule every form of righteousness, insult any pompous sophisticate or encourage listeners to call in and play characters on the air, during the skits. It was closer to theater than it was to a radio show. In a time dominated by mellow '70s hippie-DJs, Dennis came out swinging, often attacking his entire audience in ways that made everyone laugh uproariously, even if you were the target.

The shows were probably like FDR's fireside chats, but instead with celebrities gangbanging Nancy Reagan, '50s horror clips, theatrical S&M skits, tearing up disco records on the air and unabashed mockeries of televangelists and Republicans.

A regular cast of shadowy characters joined the shenanigans, and Dennis would even occasionally broadcast from places like a bus stop or the city dump, just to see what would possibly happen. He even ran for president in 1980.

The last place I ever spoke to Dennis was in the KBAY offices on San Fernando Street, right across from the Caravan Lounge. That was 2006. His old pals from KOME, Dana Jang and Jona Denz-Hamilton, have been on the air at that station for years now, and at that time, they were trying to find a way to bring Dennis back into the fold. We talked about music, old-school pro wrestling and how Clear Channel's institutionalized blandness is thoroughly corrupting the youth of America.

Dennis seemed humble about his legacy, but during his original stint at KOME, he took commercial radio to a place it had not been before—and a place it certainly won't be ever again. He brought sophistication, creativity and a theatrical, warped, stoner elegance that no radio personality, before or since, can possibly equal. He was a true original.

"He taught me everything I ever knew about how to rile up an audience," recalled Bob Calhoun, a.k.a. Count Dante of Incredibly Strange Wrestling fame. "He was a real mentor to me, but this started before I ever met him. His show on KOME put me on the path to being that unique kind of Bay Area weirdo. All of those twisted skits of his, plus the little snippets of old monster-movie dialog that he played in between AC/DC songs warped my young mind and showed me what was possible."

Dennis appreciated professional wrestling, especially back in the days before it went Hollywood and degenerated into the unwatchable garbage it is now. In fact, during the late '90s, after radio had no place for him anymore, he even jumped in the ring with Count Dante.

In Calhoun's book, Beer, Blood and Cornmeal: Seven Years of Incredibly Strange Wrestling, he recalls when Erectus, a liberal, deliberately insulted a crowd at the Fillmore, for entertainment purposes, calling them socialists, and then followed by insulting all the women in the audience, from the ring. The audience then pelted him with hundreds of tortillas and booed incessantly. A natural, it turned out he was better at the shtick than most of the big-money pro wrestlers. After that match, Erectus claimed the experience was enlightening.

"You can take any drug you want to, man, but nothing can beat that high. I've taken everything under the sun, especially working in radio back in the '70s, but making a room full of people hate you like that, making them all want to kill you, is the best high that I've ever felt."

A public memorial is being planned for later this year. Check the KOME Facebook page for information.

Traveling Man: Thollem McDonas

The only homeless musician with two degrees from SJSU's School of Music is now a published essayist. The only San Jose native to record on Claude Debussy's old piano in Brive-la-Gaillarde, France, the only one to cut a CD with William Parker and Nels Cline and also lock himself in a house with Mike Watt of fIREHOSE, has contributed to a landmark collection of writings: *Anthology of Essays on Deep Listening*, (Deep Listening Publications, $25).

Twenty years ago, pianist Thollem McDonas probably could have had a concert career. After graduating with degrees in both piano performance and composition, he could have donned a tuxedo and plied his trade in the world's greatest concert and performance venues.

Instead, McDonas decided to expound energy in grass-roots political and ecological movements. At that time, everyone thought he was bonkers for squandering his potential.

Thankfully, about eight years ago, McDonas returned to music with full focus and everyone still thought he was bonkers. After all, who could spend a life traveling and also be diverse enough to teach improvisation workshops in Mexico, play keys with political-punk bands in Italy and write essays alongside renowned contemporary composers? Who could possibly survive crisscrossing the Atlantic every year, performing in theaters, art galleries, elementary schools, concert halls, jazz clubs, festivals, warehouses, gardens, gutters, prisons and riots—and on television, radio and the Internet?

Yet this is what McDonas does. Today, with no permanent roof over his head, McDonas is experiencing a detonation of notoriety. A "peripatetic musician," this critically acclaimed pianist has, just in the last few months, released *The Gowanus Session* with jazz legend William Parker and Wilco guitarist Nels Cline.

He also spent a weekend locked in a boiling hot Texas house with Mike Watt, John Dieterich and Tim Barnes to bang out yet another CD, *You Are Always on Our Minds*, calling the group The Hand to Man Band. In the last eight years, McDonas has added 24 albums to his discography on 20 different vanguard record labels in four different countries. Legendary composer Terry Riley even wrote the liner notes for the music McDonas cut using Debussy's old piano, in partnership with the late contrabass virtuoso Stefano Scodanibbio.

What's more, McDonas also just penned an essay, "Deep Listening and the Peripatetic Life of an Improvising Musician," included in the above-mentioned anthology. His journey is an unlikely, but inspiring one.

"Perpetual travel enlightens both the traveler as well as those with whom they come into contact," McDonas writes. "I believe that traveling musicians/artists/creative and free thinkers are necessary as nongovernmental cultural ambassadors, because they represent their communities and countries and fill an important role as artist liaisons in the relations between diverse peoples."

"Deep listening," a philosophy originally developed by the pioneering 20th-century composer Pauline Oliveros, weaves Buddhist mindfulness with enhanced musical improvisation skills, distinguishing the difference between the involuntary nature of hearing and the voluntary selective nature of listening. One becomes aware of all sounds—musical, environmental, social—in order to develop a heightened sense of awareness.

In the book, the philosophy is applied to numerous contexts. McDonas, for instance, relates it to the life of a nomadic musician, constantly ingesting unfamiliar sonic palettes wherever he roams, merging them with the creative musical ideas already inside his head. A heightened awareness of constantly changing environmental sounds affects how he improvises onstage, no matter in which country he finds himself.

"The experience of being in physical motion encourages my mind to stay in motion as well," he writes. "I'm exposed to unique sounds in diverse environments that continually inform the way I hear and interact. I experience the unknown sometimes around every corner, encouraging me to keep extra aware of my surroundings and therefore putting me into a continual state of nonhabit. I feel the direct connection of the flow of my body through space with the flow of ideas through my mind as new experiences are constantly stimulating new ideas." Hail Spartans, hail!

Umberto Abronzino

A movement is afoot to build a field house at the recently reopened Watson Park to honor one of San Jose's all-time legends, Umberto Abronzino, credited not only as being the founding father of soccer in Santa Clara Valley but also as the hero that operated the Bascom Barber Shop for almost 50 years.

Originally from Italy, Abronzino, who passed away in 2006 at the age of 85, started the Peninsula Soccer League when he first came to San Jose in the late '50s. Watson Park was his main turf. Officially sanctioned by the U.S. Soccer Federation, the Peninsula Soccer League still exists today, and from 1957 until his death, Abronzino ran the league out of his barbershop.

Just about everyone who has ever played the sport in Santa Clara County owes a debt to Abronzino. He started everything. He created the royal soccer bloodline of San Jose, and his home, outside of the barbershop, was Watson Park. He was an administrator, a referee and a tireless diplomat for the game. During the 1994 World Cup in the United States, he was Italy's Ambassador to the entire tournament.

Anyone who attended the original San Jose Earthquakes matches in the old North American Soccer League (NASL) from 1974 to 1984 will remember Abronzino as the timekeeper during those games. At that time, the NASL was changing the rules of the game in order to placate confused Americans, so they actually used to stop the clock during matches. At Spartan Stadium, Abronzino was the old guy who sat there on a raised platform, on the west sideline, with a handheld cylindrical pushbutton switch to stop the game clock, upon the referee's request. Everyone knew him. He was an institution.

Watson Park closed in 2005 due to toxins in the soil—the place was originally a city dump—and Abronzino never lived to see the park undergo its new transformation. After six years of hard work, a painstaking collaborative effort finally culminated with the park reopening last year.

Along with a playground, a dog park, basketball courts, a restroom, picnic areas and other facilities, a new soccer bowl, renamed Abronzino Bowl, contains two new soccer fields, one grass and one artificial turf, both of which have lights to allow night play.

As a result, San Jose Parks Foundation and the Soccer Silicon Valley Community Foundation are now raising funds to build a field house at the park in Abronzino's honor. The field house will include restrooms, concessions, office space, storage and a permanent exhibit about Abronzino and the history of recreational soccer in Silicon Valley, curated by History San Jose.

With that, allow me to digress with a hysterical and somewhat mystical side note: last year, Team San Jose led a media tour of the old Martin Luther King, Jr., Main Library on San Carlos Street, as it was about to get demolished. The old concrete building had recently housed some the city offices that the new City Hall didn't have room for, particularly Public Works, so as we toured it, many remnants still remained inside the building, leftover from when the city employees had finally vacated the place. In one pile of garbage, I discovered the entire 60-page roll of blueprints for the new Watson Park renovation project. To save the prints from annihilation, I took the roll and donated it to History San Jose.

Perhaps it is symbolic of the endless cycles of creation and destruction that always seem to characterize San Jose's belligerent, ham-fisted suburban-planning (d)evolution: A park is built on a former city dump. Toxins close the park 50 years later, just as the City Hall moves back to downtown.

Since there isn't enough room in the new City Hall for all the employees, Public Works gets relocated to the old MLK Library building. When that building gets destroyed, no one even cares enough to save the Watson Park blueprints they'd been working on, so a newspaper columnist donates them to History San Jose, who just happens to be helping envision a new field house at the remodeled Watson Park. Welcome to San Jose, the "global epicenter of innovation," as the politicians keep telling us.

In any event, raising money for the new Umberto Abronzino Field House is a wonderful cause. Without exaggeration, he probably affected at least 500,000 people in this area, over the course of 50 years. I am certain the field house will be here to stay.

San Jose Earthquakes NASL Reunion

A few weeks ago, the Grand Council of Elders, North American Soccer League, San Jose Chapter, C.E. 1974, secretly convened in a dive bar for a very special occasion. Aside from free drinks, members of the original, and I mean original, San Jose Earthquakes reunited once again because the current club was inducting two very important folks into its Hall of Fame:

original scoring leader Paul Child, who played from 1974 to 1979, and original owner Milan Mandaric.

As a result, Jack's Bar in Japantown, where the current club's supporters regularly get hammered when they're not traveling to a road game, opened up a tab for any NASL Earthquakes alumni.

The next night, many former Quakes, from every era, were brought onto the field at halftime for the induction ceremony. The weekend proved to be yet another family reunion for many of us who grew up with the original NASL squads, which were always community-based, above all else.

The NASL team's former equipment kid, Ron Gilmore, usually organizes the reunions, which take place every five years or so, but this was a special occasion, since Child and Mandaric were being inducted. Basically, the reason many kids play soccer in Northern California, in 2012, is at least partly due to what these guys helped create, nearly 40 years ago.

Regardless of one's sports preference, this particular slice of local history remains important, because it exemplifies arguments that still rage today. In the early '70s, if one wanted professional sports, one had to drive to San Francisco or Oakland. San Jose had nothing.

Mandaric, a Yugoslavian transplant, entrepreneur in the semiconductor industry and passionate soccer fan, wanted a new soccer club in San Jose, since there was no professional sport here yet. He wanted to be the first game in town. The league's top brass at that time, including the famed Lamar Hunt, did not want the team in San Jose. They wanted it named after San Francisco because they considered San Jose to be a hick town, the redheaded stepchild of the Bay Area, or the "hinterland." Sound familiar?

Mandaric, however, pleaded his case and eventually won. The Quakes started playing in 1974. The town and media welcomed them with open arms, primarily because the team branded itself as a bunch of players who occupied exactly the same social level as their fans—all the way down to partying with everyone after each and every game.

It was a community team. Everyone in the stands had met one of the players before the team even played a single match. The players themselves hung out together off the field and caroused around in public together everywhere. As a result, the Quakes successfully sold a brand-new professional sport to what was then an unknown California suburb, one that was ready to go big time. Unfortunately, as everyone knows, the entire league collapsed 10 years later. C'est la vie.

The whole scenario raised arguments you might recognize: Is a team that prides itself on street-level connections with an entire community better for the fans than a team with high-priced rock-star players? Is the business bottom line more important than the product on the field? Is San Jose a major-league city or a hopeless minor-league wasteland?

In any event, many of these guys never left the local area. They started soccer camps, became coaches at all levels or went on to play in local over-35 leagues. In some cases, they even became bartenders when Britannia Arms opened up.

Until a few weeks ago, Mandaric had never attended the recent reunions, so it was a moving experience when they brought him out onto the field. Even though he has long since lived in England, taking the helm at clubs like Portsmouth, Leicester or Sheffield Wednesday, he referred to the Earthquakes as his hometown club. He expressed his joy that the current San Jose Earthquakes team still prides itself on being a community club.

In a nutshell, while there exist other Major League Soccer clubs with similar historical lineages, and certainly larger attendance figures, none of them have the multigenerational family that the San Jose Earthquakes have. Look for part two of this column next week, as the Quakes commence the groundbreaking ceremony on their new stadium, 40 years in the making. Cheerleaders will come out of the woodwork for that one.

San Jose Earthquakes Groundbreaking

This Sunday, the San Jose Earthquakes will break ground on a new stadium across Coleman Avenue from the Mineta International San Jose Airport. The club will aim to set a new Guinness World Record for the number of folks participating in a stadium groundbreaking. In order to beat the current mark, the club will need to enlist at least 4,533 participants to dig for two minutes.

Quite a few points will converge when the facility opens in 2014, providing a way for Quakes fans to connect with their roots. For instance, 2014 will mark the 40th anniversary of the first incarnation of the Earthquakes, back when Norman Mineta was mayor.

Soccer-wise, much has folded and unfolded since then, all of which is equally important, but 1974 will live on. Many clubs throughout the world include the year of their inception on their crests or logos, so on the back of the Quakes' jerseys, it now says, "Est. 1974."

For little tikes growing up in San Jose during that time, there was rarely anything to do except go to Frontier Village or Eastridge Mall. Except for a minor league baseball team, the town had nothing close to professional sports.

When the Quakes started, other teams in the fledgling North American Soccer League (NASL) were drawing 4,000 or 5,000 folks, tops; then San Jose started drawing upward of 16,000. Spartan Stadium became the most heralded home turf in the league, for several reasons, one of which was Krazy George, a wild man already known for instigating crowds at SJSU football games.

For every Quakes game, he would enter the field in a different manner: helicopter, ambulance, police car or camel. During the games, instead of standing on the sidelines and thus separated from the crowd, he tromped up into the stands and interacted with the audience to set off cheers, believing that if the crowd experienced a strange man sweating and screaming and bashing a snare drum right in their faces, they would be more apt to join along. It worked.

At the time, *San Jose Mercury* reporter Fred Guzman wrote a book encapsulating that first season, titled The *Great Quake of 1974*. On page 21, he describes what it was like having Krazy George on the scene, from the very first home game: "His arrival at the Earthquake opener was to establish a tradition. Just before kickoff, a garbage truck rolled onto the field and took a slow lap around the befuddled players. Out rolled George, and the crowd went crazy. He made a different arrival to each of the Quakes' games during the season and his appearance became a bigger part of the pregame festivities than the National Anthem."

If you were a kid during those years, the games were like stadium-rock shows. There was a raucous buzz right before every match. Everyone made sure to be in their seats before kickoff because they wanted to see how Krazy George was going to arrive and what he was going to do. You didn't see half the crowd trickling in during the first 10 minutes of the game, like now.

George preferred to call himself an "instigator" rather than a cheer-leader, which was fine, since the Quakes also had their own cheerleading squad, the Shakers. In what now seems like the vanishing Wild West, back in those days, the Shakers would greet the opposing team at the airport with bottles of champagne (see photo). This was before the existence of security checkpoints, so anyone could just walk up to the gate area. Along with the players, the Shakers would do promotional appearances all over the city.

Debbie Hilpert, seen in the photo at the left, was a Shaker back in the mid-'70s and still lives here. Back in those days, she says, everyone was a member of the same family—the players, the cheerleaders, the fans and the front office staff.

"It was all geared to family," she said. "That's what was so great about it. The players stopped at any given time to sign autographs, pat a kid on the head, and say, 'How you doing?' Even George, he would let kids hit his drum. That's what it was about. It was always about giving back."

With a new 18,000-seat stadium, complete with historical displays, the family will be that much bigger. I'm getting the shakes already.

Don Lattin: Distilled Spirits

A few years ago, former Bay Area religion reporter Don Lattin penned The Harvard Psychedelic Club: How Timothy Leary, Ram Dass, Huston Smith, and Andrew Weil Killed the Fifties and Ushered in a New Age for America, in which he illuminated four characters who helped bring LSD to the public forefront.

For his new book, originally conceived as a prequel to *The Harvard Psychedelic Club*, Lattin started out by investigating the previous era, specifically three men who transformed the course of 20th-century spirituality: author (*Brave New World*) and LSD enthusiast Aldous Huxley (1894–1963), the mystic philosopher Gerald Heard (1889–1971) and Alcoholics Anonymous co-founder Bill Wilson (1895–1971). While researching the book, Lattin discovered more about his own personal story, especially his own struggles with substance abuse, so the book ultimately took the form of a memoir.

Distilled Spirits: Getting High, Then Sober, With a Famous Writer, a Forgotten Philosopher, and a Hopeless Drunk ($29.95; UC-Press) weaves Lattin's personal story of recovery with the lives of Huxley, Heard and Wilson in a way that should inspire anyone. It is neither a stock drunk-to-sober story nor a preachy treatise.

As someone who wrote for the secular press for decades, surrounded by legendary *San Francisco Chronicle* alcoholics and the skid-row bars within crawling distance of the newspaper offices, Lattin learned to escape his inbred cynicism and addictions with the help of three characters from his grandparents' generation.

"Each of these men independently led an inspiring life," writes Lattin. "But it's only when we consider the three collectively, pausing at these moments where their lives intersect, that we fully appreciate their cumulative power. Huxley saw the social problem. Heard charted the spiritual course. Wilson recruited passengers for the journey."

Most readers are probably familiar with Huxley and Wilson, but Heard is something of a forgotten character, hence the book's title. Among many other identities, Heard was the first science correspondent for the BBC, wrote one of the first popular books on flying saucers and pioneered gay spirituality. He was an historian, a mystery novelist and an influence on many flavors of the human-potential movement. Heard was also the one who guided Bill Wilson during the latter's first LSD trip in the summer of 1956. The two continued a lifelong correspondence.

Among still more endeavors, Heard opened Trabuco College in the '40s, in the Southern California canyon of the same name, where Eastern philosophy met its Western counterpart, and where inquiries into comparative spirituality were the norm. The campus is now used by the Vedanta Society.

All in all, Lattin says Heard and Huxley were probably two of Western culture's last great polymaths: "In an era of increasing specialization, they were interested in everything." Religious studies scholar Huston Smith and Esalen Institute co-founder Michael Murphy are two people who continue to cite Heard as a major influence.

Lattin's own story involves a deeper descent into alcohol and drugs while treating his editors like shit and insulting them in front of the younger staff writers. Now sober more than eight years, he says writing *Distilled Spirits* was part of his ongoing recovery, reinforcing a program of rigorous honesty and teaching him the redemptive power of storytelling.

Distilled Spirits even features lurid yarns about the various reporters Lattin worked with, some nearly dead from drink but still attached to bar stools. Lattin doesn't lionize or criticize the scenario; rather, he puts it in context, looking back on a long career writing about religion from a jaded reporter's perspective.

"Newspaper reporters revel in writing about religious hypocrisy, and God knows that's never hard to find," says Lattin. "But after nearly three decades, I had to turn in my press pass. Skepticism is an honorable trait, especially for journalists, but I'd spent enough time hanging out in that dim alley where cynicism meets skepticism, looking for a little light."

As one who occupies that same alley, I can relate. In more ways than one.

Alone with Eric Fischl at the San Jose Museum of Art

The grand opera of suburban wasteland America is now unfolding like a lawn chair at the San Jose Museum of Art. The new exhibit "Dive Deep: Eric Fischl and the Process of Painting" pulls viewers into the elaborate process behind the artist's now-famous nudes of unglamorous proportions.

As soon as one enters the space, Fischl's 5-by-8-foot masterpiece, simply titled *Barbeque*, presents an awkward tension, practically screaming for a dysfunctional suburban aria.

A boy is blowing fire up in the air like a circus performer while standing in front of a bowl of dead fish. Two naked women frolic in a ridiculously geometric-shaped pool. At the same time, a beaming '80s version of Ward Cleaver works the barbecue with an orgasmic smile on his face.

The pink house in the background is one of those homogenous single-story tract-house monstrosities one sees in every California subdivision from Sylmar to San Leandro. In fact, the entire image reminds me of loopy magazine shots from 30 years ago, like something from *Good Housekeeping* gone painfully awry.

Fischl and I sauntered through the exhibit a few weeks ago. He explained, and I'm paraphrasing, that he grew up on Long Island, against the backdrop of a dysfunctional family, in the first generation of post-WWII suburban America right when the slaphappy, Eden-like euphoria of such an environment was being fetishized by tens of millions across the landscape.

He said that everyone assumed there couldn't exist a creative method of depicting such a dark operatic nightmare, but that was not the case. The naked underbelly of Eden soon emerged.

He's right, and his career proves it. Many of his paintings look like glossy magazine compositions but with characters in various states of unease. In the label text for *Barbeque*, Fischl says that, before he ever learned how to paint, the mass media inflicted on adolescents in suburban wasteland America fired up the muses and away he went: "Early influences involved exposure to characters, to figures, whatever came through television, magazines, movies, long before I saw a painting and certainly long before I understood painting. The influences were the other mediums that were pervasive in the culture. Of course, growing up in the suburbs, you went to the movies, you watched a lot of TV and you looked at magazines."

One perceives in Fischl's work an emotional distance between the all characters employed. And in some cases, they actually are employed. Sometimes, he stages live scenes with hired subjects, as in the legendary "Krefeld Project" series or in the paintings of poet Richard Price and his family. After taking massive amounts of photographs, Fischl then collages everything in Photoshop to find an adequate scene to paint.

In the show, and this is perhaps the best aspect of the experience, we see Fischl's process documented. Alongside the final paintings, we see dozens of photographs or studies illuminating his trials and errors—the path he took to the final image.

Fittingly, curator Jodi Throckmorton says that the exhibit is organized to show that Fischl did not just walk up to a blank canvas and paint these scenes. The exhibit is about process, not just the final result.

Viewers can glimpse into the universal components of the creative process—the components of failure, risk-taking and experimentation. In this way, anyone—right-brain or left-brain—should be able to identify with the procedure behind the scenes, even those who are not creatively inclined. Perfect for suburban Silicon Valley.

"We have audiences that are really interested in figurative painting, so we're hoping they can look at it from the perspective of creation," Throckmorton says. "But we're also hoping that engineers—people that may not be interested in art—can come in and see their own struggles with the creative process."

With this show, one dives deep into a dysfunctional suburban opera, replete with emotionally distant, unglamorous and awkward characters, many of whom are naked. It makes me want to write the libretto.

Two Worlds at Seeing Things Gallery

In previous crystallizations of this column, I have contemplated the San Jose condition through many a combination of polar opposites: native/exotic, luxury/gutter, urban/suburban. I would now like to take things one step further. Thanks to some new downtown San Jose establishments, this time the dichotomy is one of easy listening and hardcore punk.

We begin with the emergence of San Jose Rock Shop at 30 N. Third St., an idea long overdue. Ever since Guitar Center moved to Stevens Creek Boulevard back in the '80s, there has not been a legitimate musical instrument shop in the neighborhood. Now there is.

Located just north of a Hispanic-owned colon-cleanser retailer and around the corner from a cheap Vietnamese tailor, one finds 8,000 square feet of instruments and amplifiers, rehearsal space and repair services.

Yes, the building formerly occupied by WORKS/San Jose years ago is now reconfigured and replete with guitars, strings, keyboards, drum sets and more. Lessons are offered, consignment gear is available and bands can rent rehearsal space. Also inside is a private club, a la 924 Gilman in Berkeley, which presents all-ages live shows with no alcohol. From Third Street, one can look right through the front window and see the gear. As its moniker suggests, the place rocks.

With no effort on my part, one half of the polar opposition manifested itself. A few weeks ago, I slithered inside San Jose Rock Shop on a chilly afternoon and flipped through a stack of cheesy '70s songbooks filled with piano/organ arrangements of TV and movie themes, easy-listening hits, pop schmaltz and campy lounge classics from before there was such a genre—exactly the stuff I grew up playing on a Lowrey Genie organ and exactly the material I played while originally taking keyboard lessons at Stevens Music.

That stuff has been an integral component of my psyche ever since. My admiration of camp humor and the ridiculous side of everyday life can perhaps be traced to playing that cheesy material for years. For most of my younger years, I could not explain to any of my music circles why I was literate in and appreciative of easy-listening crooners and crappy sitcom music.

It gets even better. To exemplify how the other half operates, a previously unnoticeable door exists on Third Street, right next to San Jose Rock Shop, leading one into an adjoining room. It is there that Jai Tanju's Seeing Things Gallery now sits. I didn't even have to knock. The door was open—I searched, and I found.

Fittingly, the grand-opening party at Seeing Things Gallery this month featured the '80s hardcore-punk photography of one Mr. Bill Daniel. Gritty live-action shots of Black Flag from 1982, nearly 4-by-5-feet, exploded off the wall for everyone to see. Daniel shot the band on ancient whatever-millimeter film, and the images convey the aggressive, brutal nature of Black Flag shows back in the day.

I never saw Black Flag live, but their seminal violent masterpiece, *Damaged*, was the first punk album I ever bought, even though I snagged it right about the time hardcore was essentially dying.

Experiencing Daniel's photography of Black Flag from the *Dam-*

aged tour brought it all back. The dark, disenfranchised isolation conveyed by that slab of vinyl altered my universe, and I don't think I ever went back to popular music afterward.

When first playing that LP, I remember looking at my record shelf and thinking that none of it was interesting anymore. Black Flag was where I wanted to be. My entire identification with punk and the dark side of the quotidian world can be traced to that album, which I purchased as a teenager. Right now, at 30 N. Third St., one can look through the front window and see Daniel's photographs.

So you can imagine the two windows I'm looking through. One goes into San Jose Rock Shop, while the other goes into Seeing Things. What a concept. For all of my life, I feel like I've been trying to reconcile those seemingly opposing parts of my psyche—easy listening and punk rock—and there they were, right in my own 'hood. No need to look outside or elsewhere.

I have 30 N. Third Street to thank. A sense of integration has emerged, binary opposites are transcended and the grand synthesis is now at work.

Pong 40th Anniversary With Al Alcorn

Last week, the intersection of El Camino Real and S. Murphy Avenue presented a space-time-continuum-shattering spectacle of epic proportions. For one, Rooster T. Feathers Comedy Club invited original Pong designer Al Alcorn to grace the establishment with his presence, in celebration of Pong's 40th anniversary.

In 1972, Alcorn beta-tested the very first Pong machine in that same building, 157 W. El Camino Real, which was then Andy Capp's Tavern. With its initial success, Pong essentially launched what we now know as the video game industry.

Pong was Atari's first commercial experiment and just about everyone who's ever played a video or computer game knows it. The history endures, especially if you grew up in Silicon Valley, as there were some brief moments when Atari ruled the universe.

As the story goes, Nolan Bushnell and Ted Dabney were Atari employees one and two, respectively. Alcorn was number three. Bushnell assigned Alcorn to create a video game based on table tennis, and Pong was the result.

To test-market the idea, they installed a makeshift version in Andy Capp's Tavern in September of 1972. Right there on a borderline-rural stretch of El Camino Real, the first consumers put the first quarters into that first Pong machine. The rest is history, and the original box now sits in the Computer History Museum. Just imagine how different the last 40 years of video games would have been if Pong had never happened.

The façade of Rooster T. Feathers is virtually unchanged since the Andy Capp's days, save for a few paint jobs and a more recent sign. It remains an integral component of Silicon Valley history as well as a groovy independent business right at an intersection where a smattering of such establishments exists.

That said, the physical scenery deserves mention here as well. Most of the Sunnyvale landscape is utterly forgettable, but the complex original bouillabaisse of independent businesses right along Murphy Avenue, as one careens away from El Camino, is a retro-exotic oasis amid the more homogeneous modern strip-malls dominating the other side of El Camino. The intersection forms a suburban, old-vs.-new polarity that cannot go unmentioned.

All along that stretch of El Camino, one finds a bland, tasteless broth of faux-granite exteriors, bread-themed mall restaurants, bad stucco, ugly box-retail outlets, canned dinner-jazz fusion emanating from every external speaker and countless vitamin shops and cell-phone stores.

As always, the planners at each of the malls implemented every possible technique to discourage any possible pedestrian from ever wanting to enjoy any of it. And as always, the malls are named after whatever they destroyed, like "Cherry Orchard."

This is precisely why the Allario Center on Murphy Avenue and its neighboring center are so uplifting and refreshing to the senses as one arrives there from the generic nightmare of El Camino. Just along that stretch of Murphy, one finds Coconut Hill Indian Groceries, a Thai Massage place, the Lace Museum, an acupuncture clinic, an Aikido studio, a decades-old locksmith shop, a yarn store, a sports-card collector and a wig shop. Yeah!

It really looks like someone went out of his or her way to preserve some degree of interesting retail integrity amid the gargantuan swaths of monolithic ugliness on the main road. Just 200 feet off El Camino you feel like you're in a different galaxy entirely. That stretch of Murphy seems off the beaten path but still native, somehow.

Rooster T. Feathers, even though it's on El Camino, functions as an anchor for the rest of the interesting shops and businesses that veer off along Murphy. At least that's how I see it.

Inside the comedy club, the party opened with Alcorn taking the stage to commemorate the history, claiming he never set out to start an industry—he just had a problem to solve on a $75 TV. "Thanks for all the quarters," he quipped. "I appreciate it."

Host Erikka Innes of *Sex With Nerds* emceed the rest of the evening. "Without Pong," she said, "no one would have invented beer pong, and my parents would not have hooked up and made me."

2013

Willow Street in Willow Glen

On May 28, 1864, the San Jose City Council asked the county surveyor to measure out several new streets, including Willow. The local rag reported their commands: "He is instructed to survey a street commencing on the west line of the Monterey road on the line between the lands of Sullivan and Buck on the north, and Goodyear on the south, continuing the same on said line westerly and to extend the same on a direct line west. Said street shall be named Willow Street."

With that historical clincher in mind, the urban-blight exploration junkie fell off the wagon and recently surveyed that same stretch of road as it exists today. Ghosts of pizza joints, neighborhood bars and muffler man statues from ancient times added to an already gorgeous travelogue. As with many acts of exploration, the pillars of self, time and space underwent a profound transfiguration.

First of all, nothing on that stretch of road qualifies as "blight," so that made the junkie feel better right away. Hope emerged right off the bat, and it didn't take long to walk down Willow from First Street to the Highway 87 overpass. As with any interesting part of San Jose, it has to be experienced on foot to appreciate the historical curiosities that emerge from behind every storefront.

Decades ago, for example, this neighborhood was highly Italian in character. I was barely alive, but a quick inspection of the city directories illuminates just how thriving this working-class neighborhood actually was. It was part of what was then famously called Goosetown, and many shopkeepers lived upstairs from or near their businesses.

The whole stretch of road bubbled with activity. There were barbershops, pizza joints, retail and mini-industries of food, repair shops and service professions. Sam's Log Cabin, for example, occupied 245 Willow St. for more decades than anyone can remember.

The legendary Ricardo's Pizza occupied 218 Willow, pretty much right across the street from Sam's Log Cabin. Operated by Richard Quisenberry and featuring classic decor of red-and-white checkerboard table-cloths, wooden chairs and Italian accoutrements, Ricardo's was likewise a popular neighborhood hangout. Extra seating existed upstairs above the kitchen, and a small stage sat near the opposite wall. Circa 1970/1, a then-unknown group, the Doobie Brothers, were the house band at Ricardo's, gigging on a regular basis.

Warren Arlo Walter was the doorman at Ricardo's and still has a few of the beer signs. "The famous horn player, Chet Baker, also played often at Ricardo's on Tuesday jazz night," Walter recalled. "Chet had some substance abuse issues in those days and Richard actually kept the horn—a flugelhorn I believe it was—so it would not get pawned."

It gets better. During that same era, Babe's Muffler sat right at the southeast corner of Willow and Vine, complete with a gigantic statue similar to the one still remaining on The Alameda. That's right—Babe commanded the corner of Willow and Vine 43 years ago, just like Christ the Redeemer overlooking Rio de Janeiro. At one time, there were even three Babe statues in San Jose. I eagerly await the second coming of Babe at that corner. Someday. It will happen.

Just waltzing up and down that stretch of Willow, from the residential area to the industrial environs near the intrusive freeway, ghosts just kept emerging. At 93 Willow, for example, another legendary bar called Stella's occupied a basement as recently as the late '80s. That one I do recall seeing myself. Twenty years prior, though, it was a restaurant called Spanish Village.

Again, in those days, many of the local folks in the service industries lived just down the street, above their businesses or somewhere nearby—a true community in every respect, before decades of bumbling San Jose planners and suburban sprawl converted everyone to Walmartians.

In any event, Badalamente's Sausage is probably the last remaining Italian joint on that part of Willow left from the older generations. Even the unsightly Highway 87 could not drive it away. It will live on. The rest of this survey will continue at a later date, Babes or not.

No Regrets: The Life of Edith Piaf

In a flavor of synchronicity that now happens so often I consider it to be part of nature, two particular biographies simultaneously came into my zone of influence last month. For one, The Fractalist: Memoir of a Scientific Maverick (Pantheon), the posthumously published autobiography of Benoit Mandelbrot, arrived to remind me that disenfranchised academic researchers, those who carve their own paths outside the compartmentalized pigeonholes of established scientific fields, can eventually change the way we see the world.

Likewise, Carolyn Burke's book No Regrets: The Life of Edith Piaf (Knopf) sounded several notes, primarily that charismatic singers can rise from the slums and the abysses of alcohol and drugs to write their own lyrics, inspire other singers and thrill audiences worldwide. Turns out both Mandelbrot and Piaf spent parts of their childhood in the slum of Belleville, near Paris, and both visited San Jose at the heights of their careers.

Born in Warsaw in 1924 of Jewish Lithuanian descent, Mandelbrot overcame the horrors of World War II and was forced to relocate with his family twice before settling in southern France. The first third of The Fractalist documents those years, explaining how even though his uncle provided much guidance in his life, a certain outsider spirit and an uncontainable restlessness is what drove him.

In that sense, Mandelbrot describes his childhood as one surrounded by conflict and says that he never experienced long-term routines. Interruptions were the norm. He claims that his scientific destiny was a continuous search for a boundary-shattering problem, a "Kepler moment." Throughout his career, he seems more influenced by the academic outcasts and oddballs who crossed his path, as opposed to those who played politics within the system to remain safe.

A "general theory of roughness" as he calls it, is what resulted in the word "fractal," and once computers became fast enough, he discovered previously hidden laws of nature that no one else had cared to look for, viewable in shorelines, cauliflower heads, snowflakes, the economy and perhaps even his own career trajectory. As a result, he is now a household name.

Although not mentioned in the book, Mandelbrot did come to Silicon Valley in the late '80s, on a promo tour for a book edited by Heinz-Otto Peitgen. According to one source who was there, he bantered about feeling like a rock star, as he was often mobbed at his public appearances.

Like Mandelbrot, Edith Piaf was displaced by World War II, although the obstacles she overcame began directly as a result of a broken family situation. She either sang on the ruined streets of working-class Paris, boarded in a brothel or traveled with a circus freak show before eventually vaulting to stardom—all as a teenager.

As No Regrets explores in detail, Piaf wrote lyrics for more than 100 songs throughout her career, including several for other singers. The artist Jean Cocteau described her as an organism of "regal simplicity." When she performed, wrote Cocteau, Piaf had "the eyes of a blind person struck by a miracle, the eyes of a clairvoyant."

Spiritually, Piaf developed into an esotericist; she was an official dues-paying Rosicrucian for many years until her death. As the book observes, the American tune "Suddenly There's a Valley," when translated for Piaf, became "Soudain une vallee," with lyrics altered to reflect a Rosicrucian perspective.

What's more, a few pages later, the book notes that following several June 1957 performances at the San Francisco Fairmont, Piaf made a spiritual pilgrimage down the highway and through the hinterland to Rosicrucian Park in San Jose, where she was welcomed by her brothers and sisters.

Reading those two biographies at the same time—one male, one female—was a transformational experience, although it will be years before I figure out what any of it means. It seemed symbolic, as in ancient alchemy or Jungian psychology, when the androgynous union of opposites—male and female, yin and yang—emerged from an initial state of chaos to symbolize a magical synthesis and a more balanced situation. In this case, San Jose is the catalyzing third element, the fortifier that causes the alchemical transformation. Voila.

iLOUNGE at the ZERO1 Garage

With "innovation" already an overused, puffed-up buzzword, it feels good to see ZERO1 introduce an artist fellowship program into the mix. I get especially confident when I read stuff like this: "A platform for artistic experimentation that recognizes the artist as the ultimate provocateur, risk-taker and source of innovation."

Since the challenges of an increasingly uncertain world demand new creative strategies, the – Garage is now partnering with the Adobe Creative Technologies Lab, the Christensen Fund and Google, each of which will sponsor a particular artist's project over the course of this year.

In each case, the project will be a collaboration, a process and/or a dialog. The circuitry connecting all of the component parts is just as important as the parts themselves. Everything is connected, with the Garage functioning as part think tank, part gallery, part psychological incubator, part policy implementer and part metaphorical server room.

It sounds like snoozy academic-speak, but this is actually a pretty radical idea. Artists are the ones running the ZERO1 Garage, which is precisely what sets it apart from the shallow "innovation" talk currently boring audiences worldwide. The Garage philosophy is that if anyone in the high-tech universe really wants to solve social and cultural problems and make the world a better place, artists need to be in the conversation, since they are the true radical experimenters and the ones most comfortable with uncertainty. It's how they intrinsically operate.

At the launch event last week, ZERO1 Garage executive director Joel Slayton articulated a vision to graft artistic creativity onto any collaboration, in any context, as a vehicle for inventing a better future landscape. Each year from now on, the Garage, along with its sponsoring partners, will define particular problems requiring radically new creative approaches and then select a number of artists to implement those approaches. The artists receive a stipend and work together with the sponsors and each other. Everything and everyone will be connected.

"Imagine what this might look like in five years," Slayton said from the podium. "We'll have a very robust network of thought leaders, practitioners and creatives, from a variety of interdisciplinary fields, so that when we use this term 'artists' we're talking about artist-technologist, artist-entrepreneur, artist-designer, artist-architect, artist-urban-planner, really, this new generation of creatives that are shaping the world. And we want the Garage to be the centerpiece in Silicon Valley where those experiments come to life."

The inaugural three ZERO1 Fellows, all three of whom are Bay Area women, then presented their prospective projects. Paula Levine, a Canadian-American artist who teaches at San Francisco State University and is supported by Google, discussed the concept of empathy in a digitally connected global world: that is, mapping everybody else's suffering onto your own situation as a vehicle for understanding. The idea stemmed from her previous work, which included grafting a map of the U.S. invasion of Baghdad onto a map of San Francisco.

Cecilia Galiena, originally from Rome, presented a more mystical approach, claiming that artists provide a fresh, alternative method of inquiry, a perspective beyond the linear, objective method of science. An artist is inseparable from the audience, she said.

Initially, Galiena will focus on how indigenous peoples, through their stories and cultures, are seeking to make intellectual property serve a function besides value appropriation. Her fellowship is thanks to the Christensen Fund, a philanthropic organization integrating the arts, biodiversity and education.

The Adobe Creative Technologies Lab (CTL) kicked in for the third artist, Daniela Steinsapir, who is now given the task of developing new approaches for cross-generational collaborative communication platforms, which could include storytelling across geographical and generational boundaries, touch-screen photo editing, language translation and other developments.

Which poses one final question: Where does art criticism function in all of this? As creative paradigms continue to evolve, so must the apparatus of critique. That is an issue no one seems willing to address yet. I predict a whole new meaning for the term Garage Critic. Get ready.

San Jose Public Library Sheet Music Collection

When David Earl McDaniel donated his massive collection of sheet music to the San Jose Public Library in 1946, the library was located at Market and San Fernando streets, where the San Jose Museum of Art now sits. At that time, McDaniel probably had no idea that the collection would still remain in that celebrated institution more than 60 years later.

These days, the California Room at the King Main Library—now located at Fourth and San Fernando streets—still owns that collection of sheet music, something like 12,000 titles. Since there's no way to possibly implement public browsing of the whole collection, one must search the catalog by title and then ask the librarian to fetch the music and bring it out.

The collection includes pop standards, old torch classics, jazz, blues, novelty songs, easy listening, show tunes and all sorts of forgotten oddities from the Great American Songbook, all thanks to McDaniel.

One of the San Jose Public Library's greatest benefactors of the 20th century, McDaniel was a legendary eccentric in these parts. An amateur poet and crooner who graduated from San Jose High in 1926, McDaniel spent his life collecting thousands of books, eventually donating all of them to various departments of the library. He died in 1977, a 70-year-old bachelor, and the books he donated had a combined worth of more than $100,000. After his passing, the library even named a community room after him, the only time they had ever done such a thing.

It gets even better. McDaniel's mammoth collection of sheet music, along with an equally insane collection of records and music books, helped justify what came to be called the Music Room at the old Market and San Fernando location, an entirely separate department with its own card catalog, which opened in 1949.

Eight years later, another massive donation showed up, this one on behalf of the widow of Dr. C.M. Richards, former leader of Elks Concert Orchestra, the main gig around here before the San Jose Symphony officially launched in 1937. Richards also conducted his own men's chorus, and the donation made by his widow included an entire catalog of men's choral music, plus a large group of opera vocal scores and miniature orchestra scores.

Most of that sheet music is still located in the California Room today. For example, one file cabinet features titles from "Emaline" to "Flower of Araby." The last title in the collection is "Zoot Suit."

Eventually, as the '60s progressed, the Music Room evolved into an unprecedented multimedia endeavor for a public library. In a library document from 1964, Peggy Kraynick, then head of the Music Room, explained the facility had "record players in four of the listening booths, a piano which may be used for one hour at a time, an old Edison cylinder machine which can be used to demonstrate early recordings, a 16mm projector and screen for library use, and two slide and filmstrip projectors. The Talking Book recordings and Projected Books on 35mm film are housed and circulated from the Music Room to blind and handicapped patrons."

Continuing, Kraynick explained that the Music Room had become a charter member of the Northern California Film Circuit in 1953 and, by

1964, had owned 100 films, all the while receiving 20 titles a month from the circuit. At that time, the department also offered 400 filmstrips for circulation, complete with guides and recordings to accompany them. Eight hundred 78s and 1,500 mono LPs made up the record collection.

"The development of the Music Room has been a combination of 'learn-as-you-go' and 'do-it-yourself' experiments," wrote Kraynick in 1964. "By observing routines in similar departments in other libraries, we have developed one of the outstanding film and record lending services in Northern California."

Thanks to those librarians, the legend lives on, at least in this columnist's head. When I slithered into the main library on San Carlos Street in 2000, in order to photocopy tunes like "Satan Takes a Holiday" and "Laugh, Clown, Laugh," I had no idea those exact pieces of sheet music were donated by McDaniel decades earlier. Just like a snake eating its own tail, everything seems to be coming full circle.

Cinequest Maverick Award Winner Chuck Palahniuk

At precisely 6:26am, on Saturday, Sept. 6, 2003, four members of the San Francisco Cacophony Society pulled up to the Park Branch Library in a pickup truck. As the vehicle came to a halt at 1833 Page St., just south of the Panhandle, a fifth member met them on foot to help unload a fake plywood wall they had spent the last two days constructing.

That weekend, Chuck Palahniuk was in San Francisco to promote his new book, Diary, and was scheduled to do a reading that night in the library's rec room, on the street level, accessible through an entrance set back from the sidewalk.

At half-past-six in the morning, however, no one was around when the Cacophonists showed up. In clandestine fashion, the quintet of pranksters unloaded the fake plywood wall and began carrying it toward the entrance of the rec-room.

Diary takes place on a fictional island to which yuppies travel to their vacation homes every summer. A building contractor named Peter lives on the island and hates the yuppies, so during the off-season he infiltrates their summer homes and walls off the doorways to particular rooms— that is, he seals off the entrances. Come summer, the yuppie vacationers return to find their bathrooms gone, their kitchens gone or their living rooms gone, because Peter has walled off the rooms.

Palahniuk was a member of the Portland chapter of the Cacophony Society and a seasoned prankster himself, so, apropos of the Diary novel, members of the local chapter decided to prank his author event by sealing off the entrance to the room so no one could get into the building.

The Cacophonists constructed the wall with precise measurements, so it fit securely in front of the rec-room doors, leaving a solid white partition flush with the building, which completely sealed off the entrance.

After securing the wall, they scurried back to the truck and hightailed it east down Page Street, in search of a cheap breakfast spot, as the autumn sun began to rise in the sky.

Unfortunately, as history tells us, not all great pranks are successful. Later that morning, as soon as library employees arrived, they took the wall down. Had the wall stayed long enough for the audience and Palahniuk to show up, the prank would have been a masterpiece—for anyone who had read the book.

Therein lay the other problem. Diary was just being released—the reason Palahniuk was touring—and even though the Cacophonists managed to obtain an advance copy, no one else, including the library employees, even knew the story yet. And because the wall was removed long before Palahniuk showed up that night, not one single person even got the joke.

Now, anyone experienced in the prankster business understands that sometimes the best pranks are the ones in which the perpetrators don't get a chance to witness the result. But in this case, since neither anyone at the library nor anyone involved with producing the event had read the book yet, none of them realized the sealed-off entrance was related to the event. As a result, the perpetrators were the only ones who even knew that a prank had been played.

On Chuck's next tour, to hype his following release, Stranger Than Fiction, he appeared in L.A. but did not come back to the Bay Area. In 2005, he did a reading at Kepler's in Menlo Park, where one of the perpetrators, yours truly, presented him with "before" and "after" photos of the rec-room entrance sealed off by the Cacophony Society, apropos of Diary. Only then did Palahniuk seem to fully appreciate the prank. He definitely had a maverick spirit.

Two years later, Palahniuk returned to the Park Branch Library, divulging to the Cacophonists that the wall still existed but was stored somewhere in the back of the place. At that time, he said he was conspiring to autograph it and ship it to a storage area, to be included with numerous other artifacts sent to him by rabid fans over the years. The rec-room entrance has long since been remodeled, preventing any such prank from happening again.

Now, in 2013, Palahniuk arrives in San Jose on Saturday for the first time, to receive a Writer Maverick Spirit Award from Cinequest in connection with the film Romance, for which he did the script, based on his short story. I can't think of a better candidate.

The Circus That Ran Away With a Jesuit Priest

In 1971, a Bellarmine graduate and Jesuit priest named Nick Weber officially launched the Royal Lichtenstein Quarter-Ring Sidewalk Circus in downtown San Jose. Over the next 20 years, the circus went on to perform more than 7,000 shows at elementary schools, high schools, universities, shopping centers, community festivals and churches.

Throughout the decades, it survived fires, blizzards, robberies and thousands of miles of traveling wear and tear. The circus was Weber's dream and his ministry, although the performers came from all points of the spiritual spectrum.

Now living in Milwaukee, Weber returns to Silicon Valley next Tuesday, March 19, appearing at East West Bookstore in Mountain View to read from his 2012 book, The Circus That Ran Away With a Jesuit Priest: Memoir of a Delible Character.

On Thursday, March 21, an special reunion performance takes place in the Fess Parker Theater at Santa Clara University, at 6:30pm, featuring special guests and including guitarist Stevie Coyle and juggler Dana Smith—both alums of SCU and the Circus.

San Jose native and SCU Bronco Kevin Curdt, who toured with the group as a juggler, unicyclist and trapeze artist, slipped me a classified document titled "An Overview of Life With the Royal Lichtenstein Circus."

Typed on circus stationery from at least 20 years ago, it says the circus, at its foundation, was "a self-consciously poetic invitation to play, wonder and imagine, realized through an energetic parade-ritual of traditional circus visions. Thus a potpourri of juggling, magic, comedy, mime, acrobatics and animal acts is seen to complement and inspire hope and quality in the day-to-day life of its spectators."

Weber's book tells his life story, from a humble youth in Yuba City to his arrival at Bellarmine in 1953 to a storied career running the circus and breathing fire. The Circus That Ran Away With a Jesuit Priest is jammed with historical tidbits form the underbelly of San Jose.

For example, Weber explains the moment when he launched the ideas that eventually turned into the circus. He stood on a box in downtown San Jose's Fountain Alley, the box lettered with "Sam's Sidewalk Show," and performed balancing acts and escape tricks for the passersby.

"Those folks who gathered were midday shoppers and retired people who lived above the downtown stores," Weber writes. "They were all guinea pigs. So was I. It was a mutual test to see whether I could hold an open-ended crowd, all by myself. I had no permit, no space reservation. Such things were unneeded in San Jose those days."

Page 128 even features a photo of Weber sitting on that box in Fountain Alley in 1971. By then, Weber had graduated from the Jesuit School of Theology at Berkeley and was teaching at St. Ignatius College Prep in San Francisco. Within a few months thereafter, other folks came on board to strengthen the crew, including a then-unknown Steve Aveson.

Now a multiple-Emmy-winning newsman, Aveson claims the Royal Lichtenstein Circus on his resume, right alongside ABC News, 20/20 and Good Morning America. Photos and vignettes of Aveson appear throughout the book.

Aside from barn-burning yarns from the traveling circus life, the book functions as a sidelight on Santa Clara Valley history, especially Chapter Five: "Stretches." Here, Weber describes in vivid detail his arrival from Yuba City and new experiences at Bellarmine High School, beginning in 1953. Full tuition, plus room and board, was $1,100 per year. There were 800 students, 200 of which were resident students. Weber describes march-stepping through a meticulous daily schedule of grooming inspection, mass, meals, room cleanups, classes and study halls, all before lights went out at 9:30pm nightly.

"I immediately sensed that I was a small-town boy," writes Weber. "The skyline of downtown San Jose was a fair distance from campus but looked immense, and the neighborhood areas stretched all the way to the edge of that skyline and in all other directions as well."

We also get curious insights into same-sex school life at Bellarmine, adolescent self-doubt, bravado and sexual experimentation. I won't spoil the action for you. In any event, Weber says his pre-circus inclinations began to materialize in the form of parlor tricks and sleight-of-hand games: "It took no time at all to find a magic store downtown on First Street where I spent $1.25 of my allowance for 'The Siberian Chain Escape,'" he writes.

Start Up San Jose

For decades, what seems like the entire human race has complained about empty buildings in downtown San Jose. Many people move to or pass through the neighborhood, only to experience frustration, sadness and other psychological effects of perpetually vacant storefronts.

Every building seems empty for a different reason, which creates what I call an ecosystem of emptiness. Aside from turning fascist and regulating private property, there seems to be no way out.

But now, an idea new to San Jose has emerged: temporary pop-up retail. In our case, it might be more appropriate to call it guerrilla startup retail.

Expanding on ideas from other cities that converted empty storefronts to temporary retail spots for a weekend, San Jose City Councilmember Sam Liccardo has spearheaded and triple-tagteamed with San Jose Made and NextSpace Coworking to create Start Up Shop, a two-day pop-up installation at the Legacy Civic Tower at Second and Santa Clara streets, as part of an initiative to get property owners to drop their per-square-foot leases in exchange for permit waivers.

The 5,000-square-foot space at 75 E. Santa Clara, an abandoned corporate foyer of sorts, has been empty for many moons. Now that will change, albeit for just two days.

It's a rocking idea. Already a player in the co-working phenom, NextSpace provides physical spaces for mobile workers, laptop nomads, tiny startup teams or anyone else in a nonmonogamous relationship with his or her office. Likewise, San Jose Made already stages alternative vendor fairs featuring local creative retailers and indie businesses.

That said, on Thursday and Friday, March 21 and 22, NextSpace Co-working will migrate its operation to the space in the daytime. San Jose Made will take over at nighttime, staging a vendor fair. It's a groovy combination. We can even call it the NextSanJoseMadeSpace.

Marie Millares, one of the founders of San Jose Made, said Liccardo reached out and got the ball rolling. It came from nowhere.

"Sam emailed us and said, 'How do you feel about helping District Three put together pop-up shops in empty buildings, empty storefront locations downtown?'" Marie recalled. "I was like. 'Yeah, when do we start?' This is what San Jose Made is already trying to do, so it was great to see District Three trying to procure the space for us. ... We were ready to do it. The second someone like a councilman comes in and says, 'Let's do it together,' it's music to our ears."

Gretchen Baisa, director of business development at NextSpace, alerted her network and put the word out. Those who normally work in a coffee shop or at home can participate for two days, even if they just want to look cool checking their Facebook at Second and Santa Clara.

"It's like a field trip for my members," Gretchen said. "Whoever has a laptop and wants to come down and get some work done, they can either do it in their silo and work silently, off to the side, or they can get into it and collaborate and talk to their fellow people and hash out the best solution for their business."

While Start Up Shop is not a profound transformation that seismically alters the cultural landscape, it's a collaboration that would not have occurred two years ago. Plus, it's a great way to activate a boring, empty space, and it makes the neighborhood a better area to look at.

"The thought that five or 10 years ago, a councilmember would take a risk with a vacant space like this, wouldn't even have entered my mind," Gretchen said. "It's great to see the attitudes shifting to where we can have pop-up anything."

Marie agreed: "I think we should keep going with it. I don't think it should just involve San Jose Made. [Liccardo] should involve other groups who can change the model. I think it should be amorphous, the model for it. He should find building owners who are willing to share the space for a few days and see how the model changes, and not just be one partnership. That way the model grows quicker."

As the one who spearheaded the initiative, Liccardo will host the event, including the wrap-up party on Friday night.

Cathleen Miller: Champion of Choice

San Jose State University professor Cathleen Miller spent 10 years crisscrossing the globe to write Champion of Choice, her 500-page biography of women's advocate Nafis Sadik, and lived to tell about it.

In fact, "crisscrossing" doesn't even do Miller justice. Her path more resembled a 3D model of string art, navigating impoverished slum after slum, from the Third World to the First, and back again—all to chronicle Sadik's career as one of the 20th century's most powerful and tireless warriors for women's rights. As a work of dramatic nonfiction narrative, Champion of Choice is extensive, but accessible for everyone. Miller will talk about the book at SJSU on April 24.

For the uninitiated, Sadik, a nationalized Pakistani born in India in 1929, developed ambitions at an early age to become a diplomat and help victimized women all over the world. An obstetrician, she eventually took a post at the fledgling United Nations Population Fund in 1971, when the average global birthrate was six children per mother. By the time of her professional retirement in 2000, the average birthrate had been cut in half.

To date, her life's work as a doctor, educator and diplomat has provided women around the globe with the education and tools to control their own fertility. Her work has improved the lives of millions of women and infuriated the Vatican as a result.

In the book, Miller does not just write Sadik's story alone. That would have been too simple. Instead, she juxtaposes Sadik's career with vignettes from the trenches of female victimization in order to reveal examples of the very injustices that Sadik fights against.

She weaves in a tale from Ethiopia, for instance, where small, poverty-stricken girls are forced into pregnancy as early as 14, resulting in the gruesome circumstances of obstetric fistula. In another scene, she visits a hospital in Pakistan to interview a woman whose husband insisted on a sixth pregnancy solely because her first five were daughters.

At first, the United Nations actually asked Miller to write the book, since her previous work, Desert Flower, told the story of Somali activist Waris Dirie's worldwide plight to end female genital mutilation. The book was later adapted as a feature film and released in 34 countries, including a U.S. premiere at Cinequest in 2011.

The book sold 11 million copies in 55 languages and has played a major role in outlawing genital mutilation worldwide. It accomplished more than any group of politicians or diplomats could possibly have done.

Now, with the release of Champion of Choice, Miller says that interviewing Sadik, spending hours with her and examining her career was like getting a Ph.D. in leadership and diplomacy. In writing the book, Miller says she wanted to make sure she told the how-to and step-by-step details of how Sadik did what she did—not just what Sadik accomplished, but how she accomplished it. Thus the book also functions as a how-to manual for women who want to change history, a primer for how to raise your daughter to be a world leader.

"How many women get a chance to study with a mentor like Nafis?" Miller asked. "Not that many men have that opportunity either, but I've spent years watching this woman, meeting her, talking to her, analyzing her career under a microscope, and I wanted to pass along to women everything I've learned. That's one of the main reasons people read biography—especially biographies of successful people—to be on the fast track. We want to figure out how they did it."

For the free event on April 24, Miller says she will reveal lurid details about what's not in the book. Attendees will get behind-the-scenes vignettes about what she actually went through for 10 years. After all, the story of what happens in the author's life while writing the book is often more colorful than the published material anyway.

"I'm going to tell some funny stories about what I call the book behind the book," Miller explains. "This is a book that my friends encouraged me to write for years. ... And for years, I've been telling my friends these stories about what was happening with me while I was out there doing research on this book."

Art Boutiki Reopens

Just in time for Free Comic Book Day, one of San Jose's legendary underground bastions of zonked-out jazz, Tiki culture and graphic-novel insanity shall revive itself anew on Race Street, just off The Alameda. The circus begins this Saturday afternoon.

For a decade or more, Slave Labor Graphics (SLG) and its own Siamese Twin (a la Basket Case), Art Boutiki, operated on Market Street near Metro's offices, providing lounge lizards and comics aficionados a warehouse space in which to slither around and soak it all in.

The publishing company operated out of the warehouse, while the bands gigged on a temporary stage in the back. The gallery doubled as a retail store where said lizards could skulk around and peruse a plethora of kooky comics, plus T-shirts and other souvenirs.

At that building, Slave Labor also staged workshops, mini-flea markets and numerous other sordid affairs for discerning connoisseurs of high camp. The joint was a fixture during South First Fridays, and they even sold hockey jerseys with logos from the old Flying Pig Pub on First Street. If that's not local flavor, I don't know what is.

Now, at a prime, gritty new locale at 44 Race St., at The Alameda, SLG Art Boutiki just might possibly help anchor a new idea—that is, a reconsidered stretch of road. Two years ago, in this space, the anti-man-about-town philosophized that, with the arrival of boutiques like the Usuals as well as Black and Brown, an awesome new rebirth of that ignored thoroughfare was about to begin—that a tiny new appendage of artsy Bohemia could be in the works. Of course, he was not the only one to make this observation. It turned out quite a few others had similar visions in mind.

The Art Boutiki, in its new space, will help move that idea forward. We hope. With that perspective in mind, the anti-man-about-town creeped into the new spot last week to bask in the dust and pizza boxes while honcho Dan Vado, et al., were building the place out. His yellow Labrador, Homer, ~~jumped~~ leaped about, greeting whoever decided to ~~show up~~ announced.

As Vado walked me through the 7,000-square-foot facility, it became apparent that the building is a much better space than the previous ramshackle establishment on First Street. There is more retail area in the front, a much larger space for the gigs in the middle and gargantuan amounts of office and storage space.

In the middle space, everything was still being constructed. Various couches lay strewn about, vinyl LPs were stacked in boxes, pieces of microphone stands and amplifiers occupied various sections of the floor, and the portable stage was folded up. Plastic containers overflowed with Star Wars toys; oddball Tiki sculptures appeared in various stages of functionality; the back wall was freshly painted with the SLG Art Boutiki logo; and bamboo siding hung in front of another wall.

Miscellaneous potted plants, jars of spackling and gloriously unmatched sets of chairs sat around, as if waiting for a party. A tuned piano held its own in one corner, while a scissor lift seemed ready for action on the other side of the room.

Natural light streamed in from the roll-up door, which also allowed traffic noise from Race Street to filter through. The anti-man-about-town felt excited to see the guts of a new place from the ground up. Contemplating the entire stretch of The Alameda, one can easily envision a new Whole Foods, post-arena-artsy-madness-turned-San-Jose-Made-Boutiki, vintage clothing and comic subculture stew beginning to cook on the burner.

Vado says that unlike before, the publishing company can operate separately from the band space and vice versa. The footprint of the building facilitates his operations much better.

"Before, the bands would be in our order department. Now they can store their stuff in the back, and it's locked up. Everything is more compartmentalized. People who frequented our space will be happy to know that there are now two restrooms instead of one."

All in all, Tiki now reigns free on Race Street. Take your maroon fez and your soft blue blazer out of the closet and slither on over.

"It's Tiki but not tacky," Vado says. "We're trying for a Polynesian theme, but not to where it's overwhelming everything in the store, the stage and everything."

Nolan Bushnell: Finding the Next Steve Jobs

Nolan Bushnell and ZERO1 are putting the "rad" back in radical. So much so that Bushnell has now written a user's guide for conventional Silicon Valley managers hopelessly trying to operate in a rigid and hierarchical structure without creativity.

Published via NetMinds, a service empowering authors to publish smarter by building invested, quality teams around their books, Finding the Next Steve Jobs is a glorious, unapologetic paean to creativity and eccentricity in the workplace. It posits creativity as the most important factor in the future success of every business.

On Wednesday, May 15, Bushnell will invade the ZERO1 compound in San Jose to present his book and instruct companies on how to find, nurture and deal with creative types, in order to ensure their longevity in the ever-accelerating 21st-century business landscape.

ZERO1 makes a perfect partner, because it advocates a similar strategy. That is, if businesses are to keep up with the rapidly changing times, radical experimentation and risk-taking are necessary, and since artists are natural-born radical experimenters, their ingredients need to be incorporated into the company stew.

Bushnell, who founded Atari and Chuck E. Cheese's Pizza Time Theatre right here in suburbia decades ago, pretty much defined what it now means to be an eccentric Silicon Valley visionary. Like any creative genius, he didn't cook up a Michelin three-star meal every single time and he didn't hit a home run every at-bat, but he has first-hand knowledge about what made Steve Jobs unique, from when Jobs was a unwashed hippie working for Bushnell at Atari.

Thankfully, Finding the Next Steve Jobs does not insult the reader with belligerent dogma on how to discover unique creative talent. According to Bushnell, rules tend to ruin everything, so, instead, the book presents a series of pongs.

Unlike rules, which foolishly assume they can work for everybody everywhere, pongs apply only where the advice is helpful or needed. Instead of chapters, the book contains 53 pongs—hints toward finding and cultivating creative weirdos.

"Creativity is every company's first driver," writes Bushnell in pong #0, the introduction. "It's where everything starts, where energy and forward motion originate. Without that first charge of creativity, nothing else can take place." And then: "Openness to creativity must be present at all levels of your company. Creativity doesn't reside in one person, or even a few people. It must be planted throughout the entire company, or it won't bloom anywhere."

From there, the pongs illuminate several ideas, many of which will be second nature if you're already a polarized, right-side-of-the-brain creative type. But since most businesses are structured around rigid, hierarchical, top-down bureaucracies inimical to creativity, those businesses, if they really want the next Steve Jobs, will find the book invaluable. It's completely unlike the pedantic business-guru dreck one usually encounters.

Want to find unique creative talent? Well, Bushnell says, go to Burning Man, which he calls "an employment center disguised as a festival." Hang out at the swimming pool after the trade shows. Seek out the lurkers. When interviewing people, give them problems to solve, find out how curious they are and what books they read.

Seek out the obnoxious, the crazy, the smelly and the isolated. Never hire anyone just on his or her credentials alone. In other words, avoid the clones, the poseurs and the folks who flaunt their resumes and shine during interviews, but who can't actually do anything. At the least, test them on their curiosity and resourcefulness. Give them weird shit to figure out.

"I know of no creative who is not hypercurious," writes Bushnell. "Curious people always have a range of interests and a broad base of knowledge in many disparate fields and subjects. This trait has nothing to do with college. It has everything to do with innate intelligence."

Most of all, it isn't enough to find the next Steve Jobses and hire him, says Bushnell. You have to create a situation in which they can flourish, and then your company will too.

Tea and Synchronicity

Tea is the world's most common beverage after water. Throughout the world, 15,000 cups of tea are consumed every second. On a recent trip to Montreal, it felt like every single one of those cups was following me.

Just seconds after confessing to my hosts the muselike nature of tea in my San Jose life, and that I'd like to visit some tea-related places while in Montreal, we walked up the steps, toward the side entrance of Pointe-a-Calliere, in order to dine in the restaurant upstairs. Then, as soon as we crossed the threshold—bang!—a tea poster appeared on the wall in front of us: a shining synchronicity.

Turns out "Les Routes du the," an exhibit at Pointe-a-Calliere, explores the entire history of tea. My hosts did not originally know of my intentions to explore tea in Montreal, and I didn't know the exhibit was even happening. Synchronicities of this nature often occur when I travel (I've written about them in this space quite a few times over the years), and they usually indicate a heightened sense of creative awareness.

The tea muse was with me. I could tell because the first text panel in the exhibit finished with this: "Poetry, sophistication, and an abiding love of tea await you at every step along the way. Welcome!"

What a welcome, I thought, as I read the first panel. I was not expecting this. I saw displays and artifacts, and I read explications of tea routes throughout the Old World, plus histories of various tea methods and prominent events.

Luminous video projections constantly changed across cloth tapestries. In one area, a circular display of 12 different jars of loose-leaf tea, each with a large red button, presented themselves for sampling. All one had to do is push the button, which opened a vent and released the aroma, straight from the jar.

The Chinese character for tea also figured prominently in the exhibit; it was plastered on 10-foot-high tapestries. I read about its history. In the third century B.C.E., it was pronounced "tu," referring to a bitter herb. A later emperor ordered that the character, when referring to tea, should be pronounced "cha."

Other sections of the show documented the role of tea in Buddhism, the Victorian era and the rise of the U.S. colonies. The history of the world is the history of tea itself, it appeared.

Basically, my readers have Satori Tea Company in San Jose to blame for all of this. As a kid, I missed out on my East Indian roots, so that shop has introduced me to the lost Eastern half of myself, in a gloriously imaginative way. Full disclosure: they're friends, but technically, it's a tea bar, so the anti-man-about-town came up with his own monikers for their blends.

Ginger Citrus Guayusa is the "Hallucinogenic Rainforest Blend." I call their Vata Tea the "Elixir for a Destroyed Nervous System." I re-christened Blood Orange Rooibos as the "Alternative Antihistamine," and Ginger Pu'erh is now the "Doctor of Digestion" because it helps me digest the entire universe. Apropos of this column, I call the place, Macaron Alley.

Back in Montreal, another synchronicity unfolded at Birk's Cafe par Europea, located in Square Phillips. My Montreal pals had no idea I was interested in tea, yet Birk's, a place they were already planning on taking me to, was one of the most popular spots for high tea and macarons in the whole city.

Their blend, The sur le Nil, evoked intrigues from the Alexandria Quartet by Lawrence Durrell. I felt transported to 1940s Egypt, where "in my mind's eye the city rose against the flat mirror of the green lake and the broken loins of sandstone marked the desert's edge."

They served it to me in a heavy cast-iron teapot, austere and ritualistic in its half-Eastern, half-Western presence, so I channeled the Alexandria Quartet's plots and counterplots right there at the table.

It's the tea that seemed to conjure up these visions. The muse was doing things with me that I could not control, but the synchronicities were happy ones. I didn't go looking for the roads of tea. They found me instead.

A collective muse of 15,000 interconnected cups of tea watches over me. Every second.

Bodypainter Trina Merry

When a rock band asked her to jump onstage in her underwear and get bodypainted, Trina Merry had no idea it would lead to an international career. That was 2006, only seven years ago. A few years later, she arrived at the SubZERO Festival in downtown San Jose, and her career as a bodypainter was off and running.

A textbook example of someone who started locally and now exhibits internationally, Merry paints on human canvases for commercial clients and advertising campaigns. She builds gallery installations and motorcycles out of painted people. What a life.

She says anywhere between three to 15 people a day call her up and ask to be models. Whenever she travels, she puts out casting calls, and people come running, dying to get painted. Sometimes she doesn't even have to pay the models.

"Often people pay me to paint them—a lot of money," she told me. "I get paid to paint naked people for a living."

Again, all of this crystallized at the SubZERO Festival in San Jose, the 2013 version of which just went down last week. SubZERO, by now, is one of the most anticipated events of the year, drawing thousands of folks to a few blocks of South First Street for a European-style counterculture extravaganza of music on outdoor stages, avant-garde creativity, street performances, dancing, vendors, maker-fairing, fire-breathing, beer-tasting, high-tech, lo-tech and overall multidisciplinary circuslike atmospherics. If you haven't heard of it by now—well, you're living in a cave.

Last week, for example, Merry interpreted the Trevi Fountain in Rome on South First Street for the festival. The goddess of abundance was, well, abundant. People walked up and took pictures all night long.

Interestingly enough, in all the years of painting naked people, Merry said she is not a superhedonist like other bodypainters in the business. Art is the inspiration, above all else.

"What motivates other people to paint naked people for a living—other bodypainters that I know professionally—does not motivate me," she declared. "When I see a person that's naked or in clothes, I just see a person."

As we sat there in a coffee shop, I asked what has surprised her the most in her career to this point. What's been the shocker so far?

"What surprises me is the intimate spiritual nature of what I do," she replied. "Because you're so connecting with a person when you make art with them, in that type of environment. That's been the most surprising. And the public's reaction, internationally, virally. I've been on television, around the world, all of a sudden, in a short amount of time. That's something I'm not sure what to do with."

Now that SubZERO is over, Merry heads down south to El Segundo for a show this Saturday at ESMoA. She will construct a mock Martha Stewart country cottage with a human lamp stand, human ironing board, human coffee table and vase, plus a Tiki Room-style man cave with a human tiki statue and a bar with a live painted model pouring foo-foo drinks.

There will also be an urban condo with a human lamp stand, a two-human coffee table and a human couch, as well as a human chair that will form and reform every hour for a performance artist to sit on and relax. Outside the gallery, Merry will park an RV with a painted model camouflaged into a lawn chair and another camouflaged into the vehicle's dining-room furniture.

Every person will wear Merry's paint or that of her crewmembers. That's right, she has a crew. Hell, she may even start a franchise someday. Can you imagine? We would be the bodypainting capital of Silicon Valley.

"Our team is a really big anomaly," Merry said. "Most bodypainters don't have a team. It's just them. I work with a huge-ass team. Our casting crew is anywhere from 50 to 75 people right now—painters and models. As painters, I probably have a dozen good assistants."

Legendary Stones Manager Sam Cutler at Studio Bongiorno

Upon crossing the threshold at Studio-Bongiorno at Bellomy and Lincoln streets, a soft Santa Clara breeze follows me in. Eclectic artwork hangs on the wall. Vintage rocking chairs sit idle. Homemade candles offer themselves at various prices.

The coffee bar, surrounded by more artwork, sits behind the original teller window from San Jose's Bank of Italy Building. Classic rock blares from the stereo. Custom soaps and postcards occupy spinning circular wire racks.

Phil Bongiorno operates the joint, housed in the building formerly occupied by the California Monument Company, which manufactured headstones for the graveyard across the street. In fact, shattered granite remains of cemetery statuettes, grave-marker stencils and slabs of marble remain in the storage yard outside, along with slews of rusty paint cans from decades gone by.

Eventually, Bongiorno shepherds me into the courtyard area, where I gaze at another homemade bar, replete with wine, antiques, rusted artifacts and various donated materials from friends, artists and other eccentrics.

Across the yard, I can see more gallery space, another few rooms and still more donated materials, including a killer spinet piano. People just seem to bequeath their unwanted furniture and ephemera to Studio-Bongiorno, hoping it will add to the creative and beautifully junky atmospherics of this wonderful place.

"Random stuff shows up daily," Bongiorno tells me. "People dig the energy, and they just give me stuff, everything from handbags to watches to sheet music."

Bongiorno himself creates works out of found materials. If someone donates a rusty old stovepipe, well, it just may wind up in one of his collages.

"I'm getting a little Sanford and Son-esque with all the junk, but if something talks to me in a way, I can make art with it."

Hearing Bongiorno say that immediately brings the Sanford and Son theme into my head, and the only missing component is Chico the goat wandering over from next door. Studio-Bongiorno has that kind of effect. It's like an antique shop, a gallery space, a meeting spot for creative outcasts and a systemic recycling potlatch all in the same gorgeously ramshackle habitat. It's exactly what San Jose's art scene is desperately missing, to be honest. Good on Santa Clara.

Art shows take place each month, many of which feature artists exhibiting for the very first time, although the work is not junk in the least bit. There's obviously a degree of curatorial standards employed. Last month, for example, the highest amount a work fetched was $1,200. So far this month, says Bongiorno, that number is $675.

And there's more. Since the courtyard area holds about 50 to 75 people, Bongiorno stages numerous events between art openings, including a blockbuster hoedown set to erupt on Saturday, July 6.

Sam Cutler, former tour manager for the Rolling Stones and the Grateful Dead, will stop by to talk about his 2010 book, You Can't Always Get What You Want: My Life With the Rolling Stones, the Grateful Dead and Other Wonderful Reprobates. Cutler is in the United States for the first time in many years, and the stories will undoubtedly please any rock & roll fan.

Cutler, of course, is the dude most often demonized in the American media for the 1969 fiasco at the Altamont festival, where the Stones played their legendary free concert that resulted in the death of an audience member at the hands of a Hells Angel.

I have only read parts of the book, but Cutler does present his side of the sordid details. In one case, he relates a conversation with Jerry Garcia soon afterward; Garcia told him that none of the Hells Angels Garcia knew in San Francisco were involved with the violence. Instead, those responsible were outsider rural rubes with no connection to the Bay Area, who came just to beat the crap out of the hippies they despised. They came from San Jose, San Bernardino and Fresno, Garcia told him.

There you have it. Eclectic artwork, soap, incense, coffee, tea, booze, rusty stoves, clown paintings, aging rock legends and a great piano that's even in tune. Inspired by it all, I found myself playing Stones tunes without even trying.

School of Arts and Culture at MHP

As of right now, the School of Arts and Culture at Mexican Heritage Plaza celebrates two years of transformation on multiple levels. In 2011, after numerous phases of failure, the beleaguered plaza emerged anew when the school took it over.

Within the first year, the facility attracted thousands more kids and adults than when the City of San Jose operated the place. Now, after two years, the place exudes a sense of activity it never did before, with parents from throughout the valley sending their kids to learn music notation, dance, arts, creativity and critical thinking skills. What's more, the school's success and image has at least partly inspired the surrounding communities to ratchet up pressure on speeding, graffiti and the neglectful landlord who owns the blighted stripmall across the street.

Last week, executive director Tamara Alvarado led me in and out of classrooms and around the entire plaza, as she articulated the school's position. Especially now during summer, 1,200 children attend classes each week. Kids are the future and if we can inspire them artistically, as early as age five, they might not segue down more dangerous paths in life.

"The number one asset of the community is kids," Alvarado said. "We have to invest in their creativity and their critical thinking skills. We have to have safety in mind here, especially in this community."

As we traversed the property, Alvarado took me into several rooms to oversee, er, interrupt classes in progress. In one case, kids used papier mache and methods of Tlacuilo drawing, the pictorial language of the Aztec codices. Another room featured hip-hop dance. We randomly encountered guitar teachers and dance instructors. In another instance, Alvarado dragged me into Nauhxa Chavira's Aztec dancing class for kids aged 8-10.

"This is not glitter and glue and construction paper," Alvarado said. "This is serious arts education."

Perhaps most importantly, the plaza is a safe place to hang out. Parents are comfortable dropping off their kids. Except for myself, no suspicious characters lurked anywhere.

"It's a hundred thousand square feet of safe," Alvarado told me, as we continued walking. "With all the stuff happening these days, what parents want to know, first and foremost, is that you're safe. Until you're safe, you can't study, you can't learn how to dance, you can't learn how to think. [At the plaza], as soon as you walk in, someone's there asking who you are. But it's also welcoming."

This is true. When I first creeped into the facility, gracious employees asked my purpose for visiting. They gave me water with chia seeds, stating that the ancient Aztecs drank the concoction for energy. As I moved into the theater lobby, teenaged interns were busy sorting out School of Arts and Culture t-shirts. They were former students who had since moved up to T.A. positions. Overall, the vibe far transcended the hicktown politics I experienced at the plaza many years ago.

Under the previous reign, something exciting would unfold at the plaza, a show, company or workshop, but without remaining long-term. It seemed like short flings were the norm. Now things are different, as Alvarado has helped cement long-term relationships with several institutions. Arts organizations no longer show up as they see fit, treating the venue as if it were just a convenience. Permanent multiple partners include Opera Cultura, Future Arts Now and Mariachi Azteca, with more on the way.

All one has to do is hop across the street to see the effect in the neighborhood. The empty stripmall, a shining example of landlord neglect, sits along the northern side of Alum Rock, but is now finally cited with code violations. Fenced off, it appears ready for facade improvements. The plaza's now-constant activity and its focus on youth education have clearly increased the community's awareness and helped put pressure on powers-that-be.

"We're taking care of business," Alvarado said. "What we stand for is arts and culture. We don't stand for any of this other mess. We don't stand for violence and we don't stand for blight. We're noticing those things and we're saying, 'This isn't right.'"

Rahsaan Roland Kirk Tribute at Cafe Stritch

With the San Jose Jazz Summer Fest upon us, one particular unofficial microcosm will evince a mystical convergence of space-time continuum-shattering trajectories, all settling into play around Cafe Stritch in downtown San Jose.

Throughout the entire weekend, beginning as early as Wednesday, Aug. 7, Stritch will present a Rahsaan Roland Kirk Tribute Week, celebrating the legendary multi-instrumentalist's birthday. The celebration includes No Walls Between Us, a fantastic show of historical jazz photographs by Kathy Sloane, whose recent book, Keystone Korner: Portrait of a Jazz Club, documented her time hanging out in that legendary San Francisco joint during the 1970s. Kirk figures prominently in the book. All photos, as well as copies of the book, will be for sale, and Sloane will be present during the reception, Saturday, Aug. 10, 3-6pm. One of Kirk's collaborators decades ago, Steve Turre, will also perform two sets at Stritch Thursday through Saturday, beginning at 8pm.

That's only one aspect of the experience, one current-era slice of evidence from a multidimensional web. Since history is never linear anyway, allow me to point out that Cafe Stritch, formerly the Eulipia Restaurant, is already steeped in Kirk lore—the owners consider Kirk to be their in-house patron saint—and the connections unfold on multiple levels. Stritch takes its name from Kirk's trademark saxophone, and the place already features a mural of him on the left wall, right inside the door. The Borkenhagens first opened their restaurant Eulipia in 1977, in this same building, naming it after Kirk's, "Theme for the Eulipions." According to the owners, the spirit of Rahsaan has always lingered, especially now that a complete reinvention of their business has emerged. When Turre sets up shop this week, Betty Neals even will sit in for "Theme for the Eulipions."

Upstairs in the secret offices at Cafe Stritch, Max Borkenhagen, son of original owner Steve, articulated a quantum field of jazz trajectories and improvised history, all of which he says will swirl together like a fine cappuccino this week. As we yakked, a copy of Sloane's book occupied a music stand next to me. It seemed alive, as did a copy of Kirk's LP, The Return of the 5000 Lb. Man—the one with "Theme for the Eulipions"—sitting on Borkenhagen's desk. Since our local jazz festival is no longer a suburban commuter event, since many components of it are now integrated into the local independent business landscape, with patrons lingering around into nighttime, Borkenhagen said his hopes were high.

"Eulipia, when my parents opened it in 1977, was very similar to what we're doing now," he explained. "It was more of a cafe, a gallery, a dynamic sort of art-bohemian space. Bringing together all this history, this week, is sort of magical for us. This place began as just one idea my parents had and now there's a connection between Rahsaan, who's sort of our patron saint, and the art and music cultures of this neighborhood. And it just happens that his birthday is the same week as the jazz festival."

Kathy Sloane, whose atmospheric photos now grace all the walls of Stritch, both downstairs and upstairs, provides yet another human dimension to the quantum field revealing itself this weekend. Both she and her photos are living connections to the legacy that jazzmen like Rahsaan Roland Kirk forged, especially in regards to the civil rights movement.

"What struck me as soon as I first walked into Keystone Korner, was that this was a metaphor for the civil rights movement," Sloane told me. "It was another way of talking about freedom. I was really struck by that, and interested in learning more about the people who were making this music, where the music came from, what their lives were like trying to play this music in a not-so-welcoming environment. The jazz life is an improvised life. It's a difficult one. They don't get treated like symphony musicians."

227

For Rahsaan's birthday week celebration, guests will awaken to an interconnected multi-dimensional web of history, as only Cafe Stritch can provide. What makes any great festival is all the specific subcultures, microcosms and utopias (Eulipias) within the larger festival itself. Thanks to the patron sainthood of Rahsaan Roland Kirk, we have a perfect example.

Art Boxes in Edmonton Inspire San Jose

When I first found myself in Edmonton's Old Strathcona neighborhood three years ago, I immediately noticed the orchestrated system of 40 murals painted on utility boxes all over the area.

Painted by various artists, all of the murals seemed to reference the local community, its businesses, workers and architecture. It was clearly a comprehensive effort by many facets of civilization, and given Old Strathcona's historical yet edgy vibe, its gorgeous combination of urban underbelly, independent retail and progressive arts infrastructure, the murals fit in perfectly.

It was then that I posted shots of the utility boxes on Facebook, whining that nobody in backwater San Jose would even appreciate such an idea, yet alone try to make it happen here. Tina Morrill then apparently vamped on my negative energy and spearheaded the Art Box Project that now includes painted utility boxes all over San Jose. I am never more proud to have been more completely full of shit than when I look at those boxes around town.

As a matter of fact, when I found myself in Edmonton again last weekend, I took it upon myself to prowl around Old Strathcona. This time, I managed to corral Edmonton Historian Laureate Shirley Lowe into a coffee shop for a chat. It was she who originally led that neighborhood's effort to paint the utility boxes in the first place. Over green tea, Lowe explained how so many facets of society came together to make it happen.

For example, through a program called Community Connections, a group of five at-risk youths were rescued from dead-end environments and then employed to help design and implement the entire program. The kids measured the utility boxes to determine how much paint and supplies were needed. They recruited the artists, judged the artwork, solicited donations, and coordinated and scheduled the boxes to be painted. All of which taught them life skills they had never learned before.

"These were high-risk kids," Lowe explains. "They had no social skills. What they learned was how to organize a project, beginning to end. They had to put together a work plan, and we supervised them. Step one was to go out and find the boxes and measure them for paint, and a local store, the Paint Spot, figured out how much paint was needed and gave us the paint at wholesale prices. One of the paint companies donated the primer. The kids were in charge of finding the artists. We made it their project."

The city's job was the designate which boxes could indeed be used for the project, and then to clean them up. They also provided a few thousand dollars, with the community helping to raise additional funds. The Canadian government even supported the kids' time and participation through its Youth Employment Program.

The murals emerged in 2004 to celebrate Edmonton's 100th anniversary. Old Strathcona itself was originally a separate town before eventually amalgamating with Edmonton in 1912. To this day, Whyte Avenue is the main drag, filled with independent businesses, funky antique shops, tattoo parlors, piercing establishments, alleys, buskers, and eclectic retail—Edmonton's urban corridor for the idiosyncratic, its anti-Rodeo Drive. Several locals told me it's the only interesting area anywhere in Edmonton.

Also the home turf of the Edmonton International Fringe Theater Festival, Old Scona, as the locals call it, is a shining example of what can happen when a community comes together to save old buildings, preserve historical character, fight off belligerent urban planners and celebrate its edginess. Thirty years ago, for example, the citizens banded together to stop a hideous concrete freeway from blazing through the neighborhood, which would have destroyed many of the historical buildings.

From almost that same scenario 30 years ago, the Fringe Festival emerged, artists moved in and now, even though rents are rising, the Edmonton Fringe is the biggest one in North America. The arts community thrives here. The painted utility boxes remain just one part of the landscape. Colored brochures are even available, directing one to scour the alleys, corners and alcoves to look at every single mural. To me, the painted boxes seem like old pals.

MLK Library Time Capsule

As of right now, the current incarnation of the Martin Luther King, Jr. Main Library celebrates its 10th anniversary. The kick-off festivities begin at 11am on Sept. 5, with a remarkable event. San Jose Mayor Chuck Reed and San Jose State University President Mohammad Qayoumi will unveil the contents of a time capsule buried at the old King Library, on San Carlos Street, when that building opened in 1970.

Since the cycle of creation and destruction involved here borders on Eastern mysticism, allow me to explain: The time capsule was originally buried somewhere in front of the old MLK building, but in a quintessential San Jose maneuver, the capsule was accidentally dug up in 1987 when San Carlos was widened for the light rail. At that time, the capsule was resealed behind a plaque on the front wall of the building, facing the sidewalk. When the building was finally destroyed in 2011, the capsule was saved and transported to the new MLK Library, at Fourth and San Fernando, now celebrating a well-deserved 10th birthday.

Combining a public library with a university library was not a popular idea at first. It irked quite a few stodgy academics. They complained that a university library does not belong to the same caste as a lowly public library. The two should not be allowed to mix. That was the complaint. Obviously, at least to me, the critics were proven wrong. With the immense popularity of the place nowadays, no one can argue against the current reincarnation.

I say "reincarnation" because after all the celebrations conclude, the current era represents merely the next stage in a long cycle of library death and rebirth unique to San Jose. Since I grew up and evolved in and out of these libraries, I harbor an admittedly strange connection to the cycles of creation and destruction at play here. Which is why it's healthy to meditate on the impermanence of everything.

During the decades before the San Carlos Street location emerged, the San Jose main library was located in the old part of the building now housing the San Jose Museum of Art. My mom, a lifelong librarian, worked in that building during the 1960s. The new Main Branch debuted in 1970 on San Carlos Street, and throughout most of the next 20 years, before the next reincarnation of the convention center came along, Almaden Expressway ran all the way from Blossom Hill to Downtown, before it turned into a regular street, South Almaden Ave., and then barreled into the back of the library. From the back, one could drive right around the library to San Carlos. Nowadays, what's left of that tiny incarnation of Almaden Ave. ends behind the convention center. As a kid before Highway 87 existed, I remember riding with my mom all the way up that road, from South San Jose, in order to get to the main library. As early as age 7, I hung out in that building.

Years later, over at SJSU, two particular libraries ruled the campus: 1) the Clark Library, where I suffered through a miserable student-assistant job shelving books while hung over, and 2) the old crumbling Wahlquist Library at 4th and San Fernando. The Wahlquist Library adjoined another crumbling building that housed the financial operations of the entire university—the controller's office, payroll, accounts receivable and all that left-brain stuff. During my last year in college, I suffered through a god-awful PC tech support job in those offices. It was likewise miserable. Then, in 2003, a few years after the crumbling Wahlquist Library was demolished, the current MLK Library ushered in a new era, merging all three—the Clark, Wahlquist and former MLK libraries—each one including a piece of my own history. I felt a strange sense of poetic renewal. There's an ancient term for this: Samsara, the continuing cycles of rebirth and suffering. In fact, my whole life story seems intertwined with the endless cycles of library creation and destruction in this town, all the way through college. When I finally depart this place, I shall request my remains be placed in a time capsule, along with this column, and then buried underneath the library, to be accidentally dug up for the next cycle.

Barron Storey Presents 'Suicide'

Inside Anno Domini, the gallery already boasting one of those ominous Latin monikers, Barron Storey tells me that suicide is not a great way to promote an art show. The show is ugly, he says. Just ugly.

In Storey's case, he lost his mother, uncle, ex-wife and best friend, all to suicide. The details are too deep to include here, but as Storey began work on a graphic novel to explore his uncle's suicide, the same uncle Storey idolized as a kid, the process involved interviewing many friends who themselves had known someone that committed suicide. So Storey drew the illustrations and integrated the text in his trademark fashion. What now unfolds on the wall at Anno Domini reads like a graphic novel, depicting people who took their own lives, including quotes, lurid details, imagery, facts, figures and contemplation. One portion of the show deals with the four previously mentioned people closest to him, while the rest of the work represents the results of those he interviewed. Nothing in the show is pretty; it's a Goya-esque sprawl of self-inflicted brutality. However, the process of one lifelong artist interpreting an unusual amount of death, dealing with it through his art, results in a powerful and inspiring experience, at least for me.

"Like a lot of people who just want to hold on to their sanity, you find ways of dealing with it," Storey tells me. "Ways of categorizing it, compartmentalizing it, or something like that, so it isn't incapacitating to you. On a deeper level, it's kind of always there. And when it happened repeatedly, as it has with me, you start trippin'. I started thinking: 'What is this? Why is this something that I just have to accept? Why is this something that I can't get any details about? Why is this something my relatives don't want to say a single word about?' So it gets bottled up."

The bottle now spills all over the walls of Anno Domini. One piece depicts Storey's friend who invited everyone over for his own birthday party, and then shot himself in front of everyone. Another painting, an abstract work, represents another friend who confessed to Storey that he'd killed his own father, suffocated him with a pillow, just because his father was too weak and bedridden to do it himself, which is what the person's father had wanted.

Other works deal less with specific individuals, but more with facts and statements Storey heard from those he interviewed. "What is the most common form of suicide? Hanging."—speculates one particular drawing, although Storey admits he doesn't know if that's true or not. MEN USE GUNS proclaims another one.

Several paintings explore the ambiguous nature of overdoses, contemplating whether or not we can ever really tell if the act was intentional or not. The role of drug addiction in the suicidal impulse emerges in specific interviews, especially those related to the music business. One painting even goes into the incessant glorification of death one witnesses in the darkest corners of the death metal scene.

"For my friend who's in that scene too, the coolness of death is something that just puts it on the list of options," Storey tells me.

Beginning the section of interview pieces, one sees a tongue-and-chic dialog, a spin on Dante, with a cluster of paintings dictating to Storey that he must draw all the suicides. At the end of the entire show, another dialog emerges, one expounding on Storey's internal process of trying to get this out of his system, once and for all.

"It's not been working, but I'm trying," he confesses, adding that he wanted to cancel the exhibit, but continued at the gallery's insistence. In the process, Storey says the spirits of the deceased suicides talked back to him through the paintings. They said things like: "How dare you. How dare you use my experience for your purposes. How dare you do that. How dare you tell things that I have not given you permission to tell."

But Storey is telling the stories anyway. Permission or not.

Alchemy Museum Coming to Rosicrucian Park

In the summer of 2015, the old Rose-Croix University building at Rosicrucian Park will complete a transmutation into a newly equipped facility to showcase all aspects of the ancient art of alchemy, making San Jose home to the largest alchemy museum in the world.

There will be interactive hands-on exhibits, classroom lectures, a working alchemy laboratory, events in the auditorium and more. It will be the only facility of its kind in the United States. The Rosicrucians claim alchemy originated in Ancient Egypt, so next summer, they will stage an exhibit in the Egyptian Museum to start ratcheting up the celebration for the new facility.

Ancient alchemists in both West and East claimed to search for ways of converting base metals into gold, and their terminology contributed to the development of modern chemistry, although people for centuries have argued over the degree to which the alchemical process was mental, physical, spiritual, psychological or all of the above. Meaning, were the alchemists literally trying to convert lead into gold, or was it an allegory for personal growth? Were all those diagrams filled with coded symbology meant to suggest something quite different? That is, was all the laboratory terminology just allegory for a process of fine tuning one's own personal path, i.e., boiling away the bad elements and transforming other elements in order to sculpt a better self? Who knew what, and when?

What is common knowledge is that earlier in the 20th century, Carl

Gustav Jung brought alchemical symbolism and terminology into the practice of dream analysis and psychology, exploring how it relates to everyone's own inner journey. Ever since Jung, alchemy has been going through a period of resurgence, so to speak, even in Hollywood films.

In the 1930s, just after the Rosicrucians first set up their world headquarters in San Jose, the operation included an alchemical school of sorts, as part of the Rose-Croix University, replete with classrooms, an alchemy lab and an herborium. Much of the original facility still exists, although it hasn't been open to the public in decades. In 2015, that will change.

Dennis William Hauck is the curator of the alchemy museum. An author, consultant and lecturer, he is the de facto public face of the modern alchemy world laboratory. He wrote The Complete Idiot's Guide to Alchemy, plus another one called, The Emerald Tablet: Alchemy for Personal Transformation, and also penned, Sorcerer's Stone: A Beginner's Guide to Alchemy. Over the phone, Hauck told me that the Rosicrucians, centuries ago, were among the first ones to articulate the mental aspects of alchemy and the transpersonal components of the process, back when the protoscientists were still toiling away with beakers and furnaces. The establishment of a new alchemy museum is a natural way for the Rosicrucians to reconnect with their traditions.

"About 1500 A.D., the Rosicrucians really made a difference in alchemy," Hauck said. "They took it towards a more spiritual, evolutionary type of idea. And they posited the alchemical laboratory experience as a spiritual experience too. They were saying that the operations of alchemy apply not only in the laboratory, but also psychologically. And that thread was eventually taken up by Jung in an amazing manner."

According to Hauck, the Rosicrucian contribution to history was to expand alchemy on three levels—physical, mental and spiritual—which was a significant difference compared to just trying to convert base metals into gold and a big change from simply searching for the physical elixir of life. San Jose should be proud of that entire city block at Park and Naglee.

The new museum will even have seven different rooms of exhibits, devoted to the seven phases of alchemical transformation: Calcination, Dissolution, Separation, Conjunction, Fermentation, Distillation, and Coagulation. Each room will be filled with colors, sounds, equipment and symbolism related to each phase. Visitors will thus be able to physically walk from room to room, passing through the seven stages of the process, in proper order. Hauck says the Rosicrucians were the ones who originally deciphered the proper order of the seven stages in the first place.

"It'll be a unique place," Hauck said. "It's an exciting project."

Paul Child Inducted to San Jose Sports Hall of Fame

In 1974, San Jose was an absolute wasteland. If one was a child at that time, your parents took you to Eastridge for fun, since it had just opened a few years earlier. That or you went to Frontier Village. There was simply nothing else to do here. When Milan Mandaric launched a North American Soccer League franchise in San Jose that year, everything changed.

The original San Jose Earthquakes games jammed Spartan Stadium every single time and the players connected with everyone on a human level, giving San Jose its first ever professional sports identity. They were a community-based, working-class squad from the very beginning, a club that for many of us put San Jose on the map for the first time.

The first star striker for those original Quakes teams, a young Englishman named Paul Child, became San Jose's leading goal scorer through 1979, and subsequently San Jose's first professional soccer star. Next week he returns to get inducted into the San Jose Sports Hall of Fame, a moment long overdue.

Initially from Birmingham, Child came up through the Aston Villa football club's youth system, but by age 19 the coach had deemed him too old. Child came to the U.S. in 1972 to play in Atlanta until the team folded in 1973. He had actually gone back to England, to stay at his in-laws' flat, before Milan Mandaric talked him into making a move to San Jose for the Earthquakes' inaugural season. Now a longtime resident of Pittsburgh, Penn., Child still has fond memories of those working-class squads, the fans, the legendary players he battled against and his time in San Jose.

"The team was the only thing San Jose had," Child recalled. "That's what the great thing was—we were accepted so greatly by the people, and the fans. ... It was magic. We'd play our hearts out for the fans, you had a stadium that held 19,000 people and it was packed every game, and all you wanted to do was send those people home happy and get a victory."

At that time, the Quakes prided themselves on a working-class mentality above all else. The majority of the fans at every game had previously met some of the players already. No one on the team was in it for the big bucks, simply because there weren't any big bucks.

"We just had a bunch of hard-working guys that wanted to go out and play for the people who paid money to come watch us play," said Child. "As I look back on it now, that was the real difference. Now you have the Beckhams of the world and all these stars of the teams, but we just worked hard for each other and had great chemistry. ... And the city itself just accepted us. That was the difference."

Perhaps the best aspect of those days, either from a player's perspective or that as a youth in those crowds, was that some of the world's best footballers participated in that league during the '70s. After his coach had written him off at 19, Child was able to come to the U.S. and play against Pele, Franz Beckenbauer, Gerd Mueller, Johann Cruyff, Eusebio and George Best, essentially all the legends he'd grown up idolizing. He would never have played against those guys in England.

Child says it's all fodder for life's lessons, no matter what sport you're in. Never give up and you just may wind up in some hall of fame somewhere.

"When I left England, I felt at the bottom of the barrel," Child said. "It was the biggest downer. But then I get the opportunity to play against all those guys I'd grown up watching. ... [It's like being in a slump] but then you get out of that hole and you never quit. That's what this is all about, it's to tell the younger athletes that are coming along that you just don't quit. You keep on going, and you'll have your ups and downs, but at the end, if you just keep on trying as hard as you can, you'll come out smelling like roses."

Almaden Feed & Fuel Preserves its Barroom Mural

Thanks to a Holy Trinity characterizing San Jose for decades—real estate greed, political indifference and suburban apathy—the Almaden Feed & Fuel is no longer with us.

Formerly a stagecoach stop, a gas station, a saloon, a restaurant, a biker bar and more recently, a unique neighborhood tavern with live music, the Feed & Fuel went through several reincarnations in its century-long history. I first remember seeing the place back when Almaden Expressway didn't veer left at the Almaden Crossroads like it does now. It used to just go straight through, becoming Almaden Road, and then ease on down into New Almaden. That geography was seemingly part of everyone's high school drinking landscape.

Now the building has been destroyed, essentially euthanized, in favor of lifelessly uniform housing. Nothing new, of course. It's a familiar story: history, culture, character and uniqueness have given way to Anysuburb, USA. A small band of heroes not content with living in Anysuburb fought hard to save the building, but developers and suburban politicians were too powerful for them. Now there will be 13 more houses that look like 100,000 other houses anywhere south of Blossom Hill.

Thankfully, there's some positive news here too. Inside Almaden Feed & Fuel, there existed an old mural, if you consider 1985 as "old," which most developers in San Jose do. At that time, then-owner Blondie Barnd hired trompe-l'oeil artist John Pugh to paint a wall mural depicting bar regulars. As the building was about to get euthanized several weeks ago, it took an Englishman—someone with an intrinsic un-San Jose awareness of culture—to assume the task of saving the mural.

Roger Springall, the proprietor of Caffe Frascati in downtown San

Jose, already had a connection to Feed & Fuel, since he lives nearby and had rifled through the remains of the business when it closed for good in 2006. Right now, as one walks into Frascati, the three tables to the right, as well as the three tables on the mezzanine looking down from above, originally came from Almaden Feed & Fuel, as did the bar along the left wall. Springall says when he walked into the defunct building in 2006, in order to purchase those pieces from the owner, the place looked like a deserted movie set.

"It was like they had closed the door and walked out," Springall recalled. "There were still bottles of beer sitting on the counter, just like someone had walked out, closed the door and that was it. It was frozen in time. There were still newspapers on the tables."

But just a few months ago, after the band of heroes failed to legally save the building, Springall was allowed back, in order to salvage what he could from the inside. The guts of the place had not changed in the seven years it sat unoccupied.

"It was exactly the same as I saw it several years earlier," Springall said. "Nobody had touched anything. And the only thing I saw, what I thought we really needed to hang onto, was the mural."

Pugh's mural depicts a bygone era at Feed & Fuel. In the image, we see a female bartender and a regular standing at the opposite end of the bar. On the wall next to the bartender, we see a BART map, depicting the rapid transit system coming all the way to San Jose. But on the wall near the regular customer, we see decor from decades earlier and other accoutrements suggesting he exists years before. The wood on the bar is also much newer at his end. Thus, we're looking back in time to a regular customer left over from a previous era. Springall says Pugh recently told him this "regular" in the mural was a real person who consistently drank at Feed & Fuel and was also the same guy who went down in history as the first person in Almaden Valley arrested for being drunk on a horse. Removing the mural required chainsawing the wall out from the structure. Springall says Barnd is currently in possession of the mural and trying to find a permanent home for it.

2014

San Jose Earthquakes 40th Anniversary Celebration

For the rest of the year, the San Jose Earthquakes will celebrate a milestone. Forty years ago, Milan Mandaric started a San Jose franchise in the North American Soccer League (NASL), back when Norman Mineta was the mayor. In Mandaric's own words, it was a community team above all else, a working class unit.

To celebrate, the current version of the Quakes will rebrand their logo, crest, jersey and entire image in such a way that finally and comprehensively takes their heritage into consideration. No other team in the league is currently doing anything similar in quite this fashion. The rebranding party, open to the public, erupts on Thu., Jan. 30, at San Pedro Square Market. Former heroes from the 1970s as well as the current team, plus many players, coaches and executives from every era in-between will attend.

Rancid guitarist Lars Frederiksen, who grew up in Campbell and followed the NASL Earthquakes as a kid, even wrote a new Earthquakes theme song for one of his other bands, the Old Firm Casuals. They recorded the track, titled, "Never Say Die," with current and former Quakes players singing backup vocals. The band will perform it live at the party on Jan. 30.

This is long overdue for several reasons. First of all, the Old Firm Casuals are a working class street-punk outfit. For the uninitiated, they play British-inspired Oi! music, if I'm allowed to say so in my dirthead opinion. Since the very beginnings of that music, it has been inseparable from football. Also, with all due respect to the Earthquakes' marketing division, quite a few of their promotional schemes have been goofy or just plain embarrassing. But now, there's a world-renowned guitarist who grew up with the team, grew up with soccer, writing a song for the team, playing a style of music historically connected with football. With the team also rebranding to recognize its heritage, it finally feels like the franchise is doing something historically authentic, or at least something that resembles how it's done in the rest of the world.

What's more, throughout much of the globe, especially England, people are born with the neighborhood football club flowing through their bloodstream. And in most cases, the club has been around for a century, so the founding date is usually emblazoned on the team's crest. Historically speaking, in certain towns with absolutely nothing else to do, the club became everything to the people who grew up there, primarily because the club was all the town had. This is pretty much akin to San Jose in the 1970s. Except for prunes and a flavorless Dionne Warwick song, the town had no commercial identity.

Frederiksen said he was not commissioned by the Quakes to write the theme song. He wrote it on his own several years ago, as a fan first and foremost. Everything just came together at the right time for the band to participate in the 40-year celebration. The lyrics are about San Jose, the team, our rivalries and the working class ethic.

"The song is another extension of all the years I've gone to see the Quakes, back when I was at Spartan Stadium and at Buck Shaw," Frederiksen told me. "Buck Shaw is a place David Beckham wouldn't play at. That's fine, because he sucks. I'm glad he's gone. In fact, that's how the song goes—'This is not New York, this is not L.A.,' and the next line is, 'Our colors are black and blue, and we are San Jose.' And those are our colors, and this is our team and that's as real as it gets. We don't want a bunch of movie stars playing here."

The Old Firm Casuals recorded the track at East Bay Recorders in Berkeley. Engineer Michael Rosen, who'd previously worked with the 49ers in a similar capacity, suggested Frederiksen enlist Earthquakes players to sing back up. After finding out Quakes defender Clarence Goodson was a Rancid fan, connections were made and phone numbers were exchanged. Current and former Quakes players on the recording are Clarence Goodson, Sam Cronin, Troy Dayak, Steven Beitashour, Kelly Gray, Jason Hernandez and Jordan Stewart. All in all, it's a project worth bragging about.

Macintosh 30th Anniversary Party

Archaic manuals, programming books and thrice-generation-photo-copied pamphlets are strewn across a handful of tables in the Fireside Room of the De Anza College Campus Center. An original Macintosh computer shell, with the signatures of the original team seemingly embalmed onto the material, sits on one table like royalty.

Atop another pile of relics, a floppy disk copy of Aldus Persuasion for Windows has been converted into a letter opener. T-shirts, old equipment, computer-club programs, Verbum magazines and even more ephemera appear wherever my gaze moves. Members of the original Macintosh development team slowly file in and out of the room. This is the "Un-Conference" organized by Raines Cohen, an unofficial gathering of legends, taking place before the high-priced Macintosh 30th anniversary event in the Flint Center.

The stories are spinning me in every which direction, as original Apple characters are telling me the history of the first Macintosh, how it began entirely as research project, a secret skunkworks operation, without Steve Jobs even knowing about it. Jef Raskin liked McIntosh apples, so that was the only reason the machine eventually became known as the Macintosh, I'm told. Outside, a few wild geese are making a racket in the sunken garden area in front of the Flint Center, just as more aging legends from the original Apple era in Silicon Valley begin to mill about.

Daniel Kottke, probably the only employee who worked on the Apple I, II, III and Macintosh, who traveled to India with Steve Jobs 40 years ago and who holds a music degree from Columbia, is regaling me with stories of what it was like as the original Macintosh began to emerge. In some strange fashion, I feel outside the linear process of time, neither young nor old, but perfectly in tune.

"The Apple II was launched with big fanfare in the spring of 1977," Kottke explains, as we slide into a pair of soda-stained chairs in the Fireside Room. "But it didn't ship until summer, so the Apple II didn't have a clear birthday like the Mac did. The reason we're here is because the Mac had a very clear birthday. That's a moral for the world. If you want to celebrate your product decades later, have a clear birthday."

On that birthday, January 24, 1984, a goofy dressed-up Steve Jobs first debuted the Macintosh, on stage, at the Flint Center, with Chariots of Fire churning in the background. That presentation essentially created the ground it walked on, defining the entire next generation of the product launch as rock-star event. The PC industry was never the same afterward.

So we all sat there last Saturday, in the Flint Center, and watched a video projection of that original event, which took place on that same stage. The effect was eerie. Again, I felt outside of time but somehow completely still in the groove. I felt almost guilty about being a Commodore 64 kid and missing the original spectacle.

Most of the people who designed the original Mac, who built it, wrote the software and/or created the advertising campaign, attended the event. Three panel sessions unfolded. Technology journalist John Markoff moderated the first panel of folks talking about what led up to the Macintosh. Steven Levy moderated the next one, comprising those who wrote the original software. Bill Atkinson told stories about the origins of MacPaint, which he created. Randy Wigginton, who wrote MacWrite, likewise weaved numerous tales. All of them quipped that it took thousands of Microsoft employees to replicate what 125 Apple folks originally created.

More than 100 of those same people from the original 1984 team then took the stage for a group photo. It was a goofy yet poignant scene. I can't possibly imagine how different the world would be, now, 30 years later, had the Mac never happened. At the end of the night, Jerry Manock, originally the Mac industrial design guru, read a birthday letter to the current Mac, from the original Mac family. "Do not let vanity and compliments about your beauty stop you from always remembering your core purpose of fostering innovation and creativity in others," Manock said, reading from the birthday letter. "Don't forget to keep your sense of humor. True artists not only ship... they laugh."

San Jose Earthquakes 40th Anniversary Party

Much like the C2SV conference that held its inaugural event last year, the San Jose Earthquakes 40th anniversary celebration at San Pedro Square Market was half-punk and half-technology. When understood through that lens, it perfectly embodied the spirit of Silicon Valley, a place where disruptive creativity crosses over with engineering innovation on a daily basis.

Rancid guitarist Lars Frederiksen's other band, the Old Firm Casuals, performed the Quakes' new theme song at the end of the night. Outside in the streets, team executives livestreamed the jersey-unveiling event using the Google Glass application CrowdOpt.

For the event, the Quakes went all out, as opposed to their characteristically cheapskate methods of the past. It took them four months to put together an elaborate video montage of their entire history, going all the way back to the NASL days in the 1970s, and then they projected the video on two fronts. One projection covered the western facade of the utterly hideous SunWize building just outside San Pedro Square, while another screened on the side of the Fallon House across St. John.

Without exaggeration, probably a few thousand people congregated outside on the street to watch former NASL player Johnny Moore talk about the original 1974 squad and how the current team somehow managed to carry on the working-class, never-say-die spirit of those original teams. Moore has always been the main visual connection for the current fans to the original NASL days and also the staunch proponent in trying to convince previous misguided Quakes executive administrations to acknowledge the franchise's heritage going back to 1974. When MLS began in 1996, its hokey ersatz sports executives dismissed the NASL as a failed league, which it was, and subsequently argued those days were of absolutely no importance. They were all proven wrong, of course, and San Jose, usually the dismissed market, oddly enough became the first MLS organization to officially embody a heritage from the previous generation.

But I digress. The team's new jersey and logo were then revealed and the crowds continued to meander in and out of the market area, where several glass cases presented paraphernalia and ephemera from the NASL days, as well as Quakes teams and subsequent units that carried on between the demise of the NASL and the launch of MLS, an important and often overlooked era. Some of the 1974 team even attended and answered questions on stage from Chris Dangerfield, another NASL Quakes star from the early '80s, and one who now does commentary for the team.

The end of the night brought everything full circle. As was hyped from the very beginning, Rancid guitarist Lars Frederiksen, who grew up with the NASL Quakes, performed with his side band, the Old Firm Casuals, in the garage bar area of San Pedro Square Market. Their tune, "Never Say Die," is now the official Quakes theme song. They even played it twice. On stage, Frederiksen talked about growing up with the NASL incarnation of the Earthquakes and how George Best once came to Lars' school in Campbell, when Best played here in 1980-81. Frederiksen also devoted one song to his deceased brother, "Rocking Rob" Dapello, without whom Lars said he would never have discovered soccer or punk rock. The capper came in the form of another surprise. Gavin O'Brien, who sang for San Jose's most famous punk band, The Faction, a group that fused skateboarding and punk 30 years ago, putting San Jose on the international map a lot more than the Quakes ever did, jumped in with the Old Firm Casuals and performed two Faction songs. O'Brien has been a staple at Quakes games since the original NASL squad started in 1974.

The entire night was probably the most "San Jose" event that I have seen around here in many years. Giant video projections, Google Glass, original 1974 players, punks, metalheads, nuclear families, beer, pizza, Irish ex-mayors comparing and contrasting themselves to Krazy George, plus a 32-channel board for the monitor mix and some of the most world-renowned local punk musicians. Other teams may have more fans in the seats, but no other team in Major League Soccer has anything remotely close to the 40-year community and family that the San Jose Earthquakes have.

The First Hindu Retreat in the Western world

The Anti-Man-About-Town recently became aware of yet another slice of half-Eastern, half-Western history unique to Santa Clara County. At the Asian Art Museum in San Francisco, he was reminded that the South Bay played a major role in the history of Hinduism's foray into the West.

In the summer of 1900, the celebrated Swami Vivekananda dispatched a delegation of the Vedanta Society to the eastern side of Mt. Hamilton with the purpose of establishing a "peace retreat."

By then, Vivekananda had already lectured extensively in Chicago, New York and San Francisco, but this remote locale 15 miles southeast of Lick Observatory, in the middle of nowhere, at the far eastern portion of Santa Clara County, was the first Hindu retreat in the Western world. At least that's what the Vedanta Society says. Swamis Turiyananda and Trigunatita were among those leaders who initially helped establish and maintain the property, which blossomed into a popular retreat during the first half of the 20th century.

On its website and in its books, the Vedanta Society of Northern California documents much of the story behind the retreat's inception. A truly remarkable tale, it bears a quick summary. In 1900, a Vedanta student, one Miss Minnie C. Boock, owned nearly 160 acres of isolated property in the San Antonio Valley—that is, between Lick Observatory and where Interstate 5 would later emerge. She was in New York attending lectures and hanging out with Swami Vivekananda, who was then initially bringing the Vedanta teachings to American soil.

Vivekananda was looking for a place to establish a retreat and Boock gave him the property. Vivekananda then dispatched Swami Turiyananda, to whom he had already assigned the California chapter, to lead a contingent over Mt. Hamilton and on to the retreat area. It was to be called Shanti Ashrama. On their way up to Mt. Hamilton, they stayed at the Rita Hotel, and after a treacherous descent into then-unknown territory on the other side, they arrived at the property in August of 1900. At that time, San Jose was not yet the prune capital of the Western world.

Over the next few decades, Vedanta swamis and devotees would build living quarters, work the land and utilize the retreat for lectures and meditation sessions. The only remnant of the original compound still remaining today is the 12-by-12-foot meditation cabin, now painted white, which sits in a meadow surrounded by forested environs. Each year, swamis and devotees still visit the isolated property to engage in spiritual practice.

No San Jose history book acknowledges any of this. In Clyde Arbuckle's definitive history, he threw in a few Swedish churches that date from around the same time, but nothing on the Vedanta Society. I relayed this tale to my local experts—both in academe and in the gutters and none of them knew the story either.

Todd Perreira, who lectures at SJSU in comparative religious studies and actively researches the histories of Eastern religions and their initial forays into the local geography, said Vedanta's entrance into Santa Clara County is important.

"There were very few opportunities in those days to actually translate one's sympathy for these religions into an actual practice," Perreira told me. "So the fact that Miss Minnie C. Boock, in the summer of 1900, formally deeded her Mt. Hamilton homestead to Swami Vivekananda, the star of the World's Parliament, for the expressed purpose of setting up an ashram, the first Vedanta retreat in the Western world, casts San Jose into the role of inaugural hero during the pioneer days of religious and cultural pluralism in America."

Shanti Ashrama can be placed in the same historical context as Herman Vetterling, a.k.a. Philangi Dasa, the publisher of the first Buddhist periodical in America, who permanently settled in San Jose in 1901. Fifty years later, another hero named Jack Kerouac would stumble into the San Jose Public Library and discover Buddhism.

The exploits of Vivekananda and the Vedanta Society were seen as kooky by Americans of the early 20th century, but their practice embodied a kaleidoscopic co-mingling of spiritual paths, East and West, and in that sense they helped define an entire slice of California consciousness for the rest of the 20th century.

San Jose and Dublin Celebrate Sister City Bonds

San Jose and Dublin, Ireland, have been sister cities for 28 years now—quite an impressive scenario to say the least. Every year, the Lord Mayor of Dublin brings a delegation of colleagues from government and academia across the pond to the San Jose area for numerous meetings and activities. This year, Lord Mayor Oisin Quinn attended a San Jose Bike Party journey through the streets and even toured TechShop, since one of those fine establishments is expected to open in Dublin some time in the future.

Much more seems in the works between the two cities, so the Anti-Man-About-Town infiltrated a luncheon at City Hall to ingest some updates. At the event, the Lord Mayor hyped up some initiatives unfolding in his city, where he said a program of citywide advertising exists to help promote events and programs. After listening to the skinny on this initiative, I'm guessing it would be the equivalent of having digitally distributed banners emerge on various windows, buildings and public places throughout San Jose—from Blossom Hill Road to Berryessa, from Evergreen to Winchester Boulevard—all to help connect people in disparate parts of the landscape, so they could be more informed as to what festivals are occurring, which marathons are about to unfold or which city-sponsored events are taking place. And in Dublin, tech companies are partnering with the city to help support the infrastructure of this idea. An equivalent might benefit San Jose, especially since the landscape is so sprawled out that many people are unaware of what goes on in the rest of the city outside their own neighborhoods. It would work much better than all those amateur placards inside the buses that nobody even looks at anyway.

Concerning initiatives already in place, there's actually a scholarship exchange program between SJSU and Dublin City University (DCU), supported by Cypress Semiconductor. As of right now, Andrew Kiernan of Dublin, an engineering student, attends SJSU and sets up shop at Cy-

243

press as part of his master's curriculum. Of the 2,000-plus sister city relationships established in the U.S., the SJ-Dublin partnership is the only one incorporating a master's-level scholarship exchange program.

So, after the luncheon in the rotunda, a reception unfolded in the engineering building at San Jose State, where the entire delegation watched Kiernan and representatives from DCU, Cypress Semiconductor and the Lord Mayor speak all over again. All of them testified to the importance of travel in one's education. Andrew Wright, a veep at Cypress and an Irishman himself, even broke out the famous St. Augustine quote: "The world is a book and those who do not travel read only one page."

I can testify myself. I began traveling at 25 and never stopped, including a summer study-abroad program in Italy for five weeks that SJSU gave me credit for. It opened up entirely new avenues of creativity.

Now, if there's an engineering scholarship exchange, why shouldn't there be arts and literature exchanges between SJSU and DCU as well? After all, Dublin is a UNESCO City of Literature. Well, before I even had a chance to ask that question, it was answered. According to those who spoke at the scholarship reception, a similar academic exchange in the humanities is in the works. It's just a matter of getting the bureaucracies of the two universities to dovetail with one another.

With that, I can already think of several other ways to enhance the San Jose-Dublin relationship. Downtown San Jose has a rock & roll bar, the Blank Club, owned by an O'Brien, so there should be a sister rock club in Dublin somewhere. The neighborhood also has a great tea shop that should be twinned with its equivalent in Dublin. I can go on and on. Also, right there in the City Hall rotunda, locals gave an autographed San Jose Earthquakes jersey to the Lord Mayor, with which he posed for a picture. I can't think of anything more appropriate than a sister club in Dublin somewhere. Doesn't even have to be first division. Whichever club makes the most sense. I mean, international punk rock, tea and soccer relationships are elements no other sister city in the U.S. has going right now. That would make San Jose a much more interesting place. Silicon Valley would lead the world again.

School of Rock in San Jose

As I cross the threshold at School of Rock San Jose on Almaden Expressway, a wall of photos greets me: Kids engrossed in real-life rock & roll action shots, either on stage or in rehearsal rooms, playing bass, guitar, keys and even singing into microphones. Everyone seems to be having a rocking good time.

The rest of the lobby is business-y, but rocking. Over in the far corner, comfy leather-looking chairs occupy the floor, right in front of a Photoshop-filtered Angus Young image converted to a School of Rock poster. A check-in desk sits at the opposite side, where a few parents are signing up their kids to take lessons. There are potted plants, brand new flooring, plus School of Rock T-shirts and other merch on a clothing rack. I can hear snare drums and the laughs of children coming from somewhere down the hallways.

As I then skulk down those hallways, I see framed Agent Orange, Joan Jett and Creedence LPs gracing the walls, just outside the lesson rooms, of which there are many. I even get to prowl through two rehearsal rooms, replete with instruments, mics and soundproofing material. Throughout the building, I can hear kids running through Nirvana riffs, Concrete Blonde, as well as a complete group doing "I Melt With You" by Modern English.

A chain with locations throughout the world, School of Rock teaches guitar, bass, keys, drums and vocals to kids ages 6-18. Erik Delicath and his wife, London, opened the San Jose franchise last October in a location formerly occupied by Computerland, across the parking lot from the Almaden Britannia Arms. What differentiates School of Rock from most other music schools is that kids of all different skill levels immediately jam together. As a result, London tells me, they learn faster and have a lot more fun than if they were just taking solo lessons.

"Even as absolute beginners, we get all the kids playing together right away," says London. "Because if you're lucky enough to have music in your school when you're playing with other kids, it's usually band instruments. So with guitar, bass, or drums, you're usually taking private lessons, then you go home and sit on your bed and play. So what we're striving to create is a place where they can come and be real musicians, work on rhythm, timing, communication, cooperation and all the stuff that comes along with playing with other people."

Because of this, kids become better team players and better equipped to deal with any feelings of isolation, loneliness or disenfranchisement that may emerge later in life. Not that I'm speaking from experience.

"The kids who are shredders learn how to be mentors and be gracious when we put an absolute newbie in with them," London tells me. "The new kids have someone they can look up to and aspire to. And they tend to come along a lot faster than if we had separated them or isolated them by levels of experience. We mix them all together by design."

I can testify about all of this. I grew up with music in elementary school and I later took lessons for years, right down the street from where School of Rock now sits, but I hardly ever jammed with other people at that age. Looking back on it, I can say with all degree of certainty that doing so would have dramatically helped me, both musically, and in life. And it took prowling the hallways—in a building where people came to purchase SCSI cables at Computerland 20 years ago—to make me realize this. These kids I overheard in the rooms were awesome, perhaps already better than the cover bands who play at the Brit across the parking lot.

The kids from School of Rock San Jose have already staged one show. Their next one, a spring show, will erupt June 6 at the Montgomery Theater, benefiting the Boys & Girls Clubs of Silicon Valley. Proceeds will go toward on-site music instruction at the Gardner Community Center Clubhouse.

"Our goal is to bring music into the lives of as many kids as possible," London says.

Old-School Wrestling Photography by Shirlie Montgomery

I am ashamed and downright embarrassed to admit that I never met Shirlie Montgomery, San Jose's most legendary freelance photographer, who for decades captured celebrities, politicians and wrestlers, all for a timespan of at least 50 years. She passed away in 2012 at the age of 94, and it took this long to sift through all of what she spent the bulk of the 20th century hoarding.

Thanks to History San Jose, a remarkable photo show and exhibit, Shirlie Montgomery: Picturing San Jose Since 1938, will debut this weekend at the Leonard and David McKay Gallery at Pasetta House in History Park. Fans of '50s wrestling will especially enjoy one particular section of the show. Since Montgomery left us thousands of photos, and because she saved everything, it was a monumental task putting the show together.

Born in 1918, Montgomery was the grandniece of T. S. Montgomery, after whom the Hotel Montgomery was named and also the hero that donated the land on which the Civic Auditorium was built in the '30s. A lifelong San Jose resident who never married or had siblings, Montgomery lived a life of unequaled color. As a photographer, she worked for the Mercury-News beginning in the '40s, She was also the De Anza Hotel's house camerawoman, hired to create photographic gifts for hotel guests, while taking pictures of all the celebrities who partied in the bar during the property's heyday in the postwar era. Also a diehard wrestling fan, Montgomery took perhaps more wrestling photos than anyone who ever lived, fully documenting a then-thriving professional wrestling scene at the San Jose Civic (now City National Civic) from the '40s through the '60s, a scene often spilling over into neighborhood bars and barbecues after the matches. Legends like Gorgeous George, Lou Thesz and Ray the Crippler Stevens all came to life in Montgomery's photos. When it comes to celebrity visits, Montgomery took many iconic shots throughout the twentieth century, including Eleanor Roosevelt, Bing Crosby and Lucille Ball, some of which were taken when Montgomery worked for the original Lou's Village on San Carlos Street.

All in all, Montgomery was ahead of every curve. She helped pioneer the entire concept of the freelance photographer in the modern era, and she did quite well, especially during a time when women were rarely expected to engage in such independent pursuits. Her career as a wrestling photographer even landed her in the Slammers Wrestling Hall of Fame in the '70s.

Montgomery lived on Hester Ave in the Rose Garden area and it took a serious effort to pore through all of the materials she left behind: negatives, prints, photo albums, notebooks and other ephemera. Ken Middlebrook became one of the individuals at History San Jose whose job it was to sift through mountains of stuff to assemble the show.

"The first two rooms of the exhibit will focus on notable people, local personalities from the '40s to '60s," Middlebrook explained. "Then a side room will focus on her personal life, because she was an artistic person, who led an interesting life. ... But the biggest part of her life was when she got involved with the professional wrestling circuit. And one of the last rooms will be focused on the wrestling connection."

Since Middlebrook was kind enough to grant this columnist access to the wealth of photos ahead of time, I can surely say that, um, she left behind a monumental body of work. It would take all of 10 houses to adequately display everything. Just the wrestling photos document a time in San Jose that will never happen again, at least as long as Team San Jose prefers to have shows like Yanni and Styx at City National Civic.

Since Montgomery's most significant contribution to culture was her extensive documentation of the wrestling scene, it is also important to note that her photos do not stop with just action shots in the ring. Many of the wrestlers in the '50s and '60s, including the midgets, would show up at the Ringside tavern, a bar at First and Julian, the walls of which were covered with Montgomery's photos. Part two of this column will come off the top rope next week, presenting a space-time continuum-shattering picture of what that bar was like in those those days. Stay tuned.

'One City, One Book' Poetic Exchange: Dublin & San Jose

Once a year, the Lord Mayor of Dublin, Ireland, a UNESCO City of Literature, shows up in downtown San Jose, along with an entourage of colleagues. This time around, he informed yours truly about a Dublin initiative, "One City, One Book," that unfolds every April, when the entire city is encouraged to read the same book over the course of one month. The book is either written by a Dublin author or connected to Dublin in some way.

Other cities implement similar strategies, but since Dublin and San Jose are twinned, a chance soon materialized for me to once again suggest ways of enhancing this relationship. In Dublin's case, the "One City, One Book" program began in 2006 and this year marks the first time that a book of poetry has been chosen. If Ever You Go: A Map of Dublin in Poetry and Song is a new anthology comprised almost entirely of contemporary poets, all writing about the Dublin condition. The wide variety of work included will inspire anyone, native or exotic, to explore the main thoroughfares, neighborhoods, historical monuments, parks, slipshod alleys, libraries, pubs and other distinguishable components of Dublin's landscape. Right now, readings, recitals, film events, parties, cruises on the Liffy, guided walks, train rides and concerts are erupting all over town.

The very day I arrived, my jetlagged self infiltrated a lecture about paintings that inspired the William Butler Yeats poem, "The Municipal Gallery Revisited." The poem, written in 1937, finds the nobel laureate visiting the famous Dublin gallery and reflecting on portraits of persons related to notable events in the previous 30 years of Irish history, events in which the poet was also a part. Due to our sister city relationship, I felt like Yeats was a distant brother.

Another example: Just before I returned back home, musicians performed songs from If Ever You Go at The Church, a place of worship renovated and converted to a multi-level restaurant and bar complex. It was originally where Handel played the pipe organ, where Jonathan Swift first attended services and in which Arthur Guinness was married.

Jane Alger, one of the brains behind Dublin: One City, One Book, explained over lunch that no one knew what to expect by having a poetry book this time around. But so far, she said, If Ever You Go has been a major hit, on track to become the biggest-selling poetry book in Irish history. Everyone seems to find something within its pages. Even people normally alienated from poetry are enjoying it.

"It's not the kind of book that you read from cover to cover," Alger explained. "You buy it, or you borrow it from your local library, and you dip into it. And everybody will find a poem about a place that means something to them. ... It's a lovely gift book. It offers a view of the city that people might not necessarily engage with."

Now, I've written in this space numerous times that more local poets and creative writers illuminating the San Jose condition would make this town a zillion times more interesting to live in, on a variety of levels. Obviously, unlike Dublin, we don't have Joyce, Yeats, Oscar Wilde, or Bram Stoker, but one has to start somewhere. The time is now for a similar San Jose book. The possibilities are endless.

The day after I returned home, my jetlagged self stumbled into the San Jose Museum of Art, where newly crowned Santa Clara County Poet Laureate David Perez headed up an event with local poets reading work inspired by artwork in the museum's collection—eerily similar to the event I attended in Dublin when I first arrived. It felt like the great sister city goddess of synchronicities decided I should bookend my trip with Yeats and San Jose's own poets respectively contemplating paintings that inspired them. This is precisely what sister cities ought to be doing, and precisely how a columnist should be connecting the two, especially since April in the United States is National Poetry Month—another co-incidence. In any event, I look forward to many more poetic exchanges, literally and metaphorically, with our sister city of Dublin, Ireland.

Ao Dai Festival comes to the San Jose Fairmont

The third official Ao Dai Festival, a colorful multidisciplinary spectacle of Vietnamese history, music, dance and culture, will erupt on several levels this Sunday, both outside and inside the San Jose Fairmont.

The activities unfolding outside in the Circle of Palms are free and open to anyone who stops by, while the formal dinner inside will raise funds for the Friends of Hue Foundation, a nonprofit supporting programs such as an orphanage in Hue, Vietnam, and youth leadership programs here in San Jose. The whole shebang promises to be a ceremonious, regal affair, regardless if you're Vietnamese or not, and especially if you've got a thing for zithers.

Beginning in the Circle of Palms, and for the first time ever outside Vietnam, a traditional Vietnamese wedding ceremony will be fully recreated, replete with the groom arriving on horseback and the bride carried to the show inside a carriage. The ceremony features 100 men and women in traditional Ao Dai costumes, 20 zither players, 20 drummers, a dragon dance and women on stilts, all of which explores and articulates ancient Vietnamese stories.

As the legend goes, the bachelor returns home to his lowly village after passing a grueling test from the king, a test of his intellectual ability, without which the bride would not be allowed to marry him. After traveling for months to the king's palace to take the test, all while the would-be bride stayed home and made silk by the riverbank, the groom now comes home to a fanfare. Upon his arrival, the whole village celebrates and he can marry the bride. Centuries of Vietnamese poetry portray this story, says Jenny Do, the festival organizer.

"This story is the story of a young couple; it's a typical story at that time," Do explains. "She had already promised to marry him, but the poem goes, 'If you don't pass the test, I will never consummate the marriage,' so it put a lot of pressure on the man to pass the test. So we thought with poetry we would explain this background. The entire village would celebrate and construct the wedding, and that's when he could claim his bride."

And that's just outside the Fairmont. Inside the hotel, the formal program will then include an opulent cocktail reception, a jazz performance and a fashion promenade featuring Vietnamese and local designers. Vanessa Van-Anh Vo, a celebrated performer of the dan tranh, a traditional Vietnamese zither, is the musical director for the whole program, which also features a world premiere of "Yearning Mountain," a poetry-in-motion musical story based on another ancient Vietnamese legend.

As that story goes, a woman's husband went off to war and did not return for years, so she took their child up to the top of a mountain every day and waited for him over and over again. Eventually she turned to stone and a statue of a woman and child now sits atop a mountain in North Vietnam. It's an emotional tale known to virtually everyone in the country. Again, much Vietnamese poetry has been written based on this tale. Do says at the Ao Dai Festival, "Yearning Mountain" will be simply another spin on a classic love story.

"It's not meant to be a tragedy," says Do. "But it's pretty much a story of many Vietnamese homes. It's about the spirit and endurance and strength of the women who are always faithful."

Vo's music will bring a half-Eastern, half-Western twist to the entire story. Having already mastered several traditional Vietnamese instruments, worked with luminaries like Kronos Quartet and even won an Emmy, Vo will orchestrate an elaborate conglomeration of musicians, including Japanese taiko drummers, multilingual Moroccan vocalists and a bass player who once gigged with Prince and Sting.

"We don't want to set any limits," Vo says. "You can be anyone from any country, from any background, and be able to find something common to you. The music, the stories, the plots, will help to evoke something in your life that you can relate to. That's what we're trying to do. That's the power of music."

When Oscar Wilde Visited San Jose

Later this summer, San Jose will host the Sister Cities International Conference, expected to attract hundreds of delegates from cities across the globe, all expounding the virtues of international diplomacy.

"Sister City" is the term we use in the US, but in other countries it's also called "twinning." In San Jose's case, we're twinned with many cities, in particular, Dublin, Ireland—a relationship launched 28 years ago by then Mayor Tom McEnery and his Dublin counterpart, Bertie Ahern.

Dublin is one of the literary capitals of the world, claiming numerous legends and laureates, but the one who stands out the most for me is Oscar Wilde. He was more eccentric and dressed better than the rest, he sauntered around with a pet lobster on a leash, and he was also the only one of those legends that ever visited San Jose.

When I visited Dublin last month, I made a point of visiting the famous Oscar Wilde statue in Merrion Square, right across the street from his childhood home. Since our cities are twinned, he felt like a distant brother to me. As a result, the experience drove me to shatter the space-time continuum and research the celebrated occasion when Wilde actually came to my neighborhood 132 years ago.

Wilde first visited America in 1882 for a highly promoted lecture tour about Aestheticism that took him to about 100 cities, including San Jose.

Controversy surrounded him from the very beginning, primarily due to the way he dressed, and he was ridiculed by newspaper columnists from coast to coast. When it came to reporters, Wilde was a master of theatrical behavior and often treated interviews as performances, manipulating entire encounters just to propagandize his own notoriety. In that sense, he was decades ahead of his time.

In 1882, San Jose's population was about 13,000. The town's most lavish venue, the California Theatre (unrelated to the current California Theatre) extended one city block from First Street to Second Street, right about where San Jose Bar & Grill is now. Some city directories place it at 81 S. Second, while others say 85 S. Second. In any case, the 958-seat complex was at that time the finest facility in San Jose, before it burned down several years later.

Oscar Wilde appeared at the California Theatre on April 3, 1882—just a little more than a century before McEnery became mayor—to deliver a lecture on the English Renaissance. He also spoke about concepts of beauty and "art for art's sake." A recap in the San Jose Daily Herald opened with the following: "The High Priest of the Esthetes lectured last night to an audience which filled the dress circle of the California Theatre. All the most fashionable and cultured people of San Jose were there and the attention they paid to every word of the lecture showed how deeply they were interested in the lecturer and his subject."

With euphoric intrigue, The Herald continued by mentioning that Mr. Wilde "was dressed in the usual velvet coat, knee breeches and silk stockings, ruffled shirt, front and lace ruffs," and that we was "a tall, well-proportioned man, with a very boyish face, smooth as a woman's, and made to look more effeminate by the hair, which is long and hangs down round the face. His eyes are beautiful, shaded with long lashes and full of expression."

Unlike San Jose Bar & Grill, the theater never toyed with a dress code prohibiting neck tattoos, baggy pants or excessive gold chains. It makes me wonder what would happen if Wilde were alive today and tried to sneak into that bar with his pet lobster.

In any event, that first American tour is where Oscar Wilde honed his ideas on beauty and art, and it proved to be fertile ground for the extremes of ambiguity, sarcasm and paradox he so brilliantly employed in The Picture of Dorian Gray just a few years later. The time is right for a permanent plaque on Second Street devoted to Oscar Wilde's appearance in San Jose. I'm sure our next mayor will be cultured enough to find a way to pay for it.

Krazy George: Still Krazy After all These Cheers

The world's only decades-long full-time professional cheerleader, drum-beating lunatic and San Jose State alumnus, Krazy George Hen-

251

derson, now screams in autobiographical format. His new book, Still Krazy After all These Cheers, explodes with stories and sheer insanity. I would expect no less. You can almost hear his gravelly voice and snare drum pounding from between the pages.

Henderson was a judo star at what was then called San Jose State College in the mid- to late-'60s. After a friend introduced him to the world of cheerleading at Spartan Football games, a new paradigm began to emerge in his crackpot brain. Since he wasn't coordinated enough for the dorky choreographed movements and cheers, and felt even worse wearing dorky sweaters, Henderson developed a new approach. He had no idea that he was on the path to changing the entire professional sports landscape in America.

"Everything they would teach at cheerleading camp, I would do exactly the opposite," he writes. "They said smile at the fans and tell them how great they were. I'd pound my drum, growl at them, make mean faces and yell how pathetic they were. They would have lengthy cheers to go along with their complicated moves. My longest cheer was two words or two syllables, 'San Jose' or 'Spar-tans.'"

Henderson soon realized that physically moving up into the stands or climbing the poles at Spartan Stadium provoked the fans even more. Taking the act to the people, on their benches, elicited more excitement. The fans became one with the experience.

While teaching electronics at Buchser High School, George began to moonlight as a cheerleader for the Oakland Seals hockey team, where his talent for inciting the opposing squad to near violence began to blossom. It was all uphill from there.

When the original version of the San Jose Earthquakes started in 1974, George went pro. General Manager Dick Berg gave him $35 a game, at first. At the beginning of every match, George would enter the field in any number of ways: in a garbage truck, an ambulance, a police car, from a helicopter, hang glider or limousine, or on the back of a camel. Everyone packed the stadium to see what George was going to do. He became part of the show, bringing the crowd into the game from the very kickoff. Once the game started, there he was, all over the stands, beating the snare drum, standing on the top of the visiting team's box, leading 16,000 people in mass garish cheers and insulting all of the visiting players during the game. No one had seen anything like it, and no one in any other professional sport was doing anything remotely similar at the time. Such grandstanding techniques are commonplace nowadays, but in 1974, they were totally brand new. George was a true pioneer.

What's more, as George writes in the book, the '70s Quakes orchestrated gimmicks at Spartan Stadium that no one could possibly get away with nowadays. For example, Seattle goalkeeper Barry Walting used to keep two teddy bears in his goal for good luck. So the Quakes used their connections at Marine World to secure two real bears. When George entered the field, he brought the two bears and ran with them in front of Walting, just for a joke.

Of course, the San Jose Earthquakes only constitute one chapter in George's book, as he went on to conquer more of the NHL, plus football, baseball and even the World Cup in 1994. He undisputedly invented the Wave cheer at an Oakland A's playoff game in 1981. While working for the Houston Oilers of the NFL, George irritated Pittsburgh Steelers coach Chuck Noll so much that Noll even tried banning George from the league. That's how powerful a snare drum was.

This Saturday, George appears at the San Jose Earthquakes match, where he will sign copies of Still Krazy After All These Cheers. It should be a crazy time, indeed.

In the end, George remains a dedicated Spartan alumni.

"San Jose State is where I began the longest relationship I've had with any sports organization," he writes. "As often as possible I cheer at Spartan games and would never cheer against them no matter how much I was offered."

Blank Club Owner Shuts Venue, Opens New Club

Last week, as soon as I saw Corey O'Brien standing on the southeast corner of First and San Salvador—right outside the former F/X The Club—I knew what was happening. Through the open doors workers could be seen cleaning up some old debris and hosing things off. It was clear. After nearly 12 years of operating The Blank Club with his partners, O'Brien was about to begin a brand new live-music adventure with some new investors inside the old F/X building, which had been the Pussycat Theatre before, and The Usual, the Spy and Angels in the years following F/X's closure.

It is with a tinge of sadness, that I report The Blank Club will close for good on Jan. 31, 2015. The name will be retired and O'Brien's new, yet-to-be-named club will open by the beginning of March. It was not a sudden decision. While the Blank has been the only venue of its kind in San Jose for years, everyone knows it simply isn't big enough. While it's miraculously managed to host many legendary shows over the years, there was no real backstage, no real place to load-in and the stage itself was way too small for national touring bands. Looking back over the last 12 years, I was very lucky to see Lemmy Kilmister, the Damned, GBH and the Buzzcocks on that stage.

After awhile though, with production costs going through the roof, and with more and more national touring bands expressing grief over the less-than-ample conditions, O'Brien says he finally came to a decision. The era of the Blank Club was not going to last much longer. It must eventually come to an end and he needed to move forward on his own to find a more suitable venue. The old F/X building has been empty for seven years, and while it will be expensive, O'Brien says it will be worth it.

I had to get the skinny in person, so I showed up at The Blank Club on the afternoon of Dec. 4, during non-operating hours, to ask O'Brien what was going on. He said the place simply wasn't going to cut it anymore.

"We don't have what we need here," O'Brien told me. "The stage is too small, there's nowhere to stage gear, the green room is back behind the bar, upstairs. If we want to do major touring bands, we needed a bigger room. San Jose needs a real, mid-sized club. We don't have one here."

Opening a new live music venue in the SoFA District—in the same building where alternative music fans saw countless bands 24 years ago—will add a much-needed component to the street. The area is already making a serious comeback and opening the F/X building again is going to work wonders for music-based nightlife.

The former F/X is the only building still empty at the intersection of South First and East San Salvador—an area once referred to by San Jose nightlife junkies as "The Four Corners." Original F/X owner Fil Maresca said a new rock club in that space will be transformative: "To see that marquee lit up again is going to make a serious difference in the neighborhood."

When 400 South First Street was called F/X, from 1989-1995, it regularly jammed that building with numerous national touring acts. No Doubt, Helmet, the Melvins, Jesus Lizard and countless other bands gigged there, back when they were nobodies. This unfolded in-between huge dance nights, themed events and all sorts of performance-based revelry. It's an amazing space for all sorts of events in addition to live bands, which is why O'Brien is looking forward to opening its doors in 2015. Especially since he was one of the original regulars who drank at F/X when it first opened 25 years ago. He even DJed there.

But even though he now has over a decade of memories at 44 S. Almaden Ave., O'Brien reiterated that he is not relocating the Blank Club to another venue. The new club will be just that: a new club.

"The Blank Club is here, at this location," declared O'Brien, as we continued to stand there during non-operating hours. "To do something else, it isn't the Blank Club. The Blank Club's here. It's going to be different over there, so it needs a different name."

Alchemy Garden Opens in San Jose

Approximately 30 esotericists and others from the general public found themselves at Rosicrucian Park last Sunday–the Winter Solstice–to dedicate a new Alchemy Garden. Dakotah Bertsch, of Central Coast Wilds in Santa Cruz, designed the garden and managed its installation by the Wilds team.

After the ceremony, Rosicrucians in attendance gushed with enthusiasm at Bertsch's efforts, thanking him for transforming a relatively barren splotch of the park into four mystical gardens, representing the four alchemical elements of Earth, Air, Fire, and Water. At the center of the garden, embedded in the ground between the four planters, is the symbol for the quintessence, the mystical fifth element of alchemy.

Leading alchemist Dennis Hauck served as a consultant for the plants now being grown in the garden, since he is also curating a new alchemy exhibit that opens next year on the Summer Solstice. Hauck is also involved in efforts to design a new alchemy museum on the ground of Rosicrucian Park, which is still in the works.

For the uninitiated, the ancient alchemists claimed to search for ways of converting base metals into gold, and their laboratory-based terminology contributed to the development of modern chemistry, although for centuries people have argued over the degree to which the alchemical process was mental, physical, spiritual, psychological or all of the above. Were the alchemists literally trying to convert lead into gold, or was it an allegory for personal growth? The debate rages on.

In any case, the Renaissance-era Rosicrucians were among those who first articulated the mental aspects of alchemy and the transpersonal components of the process. In the 20th century, Carl Gustav Jung embroidered the same threads, bringing alchemical symbolism and terminology into the practice of dream analysis and psychology, exploring how it relates to everyone's own inner journey. In the 1930s, just after the Rosicrucians set up their world headquarters in San Jose, they built an alchemical school of sorts. Much of the original facility still exists, although it hasn't been open to the public in decades. The installation of a new alchemy garden with alchemical herbs is the next step in a long process that will eventually lead to the reopening of the classroom.

The garden itself features four raised planters representing each of the four elements. They're formed in the shape of the symbol that represents that garden's element. Each planter contains herbs associated with the respective element, for eventual use in the alchemy laboratory. The garden's borders are filled with tumbled recycled glass the color of each element: blue for water, white for air, red for fire and an amber color representing the earth. The borders are uplit by LEDs underneath the recycled glass, illuminating them with dramatic effect once the sun goes down.

Rosicrucian Grand Master Julie Scott led the dedication ceremony, which included a group meditation and incantation of vowel sounds related to the alchemical elements. Following the meditation, the group proceeded to each of the four sections of the garden, where an adept then stood inside the respective section and recited passages related to the respective element.

Scott also mentioned that over the last 10 years, the Rosicrucian Order has been involved in specific initiatives to reduce its massive water bills at the park. After removal of several patches of lawn that required mammoth amounts of watering, the Order earned enough credits so that the rebates from the water company paid for the entire Alchemy Garden. Now that's sustainability. Leave it to the esotericists to come up with strategies for landscape renewal. Just as the Rosicrucians travel on paths of inner-renewal, they also apply those techniques to their outer landscape.

As of now, what used to be a barren section of the park with overgrown olive trees is now a mystical garden containing hidden symbols. And it flows nicely into the fountain area, with ankh-like pathways spiraling through the garden that almost look like they were designed according to ancient Egyptian principles. A few Rosicrucians in attendance even pointed this out, asking Dakotah Bertsch, the gardener, if he designed the paths that way on purpose.

"It was just a coincidence," he said.

2015

Exhibition District Brings Colorful Murals to San Jose

Imagine 40,000 square feet of space on the sides of buildings, in any shade of jaundiced yellow, hospital gray or faded beige. Well, there's a wealth of just such space in downtown San Jose, exactly why local muralist Erin Salazar is organizing a network of professional artists to paint colorful murals on the sides of buildings throughout the neighborhood.

Endeavoring to curate this new outdoor gallery, the group is calling it, The Exhibition District. Several lead sponsors, including the San Jose Downtown Association and the Knight Foundation, are already on board. An initial fundraising gala-hoedown-spectacular will erupt at Cafe Stritch on Tuesday at 6pm, with bands, music, artists and a live auction.

Full disclosure: everyone involved here are friends of mine. But let me say this: We're not talking about a ragtag group of amateur-hour Sunday Artists. The potential line-up includes highly acclaimed local and international peeps as well as collectives already working within the city. Salazar herself recently contributed murals to the ceiling of Good Karma Vegan Cafe and the wall inside Paper Plane. As a crew, they seem to have a systemic process in place, a series of walls that have been blank and ignored for years, and even a few property owners who seem enthusiastic in allowing them to go forward.

"I think one of the most beautiful things, and one of downtown San Jose's assets, is what it doesn't have yet," says Salazar. "There's an enormous potential. A virtually unlimited potential. We're able to see what other places, like L.A., Oakland or San Francisco, have done and then cut the fat and do it right the first time."

Such an optimistic attitude is refreshing to hear from a local working artist. It was not long ago when the prevailing attitude among local artists and musicians was to equate life-success with leaving San Jose as soon as humanly possible. It was also not long ago when the city government's attitude was that San Jose doesn't need artists—(San Joseans are mostly suburban car cultists and gasoline junkies who want tidy lawns and that's why people move here, dag nabbit!)—but now certain city employees are actually listening to artists and realizing otherwise. Rocking conversations have emerged.

As a result, part of what Salazar aims to do with the Exhibition District is to function as a go-between for artists and San Jose's dysfunctional bureaucracy. And she wants to slice through the endless hick-town ego jockeying and professional jealousy between the various cultural institutions around town.

"We want to be the Switzerland of art," Salazar tells me, over peppermint tea and canned jazz at La Lune Sucree. "We want to do our best to get past all of [the bureaucracy]. ... We want to go through and cut all that red tape, so that way, when we get an artist, and it's an awesome artist, [we just want him or her] to get there and get to work. Because the system is broken when it comes to commissioning artists. And San Jose has dropped the ball for so long in not even realizing that artists live here."

Of course, it's quite easy to be skeptical. It's great that City Hall now seems to realize that artists are usually the ones making a neighborhood more interesting. And it's great that a few local property owners seem to agree. But we know what normally happens in situations like this: Conniving real estate creeps tend to view artists more like manure for the seeds of gentrification. In cities everywhere, the real estate creeps lurk in the shadows, secretly watching artists transform a bland neighborhood into something awesome. Then the real estate creeps pounce and slaughter what everyone worked so hard to create, just so they can then replace the artist culture with blandness that just happens to be more expensive than the original blandness.

Don't get me wrong. I'm still applauding the Exhibition District. Just seeing first-hand how murals have transformed other neighborhoods around the world from Winnipeg to Berlin, I can only suppress my inherent skepticism with harmonious fanfare. Let the colors bleed!

Maitri Holds Annual Gala to Combat Domestic Violence

For 24 years now, Maitri has operated as a free, local and confidential nonprofit organization helping South Asian families deal with domestic violence, emotional abuse and other forms of family conflict. Its annual gala fundraising spectacular will unfold Feb. 28 at the Computer History Museum, attracting numerous Silicon Valley entrepreneurs, C-level executives and other high rollers from the South Asian community in the Bay Area.

After years of domestic violence problems in their diaspora, Maitri began in 1991 as a call-in resource for South Asian women survivors and/ or those who may not feel comfortable approaching mainstream organizations. Since then, Maitri has grown into a multilayered support network, replete with trained volunteers and legal advisors, all overseeing a transitional house for survivors of domestic violence and a boutique for donated items. The annual gala is the organization's main event.

Sonia Pelia, Maitri's board president, has been with the organization in one capacity or another for 20 years. She told me that the cases are by no means limited to partner-on-partner physical abuse. There's so much more involved, including emotional abuse, elderly abuse or even the effects that parent-on-parent emotional abuse have on the children—a scenario I can testify to first hand. There also exist cultural dynamics particular to the South Asian community that further complicate things. Often entering the mix is emotional abuse from extended families that aren't normally understood by the American legal system. Or even more horrifying, in some cases, relatives back in India might be orchestrating the domestic violence over the phone, advising the abuser from afar. Some of which are scenarios unfamiliar to the more traditional American support systems.

"It's not simple for a mainstream system to understand what's going on," Pelia said. "So, we function not just as education and outreach for our own community, but also for the mainstream, which is very important."

Even though patriarchal and misogynist dynamics are often at the root of these issues, when I spoke to Maitri folks, they emphasized that man-bashing attitudes don't help to solve anything. In fact, more and more men are coming on board to help contribute to the cause.

"The problem is not 'he,' the problem is our culture and how we can correct this problem," said Vinita Gupta, an Indian businesswoman who's been involved with Maitri since its inception. "We want men to be equal partners in resolving the problems of domestic violence. So, when we do our gala, we want men to feel like they're part of the solution, and not people to be blamed."

Maitri is constantly at work on new ideas. For example, last September, the Maitri Boutique opened up in Sunnyvale, providing a place where men, women and children can buy used and new South Asian party clothing and accessories. The boutique supports and funds the Economic Empowerment Programs at Maitri, with supporters and guests donating all items in the shop. The boutique has served about 1,500 customers since its launch and more than 2,000 volunteer hours have gone into the store.

However, the gala fundraiser continues to be the organization's main event. This year's installment will be another star-studded affair. Pelia says the event will, as always, focus on Maitri's triumphs rather than the miserable nature of the subject matter.

"All of our galas are very positive," Pelia says. "We celebrate our successes. We try not to focus just on the sadness of peoples' lives, but we try to focus on the good things that have happened. We've grown this far, we're helping people; more people are reaching out to us and getting substantive help."

Gupta says the goal is simply to help out the community and bring the problems to the surface. Otherwise, they will never go away.

"We are very family-oriented people, yet there are a lot of issues that we keep putting under the rug and this is an opportunity to just say that we stand for solving the problem," she says. "Solutions are not always obvious, but just bringing the community together and acknowledging that we do have a problem is a major step."

'She Who Tells a Story' at Cantor Arts Center

At the Cantor Arts Center, I mistake bullets for sequins. A thousand of them, in fact. From across the gallery, a large triptych, 5 1/2 feet high and 12 1/2 feet tall, a set of three chromogenic prints on aluminum, stretches before me.

In the work, a woman lies apparently sleeping on a bed of sequins. Behind her, a wall of still more sequins backdrops the scene. Sequins are falling throughout the piece, but as I make the approach it turns out the sequins are silver and gold bullet casings.

In this piece, Moroccan-born Lalla Essaydi, a former painter who lives in New York and Marrakech, creates what looks like a 19th-century Orientalist painting but is actually an inspiration to explore her own cultural identity and her fears about the growing restrictions on women following the events of the Arab Spring. In the triptych, *Bullets Revisited #3* (2012), she uses calligraphy (a typically male art form) to suggest the complexity of gender roles within Islamic culture. Thanks to the bulleted imagery, violence just drips from the work.

Originally organized by the Museum of Fine Arts, Boston (MFA), this major new exhibition at the Cantor Arts Center, "She Who Tells a Story," presents the work of 12 leading women photographers from Iran and the Arab world. Some of them still live in the Middle East, while others have moved on to Europe or the US. In its entirety, the show ridicules Western stereotypes and preconceptions of Middle Eastern women through 79 photos and two videos, all exploring issues of identity, narrative, representation and the brutality of war in daily life. The show endeavors to end the belief that women from this part of the world are oppressed and/or powerless.

When curator Kristen Gresh originally orchestrated the show in Boston, the text panel informs us, she encountered an Iranian artist who warned her that focusing on a group of women photographers was "alarming" because it would confirm the stereotype of Arab and Iranian women as "oppressed and powerless." On the contrary, Gresh writes, the photos on view do just the opposite—they ridicule and dismiss that viewpoint, suggesting we reassess our preconceived notions.

"She Who Tells a Story," comprised almost entirely of photographs from the last 10 years, unfolds in across three main sections—Deconstructing Orientalism, Constructing Identities, and New Documentary—although most of the work blurs all three of those categories.

For example, Shirin Neshat, an Iranian born in 1957 and living in New York, overlays her photos of women with Persian scripts and/or Farsi poetry from contemporary women writers, created to evoke the role that empowered women played in the upheaval following the Iranian Revolution in 1979. In one case, a woman holds her hand over her heart, but calligraphy covers her body and face. In another instance, a woman's text-covered hand, raised to her closed mouth, implies a strong voice. "In Iran women are quite powerful, unlike their cliched image. What I try to convey through my work is that power," says the text panel.

In another section we see hysterical photos from Shadi Ghadirian's 1998 *Qajar* series, in which she depicts women in various forms of the *hijab* (headscarf), but while posing with western images like boom boxes, Pepsi cans and dark shades, or backdropped against imagery of banned books. One senses a ridicule of the polar opposition of West/East, tradition/modernity, or intimacy/distance.

In *Women of Gaza* (2009), photographer Tanya Habjouqa, a Jordanian born in 1975 who lives in East Jerusalem, recorded the experience of women in Gaza living with limited freedom. Taken over a span of two months, the images convey modest pleasures, including a picnic on the beach, a rest on a bench between university classes, or an aerobics class.

Many events related to the exhibit will unfold over the next few months. On March 5, George Washington University professor of anthropology Attiya Ahmad will discuss the photos through the lenses of gender, feminist studies and her scholarship on the Middle East. And on March 19, three of the artists—Boushra Almutawakel, Tanya Habjouqa, and Rania Matar—will participate in a panel discussing their contributions to the show.

The Legendary Video Mania

With Cinequest nearly upon us, the anti-man-about-town needs to shatter spacetime and reflect on a legendary San Jose institution that originally taught him about movies. We're not talking about academic institutions, PBS, Gill Cable, or even books. We're talking about Video Mania, the greatest VHS movie rental store in San Jose history.

Way back in the last half of the earth-shattering '80s, and located in a cookie-cutter stripmall at the northeast corner of the monolithic intersection of Branham and Almaden Expressway, Video Mania was, literally, a-maze-ing. One could easily get lost in the place and we often did. Comprising two stories—unheard of for a video store at that time—Video Mania featured thousands of movie boxes stacked floor to ceiling in a labyrinthine setup, with alleys going every which direction. It was an exotic shangri-la in the middle of suburban wasteland America.

And they stocked material no one else in the Bay Area would carry. It was at Video Mania that I first discovered *The Incredibly Strange Creatures Who Stopped Living and Became Mixed-Up Zombies*, the celebrated Ray Dennis Steckler abomination from 1964. They also carried everything by Herschell Gordon Lewis, the "Godfather of Gore," the one who singlehandedly invented the splatter flick. Stuff like *Blood Feast*, *2000 Maniacs*, *The Wizard of Gore*, and *Color Me Blood Red*—Video Mania had 'em all. I can say with a high degree of confidence that Video Mania carried more horror films than the entire total collections of most other video stores at that time. It was fantastic.

As soon as one entered the establishment, a stairway to the right led up to the second story, where they kept all the horror stuff. Worn '80s carpeting and ramshackle wooden shelving made it look like someone's grandfather had built the place out of his garage, but countless posters and all those movie boxes transformed the scene into paradise. The original movie covers sat on the shelf for anyone to look at, and then the tapes themselves were in plastic boxes behind the covers. If the plastic box wasn't there, it meant someone had already checked it out. The customers simply browsed until they found a few films they wanted, and then brought the plastic boxes with the tapes downstairs to the counter. The price was usually three movies for three days for $9.99, a smokin' deal.

"They were the first store I'd ever heard of that actually rented VCRs," recalls August Ragone, who worked at Video Mania before going on to an established path as an author and Japanese monster movie expert. "They were a one-stop shop. A lot of people remember Tower Video in the 1980s, so that sticks in their minds, but people were driving a long ways to go to Video Mania. There were people coming from Mountain View and Fremont. Because [the store] would get multiple copies of any new movies that came out."

Best of all, I could go in there, under the age of 18, and Video Mania would rent me any R-rated horror flick. They didn't seem to care. If I wanted *Dr. Butcher, M.D.* or *Jaws of Satan*, I was home free. In fact, my entire knowledge of below-budget Z-grade atrocities began with Video Mania.

Even though one of the owners was a diehard horror fan, the store also carried an obsessive science fiction collection, an entire aisle of mysterious kung-fu stuff and tons of Japanese and other foreign films. At that time, no one else stocked *Yojimbo* or *Seven Samurai*.

Older generations fondly recall how they rode their bicycles to go pick apricots from vast orchards in the previous decades. Well, I fondly recall driving my shitty, beat-up Datsun down Branham Lane, past a dive

7-11, a few vacant lots and the cultural Mecca of Orchard Supply Hardware, straight to Video Mania, just so I could snare a copy of Redneck Zombies. That store was the Promised Land.

"It was like the Xanadu of video," Ragone says. "It was this weird place you went into, and once you walked in, you were just staggered by the magic of this place, which was in this tiny strip mall, in a pocket of San Jose that most people would ignore."

The Plentiful Peach by Niloufar Talebi

Just like I'd expect from Palo Alto, the historical capital of Silicon Valley, an inspiring half-eastern and half-western collaboration will erupt this weekend.

Spacetime-continuum-channeled via Azerbaijan, Iran, San Francisco, Los Angeles, Palo Alto High and the beige corridors of SJSU's School of Music, *The Plentiful Peach* premieres Sunday at Stanford's Bing Concert Hall thanks to two unique talents: Niloufar Talebi on words and Mark Grey on music. Together they fuse the eastern and western hemispheres—a trans-hemispherical alchemy, I'll call it—with a chorus taking center stage, literally. Also included in the program are works by Henry Mollicone, George Gershwin and others.

A world premiere commissioned by the Los Angeles Children's Chorus, *The Plentiful Peach* is a coming-of-age story about a peach and the brave children who secretly grow her—against the odds. Talebi is a librettist and multiple-award-winning translator of Persian poetry who lives in San Francisco. She adapted *The Plentiful Peach* from an original story by the great Iranian writer Samad Behrangi. Grey, an acclaimed composer and sound engineer who went to Palo Alto High, as well as SJSU, wrote the choral score. (Empty disclosure: Grey and I are ancient friends; we were the equivalent of college fraternity bros, although we simply had the frat parties on stage.)

The original Samad Behrangi story, *One Peach and 1000 Peaches*, satirizes differences between the rich and poor, between privileged gluttony and poverty, between gratuitous waste and sustainability. The master takes the most fertile and watered land for himself and leaves the peasants with the unusable land while building a wall between the two worlds. A group of children employ a stealth operation to scale the wall and eat anything they can find. They stumble upon a peach, eat it, and later return to a quiet corner of the master's orchard for planting the seed. Aside from the theme of the oppressor and the oppressed, the story features viewpoints from the peach seed and the earth. Talebi was clearly moved by the original tale and I was moved just listening to her explain it over the phone.

"There's poetic line after poetic line," she said. "It's a really beautiful, lyrical story that is still relevant today, in terms of sustainability and environmentalism. And it's so rich and so lyrical and so simple and profound that it was impossible not to do something with it."

As a result, Talebi adapted the original story, which to her knowledge is not yet even translated into English, and then produced the libretto for *The Plentiful Peach*. She and Grey then discussed various narrative arcs, potential outlines, dramatic structures, compositional ideas for soloists and thematic messages they wanted to get across. During moments of the piece, Grey even sets music for children singing lines in Persian.

Talebi does not call herself a poet, but the libretto is pure poetry with multiple layers of meaning and symbolism. It really is a combo of East and West, an alchemical Sufi orchard of spiritual emotion. I'd be spoiling the peaches if I disclosed any more, but it made me want to whirl like a dervish. Or at least eat a thousand peaches.

This Sunday marks the world premiere, but this is not the first such collaboration between Grey and Talebi. In 2011, the two joined forces for *Atash Sorushan* (Fire Angels), which premiered at Carnegie Hall and later came to the Berkeley campus.

Behrangi (1939-1967), the original author of the peach story, was an interesting character who deserves much more attention in the West. A native of Azerbaijan, he was a notable Iranian writer and social critic who wrote, among other things, children's books that illuminated the struggles of the poor. His works highlighted the difference between the haves and have-nots, and he was a strong activist for children's education, arguing to reform what he saw as the failings of a state-sponsored education system. He mysteriously drowned in the Aras river at the age of 28 and it's widely suggested that his leftist, anti-State politics had something to do with it. This weekend, his work sees a new light, thanks to Grey and Talebi. I am whirling already.

Silicon Alleys 10 Year Anniversary

With *Metro*'s 30th anniversary issue coming up soon, it makes sense to reflect on the 10th anniversary of this column.

In April of 2005, *Metro* gave me some weekly space to ruminate on the San Jose condition. At the time, I had no idea what it would become. The only goal—if there was even a goal—was to provide something different every single week, so readers would never have any idea what to expect. One week, a local barbershop; the next, the use of esoteric gnosticism to analyze the intersection of Kiely and Stevens Creek. Subject-wise, nothing was out of reach: pro soccer, Zen, punk, travel, local history, union stagehands, or Manson Family members from the Cambrian District. In fact, the cover kicker on the issue containing the first Silicon Alleys said, "No one is safe from Gary Singh's new column."

A few belligerent suburban rednecks on San Jose Inside, a political blog now owned by *Metro*, immediately made fun of it. But an overwhelming majority of readers who gave feedback over the first few years said they enjoyed the column because they never knew what to expect.

As the column evolved, I began to find multiple literary appreciations for San Jose that I never knew I had. That is, a few different narrator-identities began to emerge, one being the Urban Blight Exploration Junkie. Since San Jose is essentially one gigantic off-the-radar swath of geography, just about everything here can be understood as "off the beaten path." And no previous writer had taken to the streets, literally on foot, to explore the guts of the city. I decided to do just that. The blight junkie thus became addicted to glorifying the industrial wastelands, seedy neighborhoods, rundown shopping centers, weed-infested vacant lots or any form of abandonment in San Jose. In some cases, I simply walked down Stockton Avenue, 24th Street, or Auzerais and simply wrote down whatever was there.

And here's the craziest thing: I thought I was the only one. Turns out that wasn't the case at all. I had no idea what I was tapping into with those particular columns. But readers ate it up and, in ways I never predicted, those columns became the most popular ones I've ever written. To this day, the urban blight stories contemplating the guts of San Jose, walking around and exploring the overall garbage of this town, are the ones I get the most requests to write more of. At the time, some readers even tore the column out of the newspaper and took it with them to explore the geography on their own. Some even sent me videos they made. One left me a voicemail that said, "Dude, there's this shithole over on Santa Teresa, some building, you gotta check it out. It's fucking hideous. You gotta write about it." All in all, I discovered that many San Joseans, those still here and especially those who've long since left, have a thriving connection to the seedier aspects of this landscape.

Over time, Silicon Alleys evolved and twisted and reformed itself in multiple ways. I can't write about blight every week—that would get boring. And I just don't feel the abandonment every week. So, if anything, the experiences and perspectives on San Jose tend to be deeper and more cosmic these days. The key word here is "experience," as this column reflects my own. Synchronicities, for example, have played a huge role in dozens of manifestations of this column. They can be a wonderful source of creativity. Over time, I became a love slave to the muses of synchronicity.

Finally, since my identity is half eastern, half western; half urban, half suburban; half academic, half street; and half punk, half easy listening, this is the lens through which I view San Jose. I am always prone to ridicule any ethnic category around here—Asian-American? Half-Asian-Pacific-American? *Blecccchhh!*

Which brings us to a final reduction of the perspectives behind this column. My dad was from India and my mom is Anglo, meaning, I'm "Half-Indian, Half Anglo-Willow-Glen," so the acronym is HI HAWG. The author, to his knowledge, is the only HI HAWG in San Jose. And that is why I write this column.

MACLA Celebrates 25th Anniversary

This weekend, MACLA celebrates its 25th anniversary, not only via its annual Latino Art Auction, but also with a celebration to repurpose Parque de los Pobladores across the street.

MACLA (Movimiento de Arte y Cultura Latino Americana) began as a Latino and Chicano arts advocacy group at the end of the 1980s, and it's grown into a nationally-recognized tangible institution. What's more, architect Teddy Cruz, an associate professor in public culture and urbanism at U.C. San Diego, will reveal grand plans this weekend to salvage the hideous sun-baked splotch of ineffectual concrete at the northern end of Parque de los Pobladores. The city screwed the park up a few years ago by ripping out trees and replacing them with pavement.

Expect a permanent stage plus modular and multipurpose components, transforming the space into a vibrant, multidimensional plaza of public and cultural engagement—you know, like something you'd find in any real city anywhere else. Other than that, I won't spoil it. You'll have to show up and see what transpires.

The main gig here, though, is MACLA's 25th anniversary. Around the mid- to late-1980s, seemingly endless construction began to slaughter downtown. The city was tearing up the streets to build the light rail system, driving retailers out of business left and right. Skid row areas and pockets of adult entertainment ghettos still percolated. Debates raged about the future of the city, its socio-economic makeup, housing policies and its investments in cultural life. Just a few years earlier, a Chicano-themed cultural center, the Centro Cultural de la Gente, had closed up shop.

As the '80s wore on, practically all of the city's funding for the arts went to more "vanilla" forms of cultural production and a few provocative heroes began to get sick of it, so they stepped up to the plate and made their voices heard. Maribel Alvarez was one of those people and MACLA essentially began as an advocacy organization, embroidering the threads of the civil rights, anti-poverty and Chicano movements with an ever-expanding Latino identity. Together, these threads ensured ethnic-based arts could flourish in San Jose.

"MACLA was steeped in social-change advocacy from the beginning," Alvarez told me. "In the very early stages we thought we would be more like an umbrella so we could facilitate that for other people instead of our own, but the energy was there to really bring back some of that Latino creativity and harness it."

MACLA's attitude was edgy, political, fresh, high-quality, experimental and it really did establish a movement, which later evolved into an actual physical space on South First Street. It became a repository of youth cultures, Chicano poetics, performance art, and even several other ethnic persuasions. As a group, MACLA published papers, received grants, and made itself known throughout the country. Organizations like the Andy Warhol Foundation, the Ford Foundation and several others across the USA became aware of all that MACLA had accomplished before most people in San Jose even understood what MACLA was. That's typical San Jose, of course.

But eventually, MACLA did indeed infiltrate local governments. People in positions of power actually listened to MACLA, realizing its message was real—not crusty old ethnic politics—and represented a growing tapestry of movements vastly important to the cultural landscape of San Jose. Even better, unlike other organizations, they stuck it out and refused to leave downtown.

Today, MACLA programs cutting-edge material on a regular basis. The building at 500 South First Street, formerly a '50s-era auto dealership, officially belongs to MACLA now, and after I was shown secret plans for what's in store for that two-story complex, I was quite thrilled to say the least.

Looking back on 25 years, Alvarez says she's blown away by what MACLA has accomplished since the beginning. As a movement, it paved the way a quarter-century ago and continues to do so.

"MACLA really helped redefine ethnic sensibilities," Alvarez said. "We were very sophisticated and cosmopolitan. We were very edgy and we were very traditional at the same time.

"But what is different now is that MACLA is starting to finally get that recognition, locally, and show that it has the support and the capacity to do amazing things as part of the downtown fabric."

Silicon Valley Roller Girls Serve More than Hits

Aside from beating the crap out of opponents on the flat track, Silicon Valley Roller Girls are laboring to find a new permanent home, collecting supplies for schoolkids and remaining active in social justice efforts. In short, they're everywhere.

This Saturday marks the Silicon Valley Roller Girls' (SVRG) second bout in a new temporary facility: South Hall behind the McEnery Convention Center. The squad used to practice and play its matches at San Jose Skate, way out there on the South Side, where the buses barely run. But when the landlord sold the building, the derby girls found themselves in search of a new home. South Hall will bridge the gap for the time being. Also this weekend, SVRG will be the featured volunteer organization at the eighth annual SubZERO Festival in downtown San Jose, serving suds in the beer garden and skating around to publicize the league and the June 6 bout.

But what really goes unnoticed when it comes to the derby girls, is the community service work these people do. Just to cite one shining example, former State Assemblymember Sally Lieber recently completed her annual book drive for incarcerated women and SVRG jumped at the opportunity to participate. The derby girls helped collect and donate hundreds of books to be distributed to California's state prisons. One derby girl in particular, Sasha Degrader, wrote a moving letter, a personal testimonial declaring how books helped turn her own life around, back when she was incarcerated several times.

In the letter, she describes the conditions of prison: up to seven women often sharing a locked room—pressure, anxiety, and virtually no mental exercises to even try and hone one's intellect except for books that others have donated. In cases of women trying to recover from drugs or alcohol, books are especially essential, even if it's just to improve basic skills.

"For some women," Sasha wrote, "the reading of books is the only mental exercise they will get because they stopped going to school at a young age and they are trapped in the lifestyle and economic status that led them to where they are today."

The rest of her letter is a poignant personal revelation about how she discovered *Anna Karenina* and Cormac McCarthy's *The Road* while locked up. Her roommates thought she was a nutcase for even showing emotion over such books. But the books helped her temporarily escape from the miseries of prison while increasing her mental capacity in the process—as if someone had thrown her a life raft.

When the derby girls collect books for women in prison, Sasha sees it as a perfect way of giving back. Anything to help. If a woman has more access to reading materials, even fiction, her recovery process will go better.

"By donating these books we are showing solidarity for our fellow women," Sasha wrote. "Women in prison are in the shadows of our society. Due to a broken correctional system, coupled with overcrowding, these women don't have a lot of resources. Libraries are sometimes nothing more than broom closets and storage rooms with a few shelves of tattered books."

I recently powwowed with the derby girls at Veggie Grill in Saratoga, where they skated all through the inside of the restaurant, many of them with kids in tow. One of them, who went by the name Kraken Rox, said being a derby girl had changed her life. At 53, she's the oldest skater in the entire league. She says derby is the most empowering thing she's ever done.

"When you get out there on the track, you're a totally different person," she tells me. "You could be the nicest person in the world off the track, but when you get on the track, you just beat the crap out of people and it's so much fun. And everybody loves each other. When it's all over, you hug each other and you go home. Then you come back and do it again."

Manchester United Visits San Jose

Manchester United, ranked by Forbes as the most valuable sports club in the world at $2.23 billion, will make an unprecedented visit next week to San Jose for a game against the Earthquakes. Many European clubs have played here over the last 40 years, including Real Madrid back in the 1980s, but no one as lucrative as ManU.

There is much reason to celebrate, as the two teams share some history. One of the best players ever to play the sport, and certainly the most famous ManUnited star, George Best, played for the Quakes for two seasons, in 1980-81. His story is more than well documented, but he is inarguably the most famous international sports figure ever to play for any team in San Jose, in any sport, before or since. When he passed away in 2005, I hurried over to the *Metro* office and jammed out a last-minute obituary on deadline, which later wound up in a UK-based compilation book of memories titled, *George Best: A Celebration*. His hometown of Belfast, Northern Ireland, gave him the equivalent of a state funeral. Everyone took the day off work and 100,000 people jammed the streets to watch the motorcade.

People all over this valley still tell stories of Best's time here, but his influence on the field especially crossed all boundaries. San Jose's own Brandi Chastain grew up attending Quakes games and in her 2005 book, *It's Not About the Bra*, Brandi said George Best was one of her first sports heroes.

"When I started playing soccer, I had no role models to inspire me on the field," she wrote. "No one in my neighborhood, or in my family, played the game. But the very first time I saw the professional team that would become my guiding light, the San Jose Earthquakes, I found my role model. He was George Best, and in my mind, the name fit. Watching him corkscrew bewildered defenders into the ground with his amazing moves and a smile on his face, I said to myself, 'That's what I want to do.'"

Best's legacy continues around the world. When the crew of Manchester United TV visited San Jose a few months ago, they wanted to know everything about George Best's time here. They interviewed former Earthquake Chris Dangerfield, who told them a number of stories. He and Best were teammates, pals and even housemates for a short time. After the interview, the TV crew said it was refreshing to meet a club with so much history, which makes Manchester United's upcoming visit that much more relevant.

In fact, just as I was contemplating what to write in this column, I bumped into yet another person with a George Best memory. He apparently taught people how to play darts at The Hot Pot, a nondescript bar in a nondescript strip mall on the west side. These encounters happen to me all the time. In some cases, people may not have even heard of Manchester United, but they remember George Best hanging out in San Jose or Los Gatos more than 30 years ago. In other cases, even if people from that era don't make it to the games now, they still have fond memories of George Best.

Of course, Best is not the only Manchester United connection to San Jose. Another former legend, Bill Foulkes, actually coached the Earthquakes for the 1980 season, when Best first arrived. The team was not very good, but Foulkes brought his own history with him. He was a survivor of the tragic 1958 air disaster in Munich, when 23 people died in a plane crash, including eight United players, three members of the club's staff and eight journalists.

After all these decades, it is truly remarkable for San Jose that one of the world's biggest sports clubs is now playing a match right here at the Quakes' own intimate stadium. In 1981, no one imagined such a thing would ever happen. Next week, the ghosts of George Best and Bill Foulkes will drift among the steel beams of Avaya Stadium. I think they would like the place.

Stones Manager Sam Cutler and Joel Selvin at Studio Bongiorno

Just a few years ago, Studio Bongiorno opened up in the old California Monument Building in Santa Clara, right across the street from the Mission Cemetery. For an art gallery, performance space and overall gathering spot, the joint is a nucleus of crackpot activity.

This week, two living monuments, former Rolling Stones tour manager Sam Cutler and legendary rock journalist Joel Selvin, will provide a rip-roaring conversation for anyone interested in rock history, especially Altamont.

Cutler operated with the Stones in the late '60s. From Hyde Park to Altamont, he was there, doing what was essentially a thankless job. For perhaps decades, Cutler was the dude most often scapegoated in the American media for the entire Altamont fiasco, that is, when the Stones played their ill-fated free concert that resulted in the death of an audience member at the hands of a Hells Angel. According to both Cutler and Selvin, much from Altamont has yet to be revealed. In fact, Selvin is at work on a book that should provide the final word on that dark historic event.

Cutler's own 2010 book, *You Can't Always Get What You Want: My Life With the Rolling Stones, the Grateful Dead and Other Wonderful Reprobates*, presents his side of the sordid details from Altamont. It's an amazing piece of work. The Stones essentially bailed after the whole thing was over, leaving Cutler to deal with 100 percent of the fallout. Even after Cutler illuminates the roles played by surrogate Hells Angels, the mafia, the feds, the incessant hanger-ons, groupies, lawyers, promoters and politicians, it becomes clear that the complete story still hasn't really been told. Hopefully Selvin's book will do that.

After Altamont, Cutler's book moves on to his tenure as the Grateful Dead's tour manager in the subsequent years. After the chaotic narcissistic circus of the Rolling Stones, the Dead scene was polar opposite. According to Cutler, although everyone was wasted, including himself, the adventure was much more of a family-style journey. Unfortunately, at that stage of the Dead's career, the band commanded no business sense and Cutler almost paints himself as the wise old sage just trying to right the ship in a mess of drugs and alcohol, while barely getting paid anything. Of course, this was long before the Dead rose to multimillionaire stadium rockers.

Cutler could have bashed both bands out of sour grapes. But he didn't. That would have been a terrible book. Instead, it seems like he spent some serious years grappling with how to forgive, who to forgive, and that he harbors deep respect for the Stones and the Dead, especially now in his old age and now that he's turned into a writer. Writing tends to do that to people. It makes them more self-reflective. And some damn good stories explode from the pages of his book. Not all the gaps get filled in, but it's a great rock 'n roll memoir.

This Friday will not be the first time Cutler and Selvin have co-headlined in Santa Clara. In 2013, when Cutler descended upon the States for the first time in years, the two appeared at Studio Bongiorno for a rip-roaring conversation. The stories were hysterical. One in particular featured Cutler punching out Bill Graham on the stage of the Oakland Coliseum, and then going through Jagger to essentially humiliate the famous Napoleonic promoter in his own element. According to Cutler, Graham always hated the Stones after that encounter. They were the only band he couldn't dominate.

In 2013, that event at Studio Bongiorno with Cutler and Selvin was a lightning bolt of pure magic. The crowd overflowed onto the sidewalk outside. Cutler told stories about Mick Jagger, Keith Richards, Janis Joplin, Jerry Garcia, Bill Graham, Jimi Hendrix, Syd Barrett and others I can't even recall. And he's an authoritative source. With him, sitting right there was Joel Selvin himself. Together they provided stories normally relegated to the bars after the show. Again, this was on some nondescript corner of suburban Santa Clara across from a cemetery. Who thought that would ever happen? Well, this Friday it will happen again. I guess lightning really does strike twice.

Veggielution: Constant Gardeners

Along the journey to Veggielution, a glorious audio collage envelops me. By the time I arrive at the far back corner of Emma Prusch Farm Park, I've heard roosters, geese, whistling park employees, children scampering, a few tractors and ubiquitous freeway noise from the monolithic 680/101 interchange.

As a community farm, Veggielution occupies six acres of land and generates 47,000 pounds of produce every year, but since it's buried way at the rear of Prusch Park, past a few historic houses, gates and walkways, the general park populace doesn't seem to know it's there. The entire property seems miles from the congested, motor-oil-soaked nausea of King Road outside.

"Everybody's been to the park, but hardly anyone gets all the way back here," says Veggielution interim executive director Cayce Hill, as we meet in a makeshift kitchen. "We're trying to change that."

Veggielution features many different components, so many that it's hard to keep track of them all. Hill takes me into the farm stand, where 70 customers roll in every Saturday to pick up boxes of produce intended to last for a week. Over the course of a year, another 500 youths arrive to work in the garden, which is filled with goji berries, yarrow, aster, sorrel, narcissus, chard, garbanzo beans, marjoram and zinnias. Everything is labeled in both English and Spanish. In case you wanted to know, crocus translates to azafran.

Way off in the background, I see orchards, plots of vegetable plants attached to trellises and even two greenhouses, all flanked by freeways. In the pavilion area, the ladies from Somos Mayfair are teaching kids folklorico dancing while music blasts from a boom box. The tune "El Cerro de la Silla" remains in my head for the length of my visit.

As staff and volunteers saunter back and forth in every direction, a visiting group, Filipino Advocates for Justice, arrives for a tour. Hill begins by apologizing for the traffic noise.

"The freeway forms the contour of the farm," she tells the group. "That's why it's in our logo. You're always reminded that we're in a big city."

As I infiltrate the tour, we move throughout the expanse of the farm in about 30 minutes. We visit the orchards, the potting station and the greenhouses. I learn about myriad activities occurring on a regular basis: barn dancing, yoga on the farm, environmental justice lectures, cooking classes.

But all during the journey, we're warned about Veggielution's enemy number one: feral peacocks. No one knows why or how they arrived in this part of San Jose, but they tend to hide out in the cornstalks, eating crops and creating havoc on a regular basis. Even the greenhouses are blocked off with bird netting to stop them. Peacocks are one of my favorite birds.

"They're pests," Hill says. "They can mow down a little row of seedlings in a second. And the sound they make is like children screaming."

As a nonprofit, Veggielution struggles to raise cash just like any other

501c3 outfit, which is why their Annual Bounty of Heart's Delight fund-raising dinner is this Saturday, 4:30-10pm. A grand-scale affair it shall be. The $140 ticket includes a five-course dinner on the farm with chef Matthias Froeschl of Naschmarkt in Campbell, plus hay rides, a raffle, auction and open-air dancing.

"We're hoping to get all the Veggielution regulars, as well as some people that haven't been here in a while," Hill says.

Veggielution is a full-functioning rural oasis amid one of the ugliest freeway monstrosities in all of California, a yin-yang of delicious corn orchards and Japanese eggplant juxtaposed against the perverse eyesore of suburban sprawl. In that sense, the entire scene represents the best and worst of San Jose all in one place. I would expect nothing less.

Oddball Musician Korla Pandit Gets Long-Overdue Respect

At the dawn of the television era, Korla Pandit mesmerized millions of television viewers with his dazzling talent on the Hammond organ, exotic jeweled turbans, Indian mysticism and deep penetrating eyes. He rarely spoke. He just stared into cameras throughout the 1950s, looking right into everyone's living rooms. His entire shtick was, if not the first, one of the first true TV masterpieces.

Aside from his TV work, he became the undisputed godfather of a music genre that came to be known as exotica. He was a direct antecedent of lounge lizard culture, space-age bachelor pad music, Liberace, and many flavors of high camp in the last half of the 20th century. One might even suggest Marilyn Manson, to a certain degree, ripped off Pandit's shtick.

Thanks to John Turner and Eric Christensen, a fantastic new documentary, Korla, now explores Pandit's life and career, especially the more controversial aspect of his story.

He was not actually Korla Pandit. He wasn't even Indian. He was an African-American dude named John Roland Redd from Columbia, Mo., who couldn't get a proper working gig in racist Hollywood of the late '40s. He broke in by inventing a new identity for himself and stuck to the story for the rest of his life.

That much is old news, but the documentary is long overdue and riveting at every turn. It holds your attention just the way Korla did all those decades ago. And yes, the suburban myths about Pandit are true: he did perform at Pizza and Pipes restaurants in the South Bay many times.

Turner and Christensen are Bay Area media legends—KGO employed them both for decades—so the two were well connected enough to pool their resources and shine a mystic light on Pandit's story. Christensen leveraged years of music industry connections, and Turner brought a lifelong passion for eccentric characters, oddball history and folk-art Americana to the table. Both are retired and together their efforts paid off in the documentary.

"There was a collaboration of interests," Turner said. "Eric's in music and mine in eccentric and wonderful people to celebrate. [We] met for lunch three-and-a-half years ago and started talking about projects, and I thought this Korla thing would be interesting to collaborate on and use both of our talents."

In the film, people from several walks of life rally on Pandit's behalf, including Carlos Santana, who places him on the same mystical plane as Miles Davis and Alice Coltrane. Hammond B-3 legends Dr. Lonnie Smith and Booker T. Jones testify to Pandit's unique approach to the instrument. Highball praise also comes from bands like the Cramps and the Muffs, the latter of which actually dragged Pandit out of obscurity in the early '90s to record.

On the flip side, sociologist Harry Edwards calls our attention to the fact that John Roland Redd never tried to advance the cause of racial integration. Instead, he invented another identity solely to advance his own career.

From an Eastern perspective, there is no absolute ending to this story, but the film rightly conjures up some serious questions on which the viewer will continue to meditate. Did Korla Pandit capitalize on America's insidious caricatures of the "exotic"? Did he make his family miserable by carrying on with a false identity for the rest of his life? Or should his superior musical talent and innovative keyboard play, along with his belief that music is the universal language, take precedent? I'm inclined to believe the latter.

There really won't ever be another story like Pandit's. So far, the story includes obsessive fans, crackpot genealogists, new age housewives, journalists, sociologists, lounge lizards, record collectors, B-movie freaks, organ society administrators, Eastern spiritualists and television historians. It's not crazy. It's poetic: John Roland Redd decided to go west and discovered the East instead.

The Golden State has always been home to fringe spiritualities, eccentrics, the underbelly of the entertainment industry and a place where people simply go to start over. In that sense, the journey of Korla Pandit is a truly California story. It makes me proud to be a native. And exotic.

Our Lives in This Place: Robin Lasser and Genevieve Hastings

Near the Naglee Park Garage, a portable kiosk sits on the southern side of San Carlos Street. At the kiosk, anyone can walk up and rifle through stacks of bright, artsy postcards, all printed with quotes from various community members of proposed urban village projects.

For several months now, the kiosk has traveled around the neighborhood, mostly along the East Santa Clara Street corridor, as part of a new art project titled, "Our Lives in This Place."

It's designed to help community members voice their concerns and tell the city planners what needs to be done to make the neighborhood more interesting. The plan is much larger, of course.

Over at City Hall, the Envision San Jose 2040 General Scheme includes a zillion different "urban villages" throughout the sprawling city landscape. One such village emphasizes East Santa Clara Street from Seventh to 17th Street. For the planning of this particular village, which should eventually add a few hundred more units over the next several years, the city recently did something it has never done before: A trio of artists—Robin Lasser, Trena Noval and Genevieve Hastings—were commissioned to create a new social sculpture and a social engagement project as part of the urban planning process.

As artists, the three created a series of postcards featuring reproduced portraits of specific people in the neighborhood (yes, analog art!), replete with quotes relaying their ideas for the future. Each postcard features a resident in his or her element, illustrated by artists Dax Tran-Caffee or James Gouldthorpe. Then, on the flipside, we see statements from the resident.

For example, Moses Mena, who manages the East Santa Clara Street Farmers Market, wrote that public spaces need to be saved: Half-park and half-work spaces are necessary for people, small businesses and small community-based organizations. This is what fosters real community involvement, he wrote. On another postcard, Alan Johnson of Needle in the Groove record shop remembers the word "urban" as described in rap and R&B a quarter-century ago. He wonders if another word should be used instead. In still more cases, historian Anthony Raynsford talks about the neighborhood's architectural heritage; Barbara Goldstein talks about the elderly population; Ivy Thu-Nga Vuong focuses on rooftop gardens and healthy food choices. Overall, it's a pretty good benchmark of the neighborhood's diversity.

When all was said and done, the postcards were then placed into a traveling kiosk, which, in turn, inspired more residents to voice their concerns and hopes for the future. Thus, the project became an iterative process. The artists functioned as a "connection-machine," interfacing with local residents, business folk and other community members to find out what people actually wanted from this newly defined East Santa Clara Street corridor. The result was much more interesting had everyone been forced to attend endless bureaucratic urban planning meetings.

One of the artists, Genevieve Hastings, went to San Jose State University and lives within reach of the neighborhood. As a result of this project, she became more connected and made new friends.

"We interviewed and spoke with so many incredible people along the way," Hastings says. "I feel like I have a stronger sense of community now. I also took away a far greater understanding of the urban planning process. When we started, I don't think we had any idea of the steps it takes to create these plans for urban villages. It's been a steep learning curve at times, but very rewarding."

Yet again we see artists making neighborhoods more interesting.

Twenty years ago, even 10 years ago, this wouldn't have happened. I can't imagine how utterly genteel and nauseating this process would have been, had the artists not participated. And with a public kiosk, filled up with postcards, traveling around the 'hood, giving residents a chance to chime in and learn more about their own neighbors, everyone wins.

The Chocolate Watchband Eschews Kitschy Nostalgia

The only San Jose band to share a lead singer with the Harvard-Smithsonian Center for Astrophysics is returning to its home turf this weekend. The Chocolate Watchband initially came to life 50 years ago at Foothill College, but the legendary '60s psychedelic garage-rock specialists played so many shows in San Jose that the city became their hometown. It stuck to them.

The '60s-era members went on to various other exploits. Guitarist Tim Abbott now owns KVP Studios on Lawrence Expressway. Singer David Aguilar went on teach astrophysics and write science books for National Geographic. But during its heyday in the last half of the '60s, The Chocolate Watchband carved out quite a niche, successfully blending garage and psychedelic rock, beginning with a Stones-style R&B influence, and then eventually expanding into a more experimental multi-instrumental dimension, incorporating elements of surf, jazz and '60s exotica.

Locally, the band gigged at a variety of now-forgotten venues like Napredak Hall, the Continental Roller Rink, the Spectrum in Redwood City, Homer's Warehouse in Palo Alto, and Winchester Cathedral in Redwood City. They played everywhere, almost daily, and even appeared in two films, 1967's Riot on Sunset Strip and The Love-Ins. In the former case, the B-grade counterculture exploitation masterpiece featured the Watchband playing a few songs with Rickenbackers, mod haircuts and the whole nine yards. YouTube clips are everywhere. The band only lasted about five years before falling apart, but aficionados claim the Watchband were one of the best garage-rock outfits ever.

After reforming in 1999, the band has traveled through a few more phases and returns this Saturday to the Ritz in downtown San Jose. Joining them will be Darryl Hooper from the Seeds, adding a quintessential '60s keyboard element to the band's already eclectic panoply of sonic exploration.

Remarkably, there seems to be no sense of dreamy nostalgia about any of this, no sense of reliving the past. For a bunch of dudes pushing 70, the band members don't seem to be banking on previous careers at all. Instead, they just want to offer groovy tunes that transcend generations. There's a reason why those Nuggets albums still have a cult following all the way to Europe and South America, and there's a reason why the band's recent shows in Southern California attracted a mostly younger audience. What's more, for the upcoming San Jose gig, we thankfully won't see any "50th anniversary" marketing schlock. The band is above such nonsense.

"We really don't care about that stuff," Abbott says. "People who want us and who like Chocolate Watchband music, they know we're not saying, 'Oh, let's look how long we've been together.' We just want to make music that people want to come and rock to."

As an example, Abbott says, recent Watchband gigs in Southern California and Europe elicited emotional reactions from fans who seemed thrilled to experience vibes from decades ago but not in some kitschy, nostalgic way. The music resonated beyond any possible age difference, indicating the band's influence clearly lives on.

Local guitarist Derek See, for instance, worships at the altar of '60s music. In addition to playing guitar for opening band The Gentle Cycle, he will also sit in with Watchband for a few numbers. Even though See wasn't alive during Watchband's original heyday, he discovered them on Nuggets collections and a Rhino Records compilation when he was 11 years old.

"Hearing them and hearing all that music is part of what set me up on the path of hardcore record collecting at a young age," See recalls. "One thing that set the Watchband apart from other garage bands is that their records were very good. They weren't sloppy. They were tight. They were pros. They weren't screwing around. They were the real deal."

See's participation is an example of how the music is being passed down from generation to generation in San Jose. It should be inspiring to watch.

San Jose Botches the Grateful Dead's 50th Anniversary

San Jose's City Hall didn't get much of a draw to commemorate the 50-year anniversary of the first Grateful Dead show. Last Friday at noon, almost 10 people showed up outside of San Jose City Hall to celebrate the 50th anniversary of the famous Ken Kesey Acid Test which took place in a house at 43 S. Fifth Street on Dec. 4, 1965.

This was the legendary party Tom Wolfe documented in The Electric Kool-Aid Acid Test, the same party at which the Grateful Dead first performed as the Grateful Dead. That monumental event 50 years ago was the second of several acid tests thrown by Kesey and the Merry Pranksters, the first one of which went down in Soquel a week earlier.

Thousands of Deadheads should have been there last week. Ken Babbs, whose "spread" hosted the first acid test, should also have been there. Every news station in the Bay Area could have shown up. Representatives from the Rock and Roll Hall of Fame could have documented a huge party. Of course, Bob Weir, Phil Lesh and Bill Kreutzmann should also have been there, along with Grateful Dead biographer Dennis McNally. Then there's Neal Cassady's son, John Cassady. He should have been there. Technicians from Meyer Sound, stagehands from Bill Graham Presents, and even the Hells Angels all should have been there. With all due respect to the organizers, it really felt like a major opportunity was blown.

Since the famous acid test in question went down right where City Hall now sits, last week's event came together with the purpose of declaring an official effort to place a permanent historical plaque somewhere on the property. In any real city, this would be a no-brainer. The site would vault San Jose to international recognition, as thousands of Grateful Dead fans would regularly visit the plaque, in the same way they visit Ron "Pigpen" McKernan's grave in Palo Alto. There could be concerts every single year on that date. Anyone with half a brain can imagine more ideas.

The Dead have all sort sorts of history in the South Bay, so let me digress a bit. When Bill Graham built Shoreline Amphitheatre in Mountain View, in the '80s, he and Jerry Garcia designed the entire layout of the premises to resemble the Grateful Dead's "Steal Your Face" logo. If you look at an aerial photograph of the property, you can easily see it. The oldtimers will show you.

San Jose should do something similar with City Hall: Bulldoze the wannabe-urban-chic rotunda that looks like a deodorant stick and replace it with something, anything, that pays tribute to the Grateful Dead. And since no one at City Hall had enough vision to understand the rotunda would need decent acoustics—use a microphone in the place and it sounds you're talking in an airplane hangar—the city can hire Meyer Sound to implement a better events space. Imagine Mayor Sam Liccardo holding a press conference with the Grateful Dead's Wall of Sound behind him. Now that would be something to brag about.

So, yes, of course, there should be a historical plaque. Why do we need to even advocate for it? I mean, it has nothing to do with whether or not you listen to the Grateful Dead (I don't) or if you even experienced the 1960s (I didn't). It's about significant, cultural events that happened here, monumental stuff that should be recognized. This is another instance of something that should be second nature to any culturally literate, 20th-century, even halfway-interesting city official. It shouldn't take more than a few meetings for this to get decided. Yet all of us have to scream about it for years before the bureaucracy in City Hall gets rolling. That's what really has to change around here.

But I'm not sure if it ever will. Sometimes I'm convinced that City Hall's attitude is this: If the citizens want anything interesting to happen around here, then they should fight for it. That's always been the city's mentality. If this plaque finally happens, I guess we can hope, at least for now, that when 2,000 more homogenous tech schmoes move into downtown solely because they can no longer afford Mountain View, they'll at least realize that cool and rocking history exists here.

2016

New Condos To Replace Santa Clara's Bharat Bazar

The wall of dal is about to come tumbling down. One of the oldest continuously running Indian grocery markets will soon shut its doors for the condo-pocalypse. From what little I could elicit by repeatedly grilling the dude at the register, Bharat Bazar on El Camino Real in Santa Clara will close for good at the end of this month.

The entire strip mall in which it sits will be razed for still more lifelessly uniform apartments. The Kohl's next door-the only other business left in the complex-closes Jan. 16. Welcome to the heart of Silicon Valley.

To be fair, I don't think this is a crisis. Experience tells me the stakeholders have probably known for a quite a while, but considering how Bharat Bazar first emerged in 1974, and since the anti-man-about-about-town first slithered into the place some 25 years ago, I do believe the scene is worthy of some reflection.

Journeying to the promised land of Bharat Bazar requires a pilgrimage through the destroyed stripmall wastelands of Silicon Valley. Since the complex in question sits back from the street, Bharat Bazar is tucked away in the far corner, across a perpetually empty and cracked parking lot. As a destination, the store has always felt like an exotic outlander gem, a bastion of curious international intrigue surrounded by bland suburban enclaves.

When it comes to the parking lot, every piece of it is fractured, making the whole scene look like a broken mirror. Instead of tumbleweeds, tree branches lay strewn about the landscape. Cement medians are split in half, uprooted by trees. No one has taken care of the lot in decades. Rusted shopping carts lay scattered, as if thrown away years ago.

Once across the ruptured parking lot, the traveler finds great wonders. After journeying past dilapidated facades, roadside motels leftover from the '60s, converted fast food eateries and then the final landmass of sprawling parched concrete, a spectacular Shangri-La emerges at Bharat Bazar. With shelf after shelf of moong dal, masoor dal, lentils, mustard

279

seed, cardamom, cloves, asafoetida powder, basmati rice, jars of ghee, fenugreek, black cumin, tamarind, fennel and tons more, the anti-man-about-town always felt at home. There was no need for fantasy. It was real.

The entire place went through so many different reincarnations, it was hard to keep track. At one time, videos, clothing, threads, amulets, statues and other souvenirs added to the mix of groceries. Depending on the season, I'd see tables of vegetables out front, or pallets of onions and ginger. On the weekends, it was a madhouse. Customers piled stuff into their carts while kids scampered every which direction.

Originally, there was a restaurant next door, attached at the left. It was totally homemade. If I recall correctly, I ordered from an older lady and she called to the back. Maybe a handful of plastic tables and chairs comprised the whole of it-but the food was fantastic. Nowadays, the place seems to be scaling down, so that area is for chaat ingredients, larger bags of rice and flour, and an overall warehouse-y kind of feel, plus there's still a counter for sweets and samosas, but that's it. They're clearly winding it all down for when they have to move into Bharat's other location, on Reed Avenue in Sunnyvale.

Last weekend, contemplating what's left of the entire complex proved to be a strange experience. This market opened 41 years ago. When the anti-man-about-town showed up, the only other business left in the complex was Kohl's. All the fixtures were for sale. Sauntering through, a lot of merchandise still remained, but rows and rows of mannequins, male and female, were being sold at huge discounts. Half the store was reserved to sell empty racks, displays, shelving and other fixtures. It was quite morose to walk through. It almost felt like a science-fiction novel.

Soon the condo-pocalypse will explode on this very block. For me, no matter what happens, the memory of Bharat Bazar and the Wall of Dal will always remain in my heart.

Mike McGee's Burning Tale at Studio Bongiorno

The stories and poetry of Mike McGee are like laughing yoga therapy for the terminally awkward. Several years ago, after he'd already won slam poetry contests on national and international stages, he released *In Search of Midnight*. Inside this tome we get graveyard shifts at suburban super-drugstores, love poems, humility, childhood, travel and much more.

It's a loud, boisterous celebration of life that pours out of the pages.

McGee journeys around the continent on a regular basis, and upon resurfacing in his native San Jose a year ago he wound up gigging in Santa Clara. What would possibly cause such a poetic crime to happen? Well, right across from Mission Cemetery one finds Studio Bongiorno, a monumental establishment catering to anyone outside the establishment.

It's a place preordained for poetry and storytelling. There's artwork, incense, skulls, broken sculpture, seats from Candlestick Park, a coffin, prosthetic limbs, canopies, nuts, bolts, tools and lots of artspeak emerging on a daily basis. It feels like a theater prop shop gone gloriously awry.

Studio Bongiorno is where McGee launched the Burning Tale monthly storytelling series one year ago. The next installment erupts Saturday, Jan. 23 from 6-11pm. Anyone with a tale to tell can show up and force-cram his or her soul into the ears of the audience. That's one of Mike's lines, by the way. Mike functions as the host, the bent emcee, so to speak, occasionally offering his own stories or poems in between the other participants. Weather permitting, the show takes place outside on the patio. Poetry is welcome, but the emphasis is on the story as a form.

"I tell people all the time—I can ask anyone I know—to do a poem, but nine times out of 10, they'll say, 'I'm not a poet, I don't have any poetry,'" McGee says. "But I can ask anyone to just get up and tell a story, or an anecdote, and nine times out of 10, they have one. Everyone's got a story. Tell us about that time your uncle stabbed your grandma. Tell us about that time you almost married a dog in Vegas."

In the course of putting on events, McGee says, he discovered that everyone digs storytelling, but it's not just a matter of hearing a story. People love being *told* a story. As host and performer, McGee loves how people silence themselves when their favorite storyteller in the group begins to launch another wicked tale. But the story has to be true. That's why Burning Tale can be so much fun.

"The only prerequisite for my stories, for Burning Tale, is that they have to be true, or at least as true as they can possibly be," McGee says. "And you should be the star of the story. Or you should at least be a character in the story."

It gets better. A few months back, McGee introduced a workshop component to the experience. Interested parties with stage fright or those who aren't used to speaking in front of an audience can learn how to express themselves. The featured storyteller or poet at the Burning Tale event usually leads the workshop. This time around, the workshop takes place the following day, on the afternoon of Jan. 24.

Plenty of spaces throughout the valley could host a storytelling event, but Studio Bongiorno really seems a perfect fit, not only because the graveyard sits nearby. The venue presents an eclectic, vanguard and beautifully gloomy environment in which to perform. It's not just a "space" or a "gallery." It's an environment. The props, décor and morbid accoutrements seem like part of the audience—a traditional campfire storytelling session taken to the next level.

San Jose endlessly banters about music scenes and art scenes, so it's about time to emphasize a writing scene. McGee and Studio Bongiorno go together like pen and page, like sound and fury.

"I would like writers to really discover that Studio Bongiorno is a good place to come on a Saturday or a Sunday," he says. "It's a quiet, inspiring, peaceful, weird, occult-y kind of spot for people to come, sip tea, and write their asses off."

Park Avenue Djinns

Reading about Sufi mystics in the crumbling relics of Delhi, India, triggered me to think of Park Avenue in San Jose. To be more specific, while ingesting *City of Djinns* by William Dalrymple, which is about his years in Delhi, certain passages hit close to home.

In the prologue, for example, he confesses that the ruins of Delhi are what fascinated him. No matter how often planners colluded to create new colonies of gleaming concrete, crumbling towers, old mosques, abandoned ruins or ancient tombs would suddenly appear, intruding on the city blocks, the golf courses and the roundabouts. Even though much of the old city from centuries or even decades ago had been destroyed by violence, with many people forced away after Partition, old buildings—just like spirits—often came out of nowhere, even after they were pushed out for shiny new constructions.

The physical and the temporal aspects of Delhi always seemed to merge. Despite the repeated destruction of the city, pieces of it always seemed to reincarnate.

Such has always been my attitude around here, especially when the urban blight exploration junkie typed out his greatest hits from Auzerais, Stockton Avenue or along that hideous stretch of Camden near Highway 17. This time, however, the old ghosts, the *djinns*, emerged on a weird stretch of Park Avenue heading eastward from Race Street through an old mile of forgotten San Jose. When I ingest cosmic passages like those of Dalrymple, they immediately manifest themselves as San Jose passages, whether it's through time or geography.

Venturing east from that intersection, any explorer would set his sights on Pueblo Viejo Imports. This miraculous place used to be downtown a decade ago, but, for whatever reason, it luckily escaped the city's endless crusade to convince the comfortable classes to move back downtown in search of inner-city recolonization. At that time, the Redevelopment Agency told me, new furniture places downtown—Black Sea Gallery (now Ross Dress for Less) and the original Pueblo Viejo Imports (now Original Gravity)—were "bellwether tenants," designed to kickstart retail in the neighborhood.

Predictably, that never happened and both eventually left. Now, Pueblo Viejo sits right next to another indie diamond, Bigsby House, featuring Japanese shampoo inspired by the tea ceremony. One block over, there's an abandoned building where the Vedanta folks used to give Sanskrit lessons. How's that for serendipity?

Just like in Dalrymple's *City of Djinns*, pieces of old San Jose continue to resurface in various places, if one looks hard enough. The djinns, as well as the businesses, are like spirits, which is why this particular stretch of Park Avenue is so awesome. For the non-adepts, it's half a mile south of the area of Recycle Books and Art Boutiki, both of which are also refugees from downtown for the same reasons.

Walking this stretch—and one must explore it on foot to get a proper perspective—is like experiencing five different pieces of five different eras of San Jose history, all gloriously cobbled together. It's akin to summoning the Ancients if one temporarily escapes the homogenous highrise developments not too far away.

The rest of the street, as it leads toward downtown, presents a beautifully incongruous hodgepodge of retail and residential that could only have emerged in organic fashion. No bureaucratic cabal of real estate creeps could have devised an area more interesting. It is here that odd retail sits between random Craftsman bungalows. Scattershot Victorians intersperse with a Brazilian Jiu-Jitsu training grounds and a preschool. Odd apartments sit above a corner market while other blocks feature more indie retail and still more Craftsman bungalows. There always seems to be a side parking lot leading to something else.

Finally, the entire street would be incomplete without Leather Masters, a San Jose institution for more than 20 years, and the Eritrean Community Center. Let us hope that the *djinns* of old San Jose continue to resurface. The urban blight exploration junkie will be looking for them, wherever he roams.

San Jose's Irish Assassin Pre-Dates Sister City Connection

San Jose's connection to Dublin is quite a rocking story, going back to the administration of former mayor Tom McEnery during the '80s. Soon after becoming mayor, McEnery lobbied the city of Dublin to become one of San Jose's sister cities, but no one in Ireland had heard of San Jose. The task proved daunting.

Eventually, McEnery rang up Tim Pat Coogan, a legendary Irish journalist, historian and author of numerous books.

Coogan relayed McEnery's request to Charles Haughey, then the Irish Taoiseach (pronounced tee-shook). From there, the proverbial ball began to roll and in 1986 the sister city relationship went legit. Silicon Valley companies eventually opened up shop in Ireland, exchanges were forged, and to this day the relationship is much deeper than most sister city partnerships in the U.S. Coogan mentions all of this in his book, *Wherever the Green is Worn*.

Last week, the sister city program staged an elegant reception at the Silicon Valley Capital Club to celebrate its 30th anniversary. As a concept, the Sister Cities International Organization began in 1956, following President Eisenhower's conference on Citizen Diplomacy. Not only do we now have three decades' worth of San Jose-Dublin exchanges and a 60th anniversary of the organization's founding, but 2016 will also see the 100th anniversary of the Easter Rising in Dublin.

However, I submit the relationship might go back even further. At Mission Cemetery in Santa Clara, one finds the gravesite of Michael McDonnell (1889-1950). After McEnery told me the story, it only took a few moments to unearth more details.

McDonnell, sometimes referred to as Mick McDonnell, was the first leader of "The Squad," a.k.a. "The Twelve Apostles," the assassination unit employed by Michael Collins during the Irish War of Independence. This was the group that systematically bumped off British spies in Dublin, especially members of the "Cairo Gang." Before the squad was formed, McDonnell took part in the Easter Rising of 1916 and then with the Twelve Apostles was involved in the actions on Bloody Sunday as well as several other "jobs."

McDonnell's own testimony can be found in the easily searchable Bureau of Military History Collection, a series of Irish state records documenting the years 1913-1921. In those records, McDonnell and his cohorts described in harrowing detail specific hit jobs they carried out against British operatives. From McDonnell, there's also stuff like this:

"Some time in the autumn of 1919 I was approached by Dick McKee and asked to make myself available to go to London for special duty with the object of looking the situation over in London and coming back and reporting as to the possibility of wiping out the British Cabinet, and several other prominent people including editors of newspapers, etc., who were antagonistic to this country."

Fortunately, that particular action never unfolded. In another passage, McDonnell also describes a botched attempt to execute the British Commander Lord John French. It wasn't pretty.

As the Irish Civil War began in 1922, McDonnell came to the U.S. and eventually settled in Los Gatos for the rest of his life. He died in 1950 and was buried in the Santa Clara Mission Cemetery. He even named his son Michael Collins McDonnell, who went on to serve in the Air Force during WWII, Korea and Vietnam. If one stands at the grave in Mission Cemetery, it's hard to fathom one of Michael Collins' assassins living here in his old age, but that's what happened. McEnery even recalls, as a kid, seeing his dad working with McDonnell in the same building that now houses O'Flaherty's Irish Pub.

"It's interesting to look back on, how this nice old guy sitting there with a slouch hat and smoking a pipe was one of the foremost antagonists to the British Empire," McEnery said. "And a great Irish patriot in a horrible battle for independence that forever marked his life for good and bad."

The 2016 US-All Ireland Sister Cities Mayors Summit will unfold in April, with delegations from over 60 sister cities descending upon Dublin. Any U.S. city twinned with an Irish city is invited.

San Jose Chamber Orchestra 25th Anniversary

An old wise guy from the East once said, and I'm paraphrasing, nothing in the past is ever wasted or squandered. It's all just one big stew that prepares you for what's currently unfolding. For example, don't think your college life was thrown away like last week's newspaper, just because you didn't use your degree for anything. As you evolve, it will all come back into your life somehow.

With that in my mind, the San Jose Chamber Orchestra presents its official 25th anniversary concerts this Saturday and Sunday at Le Petit Trianon Theatre. The program features world-beating premieres by retired and/or former San Jose State University School of Music faculty. For starters, Brent Heisinger will debut his new work, *EKTA III*, taken from the Hindi word for 'unity' and inspired by the African percussion teachings of another former SJSU professor, royal hartigan, who now teaches back east. This weekend, hartigan—who spells his name all lowercase—returns to play on the piece, along with bassist Wes Brown. Also on the program is a new work by SJSU professor Pablo Furman.

Of course, the spacetime continuum-shattering aspects of such a gig preclude me from any objective interpretation. In the same way that Taoists and quantum physicists might understand reality, I, as the observer, cannot separate myself from that which I observe here. Heisinger, hartigan and Furman were key influences during my decade of college, which seemed to begin right as the San Jose Chamber Orchestra did. The first two years of music theory I took at SJSU found me in Heisinger's classes. I can't even fathom how many hours I spent in the Spartan Pub studying, in particular, Wagner's use of leitmotifs in *Tristan and Isolde*, or Debussy's impressionistic pointillism in *Prelude to the Afternoon of a Fawn*. Both of those masterpieces formed a launching pad into 20th century music, which I then embraced. In Furman's case, my first semester of Sound Recording found me in a tiny upstairs studio with an old four-track recorder and quarter-inch tape, splicing the sounds of my voice into strange Dada-esque or William S. Burroughs-style sonic cut-ups. Yes, this was my first assignment.

However, in royal's case, he was my premier, half-western, half-eastern inspiration. His lifelong commitment was then, and is still, the mainstreaming of all the world's musics, whether it's Korean tunings, Balkan folk music or African percussion. He was the only SJSU prof ever to teach a semester of Indian ragas, one of the best classes I ever took. Instrumentally speaking, on a trap set, royal could play four different meters at once, all while reading the newspaper and talking about the

1979 Pittsburgh Pirates. He was also the only one who let us roll bowling balls down the aisle in the music building for a final project, with him, the teacher, as the sole bowling pin, standing at the end of the hallway. He embraced Dada. He was hip to Fluxus, Duchamp and John Cage. He was receptive when someone rode a homemade motorized skateboard through the classroom, crashing into desks while that student's compadres made a racket with synthesizers, all while the motor shorted out and filled the room with smoke, thus emptying the classroom. He was receptive if that student then hopelessly tried to justify it with French poststructuralist philosophy, as if he was some wannabe-Eurosnob grad student.

With relentless enthusiasm, he inspired hundreds of students with words of unity and freedom, both musically and politically, encouraging everyone to upset any apple cart they could find and become better at whatever they wanted to do in life.

The old wise guys from the East were right. None of those days were wasted, even though I usually was. As a result, in this column, I now get to cheerlead for some of my biggest influences in college, all of whom are still creating, composing and performing a quarter century later. Yes, they're back together this weekend to celebrate 25 solid years of new music thanks to Barbara Day Turner and the San Jose Chamber Orchestra. By my interpretation, that orchestra is San Jose. Everything cycles back, everything returns to the forefront, and I am proud to tell all my readers about such a rocking gig.

Legends Join Forces for Stirring 'Border Cantos' Opener

Richard Misrach spent years depicting the isolated, haunting landscapes of the U.S.-Mexico border areas via large-scale photographs. Guillermo Galindo builds musical instruments from debris left behind by migrants at the border. This Thursday, the photographer will join the composer and instrument builder as they both talk about their joint show, Border Cantos, at the San Jose Museum of Art.

The opening reception was one of the most enchanting events I've ever seen at the San Jose Museum of Art. Galindo and Misrach addressed the crowd, as did downtown San Jose Councilman Raul Peralez, who, in particular, delivered a poignant, heartfelt, intellectual speech about immigration and how the arts bring people together in San Jose. It seemed much more human than any speech Sam Liccardo or Cindy Chavez ever gave when they held the same position.

The real highlight of the evening came when the legend himself, Guillermo Gomez-Peña, delivered the official opening performance. A renowned author, poet and Chicano cyberpunk performance-art troublemaker, Peña is one of the all-time greats, and like any genius he has no use for categories, fences, binaries or boundaries of any sort. His entire

286

life seems like a work of performance art in of itself, however one defines "self," of course.

I remember discovering Peña's words back in the '90s when he was the first commentator to characterize Subcomandante Marcos, leader of the Zapatistas, as one of the best performance artists of the 20th century, a "consummate *performancero*." Marcos seemed to be influenced by Gomez-Peña and vice-versa. Maybe they even knew each other. Marcos seemed to operate in some strange transdisciplinary border zone of Dada, Mexican wrestling, academic socialist philosophy, recycled Che Guevara and Yasser Arafat props, and media manipulation that no other mysterious masked Mexican revolutionary ever articulated. Except for Guillermo Gomez-Peña, that is. He seemed to know exactly what Marcos was doing, and thus Peña was a pleasure to read.

But that was then. This time, there Peña was, standing in front of all the gussied-up patrons of the San Jose Museum of Art, offering an insurrectionary bilingual rant in support of all the ignored, marginalized heroes and escapees from the world's apparatus of oppression. No one else but Peña would place Berlin disco transvestites in the same struggle as the Palestinians and then use it to officially christen an art show about Mexican-American border issues. It was quite possibly the best delivery I've ever seen in that building. Together, Misrach, Peña, and Galindo seemed like the Three Musketeers.

The arts intelligentsia of the valley explored the three rooms the entire night. As an example, a series of Misrach's images depict the arduous yet arcane methods of border patrol agents clearing up dirt pathways by dragging tires, all in order to see migrants' footprints once they get past the fence. Galindo takes rusty ladders, discarded bike parts, shoes, gloves, tires and even a gigantic metal piece of the wall itself, and then wires them up, amplifies them, or even adds strings, pickups or guitar jacks. The contraptions conjure up ghosts of Marcel Duchamp's readymades or Jean Tinguely's kinetic sculptures.

While a more rudimentary dufus might simply attach a contact microphone to a piece of junk, bash on it with a hammer, and call it "sound art," such is not the case here. It's much more human and personal. Galindo is sonically and shamanistically conjuring the remaining stories of the people who discarded these items, which then function as sonic avatars of the immigrants' plight. There are ingredients from Mesoamerican perspectives, 20th century composers like Karlheinz Stockhausen and even Fluxus troublemakers like Joseph Beuys.

Together, the work of Misrach and Galindo fuses into a collaboration highlighting the human layer of the immigration issue. Gone is the belligerent hotheaded phlegm-spittle from political rallies or corporate news networks. What a relief.

What's more, a full-color brochure with curators' essays and a poem by U.S. Poet Laureate Juan Felipe Herrera is now available for free throughout the exhibition.

Music, Dance, Fashion Take Stage at Ao Dai Festival

Casual observers might know the *ao dai* as a traditional long gown worn by Vietnamese women, but it's much more than just attire. The *ao dai* symbolizes many things: liberation, struggle, empowerment and obstacles overcome.

Its history goes far outside the scope of this page, but one can go as far to say it's now a symbol of national pride and serious inspiration for artists, painters, photographers, poets and newspaper columnists.

The 2016 incarnation of the Ao Dai Festival erupts Sunday, both inside and outside the Fairmont San Jose. An elaborate multi-dimensional ceremony in the Circle of Palms area kicks off the evening, followed by the ticketed event, an even more elaborate dinner and fashion show inside the hotel ballroom. Music, dance, visuals and storytelling will rule the evening, all to benefit the Friends of Hue Foundation Children's Shelter in Central Vietnam.

Jenny Do is a long-time San Jose attorney and leader in the Vietnamese-American community who runs the Hue Foundation. She also heads up the myriad teams behind the Ao Dai Festival. Perhaps more than anyone, Do has mainstreamed the *ao dai* as a symbol of pride. So much so, that she even took a delegation to Sacramento last week to cheer on state Sen. Janet Nguyen (R-Long Beach), who helped pass a resolution to officially designate May 15 as Ao Dai Day. Nguyen was the first sitting senator ever to wear an *ao dai* on the state Senate floor. The resolution passed unanimously.

'It was so emotional when it passed, when it happened,' Do said, her voice choked with emotion. 'We were counting every single vote, watching as the votes came.'

After the fall of Saigon in 1975, Do explains in an essay, she remained in Vietnam for nine years of hunger and misery, with barely any decent clothes. While suffering through a period of so-called 'educational reforms,' intellectual erosion and being a victim of the 'new economic zone,' Do could not fathom better days. Throughout those nine years under the communist regime, she never saw Vietnamese women wear the *ao dai* anywhere on the streets.

'When I was a child, I remember my mother was very beautiful when she put on the ao dai,' Do writes. 'She looked radiant, graceful and noble in that long traditional dress. But without it, during those dark nine years, I did not find such beauty in her when she wore other torn outfits.'

Do dreamed that one day she would again see these graceful dresses beautify a city. It was a simple dream, but as every year went by, it felt further out of reach. That dream has become a reality, thanks to the senators and legions of folks helping to make the Ao Dai Festival a success.

This Sunday, the outdoor phase of the evening—free for everyone—will unfold in the Circle of Palms between the Fairmont and the San Jose Museum of Art. The 'Princess Coming-of-Age Celebration' will introduce the mythological tale of 'Son Tinh (mountain), Thuy Tinh, (water).' It features traditional Vietnamese music and the latest fashions of *ao dai* designers, and is usually a grand-scale, multisensory experience. The luminous color palette of the Ao Dai celebration—attire, props, dragon troupes, horses and the overall pageantry—blooms like a floral display amid the palm trees and surrounding beige landscape.

In the story, the princess has reached the age of marriage, so her father calls for prospective suitors (*ao dai* designers) to battle for his daughter's hand. The dressmaker who dazzles the princess with the most beautiful *ao dai* will win her heart and become her husband. Expect a rocking experience with a slew of stilt-walkers, horses, vibrant banners and zithers.

Once inside, everyone with a ticket then attends the dinner, fashion show and auction. The entire affair benefits the Hue Foundation's Children's Shelter, a very worthy cause.

The Graves of Borges and Joyce

On a soul-searching expedition in Switzerland, the anti-man-about-town found himself at the gravesites of two literary giants: James Joyce and Jorge Luis Borges. In Zurich and Geneva, respectively, I made desperate pacts with them, just as I had done with Hermann Hesse on my last trip to Switzerland.

This time, Zurich was immersed in the 100th anniversary of Dada, while Geneva unfurled itself as an international nexus of peacemaking. Both environments were fertile ground to make psychic accords with Joyce and Borges.

Baptized in Zurich, Dada was a transnational web of radical creative perspectives that forever altered the course of 20th century art and the avant-garde. Back in 1916, as the butchery of World War I and the ensuant zoological nationalism began to reconfigure Europe, a cadre of interdisciplinary artists, performers and troublemakers fled their respective countries for neutral Zurich, where they collectively set Dada in motion at the Cabaret Voltaire. A network of self-exiles, the Dadaists were the original anti-men-about-town. For the 2016 centenary, Zurich's museums, galleries, hotels and bars staged exhibitions related to Dada. Creatively speaking, I felt like an adopted child finally discovering his real parents.

Even crazier, the original Cabaret Voltaire building reopened about 12 years ago. Right now, as you read this, every morning for 165 days in a row, a particular Dadaist is being honored at 6:30am with an "offizium," a prayer of sorts. I showed up to catch the one for Tristan Tzara, which took place on his birthday. Cabaret Voltaire director Adrian Notz stood there and read Tzara's entire 1918 Dada Manifesto, in English. It was moving.

Also moving was the gravesite of James Joyce. Such visits are regular highlights of my travels, so a trek to Friedhof Fluntern was necessary before finally leaving Zurich. At Joyce's grave, I stood there and made a desperate pact with him. I said: "Alright old man, I will keep writing. You just show me how to pay the freakin' bills. Gimme a sign. Anything."

With that, Geneva emerged next, appearing before me as a global capital of humanitarianism and a transnational radiator of peacemaking vibrations. The United Nations, the World Health Organization and the International Committee of the Red Cross are all headquartered in Geneva. Unfortunately, our tour of the UN was canceled because the Syria talks were commencing that very second, so all individual visits were a no-go. But in the Red Cross Museum, we saw stockhouses of records on international prisoners of war, along with life-size projections of people talking about war-ravaged lands around the globe. Peacekeeping and all things international seemed synonymous with Geneva, its history, and its overall vibe.

And then there was CERN, a global powerhouse in of itself. At CERN, the legendary visitors' center is a giant dome 90 feet high and 130 feet in diameter. It had been closed for about a year, but coincidentally opened back up on the day I arrived. Inside we saw the very first World Wide Web server built by Tim Berners-Lee on a NeXT Machine.

Everything about Geneva seemed to exemplify connectivity across language barriers, creative disciplines or matrixes of thought, which made it all the more logical for the multilingual literary genius Jorge Luis Borges to be buried in a small cemetery, in the middle of town. As I had done with Joyce a few days earlier, I made a desperate pact. I said to him: "Alright old man, I will keep writing, just show me how to make a living. Give me a sign. Anything."

Sure enough, Joyce and Borges eventually came through and answered my call. On my way back home, I was sitting in the Zurich Airport when I received an email, offering me a Steinbeck Fellowship in Creative Writing at San Jose State University to work on my next book over the 2016/17 academic year.

Blown away, I let it sink in and then flew back home before officially accepting the offer. I already owe a very great deal to SJSU, but now I can list James Joyce, Jorge Luis Borges and the neutral matrix of Swiss peacemaking to my list of thank-yous. Everything is connected.

The Thrash Metal History of Castro Street in Mountain View

Anti-man-about-town paid for his lunch at a fantastic Indian buffet on Castro Street in Mountain View. The woman at the cashier, noticing my last name on the debit card receipt, spoke Hindi to me. When I didn't answer, she said: "You don't speak Hindi?"

I said no. She gave me a flabbergasted look and said, "Nothing? Not at all?"

To which I replied: "Look. Two buildings down is where Slayer played 28 years ago. And Exodus. And Death Angel. And bands like D.R.I. and Verbal Abuse. Each of which probably involved me, as a teenager, drinking an entire bottle of Night Train in the back parking lot and then relieving myself on the back of this very building in which we now stand. And then going inside to smash my face on the stage over and over again, or at the very least swinging my friends around in circles, while colliding with any number of drunk or drugged out metalheads and punks drenched in sweat. There were no Indian dudes hanging around during those days, so, um, I never learned Hindi. Sorry."

No, I didn't actually say that to her. But I felt like it.

For the anti-man-about-town, this was a routine example of my childhood trauma, the productive kind, returning to the surface. I say "productive" because sometimes—if one possesses the tools—the negative experiences can transform themselves into humor. After awhile it becomes natural. Now that I'm older and just barely wiser, I seem better equipped to dissolve the reactive emotions when they arise.

Before he passed away, my Dad was originally from India. My mom is Anglo, so I was born half-eastern and half-western. I've never been wholly or purely either one, but somewhere between. This was never any dramatic crisis. Rather, it just provided a rocking, thrashing metaphor for life. For example, just like San Jose, I feel half urban and half suburban. And 28 years ago, when Slayer played a few doors down from this Indian buffet, I was half thrash metal and half punk. Which is why this encounter at the cash register brought back so many memories of Castro Street in the heyday of the thrash-punk crossover era.

During the first half of the '80s, most fans of the aforementioned genres were either purely punk or purely metal. Then halfway through that decade the two scenes crossed over and merged together to create a new term, aptly called "crossover," a phenomenon that people on both sides are still complaining about. In the Bay Area, most of this went down in SF, the East Bay, or at clubs like the Keystone Palo Alto. But for a few brief years, the Mountain View Theater morphed into a makeshift venue, a beautifully decrepit sweatbox that booked these kinds of shows. All the aforementioned bands played there, in front of probably 300 people, tops.

In Mountain View, the Castro Street of 1988 was an indistinguishable suburban road connecting El Camino Real to a Caltrain Station. Nobody used email, cell phones or laptops. There were no Googlers, Tech Bros or yoga hotties. Sidewalk patio dining was nonexistent, the parking strips did not overflow with flowers and there was nothing anywhere named Weeby.

Then Slayer and Exodus showed up to sing about Satan, murder, rape, torture, cannibalism, necrophilia, rotting flesh, raining blood and lessons in violence. You know, the fun stuff. Thankfully, around the corner from the Mountain View Theater one found an unidentifiable dive bar named Mervyn's, which still exists, but for the first time in decades it now has a sign over the door, ruining all the mystery. On the way to the shows, those of drinking age would get smashed at Mervyn's while the rest of us found other ways. I distinctly remember the band Verbal Abuse praising that bar on stage during their set at the Mountain View Theater.

Unfortunately, the club only lasted a few years before going under. Nothing is permanent. In my case, I am grateful to still be here to regale you with these experiences. The rush nowadays comes not from rotgut wine and thrash metal, but instead from Aloo Gobi, chai and Bindi Masala. Even if I can't speak Hindi.

Tech Bros Forget Beat Generation's Imprint

Last week, I slithered back into the Beat Museum in San Francisco, arriving by sheer chance. Turns out the museum is currently angling to raise a cool few million so it can buy a new facility up the street.

Within minutes, director Jerry Cimino and I found ourselves venting—er, contemplating—the current generations of tech in San Jose, San Francisco and everywhere between, especially how they seem clueless to the counterculture history of these parts.

"Silicon Valley, as we know it today, wouldn't exist without The Beat Generation," Cimino said. "In many ways, Beat Generation values became Bay Area values. One of the reasons so many young people want to live here is because the Bay Area is the leading edge and the Beats made it hip."

Decades ago, Cimino worked at IBM on Cottle Road in San Jose. After he was finished with the corporate world, he launched the first incarnation of the Beat Museum in Monterey in 2003, before relocating it to North Beach a few years later.

However, one doesn't have to look very far to find local vibes and flavors these geniuses left behind. For example, Jack Kerouac first discovered Buddhism by stealing a book from the San Jose Public Library. That was the early '50s, when he often visited Neal and Carolyn Cassady, who lived on East Santa Clara Street, in a house that still exists. In addition to Kerouac, Allen Ginsberg briefly lived in a detached flat out back. Cassady also bopped around Los Gatos and other backwaters of the South Bay, along with Ken Kesey and several troublemakers from the same circles of free spirits. In fact, Cassady's son, John, still lives near these parts, as does Al Hinkle, immortalized as Big Ed Dunkel in Kerouac's *On the Road*.

And then there's Steve Jobs. When Steve and Dan Kottke tripped around India in the early '70s, one of the books they carried with them was *Dharma Bums* by Jack Kerouac. The influence of Eastern perspectives on the psyche of Steve Jobs is more than well-documented.

This may seem like free association, but there really wouldn't be a Silicon Valley without counterculture, mind-expansion and Eastern mysticism. Twenty-somethings and their blasted UX startups don't realize this. Certainly, each 12-person party of obnoxious tech bros ordering glorified slurpee drinks that take five minutes to make, and then asking for separate checks and not tipping, don't know their roots lie in compassion, altruism, Zen, poetry, green tea, antiestablishment intellectualism, ecological movements, bisexual orgies and everything else the Beats exemplified.

Which brings us back to the Beat Museum, chock-full of memorabilia, artifacts and former belongings of all the heavyweights, so much that even Jimmy Page of Led Zeppelin also recently wandered in by chance. According to Cimino, the guitarist gushed over the museum's authenticity. Alas, due to grotesque Bay Area rents, the only way to effectively operate such a museum is to own a building. So that's the grand plan.

Thus the museum's plight is a familiar one, but it should inspire the rest of the Bay Area if Cimino's plan works out. Luckily, just a few blocks away sits an abandoned bank, two stories but zoned for four. Since the building is empty, no tenants would be displaced. As a result, Cimino has now orchestrated an elaborate network of outreach to celebrities, philanthropists and politicians, all of whom understand the massive historical significance and influence of the Beats on the Bay Area. Everyone involved is hip to the gravity of the gig. The goal is to raise five million smackeroos.

"The next group of people I want to approach are Silicon Valley movers and shakers," Cimino said. "Because so many of them are following the same dream. They came out here, probably many of them not even knowing why they love this place. And I submit the reason the Bay Area is so magnificent to so many people is because the Beats made it what it is."

Surely there must be some potential heroes here in the South Bay, maybe some Valley entrepreneurs or corporate donors, with a stash to spare. What a great way to give back.

Joel Selvin Re-Explores Altamont Tragedy

In Joel Selvin's new book, *Altamont: The Rolling Stones, the Hells Angels, and the Inside Story of Rock's Darkest Day*, the veteran music journalist effectively dismantles common narratives behind the infamous December 1969 free concert at Altamont Speedway, where Hells Angels were paid $500 in beer to act as security and wound up beating people with pool cues.

One of the Angels knifed and killed a person, Meredith Hunter, although he was eventually acquitted.

The version of the story put forth by the film *Gimme Shelter* conveniently absolved the Stones, but not their manager, while also unequivocally blaming the Hells Angels and leaving everything else to chance. Over the decades, this narrative became the accepted version of the events. Turns out the film, while still one of the greatest rock documentaries ever made, did not even remotely capture what happened that day or the many moving parts that led up to the tragic final night.

Over the decades, Selvin has unearthed a landmine of details while maintaining a back-burner network of sources on the whole sordid mess. When former Stones tour manager Sam Cutler came to Santa Clara for a 2013 appearance at Studio Bongiorno, promoting his own memoir of those days, Selvin joined him on stage and the two yakked for at least an hour. It was an amazing night. From there, the book began to crystalize.

"We spent the evening plumbing [Cutler's] recollections of the event almost as if the audience wasn't there," Selvin writes. "By that time, I had already been considering this book and started collecting research, but listening to Sam that night helped me realize just how much of a story was there."

As a result, the book reads like a true crime story. It was the Grateful Dead who organized the show, at least in the beginning. The initial idea was to stage a free concert in Golden Gate Park with the Dead and Jefferson Airplane. The Stones were only to be announced the day beforehand. Since the Dead and the Airplane regularly played impromptu free gigs in the Panhandle area, and since the West Coast wanted its own Woodstock, such a scheme made sense. At first.

But as the Stones 1969 tour unfolded and the band's brain trust and operating machinery became more bloated, illegal and uncontrollable—and while the filmmakers continued to document the whole circus—the writing should have appeared on the wall. From the beginning of the tour, since Mick Jagger hated cops, he refused to allow any uniformed policemen inside the venues. This was written into the contracts with promoters.

Meanwhile, on the home front, after a mysterious person acting as the Stones' liaison botched the Golden Gate Park negotiations, the venue was moved to Sears Point Raceway, a perfect location with freeway access and a large hill for the stage. But when the owners of Sears Point demanded all distribution rights for the film, Jagger refused. So another venue had to be found, not even two days ahead of the concert. Jagger was prioritizing the film project and orchestrating a grand-scale conclusion to the tour, just for the film's sake.

Plenty of other backstories appear in Selvin's book. In one passage resembling an episode of the Andy Griffith Show, we get a glimpse at two rural cops from the only backwater substation remotely close to Altamont, both of them scrambling to comprehend a few hundred thousand wasted hippies descending on the desolate countryside east of Livermore. You can almost hear banjos while reading the pages.

In other passages, Selvin goes out of his way to corroborate Jerry Garcia's claim that the wannabe-Hells Angels and hangers-on from San Jose are the ones who ruined everything. "Prospects" are prospective Hells Angels, the aspiring members, the ones who set up chairs at meetings and stuff like that. Selvin writes that prospects from San Jose followed along to join the fracas and it was they who acted the worst. This is in addition to the San Jose Hells Angel who killed Meredith Hunter.

In the end, Selvin arrives at some very brave but logical conclusions. He lays serious blame at the feet of specific individuals, although I'd be a poor boy to spoil it for you. And there's just no place for that.

Don Buchla, RIP

Don Buchla, the legendary modular synthesizer pioneer, passed away last week at the age of 79. Anyone currently playing a synthesizer, tweaking electronics for sound generation or making any sort of modern-day electronic keyboard music has Buchla to thank, at least partly.

While Bob Moog was the first one to officially release a modular synthesizer as a commercial product, Buchla was probably the first one to envision modules with the intention of assembling them together into a live performance instrument.

As an engineer and a musician, Buchla was a daring, ornery innovator with a keen sense of what avant-garde musicians, composers and performers might want. His modular electronic music systems forever changed the way sound is created and controlled. He also built the PA rig used on Ken Kesey's Merry Prankster bus.

I never knew Buchla personally, but we were at the same party or dinner table a few times in the '90s. My music professor at San Jose State, Allen Strange, wrote the first electronic music textbook and knew Buchla for decades. They were both members of the Electric Weasel Ensemble during the '70s. The first music class I ever took at SJSU featured Allen showing us how an old Buchla system worked, using patch cords to connect oscillators, ring modulators, filters and other devices. That Buchla machine was a behemoth of an instrument, seemingly always in states of disrepair, yet it was a great intro to the guts of how commercial synthesizers worked.

As a lowly undergrad, this felt like receiving holy transmissions. The lineage of sound and noise and musical outlaw invention was being passed down, via Buchla and Allen, straight to us. The rest of the students were barely technologically literate enough to use a word processor, so those of us patching oscillators to bandpass filters using banana plugs and creating sonic rackets that shook the doors of the studio soon became the outcasts of the whole building.

On another front, this was right as Buchla was releasing his original

Lightning and Thunder alternative MIDI controllers—again, ideas way ahead of their time. This was also right at the beginning of the era when dance music people first began to culturally appropriate the term "electronic music" and co-opt it into something entirely different. But that's a different story.

Above all else, in those classes, Allen emphasized that Buchla was a contrarian troublemaker who went against the grain, a radical innovator who wasn't cut from the same cloth as "those East Coast guys." He didn't build circuits just to put knobs and keyboards on them. He was interested in non-Western tunings and musical performance interfaces that didn't yet exist. Right now, in 2016, we're probably only a few years away from augmented reality-based musical interfaces. Once that finally happens, those technologies might likewise be traced back to ideas Buchla innovated. Possibly.

My most hysterical memory of Buchla occurred in 1992, when the SJSU music department hosted the International Computer Music Conference. I rotated between sound crew, stagehand and various gofer duties. We put on two concerts a day in Morris Dailey Auditorium and almost a week's worth of tech for 100 different compositions that required different microphone arrangements, computer equipment configurations, homemade electronics, cabling, adapters and other scenarios for 16 hours a day. It probably took a year off my life.

One performance piece featured Buchla along with a few friends, and for some ridiculous reason they needed a 5-pin DIN extension cable 20 feet long. We didn't have one. Don handed me a 20-dollar bill and asked me, the student stagehand, to go to a store and find the right cable. I acted happy to oblige and scurried down to the Radio Shack on First Street—just north of where Billy Berk's is now—but they didn't have the cable. I was out of luck. So I went back to the gig, mission unaccomplished, and returned the 20 bucks. Ever since then, my memories of that Radio Shack are inseparable from Don Buchla.

Now, both are no longer with us, yet both were institutions that left a serious mark on downtown San Jose.

Dadaglobe Project Picks Up Where Tristan Tzara Left Off

Whenever I hit the road, synchronicities unfold on multiple levels. Last spring, for example, the anti-man-about-town infiltrated Zurich to experience the centenary of the Dada art movement, an international web of radical creative perspectives that forever altered the courses of 20th-century art.

Following in the footsteps of anti-establishment heroes via interviews, museum exhibits, street tours and historical research was a form of creative genealogy. Now, as you read this, certain individuals and vibes from that trip are arriving in San Francisco for the Dada World Fair, organized by City Lights Bookstore, now through Nov. 13. Talk about everything coming full circle.

One major exhibition I experienced during that Swiss adventure was *Dadaglobe Reconstructed* at The Kunsthaus Zurich, a landmark show bringing together more than 200 works originally mailed to Tristan Tzara in 1920 for his Dadaglobe book compilation. In curating that project, Tzara essentially invented what's now known as mail art. According to Tzara's specific instructions, artists sent him imagery, photo collages, warped self-portraits, poetry or texts via postal mail to be included in the book, which he intended to function as an official Dada catalog representing the radical avant-garde of post-WWI Europe. Of course, in pure Dada fashion, the book never actually happened due to financial collapse and infighting among the participants, so the original submissions were eventually dispersed into public and private collections all over the world.

Some pieces, like Max Ernst's *Chinese Nightingale*, even went on to become important in their own right, but without anyone realizing they were originally created for Tzara's Dadaglobe book.

Amazingly, about six years ago, New York-based art historian Adrian Sudhalter began tracking down all of the original submissions with the intention of reconstructing the original Dadaglobe book. It was a landmark undertaking of 20th-century art scholarship and detective work, a milestone in Dada research culminating with the Kunsthaus exhibition, which then traveled to MoMA in New York City. Now Sudhalter will talk about her research at the brand new swissnex headquarters at Pier 17 in San Francisco on Nov. 2, just one of many Dada World Fair events over the next two weeks.

Tzara was an original anti-man-about-town. Even though he was among the Magnificent Seven who co-founded Dada at the Cabaret Voltaire in 1916, he never fit into one creative category. Hailing from Romania, he wrote poetry in both his mother tongue and in French. He also orchestrated performances of "simultaneous poetry" in which participants read unrelated poems at the same time in different languages. Coming from a multi-ethnic, multi-religious, multi-political background, Tzara's creative practice was inseparable from all of those characteristics.

As Dada began to circle the drain for good, Tzara branched off to Paris where he continued to duke it out with fellow wiseass troublemakers Francis Picabia and Andre Breton, a scene that eventually led to Surrealism. But Tzara did not go away. For decades he published volumes of poetry, traveled in and out of communism, and even amassed a formidable collection of African and Oceanic art. He was a performance artist, a playwright and a scholar—a true interdisciplinary character.

"Tzara was amazing," Sudhalter said. "He was first and foremost a poet. Dada was something he did for a few years, but he was a poet for his lifetime. He was a poet before he entered the Dada scene and he was a poet after. He had a very sincere passion for poetry. And identity. And for language and the politics that are inherent in language."

When I visited Zurich last April, the current-day Cabaret Voltaire featured an offizium—a prayer or incantation of sorts—to a particular Dadaist every single morning. I attended the one for Tzara, which took place on his birthday. I didn't know ahead of time that I'd be there on Tzara's birthday. For the offizium, Cabaret Voltaire director Adrian Notz stood there and read Tzara's entire 1918 Dada Manifesto. That document was and still is one of the all-time masterpieces of oppositional defiant disorder reiterated as a strategy for creative practice. I can probably identify 100 columns in which I've tried to do the exact same thing. I owe much to Tristan Tzara. Now, thanks to City Lights, it shall continue.

Irish Revolutionary, Hired Gun Receives 100-Year Memorial

About two dozen people recently gathered at Santa Clara Mission Cemetery to stage a memorial for Irish revolutionary and legend Michael "Mick" McDonnell. Nearly 100 years ago, McDonnell was the first leader of "The Squad," a.k.a. "The Twelve Apostles," the assassination unit employed by Michael Collins during the Irish War of Independence.

The Squad systematically bumped off a number of British spies, and their story is the subject of several books, including a new one by Irish historian Tim Pat Coogan. Before the Squad was formed, McDonnell took part in the Easter Rising of 1916 and then, with the Twelve Apostles, had a hand in the actions of Bloody Sunday. As the Irish Civil War began in 1922, McDonnell came to the U.S. and eventually settled in Los Gatos for the rest of his life. He died in 1950, followed by a massive funeral at St. Mary's Church.

A few weeks ago, in commemoration of McDonnell's service to the cause of Irish independence, AmeriCeltic invited a group of Bay Area Irish history buffs to his grave for a party. AmeriCeltic is a volunteer, nonprofit organization that preserves the culture and history of Americans of Celtic descent in Northern California. They researched California's role in the Easter Rising to produce a short documentary, which led to more information about McDonnell's participation in money trails leading from San Jose back to Ireland in support of Michael Collins' activities. From there, the idea for a quaint gravesite dedication emerged.

The memorial was low-key and informal, but dramatic nonetheless. Irish flags hung suspended from a makeshift tent, as did several photocopies of old newspaper columns about McDonnell and the Squad's activities. Music stands were set up and tea was flowing. Not a cloud lurked in the sky and all I could hear was the distant sound of a lawnmower tending to the grass. One could not have asked for a more peaceful afternoon.

Sean O'Kane, president of the San Jose-Dublin Sister City Program, mastered the ceremonies with his usual booming savoir-faire. Former San Jose Mayor Tom McEnery delivered a poignant address about Mc-Donnell's life, explaining that as Michael Collins' appointed assassin, Mc-Donnell played a terrible yet crucial role in the cause of Irish freedom.

"He was probably the most significant revolutionary who ever lived in California," McEnery said. The former mayor's connection to the whole mess is more than just historical, of course. It's personal. After McDonnell arrived in the South Bay, he worked for McEnery's father at the old Farmers Union building in downtown San Jose, which is now O'Flaherty's Irish Pub, and McEnery still has childhood memories of seeing McDonnell around the business. He was a good friend of the family.

After the speeches concluded, the music commenced. Erin Thompson sang an evocative version of "The Foggy Dew." Bagpiper Phil Lenihan came next, clad in a saffron kilt, the traditional dress for formal bagpipe occasions of national importance to Irish people. Together, everyone joined in singing a rousing version of "A Nation Once Again," a song known around the world. This was perhaps the most moving part of the ceremony—local historians, musicians, a man of the cloth, a former mayor and others all paying sonic tribute to a forgotten revolutionary, backdropped by acres of headstones sprawling in every direction around us. And that distant lawnmower still plugged away.

Although no one seems to know exactly why McDonnell decided to settle in the San Jose area, as opposed to anywhere else, Tony Becker of AmeriCeltic thinks McDonnell was dispatched here to help continue an operation of sorts. At the time of the Irish Civil War, plenty of organizations existed in Northern California to raise money for the cause of Irish independence, namely the Ancient Order of Hibernians and the Friends of Irish Freedom. McDonnell became mixed up with those organizations after he settled in Los Gatos, helping to support the efforts of Michael Collins and his band of rebels, even after Collins died.

"[We] believe that is the likely reason Collins sent him here—to keep the cash flowing to the Finance Ministry of the Irish Republic headed by Collins, and not to Eamon De Valera's faction," Becker said.

An Infamous Dead Fish Performance at Marsugi's

I recently revisited one of my favorite books, *City of Djinns* by William Dalrymple, a travel book about Delhi history. In Delhi, no matter how many new businesses seem to emerge, the old legends—just like spirits or *djinns*—often come out of nowhere, sometimes decades after they were aced out.

Dalrymple portrays a city "disjointed in time, a city whose different ages lay suspended side by side as in aspic, a city of djinns."

This is also my view of downtown San Jose, where, in the SoFA District, decades of creation and destruction reverberate to the current day.

Businesses or buildings die right alongside others just beginning, seemingly merging the district's physical and temporal aspects. *Djinns* are a city's ghosts and when I see the brick building at 399 S. First St. gearing up to serve fish taco plates, I cannot help but recall when that building was Marsugi's, the best corner rock & roll dive San Jose ever had. At Marsugi's, one watched bands like Nirvana or Faith no More in front of 30 people, back when those bands were relatively unknown.

However, on one particular night at Marsugi's, things got a little fishy. At the time, we were a group of four SJSU music students gigging as an improvised noise-art fraternity of the absurd. In February of 1993, two weeks before Marsugi's was slotted to close, we played a show to maybe 12 people and I became the first one to play an amplified lawnmower in downtown San Jose. Since the club was closing in favor of mainstream upmarket riffraff, we wanted to leave our mark. The lawnmower came from my mom's house and after we loaded everything into the truck, we stopped for beer at the dumpy Lucky Supermarket downtown.

Once inside the store, I decided to buy a stack of whole fish from the seafood section. I don't remember why I did this. It was a snap decision. Nothing was premeditated.

During the show, none of my equipment was working, an occasional downside to shows with homemade electronics, so as the rest of the group proceeded to make sounds, I grew frustrated. Plus, we were angry that Marsugi's was closing, so the emotion came to a boil 10 minutes into the gig.

Enter a Briggs & Stratton lawnmower rigged with a homemade contact microphone assemblage to amplify its sounds, sitting on the beer-stained Marsugi's carpet, with gas in the tank, just waiting for me to turn it on. As the rest of the band continued to make excruciating noise for noise's sake on keyboards, bass, amplified trombone and electric guitar, I couldn't get any of my equipment to work, so I stepped onto the floor, placed my right foot on the lawnmower, and yanked the cord a few times until the machine came roaring to life. Fully amplified, the motor raged through the PA system. The sound man, already drunk and on LSD, started tweaking knobs in response. Then, I flipped the mower over so its blades violently spun in full view of the audience members and I started laughing. I just remember laughing.

Only the fish remained, so I rescued them from the Lucky's bag, theatrically taking each fish out of its plastic wrap, slow enough so the intimate crowd could realize what was about to happen. As the band played on, I threw dead fish, one by one, into the running lawnmower blades. As a result, fish guts sprayed every which direction, splattering throughout the entire club. The bar, the walls, the tables, and yours truly were covered with fish guts afterward. Some of the audience got splattered, while others tipped up tables to shield themselves from the flying fish guts. The manager immediately shut down our show, but the club smelled like fish throughout the last two weeks it remained open. The staff was never able to get rid of the smell and I had to shower several times before I stopped smelling like fish.

Skip to 2016 and the djinns of 399 S. First will resurface yet again, when a new restaurant opens next month, right where this juvenile temper tantrum went down. Space and time will merge and I can't wait for the fish tacos.

2017

Viet Thanh Nguyen Puts San Jose in Literary Spotlight

Viet Thanh Nguyen is the V.S. Naipaul of San Jose's underbelly. Or maybe the Vietnamese Nelson Algren of Santa Clara Street. His short story "War Years" conjures up exactly the right inner and outer conflicts that characterize the East-West clash of San Jose's most prominent thoroughfare. San Jose is on the literary map once again.

But first some background. Twenty-five years ago, when I'd regularly haunt the notorious Charlie's Liquors at Fourth and Santa Clara streets, right where City Hall now sits, I'd gaze in everyday wonderment at the glorious downmarket legends across the street: Lenny's Cocktails, the Quality Cafe, and New Saigon Market. In the latter case, the always-bustling mom 'n' pop grocery store was one of many Vietnamese-owned places I came to know along those several blocks of Santa Clara Street, including ABC Liquors and F&P Liquors. There were also Vietnamese hair salons and cleaners, but I didn't go to any of those.

Little did I know that, a quarter-century later, the New Saigon Market owner's offspring would win the Pulitzer Prize for fiction. *The Sympathizer*, by Viet Thanh Nguyen, came out in 2015 and won just about every award. It is truly one of the most intense books I've read in years.

Viet escaped San Jose about the time I was first discovering Charlie's Liquors. He eventually wound up with a Ph.D. in English from Berkeley and started teaching at the University of Southern California, where he remains to this day. At USC, he is the Aerol Arnold chair of English and professor of English and American studies and ethnicity, pumping out scholarship left and right, in addition to winning awards.

In 2016, Viet seemed to have a good year. *The Sympathizer* came out in paperback, and his nonfiction work *Nothing Ever Dies: Vietnam and the Memory of War*, was a finalist for the National Book Award. Viet's fiction and nonfiction, ingested together or separately, will redefine everything you think you know about the conflict Vietnamese people call "The American War."

On the local front, New Saigon Market unfortunately went by the wayside in the early 2000s. With a shiny new City Hall coming in, San Jose didn't want any downmarket riffraff across the street, so they slaughtered the entire northern side of Santa Clara Street between Fourth and Fifth streets. Gone was the glorious bottom-of-the-barrel dive Lenny's Cocktails. Gone was the $1.99 breakfast at Quality Cafe. And of course, gone was New Saigon Market. In textbook San Jose fashion, the city transformed all of it into an empty parking lot, which is still there, soon to be transformed into a Chinese-financed skyscraper.

So, just last year, in one of those classic face-palm scenarios where the city of San Jose tries to vindicate its own bumbling ineptitude, the politicians brought Viet back to town and gave him a city commendation for winning the Pulitzer Prize. Meaning, Viet Thanh Nguyen—a formidable new voice in American letters and now famous the world over—received an award in City Hall, directly across the street from where the city demolished the very market his parents built by working 12 hours a day for 20 years. Vamping on the delicious irony of it all, Viet gave a powerful speech that spoke to the loneliness and alienation of growing up as a war refugee in San Jose, seeing American businesses that didn't want his family here, always feeling out of place, never truly at home, and longing to escape the disenchantment of such a town. But thankfully, the psychological scars that San Jose left on Viet helped carve him into a Pulitzer Prize-winning author. It's one of the most heroic coming-of-age tales in local history.

Which brings us right back to the story "War Years," included in Viet's new book of short stories, *The Refugees*, which drops in a few weeks. The stories explore the effects of the refugee experience on family dynamics and relationships across the Vietnamese diaspora. In particular, War Years brings New Saigon Market to life, in all its bustling glory, like no other literary work about San Jose ever has. No matter how tall may be the skyscraper that will rise on that empty parking lot, it will always be haunted by the ghosts of New Saigon Market.

WORKS/San Jose Celebrates 40th Anniversary

This year marks the 40th anniversary for WORKS/San Jose gallery, an all-volunteer alternative arts space. Entrenched in the eastern side of the San Jose McEnery Convention Center, the gallery celebrates a long, twisted history of continuous relocation woes after moving through six downtown locations in four decades.

A microcosm of San Jose's urban redevelopment saga, the WORKS story is a unique testament to how the alternative arts can survive endless cycles of creation and destruction at the hands of greedy real estate operatives and the city planners that love them. It isn't quite David versus Goliath, but it's close.

In 1977, an adventurous group of artists and San Jose State University professors were dismayed at the more mainstream direction of the San Jose Museum of Art, so they wanted to create a community-based art gallery, a place for cutting-edge visual art, dance, performance, avant-garde books, music and whatever else came along. Most important, they wanted the venue to be democratic, with no centralized leadership, a true community-based experimental arts space. No such venue in San Jose existed at the time.

Soon enough, the group discovered an abandoned building at Vine and Auzerais, transforming the structure into San Jose's first alternative arts gallery and debuting in October 1977. In the punk spirit of the era, the artists did it themselves. In a statement with ripple effects to this day, Tony May, one of the original protagonists, would later famously recall: "We just thought San Jose would be less embarrassing if it had an art gallery."

Of the Vine and Auzerais location, another original protagonist, Jim Thomas, would later write: "The place was a wreck. Yet a bunch of energetic artists, all ersatz carpenters and house painters and too naive to realize what the hell they were getting into, still had the power to transform it."

Unfortunately, the space only lasted eight years. San Jose politicians wanted a convention center more than they wanted an art gallery, so the city eventually slaughtered the entire residential neighborhood around Vine and Auzerais in order to create what's now two lanes of Almaden Boulevard. The intersection of Vine and Auzerais is long gone.

As a result, WORKS moved into the rundown Leticia Building at 66 S. First St. for the last half of the '80s. Their rent was $400. At the time, much of downtown was still a war zone of boarded-up storefronts and nefarious activity. As light rail construction tore up the neighborhood, putting retailers out of business left and right, WORKS thrived with punk shows, edgy visual art, performances and other hijinks. It was a fantastic urban space. Mark Pauline, of Survival Research Laboratories, even showed up one year to present a lecture and video documentation. Unfortunately, 66 S. First St. was an unreinforced masonry structure, legally uninhabitable after the Loma Prieta earthquake, so the artists were once again forced to relocate.

Enter Japantown. A corrugated metal warehouse at southeast corner of Sixth and Jackson became WORKS' new home for the next six years. Several legendary troublemakers showed up to do gigs here, including world-renowned body-modification maestro Fakir Musafar. Unfortunately, San Jose history began to repeat itself and the building was demolished in favor of lifeless, uniform housing.

However, WORKS was not deterred. In 1997, the gallery moved into the Sperry Flour Building at 30 N. Third St., where it thrived more than ever, that is, until the real estate operatives again came calling. In the early 2000s, WORKS again found itself without a home.

After a brief, disastrous stint on South First Street, WORKS opened its current location at 365 S. Market just a few years ago, bringing everything full circle in cosmic fashion. Now it sits exactly on the opposite side of the Convention Center from the original defunct location at Vine and Auzerais.

As a result, much of what has transpired in downtown San Jose—when it comes to arts spaces battling the dark forces of gentrification over the last several decades—can be traced back to the pioneering avant-garde spirit embodied by the original WORKS protagonists. San Jose is much less embarrassing thanks to what they invented. Look for official 40th anniversary celebrations to unfold at WORKS later this year.

Kim Addonizio Brings New Poetry Collection to San Jose

Acclaimed poet, writer and articulator of the blues Kim Addonizio fortifies the classical poetic canon with glorious fusions of sacred and profane in her latest volume, *Mortal Trash*. Heraclitean Fire, internet dating, antidepressant medications and crappy ex-lovers appear and disappear, one after the other. She employs prosody and parody, elegy and eulogy, with equal intensity.

For this reason, Addonizio's appearance 4-5pm Friday in the Steinbeck Center, on the fifth floor of San Jose State University's Martin Luther King, Jr. Library, should make for a gala hoedown spectacular, free to the public. There will be a special cocktail hour and reading and conversation.

Addonizio's second 2016 book, *Bukowski in a Sundress: Confessions from a Writing Life*, was a memoir structured as an abstract series of essays that likewise threw a thousand emotions right in your face. Unlike poetry, you won't need to irritate the bejeezus out of the poet by asking her which stuff is true, because it's all true. Which brings us to Charles Bukowski, of course.

Apparently, some jealous critic tossed off Addonizio as "Bukowski in a Sundress" and it stuck. Whether the bozo intended this as a compliment or a snide remark doesn't matter. I'm glad it stuck.

As such, *Bukowski in a Sundress* contains more than one essay about the inquisitive prying buffoons who ask what is "real" in Addonizio's poetry, as opposed to the parts she just made up. Many good poets seem to deal with this crap. It's just part of being a poet. So, in one essay, "Pants on Fire," she comes clean and rattles off a hysterical laundry list of various poetic dimensions, that is, which material she made up and what was real, or why clueless ex-boyfriends asked her stuff in the heat-of-the-fight, like, "Why do you go into things so much?" (Only a non-writer would ask that question.) Other than that, I won't spoil it for you. Probably doesn't matter anyway, because Bukowski in a Sundress is unspoilable, if that's even a word.

Better yet, other essays in the book provide human advice for any would-be writing student who wants to know what "the life" is really like: drunken romps after boring academic writers' conferences, receiving awards at the podium while hiding the self-doubt that all writers have, or even teaching in remote backwater places and empathizing with the teenage students' pain and isolation, as they use poetry as a way out of their misery. Addonizio also goes deep into the common pitfalls of the writer's existence in regards to drugs, self-loathing, writer's block, distraction, boredom, family guilt, isolation, loneliness, destitution, nomadic inclinations, escapism via alcohol, avoiding the actual writing at all costs, and dealing with overwhelming amounts of rejection from agents, magazines or commercial publishers. You know this is part of the human condition, if you're a writer.

Thankfully, I can testify that Addonizio also writes high-quality manuals of the poetic craft. Her textbook, *Ordinary Genius: A Guide for the Poet Within*, is chock-full of exercises, meditations, discombobulations and expert lessons for grooming the practice. To make a long column short, that book was and remains a massive influence on me. Of the two dozen poems I've published in obscure journals, at least a third of them originated by doing exercises from *Ordinary Genius*. In fact, I still occasionally carry it around in my bag.

I might even owe it to Addonizio for even trying my hand at poetry on a serious level. When she came to SJSU in 2013, I bought another copy of the book and gave it to a friend of mine. In Room 255 of the main library, I stood there in the signing line with Scott Knies of the San Jose Downtown Association and Ted Gehrke, head honcho of the Fountain Blues Festival, both of whom also purchased a copy. (Poets are everywhere around these parts.) Gehrke, right then and there, booked Addonizio to perform at the Blues Festival later that year, since she's also a killer harmonica player.

This Friday, a good branding consultant would say, "Bring your own blues." It should be a rocking time.

Sholeh Wolpe Gives Epic Persian Allegory New Life

Sholeh Wolpe uses poetry to unite east and west. A few years ago, the Iranian-American poet and translator came to San Jose State University and gave a talk on Attar, the legendary Sufi mystic writer from whom Rumi acquired his entire shtick.

Attar's epic allegorical poem, *The Conference of the Birds*, had only been translated in a scholarly fashion, so Wolpe decided to translate a few passages into poetic English for her presentation at the Martin Luther King, Jr. Main Library. The experience moved her so much that she later wound up pursuing and getting a contract to translate the entire book, which just came out from W.W. Norton. Wolpe returned to San Jose State last week as part of her book launch enterprise. Once again, San Jose serves as the backdrop for a mystical convergence of East and West.

The Conference of the Birds is a grand allegory about the journey of the soul and the annihilation of the ego. The story recounts a perilous journey undertaken by the world's birds, the mystics, led by another bird, the Hoopoe, who can be understood as a sage or messenger guiding the other birds toward the truth. The journey unfolds in a series of cheeky yet profound lessons, given by the Hoopoe to the birds, followed by deceptively simple parables illustrating those lessons. The parables are funny and brash on the surface, but multiple layers of meaning emerge in almost every stanza. The path articulated is an interior voyage, with the birds learning to look for the essence within, rather than be "bamboozled by externals."

In the end, the birds realize that they are part of the Great Beloved, not separate from it. The reader need not be religious, but whatever one's path, Attar says, if you remain still, you will dry up in your own puddle.

Regarding the translation, Wolpe realized that previous English translations were not exactly simple to follow, so she pored over different versions before using the one she felt was most accurate. She also assiduously consulted scholarly analyses, all to ensure that she was providing a simple yet poetic translation rather than a verbose work of scholarship. The intense beauty and poetic nature of Attar's Persian is thus reimagined in contemporary English.

"The Persian language is a very flowery language," Wolpe says. "It's beautiful, it's very melodic and it's very flowery. Translating it carelessly would result in a very flowery cliched work in English. That it why it is very important for the translator to be recreating the work in a fresh language. ... And that's what I did, I used my poetic voice to make sure that the language itself is fresh."

As a result, the book is easy to read, yet mind-blowing in its profundity. Any imaginative reader will immediately apply the parables to his or her own predicaments or even to national events. For example, the stories of the "self-satisfied bird," driven by isolationist arrogance and devoid of wisdom, will clearly remind of egomaniacal politicians with inferiority complexes and their violent "me-first" advisers.

Another refreshing aspect of Wolpe's translation is that all gender references are removed from the story, so we get "the Beloved" or "the Ocean" as opposed to any specific god or goddess verbiage. The Persian language does not contain "he" or "she" pronouns, but since previous translators were men, they translated everything as male or "he." Not so with Wolpe's translation.

Wolpe explains: "I didn't want to turn around and make everything 'she,' to say, 'Oh, I'm a female translator.' What I did, I took it out completely. I respected the Persian language and I said, 'Well, God, the Beloved, the Almighty, there is no gender there.' So I just used different names for the Beloved."

Wolpe's pursuits don't stop with Attar. She also recently helped translate Walt Whitman's *Song of Myself* into Persian, soon to be released in Iran, now that the book finally passed the censor's approval. In this columnist's view, both of those geniuses—Attar and Whitman—provide insight into how we can improve the world by improving ourselves first.

"They're both mystic poets," Wolpe notes. "Whitman says, 'I contain multitude.' So you can see immediately, wow, that's what Attar has been saying, in a different way."

San Jose Signs Project Honors Colorful Contributions of Neon

We've all seen them. The celebrated neon signs of San Jose. We're talking Stephen's Meat Products, Western Appliance, the Sands Motel and the Wing's restaurant sign in Japantown. Signs are essential elements in the collective story of this city. They are part of San Jose's consciousness.

Thousands of natives have gushed endless praise for San Jose's old-school neon signage, with many people from out of town also showing up just to photograph the marquees. But with the majority finding solace in bland landscapes, generic signage and village after village of hideously uniform condos that no interesting person would possibly look at, someone is finally taking it upon herself to stop complaining and do something to raise awareness about San Jose's heritage of neon.

Enter Heather David, San Jose's resident expert at roadside motel architecture. David has put together a glorious and glossy tour guide called the San Jose Signs Project, a partnership between various communities, historic organizations and local businesses. The mission of The San Jose Signs Project is threefold: to educate, advocate and preserve. The physical guide is only the beginning. A gala hoedown release party is scheduled for somewhere around the end of next month and anyone is welcome to join the Facebook group for up-to-date shenanigans: www.facebook.com/sanjosesignproject.

"I strongly believe that signs are important cultural place markers, and I am not alone," David says. "Cities all over the country have been working to celebrate and protect their historic signage, and I felt that San Jose, with its notable sign inventory, should step up and do the same."

One doesn't have to venture far to understand this. In Tucson, Arizona, for instance, one finds a project called The Neon Pueblo, a large-scale effort that preserved, restored and re-installed 30 neon signs, after local heroes salvaged them from potential destruction. Tucson now incorporates the signs as part of how the city markets itself to tourists. One can acquire a massive 40-page, full-color guide to the whole project, complete with a map of all the signs. The city even revised some of the sign codes to accommodate the preservation of these unique assets, understanding that neon was part of Tucson's colorful history.

The city of Phoenix's Historic Preservation Office presents a similar concept: a two-page guide on "Mid-Century Marvels," which directs visitors to architecture and neon from the postwar era. Clearly, they understand the ways in which neon signage plays a role in the collective story of a city.

I can cite other examples—from Amarillo, Texas, to Vancouver, British Columbia—and in the latter case, the Vancouver Neon Project includes photographs of former and remaining signage all over the city, especially in its Chinatown. In the '50s, Vancouver claimed over 18,000 neon signs, second only to Las Vegas. Tasteless bureaucrats came along and outlawed the signs for decades, until the city eventually reevaluated its policies in 2000. Now the signs are back.

"Every sign has a story to tell," David says. "This story can be a reflection of the larger society's values at the time of the sign's inception and/ or it can be a story of a region's unique local history. The animated neon Wing's sign in Japantown, for example, is a place marker for one of San Jose's original Chinatowns."

The San Jose Signs Project guide includes 25 classic signs still remaining in San Jose. Included are Falafel's Drive-In, Time Deli, Y Not, Mr. T's Liquor Locker and the Kentucky Fried Chicken Bucket at 250 N. Bascom Ave. Regarding the last example, people from all over the country visit San Jose to photograph the KFC bucket because it's one of the last in the U.S. and the oldest one still standing. Similarly, the neon diving lady at the City Center Motel on Reed is one of only two original motel sign divers left in the entire state of California. They used to be everywhere, but no more.

"The long-term goal for this project is to obtain protections for as many of our historic signs as possible," David says. "The short-term goal is to conduct a professional inventory of San Jose's signs, and identify those that are indeed historic and require protection."

Chuck Barris, RIP

The former host of *The Gong Show*, Chuck Barris, passed away last month at the ripe old age of 87. His show pioneered the implementation of bad-on-purpose talent judged by drunk celebrities who gonged contestants they didn't like.

In addition to The Gong Show, Barris can also be blamed for *The Newlywed Game and The Dating Game*, going back to the '60s, helping to invent what's now called reality TV decades before the term surfaced.

Barris used game-show entertainment to embarrass his entire industry, illuminating the crass idiocy of American pop culture in the process. In that sense, he was the greatest genius in television history.

In the late '80s, Barris sold his empire to Sony, making enough to live happily ever after, so he wrote a biography claiming he was secretly a CIA hitman. The story was made into a film with the same name, *Confessions of a Dangerous Mind*.

My connection to Barris dates to January 2003, when he came to San Francisco on a book tour, appearing at the Park Branch Library on Page Street. A jampacked capacity crowd filled the room, including one dude who'd won *The Gong Show* a quarter-century earlier and even brought the trophy with him for Barris to sign.

At the time, I was regularly hanging out with the remains of the San Francisco Cacophony Society, an intentionally disorganized network of individuals united in the pursuit of experiences beyond the pale of mainstream society through subversion, pranks or any meaningless crap involving silly costumes. Collectively, about 10 of us decided to prank the Chuck Barris event by dressing up with paper bags over our heads and wearing bad '70s suits, ala the Unknown Comic, a regular from *The Gong Show*.

But there was more. That morning, we spent $50 to rent a gong from Lemon Percussion, which was then located at Willow and Bird in San Jose. A designated driver and I loaded the gong into his car and drove to San Francisco, where we secretly met the other Cacophonists upstairs at Hobson's Choice, a rum bar on Haight Street, around the corner from the Park Branch Library. After getting solidly drunk, we situated ourselves out in front of the library, put the paper bags over our heads, and then quietly carried the gong into the event, setting it up behind the audience, just as Barris began to talk. Upon our entry, everyone in the crowd turned around to look at at us, wondering what on earth we were up to. Even Barris, from the podium, asked us what was going on. But we just stood there, quiet and motionless next to the gong.

The plan from the beginning was to stand behind the crowd and not hit the gong. In this way, as the event unfolded, the entire audience would sit there, expecting us to hit the gong and ruin Chuck's talk, waiting in anticipation of when it might happen, and then we wouldn't do it. The prank was on the audience, not Chuck Barris per se. And it worked like a charm.

Throughout the event, people in the crowd kept nervously turning their heads around to see when we were going to hit the gong. And we never did. The prank came across as classy and simple, a subtle masterpiece if I should say so myself. Afterward, Barris even stood next to us for a photo, while we still had the bags on our heads. In pure Cacophony fashion, no one remembers who took the photo or what happened to it.

The next morning, back in San Jose and completely hungover, we returned the gong to Lemmon Percussion. I didn't have the ambition to explain how we'd used it.

I'm recounting this idiotic adventure not only to celebrate the life of Chuck Barris, but to encourage every reader to attend the monthly Go! Go! Gong Show! at Cafe Stritch, hosted by San Jose living legend Mighty Mike McGee. Each month, people sign up to do stupid shit on stage and the winner gets $50—exactly what we shelled out for that blasted gong at Lemmon Percussion.

Sikh Foundation Celebrates 50th Birthday

Ripple effects were felt worldwide, as the Sikh Foundation International—headquartered in Palo Alto—celebrated its 50th anniversary last weekend in grand-scale fashion. A few hundred Sikhs from around the globe dropped serious cash for a gala that took over the Asian Art Museum on Friday, followed by a free two-day conference at Stanford's Li Ka Shing Center.

Somehow, surrounded by Sikhs, I managed to avoid talking about religion for the whole weekend and only one person tried to arrange a marriage for me.

But first of all, let me introduce Narinder Singh Kapany, more commonly known around the globe as Dr. Kapany, the father of fiber optics. Kapany started the Sikh Foundation exactly 50 years ago in 1967, and he's been collecting Sikh art ever since. Over the decades, his collection has spawned several groundbreaking exhibits on several continents, including the current one at the Asian Art Museum. All of these exhibits have succeeded in foregrounding Sikh art in the contemporary museum-patron-collector nexus. On the academic front, Kapany has personally financed multiple endowments and chairs of Sikh studies at higher institutions across the country. If not for him, none of this would be happening.

Both the gala and the conference drew luminaries from a variety of backgrounds. At the conference, interfaith religious scholars, art collectors, medical technologists, and a beautifully esoteric old-school European strain of Indophile museum curator types all showed up and held court. It was fantastic.

For example, if I wanted to know which war-era descendant of which Punjabi maharajah sold a $60,000-dollar book of original Sikh-illustrated drawings of the high court to a strange collector in France, someone in the room probably had the answer. Art ruled the weekend.

The festivities also celebrated the official release of a brand new volume, *Sikh Art From the Kapany Collection*, a gargantuan 320-page hardcover art book including numerous scholarly texts by internationally recognized art historians analyzing Kapany's collection. Edited by Paul Michael Taylor, of the Smithsonian Institution's Asian Cultural History Program, and Sikh Foundation Executive Director Sonia Dhami, the book includes three main sections. The first section concentrates on the collectors and their vision, with biographical and profile information about the Kapanys and their history. The second section surveys the collection in terms of how it conveys Sikh history and ethos. The third and final section deals with stamps, coins and textiles from Kapany's collection, while also offering still more contemporary perspectives on how to preserve and exhibit the collection.

Several of the authors included in *Sikh Art* gave presentations at the Stanford conference, which unfolded over two days. The Saturday afternoon session was titled, "Sikh Arts and Heritage—Expanding Horizons," and it featured a star-studded lineup. I felt like a teenager at a rock show, in that I didn't want to leave until the last person was gone.

One of India's most distinguished contemporary painters, Arpana Caur, presented a gorgeous PowerPoint slideshow of 40 years' worth of her work, some of which featured brutal depictions of the horrors suffered during the 1947 Partition of India, albeit in abstract representations.

Author Bhupinder Singh Bance, also known as Peter Bance, came from England to present on the strange life of the last Sikh maharajah, Duleep Singh, a character who ascended to the throne in Punjab at age 5 and remained there for eight years until the British conquered Punjab and forced him into exile by bringing him back to the United Kingdom and converting him to Christianity. Once in England, Duleep became an exotic party accessory in Queen Victoria's crowd before eventually reclaiming his Sikh faith and trying to return to Punjab. To make a long story short, he wound up dying in a Paris hotel room.

Other speakers rounding out the Arts and Heritage afternoon included Dr. Jean-Marie Lafont of France, an author of many books over the last 40 years, mostly about Franco-Punjabi relations and Indo-French connections during the Sikh empire. Lafont gave a presentation about the 19th century Punjabi artist Imam Bakhsh and his illustrations for *La Fontaine's Fables*.

Among such scholarly giants of Punjab history and arts, I was blown away. Here's to another 50 years!

'The River's Edge' Brings Back Teenage Wasteland Memories

A few stories came out last week to mark the 30th anniversary of the 1987 film *The River's Edge*, based on a grotesque murder in Milpitas. The teenage killer left his victim's corpse in the woods for a few days, inviting his friends to come over and check it out. Only then was the crime finally reported.

It was a horrific incident that unleashed a national media firestorm. When the film came out, it likewise shocked the country.

The River's Edge opens with the killer sitting at the victim's body and then cuts to him and his pals trying to buy beer at a Stop 'n' Go convenience store, which were common in those days. Then we get an 80-minute window into the lives of alienated teenagers dealing with the fallout, a picture that successfully flipped the bird at all the Molly Ringwald-worshipping mallrat garbage that constituted teen films at that time. *The River's Edge* featured a then-unknown Keanu Reeves in his first major appearance. Crispin Glover and Dennis Hopper also gave legendary performances.

Directed by Tim Hunter, the film was either an abomination or a masterpiece, depending on how much denim and leather one wore as a teenager in the '80s—and to what degree one drank outside the Stop 'n' Go across from their high school. From this perspective, *The River's Edge* was a glorious paean to suburban wasteland despair, accurately depicting disenfranchised, emotionally distant teenagers blasting thrash metal from their beater cars and endlessly searching for Dennis Hopper-style wackos to buy beer for them. That was my life at that time.

Musically speaking, Slayer was still an underground band in those days—the "Reign in Blood" album had not been released as the film was being shot—so only underground troublemakers like us listened to that music. As a result, to hear Slayer in a soundtrack, to see teenagers driving around while playing that music five minutes into the movie, was just plain righteous. Seeing the film at Century 22 on Winchester, a few friends and I even showed up wearing denim and leather, just like the kids in the movie. Legends in our own minds, we did it to horrify others in the theater. I don't know if it worked.

Some more context, if you will: In 1987, a Sony Walkman was $38 at The Good Guys. Brand new CDs at Tower were $14.99. Photo Drive-Up rented VHS tapes for $1 per movie, per day. High culture in South San Jose was essentially driving or taking the bus to Record Factory and arguing with the hair-metal idiot behind the counter as to whether Maxell or TDK blank cassettes were better quality. And it only took a Dio shirt to scare the jocks and cheerleaders in high school.

There was nothing else to do except find alcohol and get wasted in parks and hillsides at nighttime. In that sense, *The River's Edge* depicted San Jose better than anything I'd seen. I'm just glad this town has a lot of parks.

Which is why, 30 years later, I just had to skulk back over to Winchester and see what's left of the Century theaters, now that Santana Row has for all practical purposes murdered them and left their corpse shells to rot in the open sun. It won't be long only until they are cannibalized by "The Row."

I got as far as the road sign. That was enough. Right there on Winchester, the old legendary Century Theater sign, familiar as my own reflection in the mirror, now says: Santana Row Customer Parking.

To that end, I guess no one should have been surprised when the Century domes were yanked off life support. The traditional cinema experience is fading. Land is expensive around here. Developers are ruthless and selfish because they know that City Hall ultimately won't care. And so we drift along in the stream of Netflix and YouTube.

All of this will produce another generation of bored teenagers filled with despair. But don't worry. They won't wind up like characters in *The River's Edge*. That would take too much work.

Recycle Bookstore 50th Anniversary

Golden anniversaries have been in the news these days, so allow me to shout from the mountaintop—or at least a street corner—about Recycle Bookstore on The Alameda. With 3,800 square feet of used books on shelves, floors, carts and boxes, the place always seems to provide a diverse literary experience.

For the last 19 years, proprietor Eric Johnson has owned and operated the store, but when Joan and Pat Hayes first started the original business in 1967, they probably had no idea it would still exist 50 years later.

Initially opening on South First Street, Recycle then moved to a location on San Fernando, where it became known for a distinguished and legendary basement. Old-timers still talk about that basement. Following the San Fernando location, the store eventually settled on Santa Clara Street for about 20 years, in the building now occupied by 2nd Story Bakeshop and Hibiscus Studio. By 1998, the store had begun to stagnate. The stock wasn't rotating like it used to and Joan Hayes began looking for a new buyer. Johnson took over the business in October of that year, but he couldn't hammer out a reasonable lease with the new landlord, so he found a new location on The Alameda, where the store sits to this day. Both Hayes and the city of San Jose backed the loan enabling Johnson to make it work.

"The city took a chance on me," Johnson says. "I don't know why, but they did. They really wanted to keep the bookstore in San Jose."

For me personally, I spent years patronizing the Santa Clara Street location, beginning in my teens, when I'd take the bus downtown to hit up Twice Read Books, Recycle and the comic shops and record stores that dotted the gritty landscape. Recycle's Santa Clara Street location was an amazing store. You'd see college students, professors, punks, drunks, scholars and everyone between. Like any great used bookstore, browsing became an adventurous expedition akin to enlightenment. One didn't need a destination, a goal, or anything to achieve. The path, the browsing, the journey itself was the destination. By the time Johnson came along and relocated the store, I was just happy the place wasn't closing.

Ever since then, Johnson says, the job has required regularly clearing out parts of entire sections and divesting specific subsections that no longer sell. He always pays attention to what customers are looking for and then adapts. By listening to what readers are asking about, by focusing on what customers are actually buying, the store remains fresh. Recycle's online presence is also substantial, increasing from 15 percent of the business many years ago to about 35 percent nowadays.

The results are noticeable. If one prowls around the store on a regular or even semi-regular basis, parts of the stock always seem to evolve, almost like an organism ejecting unnecessary ingredients and rejuvenating itself to survive. There could be a slew of antiquarian travel books showing up one month, or there might be an entire cart of sheet music lurking in the corner. Piles and piles of recently acquired European history books might sit on the floor for several weeks, while an enlarged Buddhism section could appear a few months later.

"It keeps the store a vibrant, moving, dynamic place where people are always going to see something different," Johnson says. "And that's always going to be the draw. Because once you start to get static, you're not going to last very long."

Being a used bookstore with a low overhead, Recycle was never supposed to function as a full-blown cultural hub like Kepler's, Printers Inc., or City Lights. It's a more simple business model that attracts everyone from the upper crust to the dirges of local literati.

"What I'm probably most proud of is the fact that we really don't even think about demographics," Johnson says. "I see all of San Jose come into this store. You get the suits coming in, you get the young kids, the hipsters, old people, all ethnicities. When I think of representing San Jose, I'm really happy that everybody is comfortable in that store, no matter what your demographic is. And that's pretty darn cool."

Paramount Imports 50th Anniversary

Tim Eglington doesn't remember when he first started working at Paramount Imports. It seems like one of those mystical passages of time with no end and no beginning. Within seconds, though, Stacy Sargent, the owner and decades-long manager of Paramount, jumps in the back to retrieve the answer: 1987.

Eglington is one of many with decades of Paramount experience. The time component is crucial because once again, anniversaries are exploding out of nowhere. Exactly a month from now, Paramount will throw a huge party to celebrate its 50th year at 455 Meridian Ave. Forget the Summer of Love. This is the summer of Paramount Imports.

Generations of outcasts cut their teeth at Paramount, myself included. It was the first place in the Bay Area to specialize in pipes and smoking paraphernalia before that stuff became an industry. It was also the first place in San Jose to sell Doc Martens, punk clothing, incense from India, tarot cards and black light posters of topless women. Long before local record stores popularized the rock poster phenomenon, Jim Morrison and Bob Marley posters flew off the racks at Paramount.

When original proprietor Dave Kowal first opened Paramount, it really was an imports store. He sold statuary and home decor from Mexico. Within a few years, though, pipes and posters began to fill the shelves. As the psychedelic '60s morphed into the freewheeling '70s, the stock evolved into a counterculture bouillabaisse of items. The rear half of the store turned into an exotic haven for water pipes, smoking paraphernalia and magazines. The front half evolved into a sordid mishmash of rock digs, biker oddities, crystals, counterculture books, T-shirts, black light equipment, jewelry, shoes, purses, tapestries and much more, all of which catered to the underbelly of suburban America.

Somewhere in the middle of all this, Kowal began printing his own posters out of the back of the building while running a T-shirt shop near Star Records on the East Side. But it wasn't fruitful enough. He wanted out.

Sargent, who attended Lincoln High School, met her husband, John, in the music library at West Valley College. John held a music degree from San Jose State University and was a lifelong jazz musician. They got married in June of 1980 and then bought the Paramount Imports business a few weeks later. In the 1990s, after several dramatic ups and downs, including a fire, they were able to buy the property. Even though John is no longer with us, Paramount remains a family business. Stacy's son, Casey, is set to take over the property when the time is right.

As we all congregate in the back of the place, it becomes easy for me to suggest that Paramount is the only joint of its kind in San Jose history. It has an Original Joe's degree of staying power, even if the competition seems like an entire sea of vendors selling the same thing online, offline, American made or Chinese made.

The entire paraphernalia industry has gone corporate, so I can't help but ask them why Paramount still carries on when so many other businesses have disintegrated, given up, or been replaced by hideous cookie-cutter condos.

"We're a destination," Stacy says. "We're a living, breathing place. We have super cool people working here."

Casey agrees: "We offer an experience you can't get on the internet. We've been here for 50 years, we're family-owned and we treat our customers like family."

As they issue me handwritten testimonials from other employees, I can't even sort it all out. In the end, Tim wanders over and explains that it's not just a store. The employees really feel like they're helping customers discover and celebrate new cultures and subcultures.

"Back in the 1980s, it always made me so happy to sell a kid their first Bauhaus or Sisters of Mercy shirt," Tim says. "And I could say, 'If you like them, then you'll like Christian Death.' It's almost like a rite of passage for a lot of people. At the end of the day, yeah, it's just a store, but we really try to make it more than that."

1440 Multiversity Opens in Scotts Valley

As we traverse the landscape of 1440 Multiversity in Scotts Valley, Scott Kriens of Juniper Networks talks about 800,000 pounds of Sierra granite boulders that his team gathered to build a creek bed. Along the way, he points out Indonesian teakwood chairs, custom hand-fabricated steel railings, and wooden ceiling beams air-blasted with walnut shells.

Built on a 75-acre spread formerly occupied by the abandoned Bethany Christian College, 1440 is a new learning destination, a place where numerous high-profile teachers are just now starting to book classes. People from all over the world show up to reevaluate their inner mechanisms.

Named after the exact number of minutes in a day, 1440 Multiversity is already open, but construction is still unfolding as Kriens takes me around the campus. We see yoga studios, redwood lodges, meeting and spa facilities, a lucrative organic kitchen and black limestone stairways. 1440 is a wellness center, an immersion learning destination, a cooking school, an integrative healing retreat, a hiking getaway, and a corporate meeting facility for groups who value contemplative traditions. The first shovel hit the ground summer 2014.

The entire campus, Kriens says, is the logical expansion of the work he and his wife started with the 1440 Foundation, an effort to support "compassionate communities leading generative lives" to better their relationships with themselves and others, or in other words, help people contribute to the world by creating more energy than they consume.

"Joanie and I started the foundation in 2010, not yet with any plan for all of this, but really around a belief that we still share, which is that there's a whole world of growth and learning to be developed inside of ourselves," he tells me. "In some ways it's kinda the new frontier all over again."

Some of the buildings on the campus retain elements of the abandoned Bethany campus, while other structures have been totally rebuilt. The administration building and check-in area, for example, was formerly a drab 1950s-era concrete structure. It's been taken apart and repurposed as a craftsman style building to now look like a Rocky Mountain ski lodge. Elements of Canadian cedar, stone, slate and copper give the interior an earthy vibe. Some of the wooden beams came from Melvin Belli's old Nob Hill mansion in San Francisco.

Kriens solicited numerous collaborators in the process of constructing every single component, straight down to 40-million-year-old fossils engrained in the stone masonry work, all of which was done entirely by hand, piece after piece. As we continue to trip around the property, a minute doesn't go by without him pointing out similar levels of detail at every single structure.

"To be consistent, that means building with a real staff also," Kriens says.

In another mind-blowing scenario, a building now called the Sanctuary was the original main chapel at Bethany University. The front portion of the building, formerly the choir riser, is now a retail space filled with yoga supplies, books, jewelry and gifts. Kriens points to a table made from 1,200-year-old redwood, plus chic rubber flooring and hanging lamps made from repurposed PA system horns that the church used 50 years ago. The rest of the building, formerly the main church area, is now repurposed as a studio for yoga classes, meditation, movement therapy, trauma desensitization exercises and a variety of introspective healing practices. The property goes on and on.

A teaching kitchen will feature classes, alternative food instruction and 12 stations where students can work hand-to-hand with chefs. A hi-tech lecture hall already provides hi-quality audio and video recordings for every teacher who presents here. They get copies of the video for free. The legendary Buddhist teacher Jack Kornfield recently taught a class of 300 people from 17 different countries. The list of future faculty reads like an international who's who of mindfulness, self-discovery, nutrition, growth psychology and healing arts disciplines.

"What we're out to do is to create this learning destination that invites people to both rest and recharge, but also maybe integrate some things about ourselves," Kriens says. "Not just the physical self or the intellectual self—that's what we all got taught in school—but the emotional, relational self." From that integration, he adds, we become "a little bit more whole, and then take that out, and share it with those that matter most in our lives."

A Visit to Leonard Cohen's Unmarked Grave

The Canadian poet and songwriter Leonard Cohen, the romantic sharp-dressed articulator of darkness, is buried in an unmarked grave in his hometown of Montreal, Quebec.

After a career spanning more than half a century, in which his songs, poetry and travels took him to Greece, Cuba, Nashville and a Zen monastery, Leonard finally passed away last November at the age of 82. He had just released his final album, *You Want It Darker*, in which he appears to have known he was dying.

Leonard and his home turf of Quebec, *la belle province*, have a long history in my writings for this newspaper, so I had to visit his grave when returning to Montreal last week. The resulting sequence of events was mind-blowing.

Leonard is buried alongside his family in the Jewish section at the bottom of Mont-Royal Cemetery, on the hill that gave Montreal its name. The cemetery, on its northwestern side, borders the Outremont neighborhood, a Francophone locale where stately gated mansions along Chemin de la Foret line the bottom of the hill. Regal trees arch over the streets and wide grassy parking strips. It's quite comfy.

As I skulked into the cemetery, a few maintenance workers were standing there, just inside the gate. Before I said a word, they looked at me and said, "Cohen? He's right over there." They pointed a few gravestones over. They knew exactly who I was looking for, without me even asking. In other words, I didn't have to knock, the gate was open, and the gatekeepers showed me the way. Talk about symbolism.

After arriving at the gravesite, I made a pact with Leonard Cohen. I stood there, between the rocks and the flowers, and spoke to him: "Leonard, I will keep writing, you just show me how to pay the bills. Give me a sign. Anything."

Just after I left the cemetery, a warm rain started to fall, as if Mother Nature had deliberately waited until my visit was over. With no umbrella, I then high-tailed it down Boulevard du Mont-Royal and caught a bus on Avenue du Parc back to my hotel.

The entire sequence of events brought back memories of previous stories, as this was not the only instance of cosmic serendipity unfurling itself in Quebec. In 2003, I was in Quebec City, drinking in a bar called Jules et Jim, named after the film, and we wound up conversing with all sorts of colorful characters. The scene was basically the Leonard Cohen song "Closing Time," so I later recalled this crazy night in a 2009 Silicon Alleys column, right as Leonard was going back on tour and performing at the Paramount Theatre in Oakland. Ever since he emerged from the Zen monastery, people hoped he'd someday tour again, and there he was, hitting the road at 75.

At the time of the 2009 Oakland show, no one knew Leonard would eventually come to the HP Pavilion in San Jose—now the SAP Center—for what was initially supposed to be the last show of the tour. For that gig, I wrote a cover story for *Metro*, part of which was me walking around various Montreal locales related to Leonard or his songs.

Fans from all over the world came to that gig, since no one knew the tour would get extended and everyone thought that, given Leonard's age, they would never get to see him again. Israel, Finland, Japan, Russia, Australia, Brazil, Canada and countless other countries were represented in that audience, and many of those people were walking around the arena with a copy of *Metro* in their hands. At the show, I didn't tell a soul that I was the one who wrote the story, but the person who ran Leonard's fan club later emailed me and said he handed a copy to Leonard backstage.

That was the closest I ever got to meeting the dude. Nevertheless, I can't be anything but grateful for the mind-blowing, cyclical passages of interconnectedness that San Jose and Quebec have given me over the years.

In that sense, the show must go on. Leonard may no longer be with us in physical form, but his flame still burns. He will give me a sign and I will find a way to pay the bills.

Peanuts Café Keeps It Simple

About 10 years ago I was lurking inside the legendary Peanuts Cafe on San Fernando Street, when an old-timer said to me: "If this place goes away, I'll blow up the new City Hall."

He was exaggerating, but I understood his sentiment. Thankfully, as far as I can tell, Peanuts is not going away anytime soon, and with the new academic year upon us, now is an opportune moment to celebrate the gorgeous downmarket establishment that San Jose State University (SJSU) students have frequented for eons.

You cannot call yourself a Spartan if you haven't been to Peanuts. The place soaks in its affordability. That's the point. It is not a joint for Michelin-starred chefs or a plate of chateaubriand. You go for the decades-old decor, the beer and the inexpensive omelettes.

Even better, you get Myun-Sik Chang, who has now operated the cafe for more than 35 years. Chang and his father worked as employees for the previous owner, before Myun took over the lease beginning in January 1983. Several years later he was able to acquire the property. Now, in 2017, Chang still shows up at 5am every day except Sunday, getting the place rolling for its famous dirt-cheap breakfast.

Funny thing is Chang doesn't remember why the business is called Peanuts. He says the previous owner didn't know either. What he does recall is that when he first opened, a plate of two eggs, hash browns and toast sold for 99 cents. If you wanted to add bacon, it became $1.49. Coffee tipped the scales at 35 cents.

"At SJSU, the coffee was $1.25 back then," Chang recalls. "I made mine 35 cents. I wanted to keep the customers. We got a good review in the *Spartan Daily* and the business just took off."

Chang is not the only trouper of the establishment, however. Two other employees, Juan and Raquel, have been at Peanuts for 28 years. The whole place feels like family.

"Without them, I can't run this business," Chang says, as I sit drinking a paper cup of glorious, downmarket coffee.

I can't help but notice that the only decor components updated since 20 years ago are the internet jukebox and the large flat screens in the upper corners. Everything else has remained the same over the years, with students, university staff and longtime locals continuing to roll in for breakfast or lunch. The pitchers of beer continue to flow, although the price has increased a bit and the variety has improved from the Bud draft and Amber Dark era of the 1990s. Pitchers were five bucks in those days. I can't even calculate how much beer I drank at Peanuts during my college decade.

But this is not nostalgia. If you walk inside Peanuts today, the place bubbles with activity. Framed photos and gift plaques line the walls, all given to Chang from various SJSU fraternities over the years. Hanging over the bar, there's even a historical 1952 photo of the last graduating class of San Jose High partying inside Peanuts, back when the school was located directly across the street, before it moved to its current location.

As such, the tradition continues. If you want to know where people are tearing it up during finals week, or on the last day of classes, go to Peanuts.

Chang remembers me from when I used to come in and watch soccer games 20 years ago, so we talk about how students have changed over the years. Nowadays, he observes, the masses carry smartphones, laptops, backpacks and earbuds.

"A long time ago, everyone just had backpacks," he says.

In my case, I often encounter people that haven't been to downtown San Jose in 10 or 20 years, lumbering down San Fernando Street on their way to Peanuts, just to see if it's still there. The place has a Paramount Imports flavor of staying power.

When students first move into the neighborhood, then finish college four years later, they won't remember any soulless building named "27 North" or "50 West" or "101 San Fernando." Instead, they'll remember a place like Peanuts, a place with character. If there ever emerges a true campus community, we need more places like Peanuts.

Little Italy Street Fest

Krazy George surrounds me on the walls, as does a jersey of San Jose Earthquakes legend Chris Wondolowski. Photos of former Quakes heroes like George Best, Chris Dangerfield and Landon Donovan also grace the interior of Enoteca La Storia in downtown San Jose, so much that I can almost hear George's trademark gravelly voice and decades-old snare drum.

That blasted thing has infiltrated my eardrums since 1977.

Just a few weeks ago, La Storia opened its second location, directly across the street from Henry's Hi-Life. One section of the establishment also goes by Cafe Calcio. It's a soccer-themed bar, the only one of its kind ever in San Jose.

Outside, thousands of people are crammed elbow-to-elbow along

North Almaden and St. John, milling in both directions as the Second Annual Little Italy San Jose Street Festival unfolds. Probably a dozen food booths attract lines extending every which direction. Wine is flowing as the blaring sun beats down on the pavement.

But I'm inside La Storia, tearing through a pizza, gawking at all the rocking photos. Most of them are either Italian or San Jose. One photo depicts the San Jose Earthquakes 2003 championship team, celebrating their MLS Cup win that year LA—a game I attended and covered for *Metro*. Similarly, other photos depict Italian World Cup championship teams from 1938, 1982 and 2006. Another photo of Landon, while playing for the US Nats, sits on another wall, right underneath a photo of Krazy George from the early '70s. Former Quakes keeper Joe Cannon also gets his due.

I seem to be turning Italian just sitting here. My pizza includes what seems like an entire head of garlic—a good thing. Between the garlic and sausage, I'm a bit concerned about monster breath, but it doesn't stop me from practically crawling over people at their tables, just to get a closer look at the photos.

But beyond that I find the framed jerseys of some of the all-time legends of Italian soccer gracing the opposite wall: Andrea Pirlo, Paolo Maldini and Francesco Totti. Maldini spent 25 years playing for A.C. Milan and no other team. Likewise, Totti devoted his entire 25-year career to A.S. Roma.

Krazy George, on the other hand, has spent 43 years instigating crowds at every possible incarnation of every San Jose soccer team since 1974. These are hallowed freaking walls here at Enoteca La Storia. Yeah, I should probably get jazzed by the marble elements, the wood flooring, exposed ceilings and all that stuff. But a full-blown soccer bar, half Italian and half San Jose, is decades overdue.

As the street festival rages outside, people continue to filter in and out of the bar. "Senza Luce," the Italian version of Procol Harum's "A Whiter Shade of Pale," emanates from the stereo. Opera superstar Pasquale Esposito, a graduate of San Jose State University's School of Music, then saunters in like royalty, wearing a sash colored like the Italian flag, designating him as the "Grand Marshall" of the festival. Multiple patrons rise from their tables and rush to take selfies with him.

Later around 4pm, Esposito plays the main outdoor stage, facing directly at the Little Italy gateway arch and into the throngs of people. A rock band backs him up. With a commanding set of pipes, he belts a version of "O Sole Mio" to the rafters, except there are no rafters. And he's a total charmer. In the crowd, women from ages 8 to 80 are swooning, while men are trying to figure out how they'd even compete with this dude.

Just as Esposito hits the stage, many of the vendors have already run out of food. The crowds are more than anyone expected. As I sway through the ocean of people with garlic on my breath, I see everything from blue Italian soccer jerseys to *Godfather* shirts. Old men in khaki chinos and sun hats straight from the retirement home are dancing next to teenagers. Seemingly everyone has a glass of wine, a cup of gelato or a meatball sandwich in hand. When Esposito breaks into a version of Leonard Cohen's "Hallelujah," the crowd sings along with the chorus. At that point, the evening becomes perfect. Every tune will remain in my head for days to come. All is well. *Forza Azzurri!*

William Finnegan at Cafe Stritch

William Finnegan, Pulitzer Prize-winning author of *Barbarian Days: A Surfing Life*, showed up last week at Cafe Stritch to give an articulate, crafted presentation about his life and work, after which he conversed on stage with Steve Kettmann and signed books for quite some time. It was the type of event that yet brought a recurring question to mind:

Why wasn't San Jose doing this 20 years ago?

Presented by the Center for Literary Arts at San Jose State University, the event was the second time this semester, following Viet Thanh Nguyen's near-sold-out event at the Hammer Theatre Center, that the center took strides in bringing major literary events into the urban fabric of downtown San Jose, rather than confining authors to a library meeting room.

The way I see it, this situation deserves contemplation. Ask anyone who was involved with the university 25 years ago, and they will say downtown San Jose offered nothing—certainly not a theater or a jazz club—where one could stage literary events or an after party. Nothing resembled anything "urban." If an event kept people on campus until 9pm or 10pm, there was nowhere for peeps to gather afterward, except maybe Original Joe's or Kukar's House of Pizza.

Even in recent years, the center staged the majority of its events on campus, either in the library or another building, resulting in mostly student audiences and maybe several dozen tuned-in folks on the periphery of academia. While some extraordinary author events have unfolded at SJSU every single semester, for decades, they always felt isolated from the urban fabric at large.

Now things are evolving. Plus, literary events just feel more fun when they're urban. They need to be taking place at jazz clubs with booze and bites. The famous appearance of a wasted Jack Kerouac on the Steve Allen show, with Allen manipulating the ivories, comes to mind. Jazz environs and literature just go together.

So the Center for Literary Arts seems to be reaching an inflection point. Last month, for example, *The Sympathizer* author Nguyen filled the Hammer Theatre. Those in attendance included the current and a former mayor, both members of the Bellarmine World Order just like Nguyen himself. The politicians might not aspire to Pulitzer Prizes or $650,000 MacArthur "genius" grants like the one Nguyen just received, but with people around here blathering for decades about 24-hour downtowns or upmarket student housing, it was great to see literature taking its rightful place in conversations about how the university needs to better connect with the local landscape.

I departed the Nguyen gig thinking that SJSU was finally on a path toward becoming an urban university. It won't be NYU with Washington Square Park, Greenwich Village and the entire row of cheap Indian restaurants nearby on Sixth Street, but progress is clearly happening.

Which brings me back to Finnegan.

Last week, he filled Cafe Stritch and said on stage that the gig was a "nice change from a classroom lecture hall." Like Nguyen, his work comforts the afflicted and afflicts the comfortable. The mayors didn't show, but the place was jammed. Unlike many author events where a writer spends most of his or her allotted time on stage reading from already published books, Finnegan brought several pages of prepared remarks, mostly focusing on his life as a freelance reporter or staffer at *The New Yorker* and working in dozens of ravaged countries including the worst era of apartheid in South Africa.

Finnegan illuminated the outsider life of a surfer, with its intrinsic struggle against responsibility, and how he found it difficult to "come out" as a surfer, fearing he would not be taken seriously as an international political reporter. Also, and I'm paraphrasing here, Finnegan threw light on the dichotomy of how he wants nothing to do with the 9-5 world of hierarchies, bosses, capitalist work weeks, sedentary domestication and predictable routines. He wants to remain an outsider who doesn't participate in such systems, but at the same time he still wants to tell stories and help people, speak truth to power and comfort the afflicted. It's a serious dichotomy, to which I can totally relate. I think most journalists can.

As with the Nguyen gig, I departed a little more inspired. And a little more urban. Hail Spartans, Hail!

Heather David Plumbs the Kooky History of California Motels

Heather David might know more about vibrating mattresses than anyone else in California. The proof lies in her new self-published book, *Motel California: A Pictorial History of the Motel in the Golden State*, in which she presents a fantastic taxonomy of kitsch, a hagiography of midcentury roadside motels in all their glory.

Throughout 180 full-color pages, David elevates wacky motel architecture to historical status, replete with neon signage, pools and, of course, Magic Fingers vibrating bed technology.

Like David's first book, *Mid-Century by the Bay*, this new zonked-out masterpiece is a hardbound coffee-table project chock-full of wacky ephemera from David's research over the last several years. It all began in the '20s, when developer Arthur S. Heineman opened an inn for traveling motorists in San Luis Obispo. For a while it was known as the Milestone Motor Hotel, later shortened to the Milestone Mo-Tel, believed to be the very first usage of that word. Connoisseurs of kitsch from across the globe are already demanding copies. Everyone seems to love kooky California history.

"My last orders were Switzerland, Japan, England, Germany, Australia, New Zealand," David tells me at a local coffee shop. "They're willing to pay $35 for international shipping to get this book."

From there, the book provides quirky history lessons galore, with insight into the growth of nuclear families and statewide automobile travel, plus the ways in which California's varied landscape proved fertile ground for themed motels. Mid-century swimming pool culture also comes through quite well, as does the sheer variety of innovative signage up and down the state, most of which is now gone. In that regard, fans of indie business culture will adore the book. On the other hand, if you're a jaded business traveler whose curiosity ends with how you can use your Marriott Rewards Points, well, you may adore the book somewhat less.

Speaking of which, David spent a fortune self-publishing this thing, plus hundreds of hours on the road, researching oddball accommodations and their owners, as well as amassing a collection of motel ephemera, decades-old brochures, postcards and matchbooks. All of which explode in living color.

"In terms of theme-based marketing, there's nothing like California," David says. Her face lights up when talking about cheesy motel signage from 55 years ago. "We had it all. We had the desert, we had Hollywood, we had Disneyland and all the storybook themes, we had the space race. So the only other state that has such eye candy diversity is Florida. They would be the second best, but California is number one."

Anyone with a smidgen of respect for high camp will understand that the book is not a vanity project. David doesn't care if she becomes famous. Her dedication to the subject matter is righteous and it comes through on every page.

"I just want to have a conversation about this," she tells me, her face still animated. "I mean, this is cool stuff. There's four pages on vibrating beds in there."

Which brings us to Magic Fingers. If you're old enough to remember, guests would put a coin into a ridiculous machine on the nightstand, and the bed would start doing its thing. Fifty years ago, there was even a travel guide to all the motels with Magic Fingers. David owns a copy of the guide, pictured on page 145.

"I paid seventy-five bucks for it," she says, adding that before Magic Fingers existed, Pulse-A-Rhythm vibrating beds were the norm. According to David, *Motel California* is the only book ever to document these technologies. She adds: "The thing about Pulse-A-Rhythm beds is that they promised a cure for pretty much everything. And the FDA came along and said, 'Unh unh uh' and made them pull all the devices off the mattresses and put them out of business. So after Pulse-A-Rhythm, Magic Fingers came into play."

David also learned that the Sundown Inn of Morro Bay still has a Magic Fingers bed. She even stayed the night to sample the goods.

"The woman thought I was nuts," David says. "But I needed to try it out. I can't just write about it. My Masters is in cultural anthropology and sociology. I gotta try the bed."

Leigh High School's Manson Family History

Like a lotus blooming from the mud, a seedy piece of Leigh High School history has illuminated the interconnectedness of humanity. Light has emerged from darkness. Via totally unintentional journalistic adventures in Facebook crowdsourcing, several longtime locals were reunited, even if just online.

It all began with Charles Manson.

Or, to be more precise, it began with one of his family members, Susan Atkins, who spent much of her childhood in San Jose's Cambrian Park before attending Leigh High School during the initial stages of that facility's existence in the early '60s. I have written about Atkins in this very space more than once, most recently citing passages from her book, *Child of Satan, Child of God*, in which she recalls growing up in that neighborhood. She was found guilty of seven counts of first-degree murder and died in a Chowchilla prison in 2009.

With Manson finally kicking the bucket a couple weeks ago, I felt driven to repost that story on Facebook, not even fathoming the interconnected family of connections it would spawn. Several people only a small Kevin Bacon-degree of separation from Atkins chimed in with stories—and boy, was everyone blown away.

In the thread, Facebook friends of mine claimed they had a sister who knew Atkins or that Atkins was a second cousin. Another friend said her brother used to pick on Atkins' little brother, back when all of them were kids. Still another person remembered rifling through old yearbooks at Leigh, only to see Atkins' photo cut out and removed from the book, which doesn't surprise me at all. Growing up in that neighborhood was so abysmally boring, it probably made sense for someone to become fascinated with serial killers. In any event, the same Facebook friend also recalled seeing Atkins' photo in a yearbook at Union Junior High.

But this was only part of the thread. Another friend, Shannon McKendry, jumped into the conversation to relay that her mom taught Atkins at Dartmouth Junior High and totally remembers the little Susan. This made sense, as it would follow that Atkins moved from school to school, judging by later autobiographical remarks and news stories.

Following McKendry's comment in the Facebook thread, longtime native David West, after recognizing his former teacher's surname, chimed in to say he was one Mrs. McKendry's students. He recalled her teaching him in seventh grade at Dartmouth. West remembered her being very nice and becoming a big influence in his pursuit of writing, helping lead him to a championship spelling bee victory over rival Union Junior High.

"I went on to editing literary magazines in high school, published writing in college, teaching voice and diction and work as an actor, stage and film," West wrote. "Not that she was totally responsible for all that, but she was one of the four or five teachers in my schooling that had the most effect on me."

McKendry, of course, was blown away. Edited for clarity, she wrote this in response: "My Mama was a wonderful teacher to me as well. I was reading at a very young age and was especially verbal because of her. I went on to win my fair share of spelling contests. I'm so very thankful for your fond recollection of her. She has always been a kind, loving, witty and fiercely intelligent lady. It gives me the warm fuzzies to know that she positively impacted your life. I will never forget your words."

The cosmic coincidences did not stop there. In another scenario sandwiched between the Gardner Community Center and the monolithic 280/87 interchange, a resident identified another person in the Susan Atkins comment thread as the guy she'd been receiving postal mail for at her current dwelling. Turns out he once lived in the same house she currently occupies, and he even built the garage she uses as an art studio. She'd already been researching the history of the house, its stories and former tenants. The two of them went on to share a thread of history together and discovered even more while posting comments in the thread that started about Susan Atkins.

Just as the old wise guys in the Far East used to say: From the darkest mud a lotus blooms. The dark side of Leigh High School has brought forth a new light.

Jessica Neideffer Brings Healing to City Hall

On a cold evening in front of San Jose City Hall, Jessica Neideffer sits on a rug, playing a set of a crystal singing bowls. Next to her, on the sidewalk, people lie in sleeping bags to meditate on the sounds, which are based on Vedic healing principles and amplified by a microphone to help trigger the pre-programmed pulsing light patterns of the Sonic Runway art installation.

Each bowl emits a different frequency, with Neideffer improvising to take others into deeper brain waves via sound.

Neideffer regularly appears at several places around town, such as parks, yoga studios and her private practice, Agada Energy Healing, where she does Reiki sessions and maintains a solid book of clients. But this time, right smack on a bustling corner in the middle of downtown's daily commute, other factors contribute to the overall experience. The neighborhood's perpetual ambulance sirens continue to scream. Cars honk. Skateboarders in the background attack the steps and railings outside of City Hall, as they've done for years. On the sidewalk, parents saunter by the performance with strollers. City employees, just coming off the clock, hang out and observe. Humans in various states of intoxication walk by, but no one harshes the mellow one bit.

As I stand there fumbling with my phone in order to blast the experience on Instagram, a cyclist rides up on the sidewalk and slows down to ask me: "What's with the people in the sleeping bags?" I tell him it's like meditation. Or yoga. Then he seems to understand.

A few mornings later, Neideffer and I are sitting around, shoeless, in her healing studio. There's a massage table against the wall and herbal oils on a shelf, along with books about reflexology, crystals and shamanism. She fondly talks about how wonderful it was the other night at City Hall.

"Each gathering is different people, so there's different energy and there's a different vibe from people that are there," Neideffer explains. "What I saw that night—I see things in my mind as I'm playing—I just see these beautiful pictures of people coming together and it doesn't matter where they are or what they are doing or what they believe because the sounds naturally attract people."

It didn't make a difference if passers-by were consciously familiar with the sounds. Once they arrived and began to focus on the experience—keying in on frequencies designed to speak to the mind and the body—a deeper state of awareness tends to emerge. It may not be dramatic, but the vibe was overwhelmingly peaceful. "I just saw it bringing all these wonderful people together," Neideffer says.

A San Jose native, she spent 20 years managing high-tech offices before going through some extreme symptoms of vertigo. After seeing a massage therapist who practiced Reiki, a Japanese flavor of healing and stress reduction, she realized her life's purpose was to develop a healing practice. As the saying goes, when the student is ready, the teacher will somehow appear.

As we talk, Neideffer articulates a laundry list of peeps and practices. Vedic philosophy. The Toltec lineage of Mexico. The New Thought self-help author Louise Hay. Don Miguel Ruiz and the Four Agreements. All the teachings of which emerge in the array of services she offers at her studio.

And when it comes to the practice of sound healing, it's all about intention. Neideffer likens the crystal healing bowls to any other musical instrument, in that they are extensions of the performer. Tapping into your intention is what drives how you share the sound or what you're feeling. In this case, the intention is to provide resonance to help the client overcome particular issues, both emotional and physical.

In the future, Neideffer envisions evolving her practice to work with kids on the spectrum.

"I want to expand," she says. "I want to be able to share this with people all over. And maybe creating some different classes for parents and children to come and attend. And to create at some point a really lovely community wellness center, where people can come and receive all services. Whether it's yoga or sound healing."

2018

The Formative Years of a Liquor Store Clerk

When someone asks me which part of San Jose I grew up in, I usually say the Cambrian area. But during a recent exchange, in one of those laugh-out-loud moments, I said the Cambrian era by accident. This was not a Freudian slip. It was a Jungian slip, instructing me to reinvestigate the locality and conjure up my shadow, to confront the darkness and rise above it.

That said, I recently prowled around Cambrian last week and wound up at Cask n Flask Liquors at Leigh and Camden, a bastion of darkness, a place that employed yours truly, off and on, back when I was 17 and 18 years old. This was a therapeutic experience.

Cask n Flask wasn't the first place that fired me. It was probably the second or third. The duties were stocking shelves, sweeping, dusting and other tedious drudgery. I'd show up for a four-hour shift and finish all the work in 30 minutes, after which nauseating boredom would ensue. In my admittedly fuzzy memories, I'd guess every stock boy who worked there for $3.78 an hour stole booze at one time or another, including me, but I think the statute of limitations is long gone, so I will confess my dastardly deeds right here and now. Bar managers often speak of similar scenarios, in that one has to allow for employees sneaking a few nips on the clock, so a manager just figures this into the overall finances. Write it off as spillage, they say.

Now, I've never hesitated to admit that my teenage years were characterized by a careless lack of direction, a blatant disregard for authority, or habitual attempts to satisfy cravings. In this case, the dump in question fired me out of the blue one day, only to call me back five months later because they couldn't find anyone else to come in and stock the shelves. No one wanted to work there. That's how miserable it was.

I'll give you an example. One part of the job was delivering a liter bottle of Canadian Mist to an old man that lived in a house down the street.

Every other day I'd carry the booze to his house and sometimes he'd even give me a $20 tip. I think he had the whole place to himself, because whenever I'd bring over the bottle, he'd invite me in to sit down, after which he'd talk to me for 20 minutes. I don't think he had anyone else to talk to. That's right—at 17, I was running booze to a drunk down the street for $3.78 an hour. I always wondered what happened to that dude.

These days, especially when the sun starts to set, there's an apocalyptic bleakness to the corner of Leigh and Camden. To me, as an '80s miscreant, every strip mall in that neighborhood already feels like a scene from *Repo Man* and the ancient corner strip featuring Cask n Flask is a prime example. Pieces of the sign have been missing for at least 20 years. At the opposite end, Swiss Cleaners, which was there for decades, is now abandoned and boarded up. I think there was once a computer store in there somewhere, back when retail was still necessary. Plus, it's a very congested intersection, so about a dozen cars run the red light in each direction, every cycle. You can smell the rancid burger stench from McDonald's across the street. There are no pedestrians for a mile in any direction.

Last week, when I patronized the liquor store, it didn't look any different than it did 30 years ago. I could remember exactly which shelf in 1987 featured dusty half-gallons of I. W. Harper left over from a decade earlier. After meandering around for five minutes, I bought a Twix bar. It was $1.29. And it was completely stale.

Nevertheless, I confronted my shadow, as Jung would say. Thankfully my life this week is not as aimless as it was back in those days. And I'm much less abusive of privileges. I have learned to accept my darker side and develop a much more integral outlook on life. I still sometimes feel as old as the Cambrian era, but it no longer ruins my day. Happy New Year.

Exploring the Cultural Geography of San Jose's East Side

From the King Road side of Mexican Heritage Plaza, I look west down a side street and see the top of the Fairmont Hotel in the distance. I can also see the Marriott. This is how close East San Jose is to downtown. Geographically challenged people often think of the East Side as "out there" when it really isn't.

Even worse, those who live throughout the rest of San Jose, many of whom haven't ventured east of 10th Street, mistake East San Jo for some guerrilla warfare barrio riddled with undesirables.

"This is not the set of Colors, the movie," says Tamara Alvarado, executive director of the School of Arts and Culture at Mexican Heritage Plaza, as we walk south down King Road toward San Antonio Street. "If you go up into the hills, it's like, 'Wow.' That's what gets people. There's a lot of economic and ethnic diversity."

The East Side features affluent neighborhoods and not-so-affluent neighborhoods, with Mayfair being a gloriously incongruous hodge-podge of both. I'm here to explore, Alvarado being the best tour guide. All of Mayfair—the historical markers, the social activities, community meetings, and the School of Arts and Culture—forms a nexus of self-reflection for inhabitants of the area. Stories of Cesar Chavez emerge in the churches and side streets. The School of Arts and Culture continues to play a serious role in not only activating the thrice-failed Mexican Heritage Plaza, but in steering young kids away from street gangs and into the arts.

Within moments we're heading east on San Antonio toward the fog-drenched hills, somewhat green thanks to a recent spout of rain. On the street, we spot gang graffiti but also spend time raving over the efforts of Somos Mayfair, a community group fighting for social justice, arts education and the empowerment of youth.

Of course, any visit to this area requires a pit stop at El Perrin, a lively orange-colored Mexican restaurant. We pop in just as old '70s Los Bukis tunes emanate from the system and plenty of neighborhood people are packing the place.

Our bellies filled with nopales and fiery salsa, we then arrive at Mc-Donnell Hall, in the parking lot behind Our Lady of Guadalupe Church, where Cesar Chavez first cut his chops in community organizing. A slick historical plaque, installed a few years ago, fills in the details.

Chavez used to live nearby, so we continue east down San Antonio past a few stagnant RVs and an old Mexican dude selling corn. Moving up Scharff Avenue toward Chavez's boyhood home, I can't help but appreciate the landscape. Faded tract houses dominate, but thankfully without identical manicured lawns. Each parcel seems different. Each has character. Various eras are represented, from old Victorians to new duplexes. A sense of historical continuity manifests itself—exactly what doesn't happen in many other parts of San Jose. Across the street, a red-and-white banner from Chivas, Guadalajara's legendary soccer club, hangs on a garage door. One front yard features a ramshackle Buddhist shrine bordering on avant-garde thrift store sculpture, while other lots are landscaped with gloriously downmarket assemblages from a variety of natural and man-made materials.

"It's not decoration," Alvarado notes. "It's not for people in other neighborhoods to come see. It's for us. We do this for ourselves. To show ourselves to ourselves."

And another thing. Cacti seem omnipresent.

"We grow it, we eat it, we celebrate it, we paint it," Alvarado says. "If I don't see cactus everywhere in this neighborhood, then I'll know it's all over."

The old house where Cesar Chavez once lived is designated with another historical marker. The neighbors are accustomed to weirdos rambling by to take pictures, so Alvarado and I are clear to lurk on the sidewalk. No one seems to mind. Only then do we circle back along Alum Rock to the Mexican Heritage Plaza. Alvarado says now that Mayfair has planted roots, the next step is to move beyond survival mode and into a position of hope.

"It's not necessarily because we want the west side of San Jose to come here," she says. "It's really more for internal community purposes. The more we know ourselves, the better we value ourselves, the better we value our assets, our cultural assets, our spiritual aspects, the beauty, the aesthetics of the things, and the social services agencies that are here."

Literary Inspiration at Chiang Mai Writers Club

Last week, the anti-man-about-town returned to a literary vortex of major influence. Eight years ago in Chiang Mai, Thailand, I discovered a place on Rachadamnoen Road inside the central area of town. The Chiang Mai Writers Club and Wine Bar was right down the street from the Phra Singh Temple.

Bob Tilley, a retired journalist from the UK, owned the place, along with his wife, Tong, and it functioned as the unofficial English-speaking foreign correspondents club of Chiang Mai. Every possible demographic of expat writer might be found inside. A lonesome traveling screenwriter might show up to get drunk in the corner, a journalist might pop in after filing a story, or someone may just be looking for other writers to drink with. The phrase, "you never know who you'll meet" rang true.

On the day I arrived in 2010, an antique Underwood typewriter sat on the bar. Old black-and-white photos from newsrooms of decades past hung from the walls, each inside an ancient dusty frame. Antique glass cases held fading encyclopedias, books, magazines and other literary ephemera you'd expect a lifelong worldly writer to collect. It also seemed like English-speaking travelers often came in and left gifts. It was that kind of place.

As I sat there, Tilley told me numerous stories about life as a correspondent stationed in East Germany during the Cold War. With 50 years of experiences under his belt, Tilley had serious yarns to tell, some of which jammed a small book that he sold me for seven bucks. He was a living connection to the "old days" of freelance stringing, with hundreds of assignments—some legit, others dubious—taking him all over the underbelly of various European cities and then finally Thailand. He illuminated what it was like to exist as a freelancer, writing for both upmarket and downmarket publications, supermarket gossip rags or academic journals—for whoever would write the damn checks. Such was (and is) the mercenary life of a freelancer. You straddle many different crowds of people without ever feeling truly at home in any one of them.

Which is exactly how I started years ago, so Tilley became not just an inspiration, but a beacon of assurance that a shred of the freelance journalist's life was still imaginable for me somehow, at least in theory. He told me to never give up. If you have to write for salacious outlets just to pay the bills, then do so, but don't quit trying. I was so inspired that I wrote a column about Tilley on the flight back.

Sadly, Tilley passed away a few years ago, so I never got to hang with him again, but last week when I showed up, Tong was still there. The place did not look much different. The same photos and furniture were present. The menu hadn't changed. The antique typewriter now sat like royalty on top of an old cabinet in the back corner, right next to an old communist-era dial telephone from Hungary. A maroon fez sat on top of the typewriter. A Thierry Henri soccer jersey and a San Francisco Giants pennant hung on the wall behind them. The spirit of Bob Tilley was still palpable.

The entire place was filled up with Western tourists, with no natives anywhere. As I ate my meal at a two-seater table, it only took five minutes for a tipsy Australian to walk over from the bar, and then while standing there looking down at me, bash everything that Donald Trump is all about. How could millions of people vote for this immoral degenerate piece of narcissistic garbage, he asked, eyes bugging out. The rest of the world is scared at how a dangerously illiterate lunatic could be the American president, he blurted. Calm as a monk, I agreed, adding that apologizing for Donald Trump is part of any international travel itinerary for Americans these days. Unfortunately.

Hammered Australians are ubiquitous in Thailand, so this was no big deal, really. After my meal, I bid everyone adieu and wandered back onto Rachadamnoen Road. As before, Chiang Mai was alive. Almost every single block seemed to feature bars, backpacker hostels, massage joints, artisan shops, tour companies, scooter rentals, street food carts, laundry services, beautifully crumbling ambience and very old Lanna-style Buddhist temples. Tilley made the right choice by moving here. I vowed to return.

Backwater Arts Venue Celebrates 10 Years

Backwater Arts is appropriately named. To get there, one must venture down Senter Road, in this case at nighttime, surrounded by noir strip malls of seedy karaoke joints, beauty salons, laundromats, and a VietAir freight shipping facility before turning east down Quinn Avenue.

From there, it's only a short stroll past rundown RVs, computer warehouses, trucking yards and a few characters dumping couches on the sidewalk before Quinn dead-ends at a two-story New England-style house built in 1877 and currently home to Backwater Arts.

On a chilly night, local musician Ben Henderson and the amazing female folksy trio the Wild Reeds are gigging on a cool makeshift stage out back. I am among the first to show up. A variety of tenants rent the historic house and stage a variety of events, from weddings to art shows, or, in this case, talented musicians playing for an audience of their close friends and peers. I see gloriously incongruous chairs, benches, a fire pit, a bar and eventually about 100 people bundled up for the weather. It's like any underground San Jose house party, but without the assholes. I see musicians, painters, hair stylists, yoga teachers, DJs, arts impresarios and a few downtown business owners.

The venue and creative space was founded by Anne Sconberg—who also hosts the annual Anne and Mark's Art Party. I recall writing a column about Backwater exactly 10 years ago when it originally started, yet this is my first time back since then. As a result, I confess my idiocy and embarrassment upon arrival, but no one seems to know what I'm talking about, which is probably a good thing. Others making their way in appear blown away by this historic gem of a house just off Coyote Creek and surrounded by industrial warehouse environs and former cannery remnants.

"Everything's so hidden in San Jose," says one person as he walks in, to sheer surprise at the rocking community of artists unfolding before him in the backyard.

The history of the Backwater Arts house is a feature in of itself, but I'll break it down right here and now. Quinn Avenue is named after William Quinn of Tyrone, Ireland, who came to San Jose in 1858 and eventually purchased several acres of land on both sides of Coyote Creek. A Vermont wagonmaker named Frederick G. Wool then came to the area in 1874 and acquired by trade some of Quinn's property west of the creek and built this house in 1877. He later founded the F. G. Wool Packing Co. in 1903, a family-owned and operated business straight up until 1989, making it the longest continuously operating family-run cannery anywhere in California, if not the whole country. The old brick cannery building still remains out back, as does what's left of the greenhouse and the water tower. If you talk to old-timers around town, you'll find many former employees of F. G. Wool Packing.

Subsequent generations of the Wool family spawned so many kids, grandkids and great-grandkids that it's impossible to even figure it out. But Sandy Wool, for example, was a noted county supervisor in the 1930s and '40s. The lake in Ed Levin Park is named after him. After the cannery business went kaput, the last remaining descendant of the family to remain in the house was Page Wool Hamilton, who lived there straight up until her death in 2006 at the age of 93.

Now in 2018, the house looks pretty much the same. Pieces of the original picket fence can be seen in the backyard, along with trees over 100 years old. For the Wild Reeds gig, a makeshift bar is selling beer, wine, sangria, tea and garden fresh oranges. Two-dollar peanut butter-and-jelly sandwiches sit inside a bucket. People occupy about 40 wooden chairs, bar stools and benches covered with blankets and Mexican zarapes. Everyone else is standing up. The yard is packed. Illuminating the scene are dozens of Mason jars with candles inside, all hanging from tree branches. Some people are congregating around a fire pit to stay warm. A garden sits off to one side.

After the show, it becomes obvious that Backwater still functions on so many levels. For one, you have a historic property converted into an artist colony, a phenomenon you see in many respected cities. You also have a fantastic and experiential way to introduce younger people to local history. Here's to another 10 years!

The Almaden Brit Celebrates 30 Years

Some of us were hanging out at Britannia Arms on Almaden long before Rod Stewart ever showed up. In my case, as soon as I turned 21, I drove down Blossom Hill at midnight and bought my first legal beer at the Almaden Brit. I think it was a Harp.

I was not there at the very beginning in 1988, but since this classic institution is now celebrating its 30th anniversary, the memories are spiraling back to the forefront and I can't hold back my two cents. I have more memories in that pub than at any other place south of Branham that's still left.

We'll begin with the 1990 World Cup. There was nothing close to top-flight pro soccer in the U.S. at that time, the rubes on the major networks hated the sport, and there was nowhere else for us to go watch games except Britannia Arms. 1990 was also the first time England made it to the semis since it won the tournament in 1966, so the semifinal against Jurgen Klinsmann and the Germans drew an over-capacity crowd to the Brit. Soccer fans of every nationality jammed the place. It was elbow to elbow, with Britons especially fired up.

Some context here is mandatory. In 1990, the area surrounding the Brit looked vastly different. Highway 85 did not exist yet. The vile, hideous stripmall monstrosity across Almaden was essentially an orchard. Inside the Brit, proprietors bragged about one large 10-foot TV screen in the corner with maybe two other small ones behind the bar. The most expensive item on the menu was the "combo plate" at a whopping $8.95. On tap were McEwan's, Watney's and John Courage—exotic for the time, since the current onslaught of bearded craft brew hipsters was still in diapers.

But back to the Beautiful Game. The 1990 semi-final was so emotional for the Brits that at halftime someone popped in a VHS copy of Henry V with Laurence Olivier and cued it right to the St. Crispin's Day speech, with Sir Larry leading the men off to battle. As the speech played on the large screen, many in the capacity crowd at the Brit narrated the words: "From this day to the ending of the world, But we in it shall be remembered—we few, we happy few, we band of brothers" and so on. Then at the end of the speech, everyone in the bar screamed "ENGLAND!!!" with pints raised on high. England eventually lost on penalties, but it was one of the most emotional moments I'd ever seen watching a sporting event.

During that same World Cup, the *Mercury News* sent a reporter to the Brit to document the crowds. The story still sits on the wall and some of the people mentioned are still sitting at the bar, today, 28 years later. In my view, there was nothing in domestic American sports that compared to the intensity of the World Cup and it was great to have a local place in which to escape the drabness of suburbia and watch the world's game.

Even Rod Stewart believed as much. In 1994, the World Cup finally came to the USA with several games at Stanford Stadium. Stewart, the rock singer who would have been a pro soccer player had he not chosen music instead, was in L.A. and instructed his handlers to call the Brit and inform them of Stewart's intent to come up and attend a game at Stanford. He wanted a place to watch the other games beforehand, which is exactly what ended up happening.

According to the proprietors, Stewart was down to earth, not a prima donna, and was just like one of the guys. He had a wonderful time hanging out, so much that when Brazilian legend Pele invited Stewart to join him in his luxury box at Stanford, Stewart reportedly declined, saying he'd rather just hang with his new mates from the Brit.

I was not there when Stewart showed up, but former *Metro* music editor Todd Inoue captured the festivities. The column he wrote, along with the photo of Stewart he took, still graces the wall on the way to the restroom.

Now that Britannia Arms Almaden is officially celebrating its pearl anniversary, the memories will hopefully continue. Here's to another 30 years!

Landon Donovan Returns to San Jose

Last week, Landon Donovan, one of the best soccer players ever to emerge from U.S. soil, returned to San Jose, the city that launched his career. Now 36, he plays for the Mexican team Club Leon, which battled the Quakes in a friendly game last Saturday. Landon scored the only goal and Leon won the match 1-0.

Journalism-wise, only a few of us are left from when Landon played here (2001 to 2004), so it was a poignant experience, at least for me, when he gave a press conference at the end of last week. In comparison to when we held voice recorders in front of him, 17 years ago in crumbling Spartan Stadium locker rooms, he's a more contemplative and wiser dude these days.

Landon first arrived in San Jose at the age of 19, in March 2001, just a few months after Silicon Valley Sports & Entertainment, the Sharks' business and marketing arm, had taken over as investor-operators of the team. Major League Soccer (MLS) had only existed for five years. There were only 12 teams and no one knew if the league would survive long-term. Bayer Leverkusen in the German Bundesliga owned Landon's contract, yet he could not make an impact there at such a young age, so he was loaned back to the US. In the bumbling jury-rigged machinations of MLS, the Quakes received him as an "allocation player."

I attended the original press conference announcing Landon's arrival. It was in the Compaq Center, now the SAP Center. Not yet a working journalist, I sneaked into the event, telling the security guard I was a season ticket holder. It was just like sneaking into Cactus Club 10 years earlier. I had no plans to ever be a sports writer, but later that year, a now-defunct website, Slide Tackle Magazine, started paying me $25 to write match reports.

As the story goes, right here in town, Landon morphed into the poster boy for the future of American soccer, whether he wanted that mantle or not, and it didn't unfold without drama from across the country. Certain factions wanted him in the U.S. to help save the league, while others wanted to see him back in Europe, where he'd mature amid better competition. People called him a sissy for wanting to stay and help grow the game in his own country. It seemed like he was constantly tugged in many different directions, all while being manipulated as the young savior of the American game, not something a 19- or 20-year-old usually deals with. Many issues still argued today—the MLS player versus the player with Euro league experience, the ways in which youth talent is developed here and overseas, and the resulting effects on national team quality—were thrown onto Landon's back at that time. All of which might have played a role in his battles with depression.

Aside from helping San Jose win two MLS championships, Landon left a serious legacy. It almost seems like a previous lifetime. After the 2002 World Cup, for example, he helped the United States reach the quarterfinals, the country's best-ever showing. After the U.S. was eliminated, Landon flew right back to San Jose and came onto the field for the Quakes, just 37 hours after he walked off the pitch in Korea. Before the game, a huge news conference unfolded at Spartan Stadium, and later when he entered the game as a sub, the crowd gave him a standing ovation.

The last time Landon was ever pictured in print wearing a Quakes uniform was for a 5,000-word cover story I wrote for Metro in January 2005, titled, "Earth to San Jose: Soccer Team Needs Stadium," during which then-operators, AEG, were threatening to relocate the team because they considered San Jose a backwater market, and they saw Houston as a more fruitful place to build a stadium with someone else's money. Landon was not in the story, but his likeness graced the cover.

Just last Friday, when Landon returned to San Jose for what was probably his last time playing here, barring any future old-timers games, it was a space-time continuum-shattering moment for me. As I write this column, I have nothing but gratitude for my experiences over the last 40 years of this sport in this town and Landon was a huge part of that. I feel lucky to still be here.

Power of Babel: Jaap Blonk

The Dutch master of sound poetry, Jaap Blonk, will return to San Jose for the first time in 24 years this Saturday, when he unleashes guttural phonetic madness at Anno Domini.

Now, before I go off the deep edge with this, allow me to explain that sound poetry is an artistic form emphasizing the raw sounds of the voice as opposed to syntax or semantics. We're talking pure vocal audio, the human voice as noise generator in a performance context. To the uninitiated, watching this stuff might lead you to question the person's sanity or call the paramedics, but as an art form, sound poetry traces all the way back to the dada artists in Zurich, circa 1916, and then even further back to the Italian futurists and perhaps even to "Jabberwocky," if you really want to split hairs.

In any case, this is yet another time-shattering full-circle moment reminding me that I still live in San Jose for a reason. You see, in September and October of 1994, soon after San Jose State gave me a music degree with emphasis in electro-acoustics and computer music, I went to Europe for the first time, taking three weeks to spend time with sound poets, academic computer music composers, neo-dadaists, avant-garde performance artists and troublemakers from various creative traditions—categories that often overlapped. I was studying, researching and/or performing such material and I can safely say it's what I wanted to do with my life. I didn't want to spend one more second in San Jose.

Larry Wendt, then the technician in SJSU's School of Music and the only San Josean ever to appear on a Nurse With Wound album, was also a decadeslong sound poet with a network of connections stretching across oceans. Larry was traveling in Europe at the same time, since he was doing a performance on the same bill with Jaap Blonk and many others at the Bobeobi Festival of Sound Poetry in Berlin, which took place the first weekend of October, right before I flew back. So I showed up, ran the slide projector for Larry's performance and got to drink with legendary sound poets, artists and troublemakers, old and young, from around the world, including Jaap and Henri Chopin (see photo.) Many of the artists involved could legitimately trace their creative ancestry back to dada, the lettrists, fluxus, Italian futurism or numerous other threads of the 20th century avant-garde. Some of them, like Chopin, have since passed away, unfortunately. As a first trip to Europe, the whole shebang was more than I ever imagined.

Back home at SJSU, my teacher Allen Strange, who'd traveled with me during an earlier part of the trip in Denmark, where we attended and worked at a music conference, came home to San Jose and, as a joke, told people I was staying in Europe. He said I was actually smiling all the time, enjoying myself and was not going to come back. At first, no one knew if he was serious or not.

But for whatever reason, I did come back. And so did Jaap. Later in October, just a few weeks after the Berlin festival, Jaap came to America for the first time, including a gig at SJSU. We picked him up at the airport and even took him to Super Taqueria on 10th Street. Back in those days—late '80s, early '90s—whenever Allen or Larry hosted a European artist at SJSU, they'd always take him to Super Taqueria. At the time, downtown San Jose was a total dump, but since Super Taq was still a new concept, it became an effective local place to bring Europeans who'd never eaten real Mexican food. And Coronas were about $1.75. For the gig, Jaap eventually gave a powerful, outre and hysterical performance in Room 150 of the Music Building, horrifying the opera singers out in the hallway. It was loud but, according to Allen, not as loud as when Henri Chopin was there in the '80s.

Now Jaap is returning to San Jose for what should be a memorable gig at Anno Domini this Saturday, and I am still here to write this column and tell you about it. Let the voices be heard!

VivaCalle SJ Holds Potential to be Best Yet

Last week, the city of San Jose announced the route for this year's annual Viva CalleSJ open streets initiative, which will expose tens of thousands of residents to the best and worst of San Jo, all in one afternoon. On Sept. 23, the route will start at South First and William streets in downtown San Jose, right smack in the middle of the SoFA Street Fair, where 100 bands will already be gigging throughout the afternoon.

Then the route proceeds all the way down Monterey Road, the Champs-Elysees of San Jose's underbelly, before briefly veering down Branham to Martial Cottle Park. As always, various nodes of activity will erupt at specific parts of the route.

Every year, Viva CalleSJ creates a temporary autonomous zone by closing several miles of San Jose streets and shutting them off to cars for a day. People can then walk, jog, bike, skate, exercise or play, all to explore specific neighborhoods they don't normally see, in ways they don't normally get to do. With the road closed to automobiles, everyone takes to the streets however they want, in any direction. There is no end and no beginning. Curiosity and the spirit of adventure reign free.

Forward-thinking cities all over the world stage similar open streets initiatives, in some places even once a month, and in my view, Viva

CalleSJ is one of the most inclusive, unifying events ever to emerge in San Jose. The effect of connecting isolated neighborhoods and previously disparate demographics via open streets really works. It's obvious to anyone that participates. Last year, the positive response was overwhelming. Lifelong residents explored areas of the city they hadn't seen in years.

Unfortunately, although everyone is informed of the route several months in advance, the celebration does not come without grumblings from angry suburban get-off-my-lawn types that for half a day can't drive their cars to a store two blocks away, or, more cluelessly, didn't even know the event was happening. This is expected. If Jesus Christ came back to life and gave a public sermon in San Jose, half the city would probably say, "Why didn't I know about this?"

Nevertheless, I predict this year will be the best Viva CalleSJ ever. The SoFA Street Fair will be a game-changer for the open streets party. I cannot stress it enough. From there, imagine thousands of people navigating Monterey Road without cars, past miles of crumbling junkie motels, weed-infested vacant lots, bent chain-link fences, trailer parks, hookers, pimps, recycling centers, graffiti-stained tire shops and sun-cracked parking lots, not to mention Oak Hill Cemetery. An activity hub will exist at Monterey and Umbarger, near what's left of the County Fairgrounds, possibly the most despair-ridden swath of squandered potential in the entire South Bay. These days the fairgrounds look more like a deserted movie set than anything else, but word has it county fair peeps might help orchestrate a Ferris wheel for Monterey Road, just for Viva CalleSJ. That's right, instead of clawing at each other's throats, the county and the city are actually collaborating for once, in this case to get a Ferris wheel rocking.

Monterey Road itself soaks in history. It was mythically part of the historic El Camino Real connecting the California missions. Later it became a stagecoach route and then a state highway during the decades before 101 existed. There is perhaps no street more "San Jose" than Monterey Road.

This year, the other end of Viva CalleSJ occurs at Martial Cottle Park at Branham and Snell, one of those drab intersections with no pedestrians for a mile each direction and virtually indistinguishable from any Central Valley stopover along Highway 5 to Los Angeles. Martial Cottle Park, though, is a former century-old farm beautifully reincarnated as a urban park with mucho activity space.

All in all, for this year's Viva CalleSJ, I can only say, what a combination: At least 100 bands playing live in the SoFA District. Tens of thousands of people out of their cars on the pavement of Monterey Road. Rock & roll. Suburban underbelly. Strip malls, flower beds, garbage, asphalt, sun, food, drink and San Jose's agricultural past, all in one day's adventure. It doesn't get any more local than that.

Gordon Biersch, RIP

After 28 years of operating on San Fernando Street in downtown San Jose, Gordon Biersch (GB) will close its doors for good this weekend. Every bartender and former employee that I can remember, at least those within driving distance, will descend upon the establishment for one last blowout on Saturday.

For anyone to appreciate the absurdity of this, I must take you back to an early-'90s version of downtown San Jose, before laptops, cellphones and the World Wide Web, and back when real estate syndicates were scrambling to "revitalize" the neighborhood. Much of the area was still abandoned since the '70s, while other parts of it featured crumbling retail, empty parking lots, stray halfway-house denizens, panhandling transients and fledgling obnoxious jock bars. The light rail had just gone in. Across the street was a not-yet-disastrous attempt to force-cram an upscale open-air shopping mall into the area, the now infamous Pavilion Shops. Downtown had no restaurant scene of any sort, and the entire concept of "good beer" did not exist anywhere. Although GB wasn't San Jose's first microbrewery, it was probably the first one with staying power and a key player in the next phase of downtown's perpetual state of perpetuating. At SJSU, we'd often show up after night classes in the music and art departments, since there was rarely any restaurant food obtainable past 9pm anywhere. And the beers were $3.

Even though GB came across as a privileged upmarket place—at times it was frat boy central—what made it fun was an attitude of providing the regulars with a totally different dimension of experience. As the years unfolded, as soon as any regular was deemed worthy, he or she was given a personalized stein, a half-liter German-style chalice with a pewter lid that you flipped open with your thumb. Each Steinholder had his or her name etched into the lid and also onto the museum-style cabinet in which the steins were kept behind the bar. When the bartender opened the cabinet and pulled my stein from the shelf—a shelf also with my own name—it was like being a member of a secret society. Special events like the tapping parties were initially just for the Steinholders and not for the general public. And no one else understood how to get one. We intentionally kept it a mystery. For someone that already lived in his own head most of the time, this was fantastic.

Which meant, in my case, as a Steinholder, I could walk into GB, dressed like an absolute slob, unshaven, wearing ripped-up jeans and faded t-shirt, with a mop of hair down to my shoulders, all of which elicited horrific looks from all the upmarket people. I almost could read their thoughts: "Ew, what's he doing here?" Stuff like that. Then I'd approach the bar and drink from my own personalized stein of beer, shocking the upmarket clowns all over again. Thanks to the bartenders at GB, I could

343

be a rockstar. I was a man of wealth and taste, like Mick Jagger. Confusing the crowd was the nature of my game. I confounded the mere mortals, the attorneys, the business majors, the frat boys and the suburban nuclear families, none of whom had steins. I would be around for a long, long year, stealing their souls and faiths. It was a great way to get back at the idiots that picked on me in high school.

Then the corporate pricks ruined it all. In retrospect, 2010 is about when GB began to lose its staying power, culture-wise. Many of the longtime bartenders were leaving and, like everything downtown, the food got progressively worse and more expensive. The owners began to dumb down the work culture and the Secret Holy Order of Steinholders was only a shell of its former self. Plus, a whole new generation of craft beer places began to emerge in the neighborhood, with GB, the original pioneer, seeming to lose its way. Even as the comfortable classes always filled up the dining area because they hadn't felt safe anywhere since P.F. Chang's closed, GB was never able to recapture its original vibe. The vulture capitalist owners destroyed the Mick Jagger in all of us.

Memories of Failed 'Jeopardy!' Tryouts

In 2004, Ken Jennings became the hero of trivia nerds worldwide by winning 74 games in a row on the TV quiz show *Jeopardy!* Next Tuesday, June 12, he appears in conversation at Kepler's Books in Menlo Park.

Like Jennings, I grew up watching an inordinate amount of game shows and was a full-blown trivia nerd in elementary school. I knew every baseball stadium in the U.S., every world capital and tons of rock trivia. The very presence of Ken Jennings in Silicon Valley takes me back to 1999 and 2000, when I tried out for both *Jeopardy!* and *Rock & Roll Jeopardy!* during one of the more desperate times in my life.

Here's what I remember: Late 1999, I took an 8am flight out of San Jose, wearing a gray sportcoat, a black dress shirt and a wild Italian tie. I nearly missed the 6am alarm I'd set because I was among those who'd closed Cinebar at 2am. Yet somehow I woke up, got dressed and eventually landed at LAX at 9:04am, completely still drunk from the night before. I was going broke and determined to win $40,000 or whatever it took to get me out of San Jose forever.

At LAX, I asked an old German lady at the information booth to find out which shuttle took me outside the terminals to the street buses. From there, I caught the No. 6 bus, which went straight up Sepulveda Boulevard toward Culver City. At Washington Boulevard, I transferred to the No. 1, which took me right to Sony Pictures Studios, the home of *Jeopardy!* and *Wheel of Fortune*. I was the only person dressed up on either bus.

By then, it was nearing straight-up high noon, and there was nothing in the vicinity except a lonely strip mall, where I luckily found a Thai restaurant. After a plate of spicy larb gai and two Singha beers, I wandered over to the side entrance of the Sony complex. This was L.A., and normally everyone drove, so I was a rare pedestrian walking through the gate and into the mega-campus. Various studios and buildings comprised the whole of it, but I knew where to go.

Outside the studio, I sat there on a green bench, where a crowd of maybe 20 others were congregating and also waiting to take the initial Jeopardy! test. One guy was flipping through a World Almanac, attempting to study. Another lady was going over some geography notes she had conjured up beforehand. Then a plastic SoCal Baywatch-looking dude rolled up in a motorized cart and instructed us to follow him down to Studio 16, where they filmed the show. Like lambs to the slaughter, we obliged.

Inside, we sat in the same chairs where the audience normally sat during a taping of the show, and we were given worksheets to answer the upcoming questions. A slideshow of Alex Trebek played on the screen, explaining what was about to happen. We were then bombarded with 50 questions in 13 minutes, with only a few seconds to write down each answer before the next question appeared on the screen. Whoever answered 35 out of 50 advanced to the next round of vetting. Stuff like: Who was nicknamed the Desert Fox? What country is bordered only by Russia and China? What French phrase, literally meaning "bottom of the bag" refers to a short, dead-end street? Cyrano de Bergerac was in love with who?

In the end, I didn't answer 35 questions correctly. It's much more difficult than watching it on TV.

That was December of 1999. One year later, I took the same trip to L.A. and failed all over again while trying out for *Rock & Roll Jeopardy!* I knew which band John Entwistle joined in 1962, a question many sitting next to me didn't know at all, but I couldn't answer a damn thing about Oasis. Once again, I came home rejected and forlorn.

Ken Jennings commands a staggering amount of knowledge, but, fortunately or unfortunately, by the time he came onto the scene in 2004, I had a newspaper job and a different life. I could write about laundromats, gas stations or the blighted wastelands of my hometown—a much more trivial pursuit.

Ghosts of Literary Greats in Trieste, Italy

The author James Joyce harbored a love-hate relationship with his hometown of Dublin, so he exiled himself to Trieste, a city at the tip of the Adriatic Sea, in what's now Italy. Since I've already written about Joyce's birthplace and gravesite, Trieste was the next logical destination.

Although Trieste is where Joyce wrote *Portrait of the Artist as a Young Man*, as well as *The Dubliners* and significant portions of *Ulysses*, he was not the only one whose ghost began to follow me around.

An unapologetically trans-ethnic type of place, Trieste was for centuries the main port city of the Austro-Hungarian Empire. After World War I, it became part of Italy. After World War II, it became a free independent territory administered in two different zones, one run by the Americans and the British, the other run by Tito's Yugoslavia. Then, in 1954, the two zones were split, with the northern zone going back to Italy—the current-day Trieste—and the rest going to Tito, but an area that's now part of Slovenia and part of Croatia. All of which forced generations to migrate every which direction, resulting in progressively unclassifiable flavors of nostalgia and identity. By today's geography, this is an area where Italy, Austria and Slovenia all bleed into each other with borders that make no sense to anyone. You meet Italian nationals with Slavic names or Slovenes whose mother tongue is Italian. You meet people longing for Austria who were never even Austrian and there even exist people fighting to bring back the independent Trieste.

The travel writer Jan Morris referred to Trieste's "idiosyncratic cosmopolitanism" and how it exists in a state of "permanent hiatus," terms I just love because the city seems to operate outside the linear passage of history in regards to the ways that cities are normally defined by language, authority, allegiances or relationships to larger regions. In fact, while exploring Trieste one immediately realizes the sheer idiocy of defining anyone's identity solely by nation-states or borders because such a perspective simply can't apply to Trieste. Today the city effortlessly embroiders threads of Italian, Slavic and Germanic history, as well as the politics, religion and architecture of all those demographics. It is a city where everyone's identity is formerly a part of some other identity, a place simultaneously everything and yet somehow existing between everything, a multidimensional space of intersecting transitions. It's also a coffee capital and still a major port city.

Pulled along by the flow, I walked throughout the city over the course of a few days, but James Joyce was not the only author haunting me. There were many more.

Sir Richard Francis Burton, the 19th-century explorer and blasphemous troublemaker, lived in Trieste, working as the British consulate when he translated *The Kama Sutra* and *The Arabian Nights*. While a wealth of markers and itineraries exist to re-imagine Joyce's time in Trieste, practically nothing remains of Burton's life. Nor does hardly anything remain of the provocative French novelist Stendhal, who briefly operated in Trieste, working as the French consulate.

But here's what blew me away the most. The American diplomat Alexander Wheelock Thayer wrote the first definitive biography of Beethoven, working on much of it while serving as the U.S. consulate in Trieste, likewise in the 19th century. Thayer is even buried nearby. In yet another example of synchronicity as cosmic performance art, I found out right before I traveled to Italy that Thayer's old passport, some of his correspondence, letters and artifacts, as well as his uniform from when he served as U.S. consul in Trieste, including his jacket, pants, gloves, hat and sword, are stored in the vault at the Beethoven Center at San Jose State University, in my own neighborhood, right down the street from where I live, a facility inseparable from my alma mater, the SJSU Music Department.

As a result of such spacetime continuum-shattering vibrations, I can safely say that walking around in Trieste for a few days made me want to be an international diplomat. I must have a future in foreign service. I wouldn't wear a uniform, but someday my clothes will also be acquired by the Beethoven Center. Long live an international Trieste!

The Grave of Beethoven's Biographer in Trieste

The anti-man-about-town has a long history of making mystical pacts with deceased authors at their gravesites. It usually goes along the lines of: "I'll keep writing, you just show me how to pay the bills." In fits of desperation, I have done this with Joseph Campbell, Hermann Hesse, Jorge Luis Borges, James Joyce, Leonard Cohen and a few others.

Although a recent attempt to track down Beethoven's first biographer, Alexander Wheelock Thayer (1817 to 1897), in Trieste, Italy, was not successful, the whole ridiculous adventure ultimately confirmed that I have not wasted my life.

First things first: The Ira F. Brilliant Center for Beethoven Studies at San Jose State University, aka the Beethoven Center, is loosely affiliated with the SJSU School of Music and Dance, my alma mater. By now, many have heard about the wealth of research materials, artifacts, original scores, instruments and selected resources included within the Beethoven Center's hallowed walls. It is just plain wunderbar that San Jose is home to such a facility, as Beethoven was quite a colorful and controversial character. Interest in his life and art should not be limited to music students, academics, blue-hairs, Rotarians or conservative old duffers. He was an irascible outcast, a natural genius, a revolutionary and a raging drunk. He would never survive today's music academia. They would throw him out of school in a heartbeat.

Thankfully, I did survive music academia, and I owe pretty much everything to the music department at SJSU. My professor Allen Strange was the one who put me on a path of international travel—I'd have wound up working in a record store otherwise—so I am driven to give back. That said, what the Beethoven Center didn't have were modern-day photographs of Alexander Wheelock Thayer's grave in Trieste, so when I recently visited the city, I took it upon myself to at least try and find the tombstone. What unfolded was a brilliant example of hospitality on the part of the locals.

Thayer lived in Trieste when it was still part of Austria and when he was the American Consul from 1865 to 1882. Abraham Lincoln appointed him. He worked tirelessly on Beethoven's biography, which oddly enough was translated into German and published in that language first. The complete English version was not published until decades after Thayer passed away.

To reach the graveyard, I left my hotel and hopped on the No. 10 bus at Piazza Tommaseo, directly across the street from the Adriatic Sea. Thayer was buried in the Evangelical Cemetery of the Augsburg and Helvetica Confession, one of several adjoining walled-off sections, each at progressively lower levels as they descended down a hillside, but all still near the main graveyard, the Sant'Anna Cemetery. Unfortunately, when I arrived in the late afternoon, the section containing Thayer was closed for the day and there was no way to get in. I had to fly back home the next morning, so there was no possible way to return.

The military section was the closest open area, located on the next upper level, so I walked in and spent a few minutes trying to scope a way into the evangelical section, if that was even possible. It wasn't.

Then I spotted a woman watering flowers. I scurried up and handed Maria Neva Micheli the information on Thayer, and between her English and my broken Italian, we were able to communicate. She directed me to the parking lot, where her husband, Loris Guarini, was sitting in their car. He didn't know how to access the evangelical section either, but they were both kind enough to drive me all the way around the entire graveyard complex to the main entrance to inquire at the front office. Still, there was nothing we could do. I was out of luck. Then, in a gracious act of hospitality, Micheli wrote down my email and said she would return at a later time, take photos and send them to me. Sure enough, a few days later, the photos arrived.

I relayed the images to the Beethoven Center, and they are now being considered for inclusion in a spring 2019 joint exhibit in partnership with SJSU's Steinbeck Center entitled, "Beethoven & Steinbeck: The Art of Biography." *Bravissimo!*

Neal Cassady's Old House on Santa Clara Street

A new book of lost imagery from the Beat Generation has emerged, triggering this columnist to reflect on those celebrated literary troublemakers, some of whom spent some serious time here locally. *The Beat Scene: Photographs by Burt Glinn* is a landmark collection, much of which is in color. A successful photographer on numerous fronts, Glinn took the shots between 1957 and 1960 in San Francisco and New York. All the usual suspects are included.

Now, since Neal Cassady's old house still exists at 1047 E. Santa Clara St.—the sizable den of iniquity he shared with his wife Carolyn and their three kids in the early '50s—I feel obligated to foreground the history for Metro readers who may not have flipped through Allen Ginsberg's journals, Jack Kerouac's letters or Carolyn's book, *Off the Road*. That house was legendary. If only the walls could talk.

Neal was the uncontainable genius and prime culture jammer behind much of the Beat Generation. Among many other sordid escapades, he was immortalized as Dean Moriarty in Kerouac's novel, *On the Road*, and also drove the bus for Ken Kesey's Merry Band of Pranksters. To this day, his legend lives on, with much exaggeration, all over the world.

In August of 1952, Neal and Carolyn arrived in San Jose, "a city then aptly nicknamed 'Nowheresville,'" she wrote. Neal was holding down a job at Southern Pacific Railroad while planting marijuana seeds in the flowerbeds. This was back when phone numbers were identified by two letters and five digits. Theirs was CY 7-0295.

Kerouac stayed with the Cassadys several times during the few years they lived on Santa Clara Street, with Carolyn and Jack famously having a passionate affair. Flavors of this love triangle were immortalized in Kerouac's novel, *Big Sur*, one of his best books. Decades later, Carolyn spilled the rest of the lurid yarn in *Off the Road*.

But not everything was hunky-dory. As the story goes, Neal and Carolyn were deeply engaged with the metaphysics of Edgar Cayce, which did not resonate with Kerouac, who was already looking eastward for inspiration. As a result, it was in San Jose that Kerouac stole a copy of Dwight Goddard's *A Buddhist Bible* from the San Jose Public Library, a book that became one of his first major conduits to Buddhism, leading to his embrace of the Dharma for years to come. Don't ever discount the importance of libraries.

When Ginsberg finally showed up in San Jose to stay with the Cassadys for several weeks in 1954, even more drama unfolded. The Cassadys took him to goofy hypnotist parties in Sunnyvale, and Ginsberg even wrote of meeting "spinster old lady Rosicrucians." What's more, Ginsberg was madly in love with Neal. They'd already consummated encounters going back years, and by the time Ginsberg made it to San Jose, he was scribbling masochistic fantasies. Lucky for us, Ginsberg was so bored with Nowheresville that he filled several pages in his journals.

The now-infamous interlude described in various books went down in August of 1954. As Carolyn wrote it, she walked in on Ginsberg and Neal, in Ginsberg's room, engaged in the act, after which she then retreated back to the living room, horrified. A few days later, she dropped Ginsberg off in San Francisco along with some pocket change and sent him on his way.

Nevertheless, Ginsberg wrote some seminal poems while staying at the Cassady house. He wrote, "Love Poem on Theme by Whitman," in which he fantasized about a threesome with Neal and Carolyn. "In Back of the Real," found him wandering desolate in the old San Jose railroad yard, only to equate a discarded flower with the universal struggle for beauty and hope against the wreckage of the landscape. "In Back of the Real" inspired at least a few dozen of my columns over the years.

At minimum, a plaque should be installed at 1047 E. Santa Clara St. I doubt the current owner would mind. Certainly the property value would increase. Certainly fans from around the world would visit. Will the Nowheresville City Council ever understand these things? Like Ginsberg's discarded flower, we can only hope.

Asian-American Women Novelists Return to the Steinbeck Center

If people can trace Kerouac's footsteps in North Beach or harmonize the vibes of Dashiell Hammett at John's Grill, then certainly there should be Vanessa Hua literary tours through the underbelly of Chinatown. Released last week, Hua's debut novel, *A River of Stars*, gets rolling right away when two pregnant Chinese women escape an illegal maternity clinic in SoCal before stealing a van and driving to San Francisco.

A *San Francisco Chronicle* columnist, Hua is also one of three Asian-American women, along with R.O. Kwon and Kirstin Chen, who in recent years received a Steinbeck Fellowship in Creative Writing from San Jose State University, and who released a novel to rocking fanfare in 2018. Every academic season, the Steinbeck Center at SJSU sponsors a handful of one-year fellowships for writers of any age or background to pursue a writing project while in residence at SJSU. The projects need not relate to Steinbeck, but they must be promising enough to warrant support. With Hua, Kwon and Chen all releasing books this year, a glorious convergence is afoot.

A River of Stars unfolds on multiple levels as a dark, humorous and ultimately hopeful story of two undocumented single moms struggling to overcome obstacles in the underbelly of Chinatown to achieve a piece of what it means to be American. In the book, we get to know Scarlett, pregnant with the child of a Chinese mob boss who sent her to LA in order to conceive her kid on US soil for citizenship purposes. At the illegal facility—these places actually exist—she lives under lock and key, along with many other pregnant Chinese. Scarlett then escapes with Daisy, a teenager similarly pregnant, yet longing for her boyfriend who has since disappeared. Together, they make it to San Francisco and dissolve into Chinatown, where they give birth to their children and develop an increasingly close friendship, all while struggling for work, housing and camaraderie, plus ways to achieve legal status and acceptance in the Chinese-American community.

Meanwhile, the mobster who fathered Scarlett's child scrambles to track her down, aided by Mama Fang, the woman who operated the illegal clinic. After the clinic falls apart, Fang winds up in Cupertino, running a facility that gives vitamin IV drips to schoolchildren to help them overachieve. The mob boss becomes ensnared in various other counterplots, including a scheme to secretly bankroll immortality research at Stanford.

But Hua is just one Asian-American Steinbeck Fellow from SJSU to hit the shelves this year. R.O. Kwon's book, *The Incendiaries*, is exploding onto the charts as you read this. A zillion outlets from The New Yorker all the way down to obscure book nerd portals are raving over Kwon's compact prose. In my view, *The Incendiaries* is a gorgeously bleak psychological horror novel. A college-age woman gradually gets sucked into a violent religious cult that bombs abortion clinics, yet the book is narrated in retrospect by her obsessive ex-boyfriend as he grapples to understand what happened to their lives. At just over 200 pages, *The Incendiaries* leaves an eerie aftertaste—not the type of thing one expects to see on women's lists of "summer beach reads," yet it landed on many such lists. Kwon was born in Seoul, yet grew up in SoCal and now lives in San Francisco.

The third novelist in our equation, Kirstin Chen, grew up in Singapore and even taught at SJSU for a spell. Now an adjunct professor at USF, she released her second novel, *Bury What We Cannot Take*, last spring. In yet another tale of abandonment, loss and longing, Chen placed the book in early Maoist China, late '50s, on Drum Wave Islet off the coast of Xiamen. A family rejects the new Communist regime and escapes to Hong Kong, but is forced to leave their daughter behind as proof of the family's intent to return. Chen's detailed historical research enlivens the narrative, as the daughter, a 9-year-old named San San, becomes a heroic protagonist in trying to escape her emotional isolation and reconnect with her real family. At times, it's quite sad.

All of which means we are experiencing a triple shot of Asian-American women Steinbecks, right here and now. The ol' Nobel Laureate would be proud.

Silicon Alleys Joins the '700 Club'

As of right now, this column officially joins the 700 club. That is, a total of 700 weeks have gone by since I started writing Silicon Alleys in 2005. Milestones are better than gallstones, I suppose.

The history here is two-pronged. Back when I was still sitting at Cactus Club's happy hour with the cockroaches, the washed-up strippers, the Satanists and the homeless punks, Eric Carlson was writing a *Metro* column called, "Notes From the Underbelly"—a major influence on me. He moved away in 2002, leaving serious shoes to fill.

By the time I came on board, *Metro* also featured a front-of-book column called "Biter," an irreverent dose of random alt-San Jose snark. It was a rotating column, meaning, any one of us wrote it whenever we had an idea. For my contributions, I went on the most ridiculous adventures I could find, all over the valley.

In November 2002, for example, I attended a bondage class outdoors near Leathermasters on Park Avenue. The teacher led a hands-on seminar, in broad daylight, on the grass in someone's backyard. She tied me up in front of the whole class—we all had our clothes on—and demonstrated various knots and techniques. I then wrote a Biter column comparing the experience to that of San Jose itself, how downtown had been tying itself in knots for 30 years and was undergoing yet more phases of body modification, leaving its culture on the ropes. Many creative people at the time felt tied up and strangled just having to live here.

Over the next few years, I wrote many Biter columns, embarking on similar adventures. One week I went to a pub in Campbell and entered a bachelor auction for charity, planting two women in the crowd to jack up the bidding, but the whole thing failed miserably. In other columns, I went to Los Gatos and got a spray-on tan and attended a Walmart prank at which no one showed up but the organizer. In a really dumb column, I even glorified the Asian fetishist creeps at a dubious new Vietnamese place called Sugars Coffee Bar. Thanks to my story bringing the joint above ground, the cops began shaking the place down and later closed it.

The fun didn't stop there. At the Camden Community Center, I took a class in astral projection, taught by a goofy Australian mystic. In the story, I wrote, "If I can't get my physical body the hell out of San Jose, well, at least I can get my astral body out of San Jose."

Writing those Biter columns taught me an important lesson: I had discovered a natural talent for transforming any subject into ridicule of San Jose. Not in a hostile way, but as a local scribe covering his hometown in ways no one else would possibly do. As a native, I'd grown up with all the trappings of a place that still after decades couldn't figure out if it wanted to be a big city or a suburb. At the time, every giddy feel-good project San Jose tried to implement, and the ways in which it botched every desperate scheme to achieve name recognition, only seemed to reinforce its own attention-starved identity complex. All of this was fertile ground for an overgrown snotty teenager with a killer vocabulary, so I plowed on as best I could. As a result, *Metro* gave me my own column, "Silicon Alleys," in 2005 and you're still reading it today.

With Silicon Alleys, the point from the beginning was to write something different every single week so the readers would never know what to expect. And I still try to uphold that strategy when feasible. "Alleys" just refers to anything off the beaten path—geographically, psychically or creatively.

Those Biter columns, as frivolous as they were, along with the first several years of writing the Silicon Alleys column, helped me find my own voice. I grew as a writer and as a person. Today, I no longer need to explode with juvenile tantrums, although it still happens every so often. Nevertheless, so long as the muse continues to show up each week, I will conjure words that hopefully resonate with someone, somewhere. Here's to another 700!

Jorge Luis Borges Synchronicities

Two-and-a-half years ago, the anti-man-about-town visited the gravesite of legendary author Jorge Luis Borges in Geneva, Switzerland. Borges was a unique figure at the top of 20th century literature and a major influence on me, so in Geneva I made a desperate pact with him. Standing at his grave, I said: "Alright old man, I will keep writing, just show me how to make a living.

Give me a sign. Anything." Sure enough, I was awarded a fellowship soon thereafter. I guess he was looking over my shoulder.

That was in 2016, but just a few weeks ago in downtown San Jose, Borges spun back into my orbit from multiple dimensions at once, just to make sure I was still writing and keeping up my end of the bargain. The resultant matrix of synchronicity was transformational, like walking into a hall of mirrors I didn't want to escape.

It all started on Aug. 24, Borges's birthday, of course. There in the coffee shop I sat, laptop in front of me, translating my thoughts into characters on a screen, all while distracting myself by reading quotes and bits about Borges on social media. I posted the previously mentioned column about visiting his grave, when suddenly, far away from across the street, the owner of Anno Domini responded, relaying news that the gallery's next show would include Denis Korkh's paintings inspired by Borges' book, *Labyrinths*. The creative life juice began to flow. As anyone who follows this column knows by now, I am a love slave to the muses of synchronicity, so I just knew this matrix of intrigue was nowhere near over.

Two weeks later on Sept. 6, the day before the Korkh exhibit opened, I spotted a used copy of *Labyrinths* while rifling through the shelves of books for sale at the Beat Museum in San Francisco. I didn't buy it because I thought I already owned a copy. Turned out I was mistaken. I only owned *Ficciones*, which contains several of the same short stories.

The Korkh exhibit, titled *In Borges' Labyrinths*, opened the next night, attracting the usual array of artists, patrons, stoned twenty-somethings and outré characters marveling at visuals inspired by Borges' writings. The accompanying text panels included quotes from various Borges masterpieces like, "The Library of Babel," "The Zahir" and "Tlön, Uqbar, Orbis Tertius." At presstime, several paintings had already sold.

This was more than enough serendipity to imply a heightened sense of awareness on my part, easily enough to spark more characters on a

353

screen. However, another dimension to the intrigue emerged four days later.

On Sept. 11, in what some are calling an unrelated event, the poet Stephen Kessler gave a reading at WORKS/San Jose, exactly one block over from Anno Domini. A major figure in the world of poetry, Kessler is known for many endeavors, including the years he spent translating the poetry of Jorge Luis Borges. Many of those poems are included in a large volume, still popular. Kessler also helped edit and translate an entire 300-page book of Borges' sonnets, a landmark publication several years ago.

At WORKS, Kessler sold copies of his most recent book of poetry, titled, *Garage Elegies*. I flipped it open, skipping right to page 44—a poem titled, "Translator in His Labyrinth." The poem opens with the narrator proofreading both languages and making final tunings with the dead poet looking over his shoulder. I felt like Yogi Berra Borges was telling me about *deja vu*. All over again.

Clearly I was in a Borges story, with past, present and future all becoming one and the same. Or maybe I was in a halfway house between a column and a short story, the only difference being that everything I've just written actually happened. A Borgesian theme would be: Does the author write the column or does the column write the author? Do Korkh's paintings function as translations of Borges' stories, as Borges himself would have suggested? I don't know, but two days later, I went right back to the Beat Museum in San Francisco and nabbed that copy of *Labyrinths*. To Borges I will make a necessary pact, all over again: I am still writing, please keep showing me how to make a living.

Kronos Quartet Presents Music for Change: The Banned Countries

More than any other contemporary ensemble, Kronos Quartet—David Harrington (violin), John Sherba (violin), Hank Dutt (viola), and Sunny Yang (cello)—pursues and performs music from every corner of the planet.

So last year when Donald Trump decided to implement a travel ban targeting people from specific Muslim-majority countries, the quartet responded by researching, commissioning and now presenting a program of music from those parts of the world. This Saturday, "Music for Change: The Banned Countries," takes place in Stanford's Bing Concert Hall. While the program is not limited to the countries on Trump's original list, music from Egypt, Syria, Iran, Lebanon, Azerbaijan and other countries in or near the Middle East will be emphasized.

Harrington remembers when the White House announced the travel ban. It came right before the Kronos Festival in San Francisco, when the quartet was already performing music from several of the banned countries. As a result, Harrington felt like this music, and music itself, was under attack. A logical response by the quartet would be to increase its already rich worldly repertoire by introducing American audiences even more to music from places they might not ever get a chance to visit. This became a responsibility.

"Musicians thrive, and music thrives, when we get to hear as much as we can from as many corners of the world as we can, and from as many different types of instruments and voices and viewpoints," Harrington said. "That is the strength of music. And so, at that moment, during that concert I remember thinking, 'We've got to try to counteract this kind of small thinking.'"

The program includes a few world premieres, plus works that Kronos has performed for over 20 years, and many that fall in between. Opening the program will be the haunting piece, *Mugam Sayagi*, by Azerbaijani composer Franghiz Ali-Zadeh. She first wrote it for Kronos in the early '90s. Ali-Zadeh's music combines the Persian, Turkic, Arab and Russian heritage of her home region, but with additional inspiration from 20th century avant-gardists like George Crumb and Olivier Messiaen. Harrington says the piece is a great way to open a concert. Later in the program, Iranian composer Aftab Darvishi will premiere a piece called *Winds from South*. Born in 1987, Darvishi graduated from Tehran University before getting her master's degree in the Netherlands. In another case, keyboardist Islam Chipsy, who helped Electro Chaabi music explode out of the Cairo slums, wrote a tune called *Zaghlala* which was then transcribed and arranged for string quartet by Jacob Garchik.

"Our idea is to take the listener through this kind of vast experience of musical variety and possibilities, and encourage more listening, and wider listening," Harrington said. "That's what I'm hoping this concert will do. It will kind of open some windows and some doors, and allow more music in."

Other pieces include *Wa Habibi* (Beloved), a solemn Easter-time hymn that Kronos first discovered while gigging in Lebanon. The tune is often performed in Lebanese Christian churches, but over the years Kronos discovered that the tune might have originated in France. Another tune, Yet-zav Ha-El, was inspired by early 20th-century Cantorial music usually performed in Turkish synagogues. Also on the bill is a world premiere string quartet version of a legendary Afghan folk tune, *Bia Ke Berem Ba Mazar*, arranged by Milad Yousufi.

All of which exemplifies what now after 45 years has become the Kronos life journey: a relentless endeavor to open up the world's music for everyone. If the conventional assemblage of two violins, viola and cello can be expanded by transcribing sounds from Middle Eastern instruments or Asian tunings, listeners will develop a much richer musical perspective. There are no border fences between various forms of music.

"This is the kind of thing that musicians have been doing forever,"

Harrington says. "If you hear something that magnetizes you, you want to incorporate that into the world that you're working in. And I think that's what we're finding—that there are many, many sounds we want to bring into our world. We feel it makes us stronger. It gives us a larger palate. And as a reflection of what a really well functioning society might be, this seems to me to be a good direction."

Author's Old Lowrey Genie Organ Recalls Stevens Music

There comes a time when one needs to downsize. In this case, the first musical instrument on which I ever played a campy version of "One Tin Soldier" is now headed for the great cheesemaster graveyard in the sky. The Lowrey Genie home organ my parents bought for me at Stevens Music in Willow Glen when I was 9 years old—a machine that has long since fallen into permanent disrepair—will now soon be hauled away and put out to pasture.

My entire camp humor identity began on that machine, so its demise calls for a twisted eulogy of sorts. But first, some history. Stevens Music, which existed from 1951 to 1984 at 1202 Lincoln Ave., was an institution in Willow Glen, selling and repairing instruments, plus sheet music and related products for thousands of people throughout the valley. Entire generations got their chops inside that building, operated by Tom Stevens and his son Gordon. After the main retail business closed, Reik's music eventually moved into the ground floor, with the upstairs then converting into more lesson rooms and other independent music businesses, including Stevens Violin Shop. Up until Gordon sold the building in 2013, he claimed the oldest continuously operating business license on Lincoln Avenue.

The stories from 1202 Lincoln are legendary. In the 1960s, members of rock bands like The Chocolate Watchband and Syndicate of Sound purchased gear at Stevens Music. Patrick Simmons of the Doobie Brothers bought his first guitar there. Synthesizer pioneer Don Buchla showed up and worked on equipment in the back room. And years later it was the building where I first took music lessons. At age 9 I was already walking in the footsteps of giants. Nowadays, if you walk into Black Sheep Brasserie and observe the upmarket nuclear families nibbling at their duck liver mousse, you can say that's where I first played "Love is Blue" on a Lowrey Genie.

The Genie was basically a mini descendent of larger cheesemaster-style home organs that became popular starting in the Great Depression era as people's dollars went more toward home entertainment. After the Beatles exploded in the '60s, followed by the mainstreaming of synthesizers in the '70s, nobody was buying cheesy home organs anymore. The technology was old hat, so Stevens needed to unload their inventory.

I subsequently grew up on that Lowrey Genie and then a Schafer

& Sons piano, playing sappy pop tunes, easy listening schmaltz and TV themes, or simply just butchering AM radio hits, reading off the sheet music and not even learning to gig with other people, develop my ear or play in time with additional musicians. I played everything rubato, as classical musicians would say. Some of these tunes I enjoyed, while others were awful and I just played them for camp humor purposes. Over time, though, this distinction began to fade, those polar opposites began to fuse, leaving me with a strange yet integrated taste for awful-on-purpose humor. If I fumbled through that ridiculous "Music Box Dancer" abomination, who's to say I couldn't enjoy it for its awfulness? From a Zen perspective, I took humor very seriously and I took seriousness very humorously. To me, the world was clearly not black and white, as Western thinkers wanted to believe. As a result, I can draw a direct line from those moments of easy-listening schmaltz at the Lowrey Genie right to the current day, each time I write a column glorifying some crumbling old building or if I perceive beauty in the drabness of suburbia. This is what artists do: We see beauty in the ugliness and vice versa.

I've written this before, but it's true: Music kept me away from potentially criminal paths in life. Had I not started playing keyboards, I would never have studied music in college and then come into jobs that led me to travel and become a more worldly person, which, in turn, led me to start writing. If not for arts and music education from age 9 until 29, I'd be dead.

So the old Lowrey is about to die a natural death. Like that one tin soldier riding away, my first musical instrument is off to the great perhaps and I am at peace. Fare thee well, old Genie!

The Faction and Lars Frederiksen at The Ritz

In 1983, deep in the suburban hinterland of Campbell, the punk rock photographer Murray Bowles attended a backyard party and shot several pictures of The Faction, San Jose's legendary skate punk band. A software engineer by day, Bowles was just starting a decades-long side job of capturing Bay Area punk.

In San Jose, the scene was a hodgepodge of house parties, rented halls and skate ramps because no real venues existed. As the Faction played, an 11-year-old kid named Lars Frederiksen sat on the ground in front of the drum set to keep it stationary. (See photo.)

"The cinderblock wasn't working so the kick drum kept moving and moving and moving," Frederiksen recalled. "I remember someone tried to put a 12-pack of beer in front of it, and that obviously didn't work. I think someone even said put the keg in front of it, but then everybody would have to come up when the band was playing to fill their beer. So somebody said, 'Put Lars in there.' And that's how I ended up in there."

The rest is history. Ten years later, Frederiksen joined the band Rancid, which then exploded into one of the most successful punk bands of all time, inspiring generations of fans around the world, even still.

But now, in what is probably the most spacetime continuum-shattering full-circle punk hoedown in local living memory, the Faction will first open up for Rancid in San Francisco on Thursday, and then they will headline on Friday with one of Frederiksen's other bands, the Old Firm Casuals, at The Ritz in downtown San Jose. The whole shootin' match will trigger many individuals to reflect on their own crazy journeys over the last several decades.

Over the years, Bowles' photos from that party have almost achieved folk status. He may have captured the most punk rock Norman Rockwell moment in San Jose history.

In those days, the Faction's bass player, Steve Caballero, was already a world-famous professional skateboarder with sponsorships, trophies, tour stories and the whole nine yards, all while not yet even 20. People around the world devoured skateboard magazines and then VHS videos of the Bones Brigade, of which Caballero was a key member. Thanks to what he and his crew were doing, it's not an exaggeration to say San Jose was one of the skateboarding capitals of the country. Specific street tricks and maneuvers were pioneered right here in town. As the lifestyle became inseparable from punk rock, the whole scene put San Jose on the map way more than any politician has ever been able to do. It is a travesty of justice that Caballero is not in the San Jose Sports Hall of Fame.

But I digress. With the Faction, Caballero eventually switched from bass to guitar as the band became a five-piece and then soared to even more stardom before breaking up a few short years later. After sporadic reunions over the decades, they returned to semi-regular gigging about four years ago.

Bowles' photo captures what the scene was like in those days: punks and skater kids dealing with the intrinsic boredom of suburbia. Several people in the photo are still in the area. For example, leaning on Caballero's bass amp is Denice Vaughn, wearing a pair of pink Paradise Garage creepers, shoes Caballero bought her when he was in LA for a contest.

"I threw a fit because he wanted to get me the red and black ones," Vaughn recalled. "And I said, 'No, I want the pink ones, and if I can't have those, then I want nothing.' And he drove all the way [across LA] back to Hollywood to get me those. I totally remember that. I still have them."

Bowles has since retired from the software industry, but still has a long photography career on which to reflect. His catalog of photos, now in the thousands, remains an integral component of Bay Area punk history, although he doesn't scour the scene as much as he used to.

"Nowadays everybody takes pictures with their phones," Bowles said. "It's not as though if I didn't take pictures, there'd be no pictures taken at all. Which is sort of the way it was for a lot of shows."

Al Preciado's Last Solo Show

Al Preciado is a retrospective kind of dude. A decades-long fixture in the San Jose art community and now into his 21st year of teaching at Bellarmine, he often sells his work at South First Fridays or paints canvases in front of Kaleid Gallery during the summer months, usually with his students or proteges.

The late Harry Powers showed him the ropes decades ago, and now Preciado passes the baton by teaching younger artists what he knows.

This Saturday, Preciado's latest solo show, a retrospective of large landscapes he painted mostly this year, unfolds at the Citadel Gallery, from noon until midnight. A warehouse-style building on Martha Street, the Citadel features more than 70 artist studios in addition to the gallery. Outside, Preciado tells me he knows every single crack on the sidewalk. Inside, everything is cold, off-white and almost prisonlike, but the gallery, a large open room with magnificent lighting and 20-foot-high ceilings, has for years been one of San Jose's best exhibit spaces.

"It's a very New York-style gallery," Preciado tells me. "It's the biggest space, I think, in San Jose except for the Museum of Art, and it really shows off the artists' work well. I'm a DIY kind of guy, I find that this space fits perfectly with my work because it's especially large and not tiny, so it's the best space for me because I feel like I need this kind of space to really show off my work at its best potential."

With Preciado, the stories never stop. Decades ago when attending SJSU, he says his office was at House of Pizza. The old location, he clarifies. Now at Citadel, Preciado stages retrospectives almost annually, but as we enter his studio, he claims this Saturday's show will be his last major solo exhibit.

His studio is exactly what anyone would expect: sculptures, plants, paint-spattered rugs, haphazard shelving, ancient buckets filled with brushes and art supplies, coils of bailing wire, canvases leaned up against each other, piles of milk crates high up on a shelf, scattered piles of tools, portraits of women, newspaper clippings, books crammed into a corner, plus sordid photos, sketches and even more piles of canvases jammed between everything else—all in glorious, beautiful chaos.

As we talk, two high school boys are helping Preciado clean out his studio in preparation for the show. One is from Bellarmine, the other Valley Christian. It is here that Preciado stores many of his smaller sculptures, intricate abstract compositions of foil, plastic, tape and wire. Preciado first rented a studio at the Citadel for the last half of the '80s, then returned about five years ago.

"It used to be cowboys and Indians, really Wild West," he says. "There was a lot of parties and things like that. Then they made things a lot tighter. It's more like a corporation. It's hard to get in here unless you have keys, and I feel a lot safer in this environment. It's nice, my side of the building; there's less artists so it's more quiet. I really enjoy that, because especially at night it's great to work."

Preciado's work is instantly recognizable to any longtime denizen of the local arts scene. He spent years painting the female form, including many images of ballerinas, but now he focuses on landscapes. He spent much of this year hanging out in San Jose parks, painting the greenery and the surroundings. Speaking with nuanced finality, Preciado goes back and forth as to whether this show is really indeed his last hurrah. Nevertheless, a show like this with many large canvases requires serious physical effort. He's getting older and it takes a long time to haul around a bunch of large works and then set them up for display in a huge gallery. At this point, he'd rather pass the baton to the next generation.

"Emerging young artists, it's their ball game now," he says. "I'll be happy to mentor anybody that needs it, because I think that's what you should do, as Harry Powers did with me when I was younger. He mentored me and made me realize what I had to do to make a show happen, so I'll always be thankful to him for that."

2019

Animal Houses

In the fall of 1990, I moved into a house at 361 N. 10th St. in down-town San Jose and the rest of that decade went either downhill, uphill or sideways, depending on one's perspective. In various downtown houses, I would spend the next 10 years living a dual life—half academic, half rock & roll dude—with a schizo "never the twain shall meet" identity fueling my creativity.

After leaving Tenth Street, I lived near the SoFA district, then moved to N. Sixth Street, S. Seventh Street, S. Fifth Street, S. Ninth Street and then finally a friend's living room on Second Street as Y2K emerged. Beethoven lived a similar life in Vienna, moving from place to place. Same thing with Kafka in Prague. So they've got my back.

Together, all of the dwellings served as fodder for novels I started and failed to finish, so now I'll reflect on some of the highlights I think influenced columns in the current era. At 361 N. Tenth, for example, each of the five roommates paid about $200 a month to live in the house. We converted a detached garage into a venue, where bands played at our parties. One band, The Nowhere Men, featured a pre-Rancid Lars Frederiksen along with a singer that now works at Metro.

Later, in April of 1991, I moved into a house a few blocks away from the newly-christened SoFA District. My roommates had just been issued an eviction notice right before I moved in, although they didn't tell me at first. This was back when Cactus Club, Marsugi's, Ajax, and F/X all hosted bands that would later vault to worldwide stardom. Other groups, usually the ones with no shot at stardom, would use our house for the aftershow parties. The wreckage throughout that subsequent summer rivaled any classic punk rock party house anywhere. A friend next door met her future husband somewhere in the middle of the whole mess and they are still married to this day.

After the sheriff forced us out of that house, I moved in with two female roommates at 144 N. Sixth Street. For two years, they were the sisters I never had. Even if we bickered like siblings, I either had their backs and protected them at shows when we were all wasted together, or I walked them home. Sometimes they had to walk me home.

All of this unfolded as I lived a separate life at San Jose State, in the music department, writing C code to make excruciating noise collages on SGI machines, or smashing amplified shopping carts on stage, or studying 20th century avant-garde composers like Edgard Varese, Stockhausen and John Cage—a life unknown to my friends in the rock clubs. By day I sped up drum machines to sound like machine guns or wrote Satanic lyrics for assignments in 16th Century Counterpoint class, and by night I got wasted while Urge Overkill played for 10 of us at Marsugi's.

Then everything came to a glorious peak during three years at 414 S. Seventh Street. Not to blow my own kazoo, but people still talk about that house. If you've read *Incredibly Strange Music* from RE/Search Publications, well, that book should have included our house because zillions of old tacky thrift store LPs graced the walls and we drunkenly blasted the worst easy listening music we could find. This was a block from the SJSU Event Center and we'd charge concert-goers five bucks to park in our front yard so they could avoid the parking garage. As a result, they'd buy us beer in exchange. It was creative urban placemaking long before anyone at City Hall used that term. After getting my bachelor's degree, I even walked from that house all the way to Spartan Stadium for graduation.

After losing various campus jobs and girlfriends and being the last dude left at 414 S. Seventh, I lived on Fifth, Ninth and then Second Street, but emerged with a master's degree and a traveling life that connected me to music professors, programmers and audio experimenters the world over. Not a moment was wasted, even if I usually was. Everything was preparatory material for the current moment. And the current column. Happy New Year.

American Cosmic: Jacques Vallee Returns

Publishing this week on Oxford University Press, a new book by Diana Walsh Pasulka, *American Cosmic: UFOs, Religion, Technology*, begins with Pasulka riding in a car from San Francisco to Silicon Valley. Jacques Vallee, perhaps the most well-known UFO researcher over the last 50 years, is behind the wheel. On the way, Vallee tells her, "These are the hills of Silicon Valley. There are many secrets in this valley."

Pasulka, a professor of religious studies at the University of North Carolina Wilmington, will speak about *American Cosmic* on Jan. 17 at Cubberley Theatre in Palo Alto, sponsored by the Commonwealth Club-Silicon Valley, at 7pm. She is not a current or former government agent or conspiracy theorist. Instead, she analyzes the UFO phenomenon from an academic religious studies perspective, meaning she studies the resulting effects rather than whether or not anything is true. She also takes the approach of a media archaeologist in that she uses examples of forgotten media from previous eras to help examine how the current media landscape of cinema, TV and social media exacerbates and distorts the phenomenon. More than anything, *American Cosmic* suggests that with the UFO phenomenon we are witnessing the initial stages of a new flavor of religiosity. Like Jung suggested, we're in the middle of a new myth as it's being created.

"I think of the Protestant Reformation and how it was kind of instigated by the printing press," Pasuka tells me. "So technology impacts religion, and it changes religion and creates new religious forms. So I realized that the digital environment was creating a new form of religion and it was taking the form of this kind of UFO religiosity."

But what separates *American Cosmic* apart from the current UFO hysteria is that Pasulka spends entire chapters with world-famous scientists, academics and/or high-profile public figures who believe in extraterrestrial intelligence and have been studying it for years, but who operate underneath the radar, out of the public eye. In the book they remain anonymous because of the stigma associated with UFOs. They fear being ostracized or losing their reputations.

Someone going by the name of Tyler, for example, whose public identity would most likely be known to everyone, invites Pasulka to a supposed crash site in New Mexico—not Roswell, but another site—and requires her to arrive blindfolded, only to then discover alloys and artifacts that later cannot be identified by scientists as anything created by the laws of physics. Other chapters provide specific examples of true believers whose lives are changed by their experiences with nonhuman intelligences, much in the same way that Catholic apparitions have functioned over the centuries. Yet this is a religiosity with no borders and no defined denominations.

"There are people who believe in a higher intelligence that has contacted us, or is in contact with us, or has given us these artifacts, these parts, UFO crashed parts, and we're back engineering them and they're somehow helping us evolve," Pasulka says. "So it's linked also to this concept of the evolution of the species, the survival of the species into space—this type of thing that's really, really big in Silicon Valley."

All of which, to Pasulka, seems similar enough to the early stages of Christianity in that certain people in positions of power have an interest in shaping the narrative for future's sake, and specific communities are declaring that their version of the religion is the universal version. The difference is that the UFO phenomenon can be articulated as something characterized by technology we don't yet fully understand but which many scientists are actively studying, so it feels like hanging out in Judea 2000 years ago, with researchers on board striving to prove that these events did in fact happen.

"In most religions, you have things that guide the people, faith in something unseen or unknown," says Pasulka. "And faith is what we call that relationship to something you can't prove. Well, we could possibly prove this. So there is a semblance of truth here. And since there is a semblance of truth, it gives this kind of religiosity a bit that the other religions just don't have. So we're in a new territory."

Death Before Dishonor Tattoo

Out beyond the darkness and the light, there is a milieu of Tibetan prayer flags, cholo artwork, posters, mirrors, spiritual knickknacks and demon masks. To riff on Rumi, I will meet you there. To be more specific, I speak of Paco Excel's Death Before Dishonor tattoo studio, a fixture at the otherwise constantly changing area of Third and San Carlos in downtown San Jose.

The multi-story faded brown Victorian house first housed the legendary New Skool Tattoo shop back in 1995 until a bifurcation of historic proportion spawned an offspring, Death Before Dishonor, in 2008. One room, the separate yet related Bodhidharma Gallery, will host an art show by Joe Demaree this Sunday from noon to 5pm.

Full disclosure: Many people involved here are old, old friends of mine, but I haven't been upstairs in this building for what seems like a century. As soon as I sit down in Excel's studio and await his arrival, his apprentice gives me a can of blackberry- and cucumber-flavored sparkling water. She sits at an old wooden desk in the corner, drawing ideas for tattoos while Sinatra's "My Way" plays over the system. She started five months ago, I learn.

Upstairs and away from any sidewalk sightlines, Excel's studio is a cross between a tattoo business, a '90s San Jose rock scene archive, a Victorian antique shop and a comparative religious studies classroom. I see a collection of LPs in the corner, sandwiched between Buddhist iconography, a Sharks skateboard, a High on Fire poster, antiques, figurines, artifacts of Mexican folklore and a smattering of spiritual ephemera from around the world, including a gorgeous blue and white porcelain plate from an international Buddhist union. Many of these items are gifts that clients have brought Excel from other places.

Then Excel walks in and we talk about how his studio has evolved over the years. This is not some giddy San Jose faux-urban boosterism project. The place is a bona fide sanctuary carrying a radical sympathy for time, a site specific environment, an inseparable extension of Excel's own life philosophy. It feels like an ancient shop you'd find buried away in some back alley of Bangkok or Mexico City, like something you'd see on a travel show, replete with washed-up expats, burnt-out foreign correspondents and nefarious characters lurking in the shadows for decades, not that I'm speaking from experience.

"It's a little private and nonchalant, but that's what I like about it," Excel tells me. "I'm not really into the street shop thing with people looking in the window all the time."

With subtle precision, Excel is expanding his operation toward the spiritual realm. After tattooing for 25 years, he felt he needed something else.

"My tattoo clients, they don't come around just for tattoos anymore," he tells me. "They kind of come around for something a little bit deeper than that. I've become kind of a counselor in a sense. When we tattoo people, the conversation gets really deep, there's a release of pain, it becomes very meditative, and kind of like how acupuncture touches certain nerves, releases certain toxins. I think tattooing does that, too."

As a result, Excel introduces his crew to yoga, vegan diets and non-dualism on top of everything else. Speaking of which, the Bodhidharma Gallery in the room next door to Excel's room houses a Buddhist-inspired suite of businesses thanks to Stephanie Tate, a yoga and Vipassana meditation teacher with a deep SoCal punk rock heritage. Mom's Metta Browz is her microblading business, while Mom's Metta Balm is her brand of skin care products, metta being the Buddhist concept of loving kindness. In the same room, Demaree's art show takes place this Sunday.

Back in Excel's studio, I continue to bask in the cross-pollination of Buddhism, cholo art, punk rock and Victorian artifacts. Everything is connected, but alas, nothing in life is permanent.

"The Victorian mirrors and things like that go with the building because I was brought up in Victorian buildings," Excel says. "I was raised to move old antiques. My dad collected antiques, so I like to keep antiques around me. I don't really like new stuff all that much. I'm not an IKEA guy."

Saadat Hasan Manto at Cinequest

Writing by hand in Urdu, Saadat Hasan Manto (1912-1955) left a legacy that made him one of India's most celebrated literary troublemakers. With brutal clarity, he depicted the communal violence, paranoia and psychology of Partition—the blunder from which the country was born in 1947.

Next Tuesday, March 5, Cinequest opens its 2019 festival in soaring fashion, as the illustrious Nandita Das shows up in person to present her film about Manto's life, simply titled *Manto*, at 7:15pm.

Many of Manto's stories do not conform to creative writing teacher requirements in that they don't have a resolution, an obstacle to overcome or any dramatic transformation of the protagonist. They function more as sketches or vignettes, vividly rendering the despair, displacement and madness of the Partition era. And Manto spared no one.

In 1947, Great Britain arbitrarily carved up its South Asian territory into the separate nation-states of India and Pakistan, before escaping from the scene and unleashing one of the most violent mass migrations in human history. Anywhere between 10 and 15 million people were displaced and forced to leave their ancestral lands on a moment's notice after being peaceful neighbors for millennia. Countless neighborhoods disintegrated into communal murder, rape and mutilation, with Hindus, Sikhs and Muslims massacring each other, while refugees spent months migrating between the two newly constructed countries. At least one million people lost their lives, all of which exacerbated communal hatred and religious-based distrust, which Indian politicians still exploit to this day. Manto was one the first literary figures to convey the fear, trauma and overt violence caused by Partition, as the resulting chaos unfolded around him in real time.

Throughout his short life, Manto's stories resulted in him being tried on obscenity charges five times, yet he was acquitted every time. He also went to great lengths to introduce India to Western literature. He translated both Victor Hugo and Oscar Wilde into Urdu. He wrote essays, scripts, newspaper columns and radio plays.

In the film, the legendary Nawazuddin Siddiqui (*The Lunchbox*) plays the title role in masterful fashion. Although none of Siddiqui's previous screen roles resemble anything like Manto, Das wrote the film with him in mind. It was the right choice.

When it comes to craft, *Manto* features scenes from the author's own stories like "Ten Rupees," "Khol Do" and "Cold Meat," all seamlessly juxtaposed with his real-life struggles, which sadly disintegrated into chronic alcoholism amid his displacement in Pakistan. The gritty underside of Bombay had been his beloved milieu, much in the way that Los Angeles was Bukowski's or Raymond Chandler's milieu, but then after Partition, as a Muslim, he relocated to Pakistan, after which everything went downhill. He missed the cosmopolitan flair of Bombay and could not comprehend how men could be driven to target even their friends in the wake of Partition.

Throughout the film we get historical atmospherics of Bombay and Lahore, accurate to the times. It's not a biopic per se, but more like a four-year window into the time when Manto's world began to crumble. As his mental health deteriorates, he starts hallucinating and begins to identify more with the characters in his stories than the people close to him in real life. His own fiction becomes his reality.

As such, and I won't spoil it, we also get pieces of Manto's most famous story, "Toba Tek Singh," during which the geographic split resulting from Partition is grafted onto the dislocation of the main character's psyche. In the story, Hindu, Sikh and Muslim lunatics move between asylums in India and Pakistan, much like refugees migrating between countries. Geographic displacement blurs with mental displacement.

To this day, Manto's stories resonate across India because they predict with brute force the communal, religious, political and gender-based conflicts of a country still battling itself in many ways, with identity politics, caste and freedom of expression often degenerating into to polarized black-or-white discussion with no sense of reality whatsoever. (Sound familiar?) But his predicament, as an artist, resonates far beyond India. He held up a mirror to the violence, prejudice and xenophobia of his time, and often paid the price, both financially and mentally.

Tucson Salvage at Cinequest

Thanks to Cinequest, the gritty underbellies of Cincinnati and Tucson took over downtown San Jose, in the forms of Emilio Estevez and Brian Jabas Smith, whose films depicted the margins of society without exploitation or judgment.

First of all, a trailer opened up every Cinequest film this year, with a wise man declaring that everyone who journeys through the festival will expect the unexpected. At least for me, this is already a prime characteristic of Cinequest: The unexpected experience that emerges without any possible planning. Weird connections, either professional, artistic or just plain crazy always seem to occur. Serendipitous moments of synchronicity appear on both micro and macro levels, even in a stretch of less than 24 hours.

To wit, Emilio Estevez of *Repo Man* infamy brought his latest project to the California Theatre, a film he directed and wrote, a masterpiece of social activism in which he played the lead role, a movie simply titled, *The Public*. It was one of the top five I've ever seen at Cinequest. We witness a dead-on-accurate portrayal of what it's like to work in a major city public library, in terms of the various struggling loiterers and street people who call the building home. The film takes place in the Cincinnati Public Library and Estevez plays one of the managing librarians, who is also a recovering alcoholic and former street person. Not only does his film succeed at depicting homelessness without being exploitative or judgmental, Estevez also nails what it's like from the perspective of main branch librarians, who are far from being just "librarians." They are actually social workers, first responders, job search counselors, research assistants, de facto therapists and any number of professions rolled into one. They are not "sitting around reading books all day," as some barbarians tend to suggest.

In the film, the homeless patrons of the library refuse to leave at closing time, and in protest, they demand the building be converted into a shelter due to the subzero weather outside, thus forcing a stand-off between them and the police. Emilio's character takes the side of the homeless, yet we also get Christian Slater as the insidious mayor exploiting the scenario to get votes, Gabrielle Union as a clueless TV newscaster sensationalizing the story, and Alec Baldwin as the aging musclehead detective trying to run the crisis negotiations. The film nails all of the issues: homelessness, mental health, the importance of libraries and librarians, fake politicians, fake newscasters, and the role that books play in making the world better.

After watching parts of *The Public* for a second time, I segued down the street to the Martin Luther King Jr., Main Library, a building where, except for the overnight protest, San Jose's equivalent of Emilio's film unfolds on a daily basis. On the day in question, though, a Cinequest event with *Tucson Weekly* columnist Brian Jabas Smith took over a room on the second floor. Smith writes a column, "Tucson Salvage," about the gritty underside of his hometown, columns he's now compiled into a book of the same name. Via his writing, Smith explores and chronicles local stories of alienated people and places that society has simply forgotten—everyone from legless ex-cons to recovering junkies to mentally challenged boxers.

Brian's wife Maggie created a documentary short film based on his columns, which she screened at the event, but not before he read from a column titled, "Cops and Tweakers." During the event, a few people sauntered over from the computer area of the library and said they were in some sort of homeless or close-to-homeless situation. All implied they never get to tell their stories to empathetic listeners. Each one said he or she identified with those in Smith's film. A fantastic conversation then erupted, with some great back-and-forth taking place. Via this sequence of serendipitous moments, I could not have tuned in any better to the ignored, the forgotten and the unexpected. The two films filled me up with even more gratitude for what I still have in this crazed life.

This is why longtime regulars keep returning to Cinequest. They know. It's the poetic and random connections between people, places and events that make the experience worthwhile.

Mark Grey's Frankenstein in Brussels

In Brussels last week, SJSU School of Music alumnus Mark Grey debuted his first full-length opera, a work based on Mary Shelley's novel *Frankenstein; or, The Modern Prometheus*. Over six years in the making and running two hours and 40 minutes, the opera completed a nearly sold-out run of eight performances at La Monnaie, Belgium's federal opera house. Originally slotted for 2016, the production was put back a few years due to renovations of the La Monnaie building.

The afternoon matinee on Sunday, March 17, felt particularly historical because three other School of Music alumni and former classmates of Grey's from the same era, but now living in three different countries, all descended upon the performance. Of course, yours truly was one of them, so allow me to disclose that Grey and I are old friends. We spent many months carrying on about 20th-century music at San Jose's House of Siam restaurant back in the mid-'90s.

Last week, Grey's *Frankenstein* received significant press coverage in several languages, including French, Dutch, Italian, Spanish and German, with Grey mentioning in every interview that Allen Strange, one of his musical mentors at SJSU, instilled in him an avant-garde spirit from the outset. The lengthy program booklet even included an essay about Grey's work, written by Charles Shafaieh, citing Grey's youth in Palo Alto and how he grew up alongside the technology industry taking over the valley, the dynamics of which became part of his American identity. Shafaieh even writes that the white noise and sounds of machinery Grey utilized at the opening of the opera were salutes to industrial noise acts like Merzbow and Nurse With Wound.

However, the traditionally orchestrated music Grey employed throughout the work was quite accessible and filled with color, steering the capacity crowds through a matrix of emotions from beginning to end. Collaborating with librettist Julia Canosa i Serra, he scored the work with several operatic luminaries in mind, including baritone Scott Hendricks, who played Victor Frankenstein, and tenor Topi Lehtipuu, who played the creature.

Factor in the talents of director Alex Olle of the Catalan collective La Fura dels Baus, and the Frankenstein production was a multimedia feast of dystopian bleakness at its finest. Set in the Arctic region 200 years from now, in a bizarre existence where everyone is bald, as if a colony of Buddhist monks were extracted from a botched cryonics experiment, the production utilized elaborate sci-fi settings, disregarding any stereotypes of the Hollywood Frankenstein and instead returning to the issues Shelley's novel originally explored—abandonment, isolation, self-loathing, guilt and sacrifice, with updated concerns about technology's role in society. Various video projections appeared on scrims that draped down to the stage, producing complicated visual environments that won't easily be replicated in any podunk opera house. The costumes were similarly intriguing projects. In Lehtipuu's case, it took over an hour to apply the makeup and body modifications each night.

One of the heralded opera houses of Europe, La Monnaie played a role in the Belgian Revolution of 1830, with aspiring rioters spilling out from an opera to help launch the uprising. La Monnaie also includes a separate six-story neoclassical structure housing all the ateliers and workshops. Rehearsal spaces for the singers and the orchestra accommodate a few hundred audience members. Other floors feature expansive metalworking and carpentry shops, plus a full-blown set construction workshop using the same dimensions as the stage. On the fifth floor, costume shops produce every single piece of clothing from scratch, all the way down to employing old-school bespoke shoemakers. Every person involved with the production can thus see what everyone else is working on, therefore streamlining the process, rather than having the set designers, costume designers and musicians putting the show together in separate places all over town. It's an enormous operation with 400 regular employees, notwithstanding an additional combined 800 that might show up all year to work on each particular production.

When it comes to modern-day opera, an insurrectionist spirit certainly emerged last week. Thanks to Grey, the SJSU School of Music can now claim a handful of its own alumni converged upon La Monnaie in the footsteps of the Belgian Revolution. The rest is history.

With Thierry Amsallem at the Montreux Jazz Archives

Last week, Thierry Amsallem laughed out loud while telling numerous stories about the Montreux Jazz Festival. When he gave me a tour of the Montreux Jazz digital archives on the campus of the Swiss Federal Institute of Technology in Lausanne (EPFL), his laughter evoked a true passion for all things Montreux and all things music.

"Montreux is a live recording studio with an audience," Amsallem said, emphasizing how the festival has regularly pioneered advances in audio and video recording technology. Claude Nobs launched the festival in 1967. Amsallem came on board 20 years later while still in grad school.

As he continued to tell stories, a mystical coincidence soon emerged. Neither I nor the fixers arranging our interview knew that Amsallem was among those who presented Apple Quicktime 1.0 at the San Jose Convention Center in 1991. His group helped test Quicktime by using it for a Montreux Jazz kiosk project. Similarly, Amsallem did not know in advance that I was from San Jose. Synchronicity thus drove my experience, as is often the case when I visit Switzerland. Carl Gustav Jung would be proud.

Nobs started the festival to promote a resort village on the shores of Lake Geneva, unaware that it would explode into one of the most iconic musical ecosystems on earth, resonating far beyond jazz or Switzerland. Montreux was the first live concert environment to utilize multitrack audio recording (1973), hi-def video (1991), 3D video (2010) and 4K (2012) before those technologies went mainstream.

Today, 28 years after Amsallem helped beta test Quicktime 1.0 at Montreux, he remains a part of the ecosystem, helping oversee the Montreux Jazz Digital Project, the most ambitious plan to preserve music I've ever seen. As of today, something like 11,000 hours of video recordings, 6,000 hours of high-quality audio and 80,000 photos have been digitally preserved since the project began in 2010.

"In 1967 people asked Nobs, 'Why record with video? Music is just for your ears,'" Amsallem told me with a laugh. "Even today I have people laughing at what we're doing."

Following Nobs' passing in 2013, Amsallem created the Claude Nobs

Foundation in order to sustain his legacy and continue the digital project. At that time, the archives were recognized by UNESCO and inscribed in its "Memory of the World" registry.

"UNESCO came with Obama's help," Amsallem said. "He really wanted to preserve jazz. And Hillary wrote a letter."

He then opened up the back of the server cabinets, a must-see for any tech geek. To store 50 years' worth of concerts, five petabytes on three server racks are cooled by water from Lake Geneva. Dozens of fans are also piled up, eight feet high, along the backs of the servers.

"It's noisy and consumes energy, but we want to keep the archive alive," Amsallem said, laughing. "This is how we keep it alive."

We then moved through even more areas off limits to the general public, spaces where EPFL students and researchers work on the archives. From here, audio and video are streamed to a handful of chic Montreux Jazz Cafes in places from Paris to Abu Dhabi, where patrons can literally scroll through 50 years of concert footage. Other researchers are working on various projects including an interactive 3D family tree allowing anyone to see which musicians jammed with who else over the last half century at Montreux. Also in the works is an autonomous vehicle prototype that supplies concert acoustics and video footage, transporting the cafe experience into a car.

"If you're not driving, what else are you going to do?" said Amsallem, laughing. "Watch concerts."

Later, over espressos in the Montreux Jazz Cafe on the EPFL campus, Amsallem told the story of the legendary "Swiss Movement" live LP that Les McCann and Eddie Harris recorded at Montreux in 1969. Ahmet Ertegun of Atlantic Records bought the tapes for pocket change and the LP sold millions, putting Montreux on the live recording map.

"It was great promotion for Montreux," Amsallem said. "A world of artists then wanted to play here. Now bands want to come here to be a part of UNESCO."

A Tramp Through Chaplin's World, From San Jose to Switzerland

In 1915, when Charlie Chaplin made his short film *A Night Out*, the Tramp's exploits included some footage in downtown San Jose, at the Alcantara building, the red brick structure at Post and Market streets. It wasn't Chaplin's only appearance in this neck of the woods, of course. Some 20 years later, Chaplin would also visit his good friend John Steinbeck, while the author was writing *The Grapes of Wrath* in Los Gatos.

This means without even leaving my own neighborhoods I can walk in the Tramp's footsteps. Yet this wasn't enough. It's never enough. So, last month, it was time to "expand my outreach," as the power-networking gurus say, and go straight to the source: Chaplin's World, a museum unlike

371

anything I've ever visited, in Corsier-sur-Vevey, Switzerland, on the property where Chaplin lived the last 25 years of his life before passing away on Christmas night 1977.

Inside Chaplin's World, one of the text panels gave me the best description of this column that I have ever read: "The Tramp is the eternal wanderer, at home on both country roads and in city streets. On his travels ... he mixes with all levels of society and has met thieves, drunks, fake pastors, penniless girls, insolent kids, street vendors, factory workers and the cream of society."

But there was so much more. Upon entry to Chaplin's World, one first sits in a small theater to watch a short film about Chaplin's life, after which the screen rises, allowing one to enter a mock London street environment, emulating where he grew up, with scenes from *The Kid* playing behind windows. The rest of the museum emerges in similar fashion, modeled like a series of film studios, with space after space resembling scenes from films like *Gold Rush, The Circus, Modern Times, The Floorwalker, The Great Dictator* or *The Bank*, while film montages play on screens. Text panels explain various stories behind the films, and viewers thus immerse themselves in Chaplin's World, so to speak.

The museum occupies one structure, while the second building, Manoir le Ban, where the family actually lived, is likewise transformed into a multistory exhibit space, filled up with even more photographs, exhibits, facts, figures and timelines. It is here that a wall-size multimedia display lets you click through portraits of all the 20th-century figures Chaplin befriended—everyone from Einstein to Gandhi. There's also a restaurant, aptly called The Tramp, with an old-school Hollywood vibe. It all sits on Chaplin's original 10-acre estate with amazing views of Lake Geneva and the Alps.

Of course, there's a dark side. During the McCarthyism era, Chaplin was banned from living in the United States by the conservative slobs in charge, who considered his lifelong sympathy for working class people, humanitarians and pacifism to be unpatriotic and worthy of investigation. With his family in 1952, Chaplin was aboard the Queen Elizabeth from New York to London, en route to attend the premiere of his film, *Limelight*, when the barbarians in DC revoked his return visa. After essentially building the American film industry, and living and working in the US for 40 years, he was no longer allowed to do so. To some, Chaplin was an ungrateful immigrant—an insult that slobs often hurl at various targets even today. As a result, Chaplin relocated his whole family to Switzerland, where he lived what, according to him, were his best years.

Later, Chaplin was knighted by Queen Elizabeth II in 1975. Six of his films are preserved at the National Film Registry of the Library of Congress, and to this day he holds the record for the longest standing ovation at an Oscar ceremony, at 12 minutes.

After spending time in Chaplin's World, one can even wander through the quaint village of Corsier, past markets, restaurants and theaters he frequented, and even follow placards to his gravesite. His last wife, Oona, who gave birth to eight of his kids and who died in 1991, is buried right next to him.

Standing there at the graves of Charlie and Oona, I felt nothing but gratitude for San Jose, California. At least the city hasn't thrown me out. Yet.

San Jose Theme Songs and Domei Suzuki's 1974 Tune

As part of the city of San Jose's Creative License Ambassador program, Maestra Barbara Day Turner of the San Jose Chamber Orchestra is curating a concert of original 60-second songs about San Jose, written by community members, all to be performed at City Hall on June 21. Anyone can write a song and submit it for consideration.

As part of the performances, in addition to the one-minute songs, there will be audience participation and other community crowd-sourced composition projects right there and then.

There might be some ringers, of course, which is why I'm hoping Turner resurrects the greatest song ever written about San Jose. No, I'm not talking about the Dionne Warwick abomination, the nauseating tune that even she dislikes. I am talking about a '70s jazz-rock masterpiece by the famous Japanese pop composer, Domei Suzuki (1920-2015), titled, "Yes, I Know the Way to San Jose."

Suzuki first came to San Jose in 1961. In Tokyo, he was known for producing his own hits or Japanese versions of songs by Brenda Lee and Vikki Carr. After numerous visits to the Bay Area, Suzuki fell in love with San Jose and wrote the song in 1974, with English lyrics by Tom and Cathy Clark, who were living in Tokyo. The 45 RPM single features a sweeping cover photo of '70s-era San Jose with orchards in the foreground, looking down on the valley below. Inside the single, one finds the sheet music reduction for voice and piano, as well as the lyrics. The liner notes relay Suzuki's story in his own words:

"Leaving Japan, the first place I saw on the mainland was San Francisco," he writes. "It was at night, and I shall never forget the beauty of the night scene from the plane that greeted me. I was met at the airport by my uncle and cousins, who took me straight to San Jose. I was to stay for two weeks with my uncle and his family, during which time we drove to San Francisco, Monterey, Pebble Beach, the mission at Carmel, and so on. The impression I received remains fresh in my mind. I became very fond of California. Before I knew it, I fell into the habit, like a migratory bird, of visiting San Jose at least once a year."

After making several close friends in San Jose and spending much time here, Suzuki finally made good on his promise to write a tune about the city. The intro to "Yes, I Know the Way to San Jose" sounds like something straight from *The Rockford Files*, but then it breaks into a grooving minor-key jazz-rock arrangement replete with a horn section, electric guitar, bass, trap set and swanky English language vocals by the late Tokyo chanteuse Hatsumi Shibata. The late Japanese producer Norio Maeda arranged the orchestra and recorded the track in Tokyo.

In 1976, San Jose held several events celebrating the US Bicentennial, including a multi-day jazz fair with a residency by Quincy Jones, who conducted Suzuki's tune, which was also chosen as the theme song for the San Jose City Bicentennial (1777-1977). Suzuki loved San Jose so much that he donated 14,000 of the records to the city's bicentennial commission. History San Jose still has a few copies in its archives, but otherwise you'll have to scour the antique shops on San Carlos Street or places like Needle to the Groove to even possibly track down a copy.

Upon any new listen, especially if you're a native, it's one of those, "why is this track not regularly performed" type of experiences. That a renowned Japanese jazz and easy listening giant could come here and reap enough rocking inspiration to write a song should inspire anyone else to write his or her own tune and submit it to maestra Turner's project, plain and simple. She is a genius for having this idea.

Speaking of which, at presstime a dozen artists had already submitted a tune or committed to write something. Even better, San Jose's own Jackie Gage will show up and perform her tune, "A Secret Place," written and debuted last year at the San Jose Jazz Summerfest. It doesn't get any more local than that.

Anthony Bourdain, RIP

One year ago this Saturday, we were dining on a tiny island near Grado, Italy, when we heard the news that Anthony Bourdain had passed away. It happened all of a sudden.

At the northern fringe of the Adriatic Sea, we had sailed up to a petite forested island in a small skipper boat just after lunchtime on June 8 to visit Fiuri de Tapo, an outdoor seafood restaurant. Nothing else was on the island except the restaurant and the proprietor's house, all reachable by sailing through a lagoon from the touristy hotspot of Grado, an island community two miles away. Fiuri de Tapo translates to "Flowers of Cork," after a lavender flower that blooms all over these scattered islands.

As we ventured into the outdoor seating areas, remnants of a tempest-like storm earlier in the morning dropped sporadic blankets of drizzle from the sky. Due to the weather, our group had been the only ones on the water and we were likewise now the only people in the restaurant. We were the lunch rush. Numerous picnic tables of yellow, green and blue sat empty. Their umbrellas were closed up and tied down with rope. Wind-blown leaves and twigs, plus a few trails of mud footprints complemented the overcast skies.

Within moments, the proprietor emerged from the kitchen wearing a black scarf over his head, a sweatshirt with the sleeves cut off, and a pair of blue shorts. Andrea Barchiesi was a Shakespearean "mine host," jubilant and full of life when talking about the business he built from scratch with his bare hands. He built the restaurant and even constructed a fish farm. He and his family live on the island during the high-season summer months.

As we sat down to plow through bowls of seafood soup that Barchiesi also made from scratch, a family of swallows chirped away in a nest above our table, right where the side of the building met the overhang. The birds circled in and out of the scene, on the lookout for any mosquitoes that might ruin our meal.

A menagerie of clams, mussels, crayfish and other amazing dead things I couldn't identify all floated in the soup, along with fresh sourdough bread that soaked up the bronze liquid in slow masterful fashion. Two bowls did me in.

Then we heard the news that Anthony Bourdain had committed suicide. A person in our group found out by scrolling through some notifications on his phone. Two or three of us, maybe four, responded with words like: "Huh?" "What?" "You sure?"

Silence then occurred for several seconds. Only the swallows continued to chirp.

If there ever existed a tribe to which I belonged, Bourdain was its leader. No one else would walk through the jungles of Vietnam wearing a Ramones shirt. He was one of my heroes, a travel writer of the underbelly, an international anti-man-about-town opening up the underside of the world for millions of fans—exactly the type of dream I only imagined when I first started writing 20 years ago, back when I longed to escape what was then a more bland version of San Jose. I never achieved that dream, and even today, with any type of writing life hardly lucrative to say the least, it's easy to give up. Now here was Bourdain, a renowned punk celebrity with an empathetic conscience to elevate stories of underrepresented people around the world—a dude with everything I ever wanted—and yet he still gave up.

So I walked out to the edge of the property and stared at the lagoon. The water looked glassy and eternal. The sky was clear and the storm was moving far away. No matter who died, the Adriatic Sea would always be here.

Knowing that Bourdain would have loved Fiuri de Tapo, I owed it to him to spread the word and I owed it to Anthony to carry on. I couldn't quit writing, no matter how miserable life became. Bourdain was up there, down there or somewhere, cheering me on. Others remembered where they were when JFK, Elvis or Joey Ramone died. I'd now forever recall Fiuri de Tapo as where I learned Anthony Bourdain had passed away.

Ted Gehrke and U2 at SJSU

This Saturday, the 38th Annual San Jose Fountain Blues & Brews Festival unfolds in Plaza de Cesar Chavez, once again cementing the festival's position as the longest running affair of its kind in the Bay Area.

The history is worth repeating. The birth of the festival takes us back to a version of San Jose that now seems like the vanishing Wild West, when the SJSU Associated Students Program Board oversaw a serious budget to book concerts on campus all year long. It also harkens back to a time when notorious rock promoter Bill Graham was still trying to prevent anything in San Jose from succeeding.

When a young Rick Bates first emigrated from Iowa to the Associated Students at SJSU, he hit up Ted Gehrke for a job. Gehrke assigned Bates to put up concert posters around town, but Gates eventually wound up with the title of contemporary arts chair, meaning he worked with Gehrke to book concerts.

In the spring of 1981, the prog rock band Ambrosia had just fired its manager and agent, so the group needed a gig. Working for the Associated Students, Bates booked them in the San Jose Civic Auditorium. The show sold out, giving the program board a pile of dough with which they organized the first Fountain Blues Festival, over the first weekend in May of that year.

These days, when students don't get to experience a live music infrastructure of any sort, let alone getting on the phone with national booking agencies, it seems hard to fathom a San Jose in which such activity unfolded on a regular basis. In the late '70s, for example, Bates helped book a Peter Gabriel show in the old SJSU men's gym, located in what's now Uchida Hall. Bill Graham called up Bates and tried to stop the show because Graham wanted exclusivity in San Francisco.

"At that time I was 20 years old, and he starts screaming at me," Bates recalled. "I'm a snotty little kid, and I'm going, 'Hey this is pretty cool. I must be doing something right. Bill Graham's calling me up and yelling at me.' I thought it was really pretty funny. We did another show with U2, and he did the same thing."

The U2 show, with Romeo Void opening up, is now one of the most legendary stories in San Jose rock history. On the Irish band's first US tour in 1981, Bates and Gehrke initially booked them to play a free show in the outdoor concrete amphitheater next to the Student Union. Bill Graham tried to stop the show because he wanted U2's first Bay Area gig to be at the Old Waldorf, scheduled for the next night in San Francisco. Despite Graham's threats, the free U2 show in San Jose went on. However, once it was booked and word began to explode, it was relocated upstairs into the old Student Union Ballroom, which is now a suite of antiseptic meeting facilities. Since the Brutalist-style Student Union structure was built on earthquake rollers, the over-capacity crowds po-go-dancing began to shake the building. Staff stood on both sides of the stage with ropes to prevent the speaker columns from falling over. At one point, Romeo Void's tour manager got stuck in the elevator. People were scared.

According to those who attended, even with the stage verging on collapse, the young Bono was already on a path to rock stardom. He knew how to command an audience and work a room. The show was a smashing success.

Bates went on to manage several well-known blues and roots acts, including Los Lobos, who ended up opening for U2 on the Joshua Tree tour, putting Bates back in touch with Bono. At the time, Bono still remembered the harrowing SJSU gig.

When it comes to the Fountain Blues Festival, Bates speaks fondly of the original days. At the time, it just felt like a cool project for some students to work on.

"I always feel like sometimes things are just at the right place at the right time," Bates said. "Everybody wanted to do it, and it was really successful. I never thought that it would last as long as it has."

Vietnamese Buddhist churches in far flung corners of San Jose

I went looking for Vietnamese Buddhist churches in East San Jose and found some forgotten pieces of San Fernando Street in the process. It began with a long lost text resurfacing at just the right time.

In 2002, San Jose resident Huu Do Le published *Sounds of the Bamboo Forest: Buddhist Churches of America in the Vietnamese Tradition*. A review copy showed up at Metro, and apparently I took it home with the intention of reviewing the book and then forgot about it. I have no memory of this, but after some recent domestic reorganization, I rediscovered the book. At least according to the Tibetan tradition, sometimes a key text is buried and stored away for a later date, like a time capsule, with the intention of resurfacing at the opportune karmic moment. Now is that moment.

Sounds of the Bamboo Forest features essays and exhaustive research on how the Vietnamese diaspora gradually established a Buddhist presence in the U.S., especially in California. The sections on San Jose include photos and histories of various temples in obscure residential pockets of the East Side that no one ever visits. The reader takes away important stories of how the diaspora struggled to get a foothold in swaths of suburbia that didn't always want them, often having to relocate their temples to other parts of town. Le came to San Jose in 1990 and also served as executive editor of Viet News from 1993 to 1998.

But this is not a book review. Instead, I took to the street on a Lyft bike with Le's book in the basket and went searching for the structures he wrote about. In the process I discovered additional Vietnamese temples by sheer accident. Since the book is 17 years old, many more temples have emerged since it was published. The whole adventure brought to mind numerous columns I wrote years ago in which I explored various pockets of old San Jose that no one cares about. This time, using the growth of the Vietnamese Buddhist community as a lens, I got yet another glimpse into how the city evolved over the decades, especially how various neighborhoods were annexed, cobbled together or broken up by freeways over time. This was much more fun than any San Jose tourism website.

The popular An Lac Temple, for example, sits at the corner of 34th and San Fernando streets. I'd bet most of the giddy downtown boosters have never ventured past 10th Street and thus don't even realize the intersection exists. Decades ago, this building was a residential Christian church before it was purchased and transformed into the elaborate Buddhist temple it is today. In the book, Le includes a photo of what the building looked like in 2002. It was much different.

Continuing eastward from An Lac, one can eventually discover Foss Avenue, a tiny dead-end street that follows the edge of Highway 680, going south from Alum Rock Avenue. On this short stretch of road, the Duyen Giac Buddhist Center occupies a nondescript solid brown building behind a six-foot fence. No signage exists until one turns down an unmarked cul-de-sac to see a placard at the back. No one would possibly notice the place, but *Sounds of the Bamboo Forest* mentions this organization, established in 1990. It turns out the unmarked cul-de-sac is a leftover piece of San Fernando Street from 50 years ago.

Heading back toward downtown, at 766 S. Second St., one finds the Tinh Xa Ngoc Hoa temple, likewise right in the middle of a residential block. The temple moved onto this property in 1993, after its previous location in the east hills received numerous complaints from neighbors. It's a huge two-story facility with a basement, an eat-in kitchen, a parking lot, monk's quarters and a youth facility.

In the process of riding from temple to temple, I segued down 22nd Street and by sheer chance discovered Chua Quang Duc, the Congregation of A Thousand Eyes Buddhist Temple. I didn't even have to look. It was right there waiting for me, as were other temples off Story, Tully, McLaughlin and White roads.

Who needs $4,000 temple tours in faraway countries? We got it all right here.

Dorthaan Kirk at Cafe Stritch

Dorthaan Kirk, the grand matriarch of the annual Rahsaanathon at San Jose's Cafe Stritch every August, was recently the recipient of a National Endowment for the Arts Jazz Masters Fellowship, the highest accolade our nation bestows upon jazz artists.

Each year since 1982, the program has recognized a select number of living legends whose exceptional contributions to jazz have made the USA a better place. Dorthaan was given a fellowship alongside Bobby McFerrin, Roscoe Mitchell and Reggie Workman to complete the 2020 class. In Dorthaan's case, she was awarded the A.B. Spellman NEA Jazz Masters Fellowship for Jazz Advocacy.

Dorthaan is the widow of Rahsaan Roland Kirk, the cosmic patron saint whose music, energy and spirit propel Cafe Stritch through thick and thin. This weekend will be the seventh annual Rahsaanathon and the seventh time Dorthaan has flown out from New Jersey to attend. She considers San Jose to be one of her extended families, so we got to talking.

When Stritch launched the first Rahsaan tribute gigs in August 2013, no one, especially Dorthaan, knew it would turn into an annual party, with Rahsaan's former bandmate Steve Turre flying in every year.

"It's created new listeners of Rahsaan, and exposed his music to people that probably, maybe in that area, never would've discovered him," Dorthaan told me. "Also, it brought out people who actually saw him in the Bay Area many, many years ago. So because of that, it's kept his music and spirit alive. And I'm sure a lot of people have discovered who Steve Turre is, who's kept [Rahsaan's] music alive for 40 years."

Over the last seven years, Turre has recruited some of the best players to re-create the spirit of Rahsaan at Cafe Stritch. When Dorthaan first showed up in 2013, she was skeptical. But they convinced her.

"I was very nervous the first year because Steve was using the West Coast musicians, and I didn't know them," said Dorthaan. "I was frankly nervous that they were going to be able to play [Rahsaan's] music as I know it should be played. Even though Steve had sent them the music ahead, they didn't have a lot of time to rehearse. I remember coming into the club that first time and saying, 'All right, you all better get it right.' I just kind of slyly said that. But I was amazed, really amazed, at how they nailed his music."

What's different nowadays—for good or bad—is that the Rahsaanathon no longer erupts during the San Jose Jazz Summerfest. For the few years it did, Stritch became the prime gathering joint where other living legends would show up or sit in, following their gigs elsewhere at the festival. In 2015, for example, jazz-rock fusion guitar hero Larry Coryell played a gig at the California Theatre and then afterward showed up at Stritch, where Steve Turre even acknowledged him from the stage. Sadly, we never saw him again, as Coryell passed away in 2017.

Another year, Dorthaan and I were sitting outside Cafe Stritch when Latin jazz trumpeter Jerry Gonzalez, likewise a living legend, just happened to come sauntering over. Within seconds, he and Dorthaan got to talking, the conversation spinning through 40 years' worth of stories and memories. Everyone knows Dorthaan. Sadly, Gonzalez died in a tragic house fire last year.

Rahsaan's music, though, has not passed away. His spirit will forever inhabit 374 S. First St.

"I'm amazed, because Rahsaan's been dead over 40 years, and his music still goes on," Dorthaan said. "And I don't know any musician—Sue Mingus was doing something, and there's always some activity around T. S. Monk—but there's not a lot of musicians who are no longer with us whose music is still being perpetuated as Rahsaan's is. So it's all good."

NEA fellowships aside, the Rahsaanathon remains an event that diehard fans look forward to every year, both Stritch regulars and those on the periphery.

"It is truly a bright moment, what they've done there," Dorthaan said. "Their dedication and support of Rahsaan and his music is kind of overwhelming, and I applaud them for continuing to do this event."

Emporium's 'Big E' is Being Restored to Landmark Status

One day Ted Ramos was traveling south down Monterey Road—the Champs-Elysees of San Jose's underbelly—when he spotted a faded masterpiece wasting away in a storage yard near the intersection of Live Oak Road.

At first, he thought he'd seen the "Big W," as in the film, *It's a Mad, Mad, Mad, Mad World*, but upon closer inspection, it was the "Big E" from The Emporium, the long-defunct department store at Almaden Fashion Plaza. Someone had saved the 'E' after the Emporium chain went out of business in 1996. The sign was rusty, some of the plexiglass was cracked and pieces were missing, but it was recognizable. And salvageable.

"When I looked through the little broken pieces, I could still see the neon tubing inside," said Ramos. "I was able to get a real close look at it because it was leaning up against the chain link fence from the other side. ... It looked like it had been weathered. ... But I was surprised that a lot of the plastic covering was still there. I figured that that would be all broken off, so it was a good thing to see."

His timing was perfect. Ramos' discovery of the Big E occurred soon after Heather David helped launch the San Jose Signs Project to preserve our celebrated mid-century signage, as other reputable grown-up cities across North America have similarly done. Ramos contacted David, who in turn relayed him to the epic storage facilities at History San Jose, where the Big E now sits, waiting for the next stage of restoration.

"I was willing to rent a truck myself if I had to, to get that thing transported over to History San Jose," Ramos said. "Because at that time, I wanted that thing saved."

The Emporium chain started in San Francisco in 1896. The flagship store on Market Street was a neoclassical city landmark and one of the original grand dames of West Coast retail shopping. Later, as the post-WWII suburbanization of America began to cannibalize the landscape, so did suburban shopping malls, which were often anchored by huge department stores like the Emporium and its famous Big E branding scheme. Everyone knew that 'E.'

As The Emporium continued to expand in the late '60s, it built Almaden Fashion Plaza on several dozen acres of land at Blossom Hill Road and Almaden Expressway, which was then surrounded by orchards and not much else. By the late '70s, the plaza had 52 tenants and parking spaces for 2,573 cars. In particular, this columnist grew up inside Waldenbooks and Reik's Music, a locally owned instrument retailer.

Unfortunately, The Emporium was bought out in the mid-'90s, right as Highway 85 began to emerge. Costco then opened across the parking lot, practically saving the whole complex from sheer desolation. What used to be The Emporium building is now Bed, Bath & Beyond, Diddums and buybuy BABY, although it still looks relatively similar on the outside.

Almaden Fashion Plaza was shortened to just Almaden Plaza decades ago, yet many still call it by the original name. These days, the interior open-air part of the complex looks almost exactly the same as it did 40 years ago. The same cream-colored cement trappings remain. The same brickwork patterns appear in the walkways. If you know where to look, you can see the label scar where the original Big E used to be.

Thanks to Ted Ramos, that E now is saved at History San Jose, awaiting its next reincarnation. With the recent heroic restoration of the Stephens Meat Products dancing pig sign, as well as the return of the OSH sign, maybe someone can hatch a scheme to do something.

"I've always had an interest in neon signs ever since I was a kid," Ramos said, adding that the Neon Museum in Las Vegas helped inspire him to contribute what he could locally. "When I saw all these neon signs in San Jose, I was saying, 'I wish they had something to preserve these things.' And then when I saw the San Jose Signs Project, I was like, 'Oh, awesome. I'm not the only one.'"

The Demise of NextSpace San Jose

As of this Saturday, NextSpace Coworking in downtown San Jose will bite the dust, putting an end to eight years of authentic community building. I say "community" because at NextSpace, that word meant more than anything.

NextSpace first opened in Santa Cruz in 2008, then added spaces in LA, San Francisco, San Jose and Berkeley, pioneering the concept of co-working in its original form, years before that term was culturally appropriated by shiny obnoxious companies like WeWork and thus transformed into a ludicrous buzzword.

When NextSpace started, it exemplified an idealistic if not utopian dream to unite disparate demographics so they could feed off each other, support one another, collaborate, swap professional ideas or simply find common life hacks. It was all about community. A food entrepreneur could collaborate with programmers, while a fledgling roboticist might pool resources with a UX designer. If your startup didn't need a whole office, you could rent a small corner and maybe even discover other people at NextSpace who wanted to join your team. Freelancers of any sort could roll in with a day pass and make new friends or potential clients in the process. The community manager functioned as a human connection machine, the glue that fused everyone together.

In San Jose's case, the NextSpace office in its original state didn't feel or look like anything else downtown, making it a refreshing place to hang. Even though most of the co-workers were tech-related, the vibe was nothing resembling bro culture. Beginning in 2011, the atmosphere was intentionally informal, bohemian and goofy. Orange and blue color schemes abounded. Beautifully incongruous couches, carpeting and homemade wooden tables highlighted the open spaces. Artwork by neighborhood artists graced the walls. Local non-profits rented spaces, classical musicians played during happy hours, female coding groups held meetings and disgruntled city employees dropped in to spill all the gossip.

On any given day, one became privy to financial advice presentations, entrepreneurial classes, artisan coffee tastings and numerous partnerships with local establishments. Everyone in the downtown business community either floated through to say hello or at least knew someone at NextSpace because there was no other joint like it. Former members always stopped in when they came back through town. This was precisely the point: community. It had nothing whatsoever to do with obnoxious corporate monoculture.

Unfortunately, as is the case with many freewheeling idealistic schemes in downtown San Jose, obnoxious corporate monoculture eventually won. With the rise of squeaky clean bastions of pretense like WeWork and the generation of culturally illiterate techies who love them, NextSpace wasn't making any real money, anywhere. A few years ago, the company was circling the drain for the last time when a sterile syndicate of bean counters named Pacific Workplaces saved it from certain death.

While the Santa Cruz and Berkeley offices still embody some of the original NextSpace spirit, such was never the case with San Jose after Pacific Workplaces took over. In my view, they ruined the color scheme and the goofy accoutrements by making everything gray and beige. They dumbed down the work culture, stripped away all the personality, crushed the vibe, disregarded the community manager and squandered all the goodwill established by NextSpace. It was sad and depressing to witness.

So, to reminisce and bid each other adieu, NextSpacers threw a tear-jerking final party inside the San Jose office last week. Former members from years ago stopped in and said their farewells. Food and drink overflowed. Stories came out of the woodwork. There was nothing but love in the room.

In contrast—and perhaps this is the closing irony of it all—at the same time, right up the block, a vacuous fabricated pop-up space called Backyard SJ, one of the most obnoxious flauntings of corporate artifice to hit downtown in recent memory, was duping everyone into giddy states of faux-urban euphoria. Somewhere between a phony trade-show-floor environment and a bad hipster patio bar transplanted onto a parking lot, the space featured big ugly cardboard cylinders and wood chips all over the ground, as if someone went dumpster diving outside the set of Hee Haw. BackYard SJ comes to us from—you guessed it—WeWork.

The Urban Blight Junkie Hits Spartan-Keyes

Years ago, the Urban Blight Exploration Junkie often relapsed on this very page, reporting from crumbling eyesores like Hacienda Gardens Shopping Center, the industrial wreckage of Stockton Avenue or the aromatic tire-shop wonderland of Keyes Street.

In the latter case, the junkie last explored this thoroughfare 10 years ago, but failed to elaborate on the cross streets that link this stretch of underbelly all the way to downtown. So allow me to rectify this predicament immediately.

First, some background: At least 20 years ago, the city was already drawing up philosophical schemes to expand and gentrify the downtown core southward down First Street and westward along San Carlos, some of which is now starting to happen. Meaning, the next few years might provide the last opportunity to explore the gloriously incongruous neighborhoods between 280 and the celebrated Burger Bar roadside masterpiece at First and Keyes. I'm mostly talking about the leftover commerce along First and Second streets, but any such journey also includes glorious tentacles of decaying industry that expand outward from those streets.

This whole part of town might seem like blighted throwaway trash to any high-falutin' real estate crook, but it exudes more character than any other neighborhood near downtown. Every facade is totally different, a throwback to the days when street level retail was still interesting to look at— that is, before the city started foisting all this homogenized faux-luxury crud on the rest of us.

Although a casual drive-by might suffice, any legit exploration of the area must be done on foot. You need to slither in, around and between the wreckage.

Of course, there are ghosts, or *djinns*, as the Sufi mystics might suggest. In this neighborhood, the physical and the temporal aspects of San Jose seem to merge, as old buildings—just like spirits—often appear out of nowhere, even after the real estate crooks have attempted to gentrify them out of the way.

Fifty years ago, for example, the legendary bar and restaurant, Arturo's Quiet Village, occupied the building still standing at 950 S. First St.

In recent years, the building housed T&T Aquarium and Koi Pond. Two distinct and truly wondrous crumbling old signs—one on First Street, the other at the back entrance on Second Street—provide all the intrigue you need to get started. On each sign, pieces of Quiet Village still peek through from half a century ago, while the more recent layers designating the aquarium are likewise decaying with the wind. Those two signs, together, are a microcosm of the whole neighborhood. They refuse to die.

Right next door, at 940 S. First, one finds Bruce Barton Pump Service, a family business going back nearly a century in the same building. You don't often find this stuff in San Jose.

In this neighborhood, everything crashes into everything else. Furniture stores fade into humble Mexican eateries. Rusted barbed-wire and cracked parking lots accompany businesses you wouldn't notice unless you went looking for them. Industrial yards left over from decades ago still remain, even as hipster breweries encroach down the block. In places, knee-high weeds rise from ruptured parking strips and Banda music blasts from car stereo installers. A yoga studio, a vaping place or a Vietnamese-owned auto repair business might appear, again, seemingly out of nowhere. And tire shops are ubiquitous. Just walking the sun-baked streets, you can smell rubber from the tire shops, motor oil, marijuana smoke and amazing carnitas cooking at some unidentifiable place.

Unfortunately, there's always a dark side to these journeys. These areas can be dicey at nighttime. On certain corners, low-rent hookers lobby the downtrodden johns of the underworld. Back alleys, while supposedly cleaned up over the last decade, still occasionally recall the dismal drug-addled character of downtown in the '80s.

What does it all mean? I'll tell you. As soon as the real estate syndicates succeed in gentrifying the downtown core with overpriced restaurants, banks and ping pong tables, the ignored-for-decades street riffraff will seek refuge near First and Keyes instead. That's right—First and Keyes might be the new First and Santa Clara in about 10 years. Chalk it up to progress, San Jose style.

The Urban Blight Junkie Returns to San Carlos Street

Twelve years ago on this page, the anti-man-about-town wrote a travelogue about the stretch of Stevens Creek Boulevard and San Carlos Street—from Just Leather all the way eastward to Diamond Laundry & Cleaners—identifying components of what could be understood as the Melrose Avenue of San Jose's underbelly.

Many of the places I mentioned do not exist anymore, and with developers now dumbing down the street's character with cookie-cutter housing complexes, the time was right to revisit the grand promenade.

This stretch of road takes one to a different era. The streetscapes are leftover from decades ago, when San Jose wasn't entirely filled in with suburbia and 280 didn't exist yet, so miles of connector thoroughfares with single-story retail still made sense. Don't fret, though. Interesting stuff still remains, if you just ignore all the new housing.

The emotion started right away. While riding the bus over to Just Leather, I overheard a former Del Monte Cannery employee, now 74, on his way to the 99-cent store, waxing nostalgic about how cheap it was to live here decades ago. Never again, he said. It's over.

Just Leather thankfully looked the same as when I first bought a jacket there in 1986. On the front window it still said, "Coffee is on," like it did 33 years ago. The same little Honda motorcycle sat out front in the parking space like it did in the '80s. If you don't see that bike out front, it just means the place is closed. Inside, the coffee was on and I encountered what's now the third generation running the joint. The original crew opened the store in 1967.

Across the street and just a year older than Just Leather, Falafel's Drive-in was jammed at lunchtime on a Saturday. There was a Faction sticker on the front window, right underneath the Zagat designation—a yin-yang of punk and luxury. It doesn't get any more San Jose than that.

From there, it was easy to get carried away. A slew of beautifully disfigured facades highlighted the next mile, including San Jose's celebrated row of antique shops. As always, each one featured its own janky panache and each one was doing business when I slithered in. Believe me, the experience of hearing "Green, Green Grass of Home" by Tom Jones while exploring the labyrinthine confines of a San Carlos Street antique shop is more necessary than anything WeWork will provide.

Neighborhood bars are important, too. If your hands are shaking pre-noon, like mine used to be, Alex's 49er Inn remains a highlight on this strip. Even though nearby icons like Time Deli, Thrift Village and Babyland are long gone, Alex's lives in glorious infamy, as does Bears right down the street, formerly Bella's Club. And no, I'm not forgetting the Red Stag. Even though the ancient stripmall in which it sits has been painted, fixed up and thus ruined, the Red Stag carries on. At these legendary watering holes, you will not find $17 artisan pickle sandwiches or craft brew hipsters bathing in beard oil. Instead, you'll find heroic denizens of the gritty underbelly with stories to tell.

Not too far east, one finds residue from the city's war on bowling alleys. As recently as 50 years ago, Fiesta Lanes featured a drive-through restaurant and, in later decades, a pleasantly seedy lounge that forever stank of cigarettes. Alas, nothing remains but a dark beige housing complex and a driveway named after the bowling alley.

In, around and between all of this, you'll find humble Ethiopian restaurants, tattoo shops, ginseng suppliers, vintage boutiques, a kickboxing gym and all sorts of wild places. Explore this part of town while you still can because the techie condo-pocalypse is coming. And it ain't going to stop for no one, perhaps not even O.C. McDonald and Western Billiards, both of which feature the most rip-roaring old school signs still left on that street. Someone better make sure those signs get preserved. Don't trust the developers to care. They won't.

Finally, I ended my journey at the legendary Diamond Laundry & Cleaners, right at the hideous 87 overpass. The crumbling wooden billboard is the oldest one in San Jose, and it shows. Somebody restore that masterpiece now!

Cactus Club Reunites for Benefit

On Oct. 24, San Jose's rock scene comes together at The Ritz in support of musician Matt Kolb, 49, who is fighting cancer. Bands from the early '90s Cactus Club era—including Cafe of Regret, Firme and 187 Calm—will reunite for the cause, with Kolb mustering up some Marshall amp-level strength to talk about his battle.

"I'm fighting with everything I got," Kolb said. "I can't thank my friends enough. I'm so close to survival thanks to them, their prayers and their support."

Since the organizers are billing the gig as an official Cactus Club reunion, allow me to rocksplain the history. Located at 417 S. First St., the Cactus Club (1988-2002) was San Jose's equivalent of CBGB in New York. Every club-level touring band in the country knew of the place. In its time, Cactus did everything that a rock & roll club is supposed to do: It pissed off the neighbors, it pissed off the cops, it pissed off everyone's parents, it embarrassed the politicians, it annoyed the city's Department of Building, Planning and Code Enforcement, it irritated the state Department of Alcoholic Beverage Control, and it gave San Jose name recognition across the United States of America.

When Cactus opened in December 1988, San Jose was still a backwater hick-town suburb with a pathological attention-starved inferiority complex about San Francisco, forever desperate to be taken seriously as a real city and thus finally shake the "red-headed stepchild of the Bay Area" image it was given for decades. By then, much of downtown had long since deteriorated into a black hole of skid-row atmospherics with splotches of crumbling retail left over from the '70s. The city was throwing millions at cockamamie schemes to lure the comfortable classes back downtown, while First Street south of San Carlos was the red light district, a dingy peepshow paradise where washed-up hookers went to die and trenchcoated pervs went to score bad speed. (About once a year, some clown on the street tells me San Jose needs to bring all this back, but that's another column.)

During those initial years, three other alternative music clubs existed nearby—Marsugi's, Ajax and F/X—but Cactus was San Jose's only 18-and-over venue, which meant many people no longer drove to San Francisco or the East Bay to see shows. After Cactus opened, local bands popped up everywhere. Anyone with a guitar, bass or drum set started to rehearse. Since this was before the World Wide Web, cell phones or laptops, everyone promoted shows by hand. The local rock community was much stronger than it is today, and bands supported each other much more than they do now. As a result, a thriving rock scene exploded at the corner of First and San Salvador, then dubbed "Four Corners." One didn't even need to know who was playing at which club any given night. You just headed toward that corner, found a bar or an alley in which to drink, and then went to see bands like Nirvana, Korn or No Doubt when they were nobodies. If you didn't make it inside, you'd slum it on the street and wait for whichever house party unfolded later. Everyone knew everyone else. The scene grew in organic fashion—a true, urban live-for-today spectacle of booze and rock & roll placemaking. We didn't need the Knight Foundation for anything. This wasn't a ping-pong table in Fountain Alley.

Plus, it was cheap to live downtown at that time. Band houses tended to emerge everywhere. A thrashed Victorian for five drunk roommates and their record collections went for about $1,400 a month. SJSU tuition was $700 a semester. It was Camelot.

Sadly, though, many friends from those years are no longer with us, which is why any reunion such as this becomes a poignant opportunity for reflection. One of Cactus' honchos near the end, the legendary Stikmon, told me just a few weeks ago that we have "San Jose cockroach blood." They'll never get rid of us. On a larger level, Cactus was that way, too. The club you thought would never go away is never going away, especially when one of its own needs serious help. All I can add is: Fuck cancer.

Cactus Club Reunion, Part Two

Last week, the anti-man-about-town rocksplained the history of San Jose's legendary Cactus Club, our only possible equivalent of CBGB in New York. This week, we drill down even deeper into one particular component of that glorious place that emerged near its final years: the infamous Cactus Club Happy Hour from 5 to 9pm every single day until the place closed.

Were it not for that happy hour, I would not have wound up working for *Metro* in the first place. I have Cactus to thank for it all.

Unlike jock bars that offered a happy hour from, say, 3 to 5pm or 4 to 6pm, the gig at Cactus was four hours long, catering to homeless punks, counterculture twenty-somethings and indigent old drunks from the art scene years earlier, plus a neato melange of lounge lizards, washed up strippers, transients, short-order crooks, bums, poets and *Metro* employees. In the latter case, I already wasn't living in the most healthy manner, but at least I had a few sporadic freelance writing gigs, both highbrow and lowbrow assignments. Eventually, the right person at Cactus' happy hour, Lisa Thomas, greased the skids for me to apply at *Metro*. It would never have happened otherwise.

At Cactus, Lorin Ferguson, who sadly passed away not too long ago, was one of the bartenders who supported me throughout many evenings of stale Bud drafts and Jager shots. All of which led to me spinning atrocious easy listening records every single Wednesday. It would be stretching it to say I was a "DJ" since all we did is place one beat-up turntable on top of the bar, but every freaking week I had to accost Eagle Buckett, the Cactus "technician," who is also no longer with us, for a pair of female-to-female RCA jacks just so we could pipe the turntable through the "house system," meaning, the stereo behind the bar. Yet it cranked. So until the place closed for good I spun easy listening, exotica, bad TV themes, space-age bachelor pad tunes and all sorts of nonsense, just so I could get free drinks from 5 to 9pm every Wednesday. Rockin' Rob Dapello, brother of Rancid's Lars Frederiksen, regularly came in to request the *Smokey and the Bandit* theme, which I always played. Sadly, Rob passed away in 2001, right at the height of that era.

During one particular Wednesday happy hour, when Mojo Nixon was loading in to perform later that night, he heard me spinning a ridiculous bluegrass version of "Dominique" by the Singing Nun. "You're a disturbed man," he said to me, shaking his head. I'm not making that up. In fact, I bragged for years that Mojo Nixon had called me a disturbed man.

The stories are endless. One day a Cactus security guard decided to headbutt the plate-glass window at Earl Scheib's Auto Body next door while citing passages from the Satanic Bible under his breath. The window shattered, and minutes later I saw small shards of glass protruding from his chest while the paramedics struggled to lift his heavy frame into the ambulance, all while he screamed, "Hail Satan!"

Such incidents were everyday occurrences. In my case, I was so messed up that I even rewrote an old text by occultist Aleister Crowley, a piece called *The Green Goddess* in which he waxes poetic from a New Orleans absinthe bar. I rewrote the whole thing, applying it to Cactus instead. So allow me now to finish this column with a passage from that text:

For here the stage was set for no common bards, no less than real maidens Alanis Morissette and Gwen Stefani, who soon rose to arena status. Here too played the late Kurt Cobain, Country Dick Montana, Johnny Thunders, Dee Dee Ramone and Andrew Wood of Mother Love Bone—all five of whom lived and died, giving their names to the perils of their trade. Here, authentic, and, as I imagine indignant, their ghosts do indeed stalk grimly.

And during the Cactus Club's daily happy hour as I exchange aphorisms with the bartender concerning the vanity of things, I perceive the secret of the heart of God himself; this, that everything, even the vilest urine-soaked place, is so unutterably lovely that it is worthy of the devotion of a God for all eternity.

Miss Careful is Getting Restored

Miss Careful is being restored. What many claim is the oldest billboard in San Jose—that legendary sign on the Highway 87 overpass outside Diamond Laundry & Cleaners—shall soon return to life. As you read this, local artist MESNGR, who also helped paint the crazed VTA bus on the side of Alameda Artworks, is hard at work restoring Miss Careful to her old glory by painting a brand-new sign.

Everyone who's driven along San Carlos Street as it enters downtown for the last 70 years has noticed Diamond Laundry & Cleaners because, according to the sign, Miss Careful works there. And for the last few decades of those 70 years, many local connoisseurs of underbelly have offered to help restore the sign, especially in recent times as the sign had long since deteriorated beyond repair. But now, thanks to the blessing of newly retired proprietor Mary Jane Hulbert, a team of locals have banded together to make it happen. For many years, Mary was hesitant to allow anyone to mess with the sign, but just recently she finally changed her mind.

To get the skinny, I showed up not only for Miss Careful, but also to reacquaint myself with the Diamond Laundry business in general. Upon crossing the threshold and ringing a buzzer on the side of the counter, I spoke to Peggy Sutton, who immediately appeared and told me the building used to be a gas station pre-1950.

"That's why there's three driveways out front," she said, pointing to the parking lot.

The Diamond Laundry business actually dates all the way back to 1931, to an old location on Grant Street. Then in 1950 proprietor Harold Hulbert bought the property on San Carlos Street, where the business sits today. Hulbert passed away just over 20 years ago, but Mary, his wife, worked right up until recently, even into her mid-90s. Today, her son Gary C.H. Burton along with his children, Jason and Janielle, operate the place.

As I stood there, Sutton schooled me on the history. She told me about El Patio, the bar that used to sit next door, before Highway 87 existed. Soon after Sutton graduated from Piedmont Hills High School in the '70s, she bartended at El Patio before she was even 21. Decades ago, Pete's Bakery sat across San Carlos from Diamond Laundry. The guy who ran it was the brother of the guy who ran Dick's Bakery on Meridian.

And in the back, Sutton showed me around, pointing out ancient but still functioning industrial laundry machines. Three old-school washers, like the three wise men, sat there plugging away and refusing to die. An old "mangle"—a contraption with huge rollers and cogs for pressing sheets—still functioned, although not many people needed their sheets pressed anymore. I saw an old army dryer, plus huge tumblers, various steaming equipment and other machinery I couldn't identify. There was even an old boiler from the '70s in the back corner, the heart of the whole operation, pumping steam through various pipes to all the machines in the complex.

"Without that boiler, we're dead in the water," Sutton said. "We can't work. Everything is powered by steam."

Back at the front counter, an interior remodel was underway. A new era of Diamond Laundry seemed to be around the corner. All the ancient wood-colored paneling had been replaced. The walls were painted white for the time being. On the counter, I saw red Sharpies, receipt books, collar stays and rubber stamps. Customers came in every five minutes with their own personal requests. Peggy seemed to know them all.

When it came to the staff, people tended to spend their entire lives working at Diamond Laundry. One employee, Martha Rodriguez, recently retired after 38 years. A few current workers are going on 29 years now. It's not an industry to which people beat a path looking for employment. Most people are cringing for Google jobs instead, Sutton quipped.

"We don't get that many people walking in here wanting to work for us," she said. "So we're pretty honored that these guys are still here. Every person we use, it's hard to replace him."

Murray Bowles, RIP

In 1982, when a bored suburban San Jose kid had nothing to do, the photographer Murray Bowles would sometimes be the one who drove that kid to his or her first punk rock show.

And when that kid grew older and played in a band five years later, or perhaps even 10, 15 or 20 years later, Murray still lurked in the shadows, in the pit, on the sidewalks, in the bars or somewhere nearby, showing up to shoot the gig and later publish photos. Bowles, who passed away recently at age 68 at his home in Sacto, left a serious body of work as a street-level photographer. His archive of punk rock images and negatives, numbering in the tens of thousands, played a serious role in the recent documentary *Turn It Around: The Story of East Bay Punk*.

Murray was known throughout the Bay Area and his photos were known throughout the planet, especially now in the Instagram era. His Instagram page features both current and classic shots, cementing his legacy for a new generation.

In the San Jose area, Murray made his living as a software engineer beginning in the late '70s. He also played viola in the Peninsula Symphony and in a local punk-hillbilly outfit called the Shitkickers. In that sense, he was half punk and half classical. Other band members were astounded and grateful that the legendary punk rock photographer Murray Bowles was the same guy playing viola on stage next to them. The dude was a multi-talented character.

"He had a really good knowledge of music theory," said Shitkickers guitarist Shawn Packer. "It was really interesting to listen to Murray talk parts out. He would talk them out in his head, before he played them, and then he would bust it out. It was really interesting to watch the way his musical mind worked."

As a photographer, Murray was not someone who flew around the world to shoot Metallica or the Rolling Stones. Even as recently as this year, you'd see him at various San Jose dive bars or house parties, where he'd effortlessly shoot the most fantastic gut-level pictures to help empower any fledgling punk or metal band and make them look famous. Hypothetically speaking, if you were in a band called Regurgitated Cattle Esophagus, playing on the floor at Johnny V's for a handful of sweaty XXXL-sized dudes with tall cans of Pabst Blue Ribbon, Murray just might show up. One never knew.

In fact, for 35 years, one never knew exactly where or when Murray would appear. After he passed away, literally hundreds of people chimed in with the same type of story: They were in a band years ago, some band that ultimately went nowhere, but Murray showed up one night, took photos and made them look like rock stars. Even if his subjects were just fans hanging out, Murray excelled at capturing the human element of punk scenes more than anyone else in the Bay Area. He gave people a sense of belonging they hadn't previously felt. Whether at established clubs, mountain parties or word-of-mouth shows, it went without saying that if Murray was in the building, it was going to be a good night. Legions of people all over the Bay Area have said as much for decades.

But he always showed up for his own gigs and practices. In the same way that thousands are grateful to be included in Murray's body of work as a photographer over the years, so were his bandmates. It still blows people away.

"He captures emotions. He captures moments. He has an eye," said Packer, adding that it was so much fun hanging around with a guy that made everyone laugh by just being himself. "I was super, super grateful to have that entity, to have him be a part of some art I was doing. I was so proud of that. To have this guy, who has an amazing sense of the moment, actually sharing a stage with me and working on songs with me. It was really awesome. I'm incredibly grateful that we did that."

2020

Dr. Jerry Hiura, RIP

An official Dr. Jerry Hiura table should be established at Kubota Restaurant in Japantown. In fact, there should also be an official Dr. Jerry walking tour of J-town, beginning at 90 E. Taylor and concluding at Kubota.

Hiura, who passed away on Dec. 26 at age 72, was one of the all-time legends of J-town. A dentist by trade, Dr. Jerry operated from his celebrated Taylor Street office, yet was always willing to inspect someone's teeth, even in his own driveway.

Many also knew Dr. Jerry as a relentless supporter of the arts. Not only did he help launch Contemporary Asian Theater Scene (CATS), he also at various times over the decades served as vice chair of the California State Arts Council, chair of the San Jose Arts Commission and president of Arts Council Silicon Valley—all of which led him to forever champion the plights of various cultures and diasporas in the arts, helping everyone while expecting absolutely nothing in return.

Several people in the arts community went to Dr. Jerry to get their dental work done. Always a mega-modest beacon of light and laughter, Dr. Jerry would talk to patients about art spaces, theater jobs, Asian-American struggles or issues concerning non-profit status—all while he worked on their teeth. He brought a smile to everyone's face.

"He was my dentist for years," said Tamara Alvarado, who ran MACLA from 2003 to 2008. "I loved coming in and laughing because he would ask me questions the entire time with torture instruments in my mouth. He knew I could only nod or gesture dramatically, and he laughed and I laughed."

A perfect example of the role Dr. Jerry played as a humble yet powerful networking machine emerged when he helped integrate Chopsticks Alley Art, a Vietnamese-centric arts operation, into the fabric of Japantown so that a landmark exhibit, *Salt Stained*, could take place at Ken Matsumoto's Art Object Gallery in 2018. After 40 years of the Vietnam-

393

ese diaspora enduring in San Jose, it had never once collaborated with the Japanese American community.

Trami Nguyen Cron, founder and executive artistic director of Chopsticks Alley Art, says she was previously unfamiliar with the arts community and social structure of Japantown, yet Dr. Jerry, who also became her dentist and one of her board members, functioned as a conduit to help the organization find its way. Many meetings unfolded at Kubota, where Dr. Jerry held court and even had his own tab and his own table, it seemed. Cron would sneak over and try to pay, but the staff wouldn't take her money. Jerry always covered it.

"He was very humble," Cron said. "What I liked about him ... I regret not knowing so much. Not because of lack of trying, but because he was so about other people. You go to him and it's all about you, not him. You'd try to turn it, and ask about him, his family, his life, but in his way, he'd somehow brush it off and talk about you. He was always about other people, not about himself."

Kathy Sakamoto, president of San Jose Okayama Sister Cities, agreed, adding that Dr. Jerry always responded to phone calls, whether he was in San Jose, Morocco or London. He was always trying to make light of difficult situations while working on solutions at the same time.

"He sprinkled words and checks around like fairy dust, enabling care for the arts community, the Asian Pacific and Islander community, civil rights and more," Sakamoto said. "He sincerely loved his community of family, friends and patients."

Later this summer, art shows and other events will celebrate Dr. Jerry's life and creativity, since he also wrote poetry, made jewelry and painted. Until then, though, his humble presence will be felt all over Japantown.

Buddhist Bible Author Dwight Goddard

If Dwight Goddard, the man whose book introduced Jack Kerouac to Buddhism, wound up in Los Gatos after his wife left him, then I just had to follow Rob Brezsny's astrological advice and track the guy down.

No, Goddard is not alive. He passed away in 1939, but not before authoring the seminal 1932 book, *A Buddhist Bible*, the first anthology of Buddhist teachings in English. Just over 20 years later, Kerouac was staying at Neal Cassady's house in San Jose and discovered the book in the public library.

In a now-famous story, Kerouac stole the library's copy of *A Buddhist Bible* and took it all over the US with him, scribbling down voluminous notes, leading to his embrace of the practice and forming the basis of several books, all of which inspired millions of heroic outcasts to look eastward, and inward, for the resolution of their troubles.

Nobody around here ever talks about Goddard, the man who authored *A Buddhist Bible*. That book, while still regarded as a groundbreaking publication, was the culmination of an amazing life story, one that began in engineering school before taking Goddard across China as a Christian missionary and to Zen monasteries in Japan—yet periodically filled in with itinerant spells of self-publishing in Vermont, Santa Barbara and Los Gatos, before he filed for divorce in San Jose in 1925.

Of course, an unexpected blast of serendipity had to emerge. Last week, just as I began to explore Goddard's life, *Metro*'s astrologer Rob Brezsny suggested all Aquarians should explore playfully as we conduct fun research. "Assume that you have a mandate to drum up educational experiences, and that a good way to do that is to amuse yourself with improvisational adventures," he wrote.

With that clincher in mind, off to the library I went. Luckily, I had assistance from a local Buddhist scholar who was happy to share his own research with me.

To make a long story short, Goddard's life took many trajectories. In one case, he was a mechanical engineer who made a fortune starting his own company to produce industrial machines. Sadly, his first wife, whom he deeply loved, passed away less than a year after they married.

He also graduated from Hartford Theological Seminary in 1894, after which he was posted to China on various missionary assignments to convert the natives, which ultimately didn't work. Instead, they converted him. In China, he also met his second wife, another American missionary, who bore him two children.

Years later, after more trips to China and Japan, Goddard eventually became the first American to attempt to elevate Buddhism in any substantial way, translating many of the teachings, publishing numerous books and pamphlets, and eventually producing *A Buddhist Bible*, still regarded as one of the original building blocks of Buddhism's foray into the West.

Somewhere along the line, however, Goddard had a nervous breakdown and then wound up in Los Gatos, where in 1924 he self-published a strange 16-page pamphlet, *A Vision of Christian and Buddhist Fellowship in the Search for Light and Truth*. Writing about himself in the third person, Goddard documented his Chinese travels and the impressions made upon him by the natives while also postulating a bizarre theological brotherhood combining both religions.

An item in the Jan. 25, 1925 *Oakland Tribune* also reports that Goddard filed for divorce in San Jose, separating from his second wife, who had deserted him a few years earlier. To my knowledge, no previous writings about Goddard have ever mentioned that particular detail. He later married for a third time, but once again the union was short-lived, ending in separation.

In any case, just like Kerouac, Goddard was a brutally conflicted person, forever struggling to harmonize his Catholic upbringing with his turn toward Buddhism. He was also stuck between East and West, although it appears he did indeed find peace in the end. He spent his final years in Vermont, near the forest in a house filled with Buddhist artifacts, meditating every day in total solitude.

Scott's Seafood Takes on the Curse of Casa Castillo

Right now, as Scott's Seafood prepares to migrate from way across the neighborhood into the ground level of the Twohy Building, everyone hopes the celebrated eatery can finally put an end to the ancient and perpetual cycles of creation and destruction long characterizing that corner—the notorious Curse of Casa Castillo.

The Casa in question was a very popular restaurant located at said corner for many years, but in 2001, the San Jose Redevelopment Agency booted them out of the building. Ever since then, nothing has succeeded in that space. Everything has failed. Following Casa Castillo, the likes of Zyng Asian Grill, Asqew Grill, Ruffled Feathers, Blackbird Tavern and most recently Social Policy have all opened and then imploded shortly thereafter. Hence, the Curse of Casa Castillo, as locals say.

But philosophically speaking, what if the curse went back even further? What's now the pedestrian alley, Paseo de San Antonio, used to be an actual street, San Antonio Street (see photo), that went from Plaza de Cesar Chavez all the way to SJSU. On the other side of campus, San Antonio Street has remained relatively unchanged for a century, but west of SJSU, things have been quite different. Fifty years ago, for example, one could find a curious place called Ho-Sale Gifts, plus a variety of shoe stores, jewelry shops, clothing boutiques and a slew of intriguing flophouses like the Curtis Hotel. In the immediate area, one could drink at the Gold Nugget Tavern, The Office Tavern or the Sapphire Lounge. One could shop at the radical Kaleidoscope Bookstore. Camera stores and sewing machine retailers were not far away. And at this time, the Twohy Building had not yet been repurposed with hipster apartments. Instead, one found secretarial offices, insurance companies, chiropractors, jewelers, union reps and the Alcoholics Anonymous Intergroup Central Office.

Of course, when it comes to this area, let us not forget to mention one of the most colossal failures in downtown San Jose history: the Pavilion Shops, a large open-air shopping mall, which was located across from Casa Castillo. Right now, a shuttered gym, along with Taco Mania, sit right where the entrance used to be. The entrance featured steps that went down into the lower level of the complex, where tons of retail establishments all held high hopes for an upscale version of downtown San Jo that never happened. This was 1988, right when Rod Diridon was predicting the light rail would transform San Jose into Paris, London or Zurich.

At the time, the city was throwing tens of millions at schemes to gentrify downtown with affluent people—all of which failed—and the prime hornet in their bonnet was the Pavilion Shops. The mall included, among other things, Victoria's Secret, The Sports Fan, Le Beau Monde, Looks, Musicland, a Fila store, City Sunglasses, Boudin Bakery, Bonsalls Shoes, Benetton, Belles Jambes, Art Attack, Added Touch, Teddie Ôn' Tees, plus Laura Todd Cookies, Top Ten Leather, Tish's Toys and a handful of restaurants. Since no one ever went, the whole mall eventually plummeted out of business by the mid-1990s. At street level, a few businesses remained along the perimeter, as they do now, but the open-air portion inside was closed off and the top floor was given to a server farm company.

Normally I'd offer some comic Zen perspectives to help ease the pain of such idiocy, but this week I'm in a Western mood. San Antonio Street, which I'm assuming was named after Saint Anthony, is one of the oldest streets in San Jose, going all the way back to the 19th century. Saint Anthony is also the patron saint of finding lost or stolen articles, which in this case means lost and stolen restaurants. And dive bars. And bookstores. And significant downtown retail, which we'll certainly never see again, at least not in my lifetime. So for the Catholics out there, start prayin' to Saint Anthony. The Curse of Casa Castillo could stand to be lifted.

New Ballet Moves Into Scottish Rite Temple

Led by Dalia Rawson, San Jose's New Ballet will officially open its new headquarters later this month with a gala kickoff spectacular on Feb. 29.

The company leaves its old building at 40 N. First St.—a structure loaded with historical mysteries—and travels to the Corinthian Ballroom building at 196 N. Third St., a.k.a. The Scottish Rite Temple, another architectural masterpiece filled with secrets.

The old building was a legendary structure dating back to Prohibition. In one of the offices, a bookshelf hid a secret passageway. There was also a hidden wet bar, dumbwaiters and secret staircases that allowed patrons to sneak out the back whenever the cops raided the joint. Netflix even filmed a short documentary, Nocturne, that highlighted the peculiar angles and lighting situations in the building, all using some of the most high-tech cameras in the world.

"I did love that about our old building," Rawson says. "It had a history. It had personality. Every other ballet school in the area is either in a mini-mall or a warehouse. It's converted. Every other school in Northern California is basically that. There are no ballet schools in historic buildings and I really did feel that that was something unique we had at our First Street location."

Much construction still needs to be completed at the new location, but the school is up and running on the lower level of the Scottish Rite building—the area formerly occupied by the San Jose Athletic Club. Concrete walls have been knocked down and rooms have been reconfigured. The old basketball and racquetball courts at the back of the building are now gorgeous dance studios. Where there used to be jacuzzis and locker rooms there are now dressing areas, offices and private lesson spaces.

The Scottish Rite Temple is one of the most ornate structures in San Jose. Designed by architect Carl Werner, it was first dedicated in 1925. Werner was a 33rd-degree Mason and designed most of the Scottish Rite temples in California. If one views the building from St. James Park across the street, two large marble statues can be seen above the entry portico, on top of the front columns. The statue on the left is King Solomon. The one on the right is Albert Pike (1809-1891), one of the most prominent figures in the development of American Freemasonry and a perennial target of worldwide conspiracy theories. When the building first opened, it included a 1,400-seat auditorium and the biggest stage in San Jose. There were club rooms, a library, meeting spaces and secret-ritual chambers. The kitchen and dining facilities could feed 1,000 people.

Fifty years later, after the building and the neighborhood fell into a state of disrepair, the Masons finally bailed for the suburbs, setting up shop in the Almaden and Curtner area, where they remain today. Then in 1981, with a $6-million bankroll, the building was transformed into the San Jose Athletic Club, so that a new generation of politicians, lawyers, judges, real-estate syndicates and redevelopment czars could lounge around in saunas.

Now, after years of dungeon-like emptiness, the bottom floor is once again returning to life—this time with ballet dancers. Feb. 29 will be a perfect day for the kickoff party. Ballet goes hand-in-hand with leap year anyway, and with an entire ballet company surrounded by historical Masonic vibrations and activating the space, a magical feeling is sure to emerge.

"I had really resigned myself to the fact that we were going to move into a warehouse or a mini-mall space," Rawson says, adding that the Scottish Rite Temple offers at least as much compelling history and architecture as the old location. "I think there's some continuity there and it helps us really be part of the landscape of San Jose and the culture of San Jose in a way that we wouldn't if we had moved into an old ACE Hardware building in the suburbs."

Noche de Poesia Elevates Communities Through Poetry

As an organization, ConXion operates out of a nondescript building just across Coyote Creek from where The Jungle homeless encampment used to be. The surrounding environs include Happy Hollow and the historic Ashworth-Remillard House, where the roosters meander into the Walmart parking lot.

Once inside ConXion, however, a vast array of activities become apparent, all relating to education, workforce, behavioral health and other social services for disconnected youth and adults. Murals adorn the walls. Day laborers arrive to learn computer skills, get food, or just hang out in a safe place while they look for work. Counselors, teachers and social workers tend to the needs of disenfranchised parents or kids embroiled in the child welfare system.

From this wealth of heroic services, a poetic adventure to Oakland emerged. Ashley Gomez, a cultural broker at ConXion, joined poet Rachelle Escamilla to attend a reading by Josiah Luis Alderete, a full-blooded Pocho Indio and Spanglish-speaking poet with deep roots in San Francisco's Mission District, pre-gentrification. Gomez, who runs ConXion's Parent Hub program to help decrease disproportionality in child-welfare programs, was so inspired by Alderete's performance that she organized her own poetry night for the parents and kids that regularly lean on ConXion's services. As a result, Noche de Poesia, the first event of its kind ever at the ConXion compound, erupts this Friday at 6pm.

"I wanted to create a bridge for families who don't have access to poetry nights, don't have access to workshops with fancy speakers," says Gomez, whose approach incorporates La Cultura Cura, a healing philosophy emphasizing cultural values, community and indigenous teachings. "I wanted them to have access, just to show them that there is another way, that there is creativity, and there are other communities out there that are supportive, that are healthy, and it's not like drinking or doing drugs."

On the poetry front, when Alderete isn't working at City Lights Bookstore in San Francisco, he organizes Latinx spoken word nights and performs poetry addressing a variety of social issues, from colonization to food gentrification and more. He believes Spanglish is an authentic American language.

"When he does his poetry, he's reminding us of the importance of our ancestral roots," Gomez says. "And when we get stuck in poverty, we forget about how sacred these things are. And that's why I think it's so important to bring him to these families. It's a reminder to remember your cultural roots, and not to let these things get lost with the daily grind."

Also on the bill is Brooklyn-based Chris Carr, plus ASHA, a local poet and educator, as well as Rachelle Escamilla, who hosts "Out of Our Minds," a long-running poetry radio show on KKUP. Currently based at CSU Monterey Bay, Escamilla helped book the poets due to being fed up with what she claims is the lack of representation in San Jose's poetry scene.

"San Jose used to be Chicano, there were a lot of Chicanos here," Escamilla says. "Where is the Chicano art scene? Where are the small spaces where all of the Chicano artists are working? Why does it always have to be inside of these institutional places? Why can't it be handled by people in the community that are doing it from the roots of the community? I think that's what's important about ConXion. Ashley is from the community, she's speaking to the community, she's inside of the community."

This time around, that community will hold space in the ConXion compound at 749 Story Road. Between the roosters, the sun-baked concrete, the Walmart shoppers and the Vietnamese Buddhists, revolutionary poets will inspire kids and parents alike.

"I feel very inferior compared to the poets who are going to be there," Escamilla confesses. "But all of them are heavy hitters. Their performances are strong. Everyone you're going to see at the show is someone who will make you feel fire."

Nirvana Crashed in Japantown Home

Thirty years ago, Nirvana played at the Cactus Club in San Jose and then crashed at 463 Jackson Street near Japantown. The opening act, Tad—the dude and the band—likewise slept at the house that night, Feb. 11, 1990.

"It was just a typical night at the bar: any Sub Pop band that was touring was automatically invited over," says DeAnn Caughey, who then lived at the house, along with John Graziadei and Carlos Fuentes.

Yours truly did not attend the show or the afterparty, although I did show up at the house on numerous other nights. At the time, that address was San Jose's unofficial headquarters for all things Sub Pop Records, the famed Seattle label that can be blamed for the rise of grunge. In early 1990 we weren't even calling it "grunge," but many of us owned Nirvana's *Bleach* LP or were members of the Sub Pop Singles Club, so the Cactus show was on our radar.

After the show, local fan Ken De La Cruz befriended the XXXL-sized Tad and his bandmates, then jumped in their van to show them the way to 463 Jackson. Ultimately, the party was not the usual rager that tore up the house. Only about a dozen friends hung around into the wee morning hours. Both De La Cruz and Caughey remember Kurt Cobain as the most introverted one.

"Of all the guys in those two bands, he was the least sociable," De La Cruz says. "He kind of sat in the corner and didn't talk much or interact much with anybody."

Another source claimed Cobain was shooting heroin in the house that night. Tad was also relentlessly looking to score some ice, a meth-like drug then all over the news, although he was probably joking.

But while everyone else drank and made a racket, Caughey spent an hour talking to Nirvana bassist Krist Novoselic, who was pining over a lost love.

"He was upset about a girl," Caughey says. "We sat on the couch and talked for a long time. He told me—I don't know if it's true, but he told me and I remember it—he said, 'I wrote "About a Girl."' The song was about the girl he was upset about. Maybe he was trying to show off, but I absolutely remember that conversation. It's why I was stuck on the couch with him most of the night."

Then Tad broke the loveseat.

"Tad and the band stayed in the living room," Caughey recalled. "He stayed on our loveseat. Which was so funny, because it's a love seat, so he's got his head up and his feet up. In the morning, both sides of the couch were broken-down flat."

In 1990, the rent at 463 Jackson was $750. Each of the three tenants paid $250. These were simpler times. There were no cell phones or laptops. The World Wide Web did not exist. Everyone collected records and went out to see bands multiple times a week. Drugs and alcohol were cheap. Rock and punk party houses existed all over downtown San Jose. Touring bands that came through Cactus, Marsugi's, The Oasis or F/X often needed somewhere to crash, so this night was just one regular night out of many. Nirvana wasn't yet huge, but 463 Jackson always welcomed Sub Pop bands since the tenants were big fans. Even though the house was small, floor space always became available.

"All of Nirvana were in sleeping bags in the kitchen, our beat-up old Victorian-house kitchen with a drum set in it," Caughey says. "And the bathroom was behind it, so I remember having to walk over these people in the morning to use the restroom."

Caughey was working at Costco at the time. She had just purchased a box of oranges, which she doled out to the bands in the morning, while they packed up their vehicles and hung out on the front porch. The musicians were blown away by the sunny California hospitality.

"I don't know what the weather was like where they came from, but they were super excited about the sun in their face," Caughey says.

Tony & Alba's: Pie in the Sky

The only San Jose pizza restaurant to grace the cover of *People* is also the same family business that received the first online pizza order 30 years ago.

Right now, Tony & Alba's on Stevens Creek Boulevard is knee-deep in all sorts of heroic efforts to help people get through the COVID-19 era, but their humble beginnings go back to the original Mountain View location at 619 Escuela Ave.

In the '80s, Mountain View was still a glorious bastion of old-school gritty suburbia, with a smattering of stoner apartment complexes, nefarious car washes, dive bars, stripmalls and Moffett Field employees. High-tech as we know it today was only just emerging. There was no eclectic foodie scene of any sort. When Tony and Alba Salciccia first opened their joint on a side street off El Camino Real, they had no idea what it would turn into.

"It was just a little hole in the wall," said Diana Vallorz, daughter of

Tony and Alba, who now runs the current location with her husband Al. "Early in the morning they'd be there, until late at night. My father even got a trailer so he could nap in the back, in-between. Or they'd go rent a hotel room so they could go right back to work the next morning. It was just my father, my mother, and then one employee that they hired."

In the early days, an extra large combo was $13, a sandwich was $3.50 and a salad was $2. Coffee was 50 cents with free refills. Soon enough, Joe Izzo wrote a rave review in the Mercury-News and the business sky-rocketed. People lined up all down the block and around the corner. A solid base of loyal customers emerged, the second generation of which still patronize the current Stevens Creek Blvd location.

At times, the shop even contributed pizza to Shoreline Amphitheatre, the San Jose Arena, Spartan Stadium and several other sporting events. In fact, one of the first moments I ever witnessed any example of a corporate Goliath crushing the little guy was when I worked at Shoreline in the late '80s.

Tony & Alba's supplied amazing pizza for the concession stands, but only until a nationwide conglomerate took over the operation and abandoned Tony & Alba's for a more standard and miserable kind of slop. It was a travesty of justice from which I never healed.

But I digress. At the same time, Tony & Alba's became the favorite pizza place for much of the fledgling hi-tech industries. So much so, that in 1990, nearby employees of Sun Microsystems even designed proprietary UNIX-based toolkits allowing them to order directly from their SPARCstations. Before the World Wide Web existed in its current form, Sun engineers coded up a user interface that allowed them to choose Tony & Alba's menu items and pizza toppings right from their screen, and then pipe the order to a fax protocol, which was then sent through the phone line to Tony & Alba's.

Even though the final result came in the form of a fax, it's safe to say this was the first instance of somebody ordering a pizza online, straight from their desktop workstation.

Tony Salciccia is sadly no longer with us, but Alba still remains, although Diana and Al own the business. People even recently included Tony & Alba's on the cover and inside the magazine, mentioning them in a round-up of local businesses that donate to their communities during the COVID-19 era. Tony & Alba's currently provides free pizza and delivery for quarantined seniors over the age of 70, plus the shop also donates pasta lunch bags to healthcare workers and helps out San Jose's Roma Bakery by selling their bread.

Even though the current Stevens Creek Blvd restaurant is the only remaining Tony & Alba's, customers still fondly remember the original Mountain View store decades ago. Everyone brings it up. For the most part, the business carries on just the way Tony would have wanted.

"When we started doing this thing with the seniors, I could picture my father saying right away, 'Let's do this,'" Diana said. "They were big in the community. It's exactly what my father would have done."

Silicon Alleys Celebrates 15 Years of Gratitude

In his essay, "Return to Tipasa," the Nobel Laureate Albert Camus included a line now often quoted in the COVID-19 era: "In the middle of winter I at last discovered that there was within me an invincible summer."

Meaning, maybe we will come out of this even stronger. Which is why, despite now being the official 15th anniversary of this column, I will momentarily cast aside any celebrations, or at least give them a different spin. At the moment, sickness and suffering continue to characterize society even more than usual, with heavy loads of stress, anxiety and fear collectively overshadowing any humble anniversary brags I would throw your way. So for the moment, I offer something more important: gratitude. Not just for you, the readers, but for everything this landscape has given me over the last 15 years. And gratitude will get one through a lot of hard times.

For example, while we're still allowed to exercise via long solitary walks, I went for takeout Indian food in Willow Glen. During this extended leisurely saunter, which included a few detours through empty desolate side streets, a lifetime of gratitude emerged from every direction of the landscape, both in a physical and temporal sense. I didn't plan this in advance. It just happened. As always.

By itself, Willow Street makes me feel grateful. In 2013, I wrote about Ricardo's Pizza, where the Doobie Brothers first started out as the house band 50 years ago. The same joint hosted Chet Baker on Jazz Tuesdays, but insisted he stash his trumpet in the office so he wouldn't pawn the instrument for money to buy smack. Steps away, also 50 years ago, sat Babe's Muffler, complete with a gigantic Babe statue overlooking Willow and Vine just like Christ the Redeemer overlooking Rio de Janeiro. Willow Street has given me so many stories over the years that I'm simply honored to be a native.

So when I arrived at New Indian Cuisine near Bird and Willow for some fantastic vegetable korma, I couldn't help but get a little sentimental. Just like Roy's Station in Japantown is San Jose's best Buddhist reincarnation of a gas station, New Indian Cuisine is San Jose's best Punjabi reincarnation of an auto parts store. It reminds me of this column's 10th anniversary, when I wrote about my parents. My mom, whose ethnic roots are pure Anglo, grew up in Willow Glen, while my dad was from India. Meaning, I'm "Half-Indian, Half Anglo-Willow-Glen," so the acronym is HI HAWG. To my knowledge, I am the only HI HAWG in San Jose and that is why I keep writing this column. So please patronize New Indian Cuisine for some take-out during this critical era. It's the quintessential hole in the wall with no pretense whatsoever. And they know what they're doing.

Even though I grew up across town, my mom and I spent a lot of time in Willow Glen when I was little. These days, using New Indian Cuisine as a jumping-off point, I can walk for 10 minutes in several different directions and pass by the house in which my mom grew up, houses in which her best friends grew up and/or still live in, plus the address at which I first took music lessons, my old babysitter's house and even places and/or people about whom I've written cover stories.

All in all, after traipsing down Willow from the badlands near downtown, then underneath the hideous Route 87 overpass and eventually into the more quaint neighborhoods, I felt like Albert Camus when he returned to Tipasa, a place of his youth, only to notice how different it was, yet realizing it was still a part of him. Willow Glen is not the same as it was during my own youth, but after this walk, like Camus, I am older and wiser and I can report back with near-transcendent gratitude for all the stories it has given me. The neighborhood is in my DNA. I can say this only because I remember what Willow Glen felt like before all the yuppies arrived.

In this COVID-19 era, within me there lies an invincible summer. We will get through these times. We will.

Index

Symbols

A

B

T

U

V

W

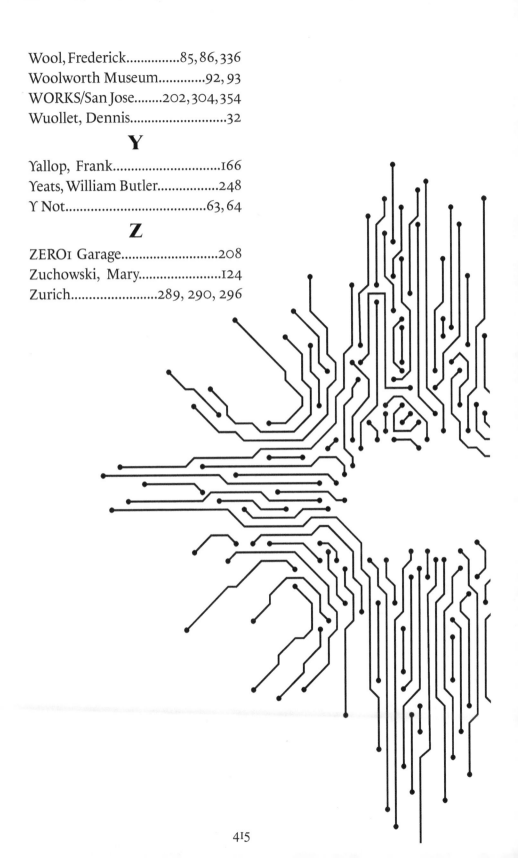

ABOUT THE AUTHOR

Gary Singh is a journalist with a music degree, a published poet and a long-time newspaper columnist at Metro Silicon Valley. His byline has appeared over 1400 times in various commercial and trade publications, including travel essays, art and music criticism, profiles, business journalism, life-style articles, poetry and short fiction. He is the author of The San Jose Earthquakes: A Seismic Soccer Legacy (2015, The History Press) and was recently a Steinbeck Fellow in Creative Writing at San Jose State University.

He still lives in San Jose.

www.garysingh.info

CPSIA information can be obtained
at www.ICGtesting.com
Printed in the USA
FSHW021500211120
76040FS